Basic and Applied Memory Research
Theory in Context
Volume 1

Basic and Applied Memory Research Theory in Context Volume 1

Edited by

Douglas J. Herrmann
Indiana State University

Cathy McEvoy
University of South Florida

Christopher Hertzog
Georgia Institute of Technology

Paula Hertel
Trinity University

Marcia K. Johnson
Princeton University

LEA LAWRENCE ERLBAUM ASSOCIATES, PUBLISHERS
1996   Mahwah, New Jersey

Lawrence Erlbaum Associates, Inc., Publishers
10 Industrial Avenue
Mahwah, New Jersey 07430

Cover design by Gail Silverman

Library of Congress Cataloging-in-Publication Data

Basic and applied memory research / Douglas Herrmann . . . [et al.],
editors.
    p.   cm.
  Includes bibliographical references and index.
  Contents: v. 1. Theory in context — v. 2. Practical applications.
  ISBN 0-8058-1542-2 (cloth : alk. paper). — ISBN 0-8058-1543-0
(pbk. : alk. paper)
    1. Memory. 2. Memory—Research. I. Herrmann, Douglas J.
BF371.B27 1996
153.1′2—dc20   95-40765
                                        CIP

Books published by Lawrence Erlbaum Associates are printed on acid-free paper,
and their bindings are chosen for strength and durability.

Printed in the United States of America
10 9 8 7 6 5 4 3 2 1

Contents

Contributors

Alan Baddeley MRC Applied Psychology Unit, Cambridge, England

Harry P. Bahrick Ohio Wesleyan University, Delaware, OH

Martin A. Conway University of Bristol, Bristol, England

Tim Curran Harvard University, Cambridge, MA

Susan T. Dumais Bellcore, Morristown, NJ

Kenneth A. Deffenbacher University of Nebraska at Omaha, Omaha, NE

Roger A. Dixon University of Victoria, Victoria, British Columbia, Canada

John Dunlosky Georgia Institute of Technology, Atlanta, GA

Jordan Grafman National Institute of Neurological Disorders and Stroke

Michael M. Gruneberg University College of Swansea, Swansea, Wales

Janine F. Hay McMaster University, Hamilton, Ontario, Canada

Douglas J. Herrmann National Center for Health Statistics, Hyattsville, MD

Paula T. Hertel Trinity University, San Antonio, TX

Christopher Hertzog Georgia Institute of Technology, Atlanta, GA

William Hirst New School for Social Research, New York, NY

Larry L. Jacoby McMaster University, Hamilton, Ontario, Canada

Janine M. Jennings McMaster University, Hamilton, Ontario, Canada

Marcia K. Johnson Princeton University, Princeton, NJ

John F. Kihlstrom Yale University, New Haven, CT

Thomas K. Landauer University of Colorado, Boulder, CO, & Bellcore, Morristown, NJ

Mark A. McDaniel University of New Mexico, Albuquerque, NM

Peter E. Morris University of Lancaster, Lancaster, England

Elizabeth Pinner New School for Social Research, New York, NY

Patrick Rabbitt University of Manchester, Manchester, England

Daniel L. Schacter Harvard University, Cambridge, MA

Paul S. Shakesby Austin Peay University, Clarkesville, TN

Robert N. Sykes University College of Swansea, Swansea, Wales

Elizabeth Valentine University of London, Surrey, England

Paula J. Waddill Murray State University, Murray, KY

Herbert Weingartner National Institute on Alcohol Abuse and Alcoholism

John Wilding University of London, Surrey, England

Barbara A. Wilson MRC Applied Psychology Unit, Cambridge, England

Qian Yang University of Manchester, Manchester, England

Preface

The world has been experiencing an economic recession for several years. Those working in the discipline of economics are responsible for developing theories and applications aimed at ending the recession. No doubt economic theory and experience are critical in promoting economic recovery. Nevertheless, science can also contribute to that recovery. Science may do so by developing new ways to improve the human condition and the world in which we live. Let us consider how this may occur.

New theoretical developments in basic research spawn new applied research and new applications. Successful application provides new information that basic research can in turn use to create more new theoretical developments. The new developments of basic research and the new applications of applied research contribute to economic recovery because they set off a series of events that stimulate economic activities.

Economic activities begin when new discoveries in basic research are selected for application, and production of a service or a product is initiated. Selection occurs when the applied world recognizes that (a) there is a practical need for a particular procedure or technology and (b) that a particular discovery from basic research might be used by applied research to develop the procedure or technology that is needed.

Once a new application is in development, several events occur. Loans are secured to finance the production, testing, and distribution of the service or product. People are hired to produce and distribute the service or product. Consumers purchase the service or product. The producer of the service or product pays taxes on profits, pays interest on the loan, and over time pays back the loan. If the service or product is very successful, production and distribution is expanded and the scope of the business cycle enlarges.

Thus, each time one of us conducts basic or applied research that leads to a new service or product that truly meets a need of others in our society, economic benefits accrue to several people. The economic benefits accrue not only to the scientist but to several others: the developers of the service or product, the distributors of the service or product, those who obtain new or better employment with the developers and distributors, and the consumers who have a previously unmet need satisfied by the service or product.

Thus, when we engage in research, we not only advance knowledge, but also may contribute to the economy because of the applications that emanate from our basic and applied research. The better our science, and the more needs that are satisfied by our applications, the greater this impact. When our research meets particular needs (e.g., improved memory performance; enhanced understanding of critical memory phenomena) it not only provides help for those who possess these needs but also helps others engaged in seeing that these needs are met.

In recent years, efforts have been made to evaluate who is doing a better job: basic memory researchers or practical memory researchers. We think that it is fair to say that any positive benefits to be gained from such debate have been attained. We believe that most memory researchers have concluded from this debate that basic and applied memory researchers are equally valuable members of the science team. Together, basic and applied researchers converge on developing the knowledge to meet society's needs.

Although basic and applied researchers are equal members on the science team, they have different job descriptions. Typically, the job of basic researchers involves investigating fundamental processes, and the job of applied researchers involves applying the basic knowledge of those fundamental processes. We propose that both of these jobs can also be described in terms of their economic impact, which is readily apparent after considering their respective roles in knowledge development of basic and applied researchers.

In identifying the fundamental principles of nature, basic research has a fundamental effect on the economy. If basic research falters, no applications will be possible and the economy will suffer as a result. If basic research succeeds, applications are possible. However, if applied research falters, no applications will be possible, the economy will suffer, and the legitimate worth of a particular piece of basic knowledge will be left unknown. Basic researchers unlock the secrets of nature; applied researchers unlock the means by which those secrets of nature can change peoples' lives. Neither basic nor applied research has an independent effect on the economy. Basic research can meet needs and improve the economy only if applied research does its job well. Applied research can meet needs and improve the economy only if basic research has provided sound basic knowledge to begin with.

Some might argue that the economic impact of our work should be regarded as a by-product of what we do, an interesting but nonessential aspect of doing science. We argue that the ultimate goal of scientists should be how we contribute to the good of society. All of us have benefited from the best of what society has to offer. Because of these benefits we are obligated to not only advance knowledge, but also to be mindful of how our work contributes to society. Given that the world economy depends at least in part on the joint effects of basic and applied research, we should be mindful of how our basic and applied work converges. If the science of memory is to make a significant contribution to society, we need to coordinate our basic and applied efforts and determine how basic and applied research complement each other.

The conference that produced this volume was designed specifically with convergence in mind. There were more basic and applied researchers attending this particular conference than at any previous memory conference. This book, which contains the invited papers presented at the Third Practical Aspects of Memory Conference, held at University of Maryland University College in August of 1994, presents the first comprehensive text on basic and applied research in the field of memory. It may be used like a textbook as part of a concerted effort to understand how to investigate memory and apply basic memory theory. It also may be used as a reference text in order to better understand certain problems in basic and applied memory research. The second volume in this series, Basic and Applied Memory Research: Practical Applications, presents more than thirty chapters, each describing research on a practical application of our understanding of human memory.

Acknowledgments

We are grateful to our families and colleagues for their encouragement and support while working on this project. In addition, thanks are due to John Gustafson, Dean of the Social Sciences at the University of Maryland University College, and to Pat Perfetto, Director of the Conference Guest Services of the University of Maryland. We also are very appreciative of the many people who volunteered to serve on the conference staff.

Conference Staff

National Communications and Publicity: Jerry Sehulster

Washington/Maryland/Virginia Communications and Publicity: Mark Palmisano, George Spilich, Ron Okada, and Richard Roberts

Grant Preparation: Douglas J. Herrmann
  Framework: Christopher Hertzog
  Finances: Gordon Willis
  Proposal: Jared Jobe
  Administration: Jonathan Schooler and Mike Toglia

Receipt of Submissions and Organization of the Program:
  Paper Abstracts: David Payne
  Poster Abstracts: John Rybash

Program Abstracts: Fred Conrad
Program Preparation: Karen Whitaker

Conference Management: Ted Schlechter, Chair
  Lodging and Meals: Joan Sander
  Information Center: Paula Lipman and Susan Schechter

Entertainment: Mary Ann Guadagno, Paul Beatty, and Kate Palmisano

Conference Financial Accounts: Mike Toglia

Exhibits: Mike Sewall
  Memory Products and Services: Peggy Intons-Peterson
  Textbooks, Societies, and Organizations: John Schulman
  Societies: Dana Plude
  Companies: George Spilich

Society for Applied Research on Memory and Cognition: David Burrows and
Ron Okada

Conference Text Editing: Cathy McEvoy, Paula Hertel, Christopher Hertzog,
and Leslie Caplan

Editing Assistant: Abby Hisey

Conference Consultants:
  Michael Gruneberg   Peter Morris   Robert Sykes
  Jordan Grafman   Lennie Poon   Martin Conway
  Richard C. Atkinson Douglas Raybeck

CHAPTER ONE

Convergence of Basic and Applied Memory Research: An Overview of Volume 1

Douglas J. Herrmann
National Center for Health Statistics, Hyatsville, MD

The first International Practical Aspects of Memory Conference was held in Wales in 1978 and the second in 1987. Those conferences were well attended and made evident the lively interest in ecologically valid and applied memory research. The proceedings of those conferences gave a "state of the art account of current research and issues in the field of applied memory" (Gruneberg, Morris, & Sykes, 1988). The success of those conferences, coupled with a continued upsurge in interest in applied memory issues, caused the organizers to decide not to wait a decade until the next conference, and the third conference was held in 1994. Because the first two conferences were held on the east side of the Atlantic, it was decided to hold the next conference on the west side—at the University of Maryland University College. This volume presents the major papers of the conference that examined broad issues concerning basic and applied memory research.

Like the previous conferences, the 1994 conference consisted of many presentations on a wide variety of applied research areas. This conference also featured many invited presentations concerned especially with seeking a convergence between basic and applied memory research, as well as empirical research on practical aspects of memory. The participants of this conference included the leading researchers in the practical aspects of memory, as well as many of the leading basic researchers, from throughout the world.

The invited and submitted papers, as well as the posters, illustrated the relevance of applied issues and findings to many fundamental theoretical issues in memory and to how theoretical ideas might be translated into practical use. In all, over 300 papers and posters were presented (see conference program, edited by Conrad, 1994). As such, this conference was the largest conference on memory held to date, basic or applied or both.

COMMON, ESSENTIAL, AND UNIQUE PROCESSES

Although basic and applied researchers are equal members on the science team, they do not have the same job descriptions. Basic researchers investigate fundamental processes, and applied researchers apply the knowledge of those processes to particular problems. However, many people do not recognize that this account of the basic and applied collaboration is a gross oversimplification. Basic memory theory almost never can be applied simply by examining the variables addressed by a theory and generating predictions about these variables for the application of interest. Other variables, perhaps unique to the application, have to be accounted for as well.

Typically, basic theory addresses variables common to most or all applications. For example, encoding is a process that must occur in all applications involving memory. Many basic memory theories assume that encoding is affected by the attributes of a stimulus, such as its familiarity or salience (Underwood, 1983; Wickens, 1970). Many memory theories also assume that certain memory mechanisms may be employed to emphasize processing of visual, acoustic, or semantic attributes of the stimulus (Baddeley, 1986; Craik & Lockhart, 1972).

However, in order to apply basic memory theory, the constructs of a theory have to be supplemented with an understanding of certain variables that are unique to an application. Variables that are essential to one application may not be involved or may only partially be involved in another application. For example, some variables that are important to advertising may be different from those variables that are important to memory for instructions given on one's job. The encoding involved in advertising is often incidental and salient on culturally relevant dimensions that may be identified by unconscious processes. The encoding involved in memory for instructions given on one's job is typically intentional, salient on social dimensions pertinent to the work situation, and based on a process of identifying what aspects of the communication pertain to the job's requirements. The unconscious process that identifies culturally relevant dimensions is essential to memory for advertising but not essential to memory for instructions given to an employee at work. Alternatively, the process of identifying what aspects of a communication pertain to a person's job is essential to memory for instructions given on the job but not essential to memory for advertisements.

In addition to supplementing basic memory theory with applied theory about essential processes, maximally effective application often necessitates consideration of certain variables that have unique values for an application. For example, almost all advertising includes a common set of variables, such as the use of models, music, endorsements, logos, and so on. However, the actual values that these variables will take differs greatly, depending on the identified market. Background music used to add memorability to a Lexus commercial, for a Lexus audience, will differ greatly from the background music used to add memorability to a Geo Prizm commercial. The interaction between this variable (background music) and other variables in the advertising of the product (logo, model, etc.) may differ depending on the unique choice of values selected for each variable.

THE BENEFITS OF CONVERGENCE OF BASIC AND APPLIED RESEARCH

This conference called for convergence between basic and applied research because it did not appear to be productive for basic and applied researchers to debate which kind of researcher was most useful to society. Because a convergence between basic and applied research had not been attempted before in the memory field, effort was taken to identify the basis for such a convergence. We believe that the convergence of basic and applied research requires consideration of the variables of interest to basic and applied research: common processes, essential processes, and unique processes. Basic research stands to benefit from a knowledge of applied research in two ways. Theoretically, an awareness of research that attempts to apply basic findings can reveal that processes thought to be basic are actually ones that are essential to some but not all applications. Likewise, an awareness of many areas of applied research can reveal processes that are so common across applications that they can be regarded as basic, and hence worthy of study by basic researchers. Methodologically, an awareness of applied research can reveal variables with large effects on memory that basic researchers can control in their studies, rather than let them vary, and hence reduce noise in their data (Mullin, Herrmann, & Searleman, 1993).

Alternatively, applied research can benefit from an awareness of basic research. Theoretically, applied researchers—who are trained in basic research—can benefit by frequently brushing up on the developments of basic theory. An awareness of basic research can sensitize applied researchers to take account of basic processes of which they otherwise might be unaware, improving the efficacy of their interventions. Methodologically, the more that an applied research knows of basic theory, the more able he or she is to control or measure variables that otherwise might confound applied research.

Thus, successful application requires firm understanding of basic memory theory, supplemented with extensive knowledge about the unique issues present in each application. The research presented in this volume focuses on how basic and applied research inform one another. Several chapters focus on the major themes or issues that must be considered as we seek a convergence between basic and applied memory research (including the chapters by Kihlstrom; Morris & Gruneberg; Bahrick; and Gruneberg, Morris, Sykes, & Herrmann). Other chapters illustrate how a convergence might be achieved by presenting the authors' work and the work of others that combine basic and applied methods to study a particular applied problem (including the chapters by Johnson; Landauer & Dumais; Rabbitt & Yang; Jacoby, Jennings, & Hay; and Baddeley). Finally, 11 chapters review the basic and applied literature in many major areas of psychology in order to discover how basic and applied research can be integrated and collaborate more effectively.

Thus, this volume is the first text of its kind to present the fundamental knowledge of theory and method to students, teachers, and researchers on how to apply basic memory research. Each chapter presents information on a wide variety of topics that will be useful to researchers and teachers alike. Anyone who reads the entire text will possess a thorough grasp of the major themes pertaining to basic and applied collaboration, how programmatic basic and applied research can be conducted on a particular memory problem, and the basic/applied work in many of the major problem areas in the field of memory. We believe that this knowledge will equip the reader to go beyond what has been done previously and to achieve better understanding of the science of human memory.

After reading this volume, we encourage you to read *Volume II, Basic and Applied Memory: Research on Practical Aspects of Memory.* The second volume provides 33 chapters that will test your understanding of the fundamental concepts covered in the first volume and further enrich your understanding of practical memory research.

REFERENCES

Baddeley, A. D. (1986). *Working memory.* New York: Basic Books.

Conrad, F. (1994). *The Third Practical Aspects of Memory Conference.* College Park, Maryland: University of Maryland, University College.

Craik, F. I. M., & Lockhart, R. S. (1972). Levels of processing: A framework for memory research. *Journal of Verbal Learning and Verbal Behavior, 11,* 671–684.

Gruneberg, M. M., Morris, P. E., & Sykes, R. N. (Eds.). (1988). *Practical aspects of memory: Current research and issues.* Chichester, England: Wiley.

Mullin, P., Herrmann, D. J., & Searleman, A. (1993). Forgotten variables in memory research. *Memory. 15,* 43.

Underwood, B. J. (1983). *Attributes of memory.* Glenview, IL: Scott, Foresman.

Wickens, D. D. (1970). Encoding categories of words: An empirical approach to meaning. *Psychological Review. 77,* 1–15.

Memory Research: The Convergence of Theory and Practice

John F. Kihlstrom
Yale University

Concern for the practical aspects of memory can be traced back at least as far as Bartlett's (1932) critique of Ebbinghaus (1885). As we all know, Ebbinghaus had hoped to do for memory and the other higher mental processes what Fechner (1860) had done for sensation and the lower ones (frankly, I loathe these terms, because they perpetuate what I consider a false distinction, but they do provide a convenient shorthand). By his invention of the nonsense syllable, and his enforcement of what Bartlett (1932, p. 8) called "a perfectly automatic attitude of repetition in the learner," Ebbinghaus hoped to prove Kant wrong, and to show that the mind could in fact be studied with the tools of modern science. And to some extent, he was successful. The establishment of what amount to psychological laws of repetition and decay was quite an achievement for 1885.

But Bartlett was unhappy, to say the least, with Ebbinghaus' reliance on the nonsense syllable and the method of reproduction. Commenting on Ebbinghaus' attempt to strip his stimulus materials of any possible variation in meaning, he wrote: "Once more [the first time was with Fechner] the remedy is at least as bad as the disease. It means that the results of nonsense syllable experiments begin to be significant only when very special habits of reception and repetition have been set up. They may, then, throw some light upon the mode of establishment and the control of such habits, but it is at least doubtful whether they can help us see how, in general, memory reactions are determined" (1932, p. 3).

Then, after several pages of detailed criticisms of Ebbinghaus's method, Bartlett continued:

I have dealt at this length with the nonsense syllable experiments, partly because they are generally regarded as occupying a supremely important place in the development of exact method in psychology, and partly because the bulk of this book is concerned with problems of remembering studied throughout by methods which do not appear to approach those of the Ebbinghaus school in rigidity of control. But most of what has been said could be applied, with the necessary change of terminology and reference, to the bulk of experimental psychological work on perceiving, on imaging, on feeling, choosing, willing, judging, and thinking. In it all is the tendency to overstress the determining character of the stimulus or of the situatiori, the effort to secure isolation of response by ensuring simplicity of external control. (1932, p. 6)

Of course, we now know that to some extent Ebbinghaus got a bad rap (Gorfein & Hoffman, 1987; Roediger, 1985; Slamecka, 1985; Tulving, 1985). Ebbinghaus had a much broader vision of memory, and a fuller appreciation of the constraints he had imposed on his own research, than he is sometimes given credit for. Ebbinghaus' achievement was not the invention of the nonsense syllable or the method of savings or even the discovery of the law of repetition; his real achievement was to show that the mind could be the object of scientific investigation, and that the combination of controlled observation and quantitative analysis could reveal the laws of mental life.

And it is also clear that Bartlett's real target was not poor Ebbinghaus himself, but rather the doctrine of associationism under which he labored. Bartlett wasn't really unhappy with the nonsense syllable. After all, he realized, as indeed Ebbinghaus did as well, that despite what the experimenter did to strip his or her materials of meaning, the subject—who after all was continually engaged in "effort after meaning" (Bartlett, 1932, p. 20)—would just put it right back in again. No, Bartlett's real target was the prevailing emphasis on the overwhelming importance of stimulus determination. Thus we get Bartlett's own doctrine, by which he attempted to save the mental in psychology against the onslaught of associationism and its evil twin, behaviorism: "The psychologist, of all people, must not stand in awe of the stimulus" (1932, p. 3).

Bartlett and his allies lost that fight, as we all know, and psychology very quickly settled down to tracking the functional relations between stimulus and response (a task that is, to some extent, still carried out by our connectionist colleagues). Fechner's Law turned into Stevens's Law. Animal learning was taken to be a satisfactory model for the human case, and was studied with a focus on the effects of different schedules of reinforcement. The study of human memory was converted into the study of verbal learning, with a concentration on interference and transfer in the acquisition of paired associates. And what we now know as the *Journal of Memory & Language* (*JML*) began life as the *Journal of Verbal Learning & Verbal Behavior* (*JVLVB*).

THE LEGACY OF THE LABORATORY

Of course, things began to change in the 1960s. In fact, the signs of change were already evident in the 1950s. From my own point of view, the signal event in the cognitive revolution in psychology—at least so far as the study of memory was concerned—was the discovery of category clustering. Bousfield (1953)—who was also one of the first to rediscover the charms of the method of free recall—observed that subjects tended to recall list items in a different order than that in which they had been presented. This was bad enough for classical association theory, but then Bousfield showed that subjects clustered list items according to superordinate, conceptual relationships that could not be predicted by the associative links between items. Bousfield's subjects were certainly not in awe of the stimulus (and neither was Bousfield, who understood perfectly well the implications of his finding). Rather, they were imposing structure on the stimulus—a structure that resided in their minds, not the environment. Of course, Bousfield built categorical relations into his word lists, and a determined environmentalist could simply say that his subjects were picking up on that structure. It was left to Tulving (1962) to clinch the point, when—in a paper that we now know he had difficulty getting published—he showed that subjects would organize a list of words into some sort of narrative (or possibly image-based) structure even if the experimenter took great pains to make sure that there were no objective interitem relations built into the list. Subjects find structure when it's there, and they impose structure when it's not—precisely the "effort after meaning" of which Bartlett wrote so affectingly.

Of course, organization theory was soon swept aside by levels of processing theory (Craik & Lockhart, 1972), but that doesn't matter. Deep processing is still something that the subject does to the stimulus, and so it only bolsters the basic point I am trying to make. The sort of associationism that Bartlett criticized in the 1930s was pretty much dead by the time the cognitive revolution was consolidated in the mid-1970s.

The cognitive revolution in psychology had quite an impact on the way we thought about memory processes. By the time *JVLVB* turned into *JML*, in 1985, the new cognitive psychology of memory had uncovered seven (plus or minus two) broad principles that characterized what was going on inside people's heads as they remembered and forgot the things that had happened to them. Barnhardt and I recently summarized these principles as follows (for full documentation, see Kihlstrom & Barnhardt, 1993; for another exposition, see Kihlstrom, 1994a; for another set of principles entirely, see Crowder, 1993):

- The Elaboration Principle: The memorability of an event increases when that event is related to preexisting knowledge at the time of encoding.

- The Organization Principle: The memorability of an event increases when that event is related to other events at the time of encoding.
- The Time-Dependency Principle: The memorability of an event declines as the length of the storage interval (i.e., between encoding and retrieval) increases.
- The Cue-Dependency Principle: The memorability of an event increases with the amount of information supplied by the retrieval cue.
- The Encoding Specificity Principle: The memorability of a event increases when the information processed at the time of retrieval was also processed at the time of encoding (or, alternatively, when the information-processing activities performed at the time of encoding are repeated at the time of retrieval).
- The Schematic Processing Principle: The memorability of an event increases when that event is relevant to expectations and beliefs about the event.
- The Reconstruction Principle: The memory of an event reflects a blend of information retrieved from specific traces encoded at the time of that event with knowledge, expectations, and beliefs derived from other sources.

I happen to think that this is not bad for 30 years' work. Only two of these principles, time-dependency and reconstruction, were well understood in Bartlett's time—and, frankly, reconstruction was not that well documented, nor for that matter accepted by anyone other than Bartlett himself. And only one of those principles that emerged subsequently, cue-dependency, even comes close to standing in awe of the stimulus. These principles reflect a thoroughgoing cognitive psychology of memory, because they move us away from stimulus structure and stimulus conditions to mental structure and processing activities—especially when you add in the details. So, for example, Hastie (1980, 1981) produced a careful analysis of the effects of mental schemata on memory, showing—quite surprisingly, I think—that events that were *in*congruent with prevailing schemata were better remembered than those that were *con*gruent. Schema-congruent events are better remembered than schema-irrelevant ones, to be sure, but the U-shaped function relating schema-relevance and memorability was a real surprise. It was definitely not what Bartlett had in mind.

Later, Hastie was able to show that the superiority of incongruent events stemmed from the subjects' attempts to explain why they occurred. And it appears that the superiority of schema-congruent events stems from the fact that the schema can serve as an internally generated retrieval cue. In the final analysis, then, the memorability of schema-incongruent events seems to reflect the elaboration principle, whereas the memorability of schema-congruent items seems to reflect the cue-dependency principle. Thus maybe there are fewer than seven principles after all. On the other hand, we might want to add other principles to characterize how events are represented in memory; thus seven plus or minus two seems like a satisfactory estimate.

Still, just as there had been signs of dissatisfaction with Ebbinghaus, there were signs of dissatisfaction with the new cognitive psychology of memory as well. Reviewing *Über das Gedächtnis* for the journal *Science*, William James was more impressed with Ebbinghaus' enterprise than with his accomplishments, writing that his laws of memory "add nothing to our gross experience of the matter" (James, 1885, p. 299). Similarly, in his keynote address at the first conference on the Practical Aspects of Memory, Neisser (1978, p. 4) offered what might be thought of as an eighth principle of memory:

- The Irrelevance Principle: If X is an interesting or socially significant aspect of memory, then psychologists have hardly ever studied X.

And then, just to rub it in, he elaborated:

You need only tell any friend, not himself a psychologist, that you study memory. Given even a little encouragement, your friend will describe all kinds of interesting phenomena: the limitations of his memory for early childhood, his inability to remember appointments, his aunt who could recite poems from memory by the hour, the regrettable recent decline in his ability to recall people's names, how well he could find his way around his home town after a thirty years' absence, the differences between his memory and someone else's. Our research, of course, has virtually nothing to say about any of these topics. (1978, p. 5)

I have to confess that although some of this critique struck a responsive chord with me, I always thought it was too extreme. For example, I have frequently taught the phenomena of infantile and childhood amnesia in my introductory psychology classes, and I have happy memories of my students wrestling with the question of whether in fact it occurred, and if so how it might be explained. They would see immediately that we need to know whether the difficulty which a 25-year-old has in remembering events from birth to age 5 is any different, quantitatively or qualitatively, from the difficulty which a 45-year-old might have in remembering events from age 20 to 25. Assuming that this is the case, I would then remind them of the principles of memory function—the sorts of principles I outlined earlier—and they would generate plausible explanations of the amnesia in terms of them. So, for example, maybe children lack the cognitive capacity, or the knowledge base, to encode retrievable memories. Or maybe they repress them, interfering with their retrieval after they're encoded. Or maybe there is an encoding-specificity effect stemming from developmental shifts in Piagetian stage. Or maybe, as Neisser (1962) himself proposed, the world of the child doesn't supply the sort of information needed to encode memories of specific episodes. My students, then, clearly saw three things: (a) that infantile and childhood amnesia were, at least in principle, explicable in terms of broad precepts developed in the laboratory; (b) that it was possible, again at least in principle, to perform formal experiments that would determine which of these precepts actually explained the effect; and (c) that it was too damn hard to conduct the necessary experiments. But at least they could see the relevance of the theoretical principles which we discussed to practical problems of everyday memory, and they got a good exercise in testing a theoretical hypothesis.

Actually, of course, they—we—were wrong on that last point. Some of the potential explanations can be ruled out by the simple expedient of asking young children what they remember of their short lives so far. If a four-year-old can tell you what he or she did at age three, but an eight-year-old cannot, that rules out some potential explanations and supports others. Such studies are now available—for example, one by Fivush and Hammond (1990)—and they tell us clearly that preschool children are, in fact, able to encode and retain their experiences, at least under certain circumstances. And it takes nothing from the investigators to say that the studies weren't *that* hard to do, after all. All that had to happen, and it turned out to be a pretty big thing, was for someone to think the subject was important enough to devote time and effort to studying it. That it took us so long borders on the criminal, and on this point we can certainly agree with Neisser.

Moreover, the detailed study of the processes underlying young children's autobiographical memory may well tell us something theoretically interesting about memory that we did not know before. For example, pioneering studies by Nelson (1993) and Hudson (1990) have suggested that autobiographical memory develops as children and their caretakers tell each other stories about the past. Findings such as these portend the emergence of yet another theoretical principle:

- The Interpersonal Principle: Remembering is an act of communication as well as of information retrieval, and so our memories of the past are shaped by the interpersonal context in which they are encoded and retrieved.

The Interpersonal Principle is important, because it suggests that memory cannot be studied with the conceptual and methodological apparatus of cognitive psychology alone. Memory is not just a matter of the acquisition, storage, and retrieval of information. When we remember our past we are telling stories about ourselves, to ourselves and to others. These stories serve personal and social purposes, and so individual and interpersonal factors become important in determining what is remembered and what is forgotten. In his wonderful textbook of social psychology, Brown (1965) made a similar point about language: It is not just a tool of thought, it is also a means of communication. Just as linguists and psycholinguists have to pay attention to the pragmatics of language, as well as to phonology, syntax, and semantics, so students of memory must pay attention to the pragmatics of remembering and forgetting, as well as to questions about the representation and processing of knowledge.

THE SOCIAL ECOLOGY OF MEMORY

Hence memory isn't just for cognitive psychologists anymore; it's also for personality and social psychologists. Bartlett (1932) knew this, too, which is why the subtitle of *Remembering* is *A Study in Experimental and Social Psychology*. As he put it then (p. 296):

> Social organization gives a persistent framework into which all detailed recall must fit, and it very powerfully influences both the manner and the matter of recall.

Neisser (1988) made a similar point in his address to the second conference on Practical Aspects of Memory. In his view, memory emerges out of social interaction, but it also supports social interaction. Neisser lamented that so little research reported at that second conference considered memory as a social activity, and he hoped to see a lot of it at the third conference, at which we are currently gathered. Based on the presentations at this third conference, I am afraid that this particular gap is still with us. It's too bad that this is the case, because the social function of memory opens up lots of possibilities of doing interesting collaborative work.

Consider, for example, the idea that memories are not just representations of prior actions and experiences, but rather *beliefs* about our past. When we tell stories about our past, we are telling about what we believe happened, partly in order to make sense of what we are now thinking, feeling, wanting, and doing. One of the functions of remembering the past is to explain the present (Ross, 1989). This is dramatically exemplified in the virtual epidemic we are currently experiencing of exhumed memories of childhood incest, sexual abuse, and other trauma. These days, exhumed memory is a common vehicle for Neisser's (1978) nightmare scenario: If we should let slip at a cocktail party that we study memory, we are likely to be surrounded and asked to explain how massive repression, and subsequent exhumation, could occur.

And Neisser's (1978) outcome is played out: We have virtually nothing to say about this topic, for the simple reason that exhumed memory seems to violate everything we know about how memory operates (for reviews, see Kihlstrom, 1994b, 1995a, 1995b; Lindsay & Read, 1994).

Actually, in my view, this is exactly what we *should* say about this topic, and not at all defensively, putting the onus on advocates of exhumed memory to produce methodologically acceptable research to support their claims. The whole point of developing a generalized theory of memory is to have a basis for constructing informed views of phenomena that have not them-selves been subject to detailed examination. A good theory is a wonderful thing to have until the experimenter comes.

Now, it could well be that a systematic study of exhumed memories will tell us something that we did not know before about how memory operates. That is certainly the hypothesis of those who are advocates for the accuracy of exhumed memories as representations of the past. These individuals, mostly clinical practitioners (some of whom have no advanced training in psychology) tell us that principles derived from laboratory studies of memory are wholly irrelevant to the case; that emotional trauma changes the prin-ciples of memory function. As evidence, they offer uncontrolled clinical anecdotes and uncorroborated self-reports from their patients. But there may be another reason why memory theory has little to say about exhumed memory: The exhumed memories may not be memories at all.

Instead, many (if not most) of the memories exhumed in the clinic appear to be *beliefs* about the past, formed as a result of persuasive communication (by therapists, e.g., or from sources in the media), and firmly held, in the absence of any actual recollection, by virtue of the power of the memories to explain the person's present circumstances—and, I believe, their value as a means of social control. Thus, for example, there is a widespread belief that anorexia, bulimia, and other eating disorders commonly occur as a result of incest or child sexual abuse—a proposition for which the evidence is in fact remarkably thin. Accordingly, individuals suffering such disorders may come to be persuaded that they were, in fact, sexually abused as children and proceed to construct memories—mental representations of the past—around such a belief. The point is that this interesting, and socially significant, phenomenon of memory cannot be explained solely in terms of principles of memory function. The only way such "memories" can be explained is in terms of principles of persuasive communication, identity formation, causal attribu-tion, and impression management; in other words, in terms of principles of personality and social psychology, not cognitive psychology. Social psycholo-gists are experts in how beliefs arise; how they are accepted; how they are transmitted, strengthened, and weakened; and what happens when they are challenged. Personality psychologists are experts in matters of identity and self-concept. If we are to make sense of the epidemic of exhumed memories, then, cognitive psychologists are going to have to make common cause with personality and social psychologists. This is because in the real world outside the laboratory, remembering is an act of communication, of self-presentation, and of social influence at least as much as it is the retrieval of a representation of the past (Kihlstrom, 1981; Singer & Salovey, 1993).

And we will want to go outside of psychology, to other social sciences such as history and sociology. Consider the question, initially raised by Halbwachs (1925/1980), of whether groups as well as individuals could be said to have memories. Bartlett (1932) doubted it, but he did believe that groups created stories about themselves just as individuals do, and for the same reasons: to conserve and reproduce their history, and to define their nature. Sometime later, of course, Orwell's futuristic novel *1984* explored the social and political control of memory in the service of conformity and stability. But it is not only political elites who convert memory into myth. Lifton (1967), in his moving study of the victims of the bombing of Hiroshima, noted that the people he interviewed tended to have very similar accounts of the event, regardless of their distance from the epicenter at the time of the explosion. Something similar might have happened in returning prisoners of war and others who fought in Vietnam.

Our colleagues in academic departments of history are very interested in collective memory and other aspects of social memory, and a few years ago the *Journal of American History* devoted a special issue (Vol. 75, No. 4, March 1989) to the problems of memory and history, which are particularly acute for those historians who rely on oral materials. The issue included an analysis by McGlone (1989) of how John Brown's children reshaped their memories of their father to create a family identity in the decades following the Harper's Ferry raid. In addition, Bodnar (1989) grappled with the differences between workers' and managers' stories of life at the Studebaker plant in South Bend, Indiana. And Thelen (1989b) provided an analysis of the memories of those involved in the discovery of the Watergate tapes, showing how each participant shaped and reshaped his story over time depending on the circumstances of the moment, while believing that his memory was accurate and unchanging. As Thelen (1989a) noted in his editorial introduction to the Special Issue:

> The fresh possibilities in the historical study of memory begin with two starting points, deeply embedded in historians' narrative traditions. . . . The first is that memory, private and individual as much as collective and cultural, is constructed, not reproduced. The second is that this construction is not made in isolation but in conversations with others that occur in the contexts of community, broader politics, and social dynamics. (p. 1119)

Collective memory is something that we psychologists haven't begun to study. But when we get around to it, I am sure that we will discover that a purely psychological analysis—that is, an analysis solely in terms of the individual's mental states—will be completely inadequate. In order to understand collective memory, we are going to have to understand how collectivities operate; and for that, we are going to have to consult our colleagues in sociology, anthropology, history, and political science.

THE REAL WORLD AND THE LABORATORY

In his address to the second Practical Aspects of Memory conference, Neisser (1988) repealed the Irrelevance Principle that he had announced almost a decade earlier. In contrast to the earlier situation, there were now (in his view) quite a few people engaged in studying interesting or socially important phenomena of memory. Based on the talks given at the present conference, one would have to say that the practical aspects of memory constitute a growth industry within psychology.

At the same time, there have arisen the inevitable critiques, of which the most prominent was that of Banaji and Crowder (1989, 1991). These authors agreed that realism is preferable to artificiality, so long as methodological rigor can be preserved. But they also argued that ecological validity neither guaranteed generalizability nor substituted for methodological soundness. They expressed doubt that studies of memory in the real world would provide information that was unavailable in the laboratory, and cautioned investigators against abandoning the precision of the laboratory in favor of mundane realism.

Banaji and Crowder's article unleashed a firestorm of protest, but frankly I think that their fundamental point is incontrovertible: It simply is not possible to learn anything about memory, *qua* memory, unless there is careful control, experimental or statistical, over the conditions of encoding, storage, and retrieval. Let me illustrate with some work from my own laboratory.

My first illustration comes from a study on autobiographical memory in a case of multiple personality disorder (Schacter, Kihlstrom, Canter Kihlstrom, & Berren, 1989). The patient, whom we called I.C., was a 24-year-old college-educated woman with a world-class talent and at least five alter egos, one of whom was a suicidal adolescent. A prominent characteristic of the dominant personality (by which I mean the one that had been known for the longest period of time to the most people) was a very dense amnesia covering the first 10 to 14 years of her life. We were able to confirm this amnesia using the Crovitz-Robinson technique, in which words are used to cue the retrieval of autobiographical memories (Crovitz & Schiffman, 1974; Robinson, 1976). In an unconstrained version of the technique, she showed a strong recency effect, with very few memories from before age 14. And when she was constrained to report memories only from the first 12 years of life, she displayed a huge number of response failures, and produced nothing at all from before age 10. This was all very interesting, and confirmed her therapist's informal assessment of memory, but without control subjects we had no idea how to interpret this effect. It turned out that control subjects, matched to I.C. for sex, age, and education, had plenty of memories from before age 14 in the unconstrained condition, and few response failures and plenty of memories from before age 10, in the constrained condition. So there really was an amnesia there after all.

Still, that was as far as we could go. Without knowledge of encoding conditions, we were left puzzled as to what it all meant. There was some evidence of childhood sexual abuse in this case, and it is possible—if one believed in such things—that I.C.'s amnesia resulted from a massive repression (or dissociation) of childhood experience from conscious recollection. Another, more intriguing possibility, was that I.C., whom we all considered to be the original personality, might actually be an alter ego who emerged when the patient was about 10 years old chronologically. The lack of memories from before age 10 would be consistent with this hypothesis, and the paucity of memories from ages 10 to 14 might reflect normal infantile and childhood amnesia affecting this newly emerging personality. It's an intriguing idea, fun to play with. But without detailed knowledge of what this person was like at that time, we'll never be able to make sense of her pattern of results. So, in the final analysis, both the practical and the theoretical significance of the case was limited by the constraints on our ability to control the conditions of encoding and storage as well as the conditions of retrieval.

Another example comes from work in my laboratory on the phenomenon of posthypnotic amnesia—the inability of highly hypnotizable subjects to remember, after hypnosis, the events and experiences that transpired while they were hypnotized (Kihlstrom, 1985). Posthypnotic amnesia occurs only if it is specifically suggested to the subject, and it can be reversed by a prearranged cue, without reinduction of hypnosis, so it is not an instance of state-dependent memory. The fact that it can be reversed at all indicates that, in contrast to the organic amnesic syndrome, whatever is going on operates at the retrieval stage of memory processing.

In the present context, posthypnotic amnesia is especially interesting because it is a phenomenon of memory that occurs naturally in the laboratory. By using standardized hypnotic procedures, in which subjects receive an induction of hypnosis accompanied by a series of test suggestions, all administered verbatim according to a prepared script and evaluated according to objective behavioral criteria, we know exactly what was said to the subjects, and how they responded, at every moment of the procedure. Thus a subject's memory for his or her experience of hypnosis might be a particularly lifelike laboratory model for studying autobiographical memory. Posthypnotic amnesia is also something that is not easy to understand in terms of the general principles I outlined earlier, so it promises to tell us something new about how memory works.

In one line of research, Evans and I were interested in the organization of memory for hypnotic experiences (Evans & Kihlstrom, 1973; Kihlstrom & Evans, 1979). I had fallen under the spell of organization theory in memory, and Evans and I had the idea that suggestions for posthypnotic amnesia might somehow disrupt the organization of retrieval processes, and thus render the memories temporarily inaccessible. Specifically, we thought that temporal sequencing was the natural form of organization for autobiographical memories, and that it was particularly vulnerable to the amnesic process. We tested this hypothesis by correlating the order in which hypnotic subjects recalled their experiences with the order in which those experiences had actually occurred during the standardized procedure, to get a measure of temporal sequencing in recall. There was a little trick in the study: We could not use our best subjects because they showed a dense amnesia, and one cannot study the organization of recall in subjects who do not remember anything. So we threw these subjects out of the experiment, and looked at temporal sequencing in the rest, testing the hypothesis that the recall of highly hypnotizable subjects, who are at least partially responsive to hypnotic suggestions, will be less organized than that of insusceptible subjects, who do not respond to them at all.

In fact, Evans and I got the temporal disorganization effect in several different studies. When the amnesia suggestion was in effect, there was less temporal sequencing in hypnotizable than insusceptible subjects. And when we eliminated the amnesia suggestion, hypnotizable and insusceptible subjects showed equal levels of temporal sequencing. Still, there were some problems. Some colleagues were highly critical of the experiments, precisely because they lacked certain experimental controls: There was no assessment of initial acquisition, for example; furthermore, the memory task was somewhat ambiguous, so it may have been unclear to the subjects what they were supposed to remember. Because of our reliance on a standardized procedure, which was by definition ecologically valid but had not been devised with this experiment in mind, we were unable to examine the fate of temporal sequencing after the amnesia suggestion was canceled. And finally, temporal sequencing was the only form of organization that we could study in the context of the standardized scales, so we couldn't test our hypothesis about temporal sequencing against alternative hypotheses concerning other forms of organization.

None of these issues could be settled within the (relatively) lifelike context of the standardized scales, and so we were thrown back on our old friend the verbal learning experiment, in which words serve as analogues of episodes of experience. Wilson and I (Kihlstrom & Wilson, 1984; Wilson & Kihlstrom, 1986) hypnotized subjects and then asked them to memorize a list of words. In this experiment we employed an incremental learning technique that virtually guaranteed that subjects would organize list items in temporal order. In another experiment, we used standard free recall learning but with a categorized word list, virtually guaranteeing that category clustering would occur. And in a third experiment, we again used free recall but with a list of unrelated words, thus forcing subjects to impose a subjective organization on the list. The results of the three experiments, taken together, nicely supported our initial hypotheses: When subjects organize experience temporally, temporal sequencing is disrupted during posthypnotic amnesia and restored when it is canceled. However, when subjects organize their experiences by conceptual or other meaning-based relationships, this organization is not disrupted during posthypnotic amnesia (for a fuller discussion, see Kihlstrom & Wilson, 1988). The amnesic process has a particular impact on the temporal relationships among memories—an important clue, I think, to the nature of the amnesic process itself.

The point is that in both cases, the most lifelike settings were not necessarily the most appropriate for addressing questions of theoretical interest. But don't misunderstand me. I'm not saying that the lifelike studies shouldn't have been done. They should have been. The point is that neither traditional nor ecological approaches to the study of memory have any privileged access to virtue. Each has its assets, and each has its liabilities (Winograd, 1988). When we first learned about I.C., we wanted to do a series of fairly traditional experiments, looking for evidence of "ego-state"-dependent memory, dissociations between explicit and implicit memory, and the like. But we couldn't get experimental control over her various personalities, and so we had to settle for a study of autobiographical memory in one of her personalities. The findings were interesting, but our inability to get experimental control over the situation prevented us from going very far. In the case of posthypnotic amnesia, I am certain that if we had begun with a traditional, verbal-learning study we would probably have looked at category clustering first, failed to find an effect, turned our attention somewhere else, and missed entirely the effects on temporal sequencing. By starting out in the naturalistic setting of the standardized scales, we discovered something interesting that we otherwise might have missed. But we were only *sure* it was interesting after we had translated the naturalistic setting into a laboratory analogue where we could get tighter control over potentially confounding variables.

THE LESSONS OF EYEWITNESS MEMORY

I think this is a common scenario. For example, it is replayed constantly in the study of eyewitness memory, one of the undisputed success stories of practical memory.

Consider first the question of memory for faces, as exemplified by the host of very interesting studies of accuracy versus confidence; biases in lineups, showups, and photospreads; cross-race accuracy in identification; and the like (for a review, see Ellis & Shepherd, 1992). The practical problem is this: Can witnesses and victims of crimes reliably identify perpetrators, live or depicted, sometime after a crime has occurred? Or, more prosaically perhaps, how well do people attach names to faces at cocktail parties? Up until 20 years ago, there wasn't much literature on this topic. There was, of course, Shepard's (1967) classic work on picture recognition, showing that memory for visual (as opposed to verbal) materials persists for a pretty long time. And, as far as putting names and faces together goes, there was that 50-year tradition of paired-associate learning. Memory for picture postcards (and for postcard-nonsense syllable paired associates) might have been taken as a satisfactory laboratory analogue of memory for faces, but nobody thought so, and for good reason: Faces are special. They are the primordial social stimulus. Babies seem to be built to find them and look at them. Studies of prosopagnosics indicate that there may be particular brain structures specialized for processing them. Thus we should accept no substitutes: We can only study memory for faces by studying memory for faces.

And in doing so, investigators imposed rigorous experimental controls on the practical question, controls that are the equal of anything that was ever done to a sophomore in a laboratory cubicle. The best studies of face memory conducted in lifelike, ecologically valid settings leave nothing to chance, they are completely controlled from beginning to end. They are, to all intents and purposes, indistinguishable from traditional laboratory experiments, except perhaps that the subjects are clerks at the local convenience store instead of volunteers from a subject pool.

Moreover, investigators turned quite quickly from purely practical questions, such as those that might be raised by judges and attorneys, to theoretical questions that are as esoteric as anything dreamed up by the inventors of ACT* or PDP. Consider, for example, the information-processing model of face recognition, proposed by Bruce and Young (1986) on the basis of both laboratory and neuropsychological studies. This is an interesting theoretical model, but I dare say that there's nothing very *practical* about it. And since this model was proposed, it has generated dozens of traditional laboratory experiments intended to test and revise its details.

Another success story from the annals of eyewitness memory research is the postevent misinformation effect documented by Loftus and her colleagues. In a study that has become a modern classic, Loftus and Palmer (1974) showed subjects a film of an automobile accident, and then asked them questions about details. By means of leading questions, the investigators were able to manipulate subjects' estimates of how fast the cars were moving. But later on, those subjects in the "fast" condition proved more likely to report broken glass than did those in the "slow" condition—when, in fact, no broken glass had been shown in the film at all. Hence subjects' memories were distorted by events occurring over the retention interval. Loftus and others have published lots of other demonstrations of the misinformation effect, usually using very lifelike stimulus materials, and nobody seems to doubt it.

Of course, there has arisen quite a controversy about the precise nature of the misinformation effect. Originally, Loftus (e.g, Loftus & Loftus, 1980) had proposed that the social construction might overwrite the original based on personal experience, which is just lost. McCloskey and Zaragoza (1985), on the other hand, concluded that the misinformation did not displace the original memory, but rather biased the memory reports of subjects who had forgotten the original for other reasons. Tversky and Tuchin (1989) attempted a compromise position, in which the two memories existed side by side, the latter interfering with retrieval of the former. So did Metcalfe (1990), who argued that the two memories are blended into a single representation that permits either one to be retrieved, depending on the circumstances. Zaragoza and Koshmider (1989) and Lindsay and Johnson (1989) suggested that the two memories might become confused because people forget their sources.

The point is that Loftus began with a very practical question that was, in fact, settled quite quickly. Yes, eyewitness memory can be distorted by leading questions. I think that everyone accepts this conclusion. Of course, the reason that everyone accepts this conclusion is that Loftus constructed her experiments very carefully, according to the traditional canons of experimental design. Her experiments were compelling because all the proper controls were in place. Put another way, she imposed laboratory conditions on a lifelike setting. Then the field turned its attention to strictly theoretical propositions about how this distortion occurred. That's what the Loftus–McCloskey debate is all about. And in the process of addressing these purely theoretical questions, the field turned to laboratory experiments of a quite traditional sort. Experiments in the McCloskey–Zaragoza vein, for example, are formally indistinguishable from the studies of modified and modified-modified free recall by which Postman and Underwood explored interference processes in paired-associate verbal learning. What goes around, comes around, in psychology as in the rest of life.

THE PARALLEL, DISTRIBUTED STUDY OF MEMORY

In some sense, the debate among memory researchers between theory and practice, and between the laboratory and the real world, is reminiscent of the "crisis" that pervaded social psychology two decades ago (e.g., Elms, 1975; Gergen, 1973; Smith, 1972). The causes of this crisis were complex, including such factors as mundane as the discovery of demand characteristics and experimenter bias and as monumental as racism and the Vietnam War, but there too the debate revolved around questions of relevance, the comparative assets and liabilities of laboratory and field research, the overreliance on college students as subjects, the question of experimentation versus description, and whether it was possible to produce a general account of social behavior that would transcend time and place (for an overview, see Jones, 1985). McGuire (1973, p. 447) captured the essence of the debate as follows:

> During the past several years both the creative and the critical aspects of [experimental social psychology] have come under increasing attack. The creative aspect of formulating hypotheses for their relevance to theory has been denounced as a mandarin activity out of phase with the needs of our time. It has been argued that hypotheses should be formulated for their relevance to social problems rather than for their relevance to theoretical issues. . . .
>
> At least as strong and successful an assault has been launched on . . . the notion that hypotheses should be tested by manipulational laboratory experiments. . . .
>
> In place of the laboratory manipulational experiment, there has been a definite trend toward experiments conducted in field settings and toward correlational analysis of data from naturalistic situations. . . .

McGuire (1969, 1973), for his part, foresaw a future paradigm for social psychology that would involve a greater balance between laboratory and field research, but that would still be oriented toward general theory rather than practical action. As he put it (1969, p. 22):

> What I am urging and predicting is that we correct the current, almost exclusive emphasis on this method by continuing the present level of laboratory manipulational work, but in addition upgrade in quantity and quality the use of natural field settings to test our basic, theoretically derived hypotheses. I am not suggesting that we abandon the physical science paradigm and stop acting like physicists. I am urging that occasionally we also start acting a bit like astronomers.

If, as Lewin argued, there is nothing so practical as a good theory, there is also nothing as good for theory as a little practicality.

One can say that as in the psychology of interpersonal relations, so in the psychology of memory. The practical memory movement, which began a decade and a half ago as a breakaway faction, or perhaps an insurgent force, has contributed much to our knowledge of memory. Investigators who were once exclusively concerned with theoretical issues and satisfied with studies of college students are now more aware of, and more concerned with, problems of practical application than they were before. And the study of memory has been opened up to new settings and new populations, compared to the norms of a decade or two ago. The practical memory movement can't claim exclusive responsibility for these changes—cognitive neuroscience, itself pretty esoteric and, except in the hands of a few investigators, not very practical, has also played an important role in these developments, as has personality and social psychology. But it can claim its fair share, and there is plenty of honor to go around.

At the same time, I sense that the breakaway or insurgent aspects of the movement are diminishing in intensity. There is real convergence occurring, in my view, and it is the result of movement on both sides. Traditional laboratory researchers are more open than they were before to what can be learned from real-life settings, special populations, and practical questions. Practical memory researchers are more interested in observing the methodological niceties, and in connecting their phenomena to more general theories, than they ever have been before.

This has got to be good for the field, in both the short and long run, because, frankly, I don't think we're headed for a situation where we'll have one set of theoretical principles to explain memory performance in the laboratory and another set to explain memory performance in the field—or, worse yet, a sort of situated memory theory in which there is a different set of principles for every different situation in which remembering occurs. Rather, I suspect that we are heading toward a situation characterized by the parallel, distributed study of memory. That is to say, theoretical and practical research, conducted in the laboratory and the real world, will proceed forward in parallel. But where once these goals and venues might have appealed to different constituencies, I think that now individual investigators will be more interested in distributing their attention more evenly across the two streams, working now on some theoretical issue, now on some practical one, now in the laboratory, now in the world outside. The result will be, I think, not an eschewing of theory but rather a real contribution of practical studies to theoretical principles.

And if I had to make a bet, it would be that the new principles would look like the Interpersonal Principle. In my view, the greatest achievement of practical memory is to remind us that the individual's mind operates in a social and cultural context. Social factors do not alter the basic principles of memory function, but as Bartlett (1932) suggested, they do affect how those principles will be instantiated. Practical memory is memory in action, and social psychologists are experts in studying mind in action. And, so, I think the greatest theoretical contribution of practical memory will come from linking cognitive psychology to personality and social psychology, and linking psychology to the other social sciences, including those concerned with the empirical evaluation of public policy (because, e.g., the cognitive and social psychology of eyewitness memory has obvious bearing on the rules of evidence pertaining to memory and testimony). When we come together for the Fourth Conference, some years hence, I hope that we will see some of those principles emerging.

ACKNOWLEDGMENTS

Closing Lecture presented at the Third Practical Aspects of Memory Conference, University of Maryland, College Park, August 5, 1994. The point of view represented here is based on research supported by Grant #MH-35856 from the National Institute of Mental Health. I thank Lawrence Couture, Elizabeth Glisky, Martha Glisky, Tim Hubbard, Katherine Insell, Shelagh Mulvaney, Victor Shames, Susan Valdiserri, and Michael Valdiserri for their comments. In this regard, special thanks are due to Chris Herzog for his detailed comments on an earlier draft.

REFERENCES

Banaji, M. R., & Crowder, R. G. (1989). The bankruptcy of everyday memory. *American Psychologist, 44*, 1185–1193.

Banaji, M. R., & Crowder, R. G. (1991). Some everyday thoughts on ecologically valid methods. *American Psychologist, 46*, 78–79.

Bartlett, F. C. (1932). *Remembering: A study in experimental and social psychology.* Cambridge, England: Cambridge University Press.

Bodnar, J. (1989). Power and memory in oral history: Workers and managers at Studebaker. *Journal of American History, 75*, 1201–1221.

Bousfield, A. K. (1953). The occurrence of clusterings in the recall of randomly arranged associates. *Journal of General Psychology, 49*, 229–240.

Brown, R. (1965). *Social psychology.* New York: Free Press.

Bruce, V., & Young, A. (1986). Understanding face recognition. *British Journal of Psychology, 77*, 305–327.

Craik, F. I. M., & Lockhart, R. S. (1972). Levels of processing: A framework for memory research. *Journal of Verbal Learning & Verbal Behavior, 11*, 671–684.

Crovitz, H. F., & Schiffman, H. (1974). Frequency of episodic memories as a function of their age. *Bulletin of the Psychonomic Society, 4*, 517–518.

Crowder, R. G. (1993). Systems and principles in memory theory: Another critique of pure memory. In A. F. Collins, S. E. Gathercole, M. A. Conway, & P. E. Morris (Eds.), *Theories of memory* (pp. 139–161). Hove, England: Lawrence Erlbaum Associates.

Ebbinghaus, H. (1885). *Memory: A contribution to experimental psychology.* Leipzig: Duncker & Humblot.

Ellis, H. D., & Shepherd, J. W. (1992). Face memory: Theory and practice. In M. M. Gruneberg & P. Morris (Eds.), *Aspects of memory: Vol. 1. The practical aspects* (pp. 51–85). London: Routledge.

Elms, A. C. (1975). The crisis of confidence in social psychology. *American Psychologist, 30*, 967–976.

Evans, F. J., & Kihlstrom, J. F. (1973). Posthypnotic amnesia as disrupted retrieval. *Journal of Abnormal Psychology, 82*, 317–323.

Fechner, G. T. (1860). *Elements of psychophysics* (2 vols.). Leipzig, Germany: Breithaus & Hartel.

Fivush, R., & Hammond, N. R. (1990). Autobiographical memory across the preschool years: Toward reconceptualizing childhood amnesia. In R. Fivush & J. A. Hudson (Eds.), *Knowing and remembering in young children* (pp. 223–248). New York: Cambridge University Press.

Gergen, K. J. (1973). Social psychology as history. *Journal of Personality and Social Psychology, 26,* 309–320.

Gorfein, D. S., & Hoffman, R. R. (Eds.). (1987). *Memory and learning: The Ebbinghaus Centennial Conference.* Hillsdale, NJ: Lawrence Erlbaum Associates.

Halbwachs, M. (1980). *The collective memory.* New York: Harper & Row. (Original work published 1925)

Hastie, R. (1980). Memory for behavioral information that confirms or contradicts a personality impression. In R. Hastie, T. M. Ostrom, E. B. Ebbesen, R. S. Wyer, D. L. Hamilton, & D. E. Carlston (Eds.), *Person memory: The cognitive basis of social perception* (pp. 155–178). Hillsdale, NJ: Lawrence Erlbaum Associates.

Hastie, R. (1981). Schematic principles in human memory. In E. T. Higgins, C. P. Herman, & M. P. Zanna (Eds.), *Social cognition* (pp. 39–88). Hillsdale, NJ: Lawrence Erlbaum Associates.

Hudson, J. A. (1990). The emergence of autobiographical memory in mother–child conversation. In R. Fivush & J. A. Hudson (Eds.), *Knowing and remembering in young children* (pp. 166–196). New York: Cambridge University Press.

James, W. (1885). Experiments in memory. *Science, 6,* 198–199.

Jones, E. E. (1985). Major developments in social psychology during the past five decades. In G. Lindzey & E. Aronson (Eds.), *Handbook of social psychology,* 3rd ed. (Vol. 1, pp. 47–107). New York: Random House.

Kihlstrom, J. F. (1981). On personality and memory. In N. Cantor & J. F. Kihlstrom (Eds.), *Personality, cognition, and social interaction.* Hillsdale, NJ: Lawrence Erlbaum Associates.

Kihlstrom, J. F. (1985). Posthypnotic amnesia and the dissociation of memory. In G. H. Bower (Ed.), *The psychology of learning and motivation* (Vol. 19, pp. 131–178). New York: Academic Press.

Kihlstrom, J. F. (1994a). Delayed recall and the principles of memory. *International Journal of Clinical & Experimental Hypnosis, 42,* 337–345.

Kihlstrom, J. F. (1994b). Exhumed memory. In S. J. Lynn & N. P. Spanos (Eds.), *Truth in memory.* New York: Guilford.

Kihlstrom, J. F. (1995a). Suffering from reminiscences: Exhumed memory, implicit memory, and the return of the repressed. In M. A. Conway (Ed.), *Recovered memories and false memories.* Oxford: Oxford University Press.

Kihlstrom, J. F. (1995b). The trauma-memory argument. *Consciousness & Cognition, 4,* 63–67.

Kihlstrom, J. F., & Barnhardt, T. M. (1993). The self-regulation of memory, for better and for worse, with and without hypnosis. In D. M. Wegner & J. W. Pennebaker (Eds.), *Handbook of mental control* (pp. 88–125). Englewood Cliffs, NJ: Prentice-Hall.

Kihlstrom, J. F., & Evans, F. J. (1979). Memory retrieval processes in posthypnotic amnesia. In J. F. Kihlstrom & F. J. Evans (Eds.), *Functional disorders of memory* (pp. 179–218). Hillsdale, NJ: Lawrence Erlbaum Associates.

Kihlstrom, J. F., & Wilson, L. (1984). Temporal organization of recall during posthypnotic amnesia. *Journal of Abnormal Psychology, 93,* 200–208.

Kihlstrom, J. F., & Wilson, L. (1988). Rejoinder to Spanos, Bertrand, and Perlini. *Journal of Abnormal Psychology, 97,* 381–383.

Lifton, R. J. (1967). *Death in life: Survivors of Hiroshima.* New York: Random House.

Lindsay, D. S., & Johnson, M. K. (1989). The eyewitness suggestibility effect and memory for source. *Memory & Cognition, 17,* 349–358.

Lindsay, D. S., & Read, J. D. (1994). Psychotherapy and memories of childhood sexual abuse: A cognitive perspective. *Applied Cognitive Psychology, 8,* 281–338.

Loftus, E. F., & Loftus, G. R. (1980). On the permanence of stored information in the human brain. *American Psychologist, 35,* 409–420.

Loftus, E. F., & Palmer, J. C. (1974). Reconstruction of automobile destruction: An example of the interaction between memory and language. *Journal of Verbal Learning & Verbal Behavior, 13,* 585–589.

McCloskey, M., & Zaragoza. M. S. (1985). Misleading postevent information and memory for events: Arguments and evidence against memory impairment hypothesis. *Journal of Experimental Psychology: General, 114,* 381–387.

McGlone, R. E. (1989). Rescripting a troubled past: John Brown's family and the Harpers Ferry conspiracy. *Journal of American History, 75,* 1179–1200.

McGuire, W. J. (1969). Theory-oriented research in natural settings: The best of both worlds for social psychology. In M. Sherif & C. W. Sherif (Eds.), *Interdisciplinary relationships in the social sciences* (pp. 21–51). Chicago: Aldine.

McGuire, W. J. (1973). The yin and yang of progress in social psychology: Seven koan. *Journal of Personality & Social Psychology, 26,* 446–456.

Metcalfe, J. (1990). Composite holographic associative recall model (CHARM) and blended memories in eyewitness testimony. *Journal of Experimental Psychology, 119,* 145–160.

Nelson, K. (1993). The psychological and social origins of autobiographical memory. *Psychological Science, 4,* 7–14.

Neisser, U. (1962). Cultural and cognitive discontinuity. In T. E. Gladwin & W. Sturtevant (Eds.), *Anthropology and human behavior* (pp. 54–71). Washington, D.C.: Anthropological Society of Washington.

Neisser, U. (1978). Memory: What are the important questions? In M. M. Gruneberg, P. E. Morris, & R. N. Sykes (Eds.), *Practical aspects of memory* (pp. 3–24). London: Academic Press.

Neisser, U. (1988). Time present and time past. In M. M. Gruneberg, P. E. Morris, & R. N. Sykes (Eds.), *Practical aspects of memory: Current research and issues. Vol. 2. Clinical and educational implications* (pp. 545–560). Chichester, England: Wiley.

Robinson, J. A. (1976). Sampling autobiographical memory. *Cognitive Psychology, 8,* 578–595.

Roediger, H. L. (1985). Remembering Ebbinghaus. *Contemporary Psychology, 30,* 519–523.

Ross, M. (1989). Relation of implicit theories to the construction of personal histories. *Psychological Review, 96,* 341–357.

Schacter, D. L., Kihlstrom, J. F., Canter Kihlstrom, L., & Berren, M. B. (1989). Autobiographical memory in a case of multiple personality disorder. *Journal of Abnormal Psychology, 98,* 508–514.

Shepard, R. N. (1967). Recognition memory for words, sentences, and pictures. *Journal of Verbal Learning & Verbal Behavior, 6,* 156–163.

Singer, J. A., & Salovey, P. (1993). *The remembered self: Emotion and memory in personality.* New York: Free Press.

Slamecka, N. J. (1985). Ebbinghaus: Some associations. *Journal of Experimental Psychology: Learning, Memory, & Cognition, 11,* 414–435.

Smith, M. B. (1972). Is experimental social psychology advancing? *Journal of Experimental Social Psychology, 8,* 86–96.

Thelen, D. (1989a). Memory and American history. *Journal of American History, 75,* 117–129.

Thelen, D. (1989b). Remembering the discovery of the Watergate tapes: Introduction. *Journal of American History, 75,* 1222–1227.

Tulving, E. (1962). Subjective organization in free recall of "unrelated" words. *Psychological Review, 69,* 344–354.

Tulving, E. (1985). Hermann Ebbinghaus's memory: What did he learn and remember? *Journal of Experimental Psychology: Learning, Memory, & Cognition, 11,* 485–490.

Tversky, B., & Tuchin, M. (1989). A reconciliation of the evidence on eyewitness testimony: Comments on McCloskey and Zaragoza. *Journal of Experimental Psychology: General, 118,* 142–147.

Wilson, L., & Kihlstrom, J. F. (1986). Subjective and categorical organization of recall in posthypnotic amnesia. *Journal of Abnormal Psychology, 95,* 264–273.

Winograd, E. (1988). Continuities between ecological and laboratory approaches to memory. In U. Neisser & E. Winograd (Eds.), *Remembering reconsidered: Ecological and traditional approaches to the study of memory* (pp. 11–20). Cambridge, England: Cambridge University Press.

Zaragoza, M. S., & Koshmider, J. W. (1989). Misled subjects may know more than their performance implies. *Journal of Experimental Psychology: Learning, Memory, & Cognition, 118*, 246–255.

CHAPTER THREE

Practical Aspects of Memory: The First 2,500 Years

Peter E. Morris
University of Lancaster
Lancaster, England

Michael M. Gruneberg
University College of Swansea
Swansea, Wales

We stand at the latest point in a very long tradition. We say "latest point" because we are confident that it is not the end of a tradition, but rather part of a new and growing beginning. In this chapter, we want to trace this tradition from its instigation in Classical times, through the Middle Ages, and up to the 1994 Practical Aspects of Memory Conference. We think that such an historical tour is valuable, as well as interesting. It exposes the roots of our endeavour—specifically, in taking part in this conference, and generally, in all of our work to extend our wider knowledge of practical aspects of memory. In particular, it raises issues concerning the factors that have always influenced the applied study of memory.

Mike Gruneberg and I are compiling this chapter because, with Bob Sykes, we convened the first two Practical Aspects of Memory conferences. The First International Conference on Practical Aspects of Memory (PAM) was held in September 1978. That we should have been interested in organizing such a conference was not, in itself, surprising. The three of us had been working on practical aspects of memory, especially mnemonic techniques, for several years. It should be emphasized, however, that like so many attending the 1994 conference, our interest in practical application developed out of what is still a continuing interest in understanding fundamental memory processes.

We initiated that first conference because we felt many psychologists studying the fundamental nature of memory processes were also interested in applying that knowledge for the general good in a practical way. We clearly judged well, as over 180 delegates attended the first Conference, presenting well over 90 papers. The conference got off to a famous start with Neisser declaring in a subsequently often-quoted statement: "If X is an interesting or socially significant aspect of memory then psychologists have hardly ever studied X." Although Neisser was willing to admit that the other 90 papers presented at the conference showed he was wrong, the importance of Neisser's address should not be underestimated. What he did was to articulate brilliantly the concerns of a large number of researchers, that the subject matter of memory research had become too confining and was failing to investigate the major issues of practical significance to the man or woman in the street. In stressing the need for ecological validity in memory research if topics of real interest were to be investigated, Neisser lit a methodological touch paper: The resulting explosion is still reverberating today.

Neisser gave his opening address not knowing of the extent of interest in practical application, but he was not the only one surprised by the involvement shown by so many eminent researchers. Baddeley and Wilkins (1984) wrote "The curious feature of the conference was that almost all the participants, like Neisser himself, believed that they were working largely in isolation against what was perceived as the dominant experimental paradigm" (p. 1).

Arguably, of as great a significance as the conference itself was the publication of the conference proceedings. We adopted a policy on publishing the proceedings (Gruneberg, Morris, & Sykes 1978), which we believed was appropriate at the time for the development of the growing interest in the area. The collection of 88 chapters from the first conference was published within four months of the conference. Because we strongly believed that rapid publication was essential to maintain interest, and because our view was, as we wrote at the time, that "the importance of the conference lies as much in terms of the questions asked as of the answers given," we tried to publish all the presentations that were methodologically adequate, especially those in which the ideas were likely to stimulate significant future research. Banaji and Crowder (1989) implicitly criticised our editing policy by attacking three papers published in the second conference proceeding on methodological grounds. We would strongly argue that, at the beginning of an academic development, ideas that stimulate new questioning are very important. Of course, the size of the 1994 conference and the maturing of applied memory research has made our original publishing strategy inapropriate for the present conference volume. Nevertheless, there are important issues here that we have discussed elsewhere (Gruneberg & Morris, 1992) and to which we will return in a later paper of this volume (Gruneberg, Morris, Sykes, & Herrmann, chap. 5).

Table 3.1 summarizes the topics covered in the first conference. It illustrates both the range of interests and the popularity of the areas, although

TABLE 3.1
Practical Aspects of Memory (Gruneberg, Morris, & Sykes, 1978)

Topics (Number of Papers in Brackets)

Opening address (1)
Arousal and stress (5)
Brain damage and clinical measurement (7)
Drugs and memory (4)
Eyewitnessing (5)
Facial recognition (6)
General educational implications (3)
Individual differences (4)
Memory aids (6)
Memory and dyslexia (4)
Memory and reading (10)
Memory in children (11)
Memory in everyday life (13)*
Memory in the deaf (3)
Strategies in memory (6)

---

*Included prospective and autobiographical memory.

it also reflects some creative editing in bringing together chapters within some of the sections that were devoted to a wide range of topics.

Of course, no new approach to memory, particularly one involving real-life investigation, sometimes at the expense of laboratory control, could go unchallenged, and this challenge duly came with Banaji and Crowder's (1989) broadside on the bankruptcy of everyday memory research. This in turn led to heated exchanges in a special issue of the *American Psychologist* on the topic—a sure sign that the Practical Aspects Movement had arrived. As the cases argued by Banaji and Crowder (1994) and Winograd (1994) show in a book that we edited recently (Morris & Gruneberg, 1994), the best balance between laboratory control and ecological validity continues to be disputable.

In the light of these disputes over the relationship of theory and practice and the value of studying memory in everyday life, it is worthwhile repeating what we said in the Preface to the first Conference Proceeding (Gruneberg, Morris, & Sykes, 1978). We stated that:

> The objectives of the Conference . . . were to examine ways in which the considerable advances recently made in our theoretical understanding of memory could be applied to "real-life" memory problems, and to examine ways in which an attack on real life problems could throw light on aspects of theoretical interest and importance. In no way was the aim of the Conference to drive a wedge between theoretical and practical aspects of memory, in a fashionable search for relevance. Nevertheless, it is our view that the practical significance of memory research has been largely ignored by psychologists,

and it is this gap that the Conference sought to stimulate psychologists to fill. (p. v)

That was the spirit in which Mike, Bob, and I approached the first and the second PAM conferences. It has always marked our personal positions and it is reflected in our recently editing two volumes, one on theoretical and one on practical aspects of memory (Gruneberg & Morris, 1992; Morris & Gruneberg, 1994). We have always believed that the success of the psychological study of memory will eventually depend on the symbiosis of theoretical and practical approaches.

That applied research gains greatly from basic research through the quality of the theories on which it can draw and the methodologies that it can modify is without question. What seems less obvious to some is the way in which applied research provides the fertile conditions within which basic research can flourish. There are many, but there is space here to mention just a few.

The key aim of the scientist is confidence in the robustness, the generalizability, of her or his theoretical account. Yet we know that much of human thought is dominated by the familiar, the easily retrieved from memory, the old problems with which the researcher has wrestled in the past. The creativity of psychological theorizing needs all the stimulation that it can get. Inevitably, any theoretical account is an explanation of the questions that the theorizer has sought to answer and encompasses the range of phenomena that he or she recognizes as being relevant. One of the ways in which applied research can help to expand the range of the basic researcher's thinking is by placing in the arena for explanation questions and phenomena that broaden but also sometimes focus the domain considered by the theoretician.

It is easy to think of scientific research as progressing independently of the attractions and pressures that shape the rest of life. However, scientists are as human as the rest of the population. It is highly likely that more theories are abandoned through changes in fashionable research topics than are shown to be invalid through data collection. There are vast opportunities for the direction of scientific research to be shaped by the choices of the researchers themselves, but even more by others, such as those controlling funding.

However, perhaps more important than the need to attract and maintain funding (vital as that is) is the need to draw the involvement of the next generation of researchers. No student faces any obligation to undertake postgraduate research on memory. They will choose to do so if it seems a more interesting and exciting prospect than the other alternatives offered in competing areas of psychology. There is an attraction in working in a flourishing group developing basic theories, but, to many, the attraction is greater still if there is a prospect of results that will benefit others. We should not underestimate the danger of research on memory declining merely because few undergraduates can see the point of devoting their lives to it.

The first Practical Aspects of Memory Conference arguably succeeded in stimulating a considerable and sustained interest in practical aspects of memory. Those attending left fired with an enthusiasm that was reinforced by the knowledge that many eminent workers in memory research shared their interest in practical questions. In subsequent years applicable research on memory blossomed, and by the mid-1980s it was clear that holding a second conference would both consolidate and stimulate this growing interest.

The Second Practical Aspects of Memory Conference was held in Swansea in 1987. Over 300 delegates attended, and about 190 papers were presented. The topics themselves had diversified, as Table 3.2 shows. Our problem at the second conference was to maintain the spirit of the first conference in a program with many more parallel sessions. Again, we decided to maintain the policy we had adopted in the first conference with respect to publication, which was to publish as many papers as possible that met our criteria of

TABLE 3.2
Practical Aspects of Memory: Current Research and Issues (Vols. 1 & 2)
(Gruneberg, Morris, & Sykes, 1988)

Opening address (1)
Action events (4)
Autobiographical memory (13)
Child witnesses (6)
Children's memory (4)
Clinical applications (4)
Drugs and memory (5)
Dyslexia (5)
Ecological perspectives (6)
Eyewitnessing (13)
Face recognition (8)
General educational implications (9)
Maintenance of knowledge (5)
Memory and aging (19)
Memory for broadcast information (3)
Memory in everyday life (18)
Metamemory (6)
Mnemonic aids (5)
Motoric memory (6)
Neurological memory deficit (12)
Prospective memory (5)
Reading (5)
Stress, illness, and memory (4)
Student learning (5)
Time of day (4)
Closing address (1)

competence and interest, in as short a time as possible. The second conference proceedings were published in two volumes, consisting of a total of 176 chapters, about five months after the conference was held.

This paper is part of the third conference on Practical Aspects of Memory. A learned Society for Application of Research in Memory and Cognition has been founded. Books and articles on many different aspects of Applied Memory are regularly published in the literature, with journals such as *Applied Cognitive Psychology* now well established. It is clear that Applied Memory Research, which 18 years ago was, to quote Neisser (1988), "barely at the margins of respectability" (p. 545) is now not so much what Neisser described as a wave of the future, but more a wave of the present.

If applied memory research is a wave of the present, we might continue that metaphor by pointing to the wake behind us, stretching back in time to the very horizon. In discussing Practical Aspects of Memory we are joining a tradition of over 2,500 years. It is an interesting, and perhaps sobering, thought that the Classical, educated Greek or Roman individual, transported forward by 2,500 years to the late 20th century would be bewildered by most that they encountered but would find it easy to understand why a conference on the study of practical aspects of memory and its improvement was being held. A training in memory improvement would have been part of the education of all upper-class Greeks or Romans, and they would recognise and be able to discuss the advantages and limitations of at least some of the techniques for memory improvement that have been investigated in modern times.

As early as 400 B.C. a document known as the *Dialexeis* contained several precepts on memory:

- A great and beautiful invention is memory always useful both for learning and for life.
- This is the first thing: if you pay attention (direct your mind), the judgment will better perceive the things going through it (the mind).
- Secondly, repeat again what you hear; for by often hearing and saying the same things, what you have learned comes complete into your memory.
- Thirdly, what you hear, place on what you know. For example . . . we place glow worm on fire and shine. So much for names. For things thus: for courage on Mars and Achilles. . . . (Yates, 1966, pp. 29–30)

Thus, 2,400 years ago, several principles that we would also commend where being emphasized. There is not just a sensible emphasis on concentration and repetition, but also a reference, with several examples in addition to those quoted above, to a sophisticated mnemonic technique. Words may be analysed for familiar semantic components and linked through them, with the semantic and perhaps imaginal links providing a basis for subsequent recall.

The above quotation from the *Dialexeis* would have been seen by the reader at the time as part of an already established approach to memory improvement even though we have to wait until Roman times for Cicero, writing in 55 B.C., to describe in his *De Oratore* the invention of the place mnemonic by Simonides. Simonides was a lyric poet who lived from around 556 to 468 B.C. There is little doubt that, as other sources confirm, Simonides was regarded in classical times as the inventor of the mnemonic system that was central to most memory improvement techniques for the next 2,000 years.

According to Cicero, Simonides chanted a lyric poem in honour of Scopas, a noble man of Thessaly, that included a passage in praise of Castor and Pollux. Scopas paid only half the agreed fee telling Simonides that he must obtain the balance from the twin gods to whom he had devoted half the poem. A little later Simonides received a message that two young men were waiting outside who wished to see him. He found no one, but during his absence the roof of the banqueting hall fell in, crushing all the guests to death in the ruins. The corpses were so mangled that the relatives were unable to identify them. Simonides, however, remembered the places in which they were sitting and was so able to identify the bodies.

Simonides drew more from the experience than the advisability of praising the gods in his poems. As Cicero said: "He inferred that persons desiring to train this facility (of memory) must select places and form images of the places they wish to remember and store these images in the places, so that the order of the places will preserve the order of the things and images of the things will denote the things themselves, and we shall employ the places and images respectively as a wax writing-tablet and the letters written on it" (Yates, 1966 p. 2).

We will never know the extent to which Simonides' discovery of the place mnemonic did follow some dramatic event as related to Cicero. What is clear, however, is that the memory improvement technique described by Cicero and traditionally ascribed to Simonides became the standard memory improvement technique for the educated individual for the next two millennia. Cicero is not the only classical writer to give an account of the place mnemonic. Some years earlier an anonymous writer had compiled, around 86–82 B.C., a textbook on rhetoric that came to be known as the *Ad Herennium*. Later, in the first century A.D., Quintilian, the leading teacher on rhetoric in Rome, also wrote at length on memory improvement techniques.

It is important to emphasise the status of memory improvement techniques in the Classical world. Today, despite our knowledge of their effectiveness, the active practitioners of memory improvement techniques based on imagery are few and often regarded as rather unusual, even if successful in their chosen area. This appears not to have been the case for the educated

Greek or Roman. They distinguished between natural and artificial memory but do not appear to have regarded artificial memory as in some way dubious. Cicero and Quintilian refer to famous feats of memory by individuals from their age and earlier. More importantly, they and the author of *Ad Herennium* place the memory improvement technique in a context that makes it both practically and theoretically attractive.

We need to recall that rhetoric—the ability to present a compelling public oration both expertly and without notes—was one of the skills expected of the educated ruling classes of Greece and Rome. Then, as now, this presented a challenge to the speaker—how to remember the points to be made? Cicero, Quintilian, and no doubt other now-forgotten teachers of the skills of oration advocated the place mnemonic that they believed had been invented by Simonides. They described how to make the most of this mnemonic method. For example, the *Ad Herennium* went into detail on the reasons for unusual images:

> When we see in every day life things that are petty, ordinary and banal we generally fail to remember them because the mind is not being stirred by anything novel or marvellous. But if we see or hear something exceptionally base, dishonourable, unusual, great, unbelievable, or ridiculous, that we are likely to remember for a long time. . . .
>   We ought then to set up images of a kind that can adhere longest in memory. And we shall do so if we establish similitudes as striking as possible. . . . (*Ad Herennium* III, xxii)

The *Ad Herennium* gives an example of a suitable image. The council for the defense, wishing to remember that the prosecutor had said that the defendant killed a man by poison to gain an inheritance and that there were many witnesses, should put in the first memory locus this image: "We shall imagine the man in question as lying ill in bed. . . . And we shall place the defendant at the bedside, holding in his right hand a cup, in his left, tablets, and on the fourth finger, a ram's testicles. In this way we can have in memory the man who was poisoned, the witnesses, and the inheritance." Perhaps a little explanation is necessary! The cup will remind the imager of the poison, the tablet of the will. But why the ram's testicles? (We assume that they are no longer attached to the ram!) Here we have the use of verbal similarity because *testes* was Latin for witnesses!

One wonders about the attitude of the student of rhetoric to these techniques. In modern times these techniques have seemed bizarre and unnatural except to those who have discovered for themselves their effectiveness. Even Frances Yates, whose *Art of Memory* (1966) has been an invaluable introduction to the history of the study of memory for many of us, frequently expressed her skepticism and sometimes her incomprehension of the mnemonics. However, research on memory improvement allows us to share with Cicero across the millennia a confidence in the methods not available even to Yates. As Cicero wrote: "Nor is it true as unskilled people assert that memory is crushed beneath a weight of images and even what might have been retained by nature unassisted is obscured: for I have myself met eminent people with almost divine powers of memory. . . ." (Yates, 1966, p. 19).

There are several reasons why the mnemonic technique is likely to have been more easily acceptable to the classical orator than it was to Yates or the modern reader. First, there was the practical demand of the task, and nothing increases the use of familiar mnemonics like the pressure to perform well. Second, the acceptance of traditional wisdom was, perhaps, greater— the vital discovery of the skepticism of the scientific method was still to come. Third, the theoretical framework within which the educated person considered memory was one in which all remembering took place in terms of mental images. It was not, therefore, a big step from the images of natural memory to the creation of artificial images, if those images could help re-membering. Finally, within the conceptual framework that structured the knowledge of the classical scholar, memory held a valued place. It was one of the three parts of prudence (memory, intelligence, and foresight), and prudence itself was one of the four parts of virtue (prudence, justice, forti-tude, and temperance) that defined the ideal person.

Looking back to Classical times, therefore, we can see that the practical techniques for improving memory had a familiarity and acceptance among the political elite that we can only envy. However, perhaps the lesson to be recognised is that the memory systems were valued because they were found to be successful and appropriate. The success of the modern practical aspects of memory movement will similarly depend on the relevance of what we can offer.

It would be misleading to imply that the place mnemonic was universally accepted. We have already seen that Cicero was obliged to defend its effi-cacy. Quintilian was more critical. Of the mnemonic he commented: "It will however be of less service in retaining the parts of a speech. For notions do not call up images as material things do, and something else has to be invented for them, although even here a particular place may serve to remind us. . . . But how can such an art grasp a whole series of connected words?" (*Institutio Oratoria*, XI, ii).

Instead of the place mnemonic, Quintilian recommended as "at once more expeditious and more effective" for the student: "to learn a passage by heart from the same tablets on which he has committed it to writing. For he will have certain tracks to guide him in pursuit of memory. . . ." (ibid, XI ii).

Hence, Quintilian recommended hard work with the aid of consistent context. We can share with him the skepticism concerning the benefits of memorizing a speech word for word. On the other hand, it has sometimes been necessary, ever since the invention of writing provided records of definitive text (cf. Hunter, 1984), to memorize verbatim.

The mention of the invention of writing justifies a brief reflection on this, the oldest practical memory aid. We tend to think of writing as the means of recording stories, histories, and definitive, sometimes sacred texts. However, the earliest written records are often much more mundane, but perhaps more illustrative of the needs of memory improvement or enhancement techniques. Many early written records are just that—records of accounts, lists of taxes, and lists of property. The technologies that were developed to supplement memory have been required where memory is weakest. They were needed for the communication of things that we do not want to change—hence the recording of the rich man's property—but later of knowledge that is valued for its alleged accuracy. The verbatim record has been the aim of the technology of storing the past that has been developed over millennia to supplement memory, from the written symbol to the video recording.

The problems that an expert in practical aspects of memory may be expected to solve are intertwined with the current technology for recording the past. It has often been pointed out (e.g., Hunter, 1979; Neisser, 1982) that the need to remember verbatim long texts came about as a result of the recording of such texts in literate societies. Earlier, even if such a problem was perceived as existing, it was unresolvable without the existence of a definitive text.

In our day, we have expectations of what should and what may not be remembered. We should remember appointments made even months or years in advance because of the use of diaries. Our colleagues expect us to converse about events that have just taken place on the other side of the world because they have been recorded and transmitted on the television. These technologies shape our expectations of our own and other's memories, define the current set of problems, and often offer theoretical frameworks for the explanation of memory itself. Perhaps many of us feel that our memories are poorer than our ancestors' because we are continually exposed to accurate records of the past ("Did I really wear clothes like that when I was a teenager?"). The perception that there are problems in remembering appointments, in the accuracy of eyewitness testimony, and so on, emerges from the expectations created by our technology for recording the past.

It has long been believed that the technologies that we invent to aid our memories will themselves modify the memory process itself. The idea that the superior memories of members of preliterate societies are neglected and destroyed following the invention of writing has been an attractive if misplaced idea. Its earliest statement is often attributed to Plato in the *Phaedrus*. He had the Egyptian god who had invented writing criticised by the king of the Egyptian gods because: "This invention will produce forgetfulness in the minds of those who learn to use it, because they will not practice their memory. . . . You offer your pupils the appearance of wisdom, not true wisdom, for they will read many things without instruction and will therefore seem to know many things, when they are for the most part ignorant and hard to get along with . . ." (Fowler, 1914, pp. 563–564).

Plato's concern was much greater than a nostalgia for a preliterate age. The obsession of the classical scholars through the Dark and Middle Ages with texts by Classical authors supports Plato's argument that the possession of a written text can obscure as much as enhance intellectual exploration and understanding. However, Plato also believed that knowledge of the truth involved remembering from before birth! Ideas of such concepts as goodness or equality had been impressed on all souls before birth. Proper education allowed the individual to recall these fundamental ideas after essential, lengthy dialogue that would be neglected by those who thought that through reading they could circumvent the process. We may not share Plato's ideas about memories from before our births, although the same idea did inspire William Wordsworth to one of his greatest poems:

Not in entire forgetfulness,
And not in utter nakedness,
But trailing clouds of glory do we come ("Intimations of Immortality")

We can, however, recognize with Plato that remembering and understanding are often intertwined and that good memory normally arises from the richest evaluation of the semantics of the particular material.

Attempts to explain the memory processes are normally framed in terms of familiar technologies for recording the past. Thus, in recent years the computer has shaped much thinking. The paradox here is that information technologies have often been developed to supplement and circumvent the limitations of our memories systems. There is, therefore, a good reason for initial skepticism over any theory that derives from technology that was itself devised because of the inadequacies of our memory. Such systems are more likely to be filling in the gaps in recording the past than mimicking the way that our memories have evolved to function.

The oldest information technology that was adopted as an explanation of memory was the wax tablet. The wax tablet was the cheap way for someone in Classical times to make temporary notes that could be erased by scraping or melting, but sealing wax was also used when permanent records of approval were made using signet rings or seals. Plato, in the *Theatetus*, had Socrates introduce the idea of memory as resembling a wax tablet. Furthermore, people differ in the wax of their memories. So: "Suppose for the sake of argument, that there's an imprint-receiving piece of wax in our minds: bigger in some, smaller in others; of cleaner wax in some, of dirtier wax in others; of harder wax in some, of softer wax in others. . . . If there is anything we want to remember . . . we hold it under the perceptions and conceptions and imprint them on it, as if we were taking impressions of signet rings" (Plato, *Theaetetus*, 191c–d).

Aristotle also explained individual differences in memory ability in terms of the wax of their memories. Thus, he commented that: "Memory does not occur in those who are subject to a lot of movement . . . just as if the change and the seal were falling on running water . . . the very quick and the very slow are also obviously neither of them good at remembering. For the former are too fluid, and the latter too hard" (Aristotle, *De Memoria et Reminiscentia*, 430a32).

As we have discussed in more detail elsewhere (Morris, 1994), this is the first template theory of memory with all the attractions and problems of template theories. One of the interesting aspects of the history of memory is the length of time over which this theory was accepted as an explanation of memory. Most classical and medieval writers on memory seem to have accepted it. Over 2,000 years later, Freud (1924/1961) was stimulated to speculate on a wax tablet metaphor for memory by the modern equivalent of the wax tablet, the child's Mystic Writing Pad that allows writing to be erased by pulling free a cover sheet for a layer to which it adheres when pressed.

Why was the wax tablet theory accepted for so long? Limitations in competing metaphors for memory must be one reason. Another was the lack of pressure from either practical requirements for a better theory or empirical observations that revealed its limitations. Yet, Plato himself had recognised that there was more to memory than matching templates. In *Theaetetus* he had also introduced the idea of retrieval and memories being available but not accessible. He compared memory to an aviary. Plato had Socrates say: "When we are children this receptacle (the aviary) is empty, and in place of the birds we must think of pieces of knowledge. Whatever piece of knowledge someone comes to possess and shuts up in his enclosure, we must say he has come to know . . ." (Plato, *Theaetetus*, 197d).

Plato then went on to draw the distinction between possessing knowledge and "having" it. One may possess it as a bird that is in the aviary but may still not be able to catch it. This same distinction between availability and accessibility was drawn 2,300 years later by Tulving and Pearlstone (1966).

Plato's famous pupil, Aristotle, was certainly familiar with the mnemonic systems and with some of the consequences of their use. He remarked that in dreams some people "seem to be arranging the objects before them in accordance with their mnemonic system." Are there similar anecdotes to be told by modern exponents of mnemonic systems?

Aristotle is frequently cited as the founder of the associationist account of memory, and there is no doubt that he had observed characteristics of free association. However, if you read Aristotle's writings on memory (i.e., *De Memoria et Reminiscentia*) seeking for an elaborate statement of the principles of associationism as they were later laid down by the British Empiricists such as Hume (1739), you may be disappointed. The section that is traditionally seen as the foundation of associationism seems to us to be as much the account of a practical method for searching our memories as the statement of an all encompassing theory. Aristotle said that when we wish to remember something: "We hunt for the successor, starting in our thoughts from the present or from something else, and from something similar, or opposite, or neighbouring. By this means recollection occurs" (451b18–20). Aristotle specifically stated "sometimes, then, people search in this way" He also said that: "Whenever someone wishes to recollect, he will do the following. He will seek to get a starting point for a change [in the memory image] after which will be the change in question. And this is why recollections occur quickest and best from a starting point. For as the things are related to each other in succession, so also are the changes. And whatever has some order, as things in mathematics do, is easily remembered" (451b22).

The centuries that followed the fall of the Roman Empire were dark days for the practical study of memory as much as other learning. In the latter days of the Roman Empire St. Augustine had written extensively on memory. However, by Charlemagne's time most of the traditional wisdom had been forgotten. When Charlemagne asked Alcuin for advice on improving his memory Alcuin could reply only with the precepts: "Exercise in memorising, practice in writing, application to study and the avoidance of drunkenness which does the greatest possible injury to all good studies" (Howell, 1941, p. 139). No doubt we should take note of this advice, but it is clear that the mnemonic methods had been lost.

The Middle Ages was marked by a growing rediscovery of the writings of classical times and their integration into the Christian world view by the scholastic philosophers. Preeminent among them were the Dominican friar Thomas Aquinas and his teacher Albertus Magnus. Writing in the early and middle years of the 13th century they reestablished the principles advocated by the classical philosophers and orators. They sought to reconcile the advice on artificial memory by Cicero with the speculations of Aristotle on the nature of memory and to place the result in an account that both acknowledged the classical analysis of virtue while being consistent with Christian philosophy.

From Albertus onward the traditional mnemonic techniques were to be familiar to the educated individual. However, Albertus was struggling with limited and corrupt texts by the Classical authors. The example images of the *Ad Herrenium* return, but was Albertus really sure what he is writing about? He recommends: "If we wish to record what is brought against us in a law-suit, we should imagine some ram, with huge horns and testicles, coming towards us out of the darkness. The horns will bring to memory our adversaries, and the testicles the disposition of the witnesses" (*Opera Omnia*, IX, p. 108).

Did Albertus understand the original example? Did he feel obliged to use it because of its ancient authority? Here, perhaps, is that great danger—the assumption that famous writers from the past must know better than we do, even if we do not understand them.

The radical scientific challenge still lay centuries in the future. One longs to ask, "Would that really work? Show me!"—questions we take for granted but that would have seemed alien ideas to most of the great thinkers of history. One wonders whether it ever occurred to Albertus and those who preceded and followed him to check the truth of his assertion that those with a melancholy temperament had better memories. The underlying theory was that of the humours. Melancholy is dry and cold and therefore receives the impression of images (cf. the wax tablet metaphor) and retains them longer than those of other humours.

Whatever the limitations we may highlight in Albertus' views, he seems to have been successful in training the memory of his pupil, Thomas, who is said to have had a phenomenal memory. He was certainly interested in memory and wrote about it extensively. In addition to reviewing the work of earlier writers, Thomas put forward his own four precepts of memory. The first is that we should choose objects to represent the things that we wish to remember that are not too familiar "because we wonder more at unfamiliar things and the soul is more strongly and vehemently held to them; whence it is that we remember better things seen in childhood." The second precept is that "a man should place in a considered order those (things) which he wishes to remember, so that from one remembered (point) progress can easily be made to the next." The third principle is that "a man should dwell with solicitude on and cleave with affection to, the things which he wishes to remember." Finally, "we should meditate frequently on what we wish to remember" (Yates, 1966, pp. 74–75).

Thus, some 750 years ago, there was a concise statement of many of the fundamental principles of memory improvement that we might give if pressed. Concrete, ordered, emotionally rich memories that are to be frequently rehearsed. These rules draw on the writings of the classical scholars, but when stated by Aquinas they have the air of rules that are recommended by someone who has put them into practice.

As the Middle Ages moved into the Renaissance, the purpose of memory improvement changed. The emphasis on memorizing became less prosaic and started to be integrated into attempts to systematize an account of the world that captured knowledge and was rich in mysticism. Yates (1966) described in detail the memory systems of Giordano Bruno and Robert Fludd. They bring memory systems into occult philosophies in the Hermetic tradition, attempting through the memory to capture within the mind the power and mysteries of the universe.

For 2,500 years the most effective memory techniques advocated had been based on mental images. These techniques had passed through the writings of the Catholic friars. To later Protestants, all images, whether in churches or in the mind, were objects of suspicion if not denigration. It is therefore not surprising that alternative techniques developed that did not depend on these questionable images and could satisfy the iconoclast.

The alternative mnemonic methods to those based on imagery have exploited the semantic connections between the items to be remembered. There was a long tradition of explaining the memory processes through associations. It is, perhaps, surprising that the suggestions that such associations could be used to help recall that were made by Aristotle were not followed up more assiduously in the following centuries, although they do seem to have been taken into account by Aquinas.

It was Ramon Lull (1235–1316), a contemporary of Thomas Aquinas, who founded the logical, semantic tradition of memory improvement. As for Aquinas, there was for Lull a strong religious basis for his interest in memory. Lull adopted Augustine's view that the Trinity was reflected in the three "powers" of the human soul: *intellectus*, the art of knowing for finding the truth; *voluntas*, the art of training the will to love truth; and *memoria*, an art for remembering truth. Once again, the interest in memory is rooted both in a reverence for its place in the virtuous aspects of humanity, and its improvement is advocated as a means of developing the individual toward a higher ideal.

Lull's method emphasized the logical structure of knowledge and the medieval universe. The nine attributes of God (goodness, greatness, power, etc.) were to be combined with the Ladder of Being that climbed from the arts and sciences through the elements and the vegetable and animal kingdoms up eventually to the angels and finally to God. Lull also represented the logical relationships underlying knowledge in the form of trees, sometimes illustrated as real trees.

With the Renaissance came the temptation to reject the arts of memory that were associated with the Middle Ages and scholastic theology. Erasmus (1512), for example, commented: "Though I do not deny that memory can be helped by places and images, yet the best memory is based on three important things, namely study, order, and care" (Yates, 1966, p. 127). No doubt this skepticism was strengthened by the association of memory techniques with the mystical Hermetic cults of Bruno and others (cf. Yates, 1966).

The rejection of the traditional, image-based arts of memory found a champion in Peter Ramus. Ramus aimed to simplify education by providing a logical analysis. Every subject was to be arranged in a hierarchical classification with dichotomized branches leading down from the general to the individual aspects. These analyses were to be memorised from this schematic arrangement. Here was the recognition that organization (e.g., Bower, 1970a) and an emphasis on semantic processing (e.g., Craik & Tulving, 1975) would ease memorizing.

Ramus had the misfortune to be a victim of the St. Bartholomew Massacre of Huguenots in 1572. No doubt this, along with his rejection of imagery in his mnemonic techniques, contributed to the popularity that his method enjoyed in Protestant countries, including England. The Ramist method found a vigorous advocate in William Perkins, a Cambridge Elizabethan Puritan, who published a number of attacks on the traditional, imagery-based memory techniques. Even Perkins (1592) admitted that "The artificial memory which consists in places and images will teach how to retain notions in memory easily and without labour." The techniques are to be rejected, not on empirical grounds because they do not work, but for two other reasons: "1. The animation of the images which is the key of memory is impious: because it calls up absurd thoughts, insolent, prodigious and the like which stimulate and light up depraved carnal affections. 2. It burdens the mind and memory because it imposes a triple task on memory instead of one; first of the places; then of the images; then of the thing to be spoken of" (Yates, 1966, p. 277).

You will recognize here two of the doubts that have always been leveled against imagery-based mnemonics—that they lead the imager into dubious mental activities and that they increase the amount to be stored in memory. Perkins referred scathingly to Peter of Ravenna who had said that he always used an image of his girlfriend, because it was sure to stimulate his memory! It certainly seems to have stimulated Perkins' imagination.

The Renaissance was also the time when printed books became available. With them came the spread of popular books on memory improvement that have continued to the present day. Whatever might be the prevailing attitude of intellectuals, there has always been a wish by the ordinary individual to improve memory. The first printed memory treatise was published in 1482. Many others followed in the 16th and 17th centuries. As with modern memory improvement books they appear to have been highly derivative from earlier works, repeating traditional rules for images, rules for places, and so on (Yates, 1966).

An interesting question is why so few memory improvement techniques have been developed. For centuries, millennia in fact, the method of loci stood alone. Lull and Ramas made a breakthrough in identifying the benefits of logical organization but did so while attempting to suppress the older technique. What limited the development of more techniques? Clearly, an intellectual tradition that relied on authority rather than experimentation played a part. Perhaps it was always going to be difficult to isolate effective techniques without an experimentally tested, theoretical framework explaining the memory processes? Perhaps those who advocated the techniques were not actually interested in using them themselves?

The professional mnemonist appears in the 17th century. Such a development must have reflected a growing interest among a wider audience in memory performance. It certainly marked a starting point in the development of an armory of practical mnemonics. The professional mnemonists were less concerned with justifying their techniques by quotations from Classical writers and very much required successful practical demonstrations. Developments in the mnemonic techniques followed.

A major advance in the applicability of mnemonics came with the introduction of the method of translating digits into letters that could then be formed into imageable words. The earliest system is attributed to Winckelman in 1648 (Paivio, 1971). The professional mnemonist, Feinaigle (1813), refined the phonetic method into the technique that is used by professional mnemonists today (e.g. Lorayne, 1957). The phonetic system allowed the traditional imagery loci mnemonic to be extended to the memorizing of numbers and the construction of pegs to replace the places themselves. The use of pegs instead of loci was begun by Henry Herdson in the mid-1600s when he replaced the memorized locations with objects that resemble numbers, such as candle for one and spectacles for eight (Higbee, 1988).

Although many professional mnemonists advocated adaptations of the classical imagery mnemonics, others developed the semantic based systems introduced by Lull and Ramas. Loisette (1896), for example, in his Assimilative Memory, provided techniques for locating and classifying associations between items to increase their memorability. He commented that "Memory is not a separate faculty" and "Memory is a Physiological and Psychological property of each mental act, and that such act retains the traces and history of its own action, and that there are as many memories as there are kinds of mental action" (Preface).

With Loisette we have crossed into the era of experimental research on memory. Ebbinghaus, for example, would have seen his research on the development of new associations and their subsequent forgetting as directly relevant to understanding the processes exploited by Loisette. The deliberate forming of images to improve memory was investigated by Kirkpatrick (1894). However, whereas in Classical times mnemonics were a part of the training of the educated person and during the Middle Ages it had been the scholars who had kept the knowledge of mnemonic systems alive, by the late 19th century academic psychologists were skeptical, if not ignorant, of the ancient memory improvement techniques. Burnham, (1888) quoting a 17th-century reference to mnemonic teachers, stated that "many there be that at this day profess the same, though they get more infamy and disrepute than gain thereby; being a sort of rascally fellows that do many times impose upon silly youth, only to draw some small piece of money from them for present subsistence" (Higbee, 1988, pp. 113–114).

Burnham went on to remark that mnemonic teachers in the late 19th century "get, not a small piece of money but a larger piece, and they sometimes impose upon others as well as silly youth." Later, Watson's rejection of imagery as part of his advocacy of behaviorism sealed the fate of research on the oldest mnemonic method until the 1960s when Gordon Bower (1970b), among others, led the rediscovery of its effectiveness. Alan Paivio (1971), one of those most responsible for reviving research on imagery, drew attention to the similarity between Watson's denouncing of imagery in his "protestant reformation" and Perkin's rejection of imagery-based mnemonics in the 16th century.

So far, we have concentrated on the history of memory improvement because it was the main focus of interest in practical aspects of memory before the 19th century. There was a major change at the end of that century. Although memory researchers largely ignored the traditional practical aids to memory, they did turn to other practical issues. Eyewitness testimony received early attention, especially in France and Germany. Binet (1900) argued for the creation of a practical science of testimony. Liszt (see Munsterberg, 1908) devised the carefully staged mock crime to investigate and illustrate the limitations on witness testimony. Liszt's "crime" was a struggle between a student with a revolver and himself during a lecture—even today hardly a common event. Stern (1904/1982) extended this technique to show the influence of expectations on witnesses' testimony when describing a more common event.

By 1909 Whipple was able to review a considerable collection of research on witness testimony. Much of this research had been carried out in Germany, and Whipple commented that the legal professions in Germany had a better appreciation of work by laboratory psychologists than was the case in the United States. Whipple was able to list 14 formulae for calculating aspects of testimony including accuracy, assurance (items reported with certainty), unreliability of oath, and so on. Many of the Classical results concerning testimony were already established, including inaccuracies in sworn statements, high error rates to neutral questions (25%), the power of leading questions, the lack of a relationship between the range of the testimony and other measures, and suggestibility in children's testimony. Forgetting was shown to be nowhere near as rapid as Ebbinghaus' results would have suggested, with Stern estimating a fairly constant decrease of 0.33% per day over three weeks. As Stern (1939) later commented wryly, he was glad to find in Bartlett's (1932) Remembering "certain methods which were familiar to me inasmuch as I had first applied them."

". . . A progressive abbreviation of the anecdotes: the story becomes less definite and more general in phrasing; each report deviates in two or three points from the proceding; the errors are confusions, substitutions, alterations of temporal and spatial setting; names and dates suffer particularly." It sounds like Bartlett's *Remembering*. It was in fact Whipple (1912) summarizing the German work on recall of stories.

One interesting feature of the early research on witness testimony was the struggle with methodological problems. Was the research really comparable with the testimony of actual witnesses? How many "mental units" does an experience contain? How do you compare the recall merely that there was "a man" with a fuller one giving his complexion and dress down to the buttons on his coat? Are all errors equivalent? And so on.

In the United States, Munsterberg (1908), in his best selling *On the Witness Stand*, brought experimental psychological research to the attention of the legal professions. He described demonstrations of the fallibility of eyewitness testimony as well as other limitations in the jurisprudence system. One consequence was that he later became the focus of sensational press coverage. He was one of the first applied psychologists to discover what many have since had to suffer to their cost—the preference of the media for a sensational story over a balanced account of facts and theories (Hothersall, 1984).

Applied psychologists kept alive the issues first investigated by Stern and his associates through the following years, but their publications were scattered, often in law rather than psychology journals (e.g., Bull & Clifford, 1979, for a review). It was not until the mid-1970s when Robert Buckhout and Elizabeth Loftus and her associates turned to witness testimony, and Graham Davies and the Aberdeen group to face recognition, that the mainstream psychological researchers returned again to the questions that the early researchers had introduced.

The 1880s and 1890s had seen the foundation of several research approaches. Sir Francis Galton (1883) had begun the study of autobiographical memory and of individual differences in memory with his questionnaire on images of their breakfast tables by 100 "adult men . . . mostly of very high repute" (p. 61) including 19 Fellows of the Royal Society. Galton devised the technique of generating autobiographical memories with cue words. He also explored composite photography as a model for the development of concepts.

Other psychologists had become interested in everyday memory. Cattell (1895) studied student memories for details of the campus, recent weather, and the content of his previous week's lecture. Recall of all of them was often very poor. The first study of "flashbulb memory" was reported by Colegrove (1899), who had asked 179 people "Do you recall where you were when you heard Lincoln was shot?" 33 years earlier, and had found that 127 could give facts such as who told them and where they were.

A more practical application of memory research had begun with Jacobs' (1887) investigation of the memory span. Only a very few years later Binet and Henri (1895) were using memory tests in their first attempts to measure intelligence. They incorporated measures of memory span, memory of geometrical designs, and memory for a short paragraph in their battery of tests. Since then measures of memory have played a part in both general intelligence testing and in more specific measures of memory ability. Binet and Simon (1905) included memory tests in the first real intelligence test, and the memory span, in particular, has since held its place in tests such as the Wechsler Intelligence Tests. It was therefore appropriate that one of the special guests at the first Practical Aspects of Memeory conference was Wechsler himself.

A review of the more recent history of memory research will not be attempted in this chapter, because we are well aware that several important areas would be omitted (some of them are included in Morris & Conway, 1993). There was the study of amnesia with, for example, the classical monograph by Ribot (1882) on diseases of memory among other early contributions. Then there is what we now call the study of prospective memory. The latter is said to have begun in the early 1920s when Lewin was holding informal discussions with students at the Swedish Cafe across the street from the Berlin Psychological Institute. Lewin noticed that the waiters recalled their customer's bills until they were paid, and then forgot them. Lewin set Zeigarnik to investigate. Yes, even coffee breaks can be justified if you are a psychologist.

We should also mention programmed instruction, which drew important contributions from Skinner, Crowder, and others. In the 1960s, programmed instruction promised a technology of learning and memory, which must surely be our aim (c.f. Kay, Dodd, & Sime, 1968). It foundered at the time on the inadequate technology for controlling the presentation of the material being studied. Information technology has since remedied that problem.

Perhaps we could end the PrePAMian review—that is, the review of the history of the study of practical aspects of memory prior to the first Practical Aspects of Memory conference—by sharing with you two references that we encountered while preparing this paper. They are the two papers by R. F. Becker listed in Young's (1961) bibliography of memory. The first (Becker, 1947) was entitled "Effect of Intermittent Exposure to 30,000 Feet Simulated Altitude on Memory in Animals." The second (Becker, Groat, & Windle) was "Study of Learning and Memory in Guinea Pigs Suffering Brain Concussion." Did Becker give up simulation for real world investigation, drop his guinea pigs, and then make the best of a bad job? At this point we realised it was time to stop the review!

Thus we return to the 1994 PAM conference, and we believe that it is a historic occasion. It is not too much to hope that a future historian of memory will be able to trace a vigorous and highly successful growth spurt in our theoretical and practical aspects of memory to this conference. Our memories are our personal histories, and the processes that shape the telling of history are often the same as those that determine our personal histories in the selection of the memories that we encode and retrieve. Without our memories all other cognition would be pointless, if not impossible. Without an awareness of our collective history as students of memory there is a related historical amnesia. As researchers of memory, we cannot know where we are going, why, or what to do unless we know what has happened in the past, how it shapes our thinking, and how it provides us with ways of looking at the world.

We have tried to use this review of the history of the study of practical aspects of memory to highlight a number of themes. One is the antiquity of the activity in which we are engaged. Another is the demonstration of the value of the scientific curiosity and skepticism that would have prevented much dutiful repetition of authoritative but false or distorted views and stimulated so much thinking if it had been available in earlier centuries. We think that the history also highlights the way in which the value placed on practical aspects of memory is always dependent on the current needs at the time, whether it is to memorize speeches or capture knowledge of the universe. Memory improvement has been valued when it has seemed relevant to the needs of powerful individuals. Another theme is the relationship between technology and the tasks set for memory experts. What is a memory problem is often intertwined with current technology and its limitations.

One major theme of this paper has been that 2,500 years ago the educated and powerful members of society regarded memory improvement as a fundamental issue. In the Middle Ages it was the educated, but no longer powerful, who continued the interest in practical aspects of memory. For many years, applied aspects of memory were neglected even by the educated. If we were able to place practical aspects of memory back within the valued knowledge of those who are currently powerful, how it would benefit the study of the Practical Aspects of Memory!

The Practical Aspect of Memory conferences were not the start of an interest in practical application. Not only had an interest in memory improvement been prominent for 2,500 years; it is clear that from the beginnings of scientific psychology other areas of practical importance such as the study of eyewitnessing and the effect of brain damage had been of considerable concern. Furthermore, the questions of the relationship between theory and practice had been as important in the first part of the 20th century, with Hugo Munsterberg in his 1913 textbook pointing to the same issues on the relationship between theory and practice that concern us at this time.

What, then, is the difference between the situation we are in and that of the middle 1970s? First, there is a much greater willingness to look at real-life memory problems in order to see to what extent they can inform our understanding of memory processes. Second, because real life phenomena are sometimes difficult to control in the conventional laboratory situation, there is more of a willingness to use laboratory approaches to deal with problems. Third is the feeling that so much is now being discovered of practical value that a communality of interest of those concerned with practical applications is growing, as shown, for example, by the new applied memory society. All of these things the previous Practical Aspects of Memory conferences facilitated. Some things, however, do not appear to have changed, such as the reluctance of the academic community to go beyond applicable research to real-life application. This will be the subject of chapter 5 by Gruneberg, Morris, Sykes, and Herrmann later in this volume. Nevertheless, we can all learn this from history: There is a time for ideas—the *Zeitgeist*. We are clearly in the middle of a *Zeitgeist* for Applied Memory Research.

ACKNOWLEDGMENT

The attendance of Professor Peter Morris at the third Practical Aspects of Memory conference was made possible through the support of the Royal Society and the British Academy.

REFERENCES

Ad Herennium. (1966). Quotations translated by F. A. Yates. *The art of memory*. London: Routledge and Kegan Paul.
Albertus Magnus. (1890). *Opera Omnia*, A. Borgnet (Ed.). Paris.
Aristotle, *De Memoria et Reminiscentia*. Quotations from the translation by R. Sorabji (1972) *Aristotle on memory*. London: Duckworth.
Baddeley, A. D., & Wilkins, A. (1984). Taking memory out of the laboratory. In J. E. Harris & P. E. Morris (Eds.), *Everyday memory, actions and absent mindedness* (pp. 1–19). London: Academic Press.
Banaji, M. R., & Crowder, R. F. (1989). The bankruptcy of everyday memory. *American Psychologist, 44*, 2185–2193.
Banaji, M. R., & Crowder R. F. (1994). Experimentation and its discontents. In P. E. Morris & M. M. Gruneberg (Eds.), *Theoretical aspects of memory Vol. II* (2nd ed., pp. 296–308). London: Routledge.
Bartlett, F. C. (1932). *Remembering*. Cambridge, England: Cambridge University Press.
Becker, R. F. (1947). Effect of intermittent exposure to 30,000 feet simulated altitude on memory in animals. *Anal. Rec., 97*, 321.
Becker, R. F., Groat, R. A., & Windle, W. F. (1961). Study of learning and memory of guinea pigs suffering brain concussion. In M. N. Young, *Bibliography of memory*. Philadelphia: Chilton.

Binet, A. (1909). La Suggestibilite. Cited in G. M. Whipple, The observer as reporter: A survey of the psychology of testimony. *Psychological Bulletin, 6*, 153–170.

Binet, A., & Henri, V. (1895). La Psychologie individuelle. *L'Annee Psychologique, 1*, 411–465.

Binet, A., & Simon, T. (1905). Methods nouvelles pour le diagnostic du niveau intellectuel des anormaux. *L'Annee Psychologique, 11*, 191–244.

Bower, G. H. (1970a). Organisational factors in memory. *Cognitive Psychology, 1*, 18–46.

Bower, G. H. (1970b). Imagery as a relational organiser in associative learning. *Journal of Verbal Learning and Verbal Behavior, 9*, 529–533.

Bull, R., & Clifford, B. (1979). Eyewitness memory. In M. M. Gruneberg & P. E. Morris (Eds.), *Applied problems in memory*. London: Academic Press.

Burnham, W. H. (1888). Memory, historically and experimentally considered: 1. An historical sketch of the older conceptions of memory. *American Journal of Psychology, 2*, 39–90.

Cattell, J. M. (1895). Measurements of the accuracy of recollection. *Science, 2*, 761–766.

Cicero, M. T. (55). *De Oratore*. Many translations.

Colegrove, F. W. (1899). Individual memories. *American Journal of Psychology, 10*, 228–255.

Craik, F. I. M., & Tulving, E. (1975). Depth of processing and the retention of words in episodic memory. *Journal of Experimental Psychology: General, 104*, 268–294.

Erasmus. (1512). *De ratione studii.*

von Feinaigle, G. (1813). *The new art of memory* (3rd ed.). London: Sherwood, Neely and Jones.

Freud, S. (1961). A note upon the "mystic writing-pad." In J. Strachey (Ed. and Trans.), *The standard edition of the complete psychological works of Sigmund Freud* (Vol. 19, pp. 227–232). London: The Hogarth Press. (Original work published in 1924)

Galton, F. (1883). *Inquiries into human faculty and its development*. London: Macmillan.

Gruneberg, M. M., & Morris P. E. (1992). Applying memory research. In M. M. Gruneberg & P. E. Morris (Eds.), *Aspects of memory: The practical aspects Vol. I* (2nd ed., pp. 1–17). London: Routledge.

Gruneberg, M. M., Morris, P. E., & Sykes, R. N. (1978). *Practical aspects of memory*. London: Academic Press.

Gruneberg, M. M., Morris, P. E., & Sykes, R. N. (1988). *Practical aspects of memory: Current research and issues* (Vols. 1 & 2). Chichester, England: Wiley.

Higbee, K. L. (1988). *Your memory: How it works and how to improve it* (2nd ed.). Englewood Cliffs, NJ: Prentice-Hall.

Hothersall, D. (1984). *History of psychology*. New York: Random House.

Howell, W. S. (1966). *The rhetoric of Charlemagne and Alcuin*. Cited in F. A. Yates, *The art of memory*. London: Routledge and Kegan Paul.

Hume, D. (1739). *A treatise of human nature* (many editions).

Hunter, I. M. I. (1979). Memory in everyday life. In M. M. Gruneberg & P. E. Morris (Eds.), *Applied problems in memory* (pp.). London: Academic Press.

Hunter, I. M. I. (1984). Lengthy verbatim recall (LVR) and the mythical gift of tape-recorder memory. In K. M. J. Lagerspetz & P. Niemi (Eds.), *Psychology in the 1990s* (pp.). Amsterdam: Elsevier Science.

Jacobs, J. (1887). Experiments on "Prehension." *Mind, 12*, 75–79.

Kay, H., Dodd, B., & Sime, M. (1968). *Teaching machines an programmed instruction*. Harmondsworth: Penguin.

Kirkpatrick, E. A. (1894). An experimental study of memory. *Psychological Review, 1*, 602–609.

Loisette, A. (1896). *Assimilative memory, or how to attend and never forget*. New York: Funk and Wagnalls.

Lorayne, H. (1958). *How to develop a super-power memory*. Preston, England: A. Thomas.

Morris, P. E. (1994). Theories of memory: An historical perspective. In P. E. Morris & M. M. Gruneberg (Eds.), *Theoretical aspects of memory* (2nd ed.). London: Routledge.

Morris, P. E., & Conway, M. (1993). *The psychology of memory* (3 Vols.). Aldershot, England: Edward Elgar Publishing.

Morris, P. E., & Gruneberg, M. M. (Eds.). (1992). *Theoretical aspects of memory* (2nd ed.). London: Routledge.

Munsterberg, H. (1908). *On the witness stand.* New York: Clark Boardman.

Munsterberg, H. (1913). *Psychology and industrial efficiency.* New York: Houghton Mifflin.

Neisser, U. (1982). *Memory observed.* San Francisco: Freeman.

Neisser, U. (1988). Time present and time past. In M. M. Gruneberg, P. E. Morris, & R. N. Sykes (Eds.), *Practical aspects of memory: Current research and issues Vol. 2*, (pp. 545–560). Chichester: Wiley.

Paivio, A. (1971). *Imagery and verbal processes.* New York: Holt, Rinehart and Winston.

Perkins, W. (1592). Prophetica sive de sacra et unica ratione concionandi tractatus. Cambridge, Sig. F viii recto.

Plato. (1914). *Phaedrus.* (H. N. Fowler, Trans.). London: W. Heinemann.

Plato. (1973). *Theaetetus.* (J. McDowell, Trans.). Oxford, England: Clarendon Press.

Quintilian. *Institutio oratoria.* Various translations.

Ribot, T. (1882). *Diseases of memory: An essay in the positive psychology.* London: Kegan Paul, Trench.

Stern, L. W. (1939). The psychology of testimony. *Journal of Abnormal and Social Psychology, 34*, 3–20.

Stern, W. (1982). *Memory observed: Remembering in natural contexts* (U. Neisser, Trans.). San Francisco: W. H. Freeman. (Originally published in 1904)

Tulving, E., & Pearlstone, Z. (1966). Availability versus accessibility of information in memory for words. *Journal of Verbal Learning and Verbal Behavior, 5*, 381–391.

Winograd, E. (1994). Naturalistic approaches to the study of memory. In P. E. Morris & M. M. Gruneberg (Eds.), *Theoretical aspects of memory Vol. II* (2nd ed., pp. 273–295). London: Routledge.

Whipple, G. (1909). The observer as reporter: A survey of the "psychology of testimony." *Psychological Bulletin, 6*, 153–170.

Whipple, G. M. (1912). Psychology of testimony and report. *Psychological Bulletin, 9*, 264–269.

Yates, F. A. (1966). *The art of memory.* London: Routledge and Kegan Paul.

Young, M. N. (1961). *Bibliography of memory.* Philadelphia: Chilton.

CHAPTER FOUR

Synergistic Strategies for Memory Research

Harry P. Bahrick
Ohio Wesleyan University

It has been 16 years since Dick Neisser (1978) gave the opening address to the first conference on practical aspects of memory. Of his many quotable remarks, the one concerning our past efforts that became most famous is the principle that: "If X is an interesting or socially significant aspect of memory, then psychologists have hardly ever studied X" (p. 4). It is not entirely surprising that scholars of memory received this commentary on their past accomplishments with less than universal acclaim. In retrospect, most would agree that Dick Neisser's address was provocative, perhaps disturbing to scholars who had spent a large portion of their professional life in the memory laboratory. It was certainly also a catalyst that gave attention and impetus to the work of those who wanted memory research to relate more directly to the neglected phenomena we encounter in our daily lives. Much has happened during the 16 years since Dick Neisser's address, and he has acknowledged (Neisser, 1988) that his assessment no longer applies to the present scene. I believe that we have moved beyond the point of wholesale disparagement of laboratory or naturalistic methods, and also beyond the point of simply advocating peaceful coexistence. My theme for this chapter is advocacy of synergy between the experimental tradition and an ecological orientation of the field. My intent is to show, in a historical perspective, that basic research directed at understanding naturalistic phenomena is succeeding in psychology as well as in other sciences. I want to stress that the emerging domains of naturalistic learning and memory research require a range of innovative strategies that combine ecological methods with traditional laboratory techniques.

At the outset I want to clarify a frequent confusion between naturalistic and applied research. The purpose of most naturalistic research is to discover general principles, and this is also the goal of basic, but not of applied, research. The goals of applied research are technological, that is, to achieve a particular endstate or endproduct. Naturalistic research explores phenomena in their natural, ecological context without reducing or modifying them to render them more amenable to laboratory study. Thus naturalistic research often involves trade-offs in which observation and correlational analyses are substituted for laboratory manipulation in order to study phenomena that do not lend themselves to laboratory control. Let me begin with what I believe to be common ground. Control is key to the discovery of regularities in nature, and the laboratory environment offers the best opportunities for control. For this reason the laboratory remains the preferred setting for investigating phenomena that permit laboratory observation. Strategies diverge when, for a variety of reasons, the phenomena of interest do not lend themselves to laboratory exploration. The required time periods may be excessive, as in investigations of acquisition and retention of complex semantic content, or of autobiographical, childhood memory content, or the variables of interest may be difficult to manipulate in the laboratory (e.g., conditions that produce intense fear, anger, pain, or deprivation).

Various kinds of rationale justified the neglect of such content within the traditional paradigm: I was taught that principles developed on the basis of list-learning experiments could be expected to generalize to more complex memory content, and therefore there was no need to examine the more complex content directly. Related rationale justified the use of metaphors, analogs, or simulated versions of the content of interest (e.g., simulated crimes), or the use of attenuated emotional or motivational conditions appropriate for the laboratory. The implicit, overriding assumption of the experimental paradigm was that laboratory methods afforded the best control and therefore yielded the best science, and that the use of nonlaboratory methods was unnecessary and undesirable because they jeopardized the scientific status of memory research.

PHYSICS VERSUS BIOLOGY

The focus on the laboratory and the assumptions of a reductionist paradigm are rooted in the model of 19th-century physics. Bruce (1985) pointed out that biology might have provided a more suitable model for psychology, because the study of naturalistic phenomena with an emphasis on individual differences was basic to evolutionary theory and therefore was an integral part of the Darwinian paradigm. In contrast, traditional memory research remained focused on average performance. Individual differences were used primarily as a basis for estimating error; they rarely became the object of inquiry. To be sure, other areas of psychological research emerging at about the same time as memory research adopted the Darwinian model, used naturalistic methods, and made important contributions to basic science as well as to technology. The entire domain of tests and measurements, the factorial analysis of intelligence into primary mental abilities, and all of the related technological contributions of aptitude testing to education and industry are based on analyses of individual differences pertaining to naturalistically acquired knowledge. In his presidential address to the American Psychological Association in 1957, Lee Cronbach (1957) deplored the schizoid division of scientific psychology into two disciplines, one using correlational methods and focusing on individual differences, the other using experimental methods and focusing on analysis of variance. It has taken many years for memory scholars to use correlational methods and to study "what humans have not learned to control or can never hope to control." In Cronbach's words: "Nature has been experimenting since the beginning of time, with a boldness and complexity far beyond the resources of science. The correlator's mission is to observe and organize the data from nature's experiments" (p. 672).

There are other lessons to be learned from psychological research that focused on individual differences. The impetus for investigating individual differences generally came from the desire to solve societal problems, for example, the failure of certain children to profit from standard reading instructions. The focus on such naturalistic phenomena and on practical concerns did not impede but facilitated the development of general theory, and the theory in turn brought about contributions to the solution of a wide range of problems of selection, placement, training, and adjustment of individuals in education, industry, and the military.

The pioneering work of Thorndike provides an excellent example of programmatic research in learning with a focus on education involving both laboratory and naturalistic investigations. Thorndike's research led to a host of practical contributions, ranging from curricular reform based on his theory of transfer, to pedagogical reforms based upon his law of effect (Thorndike, 1913), to specific instructional content changes based on ecological work such as his word counts (Thorndike & Lorge, 1944). Half a century later the impact of his contributions persists. Thorndike's work reflects the influence of functionalism and pragmatism, both inspired by the Darwinian paradigm. It is a curious fact that the Darwinian influence on traditional memory research remained minimal, although the influence on learning research was substantial. During the functionalist era learning was seen as the key to adaptation and the study of adaptation was the principal task of psychology.

The theories of Thorndike and Hull were inspired by evolutionary theory. In contrast, memory research adhered to the Ebbinghaus paradigm and remained unaffected by the Darwinian influence. The paucity of evolutionary influence on memory research is apparent from the lack of emphasis on individual differences, from the scant attention paid to motivational and emotional conditions, and from the failure to investigate the adaptive aspects of memory.

The isolation of memory research from real-world tasks has diminished, but continues to characterize much of contemporary research on information processing. Individual differences, emotional and motivational conditions, and adaptive changes or strategies remain neglected areas. Nelson and Narens (1994) pointed to the lack of a naturalistic target as one of the major shortcomings of current research. In agreement with Gruneberg, Morris, and Sykes (1991), they contended that investigations targeted at explaining naturalistic phenomena give programmatic research a common goal that facilitates and identifies cumulative progress. As Neisser (1976, p. 7) said long ago: "Cognitive psychologists must make a greater effort to understand cognition as it occurs in the ordinary environment and in the context of natural purposeful activity." In contrast, much of current memory research is oriented toward the exploration of esoteric laboratory phenomena that have no clear relation to naturalistic targets. As a result, the research frequently lacks a clear criterion for determining progress and problems are not solved. The focus simply shifts to new problem areas, or as Baddeley (1988, p. 4) described it: "Yet more experiments about other experiments." Morris (1987) concluded that the choice and development of models of human cognition seems to depend very much on the personal interest of modelers and very little on empirical and practical demands of the world.

LESSONS OF HISTORY

Research paradigms inspired primarily by a metaphoric or analogical relationship to naturalistic target phenomena may give rise to a long progression of empirical work without ever fulfilling the implied promise of shedding light on the naturalistic targets. This is a lesson we ought to have learned from our history. Pavlovian conditioning, for example, remains a valuable method of investigating the acquisition and extinction of autonomic nervous system responses, such as desensitization of phobias. The conditioning paradigm relates directly to the naturalistic target behavior in these contexts. In contrast, little of value remains from the myriad investigations of eyelid conditioning inspired by their analogical relation to complex human activities of learning, memory, or problem solving. Similarly, we no longer believe that the study of discrimination learning or maze learning in rats is the best approach to understanding human concept formation, decision making, or neurotic behavior. After years of research in which the expected payoffs did not materialize, we can conclude that in these instances the advantage of greater laboratory control did not make up for the disadvantage of a remote, analogical relation between the phenomena observed and the phenomena of primary interest. To be sure, basic research may yield serendipitous discoveries, and it is impossible to predict such gains, but the possibility of unexpected discoveries does not justify the long-term pursuit of research strategies that lack a clear relation to naturalistic targets of interest.

There are many examples of successful research in which the relation between the targeted and the investigated phenomena is direct and clear. Early in our history psychophysical scaling, the exploration of sensory processes, and investigations of rote memory come to mind. More recently, human performance theory pioneered by Donald Broadbent, Paul Fitts, Allan Baddeley, and others made important contributions to our understanding of selective attention, vigilance, working memory, and perceptual motor activities. Programmatic research in these domains contributed to general understanding of human performance in a variety of contexts, and also yielded applied benefits such as improvements in the design of displays, of work environments, and of man–machine systems.

Another historical lesson that I believe can help us to distinguish successful from unsuccessful research relates to the validity of our methods, that is, the extent to which the methods we use are capable of answering the questions we ask. When our questions can be answered by summarizing observations there is no reason to doubt the validity of methods or of conclusions, and cumulative progress is ensured. The work of Ebbinghaus illustrates a close correspondence between observations and conclusions; his conclusions did not go far beyond his observations, and his methods were clearly valid in relation to the conclusions. In contrast, when observations do not directly document conclusions, but are only compatible with them and the conclusions depend on additional unverified inferences, the methods are overextended, and cumulative progress is in jeopardy. I do not argue that we can dispense with logical inferences; I believe that inference is at the heart of creativity, but cumulative progress is ensured only to the extent that inferences are ultimately verified. Unverified inferences can lead to years of unproductive research. The early work of introspective psychologists who trained observers to identify elements of consciousness illustrates research with invalid conclusions. Elements of consciousness could not be validly identified by introspection, and the method was therefore invalid for the proposed purpose. I believe that current testing of cognitive models of memory is subject to analogous methodological difficulties (Bahrick, 1987). The available observations do not directly document a particular cognitive process. Rather, they support the inference of one or another process until minor adjustments of other models indicate that alternative processes cannot be ruled out. In order to avoid an infinite progression of indecisive research we must either develop more valid methods or defer questions that are intractable, that is, beyond the reach of current methods. Similar considerations led Watkins (1990) to reject mediationism and to recommend that theories of memory completely avoid references to unobserved processes or states.

DEGREES OF CONTROL

In order to create an appropriate perspective for synergy between naturalistic and laboratory work I now want to discuss experimental control as a decision process in memory research. In discussing available controls, I use Melton's (1963) distinction among three phases of investigations: acquisition of content, activities or interventions during the retention interval, and the retention test itself. In traditional memory research of the sort initiated by Ebbinghaus, the experimenter controls the acquisition of content and the memory test, but not the events transpiring during the retention interval. Experimental controls apply to all three phases only in memory research limited to very short time periods; for example, the Brown/Peterson paradigm, in which a filler task is used to control activities during the retention interval. The degree of control over acquisition varies, depending on the nature of content. Ebbinghaus used meaningless content in an attempt to reduce the effect of uncontrolled, preexperimental experiences on acquisition. When meaningful content is used, laboratory control of acquisition applies only to the encoding of sequential and contextual associations; the meaning of the content is established naturalistically prior to the experiment. Nevertheless, most experimentors have used meaningful content during the past 30 years of memory research because they wanted to find out how various types of meanings, organizations, or schemata affect encoding, storage and retrieval processes, and meanings, and schemata could generally not be acquired in the laboratory. My point is that the degree of control in laboratory memory research has varied from the beginning. It has involved trade-offs in which control over aspects of acquisition and the retention interval are sacrificed in order to investigate the phenomena of interest. Control over much of acquisition is sacrificed when we use meaningful material or study the effects of naturalistically acquired organization. Control over activities during the retention interval is sacrificed whenever we use intervals longer than a few minutes. Naturalistic investigations can also be described from this perspective. They usually maintain control over testing, but sacrifice control over acquisition and over the retention interval.

Now that I have dispelled the myth of a dichotomy between laboratory control versus naturalistic laissez faire, I describe how memory research can integrate the advantages of both methodologies so as to achieve a synergistic convergence. My rationale assumes that degree of control refers to a continuum and that variables that typically remain uncontrolled in memory experiments (e.g., most individual difference variables or activities during the retention interval) become part of the error term. An alternative rarely exploited in experiments involves systematic assessment of uncontrolled variables. When uncontrolled variables are assessed their relation to performance on retention tests can be established, and this offers important advantages to both laboratory and naturalistic memory research. Regression techniques can establish the effects of individual difference variables and yield estimates of conventional statistical significance, in addition to estimates of practical significance, by indicating the proportion of variance in the dependent variable accounted for by the controlled variables and the assessed variables. Finally, estimates of interactions among assessed variables can be obtained, and by including higher-order terms in the analysis, linear versus nonlinear relations are identified. Thus, the regression analysis yields much information that is not obtained in traditional memory experiments. There are limitations, of course. The regression analysis cannot yield information about causality, nor can it sort out individual effects of variables that are intrinsically confounded. It is therefore preferable to control variables in an orthogonal design when possible, and to assess and analyze through regression the effects of additional variables that would otherwise be part of the error term.

The advantages of regression analyses have been known for a long time, and have been exploited in memory experiments whenever covariance techniques were employed. Generally speaking, however, memory researchers have not availed themselves of these advantages, because they viewed correlational methods as a less scientific alternative to experiments, rather than as a supplement. My thesis is that orthogonal designs are not incompatible with regression analyses and that the integration of laboratory and naturalistic research strategies can yield innovative research designs that combine the advantages of both methodologies.

I have advocated four strategies for programmatic memory research: the identification of naturalistic research targets that relate directly rather than metaphorically to the phenomena we investigate; a focus on individual differences; designs that use experimental manipulation and regression analyses as supplementary, not as mutually exclusive options; and conclusions that are closely tied to observations without reliance on unverifiable inferences.

THE EMERGING SYNERGY

I now discuss contemporary research that exemplifies the emerging synergistic relation of laboratory and naturalistic methods. My selection is arbitrary, but it illustrates how new insights about memory have been gleaned by adopting naturalistic research targets, focusing on individual differences, avoiding unverifiable inferences, and seeking methodological controls that are tailored to the targeted phenomena, rather than imposed by adherence to an artificial dichotomy. I have chosen research on expertise as an example. Interest in superior achievement dates back to Galton's (1869) studies of genius. He measured outstanding achievements on the basis of social criteria (prizes, recognitions, etc.), defined these criteria statistically, and concluded that genius was largely innate, that is, a product of nature, not nurture. Subsequent findings of low correlations between indicants of outstanding achievement and scores on tests of general mental capacities discredited Galton's conclusions. The early research was naturalistic, that is, it focused on naturally occurring individual differences and involved no experimental analyses of performance, little laboratory testing, and inadequate controls.

During the 1950s, research on expertise changed to a laboratory setting and focused on the acquisition and retention of skills. Individuals were trained in skills such as mirror drawing or tracking moving targets. Research centered on the measurement of skill and on the identification and control of variables that affected acquisition and retention. This research advanced techniques of measurement and the development of apparatus, and it yielded information about the acquisition of skill, but it shed little light on the targeted expert behavior (e.g., piloting aircraft). In retrospect, the reasons for this limitation are clear. The expertise of professional pilots is based on several thousand hours of practice under a great variety of naturally occurring conditions, whereas most laboratory observations of skill acquisition were limited to a few hours of practice under standardized conditions. The naturalistic research targets bore only a remote relation to the skills examined in the laboratory. An integrative approach that combines the advantages of laboratory control with the examination of naturally acquired expertise began with the classic studies of chess masters by de Groot (1978). Ericsson and Smith (1991) gave an excellent account of the research that emerged from these pioneer investigations. They suggested that three stages of research strategy are involved. The first stage they described involves the identification and development of standardized laboratory-controlled tasks that capture the superior performance of the expert. Observing experts perform these tasks over a period of time is not likely to reveal significant changes due to learning, because the tasks monitor stabilized performance perfected over many years. Other evidence that the tasks capture the essence of expertise is obtained from novices who, when trained for a few weeks or months, cannot equal the performance of experts. Developing appropriate tasks usually requires programmatic laboratory research, and the strategy combines the advantages of laboratory control over testing and task development with the selection of outstanding individual performers who acquired their expertise naturalistically over a long period.

   Tasks that measure expert memory performance have played a prominent role in this phase of the research, although memory reflects only certain aspects of expertise. A wide range of domains has been researched, including chess, bridge, musical and athletic performance, electronic and computer skills, medical diagnosis, and memory expertise per se (Thompson, Cowan, & Frieman, 1993). The memory performance of experts is generally superior, but only for a narrow range of tasks and usually only for those aspects of the task that are critical for the success of experts. Thus, chess masters remember real but not random chess positions better than do novices (Chase & Simon, 1973); radiologists remember pathological but not normal aspects of x-rays better than do novices (Myles, Johnston, & Simons, 1988); and a memory expert who can recite 10,000 decimal digits of the number π performs within the normal range when memory is tested for letter rather than number sequences (Thompson et al., 1993). These findings illustrate what Ericsson and Smith (1991) described as the second stage of expertise research. This stage involves the analysis of expert performance on tasks developed in stage one in order to test hypotheses concerning the processes mediating superior performance. Thus, research on transcription typing (Salthouse, 1985) shows that with higher skill level, typists look farther ahead in the text, and this is critical to the superior typing speed of experts. Comparison of think-aloud verbalizations by experts and novices is a common method of assessing differences in the mediating processes related to the subject's level of expertise. Data based on analysis of the performance of chess masters by Chase and Simon (1973) indicate that experts have enlarged their perceptual grasp so that they can access configurations of chess pieces encoded as large chunks permitting a direct solution of problems, whereas novices must obtain solutions by a step-by-step process.
   The third stage described by Ericsson and Smith involves theoretical and empirical accounts of how the mechanisms identified in stage two are acquired through training and practice. This research determines at what levels of practice and under what conditions various aspects of performance identified in stage two are perfected. An impressive range of tasks has been examined, including expert shoplifters (Weaver & Carroll, 1985) and experts at handicapping horse races (Ceci & Liker, 1986).
   I have singled out research on expertise because this domain showed limited progress when either naturalistic or laboratory methods were used exclusively, and the recent, impressive advances reflect research strategies that pragmatically and creatively combine naturalistic and laboratory methods. The research starts by examining the unusual skills of highly trained and selected individuals who have acquired expertise naturalistically. Thus, the naturalistic target phenomena are investigated directly, not metaphorically or under reduced conditions, and with a built-in focus on individual differences. Programmatic laboratory research is typically involved in assess-

ing processes of superior performance and developing theoretical accounts of acquisition of expertise to the extent that the variables in question permit manipulation and control. If manipulation is not possible, assessment through regression analyses is substituted, as illustrated by Ceci and Liker's (1986) study of expertise in handicapping horse races. In such situations, only the testing of skills occurs in the laboratory. Our own research on the long-term maintenance of knowledge has followed this general pattern (Bahrick, 1984; Bahrick & Hall, 1991), and the methodology and results are applicable to the long-term maintenance of expertise. Our regression analyses cannot always sort out the effects of variables that are confounded; however, we have used follow-up quasi-experiments to answer unresolved questions. We found, for example, that those who take more language or mathematics courses not only retain more content as one would expect, but also retain as permastore content a much larger portion of original knowledge. More courses involve more practice and also wider spacing of practice so that the amount and the spacing of practice are inextricably confounded. In two nine-year longitudinal follow-up investigations we were able to manipulate these variables orthogonally and establish their independent contributions to the maintenance of knowledge (Bahrick, Bahrick, Bahrick, & Bahrick, 1993; Bahrick & Phelps, 1987).

Considering the length of time required for this type of study I cannot recommend it to colleagues who aspire to rapid promotions, but the research has potential benefits to society. It yields guidelines for extending the life span of knowledge at moderate expense. Given the enormous societal and personal investments in the acquisition of knowledge, it is important that memory scholars supply educators with answers to critical questions regarding the maintenance and longevity of knowledge (Schmidt & Bjork, 1992). Research on expertise yields better understanding of the structure of knowledge and skill as well as a variety of technological benefits. Among these are enhancement of expert performance and of the efficiency of training a wide range of expertise pertaining to athletic, musical, professional, and industrial skills. As a result we not only see Olympic records tumble, but tasks that once were the exclusive domain of a few select individuals are brought within the reach of many.

Several other domains of memory research now effectively combine naturalistic and experimental approaches, but this chapter is not the appropriate forum for a detailed account of their progress. Just one brief example, in the area of children's memory for stressful events, is a study by Parker, Bahrick, Lundy, Fivush, and Levitt (1994). Based on my privileged access, I know that they tested the memory of young children who experienced Hurricane Andrew. The accuracy of the children's recollections will be related to the age of the child, the degree and type of stress, and other individual difference variables. Regression analyses of such data will help us to make sense of the divergent effects of stress on memory and of the validity of children's reports of traumatic events.

We began over 100 years ago with experiments inspired by the model of physics. We made good progress in discovering regularities of memory for content acquired in the laboratory. However, these findings are of limited relevance to the concerns of educators, psychotherapists, jurists, and others who need information about the retention of semantic memory content, traumatic content, childhood memories, and other autobiographical content that cannot be acquired in the laboratory. To meet these needs and to gain a more general understanding of how memory functions we must investigate a broad range of phenomena that require a diversified methodology. I have advocated strategies that remain focused on naturalistic targets and individual differences and avoid unverifiable inferences. Our strategies must be pragmatically adapted to the phenomena of interest. This does not call for an a priori commitment to the laboratory or to naturalistic methods, but a synergistic evolution of methods perfected on an ad hoc basis. The program of the Third International Conference on Practical Aspects of Memory is proof that we are well along on this chartered course and that the future of memory research will be founded on, but not limited by, our past.

ACKNOWLEDGMENTS

Preparation of this chapter was supported by National Science Foundation Grant DBS-9119800. I thank Stephanie Berger, Darryl Bruce, Douglas Nelson, Thomas Nelson, and Eugene Winograd for their helpful comments and ideas. They are not to be blamed for the views expressed in the chapter.

REFERENCES

Baddeley, A. (1988). But what the hell is it for. In M. M. Gruneberg, P. E. Morris, & R. N. Sykes (Eds.), *Practical aspects of memory: Current research and issues* (pp. 3–17). New York: Wiley.

Bahrick, H. P. (1984). Semantic memory content in permastore—50 years of memory for Spanish learned in school. *Journal of Experimental Psychology: General, 113*, 1–29.

Bahrick, H. P. (1987). Functional and cognitive memory theory: An overview of some key issues. In D. Gorfein & R. Hoffman (Eds.), *Memory and learning, The Ebbinghaus Centennial Conference* (pp. 387–395). Hillsdale, NJ: Lawrence Erlbaum Associates.

Bahrick, H. P., Bahrick, L. E., Bahrick A. S., & Bahrick P. E. (1993). Maintenance of foreign language vocabulary and the spacing effect. *Psychological Science, 4*, 316–321.

Bahrick, H. P., & Hall, L. K. (1991). Lifetime maintenance of high school mathematics content. *Journal of Experimental Psychology: General, 120*, 20–33.

Bahrick, H. P., & Phelps, E. (1987). Retention of Spanish vocabulary over eight years. *Journal of Experimental Psychology: Learning Memory and Cognition, 13*, 344–349.

Bruce, D. (1985). The how and why of ecological memory. *Journal of Experimental Psychology: General, 114*, 78–90.

Ceci, S. J., & Liker, J. K. (1986). A day at the races: A study of IQ, expertise, and cognitive complexity. *Journal of Experimental Psychology: General, 15*, 255–266.

Chase, W. G., & Simon, H. A. (1973). The mind's eye in chess. In W. G. Chase (Ed.), *Visual information processing* (pp. 215–281). New York: Academic Press.

Cronbach, L. J. (1957). The two disciplines of scientific psychology. *American Psychologist, 12*, 671–684.

de Groot, A. (1978). *Thought and choice in chess.* The Hague: Mouton. (Original work published 1946)

Ericsson, K. A., & Smith J. (1991). Prospects and limits of the empircal study of expertise: An introduction. In K. A. Ericsson & J. Smith (Eds.), *Toward a general theory of expertise* (pp. 1–38). New York: Cambridge University Press.

Galton, F. (1869). *Hereditary genius.* New York: Macmillan.

Gruneberg, M. M., Morris, P. E., & Sykes, R. N. (1991). The obituary on everyday memory and its practical applications is premature. *American Psychologist, 46*, 74–76.

Melton, A. W. (1963). Implications of short-term memory for a general theory of memory. *Journal of Verbal Learning and Verbal Behavior, 2*, 1–21.

Morris, P. (1987). (Ed.). *Modeling cognition.* Chichester, England: Wiley.

Myles, W., Johnston, W., & Simons, M. (1988). The influence of expertise on X-ray processing. *Journal of Experimental Psychology: Learning, Memory and Cognition, 14*, 553–557.

Neisser, U. (1976). *Cognition and reality: Principles and implications of cognitive psychology.* New York: Freeman.

Neisser, U. (1978). Memory: What are the important questions? In M. M. Gruneberg, P. E. Morris, & R. N. Sykes (Eds.), *Practical aspects of memory* (pp. 3–24). London: Academic Press.

Neisser, U. (1988). Time present and time past. In M. M. Gruneberg, P. E. Morris, & R. N. Sykes (Eds.), *Practical aspects of memory: Current research and issues, 2* (pp. 545–560). Chichester, England: Wiley.

Nelson, T. O., & Narens, L. (1994). Why investigate metacognition. In J. Metcalfe & A. G. Shimamura (Eds.), *Metacognition: Knowing about knowing* (pp. 1–26). Cambridge, MA: MIT Press.

Parker, J., Bahrick, L., Lundy B., Fivush, R., & Levitt, M. (1994). *The effects of stress on memory for a natural disaster.* Paper presented at the Third Practical Aspects of Memory Conference, University of Maryland.

Salthouse, T. A. (1985). Anticipatory processing in transcription typing. *Journal of Applied Psychology, 70*, 264–271.

Schmidt, R. A., & Bjork, R. A. (1992). New conceptualizations of practice: Common principles in three paradigms suggest new concepts for training. *Psychological Science, 3*, 207–217.

Thompson, C. P., Cowan T. M., & Frieman, M. (1993). *Memory search by a memorist.* Hillsdale, NJ: Lawrence Erlbaum Associates.

Thorndike, E. L. (1913). *Educational psychology: The psychology of learning, Vol. II.* New York: Teacher's College

Thorndike, E. L., & Lorge, I. (1944). *The teacher's word book of 30,000 words.* New York: Bureau of Publications, Teacher's College, Columbia University.

Watkins, M. J. (1990). Mediationism and the obfuscation of memory. *American Psychologist, 45*, 328–335.

Weaver, F. M., & Carroll, J. S. (1985). Crime perceptions in a natural setting by expert and novice shoplifters. *Social Psychology Quarterly, 48*, 349–359.

CHAPTER FIVE

The Practical Application of Memory Research: Practical Problems in the Relationship Between Theory and Practice

Michael M. Gruneberg
University of Wales, Swansea

Peter E. Morris
University of Lancaster

Robert N. Sykes
University of Wales, Swansea

Douglas J. Herrmann
Center for Health Statistics

The Third Practical Aspects of Memory conference, and the two volumes that have come out of the conference, demonstrate that a great deal of interest exists in the practical aspects of memory. One illustration of this is that the number of papers has increased considerably from the first to the second to the third Practical Aspects of Memory (PAM) Conference, from 90 in 1978 to 190 in 1987 to 250 in 1994. Since the first conference, we have witnessed the birth of an applied journal concerned with memory and cognition, the journal *Applied Cognitive Psychology*. In recent years there have been special issues concerned with practical aspects of memory in basic research journals, such as *Memory & Cognition*. Furthermore, the American Psychological Association has recently initiated an applied journal, mainly concerned with cognition, in the *Journal of Experimental Psychology* series. Finally, as of last year, we have a formal organization to represent our interests, the Society for Applied Research in Memory and Cognition. It is fair to say that applied research in memory and cognition has come of age.

However, this chapter is not intended to recite the virtues of the practical memory movement. Substantial as the growth of the practical memory movement has been, we wish to argue that this growth has not been as great as it could have been. We believe that, although progress has been substantial, nevertheless growth is curtailed because of attitudes in the minds of many in the scientific and academic community that currently limit that growth. We believe that it is necessary to address these problems if further substantial progress is to be made.

Thus, in this chapter we review the factors that we believe threaten to limit the development of practical applications of basic cognitive theory and that also impede continued development of basic cognitive theory because of impaired communication between applied and basic researchers. First, we point out attitudes manifested by some basic researchers that make for a hostile workplace among applied researchers, those interested in developing real-life applications, and basic researchers with interests in applied work. Second, we point out that some basic researchers misunderstand the substantial intellectual challenges and difficulties involved in applied research and the application of research. Third, some of our own publication practices may unwittingly mislead readers outside the applied memory and cognition field. Fourth, we propose some recommendations for ourselves as individuals, for the Society as it represents us, and for those basic researchers who recognize that basic and applied researchers are equal servants of society. In essence, this chapter argues that technological advance has been limited by the unfavorable social context in which applied work within the basic scientific community takes place, and puts forward a number of suggestions to help overcome some of the problems.

A HOSTILE WORKPLACE: ATTITUDES THAT HINDER APPLIED RESEARCH

A scientist's workplace is the laboratory, the institution in which the laboratory exists, and the literature. Scientific developments are never fully tested until they have been expressed in the literature and other colleagues react to them. Thus, if a scientist has difficulty getting a fair hearing in the literature, and moreover is criticized for good work because this work does not conform to the current reward system, this scientist may be said to be laboring in a hostile workplace.

In this section, we point out attitudes manifested by some basic researchers that make for a hostile workplace among applied researchers, those interested in applying research, and basic researchers with interests in applied work. These factors include the assumption of some basic researchers that basic research exists for knowledge's sake only and that the duty of the scientist is to pursue knowledge for knowledge's sake only and to leave application to others; that any effort in an activity that slows the publication rate is not worthwhile; and that earning money through application is undesirable. These issues are considered in turn.

Basic Research Exists for Knowledge's Sake Only

Psychologists, being scientists, often consider that the goal of research should be the pure pursuit of knowledge. Those of us, therefore, who seek to apply our knowledge to solving problems in the real world are, ipso facto, not scientists. That line of argument was explicitly stated by Banaji and Crowder (1991) in their reply to the response of Gruneberg, Morris, and Sykes (1991) to their 1989 paper (Banaji & Crowder, 1989). This, to our mind, is the heart of the problem. Any academic psychologist who publishes a piece of work, no matter how trivial, that looks at the latest memory model, however flawed, is in a different academic league from someone who successfully applies knowledge for the use of those outside academic life—no matter how useful or how successful. We quote Banaji and Crowder (1991): "Nor do we share Gruneberg, Morris, and Sykes' (1991) confusion about what appears to us to be a clear distinction between science and invention. Our discussion was aimed exclusively at methods of scientific enquiry and not at how Edison went about inventing the light bulb or for that matter, the electric chair. We would be delighted to see a Steve Jobs of human memory technology emerge some day, but we are of the belief that our goal is to advance science and not to come up with an occasional memory aid" (p. 78).

Despite the assertions of Banaji and Crowder (1989), it seems to us that there is abundant evidence that an interaction between theory and practice is beneficial to both (see, e.g., Herrmann, 1993). Since Neisser's (1978) call to investigate real-world memory phenomena in order to enhance our understanding of memory per se, at least three areas of considerable importance to our understanding of memory have emerged (or reemerged) from almost nowhere, namely autobiographical memory, memory improvement, and prospective memory. Arguably none would have thrived in the way they have had the climate not changed to allow the investigation of real-world phenomena in nonstandard ways. These areas provide the student of memory with fundamental insight into global memory functioning through posing questions on the nature of memory mechanisms not previously systematically investigated. The interaction has also been fruitful in the other direction, with, for example, the success of the cognitive interview (see, e.g., Fisher & Geiselman, 1988) and the training of strategic behavior in slow-learning school children highly dependent on earlier fundamental basic research (Pressley, 1994, personal communication). These examples clearly illustrate that basic and applied researchers have a common interest in the success of both enterprises in order to further their own particular interest. However, to say this is to imply that basic and applied researchers are always two different animals, and this, too, is clearly a false dichotomy. Any academic psychologist interested in application has to understand the basic mechanisms he or she is dealing with, and the success or failure of any application attempt is almost certain to lead to greater theoretical insights by that individual.

The success of the three Practical Aspects of Memory Conferences clearly indicates that many academic psychologists are interested in advancing the real-life application of their own work. This does not, of course, mean that every practical application leads to advances in theory or that every theoretical advance leads to immediate practical application. As well as interacting, the two domains can lead separate lives, at least as seen at any one point in time. However, there is no telling when the two might meet. Alistair Cook once gave a talk in his "Letter from America" radio series in which he traced the development of a treatment for cancer of the prostate back 200 years to a Scottish zoologist interested only in the sex life of hedgehogs. We often forget, under the pressure to publish two or three papers a year in quality journals, that science is a long game and short-term perspectives are usually myopic. Even if, therefore, we cannot see the practical application of theories today or tomorrow, it does not follow that they will never have any use in practical application. Furthermore, it is fruitless to look at each individual aspect of our theoretical understanding of memory when what is important is that we are building up a substantial body of knowledge and understanding. What those interested in practical application need is an extensive flexible framework of understanding of the underlying mechanisms of memory. In saying this, however, one must be aware of the dangers of accepting any single framework as being the right one as opposed to being useful for particular purposes.

The argument is not, therefore, whether the pursuit of knowledge for its own sake is or is not a good idea: Both basic and applied researchers often agree that it is essential to further both ends. It is interesting to note, however, that its justification is often that, as with Alistair Cook's example, major practical applications come after discoveries made in the pursuit of pure knowledge, even in the pure sciences. As Gruneberg (1988) argued at the last Practical Aspects of Memory Conference, does anyone really believe that governments all over the world would be supporting blue skies scientific research if it was not thought that major application of a percentage of such work was likely to be forthcoming? The pursuit of knowledge for its own sake takes place within a context where the expectation is that practical consequences will flow.

In regard to these expectations, psychology, in our view, is in a weaker position than the natural sciences. Psychology is a social science, with an interest focused on the behavior of other humans. To study behavior, and to make discoveries that may help those who are funding our scientific endeavors, but to refuse to help on the grounds that this is not the job of the scientist is regrettable in a science whose aim is to further human understanding of human behavior. Let us take an example from another science. Fleming has the undying gratitude of millions because his discovery led to a major practical application—penicillin—and although he did not apply his findings directly, other eminent scientists did. Are those who were able to apply Fleming's knowledge and to have that knowledge exploited to be denied the accolade of scientists and to be regarded as mere technicians in Banaji and Crowder's terms? Without the actual application of Fleming's findings, Fleming's work would arguably have had little significance. Because of many such successes, the value of application in other sciences is not in dispute. Our problem in psychology is a much more fundamental one, especially in the area of memory research—we cannot point to a vast range of practical application, although there are some valuable successes and an increasing number of individuals outside academic life who are willing to apply research findings from memory research.

The present controversy on the value of application is by no means new. In 1914, Hugo Munsterberg wrote in his psychology text:

> Yet while it is easy to find reasons for a certain reluctance in the past, there ought to be no doubt that such detachment from life is no longer excusable for the psychology of today. Nobody imagines that physics and chemistry are desecrated by being harnessed for the technical achievements of society. We could not imagine the laws of electricity or of steam power being known in the laboratories and not being applied for railways and steamers, for lighting our houses and for cabling our news. It is no less fitting and natural that the progress of psychology, too, should become helpful to the community wherever mental life is involved in its affairs, and it is evident that the mind takes a characteristic part in every domain of social interest, of education and of religion, of politics and of law, of commerce and of industry, of art and of scholarship, of family life and of practical intercourse, of public movements and of social reform. (pp. 341–342)

It is somewhat sad to realize that in the area of memory we still seem to have the same problems as Munsterberg saw all these years ago for psychology in general.

Activities That Do Not Lead to Frequent Conventional Academic Publications Are Undesirable

Because many academic psychologists feel that we should be pursuing knowledge for its own sake, it follows that academic activities that do not result in conventional academic publications are undesirable. In other words, there is academic pressure not to involve oneself in exercises that have a low payoff in terms of frequency, level, and indeed perceived appropriateness of publication. Herrmann and Gruneberg (1993), for example, noted the different patterns of publication for applied reports and academic research. However, in the United States and the United Kingdom, for example, a department's academic quality is judged basically on the number of high-level publications in quality journals. Because real-life applied research or real-life application is time consuming and because it leads to relatively infrequent publications (often in journals, books, or book chapters read by the targeted audience rather than by psychologists), the pursuit of application can be seen as highly negative for a particular department. In other words, application of research is seen as detracting from the total departmental quality output and the individual concerned is seen simply as not pulling his or her academic weight. This is the social context that makes application difficult, particularly in the United Kingdom, because the criteria are explicit and the judgments centralized. In such a social situation academics find it difficult to carry out research that is not mainstream and will seek to carry out "pure" or at best applicable research. It might be added that such a social situation is not healthy for pure research either, because it will encourage the pursuit of hot topics and hot money rather than new and possibly innovative areas. Furthermore, by employing high-level publication as *the* criterion for creative excellence, the acts of not only application but also writing and editing books, contributing book chapters, consulting, and conference organization come to be seen as secondary activities, even second-rate activities. Indeed, it was the lack of recognition of the organization of the first two PAM Conferences as a useful academic activity that led the original organizers to consider the academic advantages of holding future conferences in the United States.

Universities are about knowledge—acquiring it, evaluating it, transmitting it, using it, and stimulating its acquisition, evaluation, and use. In other words, it is not only application that is being caught in the publication trap, but the whole future of a balanced progress of the discipline. In the United States and elsewhere, the formalization of research quality is not taken to the extremes seen in the United Kingdom. Nevertheless, the writings of such as Banaji and Crowder and others make it clear that applying memory research is to be regarded at best as the poor relation of the pure pursuit of knowledge. Because such values have been relatively unchallenged until recently, they still hold sway and still materially influence the context in which application of memory research takes place. Of course, not all applied research is published in low-level journals, and many of the eminent academic psychologists who have successfully applied memory research have done so after publishing research findings in major academic journals. Nevertheless, it is our contention that real-life application and high-level publication in quality journals do not always easily sit together. This issue is discussed further presently.

Communication With the Public Is Beneath Science

Another problem faced by those willing to apply knowledge is that of academic conservatism that results in a fear of being wrong in public, or a fear of being criticized by fellow academics if they should turn out to be wrong or if they attempt to simplify complex issues for public consumption. An example is that of Loftus' willingness to give evidence as an expert witness on eyewitnessing, despite the criticism of this by peer psychologists. Loftus has happily stood her ground, but the underlying problem is that unless academic psychologists are willing to make mistakes no progress will ever be made, because the reality of findings in the laboratory will never be tested against a real-life criterion. No science has made progress without spectacular failures—for example, no learning of organ transplant techniques could have been made without early failures, and no advance in aircraft design without accidents. Unless a climate is created within academic psychology that will allow mistakes to be made in application, without undue criticism, there will be a brake on future development. Of course, once mistakes are discovered, they need to be rectified, but making mistakes is an essential part of the development process. As a counterbalance, of course, academic psychologists have to be conscious that their views might be given undue weight by virtue of their academic position and expertise, and academics who wish to apply knowledge do have a duty of care. However, if this duty of care is taken too far, then no mistakes may be made, but no advances may come either.

Money Earned Through Application
Is Beneath Contempt

Applying research often has financial implications for those doing the applying, whether it involves court fees, copyright or patent fees, consulting fees, and so on. The earning of extra money by academic staff in the area of psychology sits uneasily with the concept of the seeker after knowledge. Even seekers after knowledge, however, in our experience, are quite happy to receive book royalties, fees for talks to outside bodies, and salary increases on promotion. Few would argue that there is anything improper in this or that money was the primary motivation for their work. For most academic psychologists who apply their knowledge, we would argue the same principle holds. Why must it be assumed that those giving evidence as expert witnesses are not primarily motivated to show the value of psychology and the usefulness of their expertise? Why must it be assumed that those who receive royalties from tests or published materials were primarily motivated more by money than by the desire to contribute to psychology by making knowledge available to a wider public? Of course there is a financial question involved, but this can be solved by universities coming to a sensible arrangement on profit sharing, rather than in criticizing those who apply psychology for being interested in the fast buck rather than demonstrating the value of psychology to a wider audience. The main point being made is that it is unfair to denigrate application because there are financial rewards, rather than to see application as the lifeblood of any science if it is to be seen as relevant to those outside. In any case, the motivation of the successful "applier" is irrelevant, in much the same way as it matters not to the world whether Beethoven wrote his fifth symphony for money or love. What matters is that useful products of psychology become available—preferably soon!

PROBLEMS IN THE PRACTICAL APPLICATION
OF MEMORY RESEARCH

In this section, we discuss some of the major practical and intellectual difficulties facing those interested in real-life application. In particular, the reasons why application takes longer than does basic research are discussed, as are the difficulties of actually conducting applied research. Finally, the difficulties involved in publishing applied research in such a way as to maximize understanding and communication between application and theory is outlined. Because these difficulties are often not appreciated by those interested in basic research, the slow progress, the seemingly "soft" scientific criteria, and the lack of large numbers of papers appearing in leading journals leads to a feeling that application is an inferior academic activity.

Applied Research Is Less Efficient Than Basic Research

One major difficulty in applying research is logistical—the time taken to interact with relevant organizations is very considerable, even if things are going well. When they are not going well, the time taken has to be multiplied. It is this aspect of developing practical application that is the real problem in many ways. In its own terms, therefore, applying research is often harder to carry out in terms of effort and time than is laboratory research, as well as producing the problem of taking away from the effort of carrying out basic research, as noted earlier.

We asked a number of eminent basic researchers who have been successful in applying memory research to indicate the kind of problems they experienced in the actual applying of their research. Their answers illustrate the kind of problems met with in the outside world. Michael Pressley (personal communication, see also Herrmann, McEvoy, Hertzog, Hertel, & Johnson, 1995) whose interest is in the application of strategic behavior in school classrooms, noted that basic research in his area involves instruction to subjects that takes a few minutes at most, and even the most ambitious basic research usually takes no more than two years from conception to final writeup. Ecologically valid research, in his case, usually took slightly longer to instruct but not much more than 20 to 30 minutes. Practical application, on the other hand, in relation to teaching strategies in real-life situations in schools, involves teaching a repertoire of strategies and involves very long-term instruction of from one to several years. Pressley reported that one of his interventions has taken five years and is not yet in print. Real-life instruction in school involves explanations, reexplanations, teacher modeling of strategy use, and extensive guided practice in using strategies learned with a variety of materials.

Barbara Wilson (personal communication) gave a number of examples from her field of memory rehabilitation, where recently she has spent a considerable number of fruitless hours with patients. One, for example, refused all help because he was, in his own view, able to cope despite great problems in everyday living. Another patient had to be abandoned because he became aggressive and refused to respond to teaching. It is not, of course, that such problems fail to occur in the laboratory, but they are usually less time consuming than in dealing with real-life problems.

Ed Geiselman (personal communication) reported that the major problem he faced was establishing what he described as user trust, cooperation, and acceptance. In other words, the suspicion of professionals outside psychology that psychology had nothing worth offering had to be overcome. His solution was the highly time-consuming one of giving workshops and talks all over the United States. He found, as have many others, that a major real-life problem in applying memory research is not the problem of inventing a better mousetrap, but of convincing end users that it really is a better mousetrap. After all, every product claims for itself the advantage of being better than its alternatives.

Graham Davies, also involved in forensic application (in this case a photofit and other identification techniques), also pointed to the difficulties involved in interacting with those outside psychology. He wrote (personal communication), "We also found it sometimes difficult to convince non-scientists of research findings, police officers in particular tend to be anecdote-driven in their decisions."

Clearly the problem here is two-fold. Those interacting with the outside world have to convince those outside of the value of application. This is often a difficult task in itself. Even where it is successful, however, it is invariably highly time consuming and seen to be in direct conflict with "appropriate" academic activities involving research grant application, laboratory experimentation, and publication in higher-level recognized psychology journals.

Applied Research Is Looser Than Basic Research

As Gruneberg and Morris (1992) noted, applied memory research is often faced with problems similar to those facing organizational psychology in terms of lack of control of critical variables. They noted three examples in which laboratory studies are likely to be limited in terms of their applicability to real life, because real life involves the interaction of variables that are difficult to control in the laboratory. One of these is the area of eyewitness research, where they pointed out that because of, for example, the impossibility of mimicking the emotional aspects of a real-life rape or murder, laboratory studies can take us only so far. Molly Johnson (1993) cautioned severely about assuming that laboratory studies can be generalized to the real world as far as eyewitness evidence is concerned. She noted a number of studies where eyewitness accuracy for actual crimes was considerably higher than might have been expected from laboratory studies.

Gruneberg and Sykes (1993) recently made the same point with reference to another aspect of eyewitnessing, the confidence–accuracy relationship. As a result of a large number of studies that fail to show a significant relationship between confidence and accuracy, a number of psychologists, such as Smith, Kassin, and Ellsworth (1989), have argued that there is no significant relationship between confidence and accuracy. Yet this is clearly a questionable conclusion, because it is based on experiments where subjects must make some errors and show some variation in their confidence ratings in order for the experimenter to employ correlational analysis. Of necessity, experiments do not cover those many real-life situations where all subjects are likely to be both confident and accurate, as, for example, when people are asked what they had for breakfast this morning. We just do not know how many confidence decisions in court are of this kind for it to be possible to advise jurors to ignore confidence judgments in all circumstances. In any event, the point made by Johnson (1993) is well known and well taken, that generalizing from the laboratory to real-life application is fraught with difficulties. Carrying out applicable research without testing against real-life conditions is simply playing at application.

Pressley also noted the difficulty in conducting properly controlled experiments when applying research in his area. He wrote (personal communication):

> In every basic and ecologically valid study of memory that I have conducted, participants were assigned randomly to conditions. That was not possible in the school-based comparative studies of strategies instruction. It takes a teacher one to two years to learn how to teach strategies, and once a teacher does, there is commitment to the approach (El-Dinary, Pressley, & Schuder, 1992): Committed teachers will not give up a preferred teaching approach for the sake of a randomized experiment. Thus, our comparative studies of in-school reading strategies instruction are quasi-experiments, with great efforts made

at the outset of the interventions to match the strategies instruction classes with control classes receiving conventional instruction.

Organizational psychologists have long had to face this kind of problem. Warr and Wall (1975), in discussing the empirical evidence on job enrichment, noted:

> The vast majority of these experimentally orientated investigations point in the same direction: the introduction of greater variety and discretion into jobs is welcomed by employees. We must not, however, allow the relative consistency of these findings to mask some important limitations. In practice, the unsuccessful experiments are less likely to be reported than those with encouraging results. And amongst the latter the evaluation of the effects of job modification has not always been entirely adequate. In relation to employee satisfaction, for instance, much of the evidence is based upon the subjective impressions of the investigators, selected verbatim reports or attitude measures which are only briefly described. Again for reasons of practicality few studies have used adequate control groups. Also, the changes introduced into jobs and the effects of these modifications on the larger organizational system, are often poorly described. This makes it difficult to identify possible causes of observed changes in employee attitudes and performance, as does the fact discussed earlier that redesigning jobs frequently involves simultaneous changes to many different aspects of the work situation. In spite of these several limitations in the research evidence we are still left with the finding that most reported correlations and experimental studies in this area support the conclusion that jobs which offer variety and require the individual to exercise discretion over his work activities lead to enhanced well-being and mental health. (p. 137)

Our view is that those wishing to apply memory research should take the lead from organizational psychology. Where it is not possible or practicable to carry out laboratory-based research, researchers should publish such research as they can carry out, clearly identifying the work's limitations. When a body of such work is built up, a meta-analysis should then be undertaken. Interpretation, however, should be conservative and where possible should be related to established and/or laboratory-based studies. Of course, mistakes might be made, but the greater mistake might be in the rejecting of such evidence as there is conservatively interpreted than in accepting it.

PUBLICATION PRACTICES BY PRACTICAL MEMORY RESEARCHERS ARE SOMETIMES ACADEMICALLY PROBLEMATIC

A major problem in relation to advancing communications through publication in applied memory research is highlighted by Leirer, Tanke, and Morrow (1993), psychologists outside academic life but who are working in the practical application of memory research. They questioned the value of academic publication and noted the difficulties facing those outside academic psychology in communicating with their academic colleagues. The requirements of the marketplace, they argued, makes academic publication difficult. They wrote:

> Publishing findings in basic or applied cognitive journals is nearly valueless for purposes of commercializing systems. Instead, it is important to use available time and resources publishing research findings in journals specific to the areas served by the product. Thus, most commercial systems development research will be published in journals that cognitive psychologists will never read. Further, because the readers of these other journals have no background or interest in cognitive psychology, little or no attention will be given to findings relevant to theoretical issues. Therefore, even though theory-relevant findings occur with regularity, they have little chance of being reported. Unless a solution to this problem is found, the flow of information between theoretical and applied researchers is likely to continue in only one direction. (p. 687)

In other words, if the arguments of Leirer et al. are to be accepted, then leaving application to those outside academic life will lead to relatively poor feedback from practice to theory, unless of course, as noted earlier, psychology journals make a point of publishing papers from practitioners. However, as Leirer et al. pointed out, those applying research are not primarily interested in publishing for academic psychologists, and hence the problem is not going to be easily solved.

However, this publication targeting, which is damaging to the communication of academics and nonacademics, is also important in the opposite direction. Academics wishing to influence fields of application must publish where they are likely to be influential. Often this will involve publishing in nonpsychology journals. Such activity is in conflict with the needs of academic psychologists to publish in high-quality psychology journals.

The "Straw-Man" Defense

It might be argued that the discussion so far is unreal and that we have been erecting "straw-men" to attack. After all, there has been an enormous increase in the production of papers on applied issues in the last 15 years. However, we do not believe that many of the papers published on applied aspects of memory *are* applied psychology; rather, they are applicable psychology.

We believe that a major distinction that must again be emphasized is that between applicable research and applied research (Herrmann & Gruneberg, 1993). Our view is that the great majority of psychologists interested in application are happy to publish applicable research, and high-level journals are often happy to publish such research. Applicable research is usually laboratory-based research that, if it were to be taken into the real world and applied systematically, would have the potential to help enhance the well-being of the community. Applied research and application, on the other hand, involve a sustained and systematic attempt to actually apply applicable research to the real world. This does not mean that applied research always involves attempts to take applicable research into the real world. This is often determined by the task demands of the particular problems being addressed. Because of the academic pressures discussed earlier, almost all academic psychologists, however much they would like to apply research in the real world, do not do so. They publish applicable research, often in major journals. This does not mean that applicable research is of no value in the application process. Many applications of research are based on, or use, information gained from studies of applicable research that show the potential for application in the real world. Examples of this are in the work of Geiselman and his colleagues, who developed their cognitive interview out of a number of pieces of laboratory research showing the effectiveness of a number of different retrieval strategies.

Pressley (personal communication), too, has based application in the classroom on applicable research. He wrote:

> The greatest lesson I have learned from this experience is that it is absolutely necessary to conduct diverse research in order to understanding fully a problem in memory (i.e., basic, ecologically valid and practical research). Most of the strategies taught in the instructional packages we have encountered in school were first validated in laboratory studies, for example, the imagery strategy so prominent in in-school strategies instructional packages of today can be traced back to research in the 1970s exploring whether imagery instructions affected memory of text, including work that I conducted (e.g., Pressley, 1976). That work in turn descended from even more basic research on imagery, such as the many studies of dual coding summarized by Paivo (1971). In addition, the direct explanation approach at the heart of the in-school instruction we have been studying owes much to many basic studies that demonstrated strategies can be taught using explanations and modelling (see Pressley, Heisel, McCormick, & Nakamura, 1982). There is no way that in-school strategies instruction would exist in anything like its current state without the previous basic research. Even so, there is no way that in-school strategies instruction could be understood based on the laboratory studies alone.

The whole point of real-life applied research, however, is that it leads to development and evaluation of a product, whether it be interview procedures for police, teaching materials for teachers, eyewitness expertise, instruments for helping the elderly, or so on. Applied research, in other words, can be either developmental (aiming to creating a product) or evaluative (aiming at assessing the effectiveness of a product), although, of course, the two interact in that evaluation is likely to lead to further modification and development. Yet even if real-life applied research is grudgingly allowed as a legitimate, if second-rate, academic exercise, the development of actual products certainly does not come within the remit of the academic psychology reward system. It is just about acceptable to carry out research that may be helpful as long as you do not actually help anyone! Ultimately, what is not rewarded will not flourish, and the whole rationale for conducting applicable and applied research will cease to exist. Although increasing involvement by those outside academic life in memory application is wholly to be welcomed, as Gruneberg (1992) argued elsewhere it is academic psychologists who are often best placed to understand principles that will make application success-ful by virtue of their knowledge of the field. In any case, the number of those outside academic psychology who are skilled, interested, and in a position to develop application is minute compared to the situation in other sciences. If we want application to flourish, there is no choice at present but to encourage real-life application by basic researchers. To those such as Banaji and Crowder who argue that this is not science, we would reply that real-life application is the lifeblood of science, and that without application there would be no science. Unless some of us, some of the time, seek to emulate Fleming, Marconi, Brunel, Stephenson, and Edison, our whole academic endeavor will come to be seen as sterile and self-indulgent.

Of course, application is happening more and more, and there have been a growing number of successes. However, we repeat again, despite the considerable progress that has been made, successful application of memory research in real life will be more limited than it needs to be unless some of the problems we have outlined are faced and overcome.

SOME PARTIAL SOLUTIONS

Finally, we propose some recommendations for ourselves as individuals, for the society that represents us, and for basic researchers interested in practical application.

What Is Successful Application?

In the first place, it is essential to address the question as to what is meant by *successful application*. In other words, what criteria should be applied to be able to claim that an application is successful? As Leirer, Tanke, and Morrow (1993) noted, the acid test of successful application is not whether it results in papers in journals of applied psychology, worthy as this is, but whether it has a major influence on those it is targeted to help. What is more important in the work of Geiselman and his colleagues: that they have published papers in the *Journal of Applied Psychology* rather than *Psycho-logical Reports*, or that police forces in many parts of the world are using the methods they have developed and verified to enable justice to be better carried out? Is the work of Leirer and his colleagues the less important because he chooses to publish in journals outside psychology, or is their work important because they have successfully marketed a product that has empirically been shown to enhance the probability of patients attending health visits and consequently receiving better quality care?

Leirer et al. (1993) argued that commercial success in the form of rapidly increasing sales of a product should be the criterion, and, not surprisingly, their product meets this criterion. However, we would wish to argue for multiple criteria for success in this area, as in the area of pure academic research. The work of Geiselman and his colleagues (e.g., Fisher & Geiselman, 1988) is used widely by police forces in the United States and the United Kingdom (and possibly elsewhere), with the consequence that information-eliciting procedures for eyewitnesses have been enhanced, leading to the likelihood of more convictions of the guilty and more acquittals of the innocent. Leirer et al.'s own product, which involves ensuring that patients attend clinics more regularly, is not just a financial saving for those who use it, it also clearly is likely to save lives, as indeed are mechanisms that remind the elderly to take their medicine. Products that are commercially successful often are so because they offer to the consumer something above and beyond financial savings.

Another outstanding example is the work of Elizabeth Loftus. Whatever the limitations in our present psychological understanding of eyewitnessing, few would argue she has *not* been highly successful in making the legal system aware of the relevance of psychology to eyewitness evidence (see, e.g., Loftus & Ketchan, 1991). Clearly, financial considerations are irrelevant here as a measure of successful application. The successful application of memory research is not one thing, such as a product or a book or the influencing of educational practice or legal procedures, nor does an application necessarily have to be widespread to be important and successful. Some diseases, for example, are rare and fatal. A researcher who finds a cure for such a disease is arguably highly successful in applying his or her knowledge. What makes for successful application in the area of memory research is that such research successfully deals with the particular social problem being targeted in a way that is as scientifically verifiable as circumstances allow. Obviously, the bigger the social problem targeted, the wider will knowledge of the successful application be and the more successful will the application be seen to be. As noted earlier, there are problems in verifying empirically whether an application is successful. Real-life application will sometimes involve making compromises with scientific standards when it comes to assessing the value of the application in terms of applied research. This will happen where controls are difficult or impossible. Clearly, what makes a successful application is multifaceted and diverse, and we appreciate that in this chapter we have done no more than point out the difficulties in making an assessment of successful application.

Modifying Journal Practices

To return to the question of how best to encourage the application of research, one obvious way is to encourage the publication of applied research that illustrates the kind of problems being addressed and the successes and failures of such application attempts. One problem in doing this concerns academic journals that claim to publish applied research. As Herrmann and Gruneberg (1993) argued, such journals should concern themselves less with academic respectability and more with generating ideas and reporting application attempts, whether or not they meet the highest standards of scientific probity, provided, of course, that the limits of the work are clearly highlighted. Furthermore, there seems to be a marked reluctance at present to publish articles that have little or no theoretical implication and are limited in scope. The problem with this approach in terms of advancing practical application is that often theoretically trivial advances can have considerable practical implications. Take, for example, the training of an incontinent Alzheimer's patient to use the toilet. Such a step might be theoretically trivial, yet can make a huge social difference to relatives and to the patient concerned. Again, a two-page paper by Morris, Jones, and Hampson in 1978 on face–name association using mnemonic strategies led to remedial programs for brain-damaged patients improving their memory performance in what is an enormously important social skill. A one-page paper by Gruneberg, Monks, and Sykes published in 1976 showing the effectiveness of the first letter search strategy in overcoming memory blocks was incorporated in 1992 into a study by Geiselman and his colleagues (Saywitz, Geiselman, & Bornstein, 1992) investigating the effectiveness of the cognitive interview.

When it comes to evaluating the value of practical application, therefore, journal editors claiming to be interested in advancing practical applications must take on board the differences involved in evaluating applied and basic research in terms of methodology, control procedures, and scope (Herrmann & Gruneberg, 1993). Now that *Applied Cognitive Psychology* has become the house journal for the Society for Applied Research in Memory and Cognition, it is the hope of the present authors that editorial policy will take account of the practical difficulties of practice–theory interaction and will publish material that, although imperfect in academic terms, is nevertheless important in generating ideas for further theory and practice. The Practical Aspects of Memory proceedings for the first two conferences that we edited had just this philosophy—and at the same time did demand conventional standards of experimentation, where appropriate. Unless some journals read by basic researchers do take this line, we do not see a rosy future for applied memory research.

Marketing Applied Research

Another important point is that there must be an appreciation on the part of the academic community that there are considerable problems in taking any application into the marketplace, and that the marketplace, whether for the general public, or psychiatrists or engineers, or whoever is the market, often involves publicity and advertising to allow those who may benefit to know of the existence of the application. This process is the antithesis of what many academics regard as their role—the quiet contemplative life, unaffected by the market place. But how otherwise can the police be made aware of the benefits of the cognitive interview, or the public know there are techniques that can help them with a number of practical memory problems they are likely to meet in everyday life? A number of basic researchers, such as Higbee (1988) and Herrmann (1991), have recently published books on memory improvement that were commercially promoted. Is it not desirable that basic researchers with expertise in the area write the books with the aim of helping the general public and students? Is it not desirable that work that can be useful to those outside psychology is interpreted by those with a deep understanding rather than only superficial knowledge? Surely those who take the trouble to make useful information available to those who need it should be seen as facilitators to the whole academic process, not as irrelevant outsiders.

Herrmann's work can be regarded as both application of research and popularization. Application is not necessarily the same as popularization. Application involves the development of ideas so that they may be of use to those outside academia. Popularization involves letting those outside know of developments that are useful but it does not necessarily involve the development of useful material per se. Both processes in our view are essential if those outside psychology are to be made aware that psychologists have carried out work that is directly useful to them. We repeat, only when those interested in the pure pursuit of knowledge are willing to acknowledge that application and popularization are directly relevant to their purpose, to the extent that application and theory cross-fertilize each other, and to the extent that letting the public know that what we do can be developed to be of direct relevance to those outside, will proper application by academic psychologists on any large scale have a chance.

Legitimatizing Applied Research

In order to legitimatize applied research and application it is necessary to have an academic reward structure that recognizes the value of application on an equal footing with basic research. It is essential to get away from a simplistic centralized system of assessing excellence, such as an undue reliance on publication in quality journals. We could, as an aside, point out that the idea that publication in high-level journals such as the *Journal of Experimental Psychology* is an indication of long-term scientific merit, is, to say the least, dubious. We examined citations of papers published in the *Journal of Experimental Psychology* in 1981 in terms of their citation rate in 1991. Only one paper was cited more than 10 times, 39% were not cited at all, and only 47% were cited more than once. This is hardly the basis for major policy decisions on what is and is not important research. Academic departments must assess individuals in terms of their contribution to society through their applied work, where appropriate. Due weight must be given in academic terms to articles published in appropriate journals rather than only in academic journals, and the contribution of actual application must be seen as a whole, not in terms of the sum of its publications. Advances in science and application of science are made in a large number of different ways, and cannot be encapsulated by one or two simplistic criteria that discriminate against real-life application.

Essentially, what is being argued is that any academic activity, if it is to be sustained, requires a reward structure that is clear and reasonable. The academic reward structure for basic researchers involved in applying research is far from clear and for the most part does not appear to exist. At present, those involved in applying research have to be satisfied with the knowledge that they are carrying out an activity that is regarded by society in general as useful. Part of the role of the new Society for Applied Research in Memory and Cognition will, in our view, be to change the academic climate such that real-life application is both academically acceptable and academically rewarded on an equal footing with purely basic or applicable research.

CONCLUDING REMARKS

The aim of this chapter has been to highlight the problems limiting the application of memory research. At present, application takes place in a social context, which in our view is detrimental to the development of applied memory research despite appearances to the contrary such as journals seemingly devoted to applied research. The third Practical Aspects of Memory Conference will go some way to emphasizing the symbiotic relationship between theory and application but, of itself, in our view the conference will have little permanent effect if the underlying academic climate and reward systems discriminate against application.

There are some hopeful signs, as noted earlier, that real-life application is developing, for example, the recent special issue of *Applied Cognitive Psychology* in which a number of nonacademic psychologists indicated the extent to which they had made a contribution to the real-life application of memory research. To our minds, this issue of *Applied Cognitive Psychology* raises real hopes that the work carried out by basic researchers can be taken up by those outside academic institutions. This issue, and the evidence that many of the nonacademic psychologists who attended the Practical Aspects of Memory conference have developed a wide variety of real-world applications, does show that practical application to real-life situations is considerable. On the other hand, the numbers, although encouraging, in no way compare with the army of technocrats and commercial organizations in other areas of science waiting to exploit academic research. For academic psychologists to assume that their work will somehow be taken up by those outside is, in our view, naive.

We do, however, wish to finish on a highly positive note. The three Practical Aspects of Memory Conferences have demonstrated beyond doubt that very many academic psychologists wish to see their work bear fruit in useful application. We have outlined a number of successes, by both academics and nonacademics, in reaching this goal. Success is clearly possible; the will is clearly there. If we can resist notions of simplistic measures of academic worth, and can carry forward the work already widespread and increasing, then what we have argued in this chapter will look as dated in 10 years' time as many of the theories and models in current use.

Both basic and applied researchers add to human knowledge and, therefore, to an understanding of memory. We wish to argue that basic and applied researchers must work together to further our science, as Munsterberg urged all these years ago. He realized that we were all batting on the same side.

REFERENCES

Banaji, M. R., & Crowder, R. G. (1989). The bankruptcy of everyday memory. *American Psychologist, 44,* 1185–1193.

Banaji, M. R., & Crowder, R. G. (1991). Some everyday thoughts on ecologically valid methods. *American Psychologist, 46,* 78–79.

El-Dinary, P. B., Pressley, M., & Schuder, T. (1992). Becoming a strategies teacher: An observational interview study of three teachers learning transactional strategies instruction. In C. Kinzer & D. Leu (Eds.), *Forty-first yearbook of the national reading conference* (pp. 453–462). Chicago: National Reading Conference.

Fisher, R. P., & Geiselman, R. E. (1988). Enhancing eyewitness and memory with the cognitive interview. In M. M. Gruneberg, P. E. Morris, & R. N. Sykes (Eds.), *Practical aspects of memory: Current research and issues* (Vol. 1, pp. 34–39). Chichester, England: Wiley.

Gruneberg, M. M. (1988). Practical problems in the practical application of memory. In M. M. Gruneberg, P. E. Morris, & R. N. Sykes (Eds.), *Practical aspects of memory* (Vol. 1, pp. 555–557). Chichester, England: Wiley.

Gruneberg, M. M. (1992). The new approach to memory improvement: Problems and prospects. In D. J. Herrmann, H. Weingartner, A. Searlman, & C. McEvoy (Eds.), *Memory improvement: Implications for memory theory* (pp. 1–7). New York: Springer.

Gruneberg, M. M., Monks, J., & Sykes, R. N. (1976). The first letter search strategy. *I. R. C. S. Medical Science: Psychology and Psychiatry, 4,* 307.

Gruneberg, M. M., & Morris, P. E. (1992). Applying memory research. In M. M. Gruneberg & P. E. Morris (Eds.), *Aspects of memory: The practical aspects* (pp. 1–17). London: Routledge.

Gruneberg, M. M., Morris, P. E., & Sykes, R. N. (1991). The obituary on everyday memory and its practical application is premature. *American Psychologist, 46,* 76–78.

Gruneberg, M. M., & Sykes, R. N. (1993). The generalisability of confidence-accuracy studies in eyewitnessing. *Memory, 1,* 185–189.

Herrmann, D. J. (1991). *Super memory.* Emmaus, PA: Rodale Press.

Herrmann, D. J. (1993). *Basic research contributions to the improvement of rehabilitation of memory.* Paper presented at the APA Annual Conference, Washington.

Herrmann, D. J., & Gruneberg, M. M. (1993). The need to expand the horizons of the practical aspects of memory. *Applied Cognitive Psychology, 7,* 553–566.

Higbee, K. L. (1988). *Your memory* (2nd ed.). New York: Prentice-Hall.

Johnson, M. T. (1993). Memory phenomena in the law. *Applied Cognitive Psychology, 7,* 603–618.

Leirer, V. O., Tanke, E. D., & Morrow, D. G. (1993). Commercial cognitive/memory systems: A case study. *Applied Cognitive Psychology, 7,* 675–690.

Loftus, E., & Ketchan, K. (1991). *Witness for the Defense.* New York: St. Martins Press.

Morris, P. E., Jones, S., & Hampson, P. J. (1978). An imagery mnemonic for the learning of people's names. *British Journal of Psychology, 69,* 335–336.

Munsterberg, H. (1914). *Psychology: General and applied.* New York: Appleton and Co.

Neisser, U. (1978). Memory: What are the important question? In M. M. Gruneberg, P. E. Morris, & R. N. Sykes (Eds.), *Practical aspects of memory* (pp. 3–24). London: London Academic Press.

Paivo, A. (1971). *Imagery and verbal processes.* New York: Holt, Rinehart & Winston.

Pressley, M. (1976). Mental imagery helps eight-year-olds remember what they read. *Journal of Educational Psychology, 68,* 355–359.

Pressley, M., Heisel, B. E., McCormick, C. G., & Nakamura, G. V. (1982). Memory strategy instructions with children. In C. J. Brainerd & M. Pressley (Eds.), *Progress in cognitive development research, 2: Verbal processes in children* (pp. 125–159). New York: Springer.

Saywitz, R. J., Geiselman, R. E., & Bornstein, G. R. (1992). Effects of cognitive interviewing and practice on children's recall performance. *Journal of Applied Psychology, 77,* 744–756.

Smith, V. L., Kassin, S. M., & Ellsworth, P. C. (1989). Eyewitness accuracy and confidence: Within versus between subject correlations. *Journal of Applied Psychology, 74,* 356–359.

Warr, P., & Wall, T. (1975). *Work and well being.* Harmondsworth, UK: Penguin.

CHAPTER SIX

Fact, Fantasy,
and Public Policy

Marcia K. Johnson
Princeton University

As suggested by Fig. 6.1, the view of cognition that I discuss is a bit like a New Yorker's view of the United States, where Manhattan takes up most of the map, and after the Hudson River there is just a small strip with a slightly larger area when you get to California. (The blank region in Fig. 6.1, just below the Mishkin fissure, is Squire's area.)

There has never been any doubt in my mind that practical applications flow naturally from the insights of cognitive psychology. In fact, the wide-ranging applicability of one idea—the gestalt notion of figure/ground—is probably what seduced me into psychology in the first place. I saw the duck–rabbit figure for the first time the summer after I graduated from high school, in an introductory psychology book (Fig. 6.2). The deep meaning of this image lit up a lightbulb in my head—there were alternative ways of seeing the world, affecting even the way our very perceptions are structured. Here, I realized, was the origin of all human conflict—misunderstandings between friends and lovers, disagreements with parents, racism, the Cold War—we were seeing the duck and the Russians were seeing the rabbit (Fig. 6.3). Although all my college courses were interesting, there was nothing so profoundly important for understanding the human condition, it seemed to me, as this idea of alternative realities—the possibilities for experience were determined by the mind as well as the world. (Now, whenever I see the duck–rabbit, I think of the impact that a good metaphor can have on a 17-year-old.)

As an undergraduate and graduate student of experimental psychology at Berkeley (with the encouragement, especially, of Geoff Keppel and Leo

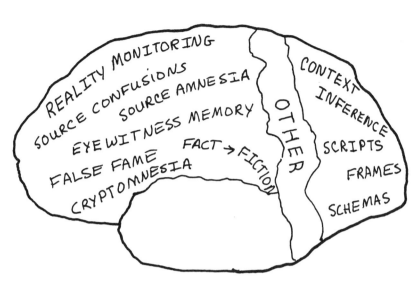

FIG. 6.1. View of mental landscape as seen from Princeton Cognition Lab.

FIG. 6.2. An ambiguous duck–rabbit figure.

FIG. 6.3. Alternative interpretations of the duck–rabbit figure.

Postman), I tried various ways of exploring the idea that the conceptual schemas available to us determine how an ambiguous environment is perceived and remembered. My first experience of the thrill of collecting empirical data was an undergraduate project in which I found that the speed with which subjects saw a familiar nonsense form embedded in an "ambiguous" environment depended on whether or not they had previously named the form. My interpretation was that subjects used preexisting conceptual categories in naming and these were likely to result in an integrated, holistic representation, whereas when subjects did not name the forms they were more likely simply to notice some distinguishing feature (e.g., a jagged point). Once the forms were embedded in many similar forms, the previously distinguishing feature would not differentiate one form from another, whereas the gestaltlike properties of a named, integrated form would cause it to "pop out" from the background. This seemed, at the time, to capture the essence of life—an inherently unstructured and ambiguous world ordered by the categories one brings to it (truly Berkeley in the 1960s). I must admit that I am still trying to fully bake some of the half-baked ideas from those years.

When John Bransford and I both arrived in 1970 as new assistant professors at Stony Brook, we had the fun and excitement of a collaboration
arising out of our mutual interest in constructive processes in comprehension
and memory. For example, we had people listen to several short stories
such as "It was late at night when the phone rang and a voice gave a frantic
cry. The spy threw the secret document into the fireplace just in time since
30 seconds longer would have been too late." On a subsequent recognition
test, subjects were likely to falsely recognize sentences that included tacit
implications of what they had heard, implications such as "the spy burned
the secret document" (Johnson, Bransford, & Solomon, 1973). Such false
recognitions were interesting because they did not simply represent para-
phrases of the information that was contained in the sentence. Rather, subjects were claiming to have heard information that was not necessarily true
given what they had actually heard (e.g., the fire may not have been lit and
the spy may have intended to hide rather than destroy the document). As
part of normal comprehension, people construct a representation or model
of the situation, drawing on general world knowledge about objects in the
environment, people's intentions and actions, and so forth. This representation runs the risk of importing information that was not part of the
actual perceptual event.

To avoid such false memories, one cannot simply turn off one's schemas
or prior knowledge. Other studies showed that when you make it difficult
for people to use prior knowledge to construct a representation of a situation,
comprehension and memory suffer greatly. Consider the following paragraph
(Bransford & Johnson, 1973):

> If the balloons popped the sound wouldn't be able to carry since everything
> would be too far away from the correct floor. A closed window would also
> prevent the sound from carrying, since most buildings tend to be well insu-
> lated. Since the whole operation depends on a steady flow of electricity, a
> break in the middle of the wire would also cause problems. Of course, the
> fellow could shout, but the human voice is not loud enough to carry that far.
> An additional problem is that a string could break on the instrument. Then there
> would be no accompaniment to the message. It is clear that the best situation
> would involve less distance. Then there would be fewer potential problems. With
> face to face contact, the least number of things could go wrong.

Comprehension and recall are much greater if people have seen the picture
in Fig. 6.4 before they get the passage than if they have not seen it or seen
it only *after* hearing the passage. Thus, in spite of the potential cost of
contextually or schematically driven inaccuracies, contextual information or
schematic prior knowledge is essential for accurate recall.

The situation is further complicated by the fact that there may be more
than one context or schema that can be brought to bear on a situation.

Consider the next paragraph about a *successful stockbroker* (Bransford & Johnson, 1973):

> The man stood before the mirror and combed his hair. He checked his face carefully for any places he might have missed shaving and then put on the conservative tie he had decided to wear. At breakfast, he studied the news-paper carefully and, over coffee, discussed the possibility of buying a new washing machine with his wife. Then he made several phone calls. As he was leaving the house he thought about the fact that his children would probably want to go to that private camp again this summer. When the car didn't start, he got out, slammed the door, and walked down to the bus stop in a very angry mood. Now he would be late.

People who read this are likely to assume that the man is getting ready for work, reading the financial page, will buy the washing machine and send his kids to camp, and so forth. Now read the passage again, but as a passage about an *unemployed man*. Now people are likely to assume that the man is getting ready for a job interview, reading the want ads, cannot afford to buy the washing machine or send his kids to camp, and so forth. That is, the passage read from these two different points of view has a quite different affective tone and quite different implications (see also Hasher & Griffin, 1978; Pichert & Anderson, 1977; Snyder & Uranowitz, 1978; Spiro, 1977; Sulin & Dooling, 1974).

We believed that the comprehension processes that our lab and others were studying and the demonstrations we concocted illustrated fundamental processes of learning and memory (see Alba & Hasher, 1983, for an excellent review of work of this period). An obvious relevant practical domain was education—as in learning to read or learning about a new content area. And, as in the case of the duck–rabbit, and the forms embedded in ambigu-ous environments, I also believed that the understandings and misunder-standings that resulted when people brought various contexts or frames to situations created the backdrop for all self-knowledge and for all social and political interactions.

But something nagged at me about such a vision of cognition and memory. If even what we see depends on what we already know, and if what we remember depends on how we interpreted what we saw, and includes the not-necessarily-true inferences we drew, then what is the relation between what we perceive and remember to *reality* (Johnson & Sherman, 1990)? Yes, the mind constructs a reality from fragments of perception and memory, but are there any constraints to what can be constructed? How trapped are we by our own schemas? Surely not all constructions are equivalent. It may be all right to remember a duck or a rabbit, but there certainly was no elephant! An organism too loosely tied to reality via perception, learning, and memory mechanisms would have never survived all those evolutionary challenges.

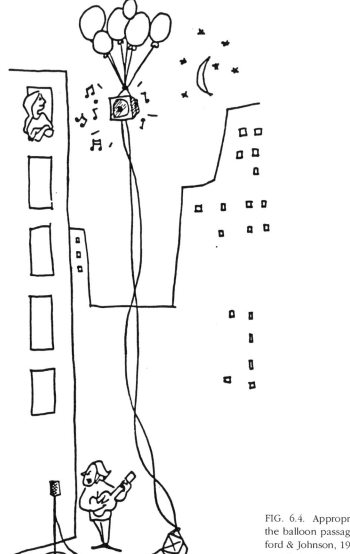

FIG. 6.4. Appropriate context for the balloon passage. (From Bransford & Johnson, 1973, reprinted by permission.)

Can we discriminate between reasonable alternative constructions of reality and fabrication? Are there some differences in the memory representations created by perceptual processes and those created by inference, imagination, fantasy, and dreams (Johnson, 1983)?

These issues were also brought home to me when, as an adult, I described a vivid childhood memory only to learn that it had not happened the way I remembered it. On a family trip, we had a flat tire and my mother, brother, sister, and I waited in the car while my father hitchhiked up the road to have the tire fixed. Evidently, as I waited in the car, I imagined that my sister went to a farmhouse to get water. The memory of my sister's interaction with the woman at the farmhouse was filled with perceptual and contextual detail and I remembered my emotions about drinking the water and not saving some for my father. Years after the flat tire incident, I mistook this remembered fantasy of my sister's visit to the farmhouse for a real event (Johnson, 1985). How could this happen? How many other memories that make up one's autobiography—one's view of oneself—are false? This thought recurred as I considered the issue of the representation of perceived and imagined information in memory. One way that I could see to explore such issues was to investigate the psychological processes by which people discriminate real from imagined events. In this research, I have had many insightful collaborators, especially Carol Raye with whom I first mapped out an initial strategy for studying the problem of what we called "reality monitoring" (Johnson & Raye, 1981).

Of course, efforts from my lab have been part of a Zeitgeist. At the same time, many others have been addressing similar issues, such as Beth Loftus and her colleagues' investigations of eyewitness testimony (e.g., Loftus, 1979), and Larry Jacoby and his colleagues' work on misattributions of familiarity (e.g., Jacoby, Kelley, Brown, & Jasechko, 1989). There are now many studies exploring reality monitoring and more general issues of source monitoring (for reviews, see Ceci & Bruck, 1993; Johnson, Hashtroudi, & Lindsay, 1993; Johnson & Sherman, 1990) in which people confuse memories for what they perceived with memories for what they imagined, or where they confuse sources of information, for example, what they saw with what they read. For example, the more often people think about a picture, the more often they think they actually saw it (Johnson, Raye, Wang, & Taylor, 1979). People, especially children, confuse what they imagined doing with what they actually did, and they confuse what they imagined someone else doing with what that person did (Foley & Johnson, 1985; Lindsay, Johnson, & Kwon, 1991). We know that confusion is related to similarity between sources in perceptual, contextual, and semantic detail (Ferguson, Hashtroudi, & Johnson, 1992). We know that the information we generate most easily, or without voluntary effort, is most likely later to be confused with what we saw (Durso & Johnson, 1980; Finke, Johnson, & Shyi, 1988). We also know that thinking or talking about imagined events maintains and perhaps embellishes their clarity—a clarity that may later be taken, mistakenly, as evidence that the event actually happened (Suengas & Johnson, 1988). We also know that thinking about emotional aspects of past events can have different consequences for memory than thinking about factual aspects (Hashtroudi, Johnson, Vnek, & Ferguson, 1994). People make judgments about the origin of events partly on the basis of whether what they remember fits with what they generally believe (e.g., [I didn't report that as my dream because] "this is not the sort of dream I ever have . . .") (Johnson, Kahan, & Raye, 1984). It is also important to note that people adopt different criteria for evaluating the sources of memories in different contexts; thus, under some circumstances confusions between what people saw and what was introduced by additional or misleading information can be eliminated by changing how the questions are asked (Dodson & Johnson, 1993; Lindsay & Johnson, 1989). And, I particularly want to emphasize that source-monitoring processes (and potential failures in source monitoring) play a critical role not only in our memories of autobiographical events, but also in our beliefs about ourselves and others, and in our opinions and knowledge about the world (e.g., Gerrig & Prentice, 1991; Johnson, 1988; Ross, 1989; Slusher & Anderson, 1987; Wilson & Brekke, 1994).

We and others have considered reality-monitoring and source-monitoring processes as they might help characterize clinically relevant phenomena such as delusions, amnesia, and confabulation from organic brain disease (e.g., Dalla Barba, 1993; Johnson, 1988, 1991; Schacter, Harbluk, & McLachlan, 1984). In the last few years, there has been some especially clever and thoughtful work done by Gail Goodman (in press; Goodman, Hirschman, Hepps, & Rudy, 1991), and by Steve Ceci and Maggie Bruck (1993) and others regarding suggestibility and source monitoring in young children. Steve Lindsay and Don Read (1994) recently wrote an excellent paper targeting the audience of practicing therapists, discussing the implications of work on reality monitoring and source confusions for understanding factors that might operate in the recovery of repressed memories.

We can understand quite a bit about source monitoring by investigating the impact of psychological processes like imagery, elaboration, rehearsal, and so forth, on source judgments. Also, as in understanding other aspects of cognition, neuropsychological evidence offers exciting possibilities. For example, the confabulations that sometimes occur as a consequence of frontal damage (Fig. 6.5), often in combination with damage to other brain regions, can be startling. A patient described by Damasio and colleagues (Damasio, Graff-Radford, Eslinger, Damasio, & Kassell, 1985) claimed to have been a "space pirate." A patient might not seem to recognize their hand and, when pressed, claim it belongs to the experimenter, and when the ring on the hand is pointed out, claim that the experimenter is wearing their ring (Joseph, 1989). In Capgras syndrome, patients exhibit a form of delusion in which they claim that someone, typically someone close or a family member, has been replaced by an impostor (Weinstein, 1991). Such examples strikingly illustrate how dependent we are on the smooth functioning of particular brain regions for the processes that ordinarily operate in reality monitoring (see also Baddeley & Wilson, 1986; Moscovitch, 1989).

FIG. 6.5. Schematic illustrating a reconstruction of frontal lobe damage (in black) from the MRI brain scan of a hypothetical patient.

Increasing efforts are being directed at characterizing patterns of confabulations and associated cognitive profiles (e.g., Dalla Barba, 1993; Johnson, O'Connor, & Cantor, 1995) and in better specifying associated locations and extent of brain lesions (e.g., Fischer, Alexander, D'Esposito, & Otto, 1994). New and improving imaging and brain mapping techniques hold out some exciting possibilities for correlating psychological and neurological levels of analysis in both brain damaged and neurologically intact individuals. For example, John Kounios is working with my lab to explore ERP correlates of memories for perceived and imagined events and of source monitoring in general.

But just as we should be able to deepen our understanding of reality monitoring by going "down" to the neurological level, we should be able to expand it by going "up" to the social/cultural level. Individual reality monitoring takes place within a social/cultural context. This cultural context helps determine what evidence should be considered, the criteria for evaluating it, and what an acceptable error rate is. The cultural context provides social support for relevant hypotheses and conclusions and affects how much evidence we feel we need. Suppose I said I am hearing strange noises; if you suggested I get an examination for tinnitus ("noises produced by the muscles governing the function of the middle ear," Saravay & Pardes, 1970, p. 237), that would be a very different social context than if you suggested it might be my angel trying to communicate with me (Johnson, 1988). Your comment may not only affect my memory for what I experienced, but the next time I hear the noise, my interpretation of it may be influenced by what you suggested as well. What might seem nutty and unlikely to be suggested in one social context might seem quite plausible in another. The impact of an individual's network of family and friends would be a rich domain for studying social aspects of reality monitoring.

I want to focus here, however, on yet another level of analysis. Consider also the reality-monitoring role that organizations and institutions serve in our culture. Think about the institutions and organizations in our society responsible for getting at or telling the truth: experts and professionals such as doctors and therapists who help people sort out real from imagined causes for their aches and problems; journalists whose role it is to dig up and report the truth; courts charged with establishing the "fact of the matter"; researchers, scientists, and educators who generate and transmit knowledge. Do we have an acceptable rate of reality-monitoring failures in our social organizations and institutions? Or do we, so to speak, have lesions in our cultural frontal lobes? Are some institutions or professional organizations suffering from anosognosia as well—that is, unawareness of deficit? (See Fig. 6.6; this is a schematic of a scan of patient U.S. As you can see, there is bilateral damage in the Washington, D.C. area, near the Congressional sulcus, with somewhat greater lesions on the right than the left.)

We have credentialing procedures for getting to participate in this cultural reality monitoring. These procedures include apprenticeships, journalism schools, professional programs, licensing exams, and so forth—the ways for transmitting the metaknowledge and reality-monitoring criteria that are to be applied along with specific domain knowledge. Scientists learn to spot confounds; journalists learn to watch for the political spin doctors; therapists learn to listen for the meaning behind the words; lawyers learn to find flaws in the other side's case; scholars and educators learn critical thinking. As in individual reality monitoring, these various institutional reality monitoring criteria are often used relatively automatically; when discriminating fact from fantasy is tough, they are used more deliberately and usually involve retrieving more information and integrating the evidence derived from multiple sources to come up with the best judgment given the available evidence. As with individual reality monitoring of autobiographical memories, there may be few conclusions that can be made with 100% certainty.

As individuals, we are often unaware of our own reality-monitoring processes until they fail. The same is true at the social level. However, we can

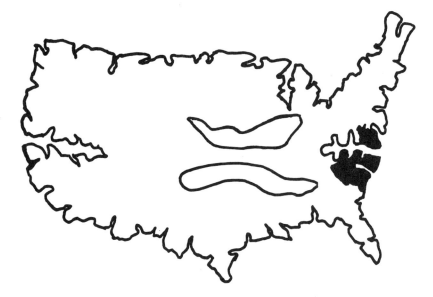

FIG. 6.6.   Reconstruction from the MRI scan of patient U.S., illustrating cultural frontal lobe damage (in black).

tell that we, as a society, implicitly count on these institutions by the surprise or shock we express when the reality-monitoring mechanisms do fail. Revelations of fictitious or composite stories reported as news shock us, as do reports of fraud in science, and perjured testimony before Congress or the courts. There are sanctions for those who violate the norms for collecting, evaluating, and reporting information; for example, you can be fired, lose your grant, lose a libel case, go to jail for perjury, or be disbarred.

In 1981, a reporter for the *Washington Post*, Janet Cooke, was stripped of a Pulitzer Prize she had been awarded for a story about an 8-year-old boy named Jimmy who had been a victim of the drug culture in which he lived. It turned out that Jimmy was fictitious, representing what Cooke saw to be the general situation she was describing (Pippert, 1989). On the other hand, in 1989, a California appeals court dismissed a libel suit by psychoanalyst Jeffrey Masson against Janet Malcolm. Malcolm had written a *New Yorker* article in which she attributed a number of phrases to Masson that he claimed were fabricated. "The court ruled that even if Masson did not say those words, Malcolm's inventions were permissible because they did not 'alter the substantive content' of what he actually said, or were a 'rational interpretation' of his comments" (Henry, 1989, p. 49). That was not the end of this case, however. The Supreme Court reversed the lower court's decision and the case was subsequently tried twice. The first resulted in a mistrial when the jury found in favor of Masson but could not agree on an award amount. The second jury found in favor of Malcolm, deciding that two disputed quotations were false and one was defamatory, but none were created with the reckless disregard for the truth required in libel cases (Margolick, 1994). The long history of the Malcolm–Masson case is testimony to the difficulty of some of the issues involved in legally differentiating fact from fiction. These two examples show reality monitoring from both within a professional community (in the case of Cooke, journalists) and (in the case of Malcolm) of one institution (the media) by another (the courts).

Journalists are now quite self-consciously worried about the implications of the rise of "reality" TV, docudramas, technologies for altering photos, and so on. They are concerned about their perceived credibility. Some argue for increasing professionalism, better and continuing training, less quoting of unnamed sources, and more attention to ethics (e.g., Belsey & Chadwick, 1992; Fry, 1985; Pippert, 1989). For individual consumers of newspapers, magazines, TV, radio, the movies, and so forth, the potential for conflating fact and fantasy information seems to be increasing exponentially because of the rapid transmission of information and the vividness of TV and movie images. In a year or so, when we think back on the O.J. Simpson case, will we be able to sort out the hard news reports of the actual facts from the inevitable docudrama embellishments?

At the individual level, we might be able to ward off some of this confusion by exercising exposure control (Gilbert, 1993) in order to prevent mental contamination (Wilson & Brekke, 1994) (see Fig. 6.7). We can try to read reliable sources and avoid sensationalized TV presentations. We can minimize or at least clearly contextualize our fantasy life. What are the analogous or appropriate controls to institute at a social level? Here we come up against some dearly held beliefs. One arises from a cultural appreciation of the importance of the duck–rabbit lesson—even when it seems perfectly obvious that something is a duck, we want to protect the right of someone to publicly suggest that it is a rabbit.

This is part of the "free press" rationale for tolerating tabloid journalism. In fact, it appears that mainstream journalism has abandoned the tabloids to the courts for reality monitoring. For example, in 1981, the comedienne and actress Carol Burnett sued the *National Enquirer* and was eventually awarded $800,000. One researcher suggested, "In the wake of Carol Burnett's successful libel suit, the tabloids are increasingly careful in their celebrity coverage; it may not all be accurate, but relatively little is defamatory" (Bird, 1992, p. 47). Bird also made the interesting observation that tabloid journalism serves an important cultural function, much like the myth-making oral or narrative tradition of earlier times. This is a more sophisticated version of the idea that tabloids are essentially entertainment. From the neuropsychological perspective, tabloids may be the cultural equivalent of the neuropsychological concept of anosodiaphoria. Anosodiaphoria is the term used

FIG. 6.7. Example of individual exposure control (Gilbert, 1993) to avoid mental contamination (Wilson & Brekke, 1994).

when a brain-damaged patient exhibits a casual acceptance of, or indifference to, an acknowledged deficit.

Well, just how serious do people find various sorts of deviations from the truth? In one preliminary study (Johnson, 1993) addressing this issue, we asked Princeton undergraduates to rate the "seriousness" of a number of situations in which falsehoods occur, on a scale ranging from 0 (not at all serious) to 10 (extremely serious). Consider the case of a tabloid newspaper printing a story about a woman who claims to have been picked up by an alien spaceship when the newspaper has no other evidence that it happened; the mean rating of 2.18 indicates that subjects thought this was only a slightly more serious falsehood than the rating of 1.58 given to a

12-year-old child telling her uncle she likes a present when, in fact, she hates it. In contrast, it was seen as a much more serious falsehood (7.68) when a TV news program sets a car on fire with explosives to have videotape illustrating that the car model has a high incidence of bursting into flames during accidents. This is interesting because it may reflect, in an indirect way, the higher procedural standard people have for the TV news than for tabloids. Presumably, the TV newspeople know of evidence indicating the car's lack of safety and just want to illustrate it. However, it is seen as a serious breach of norms and values when what appears on the screen is not authentic, even if it may depict a true state of affairs. In contrast, the tabloid has no corroborating evidence for the woman's story about the alien—it is simply a good story. It is probably false, but not too serious a breach of norms and values for the paper to publish it anyway. The staged TV video betrays a reality-monitoring trust, a trust that we do not have in the tabloids in the first place. These ratings, we think, reflect the attitude that "everybody" knows those supermarket tabloids are dumb, nobody trusts them, people read them for fun, and nobody is fooled. Hence, loose reality-monitoring criteria are acceptable in what is basically an entertainment medium.

But do tabloids only serve the function of entertaining storytelling? Or do some people get their news and reinforce their beliefs from the tabloids? And do others read them for entertainment and subsequently forget the source of what they remember? A 1990 Gallup poll found that 24% of Protestants and 34% of Catholics believed in extraterrestrial visitors (about the same percentages believe in clairvoyance). Even allowing for the possibility that the questions might have been worded oddly or misunderstood, or the individuals interviewed may have been responding to demand characteristics in the interview, these figures are worth pondering. We do not know, of course, whether tabloids reflect existing beliefs or help establish and maintain them. But a good guess is that the effects are reciprocal and iterative.

Now let's consider another illustration of the complex relations among individual reality monitoring, monitoring at the level of professional organizations, and cross-institutional monitoring—the practice of psychotherapy. There are a number of interrelated controversies raging about the possibility that certain techniques used by therapists are highly suggestive and may create false memories and beliefs in the people the therapists are attempting to help. For example, children who may be reluctant to describe abuse may be repeatedly questioned about it. However, there is some experimental evidence that children who are repeatedly asked about an event that did not happen may develop an embellished account of it (Ceci, Crotteau Huffman, Smith, & Loftus, 1994). It has been suggested that multiple personality disorder is the result of a coconstruction between the therapist and the patient—with therapists suggesting various personalities that the patient then role plays (Spanos, 1994). Likewise, a question has been raised about whether reports of ritualistic, or "satanic," sexual abuse are also products of fantasy, given the absence of documented evidence of some of the purported practices (Bottoms, Shaver, & Goodman, 1994). There is the extremely charged debate going on about whether adults ever show recovery of repressed memories—some claim that traumatic events are never repressed and others claim that this is a relatively common response to trauma, especially abuse (e.g., articles by Holmes, 1994; Horowitz, 1994).

The possibility of specific suggestion is very strong in some of the accounts of therapy or interview sessions; you wonder what the therapist could have been thinking, but certainly it was not about potential pitfalls in reality monitoring (e.g., suggesting to a child that a particular act occurred, or promising a child a prize if they "tell"). The appropriateness of particular therapeutic techniques such as hypnosis, guided imagery, or sodium amytal is under active discussion because of the possibility that these procedures may induce imagined events that later will be the sources of reality monitoring failures (e.g., Lindsay & Read, 1994).

We should also consider how therapists come to hold and sometimes change their views or at least their practice on such important issues. Obviously, those therapists who have been credentialed through some standard path (e.g., an APA accredited clinical psychology program) took courses, were supervised in clinical practice, and passed a state licensing exam. Others went through different credentialing procedures, with different philosophies or emphasis in training, for example, psychiatrists and social workers. In some states, I believe, therapy can be offered with no specific clinical credentials as long as you are careful what title you use.

Surveys of practicing clinicians suggest that few read the research literature or, if they do, few find the results of outcome research very useful (Morrow-Bradley & Elliott, 1986). I suspect that the results of research about basic cognitive and social processes are even less likely to be used than the results of outcome studies. Then how do therapists update their knowledge or expand or alter their approach after leaving training? They report learning from their own experiences and from talking to colleagues. These are, clearly, appropriate and important sources of knowledge (Hoshmand & Polkinghorne, 1992). There is a thoughtful, self-critical literature from within the academic/clinical tradition on how to improve training programs and how to increase the usefulness of research to the practicing clinician (e.g., Galassi & Gersh, 1993; Goldfried, Greenberg, & Marmar, 1990; Kazdin, 1993). A number of practitioners engage in research themselves or are open to interactions with and/or contributions from empirical researchers. But, for many therapists, like journalists, what will get their attention are the court cases that have implications for them.

For example, consider one recent case. Holly Ramona, a college student, was seeing a therapist for treatment of bulimia. During the course of therapy (including a session with sodium amytal), she began to experience what she concluded were previously unremembered memories of sexual abuse from her father. She instigated a suit under a recent California ruling that allows cases even from many years ago to be tried after abuse is remembered. The father, Gary Ramona, brought his own suit against the two therapists involved, charging that his daughter was, in effect, a victim of suggestive therapeutic techniques that lead to false memories. Mr. Ramona's case against the therapists was recently decided in his favor. According to press reports (Butler, 1994), Mr. Ramona's legal costs have been somewhere around $1.7 million; $250,000 was for five expert witnesses, some of whom testified that it is possible for people to confuse real and imagined events and that the techniques used by the therapists could well have resulted in false memories. He was awarded $475,000 in damages. It is a sobering thought that this kind of judgment against therapists may be more likely to affect future therapeutic practice than a reasoned article in a journal about the nature of memory.

Are the courts the best place for separating out fact and fantasy in this area? Is the courtroom the place to determine whether recovery of repressed memories is a real phenomenon or which therapeutic practices are prudent and which are imprudent? Professional organizations are also considering such issues, of course. For example, the American Psychological Association has appointed a task force to work on this; the American Psychiatric Association's DSM-IV (1994) warns that some clinicians are concerned that there may be overreporting of adult recovery of memories of childhood sexual abuse and notes the possibility of suggestion in assessing dissociative amnesias. A recent issue of the Harvard Mental Health Letter included two articles debating the possibility of repressed memories (Holmes, 1994; Horowitz, 1994). Clearly, there are a variety of ways professional organizations are considering these issues and attempting to keep practicing therapists informed.

Is there reason to expect that all therapists want to be aligned with the criteria of mainstream professional organizations? It has been suggested, for example, that cases of recovered memories of child sexual abuse and of ritual abuse may come disproportionately from a relatively few therapists. On this, or some other issue, the profession of psychotherapy could treat some subset of practitioners like mainstream journalists treat the tabloids, and leave them to the courts to monitor. Like libel suits against the press, negligence or malpractice suits potentially can correct flawed practice. But, like libel suits against the press, they also can have a chilling effect on unpopular ideas. And, if potential consumers do not make as sharp a distinction between mainstream and marginal therapists as they do between mainstream and tabloid newspapers, then confidence in all therapists will suffer when such incidents hit the courts.

Whom do we trust to do our social/cultural reality monitoring? A Gallup Poll (conducted March 25–27, 1994) assessing confidence in institutions found these percentages of people saying they had either a great deal or quite a lot of confidence in: the Supreme Court, 42; television news, 35; public schools, 34; newspapers, 29; and the criminal justice system, 15. (Too bad they didn't ask about therapists or researchers.) Now, admittedly, these numbers reflect many factors in addition to how confident people feel about the reality monitoring functions of these institutions. Nonetheless, these figures are interesting. For example, they suggest a large disparity between the trust people place in lower courts and the trust they place in the Supreme Court. And even the Supreme Court does not rate very high. These judgments of confidence are likely bound up with people's estimates of how much institutions are guided by shared values and defensible procedures, and how much they are guided by material rewards. I wonder, for example, how widespread are feelings such as "There is freedom of the press for anyone who can afford to publish a newspaper," or "The courts offer justice to anyone who can afford to pay for it."

The roles of individuals, groups, organizations, and institutions are intertwined in cultural reality monitoring. Regardless of whether journalists, therapists, politicians, educators, lawyers, and so forth act in good faith or purposefully deceive, their relevant professional organizations and their consumers and clients (whether other institutions or individuals) tacitly or explicitly monitor the veridicality of the information generated. And, although an individual with an intention to deceive may start out knowing the reality status of what they say, under what conditions do they come to believe their own deception? Professional organizations and individual consumers may unwittingly collude with their deceivers by not challenging information that they have reason to believe cannot be right. Silence or passive acceptance can result in a cultural *folie a deux* that produces professionals committed to ideas they only half believed to begin with. Thus, politicians might come to believe their own unrealistic stump speeches, therapists might come to believe in the efficacy of dubious practices, lawyers to believe that misleading is not lying, and journalists to believe that any source is as good as another as long as it is cited.

A consideration of reality-monitoring processes suggests a healthy skepticism about one's own memory; a consideration of social/cultural reality-monitoring processes suggests a healthy skepticism about what you read in the newspaper or see on TV; about the possibility for error in the courts; and about the suggestions of experts such as therapists, heart surgeons, and even professors and researchers. But in all of these domains, an unhealthy skepticism would be as counterproductive as no skepticism at all. That is, we cannot function either as individuals or as a culture without intact reality monitoring mechanisms that we can assume work. Can we improve our criteria for cultural reality monitoring without sacrificing values such as freedom of expression, open access to professions, or an adversarial court system? Can we distinguish between normal reality-monitoring errors and more serious signs of breakdown? In the complex interrelations among cognitions, motives, values, and material constraints operating within and among individuals, organizations, and institutions, can we identify where the lesions are likely to be that produce cultural confabulation, cultural anosognosia, and cultural anosodiaphoria?

Discriminating the origin of memories, knowledge and beliefs—reality monitoring and, more generally, source monitoring—is fundamental not only to individual cognition and social cognition, but also to what might be called "cultural cognition." Intriguing research questions and challenging issues of social values arise from considering potential applications in domains of public interest.

ACKNOWLEDGMENTS

I would like to gratefully acknowledge the support for research on reality monitoring and source monitoring that my laboratory has received over the years from the National Science Foundation, National Institutes of Mental Health, and National Institute on Aging. Thanks also to Ron Comer for helpful conversations regarding some of the issues discussed here and, especially, to Carol Raye for drawing Fig. 6.6 and Fig. 6.7.

REFERENCES

Alba, J. W., & Hasher, L. (1983). Is memory schematic? *Psychological Bulletin, 93*, 203–231.
American Psychiatric Association. (1994). *Diagnostic and statistical manual of mental disorders* (4th ed.). Washington, DC: Author.
Baddeley, A. D., & Wilson, B. (1986). Amnesia, autobiographical memory and confabulation. In D. Rubin (Ed.), *Autobiographical memory* (pp. 225–252). New York: Cambridge University Press.
Belsey, A., & Chadwick, R. (1992). Ethics and politics of the media: The quest for quality. In A. Belsey & R. Chadwick (Eds.), *Ethical issues in journalism and the media* (pp. 1–14). New York: Routledge.
Bird, S. E. (1992). *For enquiring minds.* Knoxville: The University of Tennessee Press.
Bottoms, B. L., Shaver, P. R., & Goodman, G. S. (in press). An analysis of ritualistic and religion related child abuse allegations. *Law and Human Behavior.*
Bransford, J. D., & Johnson, M. K. (1973). Considerations of some problems of comprehension. In W. Chase (Ed.), *Visual information processing* (pp. 383–438). New York: Academic Press.
Butler, K. (1994, July). Memory on trial. *San Francisco Chronicle*, p. 5.
Ceci, S. J., & Bruck, M. (1993). The suggestibility of the child witness: A historical review and synthesis. *Psychological Bulletin, 113*, 403–439.
Ceci, S. J., Crotteau Huffman, M., Smith, E., & Loftus, E. F. (1994). Repeatedly thinking about a non-event: Source misattributions among preschoolers. *Consciousness & Cognition, 3*, 388–407.

Dalla Barba, G. (1993). Different patterns of confabulation. *Cortex, 29,* 567–581.

Damasio, A. R., Graff-Radford, N. R., Eslinger, P. J., Damasio, H., & Kassel, N. (1985). Amnesia following basal forebrain lesions. *Archives of Neurology, 42,* 263–271.

Dodson, C. S., & Johnson, M. K. (1993). Rate of false source attributions depends on how questions are asked. *American Journal of Psychology, 106,* 541–551.

Durso, F. T., & Johnson, M. K. (1980). The effects of orienting tasks on recognition, recall, and modality confusion of pictures and words. *Journal of Verbal Learning and Verbal Behavior, 19,* 416–429.

Ferguson, S., Hashtroudi, S., & Johnson, M. K. (1992). Age differences in using source-relevant cues. *Psychology and Aging, 7,* 443–452.

Finke, R. A., Johnson, M. K., & Shyi, G. C.-W. (1988). Memory confusions for real and imagined completions of symmetrical visual patterns. *Memory & Cognition, 16,* 133–137.

Fischer, R. S., Alexander, M. P., D'Esposito, M., & Otto, R. (1995). Neuropsychological and neuroanatomical correlates of confabulation. *Journal of Clinical and Experimental Neuropsychology, 17,* 20–28.

Foley, M. A., & Johnson, M. K. (1985). Confusion between memories for performed and imagined actions. *Child Development, 56,* 1145–1155.

Fry, D. (1985). *Believing the news: A Poynter Institute Ethics Center report.* St. Petersburg, FL: The Poynter Institute.

Galassi, J. P., & Gersh, T. L. (1993). Myths, misconceptions, and missed opportunity: Single-case designs and counseling psychology. *Journal of Counseling Psychology, 40,* 525–531.

Gerrig, R. J., & Prentice, D. A. (1991). The representation of fictional information. *Psychological Science, 2,* 336–340.

Gilbert, D. T. (1993). The assent of man: Mental representation and the control of belief. In D. M. Wegner & J. W. Pennebaker (Eds.), *Handbook of mental control* (pp. 57–87). Englewood Cliffs, NJ: Prentice-Hall.

Goldfried, M. R., Greenberg, L. S., & Marmar, C. (1990). Individual psychotherapy: Process and outcome. *Annual Review of Psychology, 41,* 659–688.

Goodman, G. S., & Quaz, J. (in press). Trauma and memory: Individual differences in children's recounting of a stressful experience. In N. Stein, C. Brainerd, P. Ornstein, & B. Tversky (Eds.), *Memory for everyday and emotional events.* Mahwah, NJ: Lawrence Erlbaum Associates.

Goodman, G. S., Hirschman, J. E., Hepps, D., & Rudy, L. (1991). Children's memory for stressful events. *Merrill-Palmer Quarterly, 37,* 109–157.

Hasher, L., & Griffin, M. (1978). Reconstructive and reproductive processes in memory. *Journal of Experimental Psychology: Human Learning and Memory, 4,* 318–330.

Hashtroudi, S., Johnson, M. K., Vnek, N., & Ferguson, S. A. (1994). Aging and the effect of affective and factual focus on source monitoring and recall. *Psychology and Aging, 9,* 160–170.

Henry, W. A., III (1989, August). The right to fake quotes. *Time,* p. 49.

Holmes, D. S. (1994). Is there evidence for repression? Doubtful. *The Harvard Mental Health Letter* (special supplement to the July 1994 issue), 5–6.

Horowitz, M. J. (1994). Does repression exist? Yes. *The Harvard Mental Health Letter, 11*(1), 4–6.

Hoshmand, L. T., & Polkinghorne, D. E. (1992). Redefining the science-practice relationship and professional training. *American Psychologist, 47,* 55–66.

Jacoby, L. L., Kelley, C., Brown, J., & Jasechko, J. (1989). Becoming famous overnight: Limits on the ability to avoid unconscious influences of the past. *Journal of Personality and Social Psychology, 56,* 326–338.

Johnson, M. K. (1983). A multiple-entry, modular memory system. In G. H. Bower (Ed.), *The psychology of learning and motivation* (Vol. 17, pp. 81–123). San Diego: Academic Press.

Johnson, M. K. (1985). The origin of memories. In P. C. Kendall (Ed.), *Advances in cognitive-behavioral research and therapy* (Vol. 4, pp. 1–27). New York: Academic Press.

Johnson, M. K. (1988). Discriminating the origin of information. In T. F. Oltmanns, & B. A. Maher (Eds.), *Delusional beliefs: Interdisciplinary perspectives* (pp. 34–65). New York: Wiley.

Johnson, M. K. (1991). Reality monitoring: Evidence from confabulation in organic brain disease patients. In G. Prigatano & D. L. Schacter (Eds.), *Awareness of deficit after brain injury* (pp. 176–197). New York: Oxford University Press.

Johnson, M. K. (1993). Unpublished data.

Johnson, M. K., Bransford, J. D., & Solomon, S. K. (1973). Memory for tacit implications of sentences. *Journal of Experimental Psychology, 98,* 203–205.

Johnson, M. K., Hashtroudi, S., & Lindsay, D. S. (1993). Source monitoring. *Psychological Bulletin, 114,* 3–28.

Johnson, M. K., Kahan, T. L., & Raye, C. L. (1984). Dreams and reality monitoring. *Journal of Experimental Psychology: General, 113,* 329–344.

Johnson, M. K., O'Connor, M., & Cantor, J. (1995). *Confabulation, memory deficits, and frontal dysfunction.* Manuscript submitted for publication.

Johnson, M. K., & Raye, C. L. (1981). Reality monitoring. *Psychological Review, 88,* 67–85.

Johnson, M. K., Raye, C. L., Wang, A. Y., & Taylor, T. H. (1979). Fact and fantasy: The roles of accuracy and variability in confusing imaginations with perceptual experiences. *Journal of Experimental Psychology: Human Learning and Memory, 5,* 229–240.

Johnson, M. K., & Sherman, S. J. (1990). Constructing and reconstructing the past and the future in the present. In E. T. Higgins & R. M. Sorrentino (Eds.), *Handbook of motivation and cognition: Foundations of social behavior* (Vol. 2, pp. 482–526). New York: Guilford.

Joseph, R. (1989). Confabulation and delusional denial: Frontal lobe and lateralized influences. *Journal of Clinical Psychology, 42,* 507–520.

Kazdin, A. E. (1993). Evaluation in clinical practice: Clinically sensitive and systemic methods of treatment delivery. *Behavior Therapy, 24,* 11–45.

Lindsay, D. S., & Johnson, M. K. (1989). The eyewitness suggestibility effect and memory for source. *Memory & Cognition, 17,* 349–358.

Lindsay, D. S., Johnson, M. K., & Kwon, P. (1991). Developmental changes in memory source monitoring. *Journal of Experimental Child Psychology, 52,* 297–318.

Lindsay, D. S., & Read, J. D. (1994). Psychotherapy and memories of childhood sexual abuse: A cognitive perspective. *Applied Cognitive Psychology, 8,* 281–338.

Loftus, E. F. (1979). *Eyewitness testimony.* Cambridge, MA: Harvard University Press.

Margolick, D. (1994, November 3). Psychoanalyst loses libel suit against a New Yorker reporter. *The New York Times,* Section A, p. 1.

Morrow-Bradley, C., & Elliott, R. (1986). Utilization of psychotherapy research by practicing psychotherapists. *American Psychologist, 41,* 188–197.

Moscovitch, M. (1989). Confabulation and the frontal systems: Strategic versus associative retrieval in neuropsychological theories of memory. In H. L. Roediger III & F. I. M. Craik (Eds.), *Varieties of memory and consciousness: Essays in honour of Endel Tulving* (pp. 133–160). Hillsdale, NJ: Lawrence Erlbaum Associates.

Pichert, J. W., & Anderson, R. C. (1977). Taking different perspectives on a story. *Journal of Educational Psychology, 69,* 309–315.

Pippert, W. G., (1989). *An ethics of news: A reporter's search for truth.* Washington, DC: Georgetown University Press.

Ross, M. (1989). Relation of implicit theories to the construction of personal histories. *Psychological Review, 96,* 341–357.

Saravay, S. M., & Pardes, H. (1970). Auditory "elementary hallucinations" in alcohol withdrawal psychoses. In W. Keup (Ed.), *Origin and mechanisms of hallucinations.* New York: Plenum.

Schacter, D. L., Harbluk, J. L., & McLachlan, D. R. (1984). Retrieval without recollection: An experimental analysis of source amnesia. *Journal of Verbal Learning and Verbal Behavior, 23,* 593–611.

Slusher, M. P., & Anderson, C. A. (1987). When reality monitoring fails: The role of imagination in stereotype maintenance. *Journal of Personality and Social Psychology, 52*, 653–662.

Snyder, M., & Uranowitz, S. W. (1978). Reconstructing the past: Some cognitive consequences of person perception. *Journal of Experimental Social Psychology, 36*, 941–950.

Spanos, N. P. (1994). Multiple identity enactments and multiple personality disorder: A socio-cognitive perspective. *Psychological Bulletin, 116*, 143–165.

Spiro, R. J. (1977). Remembering information from text: The "state of schema" approach. In R. C. Anderson, R. J. Spiro, & W. E. Montague (Eds.), *Schooling and the acquisition of knowledge* (pp. 137–165). Hillsdale, NJ: Lawrence Erlbaum Associates.

Suengas, A. G., & Johnson, M. K. (1988). Qualitative effects of rehearsal on memories for perceived and imagined complex events. *Journal of Experimental Psychology: General, 117*, 377–389.

Sulin, R. A., & Dooling, D. J. (1974). Intrusion of a thematic idea in retention of prose. *Journal of Experimental Psychology, 103*, 255–262.

Weinstein, E. (1991). Anosognosia and denial of illness. In P. Prigatano & D. L. Schacter (Eds.), *Awareness of deficit after brain injury* (pp. 240–257). New York: Oxford University Press.

Wilson, T. D., & Brekke, N. (1994). Mental contamination and mental correction: Unwanted influences on judgments and evaluations. *Psychological Bulletin, 116*, 117–142.

CHAPTER SEVEN

How Come You Know So Much?
From Practical Problem
to New Memory Theory

Thomas K. Landauer
Bellcore and the University of Colorado

Susan T. Dumais
Bellcore

When we talk about the relation between theory and practice, we usually assume that the science comes first and enables the solution of practical problems. Thus, we speak of "applied science" and have no equally common noun phrase for direct attack on practical problems by scientific means, although "engineering research" comes close. Yet many historians, philosophers, and commentators have concluded that the historical path is more often from practice to science than from science to practice (Kuhn, 1977; Mokyr, 1990; Petroski, 1982).Technology usually advances by incremental trial, error, decomposition, simulation, and improvement, with general principle discovery and scientific theory occasionally sprouting from the process and occasionally helping to solve future practical problems. The Wright brothers perfected their wing shapes by hundreds of trials in a wind tunnel, not by calculations from aerodynamic theory. Aerodynamic theory mostly came later, to explain why the wing shapes that Wilbur and Orville chose had adequate lift and stability and to suggest new versions that, even today, need wind-tunnel testing before major investment. Fisher invented analysis of variance to help agronomists select among seed varieties, not to help biologists—much less psychologists—prove theories. On the other hand, the needs of practical problems often drive, or at least stimulate, science and theory. Navigation motivated astronomy; artillery and commerce motivated geometry and physics; medicine motivates molecular biology. Scientists try to discover the biochemical, cellular, genetic, or physiological processes that account for disease states in order to support rational cures

105

for well-known diseases more often than they take discoveries from pure science and seek diseases to which to apply them. Sometimes science is stimulated by failures of practice, by the appearance of unsuccessful or dangerous technology. The collapse of large numbers of early iron bridges was eventually *followed* by scientific investigation of the physical properties of iron beams (Petroski, 1982).

This volume's theme is theory in context. The offering that we bring is a case in which the partial solution of a practical problem in information retrieval has given rise to the germ of a theory that might resolve an empirical mystery about human memory. We start by describing the mystery, which in itself is related to a highly practical problem. We then review an apparently unrelated program of psychological engineering research, which in the end gave rise to a practically useful mathematical model and method. Finally, we show how this model can be viewed as a theory of certain aspects of human memory, report some evidence of its success as such a model, discuss how it might solve the original empirical problem, and propose tests to see whether its mechanisms should be incorporated into our general theories of memory.

THE MEMORY CONUNDRUM: CHILDREN LEARN VOCABULARY TOO FAST

The empirical problem is this: The average college graduate knows the meaning of about 100,000 distinct words. Many readers of this chapter may know twice that many. The way such numbers have been estimated is to choose words at random from a large dictionary, do some kind of test on a sample of people to see what proportion of the words they know, then reinflate. Several researchers have made such estimates (see Nagy & Herman, 1987). The varying totals they come up with are largely determined by the size of the dictionaries that they start with, and to some extent with the way in which they define words as being separate from each other. Here is one example of an estimation procedure. Moyer and Landauer (Landauer, 1986) sampled 1,000 words from *Webster's Third Unabridged Dictionary* and presented them to Stanford undergraduates along with a list of 30 common categories. If a student classified a word correctly and rated it familiar it was counted as known. Landauer then went through the dictionary and guessed how many of the words could have been gotten right by knowing some other morphologically related word, and adjusted the results accordingly. The resulting estimate was around 100,000 words. This is at the high end, but is roughly consistent with numbers from more careful studies in the literature when extrapolated to high-ability young adults.[1] It appears that

---

[1] Nagy and Anderson (1984), starting with a word list based on schoolbooks (Carroll, Davies, & Richman, 1971) and using a similar method, estimated 40,000 words for average high school seniors.

even this estimate may be somewhat low, because as many as 60% of the words found in a daily newspaper do not occur in dictionaries—mostly names, some quite common (Walker & Amsler, 1986).

Knowing 100,000 words by 20 years of age means learning an average of about 15 words a day from age 2 onward. The rate of acquisition during elementary and high school years has been estimated at between 3,000 and 5,400 words per year (10 to 15 per day), with some years showing almost twice as rapid gains as the average (Nagy & Herman, 1987; Smith, 1941). Thus, normal schoolchildren appear capable of learning at least 20 words per day over sustained periods.

Most words are learned by reading. The proof is straightforward. Spoken vocabulary is much smaller than written vocabulary. The words that individuals hear in daily intercourse with family and friends probably account for less than one fifth their reading comprehension vocabulary. Most schoolchildren spend more than a third of their waking hours in front of television sets, and the vocabulary of television discourse is even more limited. Very little vocabulary is learned from direct instruction. Most schools devote very little time to it, and it produces meager results. Authorities guess that at best 100 words a year could come from this source (Durkin, 1979).

Estimates are that the average fifth-grade child spends about 15 minutes per day reading in school and another 15 out of school reading books, magazines, mail, and comic books (Anderson, Wilson, & Fielding, 1988; Taylor, Frye, & Maruyama, 1990). If we assume 30 minutes per day total for 150 school days and 15 minutes per day for the rest of the year, we get an average of 21 minutes per day. Thus, while reading, kids are learning about one new word per minute. Combining estimates of reader and text vocabularies (Nagy, Herman, & Anderson, 1985) with an average reading speed of 165 words per minute (Anderson & Freebody, 1983; Carver, 1990; Taylor et al., 1990), we can infer that young readers encounter about three not-yet-known words per minute. Thus, the opportunity is there to acquire the daily ration. However, this is a terrifically rapid rate of learning. Consider the necessary equivalent list-learning speed. You'd have to give children a list of 60 new words and their definitions each day and expect them to permanently retain 20 after a single very brief study trial.[2] Never have we seen such a learning rate in our classrooms, laboratories, or learning theory parameter fits.

Word knowledge comes from reading, but how? Several research groups have tried to mimic the contextual learning of words. The experiments are usually done by selecting nonsense or unknown words at the frontier of the grade-level vocabulary knowledge and embedding them in carefully con-

---

[2]Remarkably, Pressley, Ross, Levin, and Ghatala (1984) reported 51% learning of word-definition pairs after only one key-word strategy learning trial. However this was for short term retention of 11 items.

structed sentences or paragraphs that imply aspects of meaning for the words. The results are uniformly discouraging. For example, Jenkins, Stein, and Wysocki (1984) constructed paragraphs around 18 low-frequency words and had fifth graders read them up to 10 times each over several days. The chance of learning a new word on one reading, as measured by a forced choice definition test, was between .05 and .10. More naturalistic studies have used paragraphs from schoolbooks and measured the chance of a word moving from incorrect to correct on a later test as a result of one reading (Nagy et al., 1985). About one out of 20 words makes the jump. Thus, experimental attempts to induce vocabulary acquisition through reading have achieved less than one sixth the natural rate when trying to simulate real reading, and less than one third even when explicitly trying to outdo nature.

So what's going on? How is it that children learn words from context at a rate much greater than we can get them to intentionally? The explanation we will offer did not occur to us until after an entirely independent research effort on information retrieval, so we will tell it in that order as well.

The Engineering Problem

In the early 1980s, four psychologists at Bell Labs were working more or less independently on techniques by which users could communicate with computers. George Furnas was collecting names for categories for an on-line classified ad prototype, Louis Gomez was creating indexes for a recipe file to use in experiments, Sue Dumais and Tom Landauer were having students name statistically derived clusters of yellow page headings, and Landauer and Kathleen Galotti were trying to find better names for text editor commands. Everyone found that nobody agreed on what to call anything. There was no consensual "natural" name for an editing command, no consensual title for a classified or yellow pages ad category, little overlap in key words assigned by cooks to the same recipe. Frustrated in our hopes to cure computer usability problems by finding natural, easy to learn terminology, we decided to study the problem before solving it. We pooled our data, gathered more from others, and did elaborate statistical analyses and simulations, leading to an incredibly long and detailed paper in the *Bell System Technical Journal* (Furnas, Landauer, Gomez, & Dumais, 1983a, 1987). In it we declared the opening of a new field of research that we called "Statistical Semantics," of which that article was the first and, as far we know, last example.

The central finding of all this effort was that although some linguists (e.g., Clark, 1987; Pinker, 1994) will tell you that there is no such thing as a true synonym, any object that you ask people to name, especially information objects like advertised items or abstracts of documents, will be referred to by about 30 different terms. If you ask for preferred terms from each of 100 people, between them they will come up with 10 to 50. Each person will think of between three and seven, and there will be little overlap among them. The chance that two people will choose the same word as their most favored moniker is somewhere between 10% and 20%.

It occurred to us that the difficulties people encounter in trying to look things up in on-line databases, or for that matter in card catalogs or back-of-book indexes, might be due to this disagreement in verbal labeling. We learned that professional indexers were aware of this problem, knew that they were unreliable in assigning keywords, and that their clients were even less to be trusted. However, they had never done the type of psychological experiments that we had, or the kinds of simulations, and were unaware of just how severe the problem was. Indeed, the common approach to its solution had been, and still is, to define and enforce a standard vocabulary for a particular domain of knowledge (e.g., chemistry or medicine) and to try to train all indexers to apply the same words. It hasn't worked. Indexers still disagree about half the time, and the untrained users who actually want the materials are hopelessly prone to ignoring the controlled vocabulary in favor of words they can think of.

We went on to study—by both simulation and direct experiment—ways to overcome the synonymy problem. We discovered that if we actually collected all the words that anybody wanted to apply to a given abstract or command, things got much better. As we went from assigning just one keyword to an item to assigning an average of 30, the chances that a user's spontaneous entry would match a desired target increased from under 20% to almost 80%. We dignified this finding in a principle that we called "Unlimited Aliasing": If users want to call something by a particular term, let them.

Libraries and publishers had never dared give each item 30 index entries before, partly because in paper the bulk would be unwieldy, and partly because they feared that extra words would lead to unwanted ambiguity. It turned out that the fear of ambiguity was largely unwarranted. Additional index words did increase somewhat the number of irrelevant things pointed to, but not nearly as much as they improved the likelihood of finding something a searcher wanted. In part this is because words that are thought of later tend to be more specific. More important, terminology is many-to-one from terms to objects—because there are many different aspects of an object that a person may want to specify—but each term tends to have only one or a few meanings in any particular domain. People tend to notice when they get things they don't want, but don't know how many things they miss. As a result, there is a pervasive overemphasis on the ambiguity (false positive) problem at the expense of the more important recall (hit rate) problem in information retrieval.

The next problem was to find a way to collect all the terms that were needed. The most effective method so far devised is "Adaptive Indexing," a technique invented by George Furnas (Furnas, 1985). It is well illustrated by an experimental prototype that he built for the on-line directory of campus services at the University of Texas. When a user typed in a keyword such as "Reproduction," the machine in its original form would come back with the response " 'Reproduction' not known." The same negative response was provoked by the keywords "Copying" and "Xerox." The frustrated user would ask around and discover that the desired department was actually called "Reprographics." She would type "Reprographics," and the machine would say, "Reprographics department does reproduction, Xeroxing, and copying. Tel. No. NNNN." Before the user could quit, the machine would ask, "Do you think the words 'reproduction,' 'Xerox,' and 'copying,' should be added to the index terms for the reprographics department?" With user concurrence, they are. The next time this user or anyone else in the community types in "Reproduction," the system will return the "Reprographics Department" among its possible choices. With repeated uses, the system acquires just those terms that most people want to apply most often to just those things that they most often have trouble finding. After a while the system will have collected a tally of how often each entered word was satisfied by particular answers. Then the system might return in response to the query Reproduction: Reprographics Department—60, Model Shop—5, Health Clinic—1. The user then chooses the most fitting option for his or her needs, with the possibility of asking for more information about each. In Furnas' field trial the system improved the probability of getting a correct answer by 50% after only a few hundred uses.

Unfortunately, in very large, rapidly changing collections, such as the medical literature, it is not satisfactory to wait for the user population to provide the necessary aliases. Many important searches may be the first ever for a particular document. Therefore, we wanted an automatic analysis method that could do some of the same job. We needed a way to discover and represent the relationship between words and the textual objects to which they might refer. The state-of-the-art technique in machine information retrieval is called the "vector method." In this approach, documents or, more properly, document surrogates such as titles or abstracts are represented as an unordered set of the words that they contain. A collection of documents is then represented as a large matrix in which each word contained in any document (absent a few hundred rare or too frequently occurring words) is a row or dimension, and each document is a column, the cells containing the number of times that a particular word occurs in a particular document. (In actual application, some transform is usually applied to the cell entries to weight most heavily those that carry the most information about which documents they are in.) A user or searcher query is construed to be the same sort of vector as a document and is compared by some pattern matching metric to each of the documents in the collection, and the system returns a list in order of the degree of match. (The degree of match is usually measured by a cosine between the document and query, for the simple reason that that measure works best, although why it does so has never been satisfactorily explained.)

Unfortunately, this method does nothing about the verbal disagreement problem. It treats each term as totally independent of every other, each as a separate dimension. A one word query—as the majority of queries are in practice—will have a zero cosine match with any document that does not contain it, even though the document may be highly pertinent and use terminology that has a very close meaning.

What we wanted was a method that would extract and represent underlying structure in a word-by-document matrix, so that words used in discussing similar topics would have similar vectors. This cannot happen as long as each word is its own separate dimension. What is needed is some analysis that reduces the dimensionality of the space and does so in an appropriate and computationally tractable way.

We chose a linear decomposition method called *singular value decomposition*, or SVD. This is a form of factor analysis, or more properly the mathematical generalization of which factor analysis is a special case. In SVD a rectangular matrix is decomposed into the product of three other matrices (see Fig. 7.1). One component matrix describes the row entities as a vector of derived orthogonal factor values, another describes the column entities in the same way, and the third is a diagonal matrix containing scaling

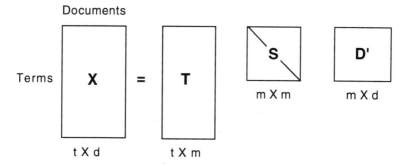

Singular Value Decomposition of the term by document matrix, X. Where:

T has orthogonal unit-length columns (T' T = I)
D has orthogonal unit-length columns (D' D = I)
S is the diagonal matrix of singular values
t is the number of of rows of X
d is the number of columns of X
m is the rank of X (<= min (t,d))

FIG. 7.1. Schematic of the singular value decomposition (SVD) of a rectangular term by document matrix. The original matrix is decomposed into three matrices each with linearly independent components.

values such that when the three components are multiplied, the original matrix is reconstructed. There is a mathematical proof that any matrix can be so decomposed perfectly using no more factors than the smallest dimension of the original matrix. When fewer than the necessary number of factors are used, the reconstructed matrix is a least-squares best fit.

SVD had several nice properties for our purpose. First, we could control the number of dimensions precisely, using as many as necessary to represent all the different word meanings in a domain but, presumably, not so many as to represent different words with similar usage as unrelated. At least that was the hope. By dropping the smallest dimensions, by hypothesis we reduce the influence of unimportant differences between words and between documents, such as which of two words of related meaning was used in a particular document.

How SVD/LSI Works

Just as in the straight vector method, a collection of documents is cast as a large matrix of words by segments of text (documents); the cells contain a weighted transform of the number of times a word occurs in a document.[3] The matrix is submitted to SVD. (Because of recent advances in sparse-matrix algorithms and computer power, collections on the order of 50,000 documents containing 70,000 useful word types can now be analyzed on popular workstations in a few hours.) The number of dimensions kept is usually determined empirically by trying a set of queries and seeing what gives the best results. For many purposes, 150–350 dimensions works well, with a gently peaked optimum. More than the optimum and SVD begins to approximate the original matrix too closely and lose the advantage of the reduced structure; fewer, and the representation lacks sufficient discrimination. [We make no attempt to rotate or interpret the dimensions; there is no need or point. They can be thought of simply as abstract dimensions of lexical usage. For more on all this, see Deerwester, Dumais, Furnas, Landauer, & Harshman (1990).]

Here is a small example that gives the flavor and demonstrates some of what the technique accomplishes. This example uses as document surrogates just the titles of nine technical memoranda produced one year on our floor at Bellcore. Five of the nine were about human computer interaction, and four about mathematical graph theory. The original matrix has nine columns, and we have given it 12 rows, each corresponding to a content word used in at least two of the titles. The titles, with the indexed terms italicized, are shown in Fig. 7.2a. The corresponding word-by-document matrix is shown in Fig.

---

[3]The usual transform we have applied, including for the analyses reported here, weights terms inversely with their entropy (i.e., -sum p log p over all documents) and cell entries as their logs.

(a)

Titles of Technical Memos

c1: *Human* machine *interface* for ABC computer applications
c2: A *survey* of *user* opinion of *computer system response time*
c3: The *EPS user interface* mangement *system*
c4: *System* and *human system* engineering testing of *EPS*
c5: Relation of *user* perceived *response time* to error measurement

m1: The generation of random, binary, ordered *trees*
m2: The intersection *graph* of paths in *trees*
m3: *Graph minors* IV: Widths of *trees* and well-quasi-ordering
m4: *Graph minors*: A *survey*

FIG. 7.2a. A sample dataset consisting of the titles of nine technical memoranda. Terms occurring in more than one title are italicized. There are two classes of documents—five about human–computer interaction (c1–c5) and four about mathematical graph theory (m1–m4).

(b)

X =

	c1	c2	c3	c4	c5	m1	m2	m3	m4
human	1	0	0	1	0	0	0	0	
interface	1	0	1	0	0	0	0	0	0
computer	1	1	0	0	0	0	0	0	0
user	0	1	1	0	1	0	0	0	0
system	0	1	1	2	0	0	0	0	0
response	0	1	0	0	1	0	0	0	0
time	0	1	0	0	1	0	0	0	0
EPS	0	0	1	1	0	0	0	0	0
survey	0	1	0	0	0	0	0	0	1
trees	0	0	0	0	0	1	1	1	0
graph	0	0	0	0	0	0	1	1	1
minors	0	0	0	0	0	0	0	1	1

FIG. 7.2b. This dataset can be described by means of a term by document matrix in which each cell entry indicates the frequency with which a term occurs in a document.

7.2b. The linear decomposition is shown next (Fig. 7.3a), and the fact that its cross multiplication perfectly reconstructs the original is illustrated. Next we show a reduction to just two dimensions (Fig. 7.3b) that approximates the original matrix. This two dimensional approximation also allows us to give a geometrical representation of the dimensional structure, as shown in Fig. 7.4. The two-dimensional vector for each document and each word defines a point on a plane for each, as shown in the figure. The same space accommodates points representing both terms and documents. (To be technically precise, the distances between terms and between documents are correct in this figure, but those between terms and documents require a scaling operation. The approximation is close enough for illustration.)

The five human computer interaction documents are all in one part of the space, and the graph theory ones in another. A query can be represented in the same way as a point in the space, and one, "*human computer* interaction," is shown. Usually, we measure the similarity of a query to the documents by the cosine, or angle of its vector with respect to those of the documents. So in the figure, the query has a cone around it containing all points with cosine greater than .9. This region cleanly separates the titles to which the query is relevant from the ones to which it is not. A notable fact is that this includes

$$X = T * S * D'$$

T=

0.22	-0.11	0.29	-0.41	-0.11	-0.34	0.52	-0.06	-0.41
0.20	-0.07	0.14	-0.55	0.28	0.50	-0.07	-0.01	-0.11
0.24	0.04	-0.16	-0.59	-0.11	-0.25	-0.30	0.06	0.49
0.40	0.06	-0.34	0.10	0.33	0.38	0.00	0.00	0.01
0.64	-0.17	0.36	0.33	-0.16	-0.21	-0.17	0.03	0.27
0.27	0.11	-0.43	0.07	0.08	-0.17	0.28	-0.02	-0.05
0.27	0.11	-0.43	0.07	0.08	-0.17	0.28	-0.02	-0.05
0.30	-0.14	0.33	0.19	0.11	0.27	0.03	-0.02	-0.17
0.21	0.27	-0.18	-0.03	-0.54	0.08	-0.47	-0.04	-0.58
0.01	0.49	0.23	0.03	0.59	-0.39	-0.29	0.25	-0.23
0.04	0.62	0.22	0.00	-0.07	0.11	0.16	-0.68	0.23
0.03	0.45	0.14	-0.01	-0.30	0.28	0.34	0.68	0.18

S=

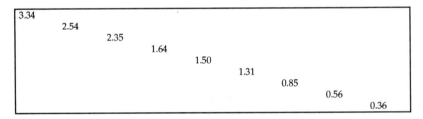

3.34								
	2.54							
		2.35						
			1.64					
				1.50				
					1.31			
						0.85		
							0.56	
								0.36

D'=

0.20	0.61	0.46	0.54	0.28	0.00	0.01	0.02	0.08
-0.06	0.17	-0.13	-0.23	0.11	0.19	0.44	0.62	0.53
0.11	-0.50	0.21	0.57	-0.51	0.10	0.19	0.25	0.08
-0.95	-0.03	0.04	0.27	0.15	0.02	0.02	0.01	-0.03
0.05	-0.21	0.38	-0.21	0.33	0.39	0.35	0.15	-0.60
-0.08	-0.26	0.72	-0.37	0.03	-0.30	-0.21	0.00	0.36
0.18	-0.43	-0.24	0.26	0.67	-0.34	-0.15	0.25	0.04
-0.01	0.05	0.01	-0.02	-0.06	0.45	-0.76	0.45	-0.07
-0.06	0.24	0.02	-0.08	-0.26	-0.62	0.02	0.52	-0.45

FIG. 7.3a. The full dimensional Singular Value Decomposition of the matrix of Fig. 7.2b.

$$
\begin{array}{rr}
0.22 & -0.11 \\
0.20 & -0.07 \\
0.24 & 0.04 \\
0.40 & 0.06 \\
0.64 & -0.17 \\
0.27 & 0.11 \\
0.27 & 0.11 \\
0.30 & -0.14 \\
0.21 & 0.27 \\
0.01 & 0.49 \\
0.04 & 0.62 \\
0.03 & 0.45
\end{array}
$$

*

$$
\begin{array}{rr}
3.34 & \\
 & 2.54
\end{array}
$$

*

$$
\begin{array}{rrrrrrrrr}
0.20 & 0.61 & 0.46 & 0.54 & 0.28 & 0.00 & 0.01 & 0.02 & 0.08 \\
-0.06 & 0.17 & -0.13 & -0.23 & 0.11 & 0.19 & 0.44 & 0.62 & 0.53
\end{array}
$$

$= X\hat{\ }$

	c1	c2	c3	c4	c5	m1	m2	m3	m4
human	0.16	0.40	0.38	0.47	0.18	-0.05	-0.12	-0.16	-0.09
interface	0.14	0.37	0.33	0.40	0.16	-0.03	-0.07	-0.10	-0.04
computer	0.15	0.51	0.36	0.41	0.24	0.02	0.06	0.09	0.12
user	0.26	0.84	0.61	0.70	0.39	0.03	0.08	0.12	0.19
system	0.45	1.23	1.05	1.27	0.56	-0.07	-0.15	-0.21	-0.05
response	0.16	0.58	0.38	0.42	0.28	0.06	0.13	0.19	0.22
time	0.16	0.58	0.38	0.42	0.28	0.06	0.13	0.19	0.22
EPS	0.22	0.55	0.51	0.63	0.24	-0.07	-0.14	-0.20	-0.11
survey	0.10	0.53	0.23	0.21	0.27	0.14	0.31	0.44	0.42
trees	-0.06	0.23	-0.14	-0.27	0.14	0.24	0.55	0.77	0.66
graph	-0.06	0.34	-0.15	-0.30	0.20	0.31	0.69	0.98	0.85
minors	-0.04	0.25	-0.10	-0.21	0.15	0.22	0.50	0.71	0.62

FIG. 7.3b. The reduced two-dimensional approximation to the matrix in Fig. 7.2b.

relevant titles that contain none of the words in the query, for example C5, *User response time* and C3, *User interface system.* The dimension reduction step has collapsed the meaning of words that appear in similar contexts to such a degree that documents that did not contain a particular term, but did contain other terms that originally occurred in similar contexts, are now predicted to be likely to have included that term.

Very roughly and anthropomorphically, SVD, with only values along two orthogonal dimensions to go on, has to guess what words actually appear in each cell. It does that by saying, "This document is best described as having so much of Factor one and so much of much of Factor two, and this word has so much of Factor one and so much of Factor two, and combining those two pieces of information (by vector arithmetic), my best guess is that word X actually appeared 0.6 times in document Y."

Comparing the rows for *human* and *user* in the original and in the two-dimensionally reconstructed matrices (Fig. 7.3) shows that although they were totally uncorrelated in the original—the two words never appeared in the same document—they are quite strongly correlated ($r = .9$) in the reconstructed approximation. Thus, SVD has done just what we wanted. It

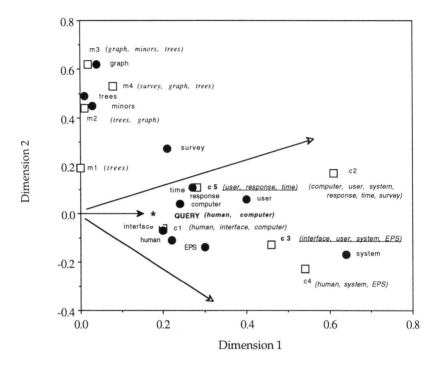

FIG. 7.4. A two-dimensional plot of 12 terms and nine documents from the sample of titles given in Fig. 7.2a and represented by the matrices of Fig. 7.3b. Terms are shown as filled circles. Documents are shown as open squares, their component terms indicated parenthetically. The query "*human computer interaction*" is represented as a pseudo-document. The cone represents the region within which points have a cosine of 0.9 or greater with the query. All documents about human–computer interaction (c1–c5) and none about graphs (m1–m4) are within this cone. In this reduced space, even documents c3 and c5, which share no terms with it, are near the query. (Axes are scaled for document–document or term–term comparisons.)

has filled in the documents with partial values for words that might well have been used in particular documents but weren't.

The shaded cell entries under m4 show this phenomenon in a slightly different way. The word *tree* did not appear in graph theory title m4. But because m4 did contain *graph* and *minor* the zero entry for *tree* has been replaced with 0.66, an estimate of how many times it occurs in titles containing *graph* and *minor*. By contrast, the value 1.00 for *survey*, which appeared once in m4, has been replaced by 0.42, reflecting the fact that it is unexpected in this context and should be counted as unimportant in matching a query. Notice that if we were to change the entry in any one cell of the original matrix, the values in the dimension reduced reconstruction would be changed everywhere.

When thus applied to information retrieval, we call the SVD technique Latent Semantic Indexing (LSI). LSI has just the property that we're looking for. It relieves the user somewhat of the need to know and produce the same words used by the author or indexer. If the user thinks of a word that has occurred in similar word contexts over the domain that was analyzed, the query will stand a good chance of matching documents of similar meaning and of rejecting documents of different meaning.

LSI's Information Retrieval Performance

How well does all this work? In the application for which it was designed, automatic retrieval of electronically stored document abstracts, it provides a significant improvement over prior methods but does not nearly solve all the problems. Its first tests were against standard collections of documents in which representative queries have been obtained and human judges have made more or less exhaustive searches of the whole database to determine which items are and are not relevant. In these standard collections LSI's performance ranged from just equivalent to the best prior method—the standard vector method with optimal term weighting—up to about 30% better. In a recent competition staged by the National Institute of Standards and Technology, LSI was compared with a large number of other research prototypes and commercial retrieval schemes. Direct quantitative comparisons among the many systems were somewhat muddied by the use of varying amounts of preprocessing—things like getting rid of typographical errors, differences in stop lists, and the amount of tweaking that systems were given before the final test runs. Nevertheless, the results appeared to be quite similar to earlier ones. Compared to the standard vector method *ceteris paribus* LSI was a 16% improvement (Dumais, 1994).

What does this mean? Approximately stated, the state of the art in information retrieval is that when half of the items you would want have been found, less than half of the items you have found were wanted. With LSI, when half of the items you want have been found, over 60% of the ones you found were wanted. Thus, although a significant step forward, LSI still leaves much room for improvement.

The LSI method has been applied in a variety of other applications, generally with results that pleased the designers and users and, where objective measures were available, has usually outperformed rival schemes. One interesting application to which no other fully automatic technique has been applied is indexing across languages (Landauer & Littman, 1990). To do this, LSI requires a training set of documents in which each is available in two or more languages. For each document a concatenated version containing all the words from both languages is constructed. Using the same number of dimensions that are required for a single language, the SVD result is a vector for each word in a common language-independent space. Given the mathematics of LSI, this would mean that any pair of words in the two languages that were used the same number of times in the same documents would have identical vectors, and that ones that are used in similar but not quite identical patterns across the documents will have similar but not quite identical vectors. Once the word vectors have been determined, they can be used for both new documents and new queries that are presented in only one of the training languages and will return appropriate documents in any language—once transformed into abstract numerical vectors, the system doesn't give a hoot which language either the query or document came from. For French and English paragraphs from the Canadian parliamentary proceedings, retrieval was as good for a query in one language finding documents in the other as it was for queries and documents in the same language. Almost as good results were obtained when going from Japanese ideographic *Kanji* characters to English words in a sample of technical abstracts.

LSI and Human Performance

The information retrieval results encouraged us to believe that LSI captures some of the underlying meaning structure of vocabulary when applied to large bodies of representative text. This presumption has been tested by predicting various aspects of the performance of human subjects dealing with textual materials.

Kintsch and his colleagues developed methods for representing text in a propositional language and have used them to analyze the coherence of discourse. They have shown that the comprehension of text depends heavily on its coherence—the continuity between the concepts expressed in one sentence or passage and the next. The Kintsch method requires difficult judgments by highly trained raters. This has limited research to very small samples of text and inhibited practical application to composition and instruction. Foltz, Kintsch, and Landauer (1993) tried applying LSI to the task. They started with a set of paragraphs about heart function that had been specifically constructed to have varying degrees of coherence, and for which comprehension measures had previously been obtained by testing students on their understanding of the texts. They obtained an LSI space by analyzing a collection of encyclopedia articles dealing with the heart. The LSI stand-in for coherence judgments was the cosine between each sentence and the following one. Fig. 7.5 shows the results. The LSI measure predicted comprehension scores extremely well, r = .93. For a control, we tried to predict comprehension using only the surface overlap of words, the first order correlation based on the proportion of word types in each sentence that were the same as those in the last. Technically this was realized as the cosine between successive sentences in the full-dimensional space, thus keeping everything constant except the dimension reduction step of the SVD analysis. This measure had almost no predictive value, $r = .18$.

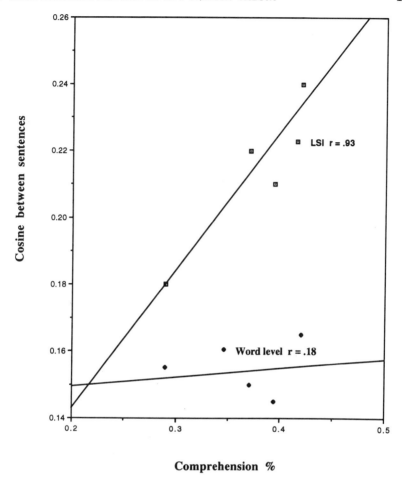

FIG. 7.5. Students' comprehension of text passages as related to their coherence. Coherence is measured either by reduced dimensional LSI similarity (LSI) or by full dimensional similarity (word level) of the words contained in successive sentences.

In a still-in-progress pilot study, Kintsch and Landauer have been trying to use LSI to match students with text at the optimal level of conceptual complexity for learning. Earlier work by Kintsch and his collaborators (see Kintsch, 1994) showed that people learn the most when the text on a topic is neither too hard, containing too many concepts with which a student is not yet familiar, nor too easy, containing too few. In a pilot study, Kintsch tested knowledge of cardiac function with a short-answer test. He then characterized the typical student's knowledge by the LSI vector for all text of correctly answered questions along with their answers. He then looked at how much students learned from reading text at varying levels of sophistication. He characterized the differentially sophisticated text by the centroid of the LSI vectors for the words it contained. When the vector point for students most closely matched that of the text, learning was greatest.

In yet another pilot study, Kintsch asked students to rate how familiar, memorable, and interesting the various paragraphs about heart function were. He found that the higher the cosine with the LSI measure of the typical student's knowledge, the more memorable, familiar, and interesting a paragraph appeared. These results are extremely preliminary and should be taken only as an additional indication that the LSI representation captures important aspects of meaning.

LSI and Synonym Tests

The initial purpose of LSI was to overcome the problem of synonymy in word usage for information retrieval. It has been our presumption and claim that the technique represents words of similar meaning in similar ways. When one compares words with similar vectors as derived from large collections, the claim is largely but not entirely fulfilled at an intuitive level. Many of the near neighbors of a word are indeed good synonyms, for example in the English–French cross-language indexing trial, the words *chambre* and *house* were quite close, as they should be in parliamentary usage. Most near neighbors, words with cosines over about .5, appear closely related in some manner. In a scaling of an encyclopedia, *surgeon, physician, patient*, and *bedside* are all close to one another. But the relationship between some close neighbors in LSI space can occasionally be quite mysterious (e.g., *verbally* and *sadomasochism* with a cosine of .8). It's impossible to say exactly why, but it's plausible that some words that have more than one meaning receive a sort of average value that signifies nothing, and that many words are sampled too thinly to get well placed. It's also possible, of course, that the "bag of words" method, which ignores all syntactical and logical entailments, sometimes misses meaning or gets it scrambled.

We were interested to see how well, compared to people, LSI captures synonymy. To do so, we measured LSI's knowledge of synonyms on a standardized test. The test was taken from the ETS Test of English as a Foreign Language (TOEFL). (It is worth noting that ETS does not use general synonym tests for ordinary verbal ability assessment because they are too easy for college students.) To make these comparisons, we first trained LSI by running the analysis on a large corpus of representative English. In various studies, we have used both collections of newspaper text from the Associated Press news wire and *Grolier's Academic American Encyclopedia*, a work intended for students. In the most successful study, we performed an SVD on segments consisting of the first 2,000 characters or less (on average, 152 words) of each of 30,473 articles in the encyclopedia. This resulted in a vector for each of 60,768 words.

The TOEFL vocabulary test consists of items in which the stem is usually a single word, and there are four alternatives, usually single word answers, among which the test taker is to choose the one most like the stem. LSI gave a prediction of the best alternative, the one with the highest cosine to the stem, in 74 of the 80 test items. For the remaining six, where LSI had never met either the stem word and/or the correct alternative, we made it guess with probability .25. Scored this way, LSI got 51.5 (64.5%) correct. Average test takers, students applying for college entrance in the United States from non-English-speaking countries, got 51.6 correct on the form of TOEFL we used. Thus, having "read" 4.6 million words from a general encyclopedia, LSI did as well as the average foreign student.

To dot some *is*, in this study we also varied the number of dimensions from 200 to 372 (the number at which the decomposition algorithm automatically terminated; see Berry, 1992). The TOEFL test results showed the weakly nonmonotonic trends we are accustomed to in information retrieval tests: 51.5 correct with 300 and 325 dimensions, and 47.5 correct with either fewer (225) or more (372) dimensions.

We also compared the pattern of errors of LSI to that of students. For each question we computed a product-moment correlation coefficient between the cosine of the stem and each alternative with the proportion of guesses for each alternative in a large sample of students. The average correlation across the 80 items was 0.70. Excluding the correct alternative, the average correlation was .44, showing that LSI confusions are somewhat like and somewhat unlike those of students. When LSI chooses wrongly and most students choose correctly, it sometimes appears to be because LSI is more sensitive to contextual associations and less to contrastive features. For example, LSI slightly prefers *nurse* (cos = .47) to *doctor* (cos = .41) as an associate to *physician*.

In an important control experiment, we chose the correct answers simply by the degree of surface co-occurrence of words in the encyclopedia passages. We did this by applying a standard vector retrieval method in which each word is treated as independent; that is, there is there is no dimension reduction. Choosing the best alternative by the highest cosine yielded just 29.5 (37%) correct answers. This demonstrates once again that the dimension reduction technique captures more than mere co-occurrence.[4] More impor-

---

[4]From an AI or linguistics perspective, one might object that first-order correlations between word types is a straw control, in that derivational and inflectional variants of words ought to be counted as equivalent. However, the point of the present endeavor is to understand or simulate how the very knowledge such relations imply is acquired by experience. LSI acquires equivalence relations about form variants in the same way it acquires those based on synonymy, by their similarity in the dimension-reduced SVD space. It seems likely that morphological similarities and morphemic combinatorics play an additional role in human learning and understanding of words, but we have not yet found a successful way to model such processes. Preliminary attempts in which we added component letter *n*-grams to the words represented in the LSI matrix produced only degradation in the TOEFL test results.

tant for our next argument, it implies that indirect associations or structural relations induced by analysis of the whole corpus are involved in LSI's success with individual words. Thus, correct representation of any one word may depend on the correct representation of many, perhaps all other words.

LSI and the Vocabulary Learning Paradox

LSI is doing a pretty good job of mimicking human performance. We like to say, only partly tongue in cheek, that it is doing real artificial intelligence. It has been learning lexical semantics entirely automatically, entirely artificially. No one has plugged in semantic information from their own heads, as is done in all other natural language understanding systems, and no preexisting humanly constructed dictionary or thesaurus is involved. The system has only a mathematical machine that it uses to run over text and extract knowledge on its own. The test of semantic knowledge that we have given it is one that is central to tests of human intelligence, vocabulary being the single measure that best correlates with overall verbal intelligence and scholastic achievement. Knowledge of words and the concepts for which they stand is at once the major foundation of human intelligence and its crowning achievement.

How does LSI's learning rate—the number of words that it "knows" as a function of how much it has "read"—compare with humans' learning rates? To know whether LSI has actually matched humans in acquisition rate, words learned per word read, we would need to know how many words of text in English the average TOEFL taker has met. This we do not know. Reading at 165 words per minute—the average for U.S. fifth graders—it would take 468 hours to read 4.6 million words. Very informal questioning of a few foreign students has suggested that they have read something like that amount of English text. An average schoolchild will have read 4.6 million words by around seventh grade. Does an average seventh grader's vocabulary equal that of TOEFL takers? We don't know. The most satisfactory answer would be obtained by testing grade-schoolers on the same items, which we have not done.

Here's another approach to the LSI—human comparison. One way a test-taker could get a word right on the TOEFL test would be by knowing the meaning of both the stem word and the correct alternative. By this model the proportion of words known is the square root of the probability correct; for our data 72%, corrected for guessing. If the TOEFL words were a random sample of words in the encyclopedia, this would mean that LSI had learned about 72% of the word types it had read, or roughly 44,000. This would give a learning rate of about one word learned per hundred total tokens read. This is about 1.6 times what children achieve naturally.

Here's yet another approach to the LSI—human comparison. If we consider only those items where LSI had met both stem and correct alternative at least once, the proportion of items correct, adjusted for guessing, was .57. By fitting Bower's (1961) one-trial learning model (which for this purpose is equivalent to many others) to the data, we estimated a learning rate, the probability of going from wrong to right on one exposure. The fitting procedure used a hill-climbing algorithm to find a learning rate parameter that, when applied to the number of occurrences of each stem and correct alternative pair for TOEFL items, gave an average proportion correct of .57. The estimated learning rate was .049, almost equal to Nagy's rough estimate of 1 in 20 for children learning from natural context in the lab (Nagy & Herman, 1987).

Despite the obviously wide uncertainty of these estimates, it seems clear enough that LSI acquires word knowledge at a clip that approaches the comparable human achievement. More important, LSI is using a mechanism for the acquisition of word knowledge that is not represented in any of our theories of memory. Notice that LSI was deprived of any use of syntax, logic, morphology, perceptual grounding, or real-world knowledge and pragmatics. Surely some of these must be of some help to humans. Suppose we were able to add these sources of information to what LSI could do. Would the high rates of learning of which humans are capable remain mysterious? We think not.

What has LSI machinery added that was undreamed of in our theories and our methods of vocabulary instruction? LSI does indirect learning. That is, it can improve its knowledge of a word in its absence and in the absence of any word that looks or sounds like it (LSI has no knowledge of what words look or sound like), the usual mechanism of positive transfer in learning theories. A vector assigned to any particular word is an average of the vectors of all the words in all the passages in which it occurs. The vectors of those words in turn are averages of all of the words with which they have kept company. The "meaning" of word X is greatly influenced by things that happen in paragraphs in which X does not appear. Indeed the occasions on which word X is actually found are a minor part of the experience by which its meaning is defined. If we imagined an LSI-like process to be working sequentially over a lifetime, experiences with other words before and after it is met, when it is not present, will have great bearing on what it "means." In laboratory attempts to teach children new words by embedding them in context, all this indirect learning is absent, or at least unmeasured. Put differently, when a child is presented with a paragraph containing one new word there may be much more learning than is measured by testing that word. There is learning about all the words in the paragraph and about their entailments with all words in the English language, or at least so the LSI model would have it.

We tested this property of the model more directly. Suppose we continue to give LSI all the documents that contain words from a particular test item, but reduce the number of other documents it sees. If there are indirect effects, the chances of a correct answer should be smaller. We reran the LSI analysis, excluding 17,394 encyclopedia articles that contained no words—either stems or answer alternatives—from 20 selected items, and had it take the test again.[5] Twelve of the 20 were correct with all the documents, only 4 with the reduced document set, (p = .01 by exact test). In other words, depriving the LSI analysis of part of the data about words not on tests of the items seriously diminished its measured knowledge of test words.[6]

This result demonstrates a kind of generalization or transfer that arises entirely from similarity relations derived from co-occurrence experience, with no contribution from or grounding in preexisting perceptual or categorical primitives, and no exogenous reinforcement of the correctness of the inferred relations among the atomic units.

The mathematical machinery of SVD is capable of making inferences based on an underlying structure in the use of words that increases learning power. Is there a similar machine in the human mind? If so, one would expect it to apply not only to the acquisition of word meanings but to the acquisition and representation of knowledge in all domains. Word meanings are particularly central, because much of what we know about any topic is contained or reflected in what we know about its vocabulary. LSI's knowledge of words is limited to analysis and prediction of the commonality of the contexts in which they occur. This seems a far cry from what we have usually imagined to be the structure of most knowledge. But is it? How much of what the average student—or average professor—knows about history, geography or botany lies in just in these same kinds of direct and indirect associations? How much of useful knowledge-based performance is knowing the right word to think or say in the right verbal context? The answer is not obvious.

As a potential theory of memory, LSI also has some intuitively intriguing qualitative properties. For one example, why do parents mix up their children's names, even when in the presence of just one child and away from home, so that the classical stimulus overload explanation falters? LSI says the reduced-dimensional representation of two siblings' names are likely to be almost identical. For another example, what, exactly, do we mean when we say that no two words have exactly the same meaning, that a word never has the same meaning on different occasions or for different people? LSI offers the hope of saying more exactly what that means.

---

[5]The selected items were those that changed scores from right to wrong or wrong to right between an analysis based on a random subset of 10,000 documents, for which the overall number correct was 39.5, and the full sample of 30,473 documents (p = .02 by exact test).

[6]The average document that did contain those TOEFL words had just 5 such words out of 152 total tokens. Thus the remaining 13,079 documents on which the reduced context TOEFL test was based still contain a great deal of information about words other than the TOEFL terms. The reduced set produced vectors for approximately 39,320 non-TOEFL word types, compared to 60,400 for the original analysis.

There are several appealing next steps in pursuing the implications of LSI as a theory of knowledge and memory. First, would be to test it rigorously in the laboratory. One might construct artificial vocabularies or artificial associative matrices (much like the ones for words and documents), expose students appropriately to the information in the matrix, and see whether their recollections fill in missing cells and alter the probability of recall of filled cells in the ways predicted by SVD analysis. Another tack would be to extend the studies done here from word knowledge to substantive knowledge in various fields, to see whether having "read" an encyclopedia or a textbook, LSI can do well on multiple-choice questions about history and geography. Still another line would be to attempt to use the theory and textual data to mimic other phenomena of human word memory, such as association norms and analogy judgments.

At this juncture, we are not yet convinced that we have hit on an important new theory of knowledge or memory, or even an important new mechanism of human memory. Nonetheless, we have identified a mechanism that can account for some of the mysterious power of the mind to acquire and represent vast quantities of information, and we have reason to believe that prior theories, which do not contain the same mechanism, are inadequate. Thus, the question is raised for memory theory: Should an indirect inferential learning mechanism similar to the one employed by LSI be considered a candidate for biological memory? Suppose the answer is yes, that natural knowledge acquisition relies to a substantial degree on similar processes. An important consequence for education would follow: It is not sufficient to teach individual unknown words or concepts in isolation; voluminous reading of rich and varied content would appear more promising.

We have come full circle. We have taken the first steps in what may be a case in which research into a practical problem—one involving the engineering of an aid for external memories—has raised issues of how internal memory works and has suggested new forms of theory for natural memory that, in turn, may imply strategies for practical memory problems.

REFERENCES

Anderson, R. C., & Freebody, P. (1983). Reading comprehension and acquisition of word knowledge. In B. Hutson (Ed.), *Advances in reading/language research: A research annual* (pp. 231–256). Greenwich, CT: JAI Press.

Anderson, R. C., Wilson, P. T., & Fielding, L. G. (1988). Growth in reading and how children spend their time outside of school. *Reading Research Quarterly, 23,* 285–303.

Berry, M. W. (1992). Large scale singular value computations. *International Journal of Supercomputer Applications, 6,* 13–49.

Bower, G. H. (1961). Application of a model to paired-associate learning. *Psychometrica, 26,* 255–280.

Carroll, J. B., Davies, P., & Richman, B. (1971). *The American heritage word frequency book.* Boston: Houghton-Mifflin.

Carver, R. P. (1990). *Reading rate: A review of research and theory.* San Diego: Academic Press.

Clark, E. V. (1987). The principle of contrast: A constraint on language acquisition. In B. MacWhinney (Ed.), *Mechanisms of language acquisition* (pp. 1–33). Hillsdale, NJ: Lawrence Erlbaum Associates.

Deerwester, S., Dumais, S. T., Furnas, G. W., Landauer, T. K., & Harshman, R. (1990). Indexing by latent semantic analysis. *Journal of the American Society For Information Science, 41,* 391–407.

Dumais, S. T. (1994). Latent semantic indexing (LSI) and TREC-2. In D. Harman (Ed.), *National Institute of Standards and Technology Text Retrieval Conference,* NIST special publication.

Durkin, D. (1979). What classroom observations reveal about reading comprehension instruction. *Reading Research Quarterly, 14,* 481–253.

Foltz, P. W., Kintsch, W., & Landauer, T. K. (1993). An analysis of textual coherence using Latent Semantic Indexing. *Society for Text and Discourse.*

Furnas, G. W. (1985). Experience with an adaptive indexing scheme. In *Proceedings of CHI'85* (pp. 16–23). New York: ACM.

Furnas, G. W., Landauer, T. K., Gomez, L. M., & Dumais, S. T. (1983a). Statistical semantics: Analysis of the potential performance of key-word information systems. *The Bell System Technical Journal, 62,* 1753–1804.

Furnas, G. W., Landauer, T. K., Gomez, L. M., & Dumais, S. T. (1987). The vocabulary problem in human-system communication. *Communications of the ACM, 30,* 964–971.

Jenkins, J. R., Stein, M. L., & Wysocki, K. (1984). Learning vocabulary through reading. *American Educational Research Journal, 21,* 767–787.

Kintsch, W. (1994). Text comprehension, memory, and learning. *American Psychologist, 49,* 294–303.

Kuhn, T. S. (1977). *The essential tension: Selected studies in scientific tradition and change.* Chicago: University of Chicago Press.

Landauer, T. K. (1986). How much do people remember: Some estimates of the quantity of learned information in long-term memory. *Cognitive Science, 10,* 477–493.

Landauer, T. K., & Littman, M. L. (1990) Fully automatic cross-language document retrieval using latent semantic indexing. In *Conference on Electronic Text Research.* Waterloo, Canada.

Mokyr, J. (1990). *The lever of riches: Technological creativity and economic progress.* New York: Oxford University Press.

Nagy, W., & Anderson, R. (1984). The number of words in printed school English. *Reading Research Quarterly, 19,* 304–330.

Nagy, W. E., & Herman, P. A. (1987). Breadth and depth of vocabulary knowledge: Implications for acquisition and instruction. In M. C. McKeown & M. E. Curtis (Eds.), *The nature of vocabulary acquisition* (pp. 19–35). Hillsdale, NJ: Lawrence Erlbaum Associates.

Nagy, W., Herman, P., & Anderson, R. (1985). Learning words from context. *Reading Research Quarterly, 20,* 223–253.

Petroski, H. (1982). *To engineer is human.* New York: Random House.

Pinker, S. (1994). *The language instinct: How the mind creates language.* New York: Morrow.

Pressley, M., Ross, K. A., Levin, J. R., & Ghatala, E. S. (1984). The role of strategy utility knowledge in children's strategy decision making. *Journal of Experimental Child Psychology, 38,* 491–504.

Smith, M. (1941). Measurement of the size of general English vocabulary through the elementary grades and high school. *Genetic Psychology Monographs, 24,* 311–345.

Taylor, B. M., Frye, B. J., & Maruyama, G. M. (1990). Time spent reading and reading growth. *American Educational Research Journal, 27,* 351–362.

Walker, D. E., & Amsler, R. A. (1986). The use of machine-readable dictionaries in sublanguage analysis. In R. Grisham & R. Kittredge (Eds.), *Analyzing languages in restricted domains: Sublanguage description and processing.* Hillsdale, NJ: Lawrence Erlbaum Associates.

CHAPTER EIGHT

What Are the Functional Bases of Individual Differences in Memory Ability?

Patrick Rabbitt
Qian Yang
University of Manchester, Manchester, England

People differ markedly in memory ability, as in all other cognitive skills. Nevertheless, there are no satisfactory accounts of individual differences in the efficiency of functional processes underlying memory, possibly because cognitive psychologists have been more impressed by massive individual differences associated with extensive, domain specific practice (Ericcsen, Krampe, & Tesch-Rohmer, 1993) or invention and use of mnemonic techniques (Ericcsen & Chase, 1982; Ericcsen & Polson, 1988). Current models for how the efficiency of the functional processes underlying memory may vary between individuals polarize between identical hypotheses, remarkably without any cross-reference. One psychometric model proposes that all cognitive skills, including memory, load on a single factor of general intellectual ability such as Spearman's (1927) "g" (for a recent discussion, see Gustafson, 1984). Interest in this somewhat dated view has been revived by the suggestion that "g" can be reified in terms of some particular performance parameter of the functional cognitive system. One suggestion has been information processing speed (Anderson, 1992; Bates & Eysenck, 1993; Brand & Deary, 1982; Eysenck, 1986; Hulme & Turnbull, 1983; Jensen, 1980; Nettelbeck, 1982; Smith & Stanley, 1983; Vernon, 1983, 1985; Vernon & Jensen, 1984). A more recent is "working memory capacity" (Carpenter, Just, & Shell, 1990; Kyllonen & Crystal, 1990). The evidence is modest, but ubiquitous correlations between performance on pencil-and-paper "intelligence tests" (IQ Test Scores, IQTS) and performance indices derived from simple laboratory tasks such as Choice Reaction Time (CRT) or tachistoscopic recognition thresholds ("Inspection Times," ITs) and supposedly more direct indices of Central Nervous System (CNS) efficiency such as latencies of early, p^{100} evoked potentials (Carly, 1994; Reed & Jensen, 1992), of thalamic events (Reed & Jensen, 1993), or complex patterns of potentials (Blinkhorn & Henderson, 1982; Hendricksen, 1982; Hendricksen & Hendricksen, 1980).

One hope has been that scores on simple laboratory tasks may provide a predictor of individual differences in general ability that is independent of education and culture. A less well-considered belief is that because these indices are derived from such simple and basic tasks they must directly reflect fundamental performance characteristics of the CNS and so reveal "biological bases of intelligence" that may be used to model inheritability of global CNS efficiency and to underpin claims of racial differences in general intelligence (Jensen, 1985; Jensen & Whang, 1993), or to explain the improvement of learning and problem-solving ability by enrichment of developmental environments in terms of faster CNS processing time (Reed, 1993). Curiously, this considerable literature makes no reference to an identical framework of explanation for the cognitive changes accompanying normal aging: that age diffusely affects the entire CNS, but the impact of these changes on all cognitive skills, including memory, occur through their effects on a single performance characteristic such as "information processing speed" (Lindenberger, Mayr, & Kleigl, 1993; Salthouse, 1985, 1994) or "working memory capacity" (Salthouse, 1991).

An opposite view is that cognitive abilities are multiplex and independent and cannot adequately be expressed in terms of any single general factor (e.g., Gardner, 1983; Guilford, 1966). In this explanatory framework it is not sensible to try to express individual differences in all cognitive abilities as the outcomes of differences in any single, "master" performance index derived from simple laboratory tasks. This is not to say that those who hold this point of view find correlations between performance on laboratory tasks uninteresting, or have failed to investigate them. While experimenters such as Brand and Deary (1982), Bates and Eysenck (1993), Jensen (1980, 1985), or Vernon (1983, 1985) have examined correlations between scores on single intelligence tests and single indices such as CRT or IT, those interested in multifactor models have, necessarily, examined correlations between scores on several intelligence tests and on many different laboratory tasks, including measures of information processing speed, memory, and learning (e.g. Horn, 1982, 1985, 1986, 1989; Horn & Donaldson, 1980; Horn, Donaldson, & Engstrom, 1981; Horn & Hofer, 1992). Horn's many substantial and meticulous investigations have repeatedly shown that no single factor of general ability adequately expresses individual variation on scores on intelligence tests or on laboratory measures of perceptual and motor speed, learning, and memory. He was among the first to point out that scores from laboratory indices of memory and speed invariably correlate with intelligence test scores

(IQTSs), and they also always fall into clearly separate factors. In Horn's analyses speed always emerges as only one of several factors, and is not necessarily the most important, nor always the most strongly associated with psychometric measures of fluid intellectual ability. Horn (1986) also discussed these data to endorse the view that different modular neuropsychological systems and processes, and thus the abilities that they support, may age at different rates (Horn, 1984). Other workers have also found similar patterns of evidence (Rabbitt, 1993).

PERFORMANCE INDICES IN LABORATORY TASKS, PUTATIVE FUNCTIONAL SYSTEM PERFORMANCE CHARACTERISTICS, AND HYPOTHETICAL NEUROPHYSIOLOGY

All these discussions have missed important differences between the levels of description that psychometricians, cognitive psychologists, and neuropsychologists use and the nature and derivation of the constructs with which they work. Psychometricians use scores obtained from many different tasks given to large numbers of people to derive the minimum number of factors that will predict variance in performance in as wide a range of tasks as possible. A limiting case was Spearman's (1904, 1927) single factor "g." Recent theories assume that these factors can be directly identified with quite different constructs, which may be called hypothetical "system performance parameters." Among these are "information processing speed" or "working memory efficiency," which are ostensively defined in terms of functional models of the human cognitive system developed by cognitive psychologists. An optimistic further assumption is that these cognitive system performance characteristics can, in turn, be directly mapped onto elementary neurophysiological indices of CNS efficiency such as "synaptic conduction rate," "rate of spread of neural excitation," or "level of random noise" (e.g., Eysenck, 1986; Salthouse, 1985).

A difficulty with these assumptions is that in cognitive psychological models the entities that define the relative efficiencies of these inferred processes do not correspond to directly measurable task performance indices such as "percent correct recall" or CRT. For example, models for CRTs treat mean CRT or CRT variance as gross indices that have little functional significance unless they are further decomposed into terms reflecting different subprocesses and their interactions (Audley, 1960; Laming, 1985; Luce, 1986; Rabbitt & Vyas, 1973; Smith, 1968; Smith, 1980; Townsend & Ashby, 1983; Vickers, 1979). To distinguish these constructs from the performance indices directly measured in laboratory tasks they may be called "system performance parameters." These derived parameters are not necessarily, or often, expressed in units of time or of information processing rate. It is interesting that in all single-factor models the mean CRT is used as an exact equivalent of information processing rate and so as an irreducibly simple and pure index of the global efficiency of the human cognitive system. However, in his original derivation of the concept of information processing rate, Hick (1952) took pains to point out that it could not be defined or understood in terms of differences in mean CRTs between individuals or conditions but only in terms of "equivocation" (i.e., trade-off) between speed and errors in paced tasks. Mean CRTs are very strongly influenced by CRT variance and by the *slowest* responses that individuals make, so that equivocation functions or speed-error trade-off functions that identify the fastest speeds at which correct decisions can be made are much more informative indices of changes in maximum processing speed with age (Rabbitt & Vyas, 1973; Smith & Brewer, 1995), with IQ test scores (Rabbitt & Goward, 1994), or with practice (Rabbitt & Banerji, 1989). Obviously, mean CRTs do vary with speed-error trade-off functions, but they are more strongly determined by the precision with which response speed can be controlled to minimize the number of unnecessarily *slow* responses that are made during a task. This quite different parameter cannot be expressed as a measure of rate or time because, besides reflecting accuracy of detection of errors and the precision with which an operator can *modify* speed from one response to the next, it may also reflect individuals' levels of confidence at the task from which it is derived (Rabbitt & Vyas, 1973). Similarly, values obtained for ITs do not solely reflect speed of perceptual integration but also the efficiency with which subjects can learn to focus their attention at the precise moment when a display appears and the extent to which they can detect and use secondary cues, such as apparent motion, to detect small differences between displays (Anderson, 1988, 1992).

Perhaps this distinction between "task performance indices" and "system performance characteristics" is most clearly seen in abstract connectionist models such as those discussed by McClelland et al. (1986). When networks are designed to yield values of the relative speeds with which they perform different tasks, these depend on complex interactions between a variety of system parameters such as the number of units in the network, the richness and architecture of connections between them, their activation thresholds, and other, more global properties such as the level of random noise in part or all of the net. The global information processing speed of a network may not be sensibly computable and, if it is, will not be diagnostic of any *single* system performance parameter. It is an outcome of interactions between a variety of different system performance parameters that, themselves, may be elementary only in the weak sense that they have to be numerically specified before a simulation can run.

Another useful heuristic analogy is between measures of CRT or information processing speed obtained from different humans and the benchmark values that are used to compare the relative power of different makes of computers. The question of how fast a particular computer can perform a particular task cannot sensibly be answered in terms of any single benchmark index, such as the number of information processing operations that its central processing unit can carry out in a second. For particular programs and machines, task execution time will be much more severely constrained by other indices such as the available memory capacity, the extent to which the architecture of the machine allows parallel processing, and other values that are not represented as units of speed or information processing rate.

For these reasons, Rabbitt (1993) argued that it is unwise to assume that any particular task performance index, such as CRT, can be equated with some inferred global performance parameter of the functional cognitive system such as information processing speed, and still less with some measurable or hypothetical index of global neurophysiological efficiency such as synaptic transmission time, level of random noise (Eysenck, 1986), or rate of spread of activation (Salthouse, 1985).

Task performance indices such as CRT or IT are not pure or irreducible indices of global CNS efficiency. As for all other performance measures obtained from laboratory tasks, their logical status is that of summary indices of complex interactions between a variety of different processes that may often include higher-order judgments and strategic planning. From this point of view, in the present state of our knowledge, there is no reason why we should find predictions of individual differences in memory ability that are made from simple measures of information processing speed more interesting theoretically or more useful in practical applications than the much stronger predictions of memory competence that can be made from more complicated tasks, such as the solution of problems in intelligence tests. It is better to return to the commonsense assumption made by the first designers of intelligence tests: In general, complex tasks are likely to modestly predict performance on a wide range of simple tasks with which they overlap in terms of only one, or a few, demands. They are also likely to strongly predict performance in other complex tasks with which they share many diverse demands. Simple tasks such as CRT and IT paradigms are likely to predict performance in a narrower range of other tasks and also, in general, to make much weaker predictions of performance than more complex tasks, such as solving intelligence test problems.

Summary

The main evidence for recent psychometric theories of the functional bases of intelligence has been modest correlations between IQTSs and laboratory speed measures such as IT (e.g., Anderson, 1988, 1992; Brand & Deary, 1982; Nettelbeck, 1982; Nettelbeck, Edwards, & Vreugdenhil, 1986) or CRT (e.g., Bates & Eysenck, 1993; Eysenck, 1986; Hulme & Turnbull, 1983; Jensen, 1980; Smith & Stanley, 1983; Vernon, 1985; Vernon & Jensen, 1984) or both (Kirby & Nettelbeck, 1989). With rare exceptions (Kail, 1992; Nettelbeck & Rabbitt, 1992), these investigations have not considered whether individual differences in information processing speed and in IQTSs can account for individual differences in efficiency of memory and learning. An influential theory of cognitive aging has also been based on weak negative correlations between individuals' ages and their performance on a variety of different indices of information processing speed and of dual task performance (Salthouse, 1982, 1985, 1991). Salthouse (1994) also recently examined how far decline in performance on laboratory measures of speed can account for a parallel decline in performance on memory tasks in age. On the other hand, he has been silent on the obvious point that age-related variance in memory and learning can be even better accounted for by performance indices derived from much more complicated laboratory tasks, including IQ tests.

Both these enterprises beg the same questions at three levels of description. The first level of these is at the level of construct validity of the performance indices on which arguments have been based. Here, the questions are whether the indices are reliable in the sense that they have acceptable levels of test/retest correlations and whether they are valid in the sense that they actually index the particular task performance indices that they are supposed to represent.

A second level of description is that of factor structures. At this level, we may test the claim that individual differences competence on all or most cognitive abilities, including memory, do indeed load on a single factor of information processing speed (Eysenck, 1986). Another related question is whether, if age is included in such analyses, it will also negatively load on this dominant speed factor (Salthouse, 1985).

A third level of description is that of decomposition of task performance indices that can be obtained from particular laboratory tasks. Cognitive psychologists invented this type of analysis to define and test functional process models of task performance by obtaining separate indices of the relative contributions to performance of hypothetically distinct and independent processes whose joint operation is necessary for task completion (Donders, 1868; Sternberg, 1969, 1973). It is possible to include indices of individual differences, such as age and IQ test scores, into such analyses to ask whether they impact on some of these processes more than others. The hypotheses of Eysenck (1986), Salthouse (1985, 1991), and others would be supported by a finding that differences in general ability and in age affect performance on memory tasks principally through their impact on information transmission speed. These hypotheses would be weakened by findings that age or general ability also impact on memory efficiency through other performance parameters, such as rate of forgetting or vulnerability to interference, which are independent of information processing speed. They would be contradicted by a finding that these individual differences impact on memory efficiency mainly through their effects on other parameters, which do not depend on, and cannot be indexed in terms of, information processing speed.

HOW WELL DO INDIVIDUAL DIFFERENCES IN INFORMATION PROCESSING SPEED ACTUALLY ACCOUNT FOR INDIVIDUAL DIFFERENCES IN MEMORY EFFICIENCY?

Salthouse (1994) reported that as successive, different, laboratory indices of speed are entered into hierarchical regression equations, so they account for increasing amounts of age-related variance in the summed standardized scores from a variety of laboratory memory tasks. He used very diverse speed indices, from CRT in easy "lights and keys" tasks to rate of letter/letter substitution coding. Easy CRT tasks make no demands on memory. In contrast, letter/letter substitution coding requires quite complex scheduling of attention to control alternate scanning of lines of code exemplars and of targets, finding the right place in each line, the ability to hold several rather than only one pair of target and code items in memory so as to minimize the number of necessary "code look-ups," rate of code learning, and efficient motor control of handwriting.

Louise Phillips (1993) empirically showed that substitution coding speed is a complex index that reflects other cognitive abilities than information processing speed. She tested 96 people aged from 60 to 79 years on a four-choice CRT task, the Baddeley (1986) semantic reasoning task, a letter/letter substitution coding task, and on four different intelligence tests: the Heim (1970) AH 4 (1) and AH 4 (2), the Cattell and Cattell (1960) "Culture Fair" IQ test, and Raven's Progressive Matrices. Table 8.1 shows correlations among these measures.

The more complex coding and semantic reasoning tasks correlated, at $r = .522$ and $.538$, respectively, with the elementary speed index, CRT, but at $r = .599$ with each other, weakly supporting the idea that as tasks become more complex so they become more likely to share a wide range of demands and to correlate more highly. If information processing speed were the sole or even the main common demand that these three laboratory tasks shared with the four intelligence tests, they should correlate with IQTS at about the same degree as they correlate with each other. In fact, average correlations with IQTSs were $r = .364$ for CRT, increased slightly to $r = .396$ for semantic reasoning, and sharply to $r = .652$ for substitution coding. Evidently, the

TABLE 8.1
Correlations Among Seven Measures Taken on Adults
From Age 60 to 79 Years*

Task	Correlation With 4-Choice CRT	Correlation With Syntactic Reasoning Speed	Correlation With Substitution Coding Speed
AH 4 (1) test	−0.383	−0.455	−0.694
AH 4 (2) test	−0.361	−0.466	−0.627
Cattell Culture Fair Test	−0.298	−0.367	−0.662
Raven's Progressive Matrices	−0.297	−0.417	−0.527
Syntactic reasoning speed	0.338	—	0.559
Substitution coding speed	0.422	0.559	—

*Adapted from Phillips (1993). Reprinted with permission.

relatively complex substitution coding task does not differ from the easy CRT task merely because it *quantitatively* greater demands on information processing speed but rather because it also involves *qualitatively* different cognitive processes which overlap, to different degrees, with the wide range of demands made by intelligence tests designed to predict performance in complex real-life situations.

Roznowski (1993) also neatly showed that indices derived from superficially similar simple laboratory tasks differ markedly both in terms of their test/retest reliability and in terms of their correlations with IQTSs. She found that test/retest reliability increased significantly and steadily with task complexity, from elementary CRT to letter/letter substitution coding. Correlations between task indices and intelligence test scores increased from between r = .23 and r = .32 for easy CRT tasks with no memory load to r = .65 for mental paper folding, r = .71 for the Sternberg memory scanning task, r = .79 for sentence/picture comparison, and r = .89 for sentence verification. Although the indices obtained from all of these tasks are expressed in units of msec, this is clearly a superficial characteristic. They are not equivalent measures of mental speed because, except for the easy CRT tasks, they also make demands on other, diverse abilities such as precision of visual imagery and dexterity of mental manipulation (paper folding), working memory capacity (Sternberg memory search), and efficiency of retrieval from long-term memory (sentence verification). This is further circumstantial evidence that as laboratory tasks become more complex and make demands on a wider range of cognitive processes so they increasingly strongly overlap with the demands of, and that predict performance at, complicated intelligence test problems.

Philips' (1993) and Roznowski's (1993) demonstrations that speed indices derived from different tasks reflected the efficiency of qualitatively different functional processes encourages us to reexamine Salthouse's (1994) finding that when individual differences in adult age and in indices of mental speed are compared as predictors of performance on memory tasks, the proportion of variance attributable to age falls as more different speed indices are included in the regression equation. Nettelbeck and Rabbitt (1992) measured ITs, CRTs letter/letter substitution coding speed, and scores on four laboratory memory tasks from 109 volunteers aged from 55 to 86 years. Standardized scores from the four memory tasks, delayed picture recognition, digit span, free recall of a list of 30 words, and cumulative learning over four trials of a list of 15 words were summed to give a gross score for memory efficiency. Table 8.2 shows that when variance in memory test scores associated with ITs, CRTs, and letter/letter coding speed was incrementally removed, the independent contribution of individual differences in age to variance in memory scores progressively declined. This is just what Salthouse (1994) found although, in this experiment, individual differences in age still accounted for significant variance in memory scores even after contributions of all three speed measures had been partialed out.

Parenthetically, apart from incommensurability of the "speed" indices derived from the tasks that he used, a statistical problem with this style of analysis is that summing indices can artifactually augment the computed strength of associations between variables. Kelley (1927) pointed out that where m is the number of tasks of type A, n the number of tasks of type B, r = the correlation between a typical type A task and a typical type B task, p = the correlation between A tasks, and q the correlation between B tasks: $r_{AB} = r\ nm/\{\ (m + (m^2 - m)p)^* \ (n + (n^2 - n)q\ \}^{1/2}$.

This radical difficulty may be left aside to make two further points from the pattern of correlations shown in Table 8.2. First, all three speed measures, taken together, account for a significant proportion of age-related variance in memory task scores, but this only amounts to a very small proportion (about 9.3%) of the entire variance between individuals. Even if we take this result at face value as a replication of Salthouse's (1994) demonstration,

TABLE 8.2
Variance Associated With Age When Speed Tests
Were Included in Regression Analysis*

Speed Test Included in Regression Analysis	Percentage of Remaining Variance Associated With Age	Significance Level of Age-Related Variance
None	9.3%	$p < 0.001$
Inspection time	8.2%	$p < 0.001$
Plus 4-choice CRT	7.4%	$p < 0.01$
Plus syntactic reasoning	4.3%	$p < 0.01$
Plus substitution coding	1.3%	$p < 0.01$

*Adapted from Nettelbeck and Rabbitt (1992). Reprinted with permission.

90% of the variance between individuals is *not* picked up by measures of information processing speed. Second, the four speed measures are very unequal predictors of memory task performance. After the 8.0% of variance predicted by substitution coding has been taken into consideration, predictions from CRT (0.2%) and from IT (0.4%) are not significant. The higher test/retest reliability of letter/letter substitution coding, shown by Roznowski (1993), may be one reason for this. Probably a more powerful factor is that substitution coding tasks make demands on other cognitive skills than speed: working memory capacity to hold and use codes; strategic list scanning; and the ability rapidly to learn and to retrieve, rather than repeatedly look up, individual substitution codes. The complexity of letter/letter substitution coding is underlined by the point that in both the Table 8.1 and Table 8.2 data sets correlations between letter/letter coding scores and scores on the Cattell Culture Fair, and the Heim AH 4 (1) and (2), are nearly as large as correlations between these three intelligence tests.

Clearly, measures of information processing speed do predict performance on memory tasks. These predictions markedly improve when the speed measures are derived from relatively complex tasks that make demands on cognitive performance characteristics other than speed, but they are never very strong. This is somewhat puzzling because a strong relationship between efficiency of recall and information processing speed is directly predicated by most functional models for memory, particularly Craik and Lockhart's (1972) and Craik and Tulving's (1975) "Depth of Processing" theory, which predicts that the more "deeply" or "elaborately" input is processed the better it will subsequently be recalled. Faster processors will be able to achieve correspondingly deeper and more elaborate encoding within a fixed study interval. Indeed Waugh and Barr (1980) and many others have directly shown that older and slower individuals can attain the same levels of recall as the young and able if they are allowed sufficiently longer study times.

The contrast between Waugh and Barr's (1980) finding that probability of recall can be directly manipulated by varying inspection time within a memory task and the relatively weak correlations found between probability of recall and information processing speed indices is provocative. It suggests that measures of speed of processes involved in particular memory tasks may strongly predict recognition or recall in those particular tasks. In contrast, as we have seen, predictions from speed indices derived from paradigms such as CRT or IT that carry no memory load tend to be quite weak. In other words, measures of information processing speed, like other aspects of task performance, may be intensely "domain specific" (Ericcsen & Chase, 1982; Ericcsen & Polson, 1987) to the tasks in which they are measured.

Table 8.3 compares correlations between memory task performance and task internal and task external speed measures obtained in various memory experiments carried out by various investigators at the University of Man-

TABLE 8.3
Correlations Among Memory Task Performance, Task-External,
and Task-Internal Speed Measures

Type of Memory Task	Correlation With Task-External Speed Measure	Correlation With Task-Internal Speed Measure
Word recognition (lists of 30 words)	2-choice CRT (lights and keys) $r = 0.21$, $p < 0.05$	2-choice classification time for words in study phase ($r = 0.38$, $p < 0.01$)
Continuous word recognition	2-choice CRT (lights and keys) ($r = 1.9$ ns)	2-choice classification time for words ($r = 0.34$ $p < 0.01$)
Word recognition (lists of 50 words)	4-choice CRT (lights and keys) ($r = 0.21$, $p < 0.01$)	Time to generate associations to words on presentation ($r = 0.42$, $p < 0.001$)
Free recall of lists of 30 nouns	4-choice CRT (lights and keys) ($r = 0.21$, $p < 0.05$) Visual search for target set of 2 target letters among background set of 24 letters ($r = 0.21$, $p < 0.05$)	Time to classify each noun as the name of a living or non-living entity ($r = 0.47$, $p < 0.01$)

chester Age and Cognitive Performance Research Centre over the last 10 years.

Although task internal speed measures always predict memory performance better than task external measures, neither do very well. At best, task internal speed measures pick up only 17% of variance between individuals. This means that up to 80% of variance between individuals remains unaccounted for by differences in speed even when the indices used are obtained from a particular functional process employed in the activity of remembering. In all experiments, all participants were also scored·on the Heim AH 4 (1) intelligence test. In all cases, when variance associated with individual differences in AH 4 scores had been taken into consideration, predictions from speed measures markedly reduced and were no longer significant. In contrast, after variance associated with speed measures had been partialed out, predictions from AH 4 scores were hardly affected and remained robustly significant.

Summary

Speed indices obtained from different laboratory tasks differ markedly in terms of their test/retest reliability and their validity as predictors of memory task performance. They also correlate at markedly different levels with intelligence test scores. It seems likely that this is because speed indices derived from complex tasks, which also involve a wide range of other cognitive performance parameters, are better predictors of performance on both memory tasks and on intelligence tests. Task internal speed indices predict performance on memory tasks better than do task external speed indices. However, even these associations are quite modest.

These findings do not support the idea that intelligence test scores predict individual differences in performance on most cognitive skills, including memory tasks, mainly because they pick up individual differences in information processing speed; (e.g., Jensen, 1985, where this argument is explicitly made). Intelligence tests certainly account for all of the variance in memory task performance that is associated with individual differences in speed, but they also appear to pick up additional variance that even task internal speed measures do not detect. This suggests that it is useful to follow Horn et al.'s (1980; 1981) style of analysis and consider relationships between memory indices, intelligence test scores, measures of information processing speed, and measures of memory efficiency at a higher level of description, that of factor structures.

FACTOR ANALYSES OF RELATIONSHIPS BETWEEN AGE, INTELLIGENCE TEST SCORES, INDICES OF INFORMATION PROCESSING SPEED, AND PERFORMANCE ON MEMORY TASKS

Before considering relationships between measures at the factor level of description it is prudent to follow Roznowski's (1993) example and check the reliability of the performance indices used. Table 8.4 shows test/retest correlations for scores from the Heim AH 4 (1) and (2) and the Cattell "Culture Fair" test. For comparison, we have also included test/retest correlations on four speed indices, a four-choice CRT task, a visual search task, a syntactic reasoning task, and a substitution coding task. Correlations are also given for four memory tasks, a free recall of a list of 15 words, cumulative learning over four trials of a list of 15 words, memory for objects, and memory for names and personal details of four imaginary people.

Test/retest correlations on these laboratory speed measures and memory tasks are lower than for psychometric tests, which are carefully designed to meet a high standard in this respect. Nevertheless, they are quite robust, can remain stable over quite long periods of time (in this case, from four weeks to three years), and so can reasonably be included into principal components analyses.

The question is how far individual variance in performance of laboratory memory tasks overlaps with variance in tests of general ability (intelligence tests) and in laboratory speed measures. A principal components analysis was carried out on scores obtained from 379 volunteers aged from 50 to 80 years who were each given three different speed tests—substitution coding,

TABLE 8.4
Test/Retest Correlations on 14 Measures

Task or Intelligence Test	Level of Test/Retest Correlation	Number of Participants
AH 4 (1) test	0.79	543
AH 4 (2) test	0.81	543
Cattell Culture Fair	0.79	367
Raven's Progressive Matrices	0.73	89
4-Choice RT	0.45	96
Inspection time	0.51	78
Visual search (2 target)	0.42	109
Syntactic reasoning	0.58	109
Substitution coding	0.65	96
Free recall (30 words)	0.45	112
Digit span	0.54	112
Cumulative recall (15 words)	0.61	112
Recall of names of 15 objects	0.53	112
Story recall (propositions correct)	0.61	112

visual search and semantic reasoning—and three different verbal memory tasks—immediate free recall of the names of 12 visually presented common objects (recall of object names, ON), immediate free recall of a list of 15 words (FR), and immediate free recall of the names of four fictitious individuals and of three items of information about each (people recall, PO). Table 8.5 gives the orthogonal transformation solution (varimax) for a principal components analysis of these data.

The first, dominant factor, which included total scores from the AH 4 (1) and (2) and Culture Fair scores as well as scores on the visual search and substitution coding task, accounts for 32% of the total variance. Scores for two of the memory tasks, free recall of names of objects and free recall of a list of 15 words, are clearly separated, and load on a second factor, which

TABLE 8.5
Results of Principal Components Analysis on Data from Three Speed Tests
and Three Verbal Memory Tasks for Adults Aged 50 to 80 Years

Task	Factor 1 (32% of variance)	Factor 2 (24% of variance)	Factor 3 (18% of variance)
Substitution coding	.788		
Visual search	.836		
Semantic reasoning	.809		
Information about people		.933	
Free recall		.828	
Names of objects			.714
Age		.932	

still accounts for substantial variance (24%). Names of objects is again clearly separate, loading on a third factor that accounts for 18% of the total variance. Free recall of 15 words is also strongly represented in this factor. The salient point is that although scores on a supposedly "pure" measure of information processing speed, substitution coding, load with intelligence test scores, memory tasks have some mutual commonality and are clearly separate from both these measures. This does not support the idea that intelligence test scores predict memory performance primarily because they pick up individual variance in information processing speed.

To examine how variance associated with age is distributed in relation to speed and memory factors, a different group of 479 volunteers aged from 56 to 78 years were tested on the Cattell Culture Fair, and on six of the speed and memory tasks described earlier: visual search, substitution coding, and the Baddeley (1986) Semantic Reasoning Task, PO, FR, and ON. Table 8.6 summarizes the orthogonal transformation solution (varimax).

This analysis shows clear commonality among the three "speed" tasks, which load, with Cattell scores, on a dominant factor that accounts for 34% of the total variance. Age, information about people, and free recall of 15 words have negligible representation on this factor, and load heavily on a second factor, which accounts for 25% of variance. Memory for names of objects loads weakly on these first two factors, and strongly on a third factor that accounts for 16% of the total variance. This does not support Salthouse's (1985, 1991, 1994) hypothesis that age decline in performance on memory tasks mainly, or entirely, reflects decline in speed of information processing. On the contrary, when loadings of age with scores from both speed and memory tasks are compared, age is found to load strongly with measures of memory but only weakly with measures of speed.

TABLE 8.6
Results of Principal Components Analyses on Data
From Cattell "Culture Fair" Test and Six Speed and
Memory Tasks for Adults Aged 56 to 78 years

Task or Source of Variation Among Individuals	Factor 1 (34% of variance)	Factor 2 (25% of variance)	Factor 3 (16% of variance)
Cattell Culture Fair	.836		
Visual search	.794		
Semantic reasoning	.822		
Substitution coding	.879		
Free recall		.856	
Information about people		.884	
Memory for names of 12 objects			.932
Age		.789	

Summary

Individual differences in speed of information processing do not account well for associations between memory test performance and intelligence test scores, nor for the decline of memory test scores with increasing age. Similar patterns of disassociations between age, general ability, speed, and performance at memory and learning tasks have often been reported before; (Horn, 1982, 1985, 1986, 1989; Horn & Donaldson, 1980; Horn, Donaldson, & Engstrom, 1981; Horn & Hofer, 1992; Rabbitt, 1993).

DECOMPOSITIONAL TASK ANALYSES TO LOCATE THE SEPARATE IMPACT OF INDIVIDUAL DIFFERENCE VARIABLES ON PROCESSES SPECIFIED IN FUNCTIONAL MODELS FOR MEMORY TASKS

Following Eysenck (1986), Salthouse (1985, 1991), and many others, we have considered correlational relationships between summary measures of information processing speed and of memory test performance such as CRTs—coding rates and total numbers of items correctly recalled or recognized. These summary task performance indices only provide rough measures of the combined efficiency of a variety of different functional processes. In terms of functional models for cognitive processes they can only be clearly understood if they can be "decomposed" to yield separate indices that represent the different contributions to task performance made by independent processes or processing stages (Sternberg, 1969, 1975). If these indices can be empirically shown to be independent it becomes possible to test whether some of the processes they represent are more affected than others by individual differences in age, general ability, practice, or by the ingestion of drugs such as alcohol (Rabbitt & Maylor, 1991; Sternberg, 1975). This decomposition provides another, convergent test as to whether or not individual differences in age or in intelligence test performance affect memory efficiency only through their effects on processes that depend on information processing speed.

Unfortunately, few functional models of memory are sufficiently well articulated to specify several distinct performance indices. An exception is Baddeley and Hitch's (1974) model for an articulatory loop system in which efficiency is defined by only two system performance parameters: the maximum rate at which the articulatory representations of a string of successively presented words can be refreshed by seriatim rehearsal (articulation rate), and the period of time during which a representation of any item will remain available if not rehearsed (decay rate). In this analysis, rehearsal rate, taken as equivalent to articulation rate, is a system performance parameter limited by information processing speed, and is indexed by differences in the intercepts of functions relating articulation rate to span. In contrast, decay rate is an independent performance parameter, is not directly related to information processing rate, and is indexed by the slopes of functions relating articulation rate to span. All empirical tests of the model have found that these two indices are independent of each other (Baddeley, 1986). The empirical basis for the model is that these functions are always found to be linear, so that memory span seems to be limited by the maximum number of phonemes that can be articulated in unit time, irrespective of how many distinct words they form.

Fig. 8.1 plots data by Goward (1987) showing relationships between articulation rates and immediate memory spans for lists of one, two, three, four, and five syllable words obtained from older and younger groups of people matched for relatively high and low scores on the Heim (1970) AH 4 (1) intelligence test.

Analyses of variance confirmed that age and AH 4 (1) test scores significantly affect the intercepts, but not the slopes of functions relating spans for words of different syllable lengths to their corresponding articulation and reading rates. In the framework of the Baddeley and Hitch (1974) and Baddeley (1986) model, this means that age and AH 4 (1) scores influence span through their effects on articulatory rehearsal rate, but have no measurable effect on trace decay rates. This is consistent with the suggestion that age and general ability alter span for pronounceable words only through their effects on information processing speed.

It is instructive to consider just how much of individual variability in performance can be accounted for in terms of the parameters defined by the Baddeley and Hitch model. In this experiment the only task performance index that picked up any individual differences was articulation rate. A first point was to test the reliability of indices. When data from all groups are combined, articulation rates and reading rates correlated at the reassuring level of $r = .715$. Significant correlations between memory spans and articulation rates and reading rates ($r = .590$) and between spans and reading rates ($r = .506$) are also consistent with the ARL model but account for at most 35% of variance between individuals. This is less than we might expect on the assumption that information processing rate is the sole individual differences variable accounting for span. Correlations between AH 4 test scores and spans are slightly higher ($r = .608$), accounting for 37% of total variance in spans. AH 4 scores significantly correlate with reading rates ($r = .648$) and articulation rates ($r = .715$). However, AH 4 scores do not predict individual variations in spans only because they are associated with these measures of information processing speed, because partial correlations between AH 4 test scores and spans remain significant both when effects of

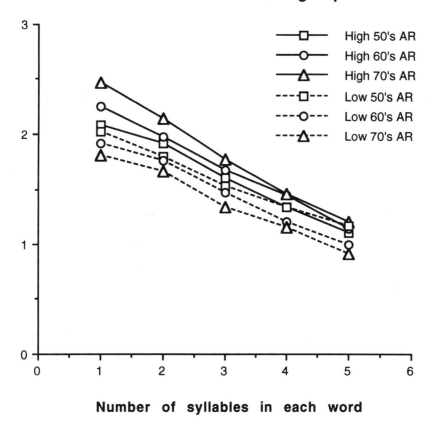

Articulation Rates for Age and AH 4 test score groups

Number of syllables in each word

FIG. 8.1. Articulation rates for age and AH 4 test score groups.

reading rate ($r = .367$, $p < 0.01$) and of articulation rate ($r = .487$, $p < 0.001$) have been taken into consideration. It seems that AH 4 test scores pick up individual differences in functional competence that significantly determine variations in spans but are independent of, and additional to, rehearsal rates. In short, over 60% of variance between individuals is *not* accounted for by measures of information processing speed, or by AH 4 test scores. This shortfall has often been found in other tests of the Baddeley and Hitch model, and is usually ascribed to involvement of processes which are functionally independent of articulation rate, such as efficient management of encoding by "chunking" of input or by detection and use of mnemonic cues. It is reasonable that test scores should pick up some of these powerful determinants of performance in this task that, collectively, clearly account for much more of variations in span with age than does slowing of information processing speed. Again it seems that speed is an important, but not the only nor necessarily the most significant, factor that mediates age-related differences in immediate memory span.

Forgetting rates are important system performance parameters in all functional models for memory, and the suggestion from Goward's (1987) data that they are unaffected by individual differences in age or IQTSs needed further investigation. The Robbins and Sahakian "CANTAB" computerized neuropsychological test battery includes a test of delayed matching of colored complex shapes to previously presented exemplars after unfilled intervals of 0, 4, and 12 seconds. Robbins et al. (1994) obtained functions relating forced choice matching accuracy to delay interval for 809 individuals partitioned into separate groups aged from 55–59, 60–64, 65–69, 70–74 and 75–79 years. Fig. 8.2 plots matching accuracy as a function of delay interval for all groups.

The main effects of age group and of delay interval approached but did not quite reach significance ($p = 0.06$). However, Fig. 8.2 suggests that this was partly because at longer delay intervals scores for older groups approached the performance "floor" of 50% chance accuracy for a binary match. Specific comparisons showed significant differences between each pair of the three youngest and between the two oldest groups ($p < 0.05$ in

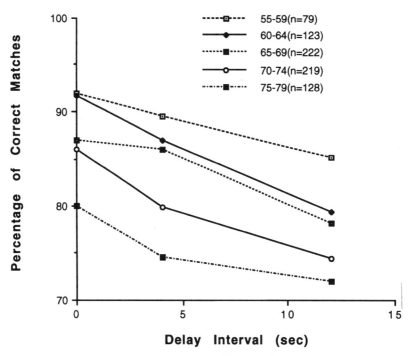

FIG. 8.2. Forgetting rates as a function of age group.

all cases). It seems that if tasks are sensitive, if recall is delayed for longer than the very few seconds covered in the Baddeley and Hitch (1974) paradigm, and if floor effects can be avoided, it is possible to detect an acceleration of forgetting rates with increasing age.

RTs for matches automatically measured and recorded in this experiment modestly but significantly predicted total numbers of items correctly identified, ($r = .21$, $p < 0.01$), but not forgetting rate indexed as the difference in numbers of corrects match at delays of 0 and 12 seconds ($r = 0.02$). Although both information processing speed and rate of trace decay significantly contribute to total recognition performance, and both significantly change with increasing age, they do not correlate with each other ($r < 0.02$) and their effects seem to be independent.

A logical difficulty in examining individual differences in forgetting rates is that age and intelligence test score groups markedly differ in their matching efficiency at the shortest delays, so that their forgetting rates must be computed from very different baselines. This is another reminder that the task performance characteristics that we measure are not illuminating unless they are interpreted in terms of hypothetical "system performance characteristics" in a functional model. For example, differences in probability of matching between groups on immediate recall may be interpreted in terms of a hypothetical system operating characteristic such as "average trace strength," with the implication that "higher initial strength" may lead to slower average decline. On these assumptions we might interpret these results as showing that rates of forgetting are inversely related to information processing rate, because younger individuals have faster information processing rates, can form stronger traces in unit time, and, as a result, will experience slower forgetting.

To test this, Yang Qian used a variant of the Brown–Peterson paradigm to compare rates of forgetting between four groups of 15 individuals orthogonally matched for age (young, aged 50–60 years, mean age = 57.2, *SD* = 1.49; old aged from 70–80 years, mean age = 75.5, *SD* = 1.89) and for scores on the Heim AH 4 (1) test (high, mean AH 4 scores = 47.1, *SD* = 4.9; low, mean AH 4 scores = 26.9, *SD* = 6.8). To equate for level of initial recall and, incidentally, to obtain a task-internal measure of encoding speed Yang presented 3 × 3 matrices of nine common nouns titrating display durations to measure the shortest interval at which each participant could report five words immediately after the display was occluded by a random mask. Yang compared immediate recall with recall after delays of 1, 2, or 4 minutes during which participants carried out a backward digit-span task. The stability of titrated exposure durations was repeatedly checked during the experiment. During the same experimental session, a task-external measure of information processing rate, four-choice CRT, was also obtained for each individual. Recall across delay intervals by two age and two AH 4 (1) test score groups are shown in Figs. 8.3a and 8.3b.

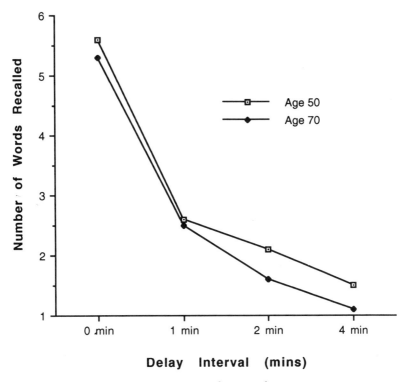

FIG. 8.3a. Decay rate as a function of age group.

Main effects of age and AH 4 score were significant, but their overall interactions with delay interval were not. However, specific comparisons showed significant interactions between age group and delay between 1 and 4 minutes, and between intelligence test score group and delay between 0 and 1 minutes. Decay rates do seem to vary with age and intelligence test performance, even when individual differences in levels of initial learning are equated.

Learning rate is another system performance parameter in memory tasks that is potentially independent of information processing rate. Nettelbeck, Rabbitt, Wilson, and Batt (in press) compared individuals' free recall on initial presentation of a list of 15 words with their subsequent rates of incremental learning of the same list over four successive presentations. Eighty-six participants were orthogonally matched for age between 55 and 86 years and for scores on the AH 4 (1) IQ test. Asymptotic functions were fitted to learning curves obtained from individual participants. This allowed comparisons of how individual differences in age, in AH 4 test scores, and in two task-independent measures of information processing time, RT and IT, affected the levels of initial recall and of subsequent learning rates. Initial

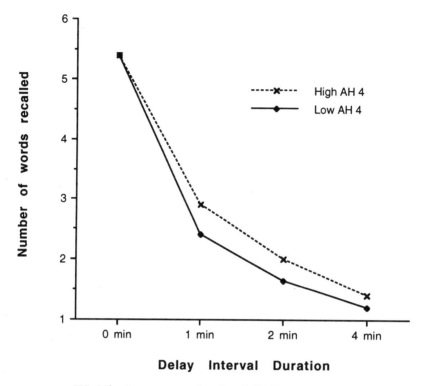

FIG. 8.3b.   Decay rate as a function of AH 4 test score group.

recall spans declined significantly with increasing age, but the correlation between age and initial span length reduced effectively to zero when variance associated with individual differences in information processing speed had been partialled out. This, of course, supports Salthouse's (1985, 1994) hypothesis that age-related differences in span directly reflect corresponding differences in information processing speed. However, Nettelbeck et al. (in press) found that individual differences in subsequent learning rates were unaffected by individual differences in age, AH 4 test scores, or CRT or IT. This suggested that task decomposition might identify independent effects of individual differences on different functional processes.

A difficulty with Nettelbeck, Rabbitt, Wilson, and Batt's (in press) data is that because lists contained only 15 words, differences in rates of learning between groups were underestimated because more able individuals approached ceiling. Yang Qian, therefore, repeated this experiment on 96 volunteers aged from 60 to 80 years, orthogonally grouped by age and high or low AH 4 test score, with lists of 25 rather than 15 words, and six rather than four list repetitions. Task external speed measures were also obtained for each individual.

People in their early 60s recalled more items than those in their late 70s or 80s, and high test scorers recalled more than low test scorers. However, changes associated with differences in age were independent of those associated with differences in AH 4 test scores. That is, differences between AH 4 test score groups were roughly the same at all ages, so that there was no evidence that individuals' higher AH 4 test scores protected them against age-related memory change. Although all subjects improved over successive trials, the younger individuals and high test scorers showed faster learning than older individuals and low test scorers. Data are plotted in Figs. 8.4a and 8.4b.

A general correlation analysis showed that measures of information processing speed were modestly and positively correlated with the total numbers of items recalled over all six trials (cumulative free recall scores; $r = 0.28$, $F = 7.81$, $df = 1,94$, $p < 0.007$). Correlations between speed measures and amounts recalled on each of the six successive trials were between $r = -0.21$ and $r = -0.31$, and were all significant at $p < 0.05$. The correlation between age and total cumulative learning scores over all six trials was also significant (-0.25, $F = 6.32$, $df = 1,94$, $p < 0.02$). After variance associated with speed measures had been partialled out the association between age and total cumulative recall scores was hardly altered ($r = -0.22$, $F = 4.86$, $df = 1,94$, $p < 0.05$). Yang's experiment, therefore, partially replicated Nettelbeck et al.'s (in press) results. She found that both age and processing speed markedly affect total cumulative learning scores, but no evidence that age-related changes in learning rates are substantially mediated by concomitant changes in processing speed.

Nettelbeck et al. (in press) suggested that total cumulative learning scores might be decomposed into at least two components: initial recall score, which was equivalent to immediate memory span for word lists; and subsequent learning rates, which were estimated by fitting hyperbolic power functions to each individual's data. Although these functions provided reasonable empirical fits to Nettelbeck et al.'s data, in Yang's data the best-fitting hyperbolic functions accounted for an average of only 64.5% of individual variance in learning rates, probably because the longer lists that she used avoided ceiling effects. However, fits of linear functions illustrated in Figs. 8.4a and 8.4b accounted for 95.3% and 94.2% of individual variance within the younger and older age groups and for 93.5% and 95.9% of individual variance within higher and lower AH 4 test score groups. Analysis of residuals with the Durbin–Watson statistic showed that the range of DW values for each of the test groups fell between 1.69 and 2.01, with $k = 1$, suggesting that linear functions do provide very acceptable fits. Participants' initial trial free recall scores correlated robustly with their free recall scores obtained in a separate part of the experiment ($r = 0.89$). Thus, initial trial free recall appears to be a reliable performance index.

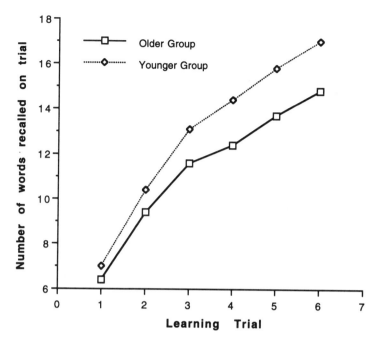

FIG. 8.4a. Learning rate as a function of age group.

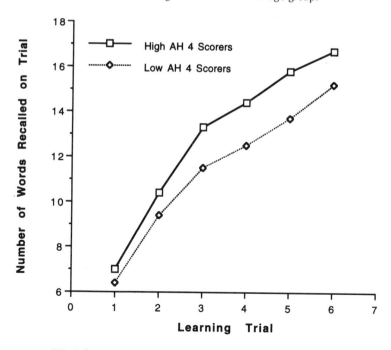

FIG. 8.4b. Learning rate as a function of AH 4 test score group.

Correlation analyses showed no significant associations between participants' initial memory spans and their learning rates ($r = 0.08$, $F = 0.68$, $df = 1{:}94$, $p > 0.1$). Participants' ages modestly and negatively correlated with both their initial memory spans and their learning rates. AH 4 test scores correlated modestly and positively only with initial memory spans but not with learning rates. Total cumulative learning scores summed over six trials correlated highly with memory spans and learning rates that, respectively, accounted for 36.3% and 23.6% (total 59.9%) of total variance between individuals.

Relationships among these variables were further explored by partial correlation analyses. Correlations between age and initial memory span reduced, and became nonsignificant, when variance associated with individual differences in speed was removed ($r = -0.18$, $F = 3.25$, $df = 1{:}94$, $p > 0.05$). The negative correlation between age and learning rate remained significant after speed was partialed out ($r = 0.22$, $df = 1{:}94$, $F = 4.5$, $p < 0.05$). This suggests that age-related differences in information processing speed affect initial memory spans but not subsequent learning rates. The negative correlation between age and total cumulative learning scores was reduced and became nonsignificant when age-related variance in initial memory span was removed ($r = -0.17$, $F = 2.40$, $df = 1{:}93$, $p > 0.05$). This also happened when age-related variance in learning rates was removed ($r = -0.16$, $F = 2.29$, $df = 1{:}93$, $p > 0.05$). When age differences in initial memory spans and in learning rates were partialed out together, the association between age and memory total score entirely disappeared ($r = -0.03$, $F = 0.10$, $df = 1{,}{:}94$, $p > 0.05$). Thus, partial correlation analyses suggest that memory span and learning rates are the main system performance parameters that account for age differences in total cumulative learning scores, but also suggest that their effects are not directly mediated by age-related differences in information processing speed.

A LISREL confirmatory factor analysis compared structural equation models for these relationships. In the first analysis the exogenous variable was age, and the endogenous variables were memory span, learning rate, total cumulative learning score, and the speed measure (CRT). The best-fitting model is shown in Fig. 8.5. The chi-square for this structure was 1.37, $df = 2$, $p > 0.50$, confirming a statistically acceptable fit. In earlier models, when memory span, rate of learning, and speed were included, the correlation coefficient for the path between age and total score of memory became very small. Thus, the path indicating a direct effect of age on total cumulative learning score was removed. Fixing the age-speed relationship at zero produced very little change in the chi-square value for the model illustrated in Figs. 8.5a and 8.5b (chi-square = 3.22, $df = 4$, $p > 0.522$, change in chi-square = 1.85, $df = 2$, $p < 0.05$). This implies that removing the path between age and processing speed did not make a significant change to the best-fitting

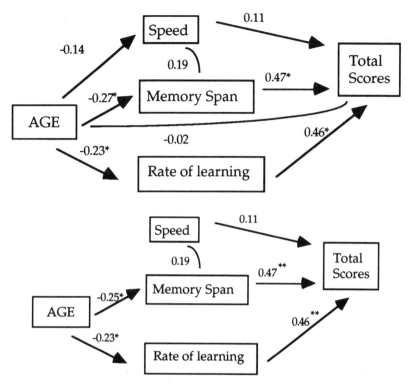

FIG. 8.5. Structural equation models for the relationships between age, memory span, learning rate, speed, and total cumulative learning (5a); with the age-speed relationship set at zero (5b).

structural model. This confirms suggestions from the partial correlation analysis that age affects total cumulative learning scores, but that its effects are not mediated by individual differences in processing speed.

For the same structural model, the chi-square value increased significantly when the relationship between age and initial span was fixed at zero (chi-square = 8.68, df = 4, p = 0.07; change in chi-square = 7.31, df = 2, p > 0.05). Similarly, when the relationship between age and learning rate was fixed as zero, the chi-square value again changed markedly and significantly (chi-square = 6.62, df = 4, p > 0.157; change in chi-square = 5.25, df = 2, p > 0.05). This suggests that age differences in initial recall span and in learning rates, taken together, are the main factors accounting for age impairment in total cumulative learning scores. Information processing speed does not seem to be an important factor mediating age changes in total cumulative learning scores.

Equivalent analyses were carried out substituting AH 4 test scores for age as the exogenous variable. Unlike age, AH 4 test scores were strongly correlated with measures of processing speed ($r = 0.66$, $F = 73.26$, $df = 1{:}94$, $p < 0.0001$) and with initial memory spans but not with subsequent learning rates. AH 4 test scores correlated significantly with initial memory spans ($r = 0.15$, $F = 2.03$, $df\,1$, $p < 0.05$) and with total cumulative learning scores ($r = 0.26$, $F = 6.78$, $df = 1{:}94$, $p = 0.01$). However, once the effects of variance in initial memory spans on total memory scores had been partialed out, the correlation between AH 4 scores and total cumulative learning scores was sharply reduced and fell below $p < 0.05$. The effects of differences in AH 4 scores on total cumulative learning scores seem to be mediated through their effects on initial memory spans. When variance associated with speed and memory span were jointly partialed out, the correlation between AH 4 test scores and total cumulative learning scores fell almost to zero ($r = 0.02$, $F = 0.26$, $df = 1$ $p > 0.05$). This suggests that the impact of AH 4 scores on total cumulative learning scores is mainly mediated by their effects on initial memory span and on speed.

Path structural analysis with AH 4 test score as the exogenous variable found that the best-fitting structural model is that shown in Fig. 8.6a (chi-square = 1.26, $df = 2$, $p > 0.53$). A first finding was that AH 4 test score is strongly related to speed, but that the direct relationship between speed and total cumulative learning score is very weak. A second finding was that the direct path between AH 4 test score and total cumulative learning score has a value close to zero, implying that the impact of AH 4 scores on total cumulative learning scores is mainly indirect. This agrees with the correlational analysis described earlier. Because the effects of speed are discounted in the best-fitting model, the remaining effective variables may either be initial memory span, or learning rate, or both. A third finding was that the relationship between speed and memory span markedly reduces after variance associated with AH 4 test scores is taken into account. Therefore, despite the good fit of the model illustrated in Fig. 8.6a the paths connecting speed and total cumulative learning score and directly connecting AH 4 and total cumulative learning score were removed. The adjusted structural model had a relatively low chi-squared value (chi-square = 2.14, $df = 4$, $p > 0.71$), indicating that it was also statistically acceptable. The difference between chi-squared values for this final model, illustrated in Fig. 8.6b, and that illustrated in Fig. 8.6a, was not significant (chi-square difference = 0.88, $df = 2$, $p > 0.05$).

The satisfactory fit of the model illustrated in Fig. 8.6a suggests that the relationship between speed and total cumulative learning score is not statistically important. For the same structural model, when the relation between AH 4 test score and learning rate was fixed as zero, the chi-squared value (chi-square = 3.51, $df = 5$, $p > 0.68$) did not significantly increase (change in chi-square = 1.37, $df = 1$, $p > 0.05$). This means that we need not assume that AH 4 test scores affect learning rates. However, the chi-squared value

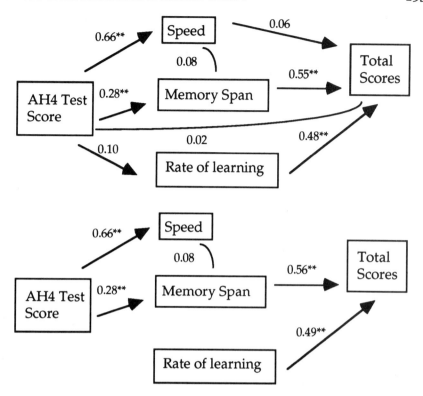

FIG. 8.6. Structural equation models for the relationships between AH 4 test scores, memory span, learning rate, speed, and total cumulative learning, with (6a) and without (6b) the paths connecting speed and total cumulative learning, and AH 4 and total cumulative learning.

increased significantly, and the model became statistically unacceptable, when the path between AH 4 test score and initial memory span was deleted (chi-square = 10.97, $df = 6$, $p = 0.09$, and change in chi-square = 7.46, $df = 1$, $p < 0.05$). The final structural model shown in Fig. 8.6b suggests that AH 4 test scores are strongly related to initial memory span and to speed, but that their effects on total cumulative learning scores are mediated by their impacts on initial memory span rather than by their impacts on processing speed.

   In sum, AH 4 scores have little or no direct effect on total cumulative learning scores. Neither do they affect cumulative learning scores indirectly through their relationship with information processing speed. AH 4 scores and speed measures both affect initial spans. Any effect that AH 4 scores or speed measures have on total cumulative learning scores is mediated by this effect on initial spans. There is no evidence that either AH 4 test scores, or speed measures, correlate with *learning rates*, as distinct from *initial spans*.

SUMMARY AND CONCLUSIONS

All these results and analyses confirm that the times that people take to carry out a variety of different tasks correlate negatively with their ages, positively with their scores on intelligence tests, and positively with the number of items that they can recall or recognize in simple laboratory tasks. The ubiquity, and the generally modest level, of these correlations are entirely consistent with nearly all previous findings in the psychometric and gerontological literature.

These relationships were examined at three levels: at the level of construct validity of summary task performance indices, such as CRT or speed at substitution coding tasks; at the level of partial correlations and of factor structure; and at the level of decompositional analysis of summary task performance indices into hypothetical system performance parameters representing the relative efficiencies of processes defined in terms of functional models of cognition.

Unsurprisingly, commonly used indices of mental speed have very different test/retest reliability. They also have very different construct validity. Simple tasks, such as easy four-choice CRT or IT, that do not demand strategic control of attention or working memory load, correlate only modestly with intelligence test scores or with performance on memory tasks. More complex tasks, such as substitution coding, that do make demands on attention, working memory, and rate of learning, correlate almost as well with intelligence tests as intelligence tests correlate with each other. In general, performance at solving intelligence test problems predicts performance on memory tasks better than any putative index of information processing speed yet examined in the literature. A simple explanation for these findings would be that the more complex a task, the wider will be the range of different cognitive processes and skills that it demands. The greater this range of demands, the more likely they are to overlap with those made by other, simple tasks and the more broadly they are likely to overlap with those made by other complex tasks. As a result, scores from complex tasks will, in general, modestly predict scores from wide ranges of other simple tasks but will much more widely, and also much more strongly, predict scores from other, equally complex tasks. From this point of view information processing speed is an important one, but only one, of a wide range of cognitive performance parameters that may vary with general ability and decline with age.

At the level of factor structures derived from summary task performance indices, scores on memory tasks loaded strongly on common factors and very weakly on factors incorporating either indices of information processing speed or intelligence test scores or both. There is no evidence that individual differences in memory ability are dominantly associated with individual differences in information processing speed, or with individual differences in any single factor of general ability derived from intelligence test scores.

At the level of decompositional analysis of task performance there was some evidence that forgetting rates were independent of encoding rates but also that, like encoding rates, they varied with age and intelligence test performance. There was also some evidence that individual differences in information processing speed associated with age and with intelligence test performance affect the total number of items acquired during six trials of a cumulative learning task, primarily by affecting the span of items recalled on the first trial and not at all by affecting the rate at which new items are acquired on subsequent trials. It seems that both age and intelligence do not affect all cognitive system performance parameters only through their impacts on information processing speed, but instead have different effects on different, apparently independent, system performance parameters.

As an explanatory construct, information processing speed cannot any longer support the starring role to which it has been assigned: that of a "master" performance parameter, in terms of which it is possible to articulate entire theories of general ability or of cognitive changes with age. The strength and uniqueness of its predictive value is unremarkable. Speed indices predict best when they are obtained as summary performance indices from complex tasks that involve a variety of demands on disparate cognitive processes, many of which, such as working memory load, involve a much wider range of system performance characteristics than speed alone. What needs to be explained is not the strength but rather the ubiquity of predictions of cognitive performances by indices of information processing speed.

In the universe of which we are a part it is not hard to find an explanation for the intrusive ubiquity of indices of rate and time in descriptions of all processes, including cognition. Processes can only be defined in terms of changes that unfold in time. It follows that duration is a necessary condition for all physical processes, including those in the CNS. Process duration can always be measured but, as is well known even from elementary physics, the relative durations of processes do not necessarily tell us anything about their relative complexities and we cannot derive useful models for processes from information about their duration alone. To model processes we need information about other properties that, although they may jointly determine their duration, cannot themselves be defined or indexed in terms of time.

Those who feel that discussions of individual differences can be carried on in terms of indices of measurement rather than in terms of functional properties of the cognitive system and of the CNS should be as content to conclude that individual differences associated with age or ability stem entirely from differences in accuracy as in speed. For easy tasks, speed is usually preferable because it can vary even when accuracy does not differ between groups or conditions. For difficult tasks, accuracy is usually a more useful measure because some humans may find some tasks impossible within any time limit, and all humans will find some tasks impossible within some time limits. Thus, because, in the human cognitive system, speed and accuracy of processes always trade off against each other, each index is necessary to interpret the other, and neither on its own will do. This still does not move us forward, because it tells us nothing about function except that information must take some time, however brief, to be transmitted, and that truncation of transmission time will reduce the amount of information transmitted, increase uncertainty, and so raise the probability of error: In short, that the mathematics of information theory can be applied to the human brain as to all other physical systems. However, when they first made this point, Hick (1952) and Miller (1957) also saw that a statement that a particular metric has a very general application to human performance is not a great advance in understanding unless it helps us towards a functional model that describes the processes whose outcomes it quantifies. The models that William Hick and George Miller proposed did not confuse performance indices with functional processes; they showed functional applications for new quantitative methods that would otherwise have remained algebraic abstractions, opened questions that would not otherwise have been asked and, having made these remarkable contributions, could be gracefully superseded because they were empirically testable. Perhaps current models for individual differences in functional memory efficiency may, at last, take note of these examples.

REFERENCES

Anderson, M. (1988). Inspection time, information processing and the development of intelligence. *British Journal of Developmental Psychology, 6*, 43–57.

Anderson, M. (1992). *Intelligence and development: A cognitive theory.* Oxford: Blackwells.

Audley, R. J. (1960). A stochastic model for individual choice behaviour. *Psychological Review, 67*, 1–15.

Baddeley, A. D. (1986). *Working memory.* Oxford: Oxford University Press.

Baddeley, A. D., & Hitch, G. T. (1974). Working memory. In G. A. Bower (Ed.), *The psychology of learning and motivation* (Vol. 8, pp. 47–90). New York: Academic Press.

Bates, T. C., & Eysenck, H. J. (1993). Intelligence, inspection time and decision time. *Intelligence, 17*, 523–532.

Blinkhorn, S. F., & Henderson, D. E. (1982). Average evoked responses and psychometric intelligence. *Nature, 295*, 596–597.

Brand, C. R., & Deary, I. Z. (1982). Intelligence and inspection time. In H. J. Eysenck (Ed.), *A model for intelligence.* New York: Springer-Verlag.

Carly, P. G. (1994). Early event-related potentials correlate with inspection times and intelligence. *Intelligence, 18*, 15–45.

Carpenter, P. A., Just, M. A., & Shell, P. (1990). What one intelligence test measures: A Theoretical account of the processing in the Raven's progressive matrices test. *Psychological Review, 97*, 404–431.

Cattell, R. B., & Cattell, A. K. S. (1960). *Handbook for the Individual or Group Culture Fair Intelligence Test.* Champaign, IL: IPAT.

Craik, F. I. M., & Lockhart, R. S. (1972). Levels of processing: A framework for memory research. *Journal of Verbal Learning and Verbal Behavior, 11*, 671–684.

Craik, F. I. M., & Tulving, E. (1975). Levels of processing and the retention of words in episodic memory. *Journal of Experimental Psychology, General, 104*, 268–294.

Donders, F. C. (1868). Die Schnelligheit psychischer Processe. *Archiv. der Anatomie und Physiologie*, 657–681.

Ericcsen, K. A., & Chase, W. G. (1982). Exceptional memory. *American Scientist, 70*, 607–615.

Ericcsen, K. A., Krampe, R. Th., & Tesch-Romer, C. (1993). The role of deliberate practice in the acquisition of expert performance. *Psychological Review, 100*, 363–406.

Ericcsen, K. A., & Polson, P. G. (1981). An experimental analysis of memory skill for dinner orders. *Journal of Experimental Psychology: Learning, Memory and Cognition, 14*, 305–316.

Eysenck, H. J. (1986). The theory of intelligence and the psychophysiology of cognition. In R. J. Sternberg (Ed.), *Advances in the psychology of human intelligence* (Vol. 3, pp. 1–75). Hillsdale, NJ: Lawrence Erlbaum Associates.

Gardner, H. (1983). *Frames of mind: The theory of multiple intelligences.* London: Macmillan.

Goward, L. M. (1987). *An investigation of the factors contributing to scores on intelligence tests.* Unpublished doctoral dissertation, University of Manchester, England.

Guilford, J. P. (1966). Intelligence: 1965 model. *American Psychologist, 21*, 20–26.

Gustafson, J. E. (1984). A unifying model for the structure of mental abilities. *Intelligence, 8*, 179–203.

Heim, A. (1970). *The AH 4 series of intelligence tests.* Stroud: NFER-Nelson.

Hendricksen, A. E. (1982). The biological basis of intelligence. Part II: Theory. In H. J. Eysenck (Ed.), *Models of intelligence.* New York: Springer-Verlag.

Hendricksen, A. E., & Hendricksen, D. E. (1980). The biological basis for individual differences in intelligence. *Personality and Individual Differences, 1*, 3–33.

Hick, W. E. (1952). On the rate of gain of information. *Quarterly Journal of Experimental Psychology, 4*, 11–26.

Horn, J. L. (1982). The theory of fluid and crystallised intelligence in relation to concepts of cognitive psychology and aging in adulthood. In F. I. M. Craik & S. Trehub (Eds.), *Aging and cognitive processes* (pp.). Boston: Plenum.

Horn, J. L. (1985). Remodelling old models of intelligence: Gc-Gf theory. In B. B. Wolman (Ed.), *Handbook of intelligence* (pp. 267–300). New York: Wiley.

Horn, J. L. (1986). Intellectual ability concepts. In R. L. Sternberg (Ed.), *Advances in the psychology of human intelligence* (Vol. 3, pp. 35–77). Hillsdale, NJ: Lawrence Erlbaum Associates.

Horn, J. L. (1989). Cognitive diversity: A framework for learning. In P. L. Ackerman, R. J. Sternberg, & R. Glazer (Eds.), *Learning and individual differences: Advances in theory and research* (pp. 61–114). New York: Freeman.

Horn, J. L., & Donaldson, G. (1980). *Constancy or chance in human development.* Cambridge, MA: Harvard University Press.

Horn, J. L., Donaldson, G., & Engstrom, R. (1981). Apprehension memory and fluid intelligence decline in adulthood. *Research on Aging, 3*, 33–84.

Horn, J. L., & Hofer, S. M. (1992). Major abilities and development in the adult period. In R. Sternberg & C. Berg (Eds.), *Intellectual development* (pp. 44–99). New York: Cambridge University Press.

Hulme, C., & Turnbull, J. (1983). Intelligence and inspection time in normal and mentally retarded subjects. *British Journal of Psychology, 74*, 365–370.

Jensen, A. R. (1980). Chronometric analysis of mental ability. *Journal of Social and Biological Structures, 3*, 181–224.

Jensen, A. R. (1985). The nature of the black–white difference on various psychometric tests: Spearman's hypothesis. *The Behavioural & Brain Sciences, 8*, 193–219.

Jensen, A. R., & Whang, P. A. (1993). Reaction times and intelligence: A comparison of Chinese-American and Anglo-American children. *Journal of Biosocial Science, 25*, 397–410.

158   RABBITT AND YANG

Kail, R. (1992). Processing speed, speech rate and memory. *Developmental Psychology, 28,* 899–904.

Kelley, T. L. (1927). Interpretation of educational measurements. World

Kirby, N. H., & Nettelbeck, T. (1989). Reaction time and inspection time as measures of intellectual ability. *Personality & Individual Differences, 10,* 11–14.

Kyllonen, P. C., & Crystal, R. C. (1990). Reasoning ability is (little more than) working memory capacity? *Intelligence, 14,* 389–433.

Laming, D. R. J. (1985). *Sensory analysis.* London: Academic Press.

Lindenberger, U., Mayr, U., & Kliegl, R. (1993). Speed and intelligence in old age. *Psychology & Aging, 8,* 207–220.

Luce, R. D. (1986). *Response times: Their role in inferring elementary mental organisation.* Oxford, England: Oxford University Press.

McClelland, J. C., Rumelhart, D. E., & the P.D.P. Research Group. (1986). *Parallel distributed processing: Explorations in the microstructure of cognition.* Cambridge, MA: MIT Press.

Miller, G. A. (1957). The magical number seven, plus or minus two. *Psychological Review, 43,* 81–97.

Nettelbeck, T. (1982). Inspection time: An index for intelligence? *Quarterly Journal of Experimental Psychology, 34A,* 299–312.

Nettelbeck, T., Edwards, C., & Vreugdenhil, A. (1986). Inspection time and IQ: Evidence for a mental speed-ability association. *Personality & Individual Differences, 7,* 633–641.

Nettelbeck, T., & Rabbitt, P. M. A. (1992). Age, intelligence and speed. *Intelligence, 16,* 189–205.

Nettelbeck, T., Rabbitt, P. M. A., Wilson, C., & Batt, R. (in press). Uncoupling learning from initial recall: The relationship between speed and memory deficits in old age. *British Journal of Psychology.*

Phillips, L. (1993). *Breaking down intelligence test performance.* Unpublished doctorate dissertation, University of Manchester, England.

Rabbitt, P. M. A. (1993). Does it all go together when it goes? *Quarterly Journal of Experimental Psychology, 46A,* 385–434.

Rabbitt, P. M. A., & Banerji, N. (1989). How does very prolonged practice affect decision speed? *Journal of Experimental Psychology, General, 98.*

Rabbitt, P. M. A., & Goward, L. (1994). Age, information processing speed and intelligence. *Quarterly Journal of Experimental Psychology, 47A,* 741–760.

Rabbitt, P. M. A., & Maylor, E. A. (1991). Investigating models of human performance. *British Journal of Psychology, 82,* 259–290.

Rabbitt, P. M. A., & Vyas, S. M. (1973). An elementary preliminary taxonomy for some errors in laboratory choice RT tasks. *Acta Psychologica, 33,* 56–76.

Reed, T. E. (1993). Effects of enriched (complex) environment on nerve conduction velocity: New data and implications for the speed of information processing. *Intelligence, 17,* 461–474.

Reed, T. E., & Jensen, A. R. (1992). Conduction velocity in a brain-nerve pathway of normal adults correlates with intelligence level. *Intelligence, 16,* 259–272.

Reed, Y. E., & Jensen, A. R. (1993). A somatosensory latency between the thalamus and the cortex also correlates with intelligence. *Intelligence, 17,* 443–449.

Robbins, T. W., James, M., Owen, A. M., Sahakian, B. T., McInnes, L., & Rabbitt, P. M. A. (1994). Cambridge Automated Test Battery (CANTAB): A factor analytic study of a large sample of normal elderly volunteers. *Dementia, 5,* 266–281.

Roznowski, M. (1993). Measures of cognitive processes: Their stability and other psychometric and measurement properties. *Intelligence, 17,* 361–388.

Salthouse, T. A. (1982). *Adult cognition.* New York: Springer-Verlag.

Salthouse, T. A. (1985). *A cognitive theory of aging.* Berlin: Springer-Verlag.

Salthouse, T. A. (1991). *Theoretical perspectives on cognitive aging.* Hillsdale, NJ: Lawrence Erlbaum Associates.

Salthouse, T. (1994, July). *Memory and Speech.* Paper presented at the International Conference on Working Memory, Magdalen College, Cambridge, England.

Smith, E. E. (1968). Choice reaction time: An analysis of the major theoretical positions. *Psychological Bulletin, 69,* 77–110.

Smith, G. A. (1980). Models of choice reaction time. In A. T. Welford (Ed.), *Reaction times.* London: Academic Press.

Smith, G. A., & Brewer, N. (in press). Slowness and age: Speed-accuracy mechanisms. *Psychology & Aging.*

Smith, G. A., & Stanley, G. (1983). Clocking "g": Relating intelligence and measures of timed performance. *Intelligence, 7,* 353–368.

Spearman, C. (1904). General intelligence objectively determined and measured. *American Journal of Psychology, 15,* 201–293.

Spearman, C. (1927). *The abilities of man.* London: Macmillan.

Sternberg, S. (1969). Memory scanning: Mental processes revealed by reaction time experiments. *American Scientist, 57,* 421–457.

Sternberg, S. (1975). Memory scanning: New findings and current controversies. *Quarterly Journal of Experimental Psychology, 17,* 1–32.

Townsend, J. T., & Ashby, F. G. (1983). *Stochastic modelling of elementary psychological processes.* Cambridge, England: Cambridge University Press.

Vernon, P. A. (1983). Speed of information processing and intelligence. *Intelligence, 7,* 53–70.

Vernon, P. A. (1985). Individual differences in general cognitive ability. In L. C. Hartledge & C. F. Telzner (Eds.), *The neuropsychology of individual differences: A developmental perspective* (pp.). New York: Plenum.

Vernon, P. A., & Jensen, A. R. (1984). Individual and group differences in intelligence and speed of information processing. *Personality and Individual Differences, 5,* 411–423.

Vickers, D. (1979). *Decision processes in visual perception.* London: Academic Press.

Waugh, N. C., & Barr, R. A. (1980). Memory and mental tempo. In L. W. Poon, J. L. Fozard, L. S. Cermak, D. Arenberg, & L. W. Thompson (Eds.), *New directions in memory and aging* (pp.). Hillsdale, NJ: Lawrence Erlbaum Associates.

CHAPTER NINE

Dissociating Automatic and Consciously Controlled Processes: Implications for Diagnosis and Rehabilitation of Memory Deficits

Larry L. Jacoby
Janine M. Jennings
Janine F. Hay
McMaster University

Sometimes we think and then act; other times we act and then make our excuses. The difference in intentionality described by this contrast has important practical consequences. Within our legal system, lawyers invest time and effort trying to convince a jury that their client did not intend to commit an illegal act or was unaware of what he or she was doing when the act occurred. Intentionality weighs heavily in the final verdict; the penalty for a criminal act is more severe when an act is judged to be intentional.

Reason (1993) discussed a criminal case involving an absent-minded elderly man that illustrates the importance of distinguishing intentionality in responding. In this case, the accused was charged with two counts of shoplifting because he had failed to pay for some of his items. When the accused was stopped and questioned, he claimed that he had overlooked the items and forgotten to pay. The defense argued that the elderly man did not deliberately intend to steal. Based on circumstantial evidence, including a prior history of "forgetting to pay" and poor performance on a cognitive failure questionnaire (which measures the frequency of self-reported action slips), the case was dismissed. For this man, intentionality made the difference between an oversight versus being charged with a criminal act.

Was justice served in this trial? Perhaps, but there is reason to question the outcome. First, was the gentleman's prior history really one of action slips (forgetting to pay) or one of deliberate shoplifting? Almost certainly, a different conclusion would have been drawn had the accused been a teenager rather than an elderly gentleman. Second, how valid are self-report

161

measures of action slips? Such questionnaires measure failures in cognitive control through the frequency of these errors. However, the correlation between responses on a cognitive failures questionnaire and memory measured in the laboratory is very low. Correlations have typically been found in the .20 to .30 range (Herrmann, 1982), which is sufficiently weak to question the validity of questionnaires.

What is needed is a more objective means of measuring cognitive control. Development of such a diagnostic tool is an important applied goal for experimental psychologists. As our population continues to age, questions of whether an act resulted from an action slip or was carried out with intent will arise more often. Questions about cognitive control are important in domains other than aging. As an obvious example, a major consequence of both frontal lobe injury (e.g., Stuss, 1991) and schizophrenia (e.g., Frith, 1987) is a deficit in cognitive control.

To adequately measure cognitive control, automatic influences of memory must be separated from consciously controlled use of memory. For example, consider a case in which an elderly executive performs quite adequately in his professional role. He is present at appointments, shows memory of prior discussions of a topic when that topic is later discussed, politely questions colleagues about the well-being of their families, and refers to their family members by name. Shortly after retiring and moving to another city, he shows symptoms of a severe deficit in cognitive control. Indeed, this retired executive could become the elderly gentleman accused of shoplifting in the previous example. The question is: Did his deficit in cognitive control have a sudden onset that coincided with his retirement, or was the cognitive deficit present prior to his retirement, but masked by automatic influences of memory (habit) supported by the structure of the preretirement environment? Answering these questions clearly requires some means of separating automatic influences from cognitive control.

Judges and juries sometimes arrive at verdicts on the basis of their ability to distinguish between intentional acts and acts that result from automatic influences. Even for a decision that has life or death consequences, these laypeople are willing to judge intentionality with the decision treated as beyond reasonable doubt. How well have experimental psychologists done in their attempts to measure intentionality? Much of the research aimed at measuring intentionality has focused on the *distinction* between automatic (unconscious) and consciously controlled processes. Little effort has been directed toward measuring the *contribution* of cognitive control to performance of a task, with the measure corrected for automatic or unconscious influences. Controversy has surrounded the validity of this distinction, and for its acceptance researchers have demanded that evidence of its validity be beyond doubt—reasonable or otherwise. For academicians, however, nothing can be proven beyond doubt. Their scepticism has swung between questioning the existence of cognitive control, as evidenced by the behaviorists (Skinner, 1971), to questioning the existence of unconscious influences, which some cognitivists deny (Brewer, 1974). While Rome burns, academicians debate whether it is justifiable to call the cause "arson" with its implication of intent.

Measuring Automaticity

Although laypeople seem satisfied with their ability to separate intentional from automatic acts, psychologists have had difficulty doing so. For some psychologists, acts committed without intention are thought to be guided by automatic influences. By the standard definition, automaticity provides a basis for rapid responding, does not require attentional capacity or awareness for the response, and does not require intent (e.g., Hasher & Zacks, 1979; Posner & Snyder, 1975). This definition has been used to construct experimental conditions and select special populations so as to investigate automaticity in memory performance. Variables that have been used include depression, the effects of drugs and alcohol, and the effects of aging and amnesia. Experimental conditions attempt to meet the goal of providing a pure measure of automatic influences by eliminating intent through a manipulation of instructions (Hasher & Zacks, 1979) or by the use of conditions (dividing attention, etc.) that do not give intent an opportunity to operate. It is assumed that one is responding on the basis of automaticity when one experiences any of the conditions or mental states cited earlier.

The manipulation of instructions to eliminate the effects of intent and, thereby, to allow automatic or unconscious influences of memory to be investigated has received a great deal of attention. Automatic influences of memory have been described as "implicit memory," which has been investigated using indirect tests for its measurement. For these tests, people are not directly asked to remember a prior event but rather to engage in a task that indirectly reflects the occurrence of that event. *Implicit memory*, as indexed by these tasks, has been defined as unintentional, the same criteria used to define *automaticity*, and thus the two terms can be considered synonymous (e.g., Jacoby, 1991). In contrast, a direct test such as recognition or recall instructs subjects to remember earlier events, and provides a measure of conscious, intentional memory.

Dissociations between performance on direct and indirect memory tests supply striking examples of effects of the past in the absence of remembering and perceptual analysis in the absence of seeing. For example, although amnesics cannot remember the earlier presentation of a word when given a test of recognition memory or recall (a direct test), they show evidence of memory by using the word more often as a completion for a stem or fragment (an indirect test) than they would had the word not been presented earlier (for reviews, see Moscovitch, Vriezen, & Gottstein, 1993; Shimamura, 1989). Similar memory dissociations are evident in people with normal functioning memory (for a review, see Roediger & McDermott, 1993). The form of dissociation found for memory is comparable to dissociations taken as evidence for unconscious perception. For example, Marcel (1983) flashed words for durations so brief that subjects could not "see" them, but could show effects of those words on a lexical decision task used as an indirect test of perception. Similarly, "blindsight" patients make visual discriminative responses without the subjective experience of seeing (Weiskrantz, 1986).

Empirical advances derived from the direct versus indirect test distinction have significantly increased our understanding of conscious and unconscious (automatic) influences (e.g., Jacoby & Dallas, 1981; Roediger, 1990; Schacter, 1987). Much of this research, however, has proceeded without confronting many of the methodological and conceptual issues that plagued earlier investigations of unconscious processes. Those issues are now resurfacing. The major difficulty for drawing a distinction between conscious versus unconscious processes is that of defining each type of process. Essential here is the relation of processes to tasks (Dunn & Kirsner, 1989). Typically, unconscious processes are equated with performance on indirect or implicit tests and conscious processes with performance on direct or explicit tests. However, this form of definition is problematic because conscious processes may contaminate performance on indirect tests (e.g., Holender, 1986; Reingold & Merikle, 1990; Toth, Reingold, & Jacoby, 1994) and, less obviously, unconscious processes might contaminate performance on direct tests (Jacoby, Toth, & Yonelinas, 1993). In addition, mapping processes onto test performance overlooks an essential aspect of any adequate definition of conscious and unconscious processes, which is that automatic and consciously controlled processes seldom operate in isolation. Further, automatic processes acting in isolation may be qualitatively different from those operating in the context of consciously controlled processes, and vice versa.

Consider the commonplace claim that in order to learn what somebody really believes, you should get him or her drunk. Drunkenness is treated as a pure measure of automaticity or true belief. The "contamination" problem is to question how drunk people have to be before their responses are no longer contaminated by consciously controlled processing. Even if one could achieve an uncontaminated test, the more serious "qualitative difference" problem is whether the test reveals people's "true" beliefs or only what they believe when drunk. It seems likely that some people's beliefs when drunk are qualitatively different from their beliefs when sober. Automatic influences in the context of consciously controlled processes, like true beliefs when sober, are of great interest. Because the indirect versus direct test distinction identifies processes with tasks, it provides no means of measuring automaticity in the presence of consciously controlled processing.

What is needed is some means of separating the contributions of cognitive control and automatic influences to behavior in a particular situation. How does the layperson do this when deciding that an act is intentional?

Celibacy Doesn't Count if You Can't Get a Date

The criterion used by psychologists to define automaticity are also used by the layperson to judge whether an act was intentional. For example, psychologists' concern with attentional variables, such as divided attention and the effects of drugs, is mirrored by legal reference to "diminished resources" when establishing in a court of law that an act was unintentional. However, the layperson does not just use information about characteristics of a static state or situation but, rather, relies most heavily on contrasting behavior across different situations to judge whether an act is intentional. For example, one is more impressed by abstinence from alcohol in a recovering alcoholic, who has previously been seen drunk at numerous parties, than in an individual who has never been seen having a drink. Clearly, the recovering alcoholic demonstrates greater evidence of intention and control. Similarly, to be given full credit for having been religiously "saved" one has to have been a blatant sinner first. Remember, it was the prodigal son who received the feast. Other examples, one of which was used as the heading for this section, are easily found.

The layperson begins by accepting the validity of the distinction between consciously controlled and automatic acts and then compares behavior in one situation with that in another to decide whether an act was intentional. Our process dissociation procedure (e.g., Jacoby, 1991; Jacoby, Toth, & Yonelinas, 1993) is a refinement of the strategy used by the layperson. We also begin by accepting the distinction between automatic and consciously controlled bases for responding, and make that distinction fundamental to our procedure. Our refinement is in the design of situations in which behavior is to be compared so as to separate the contributions of automatic influences and cognitive control.

The Process Dissociation Procedure

The process dissociation procedure measures cognitive control by combining results from a condition for which automatic and consciously controlled processes act in opposition, as in the case of action slips, with results from a condition for which the two types of process act in concert, as in the case of the well-functioning, elderly executive. The measure is the very common-sensical one of the difference between performance when one is *trying to*, as compared with *trying not to*, engage in some act or be influenced by information from some source. The difference between performance in those two cases reveals the degree of cognitive control. We later describe results to show that this objective measure of cognitive control correlates with self-report measures of recollection and of frequency of action slips.

In order to avoid the equating of processes with tasks, the process dissociation procedure separates the contributions of conscious and automatic processes to performance of a single task. The procedure builds on previous findings of task dissociations but extends the analysis to situations for which it is acknowledged that both cognitive control and automatic influences contribute to performance. Such an analytic technique seems especially important given that both types of processes are operating concurrently in most real-world tasks, and given the likely possibility that automatic (unconscious) influences are context specific and sensitive to current intentions (Jacoby, Ste-Marie, & Toth, 1993; Wegner, 1994). As illustrated by the earlier "drunk" example, it is necessary to separate processes within a task to gain a true measure of their contributions.

The strategy for the process dissociation procedure is to start with the assumption that consciously controlled and automatic influences independently contribute to performance and then design conditions aimed at meeting that assumption as well as other necessary assumptions (Jacoby, Toth, & Yonelinas, 1993). There are a number of different ways that automatic and consciously controlled influences can combine but, fortunately, each of the ways has its own earmarks (Jacoby, Yonelinas, & Jennings, in press). How can one be certain of having attained the goal of independence? One source of evidence comes from results showing that variables traditionally associated with reduced cognitive control have an effect on our estimates of consciously controlled processing (e.g., recollection) but leave automatic influences unchanged. Jacoby et al. (in press) summarized the results of 20 experiments to show that subject variables such as aging, as well as processing variables, such as divided attention and fast responding, produce that pattern of results. Averaged across those 20 experiments, the effect of factors traditionally associated with reduced cognitive control on estimates of controlled responding was .24, whereas that on estimates of automatic influences was .002. Manipulations other than those associated with cognitive control produce different patterns of results, often affecting estimates of automaticity.

However, as noted earlier, the empirical gains made possible by the procedure are bought at the expense of confronting conceptual and methodological issues that troubled, and often undermined, previous research on automatic influences. Our approach has drawn critics that question its underlying assumptions, particularly our assumption that conscious and unconscious processes *independently* contribute to performance (Curran & Hintzman, in press; Graf & Komatsu, 1994). We can convincingly counter arguments made by critics (Jacoby, Begg, & Toth, in press; Toth, Reingold, & Jacoby, 1995). For example, Curran and Hintzman (in press) argued that correlations, at the level of items, between automatic and controlled processes invalidate the independence assumption and estimates of processes. Their argument was the very reasonable one that some items are both more familiar and better recollected, and, consequently, one cannot assume that the two bases for judgments or responding are independent. Jacoby, Begg, and Toth (in press) showed that even if there is a high correlation at the item level, the bias in estimates of automatic influences would be very minor (a .01 difference) and not differential across conditions that were very different in the estimated controlled use of memory. That is, even if Curran and Hintzman were correct, the effects produced by correlations at the item level are trivial. What is often made clear by comments of critics is that the word *independence* has many meanings, only some of which are relevant to our purposes. Correlation does not mean lack of independence (see Jacoby, Begg, & Toth, in press, for this argument).

The best response to critics is to show the success of our approach. In the following section, we illustrate the process dissociation procedure by describing its use in several experiments done to analyze age-related deficits in memory. Although the focus is on effects of aging, we have found that manipulations such as dividing attention, speeded responding, and fast presentation rate mimic the elderly's pattern of performance. Then, in the final section, we address applied issues for which it is important to separate automatic and consciously controlled uses of memory. We return to examples there, such as our elderly shoplifter, to question the relation between subjective reports of awareness, and the objective measure of cognitive control supplied by our process dissociation procedure. We also describe the utility of our procedure for diagnosis and treatment of memory deficits. Designing effective, special environments that provide support to compensate for memory deficits, and designing programs aimed at rehabilitating memory, require that one separate the contributions of automatic and consciously controlled processes.

MEMORY EFFECTS OF AGING

Action Slips: Separating Habit and Recollection

The interplay between consciously controlled and automatic processes can be seen in daily life through the action slips that people commit. These errors in performance occur when automatic responding and current intention are opposed, leading to conflicting responses (e.g., Norman, 1981; Reason, 1979). Automaticity, in this case, is expressed in the form of a habit that overcomes our intended behavior. These errors can be illustrated with a story about an aging math professor at the University of Manitoba who went to a conference in Chicago and was unable to find his airline ticket when he was ready to return home. After an extensive search for the ticket, he bought another and, upon arriving in Winnipeg, called his wife to pick him up at the airport. She responded that she would be unable to do so because they only had one car and he had driven it to Chicago!

The professor's action slip is useful to highlight the distinction between automatic and controlled influences of memory. It is likely that he typically flew to conferences, and his action slip was a result of habit gained from prior conferences dominating recollection for having recently driven. That is, his error reflects proactive interference from memory for earlier trips, and automatic influences served as the source of that interference.

Action Slips and Aging. Does aging increase the likelihood of action slips? Our story about the math professor suggests this is the case and, in fact, there is anecdotal evidence that the elderly are more likely to commit action slips than are younger subjects. We (Jacoby & Hay, 1993) addressed this question more directly by examining memory performance in a lab situation where habit and intention act in opposition.

The first phase of our action slip experiment was designed to create habits of a specific strength. Words were presented paired with a fragment of a related word, and subjects were to predict how these fragments would be completed. One of two possible completions for each fragment was shown, with a "dominant" completion being shown twice as often as the other. For example, 12 times out of 18 (67% of occurrences) when knee b_n_ was shown, the fragment was completed with the word *bone* (the dominant item) whereas for its other 6 presentations (33% of occurrences) it was completed with the word *bend* (the nondominant item). The habit of producing the dominant completion should be stronger than habit for the nondominant completion. Our intention was to build a habit or automatic response in a manner similar to having our math professor fly to two thirds of the conferences he attends.

The second phase of the experiment created a situation that was meant to resemble recollecting the mode of transportation to a current conference. In that second phase, people were presented with a list of nine word pairs, and then tested by presentation of the first member of each pair and a fragment of the second word (e.g., knee-b_n_). Subjects were to complete the fragment by recalling the word that was paired with the cue word in the short list they had just studied. Subjects studied and were tested in this manner for several lists. The trick, of course, is the completion word presented in the study list was not the word made dominant in Phase 1 (e.g., the study pair was *knee-bend*, rather than *knee-bone*). Consequently, relying on habits established in Phase 1 would produce an action slip of completing the fragment with the stronger habitual response in Phase 1, although the weaker response was appropriate.

TABLE 9.1
Probability of Responding with a Dominant Item and Estimates
of Recollection and Automatic Influences for Young and Elderly Adults

	Test Condition		Estimates	
	Facilitation	Interference	Recollection	Automatic
Young	.80	.35	.44	.63
Elderly	.73	.44	.29	.62

If the elderly are more susceptible to action slips, they should mistakenly give the dominant items from training more often than do younger adults. Those were the results that were obtained (see interference condition, Table 9.1). How should the greater probability of an action slip be understood? One interpretation is that the elderly are more susceptible to interference from prior learning. Indeed, there is a large amount of literature to show that the elderly are more vulnerable to proactive interference effects than are younger subjects (e.g., Winocur & Moscovitch, 1983), and several authors have argued that interference effects stem from the elderly's inability to inhibit irrelevant information (e.g., Hasher & Zacks, 1988). Our evidence thus far could suggest that the elderly are less able than the young to inhibit responding on the basis of habit and, therefore, may have deficient inhibitory mechanisms.

If this is the case, we should be able to demonstrate that the elderly perform as well as the young when recollection and automatic processing act in concert to produce the same response. That is, the elderly may do as well as, or even better than, the young if habit is a source of facilitation rather than interference. In that circumstance, a failure to inhibit effects of habit would be to one's advantage. Think back to the aging math professor. Had he flown to the conference in Chicago, as he usually did, habit would have helped him on his way home. In this case, habit and recollection work together to facilitate performance.

In the experiment just described, a facilitation condition was also used to compare performance of young and elderly adults. This time, the dominant items from the training phase appeared on the study list. At test, if subjects could recollect that the word was just presented, they would give the correct response. Alternatively, if they failed to recollect the item, they could produce the correct answer by relying on habit. Unlike the interference condition, subjects did not need to inhibit habitual responses; consequently, if the inhibition hypothesis is adopted, one must predict that age deficits will be eliminated.

The results did not support this prediction (Table 9.1). Older adults were *less* likely than the young to correctly recall an item in the facilitation condition.

This finding is difficult to understand if the source of memory deficits in the elderly stems from poor inhibition. Given that the elderly were less likely to correctly recall an item when habit was a source of facilitation, as well as a source of interference, some other explanation is required. However, we would not have recognized the inadequacy of the inhibition hypothesis if we had only examined the interference condition. To truly understand performance, responding in both the interference and facilitation conditions must be considered. To see that this is the case, think of our experiment as being analogous to an investigation of recognition memory. The role served by facilitation test items is analogous to that served by "old" words and the role served by interference test items is analogous to that served by "new" words on the recognition test. For recognition memory, of course, one has to compare performance on old and new items to separate correct responding that reflects memory from that due to guessing. Rather than memory and guessing, however, we want to separate the contributions of recollection and automatic influences. The situations are similar in that automatic influences can serve as the basis for guessing. We return to this point later.

Rather than inhibition, a better explanation of our results is that the elderly are deficient in their ability to consciously recollect an earlier event and, consequently, more vulnerable to misleading effects of habit. To investigate this possibility we need to separately examine automatic and consciously controlled influences on performance. Jacoby's process dissociation procedure (Jacoby, 1991) allows us to separate out and measure the contributions of habit and recollection within a given task, and determine the effects of aging on each process. We first illustrate this procedure in the context of our action-slip experiment.

Estimating Automatic and Consciously Controlled Influences

For the facilitation condition in the action slip experiment, subjects can give the correct answer at test either by recollecting (R) the item presented in the study list, or by relying on habit or automatic influences (A) when recollection fails $(1 - R)$. We assume that these two bases for responding act independently; recollection can occur with or without responding on the basis of automatic influences and vice versa. Consequently, the probability of a correct response, which would be to respond with the "dominant" item, in the facilitation condition (Fac) is:

$$\text{Prob (dominant item)} = R + A (1 - R)$$

In contrast, for the interference condition, responding with the dominant item is an action slip. Such an action slip will occur only if subjects fail to recollect the nondominant response that appeared in the study list. If subjects fail to recollect the nondominant response $(1 - R)$, an action slip will occur with a probability that reflects automatic influences (A). The probability of an action slip in the interference condition (Int) is:

$$\text{Prob (dominant item)} = A\,(1 - R)$$

By using these two equations we can compute estimates of automatic influences and recollection. Subtracting the probability of an action slip on interference trials (Int) from the probability of a correct response on facilitation trials (Fac) provides an estimate of recollection:

$$R = \text{Fac} - \text{Int}$$

Given an estimate of recollection, an estimate of automaticity or habit can be computed by simple algebra, dividing the probability of an action slip in the interference condition (Int) by the estimated probability of a failure in recollection:

$$A = \text{Int}/(1 - R)$$

When we calculate these estimates, we find that the poor memory performance of the elderly was not because of a failure to inhibit automatic influences or habit. The estimated contributions of automatic influences were near identical for the elderly and the young (see Table 9.1). Furthermore, these estimates of automatic influences reflected the probability with which fragments were completed with dominant items during training. That is, there was a .67 probability that a dominant item would appear on any given trial during training, and the estimates of automatic influences obtained by using the process dissociation procedure were .63 for the young and .62 for the elderly.

In contrast, estimates of recollection revealed pronounced age-related deficits; the elderly showed much poorer consciously controlled processing (.29) than did the young adults (.44). It is this deficit that was responsible for the larger number of action slips committed by the elderly in the interference condition, and for their poor performance when habit and recollection were acting in the same direction (in the facilitation condition). Factors other than aging also increase the likelihood that action slips will occur. We have found that forcing young adults to respond quickly at test or rapidly presenting information at study increases the probability of such errors (Jacoby & Hay, 1993). Similar to aging, the effects of speeded responding and rapid presentation serve to reduce recollection and leave automatic influences in place.

This invariance in estimates of automaticity does not reflect a general insensitivity of that measure. We have carried out other action-slip experiments to show that varying the number of presentations of a pair during training (i.e., the "strength" of a habit) influences estimates of automaticity but leaves recollection unchanged (Jacoby & Hay, 1993). As discussed earlier, manipulations that affect one process while leaving the other intact provide evidence to support the assumption of independence between intentional and automatic responding. Those later experiments also revealed probability matching, as did the experiment described previously, which suggests that probability matching can be used as a measure of implicit learning (cf., Estes, 1976; Reber, 1989). It seems likely that the observed probability matching qualifies as implicit knowledge, because probability matching was found when conscious recollection of list structure would be nearly impossible (i.e., rapid responding). Probability matching, as a measure of implicit learning, holds important advantages over other procedures. Foremost, probability matching measures implicit learning in the context of intentional use of memory, and adoption of the process dissociation procedure eliminates concerns that the measure of implicit learning is contaminated.

Automatic and Intended Influences of Memory for a Prior Event

The distinction between behavior driven by habit versus behavior driven by recollection is really the difference between automatic and intended influences of memory for a prior event. In the case of habit, the automatic influence was built up by multiple presentations of a stimulus; however, automatic influences of memory also arise from a single presentation of an item. A series of "false fame" studies illustrates this effect (Dywan & Jacoby, 1990; Jacoby, Kelley, Brown, & Jasechko, 1989; Jacoby, Woloshyn, & Kelley, 1989).

In this paradigm, subjects read a list of nonfamous names and then performed a fame-judgment test consisting of old names, new nonfamous names, and famous names. Subjects were correctly informed that the study names were nonfamous, and if they recognized a name from that list they could be certain it was not famous. Because prior presentation of a name increased its familiarity, subjects could misattribute this familiarity as fame, by mistaking old names for famous ones (the false fame effect). However, if subjects could recollect the source of the name, any automatic influence of familiarity would be opposed, and subjects would correctly identify the name as nonfamous. This task is, in essence, an interference condition, similar to the one described earlier where habit and recollection were placed in conflict.

Elderly adults show the false fame effect (Dywan & Jacoby, 1990; Jennings & Jacoby, 1993a) as do amnesics (Cermak, Verfaellie, Butler, & Jacoby, 1993; Squire & McKee, 1992) and patients who have suffered a closed-head injury (Dywan, Segalowitz, Henderson, & Jacoby, 1993). Subjects in each of these special populations were more likely to mistakenly respond "famous" to old names as compared to new, nonfamous names, whereas the opposite was true for younger subjects with normal functioning memory. This finding suggests that these populations suffered a lessened ability to engage in recollection; however, automatic influences of memory were preserved. Jennings and Jacoby (1993a) have used the process dissociation procedure to show that this is the case; automatic influences of memory (familiarity) on fame judgments were the same for elderly and young adults despite large age differences in recollection. In experiments to be described later, we used a misleading effect of familiarity, much like false fame, to diagnose deficits in recollection and design a training procedure to rehabilitate recollection.

Automatic influences based on a single presentation, such as those seen in the false fame effect, have typically been studied with indirect tests of memory. As discussed, however, it is better to separate the effects of automatic and consciously controlled influences within a task. In the action-slip experiment described earlier, we accomplished this by manipulating materials to construct facilitation and interference conditions. However, the same goal can be achieved by manipulating task instructions.

Measuring Recollection. Jacoby, Toth, and Yonelinas (1993) used a manipulation of inclusion versus exclusion instructions with a stem completion task to separate recollection from automatic influences of memory. Young adults first studied a list of words either under conditions of full or divided attention. In both conditions, subjects read study words aloud. However, subjects in the one condition were allowed to give full attention to their study of those words, and were warned of a later memory test. Subjects in the second condition were not warned about the later test, and were required to engage in a second task while reading the words aloud. They were told to give as little attention as possible to the reading task. Our goal was to show that reducing attention could produce memory results that were the same as found with elderly subjects or amnesics. That is, by manipulating attention, we attempted to produce a deficit in later recollection (a controlled use of memory) but leave automatic influences unchanged.

The inclusion versus exclusion test instructions were important for separating the contributions of controlled and automatic influences of memory. For both types of test, subjects were presented with word stems that they were told to use as cues for recollecting earlier-studied words (e.g., mot_, as a cue for recall of *motel*). For the inclusion test, subjects were instructed to complete stems with recollected words or, if they were unable to do so, complete stems with the first word that came to mind. The inclusion test is the same as a standard direct test of memory with instructions to guess. For the exclusion test, in contrast, subjects were told to complete stems with words that were *not* presented earlier. The exclusion test is akin to testing people's ability to keep secret their memory for the earlier studied list. They were to recall studied words so as to avoid giving them as responses, just as one might recall a secret to avoid disclosing it. Completing an exclusion test item with an old word would be an action slip of the same sort as described for our math professor.

Not surprisingly, on the inclusion test subjects showed higher recall in the full than divided attention condition (see Table 9.2). However, even after divided attention, the probability of completing a stem with an old word was well above base rate (the probability of completing the stem with a target word when that word was not presented). Subtracting false recall from correct recall (subtracting base rate from the total number of words completed) is a standard way of measuring recollection. But is that method accurate? Does above-base rate performance reflect subjects' ability to recollect earlier presented words or does it reflect automatic influences? This question is important because several experiments have shown that amnesics sometimes perform nearly as well as normals on direct tests of memory (e.g., Bowers, Verfaellie, Valenstein, & Heilman, 1988). In those cases, are the amnesics truly able to recollect, or does their correct responding reflect guessing that is informed by automatic memory influences?

Performance on inclusion and exclusion tests can be used to estimate the separate contributions of recollection and automatic influences of memory, just as was performance on facilitation and interference test items in the action slip experiment. Indeed, the inclusion test is a facilitation test. Subjects could respond correctly on an inclusion test either because they were able to recollect (R) an earlier-studied word, or because although recollection failed ($1 - R$), automatic (A) influences were sufficient to result in the word being given as a guess: $R + A(1 - R)$. The exclusion test is an interference test. For an exclusion test, an earlier-studied word will be given as a response (an action slip) only if subjects fail to recollect the earlier-studied word, but automatic influences are sufficient for the word to be given as a guess: $A(1 - R)$. As should be apparent, these are the same equations as used to separate recollection and automatic influences in our action slip experiment, and estimates are gained in the same manner.

TABLE 9.2
Probability of Correct Stem Completion and Estimates of Recollection and
Automatic Influences of Memory as a Function of Attention

	Test Condition		Estimates	
	Inclusion	Exclusion	Recollection	Automatic
Full	.61	.36	.25	.47
Divided	.46	.46	.00	.46

Note: The baseline completion rate for items not presented at study was .35.

Estimates of recollection and automaticity (Table 9.2) show that dividing attention during study produced effects that were the same as those produced by aging. Recollection was reduced to 0 by dividing attention. We were successful in making our undergraduates totally amnesic! However, estimated automatic influences after divided attention were near identical to those after full attention. This shows that, after divided attention, correct responding on the inclusion test stemmed totally from correct guessing informed by automatic influences. The same is likely true when amnesics are sometimes found to perform as well as normals on a direct test of memory. Had we used the standard means of correcting for guessing, we would have mistaken automatic influences of memory for recollection. The two bases for responding are different in important ways. For example, automatic influences of memory would result in one mistakenly disclosing a secret (exclusion test), whereas recollection would allow the secret to be withheld. Are elderly subjects less likely to be able to keep a secret? Craik (1982) suggested that age-related differences in memory are the same as those produced by dividing attention.

Special Populations and Recollection. Jacoby (1992) used an inclusion and exclusion test procedure to examine age-related effects of memory. That experiment used the same materials as did the full- versus divided-attention experiment, but the procedure was slightly different. Study and test items were intermixed, and the number of items intervening between the study presentation of a word and its test (spacing) was varied, as was the nature of the test.

When an inclusion or exclusion test immediately followed presentation of its completion word (0 spacing), performance of the elderly and of the young was near perfect. This finding is important because it shows that the elderly were able to understand and follow instructions. They were able to include and exclude old words when tested immediately after studying those words. In contrast, when a large number of items intervened between the presentation of a word and its inclusion or exclusion test (48 spacing), the elderly performed much more poorly than did the young (Table 9.3).

TABLE 9.3
Probability of Correct Stem Completion and Estimates of Recollection and
Automatic Influences of Memory as a Function of Age

	Test Condition		Estimates	
	Inclusion	Exclusion	Recollection	Automatic
Young	.70	.26	.44	.46
Elderly	.55	.39	.16	.46

Estimates of automaticity and recollection (Table 9.3) provide evidence that the elderly suffered a deficit in recollection as compared to younger participants but that automatic influences of memory were unchanged. This correspondence between age-related differences in memory and effects of full versus divided attention supports Craik's (1982) claim that dividing attention during study can mimic the effects of aging on memory.

The same pattern of dissociations has been found with a closed-head injured population using the lag procedure described earlier. They, too, show deficits in recollection but intact automatic processing (Ste-Marie, Jennings, & Finlayson, in press). For both populations declines in recollection are pronounced, appearing when only a few items have intervened between presentation and test. The lag paradigm produces consistent results across populations and is highly sensitive as a measure of memory deficits. To truly test memory, one has to measure both a person's ability to intentionally deliver a message (inclusion test) and ability to keep a secret (exclusion test). In some regards, keeping a secret is a greater memory accomplishment than is delivering a message. We later exploit these characteristics in our attempt to diagnose and train recollection.

All the research described thus far serves to illustrate the process dissociation procedure and demonstrate its utility for separating automatic and consciously controlled memory processes. In the following sections we describe application of the procedure as a potential diagnostic test, and highlight the importance of separating automatic and consciously controlled processes for the diagnosis and treatment of memory impairments. An important issue in this regard returns us to our elderly shoplifter to question the relationship between cognitive control as measured objectively by the process dissociation procedure versus subjective reports of memory performance.

APPLIED ISSUES

Relation of Subjective and Objective Measures of Memory

As described in conjunction with our elderly shoplifter, there is usually a very low correlation between performance on standard laboratory tests of memory and performance on cognitive failures questionnaires. The latter test relies on self-reports of memory failures. What is the relation between memory used as a means of cognitive control for performance and memory used as a basis for self-report of remembering? The process dissociation procedure acts as an objective means of measuring cognitive control. For the experiments just described, recollection was measured as the difference between when one is trying to as compared to trying not to engage in some act. But to what extent are people aware and able to self-report that they are recollecting? Recently, Jennings (1995) addressed this question by asking people to make subjective memory judgments in an adaptation of the remember/know procedure introduced by Tulving (1985) and used extensively by Gardiner and colleagues (Gardiner, 1988; Gardiner & Java, 1991; Gardiner & Parkin, 1990; Parkin & Walter, 1992).

During a test of recognition memory, subjects were asked whether they "remembered" an item as being presented earlier (recollected some specific detail of seeing the word), or they just "knew" that the word had occurred, or thought the word was "new." This "remember/know" paradigm relates well to the process dissociation procedure in that recollection appears to drive "remember" responses whereas automatic influences seem to underlie "know" responses. However, there is an essential difference between the two procedures. The original "remember/know" procedure assumes that the two processes are mutually exclusive (i.e., exclusivity assumption). Subjects can only respond "remember" or "know" for any given item, so the processes that underlie these responses can never occur together. In contrast, we assume that automatic influences and recollection act independently, such that each process can occur with or without the other.

Estimating Processes. Applying the independence assumption to the "remember/know" procedure allows us to estimate recollection and automaticity in a manner similar to that used in the process dissociation procedure. "Remember" responses map directly onto recollection, as long as a subject only responds "remember" if he or she recollects specific information about an item. However, "know" responses do not map directly onto automatic influences estimated by the process dissociation procedure but, instead, resemble the exclusion condition. In both cases, subjects give a response based on automatic influences in the absence of recollection $[A(1 - R)]$. An estimate of automatic influences can then be calculated as the proportion of "know" responses divided by a failure in recollection: $A = \text{Know}/(1 - R)$.

Applying this procedure with elderly adults allows us to investigate the correspondence between objective and subjective measures of memory. Using the process dissociation procedure, it has been demonstrated that aging produces a decline in recollection but leaves automatic influences intact. If awareness and cognitive control are related, we should be able to demonstrate the same pattern of results using subjective report.

According to both the independence and exclusivity assumptions, "remember" judgments are equivalent to conscious recollection and, as shown in Table 9.4, these "remember" responses decreased with age. However, comparing "know" responses with our automaticity estimates distinguishes the exclusivity and independence assumptions. Taking the "know" responses as a measure of automatic influences suggests that the elderly "remember"

TABLE 9.4
Probability of Responding "Remember" or "Know" and Estimates
of Recollection and Automatic Influences of Memory as a Function of Age

	Test Responses		Estimates	
	Remember	Know	Recollection	Automatic
Young	.56	.22	.56	.50
Elderly	.35	.33	.35	.47

less but "know" more than the young (for similar results, see Parkin & Walter, 1992). Although it is comforting to think that we know more as we become older, that result is surprising if one identifies knowing with the use of familiarity as a basis for recognition memory. Based on the earlier reported study of fame judgments, one might expect familiarity to be a more automatic basis for recognition that is not influenced by aging. Indeed, when estimates of automaticity are calculated assuming independence (i.e., $A = K/(1 - R)$), they again show that recollection declines with age, but automatic influences are unchanged. Evidence supporting the assumption of independence over exclusivity has been discussed elsewhere (see Jacoby, Yonelinas, & Jennings, in press) and will not be reviewed further here.

In summary, the findings of the present "remember/know" experiment showed the same pattern of results that has been found using our more objective measure: "Remember" responses declined with age, but automatic influences were invariant (see Table 9.4).

This latter pattern of results found with subjects' reports suggests that there can be a high degree of correspondence between objective and subjective measures of memory, and that both young and elderly adults can be aware of using recollection. However, evidence to support the correspondence between objective and subjective measures of memory would be more compelling if similar estimates were obtained when both types of measures were compared for the same subjects within a common task. We investigated this possibility in the action slip experiments, by asking young and elderly adults to make subjective memory judgments after completing a fragment during the test phase (Jacoby & Hay, 1993). Subjects were told to say "recall" if they could remember that their response came from the preceding study list. "Recall" responses resemble the "remember" responses from the previous experiment and, thus, the probability of completing a fragment correctly and saying "recall" served as a subjective measure of recollection.

The results of this experiment again revealed that recollection and subjective remembering declined with age. Comparing the subjective and objective measures of recollection revealed near identical results for both the young (.44 vs. .44) and the elderly adults (.24 vs. .29). In addition, these estimates were significantly correlated for both groups, with coefficients of .71 and .81 for young and old, respectively. Clearly, the agreement between subjective and objective measures of memory did not differ with age. Both young and elderly subjects were very accurate in their ability to assess whether they were recollecting. Of course, this may not always be true. Comparing effects on objective and subjective measures of recollection provides a means of detecting discrepancies between the two. One of our goals is to determine whether there are situations in which the elderly underestimate their ability to recollect.

Memory in the Real World Versus Lab Performance

Given the close relation between objective and subjective measures within the lab, one may also expect a close correlation between objective lab tasks and subjective reports of everyday memory, as measured by self-report questionnaires. However, based on the current literature (see Herrmann, 1990, for review) this does not seem to be the case. Many different questionnaires examining everyday memory failure have been reported in the literature (e.g., Broadbent, Cooper, Fitzgerald, & Parkes, 1982; Reason, 1993), yet responses on these instruments correlate weakly with laboratory tests of memory (Herrmann, 1982).

The lack of convergence between memory performance in the lab and self-report of memory as measured by questionnaires has been a source of disappointment for those investigating memory and aging. Some researchers have interpreted these findings as evidence that older adults are unaware of their everyday memory performance, overestimating or underestimating their abilities depending on the situation (Rabbitt & Abson, 1991). Others have used the poor correspondence between performance in the lab and subjective estimates of everyday memory to question the ecological validity of laboratory measures (e.g., Broadbent et al., 1982). It has been proposed that laboratory tasks do not reveal true memory capabilities, but merely reflect the task demands of unnatural situations in which specific memory strategies are induced.

We believe the fundamental problem with the literature comparing memory in laboratory tasks with questionnaire reports has been the failure to separate automatic and consciously controlled influences within the lab. Given that age-related deficits are found in recollection but not automatic influences, we expect questionnaires of everyday memory to relate only to recollection. This being so, it is not surprising that others who have failed to separate out the two memory processes have found very low correlations.

We wanted to determine whether subjects who showed poor recollection in our experiments would report a high frequency of memory failures in daily life. That is, would our elderly shoplifter and our aging math professor demonstrate poor recollection in our experimental tasks? To explore this issue, we (Jennings & Hay, 1994) designed a memory questionnaire focusing on everyday situations that relied on recollection, and compared the results to lab performance. Some questions were taken from existing questionnaires (Broadbent et al., 1982; Reason, 1993), whereas others were created specifically for our study. Subjects were asked to rate the frequency of everyday memory errors, such as the likelihood of forgetting to take medication or turn off the stove. These same subjects also performed in the "remember/know" experiment described earlier, allowing us to estimate their ability to use recollection in the lab.

The results of this study revealed that memory complaints were highly correlated with recollection ($r = .56$), but uncorrelated with automatic influences ($r = .08$). Furthermore, when we examined the correlation between the questionnaire and overall recognition performance on the lab task (when the contributions of the two processes were not separated), we found a much weaker correlation ($r = .33$). These results suggest that prior findings of low correlations between memory complaints measured by questionnaires and performance on laboratory tasks were not due to the poor ecological validity of the lab tasks. Instead, low correlations resulted because the lab tasks contained both controlled and automatic influences. Given that recollection alone correlates with everyday memory complaints, failing to examine the effects of recollection separately from automatic influences dilutes this relationship.

The rationale underlying the process dissociation procedure holds that recollection serves as a basis for control. This being so, it should not be surprising that recollection can be revealed by self-report in the "remember/know" procedure and through questionnaire responding. However, it is important to realize that although awareness and control can be highly correlated, they need not always coincide. There will be occasions when awareness and control diverge.

The dissociation between awareness and control can be seen in the behavior of patients with schizophrenia and other frontal dysfunctions when they perform the Wisconsin Card Sorting Task. This task requires subjects to sort cards according to constantly changing categories in response to verbal feedback. Schizophrenics and frontal patients typically achieve a small number of categories and continue to sort by the same criterion, despite feedback indicating they are incorrect. The behavior of these patients illustrates that they can often explicitly state the underlying principles of the task, indicating awareness, yet fail to utilize these principles in their actual performance (e.g., Cohen & Servan-Schreiber, 1992; Goldberg & Weinberger, 1988; Stuss & Benson, 1984).

Questions about the relation between awareness and control touch on a number of applied issues. Perhaps there are situations in which we have more cognitive control than we are able to report. We may find cases for which elderly subjects' recollection, as measured by their objective performance, is higher than indicated by their subjective reports. Other times, subjective reports may claim more control than is evidenced by objective behavior. These discrepancies may arise because we sometimes do act and then make our excuses (e.g., Jacoby, Kelley, & Dywan, 1989) or, as with frontal-lobe patients, awareness is not always translated into a basis for cognitive control of behavior. Further, subjective experience is highly important for purposes of training performance, as discussed by Jacoby, Bjork, and Kelley in a report for the National Academy of Sciences (1994).

Diagnosing Age-Related Deficits in Recollection

The evidence, thus far, suggests that elderly adults experience pronounced declines in their ability to recollect, which can lead to dramatic action slips. But can we identify elderly adults who are more prone than others to these action slips? That is, can we diagnose individuals who suffer from extremely poor recollection? One common complaint about the elderly is their propensity for repeatedly telling the same story to the same audience. This error is produced in a similar manner as action slips—automatic influences of memory that push toward repeatedly telling a story are not successfully opposed by recollection for having previously told the story to the same individuals. Rather than serving as a basis for recognition of a story as previously told, automatic influences that result from an earlier telling might be misattributed to the story being particularly appropriate for the present audience. As a related example, it sometimes happens that we see a friend and think of a funny story that we are sure she would enjoy. After relating the story to our friend, she tells us that she did enjoy it, and that is why she earlier told it to us. Similar errors happen in professional settings, but are sometimes much less humorous. For example, a person presents a new idea for an experiment to another person but is discouraged from doing the experiment. Later, the critic presents the same idea as his own to the person from whom he unintentionally stole it. Not only can errors of this sort signify a deficit in recollection, but they can also indicate the severity of that deficit. For example, one would be less concerned about a colleague who repeats a story or idea one month later than a colleague who repeats a story or idea after five minutes.

We (Jennings & Jacoby, 1993b) designed a lab situation that mirrors this real-life example and allows us to determine the magnitude of change in recollection with age. The task we developed is similar to the fame task (Jacoby, Kelley, Brown, & Jasechko, 1989; Jacoby, Woloshyn, & Kelley, 1989) in producing misattributions of familiarity and draws on the lag paradigm originally used with stem completion. Young and elderly adults were asked to study a list of 60 words followed by an inclusion and exclusion test. Both tests consisted of old and new words. The old words were given only a single presentation, but each new word was repeated once after 0, 3, or 12 intervening items. The second presentation of new words can be referred to as "catch items" (see later in this chapter) and are critical for assessing a misattribution of memory of the same sort that underlies repeated telling of a story.

For the exclusion test, subjects were asked to identify study words; they were to respond "yes" to old words but to respond "no" to new and catch items. The first presentation of catch items should increase their familiarity (Fischler & Juola, 1971; Underwood & Freund, 1970)—somewhat like telling a story once increases its chance of coming to mind again—and subjects could misattribute this familiarity to the prior study phase, confuse catch words with old ones, and mistakenly respond "yes." However, if subjects could recollect the source of a word's initial presentation (study vs. test), or recollect that they had already responded to a word, then any influence of familiarity would be opposed, and subjects would avoid responding "yes" (much like refraining from repeating a story). Telling subjects to respond "no" to catch words placed the automatic influence of familiarity and recollection in opposition; a catch word would elicit a "yes" only if it was sufficiently familiar (F) and not recollected as presented at test $(1 - R)$.

In contrast, on the inclusion task, we told subjects to respond "yes" to *any* words they had seen before (words they had read aloud and catch words). In this case, both recollection and familiarity would lead to correctly responding "yes" to catch words. For an inclusion test, subjects could respond "yes" to a catch word either because it was recollected as being on the test list (R) or because, although recollection failed, the word was sufficiently familiar $[F(1 - R)]$. The process dissociation equations then allowed us to estimate the probability of basing a decision on recollection and automatic influences (familiarity) at each lag interval. Based on the example of repeating a story after five minutes, we wanted to determine the length of the interval between study and test necessary to show age differences in recollection; if this interval proved to be very short we could consider age deficits to be very strong.

Age-related declines in recollection proved to be surprisingly pronounced (see Table 9.5). Older adults revealed significantly worse recollection than young adults when only *three* items had intervened between the first and second presentation of a catch word, a time interval of less than 10 seconds! Moreover, performance continued to decline as the lag intervals increased. In contrast, automatic influences revealed no significant effect of age or delay (Table 9.5), although it should be noted that the elderly showed slightly higher estimates of familiarity than the young. This discrepancy stemmed from the elderly's tendency to show a higher level of base rate

TABLE 9.5
Probability of Basing a Decision on Recollection
and Familiarity in a Recognition-Lag Task

	Recollection			Familiarity		
	0	3	12	0	3	12
Young	.96	.90	.83	—	.64	.66
Elderly	.94	.71	.51	—	.67	.74

Note: Estimates of familiarity could not be calculated at Lag 0. Because most subjects had a probability of correctly responding "yes" in inclusion of 1.0, and a probability of mistakenly responding "yes" in exclusion of 0, recollection equals 1.0, making the estimate of familiarity undefined.

responding "yes" to new items (.16), relative to the young (.10), inflating their estimates of automatic influences. When base rate is removed from these estimates, the difference between young and elderly is inconsequential.

This lag paradigm has provided us with a useful procedure for revealing deficits in recollection at short intervals. Moreover, this technique can easily be developed into a format that acts as a diagnostic tool. For example, deficits in recollection after only one or two intervening items or performance levels below the mean (i.e., greater than 25% errors) at longer intervals may act as warning signals for dementia.

Effects of Environmental Support on Memory Performance

Is nature so perverse that we are more likely to repeat a "stolen" story or idea to the person from whom we stole it than to anybody else? Perhaps. Consider the effects of reinstating context on automatic influences of memory. A person, originally from Scotland, enters a pseudo-Scottish pub in a North American city in which he has lived for a large number of years. Upon doing so, his Scottish accent becomes so "thick" that he cannot be understood by those accompanying him, and with some embarrassment he has to explain that he just asked if they would like to buy him a beer. A more important consequence of reinstating context can be seen in one condition of parole for ex-criminals. Upon release, they are not allowed to return to the environment that surrounded their crime. The belief is that returning to their old environment will cause them to reassume their automatic, antisocial ways of responding.

The distinction between controlled and automatic influences of reinstated context is important for treating those who have suffered a severe deficit in memory. What can be done about memory impairment? One approach is to design special environments that offer external cues and support to assist memory performance (Park, 1992). The idea of environmental support was originally suggested by Craik (1983, 1986) to account for different patterns of age-related declines in a variety of memory tasks. Age differences in free recall are usually large, whereas differences in recognition are typically small (Craik & McDowd, 1987). To account for these differences, Craik suggested that memory and other cognitive tasks vary in the extent to which external context induces or supports the mental operations appropriate for the specific situation. Furthermore, he suggested that older adults are more reliant on such environmental support and can perform relatively well if support is present. The poor performance of the elderly in the absence of environmental support is said to result from their lessened ability to engage in self-initiated processing.

When the idea of environmental support is applied generally, it suggests that improving encoding or retrieval conditions should produce a pattern of compensation, with older people deriving more benefit from improved conditions than younger people, whose self-initiated processing is unimpaired. This pattern was observed in some early experiments reported by Craik and Byrd (1982); however, other studies have shown that older subjects benefited to the same extent as did their younger counterparts, or that younger subjects benefited more (Craik & Jennings, 1992; Light, 1991). How can these contradictory patterns of results be understood? One possible explanation is that environmental support may enhance only consciously controlled processes in some cases or only automatic processes in other circumstances, or improve both processes simultaneously. Consequently, the pattern of results may be dependent on the type of processing affected.

To truly understand the effects of environmental support, it is necessary to separate the contributions of automatic and controlled processes. Recent research using the process dissociation procedure has examined the effects of environmental support in the form of reinstating context across study and test conditions (Jacoby, in press). Subjects studied word pairs under conditions of full or divided attention. At test, subjects were asked to complete fragments corresponding to the second member of each pair under inclusion and exclusion instructions. For half of the test items, study context was reinstated. The results show that reinstating context increased estimates of automatic and consciously controlled processing for both groups (see Table 9.6).

However, there was a strong interaction between group and process. Automatic processing was equally enhanced for both full and divided attention subjects, whereas consciously controlled processing showed greater improvements in the full attention condition. Although these data do not shed light directly on the confusing pattern of results found in the aging literature, they do suggest that effects of environmental support on both automatic and consciously controlled processing must be considered.

TABLE 9.6
Estimates of Recollection and Automatic Influences as a Function
of Reinstating Context for Full and Divided Attention

	Recollection	Automatic
Same context		
Full attention	.32	.45
Divided attention	.15	.46
Different context		
Full attention	.09	.37
Divided attention	.04	.38

Note: The baseline completion rate for items not presented at study was .32.

Although environmental support has the potential to facilitate memory performance in older adults, relying on highly structured environments can also have negative consequences. Research carried out by Langer (1981) suggests that oversimplifying or routinizing environments for the elderly can limit the potential stimulation for active, conscious information processing leading to "mindlessness." Environmental support is a two-edged sword, with the potential to both help and harm older adults. A similar paradox is reflected in childrearing. To parent effectively, one wants to structure the environment to encourage desirable behaviors but not completely rob a child of control or autonomy when eliciting such conduct; one wishes to be caring but not overbearing. Similarly, with older adults, incapacititating consciously controlled processing with highly structured environments can lead to self-induced dependence, perceived loss of control, and poor mental health (Langer, 1981).

Rehabilitating Recollection

Rather than structuring the external environment to aid memory, a more internal approach lies in the rehabilitation of memory through training. Typically, efforts to improve memory in the aged have focused on elaborate encoding schemes (for a review, see Kotler-Cope & Camp, 1990), such as pegword mnemonics (Wood & Pratt, 1987) and method of loci (Kliegl, Smith, & Baltes, 1989; Robertson-Tchabo, Hausman, & Arenberg, 1976). Although some improvement has been demonstrated, these effects are usually task specific and shortlived (Scogin & Bienias, 1988; Wood & Pratt, 1987).

More recently, rehabilitation has focused on training automatic retrieval processes. The spaced retrieval technique (Camp & Schaller, 1989; Landauer & Bjork, 1978; Schacter, Rich, & Stampp, 1985) and method of vanishing cues (Schacter & Glisky, 1986) are designed to create habits or automatic responses through repeated rehearsal, allowing memory-disordered subjects to acquire a limited amount of new information. Unfortunately, these techniques are open to error. If the strongest automatic response that comes to mind during training is erroneous, then the wrong habit may be strengthened (Baddeley & Wilson, 1994). One means for avoiding this drawback, which we are currently exploring, involves training controlled uses of memory (i.e., recollection).

We believe that training recollection may be possible with memory-impaired individuals who retain some consciously controlled processing, such as the elderly, and patients with mild to moderate memory deficits. It is this approach for improving memory performance that we are currently attempting to use with older adults. In the experiments described earlier, elderly adults showed some degree of spared recollective processing. We (Jennings & Jacoby, 1993b) want to train that ability by placing the elderly in a situation in which recollection is easy, and then, by gradually increasing the difficulty, shape recollective processing. Slowly moving the elderly from a situation in which they can perform competently may allow them to adapt their recollective process to more demanding situations.

The rationale underlying our attempt to train recollection harks back to the example of an elderly adult repeatedly telling the same stories. Even if memory is badly impaired, the elderly adult is quite unlikely to immediately repeat a story. What if we could train him or her to extend that delay? What is needed are many stories along with some method of controlling the opportunity for retelling a story so as to "shape" recollection. The methodology employed for the recognition lag paradigm described earlier has been adapted for training, although only the *exclusion* condition was used. Because this condition sets familiarity (automatic influences) and recollection in opposition, we can infer recollection, or lack thereof, through errors (responding "yes" to catch words). Moreover, we can reinforce responses that are based on recollection (responding "no" to catch words). During training, elderly subjects had to recollect catch words shortly after their initial presentation when recollection was easy (i.e., one intervening item). Positive feedback followed each correct response. The test intervals increased slowly across the training sessions as performance improved. Ideally, with repeated practice and feedback, the elderly should show accurate recollection across longer and longer delays.

The critical question was whether recollection could be improved by shaping across a small number of training sessions. Elderly subjects received four training sessions a day for seven days, and each training session was a miniature exclusion task. For each session, subjects were asked to read aloud and learn a list of 30 words. They were then given a training phase in which they were shown the 30 words they had seen at study and 30 new words, and the 30 new words were repeated at one of two lags. Subjects were asked to respond "yes" to the study words, but "no" to the new and catch items, and were given positive feedback whenever they responded correctly. See Table 9.7 for the method.

TABLE 9.7
Example Training Session

Study Phase:
  30 words read aloud and studied (2 sec rate)
Test Phase:
  Yes/no recognition test
  30 old words
  30 new words, each presented twice after one or two intervening items (Lags 1 & 2)
  Respond "yes" to old words only
  Respond "no" to new words for both presentations
  Positive feedback for correct responses
Remaining Sessions:
  Same procedure but lag intervals increase when performance reaches criterion
  Lag conditions can increase from 1 and 2, to 1 and 3, to 2 and 4, and so on to 16 and 40

The shaping procedure was implemented through the lag conditions. In Session 1 words were repeated after one or two intervening items. If subjects performed to criterion, then in Session 2 the lag conditions increased to one and three items. If subjects again performed to criterion, the lags increased to 2 and 4 items, and so on to 16 and 40. These lag pairs were chosen so that subjects were always working at one lag interval they had mastered and was therefore easy, and a second interval that was new and more difficult. Criterion performance was the level of performance shown by young adults in our previous experiment. If subjects did not achieve the criterion at both lags, they continued to work at those lag intervals for as many sessions as required to reach it. Once the criterion was met, the lag intervals increased. Improvements in performance were gauged by comparing the length of the interval in which subjects reached criterion on the first and last day of training. If interval length increased significantly during training, then we improved recollection.

Because the experiment is still in progress, our data are preliminary. Six of the seven experimental subjects revealed a dramatic improvement in recollection during training. Examining the group results, one can see those gains. On the first day of training, subjects performed below criterion when only one item intervened between the first and second presentation of a word. After training, however, these subjects performed to criterion when 28 items occurred.

In order to ascertain whether these effects stemmed from our shaping technique or merely arose from practice or bias effects, we tested a group of control subjects. These subjects were given the same amount of training as our experimental subjects without the shaping procedure. Rather than gradual increases in the lag intervals, control subjects were presented a randomly ordered set of lag pairs across sessions. If they did not show significant improvements, we could be more confident that any gains in performance by the experimental group were due to training.

The control subjects did not show the same level of improvement found with the experimental subjects. Two control subjects demonstrated gains in performance, whereas the other three subjects showed no improvement. The group data thus indicated moderate positive change, which suggests that the control subjects experienced a practice or training effect that was unrelated to the shaping procedure. In contrast, the experimental group's results, which exceeded the control group's gains, suggest that shaping has some additional influence on performance. The results of our training procedure appear encouraging thus far, but this experiment was only meant to be a preliminary attempt at training. Future work will capitalize on these results and involve changes designed to increase training effects, produce transfer from these effects to real life, and maintain long-term performance.

SUMMARY AND CONCLUSIONS

Among the most important practical problems faced by psychology is that of measuring cognitive control. Everyday life is replete with examples showing the necessity of distinguishing between automatic and consciously controlled influences of memory. To understand errors such as action slips and repeated telling of a story, it is necessary to separate the contributions of these processes within a task, rather than identifying each type of process with a different task, as is done by the implicit and explicit memory distinction. The process dissociation procedure accomplishes this goal by combining results from a condition for which automatic and controlled processes act in opposition with results from a condition for which the two types of processes act in concert. Doing so provides the intuitively appealing definition of cognitive control as the difference in performance between when one is trying to versus trying not to engage in some act or be influenced by information from some source.

Results from use of the process dissociation procedure are highly encouraging. Factors traditionally associated with reduced cognitive control, such as divided attention and age-related deficits in memory, have the effect of reducing recollection but leave automatic influences unchanged. The effects on estimated recollection are sufficiently large and reliable to enable the procedure to be used as a diagnostic tool. Moreover, the process dissociation procedure offers advantages over traditional measures of recollection, which are inflated by guessing that reflects automatic influences of memory. Further, subjective reports of memory deficits are in good accord with the objective measure of cognitive control provided by the process dissociation procedure, suggesting that a diagnostic test based on this procedure would reflect capacities relevant to real life. Finally, use of the process dissociation procedure to analyze the effects of reinstated context showed effects on automatic influences that are separate from effects on controlled use of memory. That there are two effects of reinstating context is important for the design of special supportive environments to diminish consequences of memory impairment. However, a more ambitious goal for memory remediation is to devise techniques for rehabilitating recollection. Such techniques would complement attempts to exploit preserved, automatic influences of memory through training or special environments (e.g., Baddeley & Wilson, 1994).

The layperson refers to cognitive control by using terms such as *will* that have long been in disrepute because of their philosophical implications but are important for society. Recently, the philosophical issues surrounding consciousness and intention have again gained prominence in psychology. Psychologists can contribute to those discussions by showing the *practical* importance of the distinction between automatic and controlled processes. This distinction can be applied to improve methods for the diagnosis and treatment of memory deficits. A failure to do so reflects a lack of will.

REFERENCES

Baddeley, A., & Wilson, B. A. (1994). When implicit learning fails: Amnesia and the problem of error elimination. *Neuropsychologia, 32*, 53–68.

Bowers, D., Verfaellie, M., Valenstein, E., & Heilman, K. M. (1988). Impaired acquisition of temporal information in retrosplenial amnesia. *Brain and Cognition, 8*, 47–66.

Brewer, W. F. (1974). There is no convincing evidence for operant or classical conditioning in adult humans. In W. B. Weimer & D. S. Palermo (Eds.), *Cognition and the symbolic processes* (pp. 1–42). Hillsdale, NJ: Lawrence Erlbaum Associates.

Broadbent, D. E., Cooper, P. F., Fitzgerald, P., & Parkes, K.(1982). The cognitive failures questionnaire (CFQ) and its correlates. *British Journal of Clinical Psychology, 21*, 1–16.

Camp, C. J., & Schaller, J. R. (1989). Epilogue: Spaced retrieval memory training in an adult day-care center. *Educational Gerontology, 15*, 641–648.

Cermak, L. S., Verfaellie, M., Butler, T., & Jacoby, L. L. (1993). Attributions of familiarity in amnesia: Evidence from a fame judgment task. *Neuropsychology, 7*, 510–518.

Cohen, J. D., & Servan-Schreiber, D. (1992). Context, cortex, and dopamine: A connectionist approach to behavior and biology in schizophrenia. *Psychological Review, 99*, 45–77.

Craik, F. I. M. (1982). Selective changes in encoding as a function of reduced processing capacity. In F. Klix, J. Hoffman, & E. van der Meer (Eds.), *Cognitive research in psychology* (pp. 152–161). Berlin: Deutscher Verlag der Wissenschaffen.

Craik, F. I. M. (1983). On the transfer of information from temporary to permanent memory. *Philosophical Transactions of the Royal Society, B302*, 341–359.

Craik, F. I. M. (1986). A functional account of age differences in memory. In F. Klix & H. Hapendorf (Eds.), *Human memory and cognitive capabilities, mechanisms and performances* (pp. 409–422). Amsterdam: Elsevier.

Craik, F. I. M., & Byrd, M. (1982). Aging and cognitive deficits. The role of attentional resources. In F. I. M. Craik & S. Trehub (Eds.), *Aging and cognitive processes* (pp. 191–211). New York: Plenum.

Craik, F. I. M., & Jennings, J. M. (1992). Human memory. In F. I. M. Craik & T. A. Salthouse (Eds.), *The handbook of aging and cognition* (pp. 51–110). Hillsdale, NJ: Lawrence Erlbaum Associates.

Craik, F. I. M., & McDowd, J. M. (1987). Age differences in recall and recognition. *Journal of Experimental Psychology: Learning, Memory, and Cognition, 13,* 474–479.

Curran, T., & Hintzman, D. L. (in press). Violations of the independence assumption in process dissociation. *Journal of Experimental Psychology: Learning, Memory and Cognition,*

Dunn, J. C., & Kirsner, K. (1989). Implicit memory: Task or process? In S. Lewandowsky, J. C. Dunn, & K. Kirsner (Eds.), *Implicit memory: Theoretical issues* (pp. 17–31). Hillsdale, NJ: Lawrence Erlbaum Associates.

Dywan, J., & Jacoby, L. L. (1990). Effects of aging on source monitoring: Differences in susceptibility to false fame. *Psychology and Aging, 5,* 379–387.

Dywan, J., Segalowitz, S. J., Henderson, D., & Jacoby, L. L. (1993). Memory for source after traumatic brain injury. *Brain and Cognition, 21,* 20–43.

Estes, W. K. (1976). The cognitive side of probability learning. *Psychological Review, 83,* 37–64.

Fischler, I., & Juola, J. F. (1971). Effects of repeated tests on recognition time for information in long-term memory. *Journal of Experimental Psychology, 1,* 54–58.

Frith, C. D. (1987). The positive and negative symptoms of schizophrenia reflect impairments in the perception and initiation of action. *Psychological Medicine, 17,* 631–648.

Gardiner, J. M. (1988). Functional aspects of recollective experience. *Memory and Cognition, 16,* 309–313.

Gardiner, J. M., & Java, R. I. (1991). Forgetting in recognition memory with and without recollective experience. *Memory & Cognition, 19,* 617–623.

Gardiner, J. M., & Parkin, A. J. (1990). Attention and recollective experience in recognition memory. *Memory & Cognition, 18,* 579–583.

Goldberg, T. E., & Weinberger, D. R. (1988). Probing prefrontal function in schizophrenia with neuropsychological paradigms. *Schizophrenia Bulletin, 14,* 179–183.

Graf, P., & Komatsu, S. (1994). Process dissociation procedure: Handle with caution! *European Journal of Cognitive Psychology, 6,* 113–129.

Hasher, L., & Zacks, R. T. (1979). Automatic and effortful processes in memory. *Journal of Experimental Psychology: General, 108,* 356–388.

Hasher, L., & Zacks, R. T. (1988). Working memory, comprehension, and aging: A review of a new view. In G. K. Bower (Ed.), *The psychology of learning and motivation* (Vol. 22, pp. 193–225). New York: Academic Press.

Herrmann, D. J. (1982). Know thy memory: The use of questionnaires to assess and study memory. *Psychological Bulletin, 92,* 434–452.

Herrmann, D. J. (1990). Self-perception of memory performance. In W. K. Schaie, J. Rodin, & C. Schooler (Eds.), *Self-directedness and efficacy: Causes and effects throughout the life course* (pp. 199–211). Hillsdale, NJ: Lawrence Erlbaum Associates.

Holender, D. (1986). Semantic activation without conscious identification in dichotic listening, parafoveal vision, and visual masking: A survey and appraisal. *Behavioral and Brain Sciences, 9,* 1–23.

Jacoby, L. L. (1991). A process dissociation framework: Separating automatic from intentional uses of memory. *Journal of Memory and Language, 30,* 513–541.

Jacoby, L. L. (1992, November). *Strategic versus automatic influences of memory: Attention, awareness, and control.* Paper presented at the 33rd Annual Meeting of the Psychonomic Society, St. Louis, MO.

Jacoby, L. L. (in press). Dissociating automatic and consciously-controlled effects of study/test compatibility. *Journal of Memory and Language.*

Jacoby, L. L., Begg, I. M., & Toth, J. P. (in press). In defense of independence: Violations of assumptions underlying the process-dissociation procedure. *Journal of Experimental Psychology: Learning, Memory, and Cognition.*

Jacoby, L. L., Bjork, R. A., & Kelley, C. M. (1994). Illusions of comprehension, competence, and remembering. In D. Druckman & R. A. Bjork (Eds.), *Learning, remembering, believing: Enhancing human performance* (pp. 57–80). Washington, DC: National Academy Press.

Jacoby, L. L., & Dallas, M. (1981). On the relationship between autobiographical memory and perceptual learning. *Journal of Experimental Psychology: General, 3*, 306–340.

Jacoby, L. L., & Hay, J. F. (1993, November). *Action slips, proactive interference, and probability matching.* Paper presented at the 34th annual meeting of the Psychonomic Society, Washington DC.

Jacoby, L. L., Kelley, C. M., Brown, J., & Jasechko, J. (1989). Becoming famous overnight: Limits on the ability to avoid unconscious influences of the past. *Journal of Personality and Social Psychology, 56*, 326–338.

Jacoby, L. L., Kelley, C. M., & Dywan, J. (1989). Memory attributions. In H. L. Roediger & F. I. M. Craik (Eds.), *Varieties of memory and consciousness: Essays in honour of Endel Tulving* (pp. 391–422). Hillsdale, NJ: Lawrence Erlbaum Associates.

Jacoby, L. L., Ste-Marie, D. M., & Toth, J. P. (1993). Redefining automaticity: Unconscious influences, awareness, and consciousness. In A. D. Baddeley & L. Weiskrantz (Eds.), *Attention, selection, awareness, and control: A tribute to Donald Broadbent* (pp. 261–282). New York: Oxford University Press.

Jacoby, L. L., Toth, J. P., & Yonelinas, A. P. (1993). Separating conscious and unconscious influences of memory: Measuring recollection. *Journal of Experimental Psychology: General, 122*, 139–154.

Jacoby, L. L., Woloshyn, V., & Kelley, C. M. (1989). Becoming famous without being recognized: Unconscious influences of memory produced by dividing attention. *Journal of Experimental Psychology: General, 118*, 115–125.

Jacoby, L. L., Yonelinas, A. P., & Jennings, J. M. (in press). The relation between conscious and unconscious (automatic) influences: A declaration of independence. In J. Cohen & J. W. Schooler (Eds.), *Scientific approaches to the questions of consciousness.* Hillsdale, NJ: Lawrence Erlbaum Associates.

Jennings, J. M. (1995). *Age-related changes in automatic and consciously controlled memory processes.* Doctoral dissertation, McMaster University, Hamilton, Ontario.

Jennings, J. M., & Hay, J. F. (1994, June). *Predicting everyday memory failure in older adults.* Poster presented at the 1994 Canadian Aging Research Network (CARNET) Conference, Toronto, ON.

Jennings, J. M., & Jacoby, L. L. (1993a). Automatic versus intentional uses of memory: Aging, attention and control. *Psychology and Aging, 8*, 283–293.

Jennings, J. M., & Jacoby, L. L. (1993b, August). *The effect of aging on consciously-controlled memory processing.* Paper presented at the 1993 American Psychological Association Conference, Toronto, ON.

Kliegl, R., Smith, J., & Baltes, P. B. (1989). Testing-the-limits and the study of adult age differences in cognitive plasticity of a mnemonic skill. *Developmental Psychology, 25*, 247–256.

Kotler-Cope, S., & Camp, C. J. (1990). Memory intervention in aging populations. In E. A. Lovelace (Ed.), *Aging and cognition: Mental processes, self-awareness and interventions.* Amsterdam: Elsevier.

Landauer, T. K., & Bjork, R. A. (1978). Optimum rehearsal patterns and name learning. In M. M. Gruneberg, P. E. Morris, & R. N. Sykes (Eds.), *Practical aspects of memory* (pp. 625–632). New York: Academic Press.

Langer, E. J. (1981) Old age: An artifact? In J. L. McGaugh & S. B. Kiesler (Eds.), *Aging—biology and behavior* (pp. 255–281). New York: Academic Press.

Light, L. L. (1991). Memory and aging: Four hypotheses in search of data. *Annual Review of Psychology, 43*, 333–376.

Marcel, A. J. (1983). Conscious and unconscious perception: Experiments on visual masking and word recognition. *Cognitive Psychology, 15*, 197–237.

Moscovitch, M., Vriezen, E. R., & Gottstein, J. (1993). Implicit tests of memory in patients with focal lesions or degenerative brain disorders. In H. Spinnler & F. Boller (Eds.), *Handbook of neuropsychology* (Vol. 8). Amsterdam: Elsevier.

Norman, D. A. (1981). Categorization of action slips. *Psychological Review, 88*, 1–15.

Park, D. C. (1992). Applied cognitive aging research. In F. I. M. Craik & T. Salthouse (Eds.), *The handbook of aging and cognition* (pp. 449–493). Hillsdale, NJ: Lawrence Erlbaum Associates.

Parkin, A. J., & Walter, B. M. (1992). Recollective experience, normal aging, and frontal dysfunction. *Psychology and Aging, 7*, 290–298.

Posner, M. I., & Snyder, C. R. R. (1975). Attention and cognitive control. In R. L. Solso (Ed.), *Information processing in cognition: The Loyola Symposium* (pp. 55–83). Hillsdale, NJ: Lawrence Erlbaum Associates.

Rabbitt, P., & Abson, V. (1991). Do older people know how good they are? *British Journal of Psychology, 82*, 137–151.

Reason, J. (1979). Actions not as planned: The price of automatization. In G. Underwood & R. Stevens (Eds.), *Aspects of consciousness, volume 1, psychological issues* (pp. 67–89), Nottingham, England: Academic Press.

Reason, J. (1993). Self-report questionnaires in cognitive psychology: Have they delivered the goods? In A. Baddeley & L. Weiskrantz (Eds.), *Attention: Selection, awareness, and control* (pp. 406–423). Oxford, England: Clarendon Press.

Reber, A. S. (1989). Implicit learning and tacit knowledge. *Journal of Experimental Psychology: General, 118*, 219–235.

Reingold, E. M., & Merikle, P. M. (1990). On the inter-relatedness of theory and measurement in the study of unconscious processes. *Mind and Language, 5*, 9–28.

Robertson-Tchabo, E. A., Hausman, C. P., & Arenberg, D. (1976). A classical mnemonic for older learners: A trip that works! *Educational Gerontology, 1*, 215–226.

Roediger, H. L. (1990). Implicit memory: Retention without remembering. *American Psychologist, 45*, 1043–1056.

Roediger, H. L., & McDermott, K. B. (1993). Implicit memory in normal human subjects. In H. Spinnler & F. Boller (Eds.), *Handbook of neuropsychology* (Vol. 8). Amsterdam: Elsevier.

Schacter, D. L. (1987). Implicit memory: History and current status. *Journal of Experimental Psychology: Learning, Memory, and Cognition, 13*, 368–379.

Schacter, D. L., & Glisky, E. L. (1986). Memory remediation: Restoration, alleviation, and the acquisition of domain-specific knowledge. In B. Uzzell & Y. Gross (Eds.), *Clinical neuropsychology of intervention*. Boston: Martinus Nijhoff.

Schacter, D. L., Rich, S. A., & Stampp, M. S. (1985). Remediation of memory disorders: Experimental evaluation of the spaced-retrieval technique. *Journal of Clinical and Experimental Neuropsychology, 7*, 79–96.

Scogin, F., & Bienias, J. L. (1988). A three-year follow-up of older adult participants in a memory-skills training program. *Psychology and Aging, 3*, 334–337.

Shimamura, A. P. (1989). Disorders of memory: The cognitive science perspective. In F. Boller & J. Grafman (Eds.), *Handbook of neuropsychology* (Vol. 3, pp. 35–73). Amsterdam: Elsevier.

Skinner, B. F. (1971). *Beyond freedom and dignity*. New York: Knopf.

Squire, L. R., & McKee, R. (1992). Influence of prior events on cognitive judgments in amnesia. *Journal of Experimental Psychology: Learning, Memory, and Cognition, 18*, 106–115.

Ste-Marie, D. M., Jennings, J. M., & Finlayson, A. J. (in press). The process dissociation procedure: Memory testing in brain-damaged populations. *Clinical Neuropsychologist*.

Stuss, D. T. (1991). Self, awareness, and the frontal lobes: A neuropsychological perspective. In J. Strauss & G. R. Goethals (Eds.), *The self: An interdisciplinary approach* (pp. 255–278). New York: Springer-Verlag.

Stuss, D. T., & Benson, D. F. (1984). Neuropsychological studies of the frontal lobes. *Psychological Bulletin, 95*, 3–28.

Toth, J. P., Reingold, E. M., & Jacoby, L. L. (1995). A response to Graf and Komatsu's (1994) critique of the process dissociation procedure: When is caution necessary? *European Journal of Cognitive Psychology, 7*, 113–130.

Toth, J. P., Reingold, E. M., & Jacoby, L. L. (1994). Towards a redefinition of implicit memory: Process dissociations following elaborative processing and self-generation. *Journal of Experimental Psychology: Learning, Memory, and Cognition, 20,* 290–303.

Tulving, E. (1985). Memory and consciousness. *Canadian Psychologist, 26,* 1–12.

Underwood, B. J., & Freund, J. S. (1970). Testing effects in the recognition of words. *Journal of Verbal Learning and Verbal Behavior, 9,* 117–125.

Wegner, D. M. (1994). Ironic processes of mental control. *Psychological Review, 101,* 34–52.

Weiskrantz, L. (1986). *Blindsight: A case study and implications.* Oxford: Oxford University Press.

Winocur, G., & Moscovitch, M. (1983). Paired-associate learning in institutionalized and non-institutionalized old people: An analysis of interference and context effects. *Journal of Gerontology, 38*(4), 455–464.

Wood, L. E., & Pratt, J. D. (1987). Pegword mnemonic as an aid to memory in the elderly: A comparison of four age groups. *Educational Gerontology, 13,* 325–339.

CHAPTER TEN

Applying the Psychology of Memory to Clinical Problems

Alan Baddeley

MRC Applied Psychology Unit, Cambridge, England

Over the last 30 years, the study of memory deficits in brain-damaged patients has helped revolutionize our theoretical approach to human memory. Examples included the demonstration of pure and specific long-term memory deficits in amnesic patients (Milner, 1966), deficits that fitted neatly into the distinction between long- and short-term memory emanating from the literature on normal subjects (Baddeley & Warrington, 1970), a distinction that was given further support by evidence from patients with deficits to short-term phonological memory (Shallice & Warrington, 1970). Analysis of such short-term memory deficits was highly influential in the development of the concept of working memory in general, and more specifically in the development of a concept of a phonological loop that has evolved as a system for the acquisition of language (Baddeley, 1992; Gathercole & Baddeley, 1993).

In the case of long-term memory, the distinction between implicit and explicit memory that has dominated the recent literature was originally driven by the observation that amnesic patients showed a wide range of preserved learning capacities despite grossly impaired memory (Brooks & Baddeley, 1976; Cohen & Squire, 1980; Warrington & Weiskrantz, 1968). Finally, although the distinction between semantic and episodic memory did not originate in the neuropsychological clinic, having reached something of an impasse in the psychological laboratory (Kintsch, 1980), the area is currently being rejuvenated by the study of semantic memory deficits in neuropsychological patients (see Patterson & Hodges, 1995, for a review).

Although cognitive psychology has gained immeasurably from neuropsychological patients, it is far from obvious that the patient has gained very much in return. Although it is not, of course, the job of the cognitive psychologist to deliver therapy, or indeed to counsel the patient, there is a case for suggesting that if we are to continue to have the wholehearted cooperation of our clinical colleagues, then it would be helpful if we could offer something in return. Clearly, a better understanding of the nature of the underlying deficit is one way in which we can make a contribution. An even greater contribution, however, could result if we can build our laboratory-based technical and conceptual developments into the clinical tools available to the clinical psychologist and therapist.

On the whole, cognitive psychology has not been a major source of such practical help. Although the concepts and techniques of cognitive psychology have been applied with great success and ingenuity to the analysis of individual cases (see Shallice, 1988, for a review), with some notable exceptions, clinical assessment in neuropsychology still relies principally on test batteries developed in a psychometric tradition that typically predates recent developments in cognitive psychology.

There are, of course, very good reasons for this apparent conservatism. The usefulness of a test is at least partly dependent on prior experience with that test, built up over many years of clinical experience. Such experience needs, of course, to be supplemented by adequate population norms. Collecting adequate norms is an expensive and time-consuming activity that uses psychometric skills and techniques that tend not to feature prominently in the career development of cognitive psychologists. Such skills tend to be tolerated within cognitive psychology rather than embraced with enthusiasm. In short, as cognitive psychologists we are good at inventing new methods, but less good at turning them into a clinical usable technology. I hope, in the pages that follow, to persuade you that this is a pity; to argue not only that is it useful to develop such a technology, but also that it can provide a very enjoyable activity that complements an interest in the basic understanding of human cognition.

I describe three attempts to apply the cognitive psychology of memory to clinical neuropsychological questions, one concerned with semantic memory, one with episodic memory, and one with implicit learning. Each will be based on a different strategy; the first simply exploits methods developed in the laboratory so as to provide clinical tools, the second involves attempting to develop a new test, and the third tries to utilize recent theoretical advances in order to improve the treatment of patients with memory disorders.

RAIDING THE COGNITIVE ARMORY

Most current clinical tests of memory use procedures that originated in the laboratory. Hence, they typically involve paired associate learning or reproduction of figures or of paragraphs of prose, all techniques that have formed part of the study of memory for at least 50 years. It seems likely that such techniques will continue to be useful, just as they have been within the laboratory, but that does not, of course, mean that we should not be constantly on the lookout for new methods that might allow the clinician to ask new questions. As an example of this, I would like to describe the development of a test concerned with semantic memory, entitled the Speed and Capacity of Language Processing (SCOLP; Baddeley, Emslie, & Nimmo-Smith, 1992).

The SCOLP involves two subtests. One is concerned with speed of comprehension, and is highly sensitive to any cerebral insult or stressor that compromises the speed of semantic processing. A second subtest relies on accuracy of lexical decision and aims to provide a robust estimate of crystallized verbal intelligence, a measure that is relatively insensitive to changes in the level of current cognitive functioning. The two between them, therefore, provide an indication of both current and premorbid language processing capacity.

Silly Sentences: A Measure of Speed of Comprehension

The speed of comprehension test originated in the classic study by Collins and Quillian (1969) that attempted to test Quillian's computational model of semantic memory. You may recall that this model made strong assumptions about the way in which information is stored in semantic memory, and attempted to test this assumption using a task in which subjects were required to verify statements about the world such as "Canaries are yellow," or "Canaries have skin" as rapidly as possible. The initial study provided results that appeared to support the model, and rapidly earned a place in cognitive psychology textbooks. Unfortunately, however, doubts were cast on the extent to which the original study had adequately sampled the material tested (Clark, 1973), and a subsequent study by Conrad (1972) that used a more representative sample of material failed to support the model.

Graham Hitch and I were developing our working memory model at the time when the Collins and Quillian sentence verification task appeared to be opening up exciting new avenues to the understanding of semantic memory. As part of the process of exploring the role of working memory in comprehension, we adopted the Collins and Quillian sentence verification task and produced an extensive and carefully constructed set of sentences. We found the task to be readily usable, and to be sensitive to the concurrent load on working memory (Baddeley, Lewis, Eldridge, & Thomson, 1984), but, like Conrad, failed to observe the crucial relationship between the structure of the material and verification time predicted by the Quillian model. We had, however, begun to use the test more widely, finding that it provided a rapid and sensitive measure, not only of concurrent load but

198   BADDELEY

also of stressors such as alcohol or high pressure (Baddeley, 1981; Logie & Baddeley, 1985).

We were left, therefore, with a test that no longer provided an elegant estimate of an important theoretical construct, but that could instead be regarded as providing a very sensitive measure of language comprehension, albeit a theoretically imprecise measure that reflected the diversity and complexity of comprehension. The multifaceted nature of the test was reflected in a series of correlational studies in which we showed that speed of sentence verification correlated with performance on a range of other semantic memory tests, both unspeeded tests such as recognition vocabulary, and speeded tests including verbal fluency and speed of category judgment. Like category judgment, our sentence verification test also had a speed component, correlating with the letter categorization task developed by Posner and his colleagues in which subjects match pairs of letters for either having the same physical characteristics (in which case Aa would be judged not to match), or name matching in which the two would evoke a "yes" response (Posner, Boies, Eichelman, & Taylor, 1969).

It appears then that Collins and Quillian were correct in assuming that their test was a measure of semantic memory. However, this was clearly not the whole story, because the test correlated just as highly with a test of syntactic processing in which subjects attempted to verify statements about the order of two letters A and B, a test that utilized repeatedly an extremely limited semantic domain. The test involves both simple active declarative sentences ("A follows B—BA") as well as more complex sentences involving passives and negatives ("B is not followed by A—BA"), is sensitive to stressors (e.g. Logie & Baddeley, 1985), and correlates with verbal intelligence (Baddeley, 1968).

As with the original Collins and Quillian study, negative items in our semantic processing test are generated by combining the subject and predicate of two different sentences. Hence, "Bishops hold a religious office" and "Shoes are sold in pairs" might be recombined to produce "Shoes hold a religious office" and "Bishops are sold in pairs." Because of the bizarre nature of the negatives, the test is often referred to as "Silly Sentences." In the standard test version, after a brief practice session, subjects complete as many sentences as possible in two minutes. A normal subject takes about two seconds per sentence, with an error rate of less than 5%. Speed of processing is very sensitive to the effects of both environmental stressors (Logie & Baddeley, 1985) and brain damage (Baddeley, Harris, & Sunderland, 1987), whereas error rates typically remain very low. One exception to this generalization occurs in the case of schizophrenic patients, who sometimes make a much higher percentage of errors, probably reflecting a semantic memory deficit, evidence of general thought disorder, or possibly both (McKenna, Clare, & Baddeley, 1995).

Subjects seem to enjoy performing the test, and it is readily accepted even by patients who have substantial cognitive impairment. This is probably because they feel that they are able to do the test successfully, as indeed they are; impaired performance is typically reflected in longer latencies rather than errors.

Although the standard mode of testing involves paper and pencil, the test can, of course, be adapted to be presented by computer, or indeed by auditory presentation, allowing it to be used with subjects with literacy problems. This form also lends itself to testing at a distance using a telephone link. Using this mode, Jackson, Louwerens, Cnossen, and de Jong (1993) found it to be a highly sensitive measure of the effects of a tranquilizer drug.

The nature of the original material makes it unsuitable for use with young children, or indeed with people from nonwestern cultures. For that reason, a new version was recently developed for testing third-world children. It uses auditory presentation to avoid the need for the subjects to be literate, and limits itself to statements about the world that are likely to be truly cross-cultural, such as "Fire is hot" or "The sun shines at night." In a recent study carried out in Jamaica, the revised version of the test was found to be highly reliable and correlated with performance on the reading, writing, and arithmetic subscales of the Wide Range Achievement Test (Baddeley, Meeks-Gardner, & Grantham-McGregor, 1995).

Spot-the-Word: An Estimate of Premorbid Intelligence

Suppose we assess a patient on the semantic processing test and find that he or she performs rather slowly. How are we to know whether this indicates someone who has always been rather slow in comprehension, or someone who was previously a rapid comprehender but has subsequently shown marked impairment as a result of brain damage? One way is to attempt to use a "hold" test, that is, a test in which performance is assumed to remain relatively constant despite a general impairment in cognitive functioning. The most commonly used test in this connection is the National Adult Reading Test (NART) in which the subject is required to read out a series of words, all of which have in common the fact that they are irregular in their spelling-to-sound correspondence. The words range from common to rare, and the number pronounced correctly is used as an indication of the subject's premorbid verbal intelligence (Nelson, 1982). The test is used widely, and provides a useful clinical tool. It does, however, have a number of limitations. It may not be suitable for patients with perceptual problems, and clearly cannot be used when patients' reading is disordered. It is not, of course, usable in languages that have regular orthographies, and may give a misleading indication of level of verbal intelligence in patients whose education is limited, or those who have acquired their vocabulary largely through reading, who may be quite familiar with some of the rarer words, fully understanding their meaning, but nonetheless be unaware of the correct pronunciation. Finally, some subjects find the test slightly humiliating, because it almost invariably ends up by requiring them to demonstrate their ignorance by failing to read a word out loud, something that most of us have not done since primary school.

We therefore developed an alternative test that capitalized on the fact that even patients with reading problems are often able to recognize whether or not a string of letters constitutes a real word. Subjects are presented with pairs of items, comprising one real word and one pseudoword, and are invited to "spot the word." Lexical decision is relatively robust, presumably because the choice can be made on the basis of any of a number of features, ranging from recognition of meaning through identification of a familiar orthographic or phonological pattern to a simple general sense of greater familiarity for one item than the other, possibly based on a small contribution from several of these sources. Subjects readily accept the task, which can, if necessary, be presented auditorily.

The validity of the test is indicated by a number of studies in which it has been shown to correlate in the region of .8 to .9 with vocabulary, NART, and WAIS (verbal) (Baddeley, Emslie, & Nimmo-Smith, 1993). The robustness of the measure is still being explored. A preliminary study required two groups of elderly patients to perform both NART and spot the word. One group was diagnosed as suffering from dementia, whereas the others were diagnosed as depressed but not demented. As Fig. 10.1 shows, patients categorized as suffering from dementia showed poorer performance on both spot the word (which was tested twice using parallel forms) and on NART.

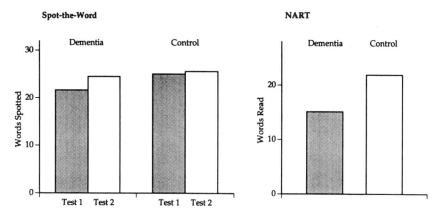

FIG. 10.1. Performance of patients classified as suffering from dementia or depression on two tests that aim to reflect premorbid verbal intelligence, the NART and spot the word. (Data from Emslie, Pearson, & Baddeley, in preparation.)

A second test involved correlating performance on spot the word and NART with a measure of dementia, the Mini Mental State Examination (MMSE). In the case of NART, a significant positive correlation occurred between NART and MMSE, calling into question the capacity of NART to give an unbiased measure of premorbid verbal intelligence. In the case of spot the word, the correlation was lower and failed to reach significance, suggesting that it might possibly provide a more robust estimate of premorbid IQ than NART; however, considerably more work needs to be done before this conclusion can be drawn with any confidence. In general, it seems unlikely that any test will be totally robust; however, spot the word does offer a rapid estimate of verbal IQ that is likely to be less sensitive to subsequent brain damage than most current intelligence tests. Combining the two components of SCOLP thus provides a measure of current cognitive processing capacity, together with a rapid and patient-friendly estimate of premorbid IQ, that together give an estimate of the magnitude of cognitive deficit (Baddeley, Emslie, & Nimmo-Smith, 1992).

DEVELOPING A NEW TEST OF EPISODIC MEMORY

Whereas spot the word and Silly Sentences involve capitalizing on methods from the cognitive psychology laboratory to provide new tests, one area in which large numbers of tests already exist is that of episodic memory. Why, then, is another test needed? The reasons are spelled out in a recent assessment of available memory tests by Mayes (1995). The characteristics regarded as desirable by Mayes include the need for a relatively pure measure of various memory subsystems, with separate assessment of recall and recognition, visual and verbal memory, learning and forgetting. In addition, it is important to be able to ensure that any performance decrement is due to memory deficit, and not to problems of perception or response production. Finally, it is desirable to have a range of scores that allows both severely amnesic patients and healthy normals to be tested without performance being unduly restricted by floor or ceiling effects. Mayes concluded that none of the available tests achieves this.

Consider, for example, the most widely used clinical memory test, the Wechsler Memory Scale (WMS), and its recently revised version (WMS-R). The original WMS had the highly unfortunate characteristic of producing a general memory score that was based on combining subtests that reflected quite different cognitive systems. In particular, the test involved both tests of relatively standard episodic memory, such as paired associate learning, with measures of "concentration" involving such information processing tasks as backward counting and digit span, tests that involved systems that are quite separate from those typically involved in episodic memory. The latter tests tend to correlate with intelligence, with the result that a highly intelligent patient with a dense but pure amnesia might score within the normal range because his or her bad episodic memory would be balanced by good short-term memory and attention. The WMS-R avoids this problem, but does so by giving a series of separate measures, which unfortunately loses the advantage of a single, broadly based robust test of episodic memory. Other problems pointed out by Mayes include inadequate testing of recognition, and doubts as to whether it adequately separates visual and verbal memory.

Finally, the fact that the visual tests require the subject to draw from memory a series of previously observed patterns confounds memory deficits with problems of perception and motor control. The WMS and its successor, the WMS-R, have served neuropsychology well, but they are essentially based on the methods and concepts of the 1950s when the WMS was first designed, suggesting that the time has come to develop alternative tests that take advantage of subsequent developments.

Confessions of a Door Bore

The new test began life at a meeting of the Scientific Committee of the Amnesia Association, an organization of caregivers and professionals with a common interest in trying to help amnesic patients. It was agreed that despite a very wide range of clinical tests, diagnosis of memory disorders was still a problem, partly because, in Britain at least, there are relatively few clinical psychologists, and virtually no tests that can be successfully given by nonpsychologically trained professionals. It was noted that visual memory was an area that was particularly devoid of good tests, and I volunteered to try to come up with a simple visual memory test that was easy to administer and score, and readily acceptable to the patient. I had previously been intrigued by a poster entitled "The Doors of Dublin" that consisted of a large number of colored photographs of elegant front doors from the Georgian squares of Dublin. It had struck me on seeing it that it would make beautiful material for a visual recognition test, but because I was not seeking to create such a test at the time, had not taken the matter further.

By this time, "The Doors of Dublin" appeared to have vanished, but I was able to obtain door posters from various other locations and began to put together a test, with the help of a colleague, Hazel Emslie. We decided to opt for a four-alternative forced-choice situation, because two alternatives gave a high guessing rate that would then require a rather large set of items in order to obtain reasonable discrimination. This unfortunately meant that we needed sets of four doors that were relatively similar, and it rapidly became clear that the available posters were insufficient to provide this. I asked our Unit photographer to photograph local doors, and having just got a new camera, started to take door photographs myself. I was on the slippery slope and have been photographing doors ever since. I began in Cambridge, noticing the way in which doors vary as a function of the period and type of architecture. Victorian terraces, for example, have doors that are usually structurally similar, and in some cases are painted identical colors, making them ideal for difficult items. At the other extreme are doors like that of a signwriter who painted little pink clouds all over his. I took my obsession with me on holiday, and discovered intriguing differences in door patterns from one French village to another, together with magnificently ornate doors in Amsterdam, or, probably the climax for a door bore, the Moorish doors of the Alhambra in Grenada. Beware the lure of the door!

To return to the test, we decided to split it into two halves, one easy and the other more difficult, so that patients who had difficulty with the first set would not have to experience the stress of obvious failure. In practice, it turns out that subjects are not excessively threatened by their inability to decided which of four almost identical doors they have seen before, so our fears of distressing subjects proved unfounded, although ensuring that subjects all begin with a relatively easy test is probably still a good idea. The first test involves presenting 12 doors, 1 at a time, followed by 12 sets of 4, with the subject instructed to pick out the door that has been seen before. Difficulty ranges from very easy to extremely difficult, which means the test can be used for a wide range of subjects, from elderly dementia patients to bright young graduate students (Baddeley, Emslie, & Nimmo-Smith, 1994).

One of the problems with tests of visual memory is the avoidance of a reliance on verbal coding. One solution is to attempt to use abstract figures that are not readily nameable. Unfortunately, this tends to challenge subjects to come up with some form of verbal code, which not only adds a verbal dimension, but furthermore a strategy effect that probably reflects the subject's general intelligence. In choosing doors, we opted for an alternative solution employed by Bahrick and Boucher (1968), who avoided the problem of verbal labeling by selecting items to be remembered that all had the same verbal label, for example, all cups. In order to further minimize the usefulness of verbal labeling, the experimenter explicitly provides a label while each item is presented (e.g., "a boathouse door," "a French barn door"), always ensuring that the label provided will be true of all four items presented at recognition. Poor performance could, of course, reflect impaired perception rather than memory. This can be checked by retesting the subject under conditions whereby the target and four-alternative test set are presented simultaneously. Failure under these conditions would clearly indicate a perceptual deficit.

Having developed our visual recognition test, it occurred to us that it would be desirable to have an equivalent verbal recognition test. We wanted to avoid a situation in which the subject would code in terms of semantic or visual imagery, and hit on the idea of using names. Although names are often readily encodable in visual or semantic terms, such codes are usually quite arbitrary and inappropriate. One does not expect Mr. Green to differ in any obvious way from Mr. Brown, and on meeting Mrs. Thatcher, would not expect to see straw in her hair or other signs of her association with a traditional rural craft. We therefore hope that this, together with the relatively rapid presentation of names and the requirement that the subject pronounce them, would maximize acoustic or lexical coding and minimize the role of visual or semantic codes in our verbal recognition test. The use of such supplementary codes was also rendered less helpful by careful selection of foils. Hence, "Henry Bridgeman" might be combined for recognition purposes with "Henry Bridgestock," "Henry Bridgewater," and "Henry Bridgeworth." We selected the names from the Cambridge Telephone Directory and, in a series of pilot studies, gained some insight into what appears to make names difficult or easy to recognize, once again ending up with 2 sets of 12, 1 relatively easy and 1 relatively hard. Easy names tended to be those that were distinctive, such as "Jeakins" or "Diddel," whereas difficult names were those that had highly similar distractors, as given earlier, or that were very common such as "Johnson," "Jackson," "Wilson," and "Watson."

Having arrived at our visual and verbal recognition tests, it seemed appropriate to supplement them with recall tests, and to include a learning component, and a delayed recall, which would allow any differences in rate of forgetting to be detected. For the verbal test, we again chose names, presenting pictures of four people, a doctor, a minister, a newspaper boy, and a postman, and giving the subjects up to three learning trials to master the first and second name of each, followed by a delayed recall test. Unlike the recognition test, which concentrated on the surnames and held the forename constant, recall involved learning both names and pairing them appropriately.

The visual recall task was somewhat more difficult, because we could obviously not expect our subjects to demonstrate recall by producing an accurate colored drawing of each photograph of a door. We therefore chose stimuli that could be drawn very easily—four versions of the cross—of which very many designs exist. The four that we selected differed in overall shape (square or rectangular), the features at the end of the arms, and the presence or absence of a feature at the point where the arms crossed. Although the four cross types do have names (potent, pommee, quadrate, and celtic), we have not so far come across anyone who knows them. The initial learning trial requires the subject to copy each cross, hence ensuring that perception and production are adequate, or, if not, providing an appropriate baseline against which the recalled crosses can be compared. Again subjects are given up to three learning trials to reach criterion, and are tested after a delay, during which other parts of the test are given.

Having designed our test, we tried it out on a group of elderly patients from a hospital serving a largely rural community. The patients were attending a day center and were diagnosed as suffering from either dementia or depression. Our initial discovery was that our test was too hard for the dementia patients. Fortunately, by this time we had accumulated a large array of doors and names, and were able to modify the test and try again. This time we were successful in that subjects were all scoring above chance, with a highly significant advantage to those patients diagnosed as depressed rather than suffering from dementia. We did not find a perfect association between test score and the diagnosis of the psychogeriatrician, but diagnosis in this group is inherently uncertain. We tested the patients on some half-dozen tests that were assumed to be diagnostic of dementia, and found that none of the tests entirely agreed with the psychogeriatrician, nor indeed with each other. At the very least, our new test looked promising.

Our next question concerned the suitability of the test for detecting much milder deficits in a much more sophisticated population. To explore this, we carried out a study using the Subject Panel of the Applied Psychology Unit, comparing middle-aged panel members with elderly members. The panel comprises volunteers who come along to take part in experiments on cognitive psychology, typically involving memory or attention or concerned with applied issues such as the utilization of computers. The panel in general tends to be above average in both intelligence and educational level, and this is particularly true of the elderly subjects. Most 70-year-olds do not voluntarily submit themselves to tests of memory, attention, and computing. In order to offer a brief comparison, we also tested subjects on Warrington's (1984) Recognition Memory Test, which involves both verbal and visual subtests. The verbal test requires the subject to judge the pleasantness of 50 words, which must then be recognized from 50 word pairs, whereas the visual subtest involves a similar judgment and recognition of 50 faces. The study produced encouraging results, which are discussed later. We went on to collect stratified norms in which equal numbers of men and women were sampled from each age band between 16 and 80, with each sample comprising a balance of subjects from different socioeconomic backgrounds. As expected, there was a systematic decline with age on all four tests, with the decline appearing to be somewhat more marked for recall than for recognition, as is assumed to be typically the case for memory and age. A factor analysis of the overall data set indicated one major factor together with a secondary factor that appeared to reflect the visual–verbal difference.

For the next stage, we enlisted the help of our colleague Ian Nimmo-Smith to derive age-scaled norms. This is a procedure whereby curves are fitted for each age band expressing the distribution of scores across the population sampled. This can then be expressed either as percentiles or as z-scores, which can in turn be expressed as conventional scaled scores, where a scaled score of 10 represents the mean for the population, and each scaled point above or below represents one third of a standard deviation away from that mean. Hence, a subject with a scaled score on a subtest of 4 would be two standard deviations below the population mean. The advantage of scaled scores, of course, is that they allow data to be compared across tests, or indeed combined in specified ways to allow a range of different comparisons to be made.

The four subtests can be combined to give a single overall memory score, or used in subgroups to provide separate measures of recall and recognition and of visual and verbal memory, whereas other scaled scores allow the magnitude of any visual–verbal or recall–recognition discrepancies to be evaluated. Most normal subjects show little or no forgetting, but should forgetting be observed then its magnitude can be assessed against the population norms, as can rate of learning or indeed accuracy in copying. The doors and people test, therefore, offers on the one hand a robust broadly based general measure of explicit memory, which on the other hand can, if necessary, be analyzed to give a much more detailed profile. Each conclusion is based on at least two subtests, so as to minimize the risk of misinterpreting a brief lapse of attention.

We moved on to the issue of validating the test. Such validation needs to demonstrate that the test is reasonably sensitive and preferably correlates with other existing memory measures. Furthermore, it would clearly be highly desirable if the visual–verbal component could be validated against suitable patient groups. Finally, if the subcomponents are to be useful, then it is important to demonstrate that different groups will show different patterns so as to rule out the possibility that the various subscores simply measure a common factor with differential degrees of sensitivity.

Returning to the results from the previously described study of middle-aged and elderly members of the APU Subject Panel, as Fig. 10.2 suggests, although the *age-scaled* score shown in the upper-left panel indicates that both groups were, as expected, slightly above average in performance, in terms of *unscaled* overall score shown in the lower-left panel the groups are highly significantly different, suggesting that for this group, at least, our test is substantially more sensitive than the Warrington visual or verbal recognition memory tests. In terms of the memory profile, across the four subtests, as Fig. 10.2 suggests in the rightmost portions, there was a significant tendency for the older group to show a visual–verbal discrepancy that appears to reflect their greater difficulty with names, not an unsurprising conclusion to the average elderly person. It is however, worth bearing in mind that data from IQ tests show the opposite, with verbal intelligence being more robust to the effects of age than visual, a result that has on occasion been interpreted as suggesting that the right hemisphere ages more rapidly than the left. A much more plausible interpretation would seem to be that

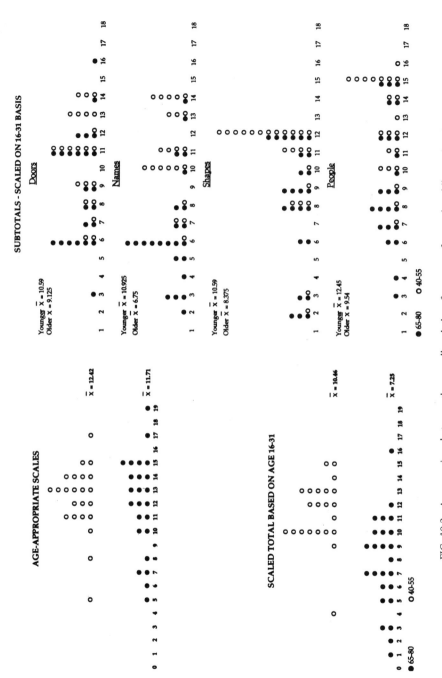

FIG. 10.2. A comparison between the overall scaled performance of normal middle-aged and normal elderly groups on the doors and people test and its four constituent subtests.

the WAIS language tests rely more on crystallized intelligence reflected in relatively robust measures such as vocabulary, whereas the nonverbal subtests appear to rely more on fluid intelligence and the solving of novel problems, capacities that are known to be sensitive to aging.

Fig. 10.2 shows another way in which the norms may be used to assess the results of this study. Rather than compare a middle-aged and elderly group, we can compare both groups with the general population, deriving from each subject a scaled score that would have been obtained were the subject in his or her early 20s. Fig. 10.2 shows the results obtained, together with the appropriately scaled scores for the two groups. They indicate that, first of all, the groups are on the whole above average in their performance, given their age, as indeed we would expect from the self-selected nature of the Subject Panel. However, when compared to young subjects, both the middle-aged and elderly groups are impaired, with the elderly more severely impaired, exactly as one would expect. Finally, the discrepancy is particularly marked in recall and recognition of names.

Although our study successfully demonstrated the sensitivity of the doors and people test to the effects of age, it does not, of course, allow validation of the visual–verbal subtests. For this, we were fortunate in being able to collaborate with Robin Morris and his colleagues at the Institute of Psychiatry in a study that compared patients who had undergone left or right temporal lobectomy as a treatment for epilepsy (Morris, Abrahams, Baddeley, & Polkey, in press). Such patients form perhaps the only group for which a clear visual versus verbal memory distinction can be guaranteed (Smith & Milner, 1989). The results of the temporal lobectomy study are shown in Fig. 10.3, from which it is clear that the test does successfully distinguish between the two groups, with left-hemisphere patients showing a clear verbal memory deficit, whereas the opposite is shown by patients with right-temporal lobectomy. As the scaled scores suggest, both groups show

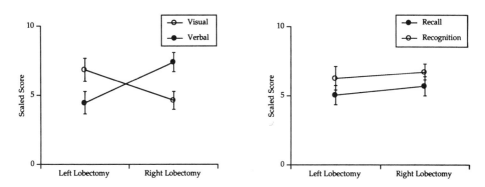

FIG. 10.3. Performance of left- and right-temporal lobectomy cases on the doors and people test.

SCHIZOPHRENIC PATIENTS

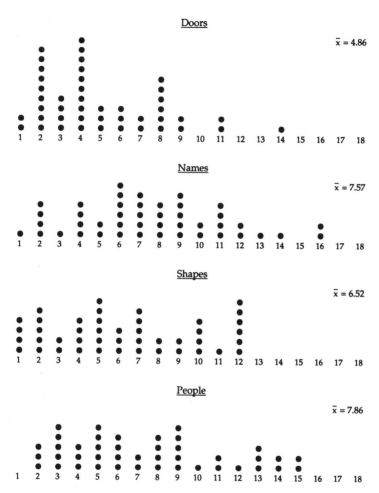

FIG. 10.4. Performance of schizophrenic patients on the doors and people test.

an overall memory deficit, with a tendency for both to show a more marked deficit in recall rather than recognition.

Having established the validity of this aspect of the test, we were able to use it to explore the memory of another patient group, schizophrenics, for whom claims of hemispheric imbalance have often been made. Fig. 10.4 shows the results, from which it is clear, first of all, that the most sensitive subtest for this group appears to be the recognition of doors. When subjects are assessed in terms of visual–verbal discrepancy, then a subgroup of schizophrenic patients occurs who do appear to have a particular problem in visual memory, suggesting, for some patients at least, the possibility of a more marked right-hemisphere impairment.

Considered overall, therefore, the new test appears to be reasonably sensitive and to provide both an overall measure of memory performance and also a pattern of subtest performance that differs from one group to another. Visual memory is impaired in right-hemispherectomy patients and verbal in left. Normal elderly subjects seem to be particularly sensitive to problems of name memory, whereas schizophrenic patients appear to be more sensitive to deficits in visual recognition. We have not so far studied groups for which a clear recall–recognition difference would be expected; a contrast between Huntington's and Alzheimer patients might be helpful here (see Brandt & Rich, 1995), or possibly between patients with memory deficits resulting from frontal lobe damage, in contrast to patients whose damage reflects temporal lobe impairment (Mayes, 1995).

We have, however, already established that the test has a number of advantages, including the range of performance over which it is usable and its capacity to give a broad-based overall score that can then be unpacked into a number of more analytic measures. One final advantage is its user friendliness; it is a challenging test, but one that even memory-impaired subjects appear to enjoy. It has already achieved more than we anticipated when we first began to cut up posters of doors, but how useful it will ultimately prove to be, only time and experience will tell.

IMPLICIT MEMORY AND REHABILITATION

The examples I have given so far have been cases in which existing methods were taken and applied to the problem of assessing cognitive and memory deficit in neuropsychological patients. My final example comes from an attempt to apply a theoretical advance in cognitive psychology to the development of methods for helping patients cope with their memory problems. The theoretical advance concerns the separation of implicit and explicit memory, which itself stemmed initially from neuropsychological evidence for such a dissociation in amnesic patients. The drive for the work in my own case came from the frustrating paradox that although more and more investigators were producing evidence that amnesic patients were capable of learning more and more things, nevertheless it seemed to be extremely difficult to turn this theoretical insight into improved rehabilitation. One clear exception to this was the series of experiments by Glisky, Schacter, and Tulving (1986), who used the stem completion method of cuing recall to help memory impaired patients learn computing skills. However, although the method was certainly helpful, it does not appear to have led to any general principles that might be taught to therapists attempting to help patients with memory problems.

The clear implication is that explicit or episodic memory, of the type that is grossly impaired in amnesia, plays an important role in new learning over and above that of providing conscious recollection of the past. This point was brought home to us particularly clearly in a study that aimed to teach amnesic patients the simple skill of using an electronic memory aid. Subjects were required to learn to enter the date and time into a device, a process that involved six simple steps. Although this might seem to be a procedural task, making no apparent demands upon the subject's capacity for recollection, performance nonetheless correlated extremely highly with explicit memory performance as measured for example by the Rivermead Behavioural Memory Test. It appeared to be the case that six steps exceeded the memory span of virtually all subjects, hence requiring more than one learning trial. In subsequent trials, patients with normal memory recollected their errors and were able to avoid repeating the same mistake again. Amnesic patients, on the other hand, who lack this source of mnemonic evidence, tend to make the same mistakes repeatedly. Considered more generally, this hypothesis suggests that one crucial function of explicit episodic memory is to allow people to review the past and use this information in order to avoid making errors in the future. It follows from this that amnesic patients are likely to show comparatively preserved learning on error-free tasks for which performance is measured in terms of time rather than errors, an observation that had been previously made by Brooks and Baddeley (1976). Furthermore, it should prove possible to enhance the learning of amnesic patients if the situation is structured so as to prevent errors occurring. In fact, work in the behavioral tradition had already demonstrated that errorless learning could be an efficient way of training a pigeon to perform a visual discrimination task (Terrace, 1963), and had indeed been adapted for use with handicapped human subjects (Sidman & Stoddart, 1967). The method has not crossed over into neuropsychology, however, and even in the animal literature appears to have largely dropped from view.

Barbara Wilson and I decided to test this hypothesis in a study in which amnesic patients attempted to learn under conditions where errors were either initially encouraged or avoided (Baddeley & Wilson, 1994). We chose stem completion as our learning task, to ensure that the amnesic patients would be able to learn, but even so, were forced to use lists of only 5 words, compared to 10 words that were learned by the control groups. These comprised both a group of young subjects, and an elderly group who were likely to make sufficient errors to avoid the problem of ceiling effects.

The "errorful" condition involved presenting the subjects with the first two letters of a word and encouraging them to guess the word. "I am thinking of a word and the first two letters are *BR*. Can you guess what the word is?" The subject might then generate *BRAIN*, *BREAD*, and *BROWN*, each of which the experimenter would reject before providing the "correct" response *BRING*, which the subject was then asked to write down. The initial learning phase of the experiment involved going through the list three times, with each test ending with the subjects writing down the correct response. This was immediately followed by the second phase of the experiment, in which the first two letters of each word were presented and the subject was invited to provide the appropriate completion, being corrected immediately if the wrong response were produced. The errorful condition is therefore one in which every effort is made to inject errors at the start of the learning session, so that the fate of such errors can be studied over the subsequent learning session.

The "errorless" condition involved an equivalent set of words, but in this case the subject was given no chance to guess. Hence, the experimenter would say "I am thinking of a word beginning with *BR* and that word is *BRING*. Please write that down." The procedure was otherwise identical to that used in errorful learning, with three learning trials in Phase 1, followed by a second phase comprising nine subsequent test trials. The test trials were run in groups of three, with a five-minute rest between.

The results of the study are shown in Fig. 10.5, where errorless and errorful learning are shown on different panels. In the case of errorful learning, the amnesic patients are clearly at a disadvantage, even though they are learning only five words. This may at first sight seem surprising, because stem completion has been shown to be unimpaired in amnesic subjects. It is, however, crucial to note that the method used here is not the standard one in which amnesic and control subjects are encouraged to produce the first word that comes to mind. In the present instance, the word required is the one that was presented by the experimenter, an explicit rather than an implicit instruction. The amnesic subjects are also somewhat impaired in learning using errorless learning, but there is considerably less difference.

Once the subjects enter Phase 2, in which errorless learning is replaced by trial and error learning with correction, the amnesic patients virtually cease to improve, because increments that occur within three-trial blocks are lost by forgetting over the five-minute interblock interval. This might seem surprising because, in general, once an amnesic subject has learned then rate of forgetting is generally regarded as normal (Huppert & Piercy, 1978; Kopelman, 1985). It seems likely that what we are observing is a priming effect that dissipates over time, rather than an example of durable explicit learning. However, this in turn raises the further, more detailed question of whether the poor performance shown by amnesic patients results from failure to learn or greater susceptibility to forgetting. One way of answering this question is to utilize a Markov chain model in order to provide a more detailed account of the learning and forgetting process. Such a model

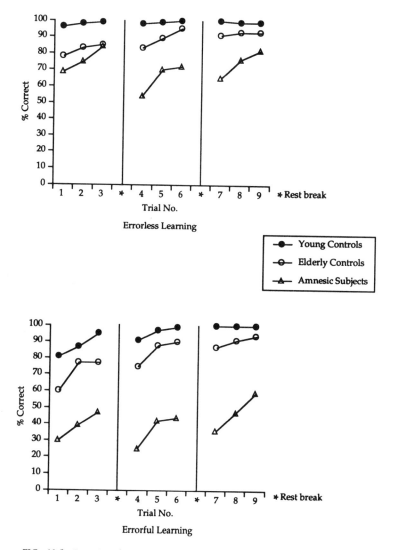

FIG. 10.5. Learning function for the three groups of subjects tested using errorless or errorful learning procedures.

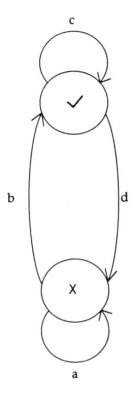

FIG. 10.6. Representation of a simple two-state Markov chain model used to analyze the learning data: (a) represents the probability of an unlearned item remaining unlearned, (b) of it being learned, (c) of a learned item being retained, and (d) of its being forgotten and returning to the unlearned state.

takes the sequence of responses and categorizes them as correct or incorrect. A response that begins incorrect and hence unlearned may either remain incorrect or become correct, and subsequently the correct response may either remain correct or be forgotten, reverting to the previous incorrect state. The sequence of responses produced by a subject can be used to compute the probability of these various transitions, as shown in Fig. 10.6, where (a) represents the probability that an unlearned response will remain unlearned, (b) that it will be learned, whereas (c) represents the probability of a learned response being retained, and (d) the probability that it will be forgotten. If the errorless condition leads to better learning than the errorful, then it should be reflected in the magnitude of probability (b).

Fig. 10.7 shows the performance of the amnesic subjects in terms of this learning probability. The x-axis reflects the probability of learning under errorful conditions, and the y-axis the errorless condition, with each point representing one patient. If errorless learning is advantageous for that subject, then his or her point should rest above the diagonal, as indeed it does for all 16 amnesic subjects tested. The second panel of Fig. 10.7 shows the equivalent plot for normal elderly subjects; although there is a tendency for errorless learning to be helpful, this is by no means universally the case. Note also that the difference between these two groups is not simply due

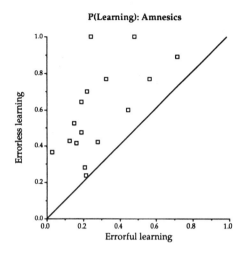

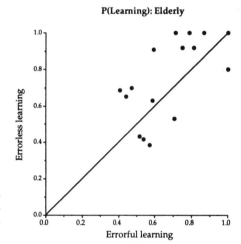

FIG. 10.7. The relationship between errorless and errorful learning for amnesic and elderly subjects.

to ceiling or floor effects; at comparable overall learning probabilities, the
amnesic patients clearly perform better with errorless learning, whereas this
effect is much less marked in the normal elderly. Performance of the young
was too near ceiling to allow a useful comparison.

Our result was certainly consistent with the prediction that errorless learning would be advantageous for amnesic patients, but leaves open a number
of more detailed hypotheses as to the mechanism involved. We considered
three possibilities. The first assumes an active process involving the episodic
recollection of errors and avoidance of their repetition. The second assumes
a more automatic process analogous to the classic concept of proactive

interference (PI). On this interpretation amnesic patients show poorer learning because they are more susceptible to PI than controls, an explanation similar to that proposed and subsequently rejected by Warrington and Weiskrantz (1982). Both of these make the same prediction with regard to intrusion errors; a higher proportion of errors made by amnesic patients should be repetitions of prior errors, rather than novel responses that have not been made before.

A third hypothesis would make a somewhat different prediction. Suppose we assume that performance may be based either on an explicit episodic memory system that is impaired in amnesia or on a preserved implicit memory system that is common to amnesic and control subjects. If the episodic system provides the correct response then it will be made, leading to a clear advantage for the control subjects. However, if no response is forthcoming from this source of evidence, then implicit memory will be used to generate a response; because this system is poor at eliminating errors, it will produce a mixture of repetitions of earlier errors and new intrusions. On this hypothesis, once episodic memory has failed, the two groups are equivalent in relying on the same implicit system. The proportion of intrusion errors that are repetitions should therefore also be the same for amnesic and control subjects. As Fig. 10.8 shows, this is what happens, supporting Warrington and Weiskrantz's (1982) decision to abandon the classic interference theory interpretation of amnesia.

Our experiment, therefore, appears to have supported the hypothesis that amnesic patients have difficulty in dealing with errors, suggesting that errorless learning may be a valuable principle to incorporate into the methods used by therapists attempting to rehabilitate patients with memory deficits. It is important to note that such a principle would be a genuine departure from current practice, where it is common for the therapist to encourage the patient to guess on the grounds that this would take full advantage of any minimal information present.

However, before suggesting that clinical practice should be changed, it is clearly important to validate our conclusions using a range of more realistic tasks than attempting to learn a list of unrelated words. The first stage of this has already been completed, using a series of single-case studies to teach tasks ranging from the use of an electronic memory aid, through reteaching spelling to an acquired dyslexic patient, to learning the names of therapists and ward staff (Wilson, Baddeley, Evans, & Shiel, 1994). Although it is clear that there is a good deal more to be learned about the method, including optimal size of learning chunk and methods of avoiding excessive forgetting, it is already becoming clear that the method has great promise and in each case has proved more effective than existing trial-and-error methods. Perhaps the most encouraging sign was the observation of the occupational therapist, who had been running a number of single-case errorless learning studies on a neurological

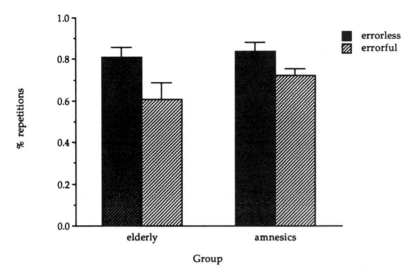

FIG. 10.8. Proportion of intrusion errors that are repetitions of prior erroneous responses for amnesic and control subjects.

ward, that the ward staff had observed the success of the methods and were beginning to use them spontaneously.

CONCLUSION

In recent decades, the study of human learning and memory has shown vigorous development, both conceptual and methodological. A good deal of the impulse for this development has come from a growing willingness to tackle problems beyond the laboratory, with the result that it is now commonplace for the memory theorist to be influenced by results obtained in the clinic, or indeed in the world outside. We are now in a position to begin to repay some of these debts, not only by providing models that offer a better understanding of the phenomena concerned, but also by developing tools that will enable the therapist or educator to operate more effectively. There is little doubt that the process of developing such tools will, in turn, enrich both our methodology and our basic models of cognition.

REFERENCES

Baddeley, A. D. (1968). A 3-min reasoning test based on grammatical transformation. *Psychonomic Science, 10,* 341–342.

Baddeley, A. D. (1981). The cognitive psychology of everyday life. *British Journal of Psychology, 72,* 257–269.

Baddeley, A. D. (1992). Working memory. *Science, 255,* 556–559.

Baddeley, A. D., Emslie, H., & Nimmo-Smith, I. (1992). *The Speed and Capacity of Language Processing (SCOLP) Test.* Bury St. Edmunds, Suffolk: Thames Valley Test Company.

Baddeley, A. D., Emslie, H., & Nimmo-Smith, I. (1993). The Spot-the-Word test: A robust estimate of verbal intelligence based on lexical decision. *British Journal of Clinical Psychology, 32,* 55–65.

Baddeley, A. D., Emslie, H., & Nimmo-Smith, I. (1994). Doors and people: A test of visual and verbal recall and recognition. Bury St. Edmunds, Suffolk: Thames Valley Test Company.

Baddeley, A. D., Harris, J., & Sunderland, A. (1987). Closed head injury and memory. In H. S. Levin, J. Grafman, & H. M. Eisenberg, (Eds.), *Neurobehavioral recovery from head injury* (pp. 295–317). New York: Oxford University Press.

Baddeley, A. D., Lewis, V., Eldridge, M., & Thomson, N. (1984). Attention and retrieval from long-term memory. *Journal of Experimental Psychology: General, 113,* 518–540.

Baddeley, A. D., Meeks-Gardner, J., & Grantham-McGregor, S. (1995). Cross-cultural cognition: Developing tests for developing countries. *Applied Cognitive Psychology, 9,* Special Issue, S173–S195.

Baddeley, A. D., & Warrington, E. K. (1970). Amnesia and the distinction between long- and short-term memory. *Journal of Verbal Learning and Verbal Behavior, 9,* 176–189.

Baddeley, A. D., & Wilson, B. A. (1994). When implicit learning fails: Amnesia and the problem of error elimination. *Neuropsychologia, 32,* 53–68.

Bahrick, H. P., & Boucher, B. (1968). Retention of visual and verbal codes of the same stimuli. *Journal of Experimental Psychology, 78,* 417–422.

Brandt, J., & Rich, J. B. (1995). Memory disorders in the dementias. In A. D. Baddeley, B. A. Wilson, & F. N. Watts (Eds.), *Handbook of memory disorders* (pp. 243–270). Chichester, England: Wiley.

Brooks, D. N., & Baddeley, A. D. (1976). What can amnesic patients learn? *Neuropsychologia, 14,* 111–122.

Clark, H. H. (1973). The language-as-fixed-effect fallacy: A critique of language statistics in psychological research. *Journal of Verbal Learning and Verbal Behavior, 12,* 335–359.

Cohen, N. J., & Squire, L. R. (1980). Preserved learning and retention of pattern analyzing skill in amnesia: Dissociation of knowing how and knowing that. *Science, 210,* 207–210.

Collins, A. M., & Quillian, M. R. (1969). Retrieval time from semantic memory. *Journal of Verbal Learning and Verbal Behavior, 8,* 240–247.

Conrad, C. (1972). Cognitive economy in semantic memory. *Journal of Experimental Psychology, 92,* 149–154.

Gathercole, S. E., & Baddeley, A. D. (1993). Phonological working memory: A critical building block for reading development and vocabulary acquisition. *European Journal of Psychology of Education, 8,* 259–272.

Glisky, E. L., Schacter, D., & Tulving, E. (1986). Computer learning by memory impaired patients: Acquisition and retention of complex knowledge. *Neuropsychologia, 24,* 313–328.

Huppert, F. A., & Piercy, M. (1978). Dissociation between learning and remembering in organic amnesia. *Nature, 275,* 317–318.

Jackson, J. L., Louwerens, J. W., Cnossen, F., & de Jong, H. T. (1993). Testing the effects of hypnotics on memory via the telephone: Fact or fiction? *Psychopharmacology, 111,* 127–133.

Kintsch, W. (1980). Semantic memory. In R. S. Nickerson (Ed.), *Attention and performance VIII* (pp. 595–620). Hillsdale, NJ: Lawrence Erlbaum Associates.

Kopelman, M. D. (1985). Rates of forgetting in Alzheimer-type dementia and Korsakoff's syndrome. *Neuropsychologia, 23,* 623–638.

Logie, R. H., & Baddeley, A. D. (1985). Cognitive performance during simulated deep-sea diving. *Ergonomics, 28,* 731–746.

Mayes, A. (1995). Tests of memory. In A. D. Baddeley, B. A. Wilson, & F. N. Watts (Eds.), *Handbook of memory disorders* (pp. 367–391). Chichester, England: Wiley.

McKenna, P. J., Clare, L., & Baddeley, A. D. (1995). Schizophrenia. In A. D. Baddeley, B. A. Wilson, & F. N. Watts (Eds.), *Handbook of memory disorders* (pp. 271–292). Chichester, England: Wiley.

Milner, B. (1966). Amnesia following operation on the temporal lobes. In C. W. M. Whitty & O. L. Zangwill (Eds.), *Amnesia* (pp. 109–133). London: Butterworths.

Morris, R. G., Abrahams, S., Baddeley, A. D., & Polkey, C. E. (in press). Doors and people: Visual and verbal memory following unilateral temporal lobectomy. *Neuropsychology.*

Nelson, H. E. (1982). *The National Adult Reading Test (NART).* Windsor, England: NFER-Nelson.

Patterson, K., & Hodges, J. (1995). Semantic memory disorders. In A. D. Baddeley, B. A. Wilson, & F. N. Watts (Eds.), *Handbook of memory disorders* (pp. 167–186). Chichester, England: Wiley.

Posner, M. I., Boies, S. J., Eichelman, W. H., & Taylor, R. L. (1969). Retention of visual and name codes of single letters. *Journal of Experimental Psychology, 79,* 1–16.

Shallice, T. (1988). *From neuropsychology to mental structure.* Cambridge, England: Cambridge University Press.

Shallice, T., & Warrington, E. K. (1970). Independent functioning of verbal memory stores: A neuropsychological study. *Quarterly Journal of Experimental Psychology, 22,* 261–273.

Sidman, M., & Stoddart, L. T. (1967). The effectiveness of fading in programming simultaneous form discrimination for retarded children. *Journal of the Experimental Analysis of Behavior, 10,* 3–15.

Smith, M. L., & Milner, B. (1989). Right hippocampal impairment in the recall of spatial location: Encoding deficit or rapid forgetting? *Neuropsychologia, 27,* 71–81.

Terrace, H. S. (1963). Discrimination learning with and without "errors." *Journal of Experimental Analysis of Behavior, 6,* 1–27.

Warrington, E. K. (1984). *The Recognition Memory Test.* Windsor, England: NFER-Nelson.

Warrington, E. K., & Weiskrantz, L. (1982). Amnesia: A disconnection syndrome. *Neuropsychologia, 20,* 233–238.

Warrington, E. K., & Weiskrantz, L. (1968). New method of testing long-term retention with special reference to amnesic patients. *Nature, 217,* 972–974.

Wilson, B. A., Baddeley, A. D., Evans, J. J., & Shiel, A. (1994). Errorless learning in the rehabilitation of memory impaired people. *Neuropsychological Rehabilitation, 4,* 307–326.

CHAPTER ELEVEN

Implicit Memory and Perceptual Brain Mechanisms

Tim Curran
Daniel L. Schacter
Harvard University

Implicit memory refers to the influence of a previous experience on subsequent behavior without conscious recollection of that experience (Graf & Schacter, 1985; Schacter, 1987). In contrast, explicit memory denotes conscious recollection of a previous experience. Much of the current interest in implicit memory is attributable to its relative immunity to conditions that cause profound changes in explicit memory. Examples of special populations who have shown normal performance on certain implicit memory measures despite significant explicit memory impairment include subjects with amnesia attributable to Korsakoff's disease or medial temporal lobe injury (e.g., Cermak, Talbot, Chandler, & Wolbarst, 1985; Graf & Mandler, 1984), Huntington's disease (e.g., Heindel, Salmon, Shults, Walicke, & Butters, 1989), and Alzheimer's disease (e.g., Keane, Gabrieli, Fennema, Growdon, & Corkin, 1991; Partridge, Knight, & Feehan, 1990).

A better understanding of the psychological and neural mechanisms that underlie amnesics' spared implicit memory could guide the rehabilitation of such patients. An example of how developments in basic and applied research can be mutually beneficial is provided by Glisky and Schacter (1987, 1989), who successfully trained a densely amnesic woman to learn a number of computer commands and skills that were necessary for employment in a data entry position. Previous research had shown that amnesics' retrieval of familiar words could be implicitly influenced by prior learning when the patients were cued with the first few letters of a word (e.g., Graf, Squire, & Mandler, 1984; Warrington & Weiskrantz, 1974). This finding led Glisky and

Schacter (see also Glisky, Schacter, & Tulving, 1986b) to develop the "method of vanishing cues" for teaching subjects to give the name of a computer command (e.g., SAVE) in response to its definition ("to store information on a disk"). Subjects were given as many initial letters as necessary to retrieve the name of the command that corresponded to the defined computer operation (e.g., SAV_). The number of letters decreased across subsequent trials (SAV_, SA_, S_) until the patient was able to give the command in response to the definition alone.

These efforts to teach computer operations to memory-impaired patients also have theoretical implications. Even when patients became quite accurate at producing the computer commands from definitions, they were typically unable to produce the command when the wording of the definition was changed. This inflexibility suggested that amnesics' memory was "hyperspecific" to the conditions of learning (Glisky, Schacter, & Tulving, 1986a; Schacter, 1985). Basic research on the hyperspecificity of implicit memory soon followed. In contrast to hyperspecificity observed in the studies of computer learning, Shimamura and Squire (1988) found that amnesic patients, after learning to recall the last word of a sentence when cued with the beginning of a previously studied sentence, were able to generalize this knowledge to paraphrased sentences as well as control subjects. Further research on learning the names of business-related documents suggests that such generalization ability increases with the amount of study and may depend on the familiarity or meaningfulness of the to-be-learned material (Butters, Glisky, & Schacter, 1993; see also Tulving, Hayman, & Macdonald, 1991).

The development of techniques to teach computer operations and other kinds of practically useful new knowledge to memory-impaired patients is, of course, limited by our currently incomplete understanding of the memory processes that are spared in amnesia. Although the method of vanishing cues was inspired by the effectiveness of partial cuing, we believe that the development of even more effective approaches will depend on a deeper understanding of those aspects of memory that are spared in amnesia. In what follows, we outline a cognitive neuroscience approach that promises to better specify the brain mechanisms of implicit memory.

PERCEPTUAL REPRESENTATION SYSTEM AND IMPLICIT MEMORY

Our approach to studying implicit memory begins with the hypothesis that many manifestations of implicit memory reflect changes in perceptual brain mechanisms. This general idea has been dubbed the Perceptual Representation System (PRS) hypothesis (Schacter, 1990, 1992, 1994; Tulving & Schacter, 1990), and it is similar to other theoretical accounts of implicit memory that have emphasized the importance of perceptual processes (Keane et al., 1991; Roediger, 1990; Squire, 1992, 1994). It is well established that different brain mechanisms control different perceptual domains such as the perception of objects (Humphreys & Riddoch, 1987; Kosslyn, Flynn, Amsterdam, & Wang, 1990) versus perception of words (Caplan, 1992; Coltheart, Sartori, & Job, 1987). As we discuss later, word perception can be further subdivided according to input modality, and these kinds of distinctions have implications for understanding implicit memory. The current review is limited to implicit memory for words, and its relationship to lexical brain mechanisms.[1]

Our review is also limited along another dimension. A number of investigators have suggested that a distinction must be drawn between perceptual and conceptual tests of implicit memory (cf., Blaxton, 1989; Roediger & McDermott, 1993; Roediger, Weldon, & Challis, 1989; Tulving & Schacter, 1990). In a typical implicit memory experiment subjects are presented with a list of words (the "study" or "presentation" list), and are induced to study these target materials by making a particular type of encoding judgment, such as rating the pleasantness of the words or counting the number of vowels. Later in the session the subjects are asked to perform a task that is ostensibly unrelated to the study list. For example, subjects might be given a series of words stems (APP_; e.g., Graf & Schacter, 1985) together with instructions to provide the first completion that comes to mind (APPLE). The test list is designed such that studied words can serve as answers to some of the test cues. *Repetition priming* refers to the increased probability of responding to test cues with target materials as a consequence of prior exposure to them. Stem completion is typically considered to be a perceptually driven test because the letter cues provide a perceptual cue for correct responses. Other perceptual implicit tasks include word fragment completion (A_P_E; e.g., Roediger, Weldon, Stadler, & Riegler, 1992; Tulving, Schacter, & Stark, 1982), and perceptual identification of words that are presented for very brief durations (e.g., 35 msec; Jacoby & Dallas, 1981). As discussed later, repetition priming in perceptual implicit tasks is typically sensitive to variables that influence the manner in which words are physically perceived, but insensitive to differences in semantic analysis. In contrast, conceptual implicit tasks are typically insensitive to perceptual variables but sensitive to semantic variables. Conceptual implicit tasks provide cues that are conceptually or semantically related to primed words. Conceptual implicit tasks include category instance production (FRUIT - ?; Srinivas & Roediger, 1990) and answering general knowledge questions (What is red and grows on trees?; Blaxton, 1989).

---

[1]The perceptual representation system hypothesis has also been advanced to account for visual object priming (Cooper, Schacter, Ballesteros, & Moore, 1992; Schacter & Cooper, 1993; Schacter, Cooper, & Treadwell, 1993).

PERCEPTUAL PRIMING

Research with college students has suggested that repetition priming on many implicit memory tasks is a presemantic phenomenon that is greatly influenced by perceptual variables. One important source of evidence for this conclusion is the finding that, unlike performance on explicit memory tests, many measures of implicit memory are uninfluenced by manipulating the level of semantic analysis. On typical explicit memory tests such as free recall or recognition, memory benefits from encoding tasks that focus subjects on the meaning of the to-be-remembered stimulus rather than on its physical attributes. This advantage of semantic encoding is the well-known levels-of-processing (LOP) effect (e.g., Craik & Tulving, 1975). In contrast, LOP manipulations typically do not affect priming on implicit tasks such as perceptual identification (Jacoby & Dallas, 1981), and word-fragment or word-stem completion (Roediger et al., 1992). Although small LOP effects are sometimes seen in implicit memory experiments (Challis & Brodbeck, 1992), in all likelihood they reflect the performance of some subjects who adopt explicit retrieval strategies (Bowers & Schacter, 1990; Roediger et al., 1992; Schacter, Bowers, & Booker, 1989). Whereas the foregoing results have been obtained with visual implicit memory tests, recent work on auditory identification and completion tasks indicates that auditory priming is little affected or unaffected by LOP manipulations that have large effects on explicit memory (Church & Schacter, 1994; Schacter & Church, 1992).

A second important finding is that repetition priming, but not explicit memory, is consistently reduced when the perceptual modality of the studied target is different from the tested stimulus. Priming on visual implicit tests such as word-fragment completion, word-stem completion, and word identification is reliably greater after visual presentation of words than after either auditory presentation or presentation of pictures (cf., Graf & Mandler, 1984; Jacoby & Dallas, 1981; Rajaram & Roediger, 1993; Schacter & Graf, 1989; Weldon & Roediger, 1987). Conversely, priming in auditory tasks such as auditory stem completion is greater after auditory than visual study (Bassili, Smith, & MacLeod, 1989; Jackson & Morton, 1984).

There has also been considerable interest in the question of whether priming depends on within-modality perceptual information—that is, whether priming is influenced by changing specific perceptual features of target items between study and test, such as the typefont of a word in the visual domain or the speaker's voice in the auditory domain. A primary theoretical motivation for studying the perceptual specificity of repetition priming concerns the differing predictions made by "abstractionist" versus "nonabstractionist" theories of repetition priming (e.g., Richardson-Klavehn & Bjork, 1988). Abstractionist theories contend that repetition priming of words operates at an abstract lexical level, such as orthographic or phonological representations of words, that is insensitive to the exact perceptual form in which words are presented (e.g., Carr, Brown, & Charalambous, 1989). Nonabstractionist theories posit that repetition priming reflects the retrieval or reinstatement of unique episodes from memory, and that retrieval of these episodes is dependent on the match in perceptual cues available at study and test (e.g., Jacoby & Brooks, 1984; Kolers & Roediger, 1984). Strongly abstractionist views cannot account for the aforementioned finding that priming is greatest when modality and other perceptual features of target stimuli are held constant between study and test. On the other hand, it has often been found that even when priming is reduced by a modality shift or attribute change, it is not entirely eliminated. The observation of significant cross-form priming undermines theories that exclusively rely on retrieval of perceptually specific episodes. In an attempt to resolve these disparities, Kirsner, Dunn, and Standen (1989) suggested that priming may reflect the independent contribution of separate form-specific and nonspecific mechanisms. We believe that Kirsner et al.'s distinction is heuristically valuable for emphasizing that perceptually specific mechanisms play an important, although not exhaustive, role in repetition priming. This allows us to move beyond the debate over abstractionist versus nonabstractionist theories to pose questions about the nature of the perceptual mechanisms that do have an influence on repetition priming.

Although the observation of modality effects suggests that visual and auditory perceptual systems make unique contributions to repetition priming, the evidence is mixed concerning the effects of within-modality manipulations of perceptual features. In the visual domain this issue has often been investigated by manipulating the typefont or case of visual words. Some studies have found priming to be sensitive to these variables (Jacoby & Hayman, 1987; Kolers & Roediger, 1984; Roediger & Blaxton, 1987), whereas others have not (Carr et al., 1989; Clarke & Morton, 1983; Rajaram & Roediger, 1993).

Recent studies have helped to better delineate the conditions under which such changes in typography might influence visual priming. Graf and Ryan (1990) obtained typographic sensitivity only when the orienting task required subjects to focus on the perceptual attributes of the primes. Graf and Ryan used atypical fonts in their experiments, and subsequent research has suggested that this may be an important factor. Brown and Carr (1993) found typographic sensitivity in lexical decision and speeded naming tasks only when the second occurrence of the word was in an atypical, handwritten form. They argued that subjects are more likely to access an abstract lexical representation when tested with typical typography, whereas atypically typography serves as a unique perceptual cue for retrieving a specific prior episode. Finally, Marsolek, Kosslyn, and Squire (1992) found modality and typographic sensitivity when word stems were presented to the left, but not the right, visual field. These visual field differences were presumed to reflect differences in the brain mechanism underlying priming in the cerebral hemispheres contralateral to the field of presentation. Marsolek et al. suggested that the perceptually sensitive priming effects arising from left visual field presentation reflect form-specific representation of words in the right hemisphere. In contrast, a left-hemisphere mechanism may represent words in an abstract form that is insensitive to these perceptual changes. Taken together, typography seems most likely to influence priming when perceptual features are attended at study (Graf & Ryan, 1990), the test typography provides a relatively unique perceptual cue for a prior episode (Brown & Carr, 1993), and processing of the target is biased toward right-hemisphere mechanisms (Marsolek et al., 1992).

Research on the typographic specificity of priming has recently been extended to amnesic Korsakoff's patients (Kinoshita & Wayland, 1993). When study/test typography was manipulated in a word fragment completion experiment, control subjects, but not amnesics, showed significantly greater priming when study/test typography was the same than when it was different. Interpretation of this study is limited by the lack of an explicit memory test, and the possibility that group differences reflect explicit retrieval by control subjects. However, this lack of specificity may reflect important differences in priming between amnesics and normal subjects. Though modality specificity has been previously observed in amnesics (Graf, Shimamura, & Squire, 1985), the lack of typographic specificity may reflect a medial temporal lobe contribution to within-modality specificity effects in normal subjects, a point to which we return when considering recent neuroimaging studies of priming.

Schacter and Church (1992) recently began to examine similar questions of within-modality specificity in auditory priming. Auditory repetition priming was examined by asking subjects to identify words that were masked by white noise (Experiments 1 and 2) or to complete single-syllable auditory word stems (Experiments 3, 4, and 5). Priming was measured as the difference in completion or identification rate for previously studied versus nonstudied words. Perceptual specificity was tested by varying the speaker's voice at study and test. All words were said in either a male or female voice, and the voice could be the same or different from study to test. Voice specificity effects were obtained in the stem completion tasks (Experiments 3 & 4), but not in the noise-masked word identification task (Experiments 1 & 2). In Experiment 5, the voice specificity effect on stem completion was eliminated when stems were masked with white noise. Thus, it appeared that the white noise interfered with the processes underlying voice specific priming. These results suggests that auditory priming can be sensitive to voice-specific information.

Subsequent research used a auditory identification task in which words were degraded by a low-pass filter to avoid the previously documented white-noise interference on voice specificity effects (Church & Schacter, 1994). Priming of low-pass filtered words was sensitive to study/test changes in speaker gender, emotional intonation, and fundamental frequency. These same variables had little or no effect on tests of explicit memory. The effects of fundamental frequency were extended to auditory stem completion priming, whereas study/test changes in loudness affected neither implicit stem completion nor explicit cued recall. These results suggest that the perceptual mechanism(s) underlying auditory priming include a representation of fundamental frequency or pitch.

Studies of auditory priming have recently been extended to amnesic patients. Schacter, Church, and Treadwell (1994) found that amnesics exhibited entirely normal priming effects on the identification in white noise task used previously by Schacter and Church (1992). Consistent with Schacter and Church's findings with college students, priming in both amnesics and control subjects was unaffected by study-to-test changes in speaker's voice. More recently, Schacter, Church, and Bolton (1995) examined auditory priming on the low-pass filter identification test, in which voice change effects have been observed in college students. Schacter et al. found that amnesic patients failed to exhibit more priming in a same-voice condition than in a different-voice condition, whereas matched control subjects did exhibit voice-specific priming. These observations, just like Kinoshita and Wayland's finding that amnesics did not exhibit font-specific visual priming, raise the possibility that some perceptual specificity effects in priming depend on brain systems that normally are associated with explicit memory.

In summary, research on repetition priming has suggested that it is largely a presemantic and modality-specific phenomenon. Although priming transfers to some extent from one modality to another, repetition priming is consistently greater within than between modalities. These and other features of priming suggest several characteristics of the brain mechanisms that play an important role in perceptual priming. First, data showing spared priming in amnesia suggests that the brain mechanisms of perceptual priming are largely independent of the medial temporal lobe structures that are typically damaged in amnesia. However, the evidence of abnormal perceptual specificity effects in amnesics (Kinoshita & Wayland, 1993; Schacter et al., 1995) raises the possibility that some kinds of priming may depend on hippocampus and related structures. Because amnesic patients show normal modality effects in priming (Graf et al., 1985), it seems likely that any role for the hippocampus in priming would be restricted to highly specific, within-modality perceptual information. Second, the brain mechanisms that support priming cannot be heavily involved in semantic processing or representation.

Recent neuropsychological and neuroimaging research that we consider next has suggested functional brain areas that meet these requirements.

BRAIN MECHANISMS OF LEXICAL PERCEPTION

Current neuropsychologically inspired models of word recognition (e.g., Coltheart, Curtis, Atkins, & Haller, 1993; Ellis & Young, 1988) suggest that separate functional modules are responsible for recognizing perceptual and semantic attributes of words. Neuropsychologists have described cases in which brain-damaged patients are able to analyze words in terms of their perceptual characteristics, but show impaired semantic analysis. Patients with "transcortical sensory aphasia" are often able to read visual words and repeat auditory words that they fail to comprehend (Coslett, Roeltgen, Rothi, & Heilman, 1987). This observation suggests that the perceptual analysis of words does not necessarily rely on semantic information. Other cases have shown that such neuropsychological dissociations between perceptual and semantic analysis can be modality specific.

In the visual domain, one patient was able to read aloud visual words, but was unable to sort them into semantic categories or match them to pictorial referents (Schwartz, Saffran, & Marin, 1980). Her reading extended to words with both regular and irregular grapheme–phoneme correspondence, suggesting that she retained access to the visual form of words rather than merely reading through a superficial process of grapheme-to-phoneme conversion. Funnel (1983) described a patient who was unable to make semantic relatedness judgments about words that she could read aloud. A similar patient could read visual words but was unable to sort them into semantic categories (Sartori, Masterson, & Job, 1987). Neither of the latter two patients could read pronounceable nonwords, so their word reading was probably not accomplished through grapheme-to-phoneme conversion. These patients suggest that distinct areas of the brain process visuoperceptual versus semantic information about visually presented words. We refer to the brain mechanism(s) responsible for processing the visual attributes of words as the *visual word form system* (following Warrington & Shallice, 1980).

An analogous, presemantic *auditory* word form system has been hypothesized to process the perceptual attributes of auditory word forms. Patients with "word-meaning deafness" show a specific impairment in comprehending spoken words. Kohn and Friedman (1986) described two word-meaning deafness patients who would sometimes fail to comprehend spoken words that they could repeat aloud. Despite this auditory comprehension deficit, they were able to comprehend the written form of the same words. These patients demonstrate a dissociation between the perceptual and semantic analysis of auditory word forms.

Converging evidence that separate neurological modules are involved in processing perceptual versus semantic attributes of words has been derived from modern functional imaging research using positron emission tomography (PET; for review, see Petersen & Fiez, 1993; Wise, Hardar, Howard, & Patterson, 1991). PET has suggested that the orthographic analysis of visual word forms depends significantly on a medial extrastriate region of the left occipital cortex and a left posterior region of the middle temporal gyrus (cf., Howard et al., 1992; Petersen, Fox, Snyder, & Raichle, 1990). In the auditory domain, PET studies suggest that left, posterior temporal/temporoparietal cortex activation is related to auditory or phonological processing of words (Howard et al., 1992; Petersen & Fiez, 1993; Petersen, Fox, Posner, Mintun, & Raichle, 1989; but see Wise et al., 1991, for a slightly different interpretation). PET research has also supported the neuropsychological inference that distinct functional/anatomical mechanisms support the semantic processing of words. Left lateralized areas of the medial frontal lobe become active when subjects briefly attend to the meaning of words (Petersen, Fox, Snyder, & Raichle, 1990), and some left temporal areas show increased activity with longer, more sustained semantic analysis (Demonet et al., 1992; Friston, Frith, Liddle, & Frackowski, 1991; Raichle et al., 1994). Although PET investigations of cognitive function are relatively young, and a variety of key methodological and conceptual issues still need to be worked out (for discussion, see Demonet, Wise, & Frackowiak, 1993), these studies suggest an emerging outline of the functional neuroanatomy of various kinds of word processing and representation.

In summary, neuropsychological and neuroimaging research has suggested that the perception of words is carried out by distinct, modality-specific, presemantic mechanisms: the visual and auditory word form systems. The PRS hypothesis asserts that these word form systems are involved in the perceptual priming phenomena reviewed earlier.

RECENT EVIDENCE LINKING PERCEPTUAL PRIMING TO LEXICAL BRAIN MECHANISMS

The hypothesis that the brain mechanisms controlling word perception may also be responsible for repetition priming has recently found some more direct support. The brain mechanisms of perceptual priming have begun to be investigated on neuropsychologically impaired patients, other than amnesics, who have difficulty with certain aspects of word perception and recognition. Other relevant evidence has come from PET.

PET was used to investigate the brain mechanisms of priming in a stem completion task (Squire et al., 1992). The effects of priming were assessed by measuring the blood flow difference between a baseline condition in which stems could not be completed with previously studied words compared to a priming condition in which half of the stems could be completed with previously studied words. The priming condition elicited a significant reduction in right posterior blood flow compared to the baseline. It is likely that this area of priming-sensitive activation corresponds to an area that previous PET research has suggested is involved in processing the preorthographic visual features of words (Petersen et al., 1989, 1990). Unexpectedly, Squire et al. also found that right, hippocampal activity increased in the priming task. Interpretation of this experiment is somewhat problematic, however, because primed stem completion rates (71.5%) were unusually high—in fact, nearly as high as the completion rates in an explicit cued-recall task (76.4%). Therefore, it is likely that the results are contaminated by the use of explicit retrieval strategies.

Direct evidence on this latter point is provided in a recent PET study of stem completion priming by Schacter, Alpert, Savage, Rauch, and Albert (in press). Schacter et al. used a shallow, nonsemantic encoding task in an attempt to weaken explicit memory, and thereby reduce the explicit contamination that apparently occurred in Squire et al.'s experiment. The general hypothesis was that with explicit contamination removed, the hippocampal activation reported by Squire et al. would no longer be observed, whereas the blood flow reduction in right occipital cortex would continue to be seen. Schacter et al. did indeed observe a much lower level of primed stem completion performance than did Squire et al. (approximately 30%), and internal analyses provided further evidence that explicit memory contamination did not occur. Most important, the major hypotheses were confirmed: Priming was associated with a significant blood flow reduction in right extrastriate occipital cortex (Brodmann area 19), together with no detectable changes in the hippocampus. These findings provide strong support for the general hypothesis that priming depends on perceptual brain mechanisms.

In a more recent experiment following up on Squire et al.'s (1992) initial stem completion priming results, Buckner et al. (1995) varied the case of target words between study and test—words were studied in lower case and tested in upper case. Although a semantic encoding task was used, as in the previous experiment, priming levels were considerably lower than in the same-case condition used in the Squire et al. (1992) experiment. This observation suggests that there was less of an explicit contamination effect in the different-case experiment than in the same-case experiment. Under these conditions, Buckner et al. replicated their earlier finding that priming was associated with a right-occipital decrease, but failed to observe any hippocampal activation. In addition, they also observed a priming-related decrease in a left extrastriate occipital region. However, they also noted that further analysis of the Squire et al. results revealed a left-occipital decrease as well. Schacter et al. (unpublished data), too, observed that priming was associated with a small decrease in left-occipital extrastriate cortex.

Schacter (1994) speculated that the foregoing PET data imply that the hippocampus plays some role in perceptual specificity effects in priming. The suggestion rests on the finding that (a) the hippocampus was activated after semantic encoding in a same-case condition (Squire et al., 1992) but not in a different-case condition (Buckner et al., 1995), and (b) the hippocampus was not activated in a same-case condition after nonsemantic encoding (Schacter et al., unpublished data). Taken together, these results imply that the hippocampal activation (or, more specifically, right hippocampal activation) occurs during primed stem completion when a "strong" episodic memory trace has been established by semantic encoding, and when a perceptually matching cue is provided, as in the same-case condition. Schacter (1994) further speculated that such hippocampal activation may be largely involuntary. As Moscovitch (1994) emphasized, the hippocampus can be viewed as a relatively "dumb" module that automatically provides outputs when cued with appropriate inputs. Thus, to the extent that the hippocampus plays a role in some perceptual specificity effects in priming, such effects may involve involuntary explicit memory (Schacter, 1987) rather than implicit memory. This idea is consistent with the previously mentioned failures to observe perceptual specificity effects in amnesic patients, which also imply some hippocampal or medial temporal involvement in this aspect of priming (for further discussion, see Schacter, 1994; Schacter et al., 1995).

The foregoing considerations indicate that any exclusive equation of perceptual priming with the activity of a visual word form system is probably too simplistic. In addition to the possible involvement of the hippocampus in some kinds of perceptual specificity effects, the fact that the strongest priming-related changes in the aforementioned PET studies were in right-occipital cortex contrast with other findings suggesting a left-hemisphere locus for visual word form processing (Howard et al., 1992; Petersen et al., 1990). As noted earlier, right-occipital extrastriate cortex appears to be involved in a kind of preorthographic visual analysis (Petersen et al., 1990). It appears that both left- and right-occipital subsystems can be involved in visual priming, but the exact nature of their contribution, and the conditions under which they contribute more and less to priming, remains to be elucidated.

Marsolek et al.'s (1992) experiments on visual hemifield priming that were discussed earlier also bear on these points. Their results suggested that a typographically sensitive priming mechanism may operate in the right hemisphere, whereas a mechanisms sensitive to abstract orthographies may control left-hemisphere priming. Although we suspect that the right hippocampus may be involved in these specificity effects, these results highlight again that different aspects of visual perceptual priming may depend on different subsystems associated with the left and right hemispheres.

Evidence concerning the brain systems involved in visual word priming has also been provided by studies of patients with reading deficits. Repetition priming has recently been investigated in a dyslexic patient, A.M., who had a left-occipitotemporal lesion and appeared to have impaired access to the visual representation of words (Carlesimo, Fadda, Sabbadini, & Caltagirone, 1994). A.M. showed impairments in reading and visual lexical decision despite preserved oral repetition and auditory lexical decision. Word comprehension seemed to rely on accessing semantics through phonology, because A.M. had great difficulty in discriminating between visually presented homophones (e.g., ATE and EIGHT). Priming was tested with a visual perceptual identification task, a visual stem completion task, and an auditory stem completion task. Little or no priming was observed in the two visual tasks, but auditory stem completion priming was normal. These results are consistent with the hypothesis that visual priming depends in part on a left-occipitotemporal brain mechanism that is crucial for the identification of visual words.

A different pattern of results was observed in a study of a patient who exhibited the phenomenon of letter-by-letter reading (Schacter, Rapscak, Rubens, Tharan, & Laguna, 1990). Letter-by-letter reading has been hypothe-sized to reflect either a visual word form deficit (Warrington & Shallice, 1980) or a deficit in the parallel transmission of information about individual letters to an intact visual word form system (Patterson & Kay, 1982). War-rington and Shallice (1980) suggested that letter-by-letter reading is accom-plished by a "reverse spelling" process that bypasses the damaged word form system. Schacter et al. (1990) reasoned that P.T. did not rely on reverse spelling because her spelling, but not her reading, was worse for regular than irregular words. This dissociation of P.T.'s spelling and reading sug-gested that Patterson and Kay's hypothesis of serial letter transmission to an intact visual word form system was more likely to account for her reading performance than was a reverse spelling process.

Schacter et al. (1990) assumed that P.T.'s visual word form system was intact, and therefore it was predicted that she would show normal visual priming despite her reading impairment. As predicted, P.T. consistently showed priming in a perceptual identification task. The results were unlikely to be contaminated by explicit memory because priming was sensitive to modality changes, whereas her recognition memory was modality inde-pendent. Finally, it was argued that her spared priming operated at the level of visual word forms rather than individual letters because she showed no priming of orthographically illegal nonwords. Based on the hypothesis that the visual word form system contributes to priming, these results suggest that letter-by-letter reading does not necessarily reflect an impaired word form system.

A recent study of repetition priming with a word meaning deafness patient, J.P., has provided direct support for the hypothesis that auditory priming does not depend on normal semantic analysis of auditory words (Schacter, McGlynn, Milberg, & Church, 1993). Similar to previously described word meaning deafness patients (e.g., Kohn & Friedman, 1986), J.P. had impaired auditory comprehension despite spared visual comprehension. However, he was able to process auditory words to an extent that allowed him to repeat them aloud and write them down. This pattern of linguistic functioning suggested intact presemantic processing of auditory word forms and, therefore, Schacter, McGlynn, et al. (1993) predicted that auditory priming would be normal. Priming was measured in two versions of the auditory identification task in which words were degraded either with white noise (Experiment 1) or with low-pass filtering (Experiment 2). J.P.'s priming was not significantly different from controls in both experiments. Although baseline differences between J.P. and controls cloud interpretation, these results are consistent with the PRS hypothesis and represent a promising first step in the study of the brain mechanisms of auditory priming.

PRACTICAL APPLICATIONS

As a whole, the research linking perceptual brain mechanisms to implicit learning is in it infancy, and many problems and paradoxes remain to be solved. Nevertheless, we think that the early work reviewed here is quite promising. We believe that the foremost practical application of this work is its potential as a foundation for the development of therapeutic techniques that would help neuropsychologically impaired patients compensate for their cognitive deficits. The basic theoretical idea of the existence of multiple forms of memory suggests that therapy for a patient with damage to one system should be tailored towards the forms of memory that are spared. This was the approach taken by Glisky and Schacter (1987, 1989; Glisky et al., 1986a, 1986b) in their attempts to teach complex new knowledge to amnesic patients.

Research on perceptual priming may not aid the advancement of techniques to teach patients to associate computer commands with their definitions because this is, by definition, a form of conceptual or semantic learning. However, research on the perceptual specificity of perceptual priming may, in retrospect, provide perspectives on why amnesic computer learning seemed to be hyperspecific. One possibility is that amnesics rely heavily on the output of PRS when they acquire new knowledge, whereas control subjects rely more on elaboratively encoded episodic information. Because amnesics depend more on a presemantic system to learn the task, their knowledge is often less flexible than is the knowledge acquired by control subjects.

Another intriguing possibility is raised by the idea that some perceptually specific forms of priming rely on involuntary explicit memory that depends on the hippocampus. Because the hippocampus and related structures are typically damaged in amnesic patients, and because the hippocampus also plays a role in encoding of episodic information (e.g., Squire, 1992), any episodic traces that are laid down by amnesic patients are probably quite weak or impoverished. Given such impoverished memory traces, amnesics may not find it useful to engage in voluntary or intentional retrieval of episodic information, and may instead rely on the degraded but involuntary and automatic outputs of the impaired hippocampal system. According to the speculations that we offered earlier, such dependence would also work toward "hyperspecific" learning in amnesic patients, because the hippocampus—even an impaired one—may only produce outputs in the presence of highly specific, matching cues. The method of vanishing cues, modeled after a stem completion task, likely encouraged a form of perceptually based learning, and hence may have encouraged hyperspecificity for both of the foregoing reasons. Subsequent research on amnesics' ability to generalize across semantically similar cuing conditions suggests that generalization ability may depend on how readily the to-be-learned information can be incorporated into the patient's preexisting knowledge base (Butters et al., 1993; Shimamura & Squire, 1988). Therefore, generalization may improve if the encoding task focused subjects on the relationship between the computer command and relevant preexisting knowledge.

Priming research may also have useful applications in patients with damage to cortical perceptual systems that subserve aspects of priming. To the extent that perceptual priming reveals the manner in which lexical and perceptual brain mechanism learn from and adapt to environmental events, a better understanding of the learning capabilities of different lexical/perceptual brain mechanisms may help patients such as Schacter et al.'s (1990) letter-by-letter reader, P.T., and Carlesimo et al.'s (1994) dyslexic, A.M., to learn compensatory reading strategies to help overcome their reading disabilities. Letter-by-letter reading is itself a compensatory strategy (Shallice, 1988). A.M. appeared to rely on a compensatory strategy of trying to comprehend visual words by accessing semantics through phonology. This was evidenced by his difficulty in discriminating between the meanings of visually presented homophones. More complete models of word recognition along with a better understanding of the learning capabilities of the component modules would be an invaluable aid to remedial therapy for patients with neuropsychological language impairments.

Although we have focused on priming in this paper, it is important to remember that other forms of implicit memory have also been studied and are potentially relevant to practical interventions in cases of memory disorders. It is known, for instance, that amnesic patients can learn various kinds of motor and cognitive skills in a normal or near-normal manner (for review, see Schacter, Chiu, & Ochsner, 1993; Squire, 1992, 1994). Moreover, motor skill learning is typically normal even in patients with Alzheimer's disease (e.g., Heindel et al., 1989) who exhibit severe explicit memory deficits and a rather mixed pattern of spared and impaired priming (cf., Albert & Moss, 1992; Huppert, 1991; Hyman, Damasio, Damasio, & Van Hoesen, 1989; Keane et al., 1991; Kopelman, 1992; Salmon & Heindel, 1992). However, there have been few systematic attempts to exploit these preserved mechanisms to help afflicted patients to acquire skills relevant to everyday activities (e.g., Dick, 1992). The need for such interventions is particularly acute in Alzheimer's disease, which afflicts 2% to 5% of the population over age 65, and results in economic costs in the United States that have been estimated at over $30 billion a year (Hyman et al., 1989). Although behavioral interventions cannot prevent the inevitable decline of Alzheimer patients, they might ease the burden on caretakers for significant portions of time (Dick, 1992). Perhaps this will be one of the new frontiers in which basic research on implicit memory and the brain is usefully applied to the practical concerns of everyday life.

REFERENCES

Albert, M. S., & Moss, M. B. (1992). The assessment of memory disorders in patients with Alzheimer's disease. In L. R. Squire & N. Butters (Eds.), *Neuropsychology of memory* (pp. 211–219). New York: Guilford.

Bassili, J. N., Smith, M. C., & MacLeod, C. M. (1989). Auditory and visual word-stem completion: Separating data-driven and conceptually driven processes. *Quarterly Journal of Experimental Psychology, 41A,* 439–453.

Blaxton, T. (1989). Investigating dissociations among memory measures: Support for a transfer-appropriate processing framework. *Journal of Experimental Psychology: Learning, Memory, and Cognition, 15,* 657–668.

Bowers, J. S., & Schacter, D. L. (1990). Implicit memory and test awareness. *Journal of Experimental Psychology: Learning, Memory, and Cognition, 16,* 404–416.

Brown, J. S., & Carr, T. H. (1993). Limits on perceptual abstraction in reading: Asymmetric transfer between surface forms differing in typicality. *Journal of Experimental Psychology: Learning, Memory, and Cognition, 19,* 1277–1296.

Buckner, R. L., Petersen, S. E., Ojemann, J. G., Miezin, F. M., Squire, L. R., & Raichle, M. E. (1995). Functional anatomical studies of explicit and implicit memory retrieval tasks. *The Journal of Neuroscience, 15,* 12–29.

Butters, M. A., Glisky, E. L., & Schacter, D. L. (1993). Transfer of new learning in memory-impaired patients. *Journal of Clinical and Experimental Neuropsychology, 15,* 219–230.

Caplan, D. (1992). *Language: Structure, processing, and disorders.* Cambridge, MA: MIT Press.

Carlesimo, G. A., Fadda, L., Sabbadini, M., & Caltagirone, C. (1993). Visual repetition priming for words relies on the access to the visual input lexicon: Evidence from a dyslexic patient. *Neuropsychologia, 32,* 1089–1100.

Carr, T. H., Brown, J. S., & Charalambous, A. (1989). Repetition and reading: Perceptual encoding mechanisms are very abstract but not very interactive. *Journal of Experimental Psychology: Learning, Memory, and Cognition, 15,* 763–778.

Cermak, L. S., Talbot, N., Chandler, K., & Wolbarst, L. R. (1985). The perceptual priming phenomenon in amnesia. *Neuropsychologia, 23,* 615–622.

Challis, B. H., & Brodbeck, D. R. (1992). Levels of processing affects priming in word fragment completion. *Journal of Experimental Psychology: Learning, Memory, and Cognition, 18,* 595–607.

Church, B. A., & Schacter, D. L. (1994). Perceptual specificity of auditory priming: Implicit memory for voice intonation and fundamental frequency. *Journal of Experimental Psychology: Learning, Memory, and Cognition, 20,* 521–533.

Clarke, R., & Morton, J. (1983). Cross modality facilitation in tachistoscopic word recognition. *Quarterly Journal of Experimental Psychology, 35A,* 79–96.

Coltheart, M., Curtis, B., Atkins, P., & Haller, M. (1993). Models of reading aloud: Dual-route and parallel-distributed-processing approaches. *Psychological Review, 100,* 589–608.

Coltheart, M., Sartori, G., & Job, R. (Eds.). (1987). *The cognitive neuropsychology of language.* London: Lawrence Erlbaum Associates.

Cooper, L. A., Schacter, D. L., Ballesteros, S., & Moore, C. (1992). Priming and recognition of transformed three-dimensional objects: Effects of size and reflection. *Journal of Experimental Psychology: Learning, Memory, and Cognition, 18,* 43–57.

Coslett, H. B., Roeltgen, D. P., Rothi, L. G., & Heilman, K. M. (1987). Transcortical sensory aphasia: Evidence for subtypes. *Brain and Language, 32,* 362–378.

Craik, F. I. M., & Tulving, E. (1975). Depth of processing and the retention of words in episodic memory. *Journal of Experimental Psychology: General, 104,* 268–294.

Demonet, J. F., Chollet, F., Ramsay, S., Cardebat, D., Nespoulous, J. L., Wise, R., Rascol, A., & Frackowiak, R. S. J. (1992). The anatomy of phonological and semantic processing in normal subjects. *Brain, 115,* 1753–1768.

Demonet, J. F., Wise, R., & Frackowiak, R. S. J. (1993). Language functions explored in normal subjects by positron emission tomography: A critical review. *Human Brain Mapping, 1,* 39–47.

Dick, M. B. (1992). Motor and procedural learning in Alzheimer's Disease. In L. Backman (Ed.), *Memory functioning in dementia* (pp. 135–150). New York: North-Holland Elsevier.

Ellis, A. W., & Young, A. W. (1988). *Human cognitive neuropsychology.* London: Lawrence Erlbaum Associates.

Friston, K. J., Frith, C. D., Liddle, P. F., & Frackowski, R. S. J. (1991). Investigating a network model of word generation with positron emission tomography. *Proceedings of the Royal Society of London, 244B,* 101–106.

Funnel, E. (1983). Phonological processes in reading: New evidence from acquired dyslexia. *British Journal of Psychology, 74,* 159–180.

Glisky, E. L., & Schacter, D. L. (1987). Acquisition of domain-specific knowledge in organic amnesia: Training for computer-related work. *Neuropsychologia, 25,* 893–906.

Glisky, E. L., & Schacter, D. L. (1989). Extending the limits of complex learning in organic amnesia: Computer training in a vocational domain. *Neuropsychologia, 27,* 107–120.

Glisky, E. L., Schacter, D. L., & Tulving, E. (1986a). Computer learning by memory-impaired patients: Acquisition and retention of complex knowledge. *Neuropsychologia, 24,* 313–328.

Glisky, E. L., Schacter, D. L., & Tulving, E. (1986b). Learning and retention of computer-related vocabulary in amnesic patients: Method of vanishing cues. *Journal of Clinical and Experimental Neuropsychology, 8,* 292–312.

Graf, P., & Mandler, G. (1984). Activation makes words more accessible, but not necessarily more retrievable. *Journal of Verbal Learning and Verbal Behavior, 23,* 553–508.

Graf, P., & Ryan, L. (1990). Transfer-appropriate processing for implicit and explicit memory. *Journal of Experimental Psychology: Learning, Memory, and Cognition, 16,* 978–992.

Graf, P., & Schacter, D. L. (1985). Implicit and explicit memory for new associations in normal and amnesic subjects. *Journal of Experimental Psychology: Learning, Memory, and Cognition, 11,* 501–518.

Graf, P., Shimamura, A. P., & Squire, L. R. (1985). Priming across the modalities and priming across category levels: Extending the domain of preserved function in amnesia. *Journal of Experimental Psychology: Learning, Memory, and Cognition, 11,* 386–396.

Graf, P., Squire, L. R., & Mandler, G. (1984). The information that amnesic patients do not forget. *Journal of Experimental Psychology: Learning, Memory, and Cognition, 10,* 164–178.

Heindel, W. C., Salmon, D. P., Shults, C. W., Walicke, P. A., & Butters, N. (1989). Neuropsychological evidence for multiple implicit memory systems: A comparison of Alzheimer's, Huntington's, and Parkinson's Disease. *Journal of Neuroscience, 9,* 582–587.

Howard, D., Patterson, K., Wise, R., Brown, W. D., Friston, K., Weiller, C., & Frackowiak, R. (1992). The cortical localisation of the lexicons: PET evidence. *Brain, 115,* 1769–1782.

Humphreys, G. W., & Riddoch, M. J. (1987). *Visual object processing: A cognitive neuropsychological approach.* London: Lawrence Erlbaum Associates.

Huppert, F. A. (1991). Age-related changes in memory: Learning and remembering new information. In F. Boller & J. Grafman (Eds.), *Handbook of neuropsychology* (pp. 123–147). New York: Elsevier.

Hyman, B. T., Damasio, H., Damasio, A. R., & Van Hoesen, G. W. (1989). Alzheimer's Disease. *Annual Review of Public Health, 10,* 115–140.

Jackson, A., & Morton, J. (1984). Facilitation of auditory word recognition. *Memory & Cognition, 12,* 358–574.

Jacoby, L. L., & Brooks, L. R. (1984). Nonanalytic cognition: Memory, perception, and concept learning. In G. H. Bower (Ed.), *The psychology of learning and motivation* (pp. 1–47). New York: Academic Press.

Jacoby, L. L., & Dallas, M. (1981). On the relationship between autobiographical memory and perceptual learning. *Journal of Experimental Psychology: General, 110,* 306–340.

Jacoby, L. L., & Hayman, C. A. G. (1987). Specific visual transfer in word identification. *Journal of Experimental Psychology: Learning, Memory, and Cognition, 13,* 456–463.

Keane, M. M., Gabrieli, J. D. E., Fennema, A. C., Growdon, J. H., & Corkin, S. (1991). Evidence for a dissociation between perceptual and conceptual priming in Alzheimer's disease. *Behavioral Neuroscience, 105,* 326–342.

Kinoshita, S., & Wayland, S. V. (1993). Effects of surface features on word-fragment completion in amnesic subjects. *American Journal of Psychology, 106,* 67–80.

Kirsner, K., Dunn, J. C., & Standen, P. (1989). Domain-specific resources in word recognition. In S. Lewandowsky, J. C. Dunn, & K. Kirsner (Eds.), *Implicit memory: Theoretical issues* (pp. 99–122). Hillsdale, NJ: Lawrence Erlbaum Associates.

Kohn, S. E., & Friedman, R. B. (1986). Word-meaning deafness: A phonological-semantic dissociation. *Cognitive Neuropsychology, 3,* 291–308.

Kolers, P. A., & Roediger, H. L. (1984). Procedures of mind. *Journal of Verbal Learning and Verbal Behavior, 23,* 425–449.

Kopelman, M. D. (1992). The "new" and the "old": Components of the anterograde and retrograde memory loss in Korsakoff and Alzheimer patients. In L. R. Squire & N. Butters (Eds.), *Neuropsychology of memory* (pp. 130–146). New York: Guilford.

Kosslyn, S. E., Flynn, R. A., Amsterdam, J. B., & Wang, G. (1990). Components of high-level vision: A cognitive neuroscience analysis and accounts of neurological syndromes. *Cognition, 34,* 203–277.

Marsolek, C. J., Kosslyn, S. M., & Squire, L. R. (1992). Form-specific visual priming in the right cerebral hemisphere. *Journal of Experimental Psychology: Learning, Memory, and Cognition, 18,* 492–508.

Moscovitch, M. (1994). Memory and working-with-memory: Evaluation of a component process model and comparisons with other models. In D. L. Schacter & E. Tulving (Eds.), *Memory systems 1994* (pp. 269–310). Cambridge, MA: MIT Press.

Partridge, F. M., Knight, R. G., & Feehan, M. (1990). Direct and indirect memory performance in patients with senile dementia. *Psychological Medicine, 20,* 111–118.

Patterson, K., & Kay, J. (1982). Letter-by-letter reading: Psychological description of a neurological syndrome. *Quarterly Journal of Experimental Psychology, 34A,* 411–441.

Petersen, S. E., & Fiez, J. A. (1993). The processing of single words studied with positron emission tomography. *Annual Review of Neuroscience, 16,* 509–530.

Petersen, S. E., Fox, P. T., Posner, M. I., Mintun, M., & Raichle, M. E. (1989). Positron emission tomographic studies of the processing of single words. *Journal of Cognitive Neuroscience, 1,* 153–170.

Petersen, S. E., Fox, P. T., Snyder, A., & Raichle, M. E. (1990). Activation of extra-striate and frontal cortical areas by visual words and word-like stimuli. *Science, 249,* 1041–1044.

Raichle, M. E., Fiez, J. A., Videen, T. O., MacLeod, A. C., Pardo, J. V., Fox, P. T., & Petersen, S. E. (1994). Practice-related changes in human brain functional anatomy during nonmotor learning. *Cerebral Cortex, 4,* 8–26.

Rajaram, S., & Roediger, H. L. (1993). Direct comparison of four implicit memory tests. *Journal of Experimental Psychology: Learning, Memory, and Cognition, 19,* 765–776.

Richardson-Klavehn, A., & Bjork, R. A. (1988). Measures of memory. *Annual Review of Psychology, 39,* 475–543.

Roediger, H. L. (1990). Implicit memory: Retention without remembering. *American Psychologist, 45,* 1043–1056.

Roediger, H. L., & Blaxton, T. A. (1987). Retrieval modes produce dissociations in memory for surface information. In D. S. Gorfein & R. R. Hoffman (Eds.), *Memory and cognitive processes: The Ebbinghaus centennial conference* (pp. 349–379). Hillsdale, NJ: Lawrence Erlbaum Associates.

Roediger, H. L., & McDermott, K. B. (1993). Implicit memory in normal human subjects. In H. Spinnler & F. Boller (Eds.), *Handbook of neuropsychology* (pp. 63–131). Amsterdam: Elsevier.

Roediger, H. L., Weldon, M. S., & Challis, B. H. (1989). Explaining dissociations between implicit and explicit measures of retention. In H. L. Roediger & F. I. M. Craik (Eds.), *Varieties of memory and consciousness: Essays in honour of Endel Tulving* (pp. 3–41). Hillsdale, NJ: Lawrence Erlbaum Associates.

Roediger, H. L., Weldon, M. S., Stadler, M. A., & Riegler, G. L. (1992). Direct comparison of two implicit memory tests: Word fragment and word stem completion. *Journal of Experimental Psychology: Learning, Memory, and Cognition, 18,* 1251–1269.

Salmon, D. P., & Heindel, W. C. (1992). Impaired priming in Alzheimer's disease: Neuropsychological implications. In L. R. Squire & N. Butters (Eds.), *Neuropsychology of memory* (pp. 179–187). New York: Guilford.

Sartori, G., Masterson, J., & Job, R. (1987). Direct-route reading and the locus of lexical decision. In M. Coltheart, G. Sartori, & R. Job (Eds.), *The cognitive neuropsychology of language* (pp. 59–78). London: Lawrence Erlbaum Associates.

Schacter, D. L. (1985). Multiple forms of memory in humans and animals. In N. M. Weinberger, J. L. McGaugh, & G. Lynch (Eds.), *Multiple forms of memory in humans and animals* (pp. 351–379). New York: Guilford.

Schacter, D. L. (1987). Implicit memory: History and current status. *Journal of Experimental Psychology: Learning, Memory, and Cognition, 13,* 501–518.

Schacter, D. L. (1990). Perceptual representation systems and implicit memory: Toward a resolution of the multiple memory system debate. In A. Diamond (Ed.), *The development and neural bases of higher cognitive functions* (pp. 543–571). New York: Annals of the New York Academy of Sciences.

Schacter, D. L. (1992). Priming and multiple memory systems: Perceptual mechanisms of implicit memory. *Journal of Cognitive Neuroscience, 4,* 244–256.

Schacter, D. L. (1994). Priming and multiple memory systems: Perceptual mechanisms of implicit memory. In D. L. Schacter & E. Tulving (Eds.), *Memory systems 1994* (pp. 233–268). Cambridge, MA: MIT Press.

Schacter, D. L., Alpert, N. M., Savage, C. R., Rauch, S. L., & Albert, M. S. (in press). Conscious recollection and the human hippocampal formation: Evidence from positron emission tomography. *Proceedings of the National Academy of Sciences.*

Schacter, D. L., Bowers, J., & Booker, J. (1989). Intention, awareness, and implicit memory: The retrieval intentionality criterion. In S. Lewandowsky, J. C. Dunn, & K. Kirsner (Eds.), *Implicit memory: Theoretical issues* (pp. 47–65). Hillsdale, NJ: Lawrence Erlbaum Associates.

Schacter, D. L., Chiu, C. Y. P., & Ochsner, K. N. (1993). Implicit memory a selective review. *Annual Review of Neuroscience, 16,* 159–182.

Schacter, D. L., & Church, B. A. (1992). Auditory priming: Implicit and explicit memory for words and voices. *Journal of Experimental Psychology: Learning, Memory, and Cognition, 18,* 915–930.

Schacter, D. L., Church, B. A., & Bolton, E. (1995). Implicit memory in amnesic patients: Impairment of voice-specific priming. *Psychological Science, 6,* 20–25.

Schacter, D. L., Church, B., & Treadwell, J. (1994). Implicit memory in amnesic patients: Evidence for spared auditory priming. *Psychological Science, 5,* 20–25.

Schacter, D. L., & Cooper, L. A. (1993). Implicit and explicit memory for novel visual objects: Structure and function. *Journal of Experimental Psychology: Learning, Memory, and Cognition, 19,* 995–1009.

Schacter, D. L., Cooper, L. A., & Treadwell, J. (1993). Preserved priming of novel objects in patients with memory disorders. *Psychological Science, 4,* 331–335.

Schacter, D. L., & Graf, P. (1989). Modality specificity of implicit memory for new associations. *Journal of Experimental Psychology: Learning, Memory, and Cognition, 15,* 3–12.

Schacter, D. L., McGlynn, S. M., Milberg, W. P., & Church, B. A. (1993). Spared priming despite impaired comprehension: Implicit memory in a case of word meaning deafness. *Neuropsychologia, 7,* 107–118.

Schacter, D. L., Rapscak, S. Z., Rubens, A. B., Tharan, M., & Laguna, J. (1990). Priming effects in a letter-by-letter reader depend upon access to the word form system. *Neuropsychologia, 28,* 1079–1094.

Schwartz, M. F., Saffran, E. M., & Marin, O. S. M. (1980). Fractionating the reading process in dementia: Evidence for word-specific print-to-sound associations. In M. Coltheart, K. Patterson, & J. C. Marshall (Eds.), *Deep dyslexia* (pp. 259–269). London: Routledge & Kegan Paul.

Shallice, T. (1988). *From neuropsychology to mental structure.* Cambridge, England: Cambridge University Press.

Shimamura, A. P., & Squire, L. R. (1988). Long-term memory in amnesia: Cued recall, recognition memory, and confidence ratings. *Journal of Experimental Psychology: Learning, Memory, and Cognition, 14,* 763–770.

Squire, L. R. (1992). Memory and the hippocampus: A synthesis of findings with rats, monkeys, and humans. *Psychological Review, 99,* 195–231.

Squire, L. R. (1994). Declarative and nondeclarative memory: Multiple brain systems supporting learning and memory. In D. L. Schacter & E. Tulving (Eds.), *Memory systems 1994* (pp. 203–231). Cambridge, MA: MIT Press.

Squire, L. R., Ojemann, J. G., Miezin, F. M., Petersen, S. E., Videen, T. O., & Raichle, M. E. (1992). Activation of the hippocampus in normal humans: A functional anatomical study of memory. *Proceedings of the National Academy of Science, 89,* 1837–1841.

Srinivas, K., & Roediger, H. L. (1990). Classifying implicit tests: Category association and anagram solution. *Journal of Memory and Language, 29,* 389–412.

Tulving, E., Hayman, C. A. G., & Macdonald, C. A. (1991). Long-lasting perceptual priming and semantic learning in amnesia: A case experiment. *Journal of Experimental Psychology: Learning, Memory, and Cognition, 17,* 595–617.

Tulving, E., & Schacter, D. L. (1990). Priming and human memory systems. *Science, 247,* 301–305.

Tulving, E., Schacter, D. L., & Stark, H. A. (1982). Priming effects in word-fragment completion are independent of recognition memory. *Journal of Experimental Psychology: Learning, Memory, and Cognition, 8,* 336–342.

Warrington, E. K., & Shallice, T. (1980). Word-form dyslexia. *Brain, 103,* 99–112.

Warrington, E. K., & Weiskrantz, L. (1974). The effect of prior learning on subsequent retention in amnesic patients. *Neuropsychologia, 12,* 419–428.

Weldon, M. S., & Roediger, H. L. (1987). Altering retrieval demands reverses the picture superiority effect. *Memory & Cognition, 15,* 269–280.

Wise, E., Hardar, U., Howard, D., & Patterson, K. (1991). Language activation studies with positron emission tomography. In *Exploring brain functional anatomy with positron emission tomography* (pp. 218–234). Chichester, England: Wiley (Ciba Found. Symp. 163).

CHAPTER TWELVE

Memory and Attention

William Hirst
Elizabeth Pinner
New School for Social Research

We find ourselves in a definitional nightmare. As we conceive of our task, we are to chart the relation between attention and memory or, more narrowly, to determine whether attention is necessary for memory and, if it is, how attending affects memorizing and remembering. Our problem is that there is simply no consensus on the nature of either memory or attention. It is not merely that there are variations on a theme; rather, different researchers depict extreme opposites. If we are ever to make headway on our main task of mapping the relation between attention and memory, then we must unravel some of this confusion, or at least firmly stake claim to the theoretical territory in which we feel most comfortable. Hopefully, in doing so, we can proceed with charting the relation between memory and attention without becoming caught in a murky swirl of competing theories.

ATTENTION

Let us begin by considering attention. In his brilliant classic *The Principles of Psychology*, William James (1950) wrote "Everyone knows what attention is. It is the taking possession of the mind, in clear and vivid form, of one out of what seems several simultaneously possible objects or trains of thought. Focalization, concentration, of consciousness are of its essence." Psychologists have been able to capture James' phenomenological description of attention in various widely used experimental paradigms. For instance, they have contrasted conditions in which subjects reliably report either states of attention or inattention (see Holender, 1986, for a review). Alternatively, they have created states of attention and inattention by presenting subjects with two concurrent messages and then giving the subjects a demanding task to perform on one of the messages. If subjects follow these instructions, they can attend only to the task-relevant message (again, see Holender, 1986). The problem, then, is not with measuring attention or realizing it experimentally; rather, dissension surfaces when translating James' seemingly straightforward phenomenological description into precise cognitive terms.

There are two radically different ways of talking about the phenomenon of attention (see Hirst, 1986, 1994 for reviews). These two approaches adopt distinct ontological stances. In one case, the approach assumes that attention is something that people have. Scholars adopting this perspective usually try to find some mental mechanism or structure to associate with attention. They view mental resources as fuel that drives processing (Kahneman, 1973; Norman & Bobrow, 1975), or as mechanisms with limited capacities, such as short-term memory (Wickens, 1980, 1984). They treat attention as the device people use to place the outside world on a Cartesian stage, to use Dennett's (1991) term, envisioning it as a flashlight (Schulman, Remington, & McLean, 1979), an enhancement of neural activity (Desimone, Albright, Gross, & Bruce, 1984), or a filtering or attenuation of unwanted stimuli (Broadbent, 1958; Treisman, 1969). According to this perspective, people cannot attend to two things simultaneously because they have limited resources or mental mechanisms of finite capacity. Performance breaks down when a task requires more resources than an organism has available. The point we want to emphasize here is that such theorizing equates attention with something people have—be it a pool of resources or a collection of mechanisms.

Now consider an alternative approach to attention. Here it is claimed that attention simply does not exist as a mechanism, structure, or faculty; rather, it is a consequence of forms of processing other than those that might be distinctly labeled attentive, for instance, perceptual or motoric processing. The phenomenological experience of "attending" to something is simply the outcome of seeing, feeling, smelling, tasting, or acting, not of training a flashlight, activating a filter, or enhancing the firing of a neuron. When you attend to a flower and not to other objects in the garden, you simply are seeing the flower. What aspects of the flower you see will depend on your intentions or goals and the perceptual skills you possess. You may attend more to its color than its shape because you are concerned about the garden's color scheme. And you may fail to attend to its stamen or the texture of its leaves because you are basically an inexperienced gardener without the necessary skills to notice these subtleties. A more botanically astute gardener might hone in on just these features.

In this view, what one attends to depends at least on (a) the implicit or explicit goals individuals might face and (b) the cognitive skills they have available to accomplish these goals. These are what should be considered by a theorist of attention, not some putative "attentional mechanism." People have difficulty attending to two things at once because they do not possess the necessary skills to process the two tasks simultaneously (see Hirst, 1986; Hirst & Kalmar, 1987; Hirst, Spelke, Reaves, Caharack, & Neisser, 1980; Neisser, 1976). They can overcome these apparent limits on divided attention by acquiring new cognitive skills. In doing so, they can learn to performing mind-boggling feats, as when a cocktail pianist talks with customers as she plays their requests (Allport, Altonis, & Reynolds, 1972) or when a specially trained student reads and writes simultaneously (Hirst et al., 1980). These achievements reflect not a change in or circumnavigation of internal mechanisms, but the acquisition of new and relevant skills.

It is incorrect to think in these instances that people are developing general attentional skills. The skills people learn in such situations are incredibly specific. They might learn to attend selectively or more accurately, to see the distinctive features of a Rothko painting but not those of a Pollack, to hear their name over the hubbub of a party but not the name of their cousin, or to type and talk simultaneously but not to type and sing at the same time. When one speaks of attentional skills, one is not referring to a generalized ability to attend, but to a specific ability to "read" a Rothko, hear a specific name, or type while talking.

Thus, attention could simply be a matter of responding to task demands with the appropriate cognitive skills. To attend is to see, hear, taste, smell, or act. One attends to what one sees, hears, tastes, smells, or acts upon, and limits on selective and divided attention depend on the available skills. Logan (1988) offered a precise realization of this general approach in his discussion of automaticity. He argued that a new memory trace is formed every time a task is performed. Consequently, the processes underlying the performance of a task are multiply represented after practice. Under these circumstances, people do not need to construct the processes needed to perform the task; rather, they merely have to look them up in memory. They perform a task automatically when they can completely rely on a rapid retrieval of the needed processes from memory. From this perspective, attention is related to the process of constructing how to carry out a task.

One final comment: Our discussion up to now has treated attention as an all-or-none phenomenon—you either attend to stimuli or you do not. But you can attend in degree—intentionally or absentmindedly, with concentration or without. From a structural perspective, the degree to which you attend depends on the mechanisms you engage or the resources you employ. In the case of partial attention, you are only partially using the available and relevant mechanisms or resources. From a process perspective, you are not partially using a mechanism, but employing different processes. The phenomenological experience of only partially attending should directly reflect the engaged processes.

MEMORY

The field of attention, then, swirls around two extremes: a search for mechanisms and a denial of the existence of a mechanism. The field of memory may not be quite as tumultuous, but it also nightmarishly swings between seeming polar opposites. To some extent, the struggles in the domain of attention are echoed in the definitional crises psychologists face when confronting memory. These crises revolve around an intense debate over whether memory should be properly thought of as a structure or a process. The issue has been most clearly engaged in investigations of short-term and long-term store (see Klatzky, 1980, for an introductory review), but the same issue figures in debates about long-term memory, the main interest of this paper.

It is now widely accepted that we must "divide" long-term memory, in part because performance on direct and indirect tests of long-term memory clearly differs (Schacter, 1989, 1992; Squire, 1992). For instance, performance on a direct memory task is subject to the effects of interference and depth of processing and is disrupted in amnesics, whereas performance on an indirect memory task is relatively free from the effects of interference and depth of processing and remains intact in amnesics (see Schacter, 1989, for a review).

We can characterize the needed division of long-term memory by distinguishing between *memory images* and *memory beliefs* (Hirst, 1990, 1994; also Johnson, Hashtroudi, & Linsday, 1993; Johnson & Hirst, 1991). In both the direct and indirect memory tasks, the image of, for example, a previously presented word, may come to mind. This memory image may be vivid and detailed, or faint and fragmented. It may be elaborated, with information about the spatiotemporal context in which the word occurred, the orthography of the word, the color of the background, and so on, or it may be impoverished, with the only available information being the word itself. People can assign to a memory image a memory belief that the image refers to an event from the personal past. A stem completion task, for instance, does not require them to make this assignment, but a cued recall task does: For the stem completion task, one need only say what comes to mind; for the cued recall task, one must not only say what comes to mind, but also assert that it appeared at a specific time and place in the personal past.

Thus, the experimental results suggest that there are two kinds of memories: those consisting of both a memory image and an associated memory belief, and those consisting of the memory image alone. Psychologists locate the origin of such memory beliefs in different mental spaces, some using a structural framework to guide their theorizing (Squire, 1992; Tulving & Schacter, 1990), others employing a processing framework (Hirst, 1993; Johnson & Hirst, 1991; Roediger, 1990). According to structure-oriented researchers, two discrete, encapsulated systems exist, for example, an explicit memory system that endows a memory image with a memory belief and an implicit memory system that does not (Schacter, 1987). Memory beliefs are inherent features of retrieval from explicit memory, whereas they do not accompany the retrieval of an implicit memory. The experimental results are accounted for by assuming that these two memories have different properties. Explicit memory is affected by the depth with which information is encoded and is susceptible to interference, whereas implicit memory is not. Moreover, explicit memory is mediated by the brain structures destroyed in amnesic patients, whereas implicit memory is mediated by brain structures that remain intact in amnesic patients.

Alternatively, process-oriented researchers posit that a memory belief is constructed out of the features of the memory image. People must endow the memory image with a memory belief. The belief is an adscititious feature of the retrieval of a memory image, growing out of not a mental structure, but myriad judgmental processes. People construct the belief by judging that the image contains sufficient spatiotemporal information, is vivid or rapidly retrieved, or follows from other recollections (Kelley & Linsday, 1992; Manier & Hirst, 1994; see also Whittlesea, Jacoby, & Girard, 1990). Inasmuch as the content of a memory image can differ from instance to instance, the degree to which people can justifiably construct a memory belief also will differ from instance to instance. Researchers adopting a processing perspective explore the relation between the content of a memory image, the conditions that affect this content, and the processes underlying the construction of a memory belief (Johnson et al., 1993; Johnson & Hirst, 1991). Careful analysis of task demands is particularly important. Such analysis is sufficient to explain the dissociation between performance on indirect and direct tests of memory. For instance, a stem completion task does not demand that subjects build a richly elaborated memory image, nor does it demand that subjects construct from the image a memory belief. As a result, performance on this task, and presumably other indirect tests of memory, should not depend on the depth with which the material was originally encoded. On the other hand, a cued recall task does demand that people make a memory judgment and, consequently, motivates subjects to construct richly elaborated memory images. Success at this task should depend on the depth with which the material was originally encoded. Moreover, if one posits that amnesia disrupts the encoding of elaborate mnemonic representations, as several researchers have (Hirst, 1990, 1993; Johnson & Hirst, 1991), then one would expect amnesia to depress performance in direct memory tasks, but not performance in indirect memory tasks. Clearly, one does not have to posit separate memory systems to account for the extant experimental data.

RELATING ATTENTION AND MEMORY

The way we envision the relation between attention and memory—indeed, even the questions we ask about attention and memory—will depend on where we place ourselves in this tortuous landscape of definitional confusion. For instance, from the perspective of a structuralist, a central problem in charting the relation between memory and attention is: Why does the employment of an attentional mechanism—the machinery that brings an object or train of thought into mental focus—benefit memory? This question does not arise if one adopts a processing approach, inasmuch as attentional mechanisms simply do not exist. Rather, from a processing point of view, we need to concentrate on the skills or processes employed in different tasks and how these skills might benefit memory.

Presently, no definitive evidence exists supporting one approach over another. We cannot safely opt for a structural or process approach by confidently turning to the extant empirical work. Rather, if we want to avoid a nightmarish tangle of conflicting questions and presuppositions and proceed with clarity in our exploration of the relation between attention and memory, then we simply must make our theoretical biases clear and proceed from there. Thus, with some apology, we build the rest of the chapter around a processing rather than structural approach to attention and memory. We choose this option because, as we hope becomes clear, we think that it perspicaciously highlights many interesting connections between memory and attention. In particular, as noted, we ask how the processes eliciting a sense of attending relate to the processes that lead to good retention. In order to answer this question, we make six assumptions, which to a large extent define our processing approach to attention and memory. We list them here without much comment; their relation to issues of memory and attention are worked out in the next section.

First, we assume that the processing people undertake is motivated by the goals they adopt or the demands of the task at hand. The claim that human behavior is goal directed has a long history and, although it is not universally embraced, it has been a working assumption in many psychological theories.

Second, we assume that attention is a consequence of processing, not the application of a mechanism. As we have already acknowledged, there is no firm way to empirically and definitively support this claim. It is our working assumption or postulate. In what follows, we use *attention* as a shorthand term, a generic label, for seeing, hearing, touching, smelling, thinking, and so on. Our use of the word *attention* should not be read as referring to a mechanism, but cognitive processes involved in acts such as perceiving, thinking, or imagining.

Third, we assume that not all processing leads to the phenomenological experience of attending. The next few assumptions articulate which processing creates a feeling of attending.

Thus, fourth, we assume that although the specification of which processes elicit a sense of attending is, to a large extent, an empirical issue, some general principles are possible. Specifically, what people attend to depends on the extent to which the product of any line of processing is central to the goal. The processing people undertake is often hierarchically structured. They may have the goal of inspecting a garden, but this goal involves many subgoals, including looking at flowers. The subgoals may involve sub-sub-goals, for example, the analysis of the shape of the petals and the height of the plant. We say that the processing is hierarchically structured because each goal in the hierarchy has associated with it a process or set of processes. A core claim of our processing approach to attention, and one that we believe accords with phenomenological experience, is that inasmuch as the goal of seeing the flowers is closer to the main goal of inspecting the garden than the subgoal of analyzing the petals and leaves of the flowers, people are more likely to have the phenomenological sense of attending to the flower than attending to the petals or leaves. Along the same lines, when faced with the goal of putting on their shoes, people may attend to tying a shoelace, but not to the specific motor activity of their fingers. That is, they are less likely to attend to features that are products of processing lower down in the hierarchy. The assumption has an almost tautological flavor to it. If the goal is to look at the flower, then, of course, what one sees or attends to is the flower, not necessarily its stamen. However, if the goal is to look at the stamen, then that is just what one attends to.

Fifth, we assume that the elaboration of material usually requires processes that elicit a sense of attending. Without the conscious awareness that accompanies such states, people can only form a fairly shallow representation of the world. This claim is crucial to our discussion. Since the early work of Poetzl (1917), psychologists have tried to determine how deeply we process subliminally presented stimuli. The first author has reviewed this evidence elsewhere (Hirst, 1986; Hirst, 1994; see also the discussion of Greenwald, 1992). As far as we can determine, when a rigorous criterion for subliminal perception is adopted—a so-called objective threshold (Cheesman & Merikle, 1984, 1986; Merikle, 1992)—it is difficult to obtain reliable evidence for unconscious semantic processing. However, as the criterion is loosened and material is presented in what might be called the "twilight of consciousness," processing the meaning of the presented material is possible. There is no evidence that even with this weaker criterion subjects elaborate on the material, going beyond its meaning to form associations with prior knowledge.

Finally, we assume that how easily people construct a memory belief depends on how elaborately and deeply they encoded the stimuli. The more information subjects have about the origin of a memory image, the more justified they feel in constructing a memory belief (Hirst, 1990; Kelley & Linsday, 1992; Manier & Hirst, 1995). It follows, and the empirical evidence verifies this point, that depth of processing affects memory images with an associated memory belief, so-called explicit memories, more than the elicitation of memory images per se, so-called implicit memory. Consequently, how easily a memory image is elicited should be not terribly dependent on how elaborately or deeply it was initially encoded.

From a processing perspective, then, attending to an object or train of thought should benefit the construction of a memory belief to the extent that the processing eliciting this sense of attending requires deep or elaborative encoding of the material. When one is attending to the wrong aspects of the target (e.g., the number of *es* in a target word rather than the word's meaning), no matter how intensely a person feels that he or she is attending, memory will suffer. Moreover, one may not be able to process things deeply or elaboratively without eliciting the sense of attending. In states of inattention, processing is at best shallow. It is easy, then, to see why common sense dictates that memory—at least, so-called explicit memory—requires attention: A state of inattention ensures shallow processing, which in turn ensures that it will be difficult to justify a memory belief. This does not mean that memory images cannot be formed under conditions of inattention. It may be possible to form memory images without accompanying memory beliefs—implicit memories—without processing stimuli to a level that elicits a sense of attending. Deep or elaborative encoding is less important for implicit memories.

APPLYING THE PRINCIPLES

In this section, we want to follow up on our predictions and explore memory and attention in three different contexts: subliminal learning, implicit learning, and explicit learning and implicit evocation.

Subliminal Learning

We begin by examining an experimentally contrived instance of inattention. Here material is presented to subjects so quickly that they claim not to see it. Is any information retained under such conditions of inattention, that is, is there any evidence of *subliminal learning?* According to our assumptions, whatever information is retained, it should not be elaborately enough represented to support recognition or recall. And this appears to be the case: Subjects fail to report even seeing it, let alone remembering it after a delay. The challenging question is: Does the subliminally presented material form enough of a mnemonic trace to support the formation of a memory image, even if it is not rich enough to support the construction of a memory belief? Or, to put it another way, can the subliminally presented material form an implicit memory? We would predict that the answer is "yes." Inasmuch as the subjects are not attending to the material, the representation formed of the material is at best unelaborated (by Assumption 5). Such a shallow representation would make constructing a memory belief difficult, if not impossible (by Assumption 6). The representation, however, could, at least theoretically, support the elicitation of a memory image (again, Assumption 6).

The extant evidence suggests that subliminally presented material can form an implicit memory. Marcel (1983a, 1983b) showed that the subliminal presentation of a semantic associate can facilitate semantic priming of a superliminal target. For priming to occur, some retention is necessary, inasmuch as there is a delay between the preceding associate and the target. The delay is usually quite short, however—in the range of a second or two in the Marcel studies. What about the long-term retention of subliminally presented material?

The *mere exposure effect* offers an example of this kind of subliminal learning. A brief exposure to an item will increase subjects' preference for that item not just for a few seconds, but for minutes or more (Kunst-Wilson & Zajonc, 1980). The exposure need not be conscious, although the effect may be more robust if it is conscious (Bornstein, 1993; Kunst-Wilson & Zajonc, 1980; Mandler, 1985; Mandler, Nakamura, & Van Zandt, 1987). For example, when visual figures such as irregular octagons were flashed several times to subjects so fast that the subjects could not subsequently recognize them, the subjects still chose the target figure in a preference test more often than they would have without the prior presentation. The memory established during the presentation phase of the experiment could support a preference judgment, but not a recognition judgment. It would appear that implicit, but not explicit, memories can be formed when material is presented below the threshold of awareness.

Implicit Learning

Sometimes people may clearly see stimuli, but fail to notice features or relations between and within the stimuli. Subliminal perception is not involved. People claim not to notice what if pointed out to them they could unquestionably see. Do subjects in such circumstances form memories of these unnoticed relations, what we will call *implicit learning?* The answer, of course, depends on how deeply they encode the material. If they are truly not attending to the relations or features, then according to our assumptions, they may form mnemonic representations. These representations may be elaborate enough to support the formation of a memory image, but not the construction of a memory belief.

Several lines of experimentation have documented implicit learning. In studies of artificial grammar, subjects appear to learn grammatical rules generating structured strings of letters, even if they cannot articulate these rules (Reber, 1967, 1989; Reber & Allen, 1978). Similarly, in studies in which subjects must learn about the principles governing a transportation system, learning appears to be implicit: Subjects learn the principles without being able to articulate them (Berry & Broadbent, 1968; Broadbent, Fitzgerald, & Broadbent, 1986).

Lewicki, Hill, and Bizot (1988) and Lewicki, Hill, and Czyewska (1992; see also Bargh, 1993) demonstrated the implicit learning of contingencies in social judgment tasks. They presented subjects with pictures of women with short or long hair. Subjects heard short stories about each woman, indicating that they were either kind or capable. Personality and hair length were contingent; for example, long-haired women were always kind. Following this presentation, subjects judged the personality of unfamiliar women in a new set of pictures. Although subjects did not notice the relation between hair length and personality, they nevertheless used the contingency when making subsequent social judgments.

Nissen and Bullemer (1987) used a dual-task methodology to examine the effects of attention on memory. Subjects practiced a serial reaction time task, in which the position of an asterisk on a screen signaled which of four corresponding buttons subjects should press. Successive positions of the asterisk were either random or followed a repeating, 10-step sequence (DBCACBDCBA). The sequence was repeated without pause, so that there was no indication of when one sequence ended and another began. In some conditions, subjects also performed a concurrent task. Nissen and Bullemer measured learning by tracking decreases in response time. Subjects learned the repeating sequence more rapidly than they did the random sequence, indicating that they had picked up the organization in the series. Moreover, the presence of a secondary task did not interfere with learning. This latter result suggests that attention was unnecessary for this kind of learning. Interestingly, Nissen and Bullemer also found that amnesic patients learned the repeating sequence faster than they did the random sequence, but they could not verbalize their knowledge.

Finally, Manier and Hirst (1995) showed that subjects can guide recognition by utilizing information about an unnoticed contingency between the spatial location of a word on a CRT screen and its membership in one of four semantic categories. Subjects were not consciously using the contingency when making a positive recognition judgment, inasmuch as they were not even aware that the contingency existed. Nevertheless, its unconscious influence led to a conscious sense of recognition, even for semantically related distractors.

In each of these cases, subjects consciously processed part of the stimulus array, but not other parts. In many cases, the implicit knowledge they acquired clearly involved at most the formation of simple associations or the encoding of exemplars. In the work of Lewicki and his colleagues, for instance, subjects only needed to form simple associations between hair length and personality trait. Similarly, in Manier and Hirst subjects had to form simple associations between spatial location and semantic category.

The learning observed in Nissen and Bullemer (1987) also may only involve "simple associations." Curran (1994) contrasted the learning of two structured sequences. One sequence type involved simple associations: One element of the sequence predicted the next element. These sequences resembled those of Nissen and Bullemer. The other sequence type involved hierarchical associations: One could never predict on the basis of a single element what the next element would be, but one chunk of a randomly arranged sequence predicted the appearance of another chunk of randomly arranged sequence. This structure rests not in a relation between an element and its neighbor, but between chunks of elements. Curran found that a secondary task interfered less with the learning of the sequences of simple associations than with the learning of the sequences of hierarchical associations. Moreover, although amnesics could learn the sequences of simple associations at normal rates (but could not articulate what they had learned) they could not learn normally the sequences of hierarchical associations.

Finally, Perruchet and his colleagues (Perruchet, Gallego, & Savy, 1990; Perruchet & Pacteau, 1990) established that even the work on artificial grammars may not involve learning hierarchical or complex associations, rules if you like. Rather, they demonstrated that subjects in these experiments could make the necesssary grammatical judgments about a string of letters purely on the basis of the proximity of this string to previously presented exemplars of grammatical and ungrammatical strings.

Thus, implicit learning appears possible only when subjects need to encode exemplars or simple associations. When a more elaborated representation is needed, then learning must take place under conditions admissible to the formation of an explicit memory.

The literature on automatic and effortful encoding is related to the literature on implicit learning in that automatic acts are usually thought to occur without attention. Hasher and Zacks (1979) established four criteria by which to separate automatic and effortful encoding: Unlike effortful encoding, automatic encoding is not disrupted by the performance of a concurrent tasks; is as good under incidental as under intentional learning conditions; is not affected by education, IQ, or mental states such as depression; and remains stable with development. Automatic encoding is a process that does not require attention, whereas effortful encoding, as the name suggests, is a process that does.

Hasher and Zacks reviewed a substantial number of studies that suggest that the encoding of information about frequency of occurrence, spatial location, and temporal order was automatic. For instance, when subjects were asked to study a list of words, which were repeated throughout the list with varying frequency, subjects' memory of the words was affected by the instructions they were given, with intentional learning better than incidental learning; was diminished when they were forced to perform a concurrent task; varied with their education, IQ, and mental health; and showed a clear improvement as children grew into adulthood. On the other hand, subjects' memory for the frequency of occurrence of the words showed no such trends: It was as good under incidental as intentional learning conditions; remained stable even as subjects performed a concurrent task; was unaffected by education, IQ, or mental health status; and showed no developmental trends.

Recently, Hasher and Zacks' framework for discussing these results has come under question. Several theorists have argued that one need not posit a qualitatively different form of processing to account for Hasher and Zacks' results. For instance, Hanson and Hirst (1989) built on the observation that processing is often hierarchical and, hence, the initiation of one process may "bring along" other processes. People usually see an object as occupying space. Consequently, if they attend to and effortfully encode the form of an object, they will inevitably encode the spatial location. Hintzman (1988) advanced a different but related argument: If people encode a different mnemonic trace each time they encounter an item, then there would be sufficient information in memory on which to base a frequency of occurrence judgment.

Thus, even when considering the distinction between automatic and effortful encoding, it may be more telling to examine the exact processing underlying an act of encoding, the resulting representation, the hierarchical nature of the processing, and task demands rather than to simply classify acts of encoding as automatic or effortful. The significant difference between automatic and effortful encoding may be not that one requires attention, but what subjects look at.

Explicit Learning and Implicit Evocation

So far we have concentrated on the effect of inattention on memory. Let us turn to experimental conditions in which subjects report that they are attending to the relevant stimuli. In such instances, we will say that subjects have the possibility to *explicitly learn* the relevant material. As the qualifier *possibility* suggests, subjects need not elaborate on to-be-remembered material when they report they are attending to it. Indeed, having the sense of attending when memorizing does not in and of itself guarantee the ready construction of a memory belief when remembering. As noted at the beginning of the chapter, subjects may attend to the wrong things. People can devote their full attention to the number of *e*s in a word and end up remembering the material much less effectively than if they only cursorily attended to the material's meaning. The success subjects will have in eliciting the desired memory image and the degree to which they can justifiably construct a memory belief depends not on whether they are attending, but how they are attending.

In some instances, subjects may explicitly learn the material and even form an elaborated representation, but they will subsequently fail to construct a memory belief when the memory image is evoked. We refer to such instances as *implicit evocation.*[1] Repetition priming is an intensively investigated example of implicit evocation. Unlike instances of subliminal learning or implicit learning, here subjects attend to the material that they subsequently evoke implicitly. We believe that such situations are better understood in terms of task demands rather than in attentional terms. To the extent that inattention is an issue at all, it occurs at the point of retrieval. Some investigators refer to implicit evocation as *memory without awareness,* but they do not mean to imply that subjects are not attending to the memory image. In instances of priming, for instance, subjects are aware of the memory image, but for one of two reasons do not construct a memory belief: Either they are *not* attending to the features of the memory image that would justify constructing a memory belief—a situation of inattention we believe rarely occurs—or, more likely, the task demands do not guide them to retrieve the kind of information that would justify constructing a memory belief. In this instance, the task demands at the time of retrieval and not the way in which the information was originally encoded affect the construction of a memory belief. It is not attention per se, but the demands of the task, that determine what is remembered.

CONCLUDING COMMENTS

In this chapter, we treated attention as a consequence of processing rather than as a mechanism, structure, or faculty. People do not apply attention in order to bring something into focus or place it in the center of the footlights of consciousness; rather, they see, hear, touch, smell objects in the world

---

[1]We choose the term *evocation* instead of *remembering*, because the latter implies explicit recollection.

or think certain trains of thought. The sense of attending arises from the execution of these cognitive acts rather than from the application of some ingredient to the acts. Memory is also a product of processing: Performance on an explicit memory task is affected by the depth with which the to-be-remembered material was processed, whereas the performance on an implicit memory task is not. As a consequence, attention may be a necessary ingredient for good performance on an explicit memory test, but is less important (if important at all) for good performance on an implicit memory test. From this perspective, attending per se impacts on memory indirectly, not directly, inasmuch as attention's influence on memory performance depends on what a person does when memorizing and remembering and the task demands that guide memorizing and remembering.

We can now return to our original question: Is attention necessary for memory and, if it is, how does attending affect memorizing? The answer appears to be that it depends on what you require for something to be a memory—simply a memory image (i.e., merely an implicit memory)—or a memory image and an associated memory belief—an explicit memory. Following is a list of several of our conclusions (we state them in terms of visual attention, but they can be easily extended to other modalities):

1. When material is presented so quickly that people cannot undertake the elaborative processing that gives rise to attention, they may subsequently build a memory image, but cannot justify a memory belief—in other words, they can form an implicit, but not an explicit, memory.

2. When something is presented long enough to permit perception, but subjects nevertheless do not report seeing it, they again will form a mnemonic representation that will support the construction of a memory image, but not a memory belief.

3. When people report seeing the material, they can potentially build a deep enough representation to support both the evocation of a memory image and the construction of a memory belief. However, what is important is not whether they attend to the material, but what they do with the material—not if they attend, but how they attend.

4. The automatic encoding of information is *not* a qualitatively distinct form of encoding; rather, people automatically encode information about frequency of occurrence or spatial location of objects or the temporal order of events because such encoding is inevitably entailed in the encoding of the objects or events themselves.

Two practical suggestions follow on this approach. First, one can indirectly shape memory even under extreme conditions of inattention. This effect may not be as strong as it would be if subjects were attending to the material, and it may not apply to the construction of a memory belief, only the evocation of a memory image. Nevertheless, such indirect shaping of memory is possible. Second, and more interesting, telling people to attend to something will not in and of itself lead to better performance on direct tests of memory. In fact, one is better off telling someone how to encode and how to retrieve rather than teaching someone to attend. If attention is a consequence of processing rather than an ingredient one adds to processing to enhance it, then it makes little sense to try to teach someone a generalized skill of attending. One teaches skills of memorizing lists of words, speeches, pictures, and so on. As one employs these newly acquired skills, one attends to the mnemonically salient features of the stimuli, and memory improves.

ACKNOWLEDGMENTS

This research was supported by grants from the National Institutes of Health and a grant from the McDonnell Foundation.

REFERENCES

Allport, D. A., Antonitis, B., & Reynolds, P. (1972). On the division of attention: A disproof of the single channel hypothesis. *Quarterly Journal of Experimental Psychology, 24*, 225–235.

Bargh, J. A. (1993). Being unaware of the stimulus versus unaware of how it is interpreted: Why subliminality *per se* does not matter to social psychology. In R. F. Bornstein & T. S. Pittman (Eds.), *Perception without awareness* (pp. 236–255). New York: Guilford.

Berry, D. C., & Broadbent, D. E. (1988). Interactive tasks and the implicit–explicit distinction. *British Journal of Experimental Psychology, 79*, 251–272.

Bornstein, R. F. (1993). Subliminal mere exposure effects. In R. F. Bornstein & T. S. Pittman (Eds.), *Perception without awareness* (pp. 191–210). New York: Guilford.

Broadbent, D. E. (1958). *Perception and communication.* London: Pergamon.

Broadbent, D. E., Fitzgerald, P., & Broadbent, M. H. P. (1986). Implicit and explicit knowledge in the control of complex systems. *Journal of Experimental Psychology Monographs, 80*(2, Pt. 2), 1–17.

Cheesman, J., & Merikle, P. M. (1984). Priming with and without awareness. *Perception and Psychophysics., 36*, 387–395.

Cheesman, J., & Merikle, P. M. (1986). Distinguishing conscious from unconscious perceptual processes. *Canadian Journal of Psychology, 40*, 343–367.

Curran, T. (1994, March). Paper presented to Cognitive Neuroscience Society, San Francisco.

Dennett, D. (1991). *Consciousness explained.* New York: Little, Brown.

Desimone, R., Albright, T. D., Gross, C. G., & Bruce, C. (1984). Stimulus-selective properties of inferior neurons in the macaque. *Journal of Neuroscience, 4*, 2051–2062.

Greenwald, A. G. (1992). New look 3: Unconscious cognition reclaimed. *American Psychologist, 47*, 766–779.

Hanson, C., & Hirst, W. (1989). Representation of events: A study of orientation, recognition and recall. *Journal of Experimental Psychology: General, 118*, 136–147.

Hasher, L., & Zacks, R. T. (1979). Automatic and effortful processing in memory. *Journal of Experimental Psychology: General, 108*, 365–388.

Hintzman, D. L. (1988). Judgment of frequency and recognition in a multiple-trace memory model. *Psychological Review, 95,* 528–551.

Hirst, W. (1986). The psychology of attention. In J. E. LeDoux & W. Hirst (Eds.), *Mind and brain: Dialogues in cognitive neuroscience* (pp. 105–141). New York: Cambridge University Press.

Hirst, W. (1990). On consciousness, recall, recognition, and the architecture of memory. In K. Kirsner, S. Lewandowsky, & J. C. Dunn (Eds.), *Implicit memory* (pp. 33–46). Hillsdale, NJ: Lawrence Erlbaum Associates.

Hirst, W. (1993). On the nature of systems? In G. Harman (Ed.), *Conceptions of the mind* (pp. 13–37). Hillsdale, NJ: Lawrence Erlbaum Associates.

Hirst, W. (1994). Cognitive aspects of consciousness. In M. S. Gazzaniga (Ed.), *The cognitive neurosciences* (pp. 1307–1319). Cambridge, MA: MIT Press.

Hirst, W., & Kalmar, D. (1987). Characterizing attentional resources. *Journal of Experimental Psychology: General, 116,* 68–81.

Hirst, W., Spelke, E. S., Reaves, C. C., Caharack, G., & Neisser, U. (1980). Dividing attention without alternation or automaticity. *Journal of Experimental Psychology: General, 109,* 98–117.

Holender, D. (1986). Semantic activation without conscious identification in dichotic listening, parafoveal vision, and visual masking: A survey and appraisal. *Behavioral and Brain Sciences, 9,* 1–23.

James, W. (1950). *The principles of psychology.* New York: Dover. (Original work published 1890)

Johnson, M. K., Hashtroudi, S., & Lindsay, S. (1993). Source monitoring. *Psychological Bulletin, 11,* 1–26.

Johnson, M. K., & Hirst, W. (1991). Processing subsystems of memory. In H. J. Weingartner & R. Lister (Eds.), *Perspective on cognitive neuroscience* (pp. 197–217). New York: Oxford University Press.

Kahneman, D. (1973). *Attention and effort.* Englewood Cliffs, NJ: Prentice-Hall.

Kelley, C. M., & Lindsay, D. S. (1992). *Remembering mistaken for knowing: Ease of retrieval as a basis for confidence in answers to general knowledge questions.* Manuscript submitted for publication.

Klatzky, R. (1980). *Human memory: Structures and processes.* San Francisco: Freeman.

Kunst-Wilson, W. R., & Zajonc, R. B. (1980). Affective discrimination of stimuli that cannot be recognized. *Science, 207,* 557–558.

Lewicki, P., Hill, T., & Bizot, E. (1988). Acquisition of procedural knowledge about a pattern of stimuli that cannot be articulated. *Cognitive Psychology, 20,* 24–37.

Lewicki, P., Hill, T., & Czyewska, M. (1992). Nonconscious acquisition of information. *American Psychologist, 47,* 792–801.

Logan, G. D. (1988). Towards an instance theory of automatization. *Psychological Review, 95,* 492–527.

Mandler, G. (1985). *Cognitive psychology: An essay in cognitive science.* Hillsdale, NJ: Lawrence Erlbaum Associates.

Mandler, G., Nakamura, Y., & Van Zandt, B. J. S. (1987). Nonspecific effects of exposure on stimuli that cannot be recognized. *Journal of Experimental Psychology: Learning, Memory, and Cognition, 13,* 646–648.

Manier, D., & Hirst, W. (1995). *On the origins of memory.* In preparation.

Marcel, A. (1983a). Conscious and unconscious perception: An approach to the relations between phenomenal experience and perceptual processes. *Cognitive Psychology, 15,* 238–300.

Marcel, A. (1983b). Conscious and unconscious perception: Experiments on visual masking and word recognition. *Cognitive Psychology, 15,* 197–237.

Merikle, P. M. (1992). Perception without awareness: Critical issues. *American Psychologist, 47,* 792–795.

Neisser, U. (1976). *Cognition and reality.* San Francisco: Freeman.

Nissen, M. J., & Bullemer, P. (1987). Attentional requirements of learning: Evidence from performance measures. *Cognitive Psychology, 19,* 1–32.

Norman, D. A., & Bobrow, D. G. (1975). On data-limited and resource-limited processes. *Cognitive Psychology, 7,* 44–64.

Perruchet, P., Gallego, J., & Savy, I. (1990). A critical reappraisal of the evidence for uncosncious abstaction of deterministic rules in complex experimental situations. *Cognitive Psychology, 22,* 493–516.

Perruchet, P., & Pacteau, C. (1990). Synthetic grammar learning: Implicit rule abstraction or explicit fragmentary knowledge. *Journal of Experimental Psychology: General, 119,* 264–275.

Poetzl, O. (1917). The relationship between experimentally induced dream images and indirect vision. In J. Wolff, D. Papaport, & S. H. Annin (Eds.), *Psychological issues* and trans. 2, (#3, Monograph 7): 41–120.

Reber, A. S. (1967). Implicit learning of artificial grammars. *Journal of Verbal Learning and Verbal Behavior, 6,* 855–863.

Reber, A. S. (1989). Implicit learning and tacit knowledge. *Journal of Experimental Psychology: General, 118,* 219–235.

Reber, A. S., & Allen, R. (1978). Analogy and abstraction strategies in synthetic grammar learning: A functional interpretation. *Cognition, 6,* 189–221.

Roediger, H. L. III. (1990). Implicit memory: Retention without remembering. *American Psychologist, 45,* 1043–1056.

Schacter, D. L. (1987). Implicit memory: History and current status. *Journal of Experimental Psychology: Learning, Memory, and Cognition, 13,* 501–518.

Schacter, D. L. (1989). On the relation between memory and consciousness: Dissociable interactions and conscious experience. In H. L. Roediger III & F. I. M. Craik (Eds.), *Varieties of memory and consciousness: Essays in honor of Endel Tulving.* Hillsdale, NJ: Lawrence Erlbaum Associates.

Squire, L. R. (1992). Memory and the hippocampus: A synthesis from findings with rats, monkeys, and humans. *Psychological Review, 99,* 195–231.

Treisman, A. (1969). Strategies and models of selective attention. *Psychological Review, 76,* 282–299.

Tulving, E., & Schacter, D. L. (1990). Priming and human memory systems. *Science, 247,* 301–306.

Whittlesea, B. W., Jacoby, L. L., & Girard, K. (1990). Evidence of an attributional basis for feelings of familiarity and perceptual quality. *Journal of Memory and Language, 29,* 716–732.

Wickens, C. (1980). The structure of attentional resources. In R. S. Nickerson (Ed.), *Attention and performance* (Vol. VIII, pp. 239–256). Hillsdale, NJ: Lawrence Erlbaum Associates.

Wickens, C. (1984). Processing resources in attention. In R. Parasuraman & D. R. Davies (Eds.), *Varieties of attention* (pp. 63–98). Orlando, FL: Academic Press.

CHAPTER THIRTEEN

A Combinatorial-Binding and Strength (CBS) Model of Memory: Is It a Better Framework for Amnesia?

Jordan Grafman
National Institute of Neurological Disorders and Stroke

Herbert Weingartner
National Institute on Alcohol Abuse and Alcoholism

All the time the Guard was looking at her, first through a telescope, then through a microscope, and then through an opera-glass. At last he said, "You're traveling the wrong way. . . ."

—Carroll (1875)

INTRODUCTION

Since the cognitive revolution began, the goal of researchers concerned with human memory has been to identify and describe the functional and neurobiological basis of the various memory systems (Squire, 1992; Squire & Butters, 1992). A wide variety of methods have been used in the attempt to achieve this broad goal, and these include: behavioral studies of normal volunteers in the human learning laboratory; neuropsychological studies of cognitively impaired patients; studies of normal volunteers, as well as patients, following the administration of drugs that can produce graded reversible brain lesions; as well as studies in other animals ranging from nonhuman primates to simple organisms such as aplysia. The findings from all of these types of studies have been used to build models of memory that would account for the components and operations that are necessary for acquiring and encoding information, consolidating it in memory, and then retrieving it under various conditions. In this chapter, the use of the word *system* refers to a collection of neural structures and cognitive operations that have a

259

similar memorial purpose. The use of the word *process* refers to the activation of those cognitive and neural operations. The words *function* or *form* are interchangably used in the text and refer to the observable performance of subjects on memory tasks.

Some of the distinct forms of human memory that have been described include: memory functions that require subjects to be aware of the source or context of remembered information (explicit memory; Appollonio et al., 1994; Tulving, 1985; Tulving & Schacter, 1990); remembering that can be inferred on the basis of subject's behavior rather than what can be directly retrieved from memory, where the subject need not be explicitly aware of what is in memory (implicit memory; Schacter, 1987; Tulving & Schacter, 1990); memory and learning of rules and procedures (procedural memory; Grafman, Weingartner, Newhouse, Thompson, et al., 1990; Pascual-Leone et al., 1993); memory of knowledge, such as semantic information, that can be dissociated from the context in which that information was acquired (semantic memory; McKenna & Warrington, 1993; Weingartner, Grafman, Boutelle, Kaye, & Martin, 1983); memory functions that require sustained concentration and attention (effortful memory) in contrast to memory functions that can be carried out in parallel with other operations (automatic memory; Grafman, Rao, Bernardin, & Leo, 1991; Grafman, Weingartner, Lawlor, et al., 1990). Other forms of memory that have been identified and described both functionally and in terms of underlying neurobiological mechanisms include associative learning and memory based on pairings of simple stimulus–response relationships, that is, simple conditioning paradigms (simple associative conditioning); and processes involved in the development of a permanent record of experience (memory consolidation). Even this listing of proposed human memory processes and forms is by no means exhaustive (Boller & Grafman, 1989, 1993; Jacoby, 1991; Moscovitch & Umilta, 1991; Roediger, Rajaram, & Srinivas, 1991), but see Roediger for a more cynical view of this parcellation of memory (Roediger, 1990).

One of the most consistent features of many of the neuropsychological models of human memory has been the assumption that because some aspects of memory are spared and others impaired by some "treatment" that this is evidence for different types of memory systems (Collins, Gathercole, Conway, & Morris, 1993). We would argue that this is neither a useful conclusion nor an effective strategy for organizing the wealth of data that is available about memory. Instead, we have concluded that many of the patterns of dissociations of memory (patterns of spared and impaired memory functions) are interpretable as differences in the expression, that is, retrieval, of one of only two forms of memory rather than a multitude of different memory systems. One aspect of memory that there is strong evidence for is within-network representational strength. This strength variable (often referred to as *consolidation*) is a combination of exposure to, and/or activation of, the unit of information that is stored within a network along with the interactive relationship (along an inhibition-facilitation axis) of that unit of information to other units within its psychological–neurobiological neighborhood in that particular network. The presumption is that there are many networks in the brain that have a common within-network cognitive architecture—yet each network would be devoted to a distinctive cognitive representation-operation.

Another aspect of memory that there is strong evidence for is that information in memory is associated, or bound, to the time, sequence, and context in which it was acquired. This memory process is often referred to as *episodic memory*. It is our interpretation of the current neurobiology of memory literature that the hippocampus and related structures have a unique role in the binding of disparate information in time as well as to the context in which that information was acquired in order to form an episode (Cohen & Eichenbaum, 1993). Memory must benefit from individuated records of information that have enormous flexibility in how they can be linked to one another to fashion various distributed neural networks. The facets of knowledge that are elicited during retrieval are at least partly determined by how these individuated records, contained in local neural networks, are bound together across local networks. It is the expression of these "bound records" that we believe is often misinterpreted as evidence of different memory systems.

THE NEUROPSYCHOLOGY OF MEMORY

The variety of ways in which memory functions can be selectively altered has been well described under many different conditions, and is a database that is familiar to all memory researchers engaged in neuropsychological investigation (Boller & Grafman, 1989, 1993; Squire & Butters, 1992). We would argue that although the memory findings themselves are clear and indisputable, how they should be organized and interpreted and their implications for theories of memory are open to reconsideration and further review. For example, the fact that some memory-impaired patients cannot remember information explicitly, but nevertheless behave as if they remember some aspect of the previously processed experience implicitly, does not mean that explicit and implicit memory are different memory processes or reflect different memory systems.

Likewise, the fact that amnesic subjects may demonstrate that they can take advantage of, or "remember," previous skill training, but do not recall the fact that they have had such experience, need not imply that remembering rules and procedures is a distinct memory system. Should we invoke a totally different memory system for each instance of remembering? The point we are reiterating is that stimulus-specific retrieval failure does not, in and of itself, constitute evidence of the existence of separate kinds of memory.

It is our thesis that the new challenge of cognitive neuroscience is to consider whether such "instances" of memory are unique memory systems or processes or whether they represent varying bindings of representational knowledge. Either choice implies a different set of methods to examine, and conclusions about, memory.

Specific Forms of Memory Impairment in Cognitively Impaired Patients and in Response to Drug Treatments

Almost 10 years ago, we published a paper in *Science* (Weingartner et al., 1983) that argued that the simple dichotomy in memory processing between episodic and semantic memory distinguishes the impairment in memory that is expressed in patients suffering from dementia from that seen in amnesia. That conceptual distinction was driven by both the contemporary theoretical and reductionist zeitgeist (Tulving, 1985) as well as the behavioral–clinical data we and others had collected. In our paper we demonstrated that amnesic Korsakoff disease (KD) patients had impaired episodic memory but spared semantic memory, whereas a similarly recent memory-impaired sample of Alzheimer's disease (AD) patients expressed both episodic and semantic memory deficits. We argued that in the case of the AD patients, their episodic memory deficits could be at least partially explained by the severity of their semantic memory deficits. Although the episodic–semantic distinction at the time appeared to capture the behavioral findings of the experiments, it has been more recently challenged by other conceptual theories of memory exemplified by the explicit–implicit (Moscovitch, Vriezen, & Gottstein, 1993), procedural–declarative (Pascual-Leone et al., 1993), and transfer–appropriate processing (Tenpenny & Shoben, 1992) frameworks.

The current distinction between explicit and implicit memory now serves as the basis for operationalizing what is meant by an *amnesia* (Moscovitch et al., 1993). Scores of studies have demonstrated that amnesic patients can retain, and implicitly remember, certain forms of information even if they are not aware of the source of their training or knowledge. For example, if amnesics are shown a set of pictures to remember and later asked to recall or recognize those pictures explicitly, they are unable to do so. If, however, they are simply asked to name the pictures without reference to a previously shown list, they will more quickly name those pictures shown to them earlier compared to a new set of pictures. This finding suggests that some critical aspects of the pictures themselves were correctly encoded, retained, and retrieved, and that this information, which is in memory, influenced the patient's perception and expression of knowledge (in this case, the ability to name the picture correctly). If this description of the performance of a typical selectively amnesic patient was given to a "woman in the street," she would be dumfounded that such an individual would be called memory impaired. That is, amnesics can attend to information, can encode information, consolidate it, retain it in memory over long periods of time, and then remember it as well as normal controls under certain conditions.

Drugs have also been used as a tool for exploring memory because they can induce highly specific, but reversible, forms of memory impairment (Lister & Weingartner, 1987; Warburton & Rusted, 1992; Weingartner, Eckardt, Molchan, Sunderland, & Wolkowitz, 1992). Scores of studies have demonstrated that different classes of drugs can have highly specific memory effects that can model the different types of memory impairments that are expressed in different neuropsychological disorders (Wolkowitz, Tinklenberg, & Weingartner, 1985). For example, benzodiazapine effects simulate the form of memory impairment expressed in the selectively amnesic patient (Curran, 1986; Curran, Schiwy, & Lader, 1987; Danion, Zimmermann, Willard-Schroeder, Grange, & Singer, 1989; Fang, Hinrichs, & Ghoneim, 1987; File, Sharma, & Shaffer, 1992; Ghoneim, Dembo, & Block, 1989; Hommer et al., 1986; Hommer, Matsuo, Wolkowitz, Weingartner, & Paul, 1987; Lister, Weingartner, Eckardt, & Linnoila, 1988; Weingartner, Hommer, Lister, Thompson, & Wolkowitz, 1992). That is, both recognition and recall are impaired following the administration of a benzodiazapine. These anterograde amnesic effects are dose-dependent. The benzodiazapine-induced impairments in explicit memory are confined to remembering information presented minutes earlier but not for remembering information that had been presented seconds earlier. Thus, benzodiazapines do not impair the ability of subjects to retain information in working memory as measured by digit-span tests.

In contrast, retrieval of information already stored in memory is unaltered by benzodiazapine treatment in much the same way that this facet of memory is generally spared in the amnesic patient. Memory for information that is part of knowledge memory (e.g., the ability to generate category exemplars) is retrieved just as effectively as under placebo conditions. Furthermore, as is the case in amnesic patients, benzodiazapine-treated subjects show no impairments on a large variety of tasks that require implicit memory functions such as learning and remembering procedures, learning and recalling how to solve problems that require perceptual integration, concept formation, and use of semantic processes. Benzodiazapines allow a subject to encode information, consolidate it, retain it in memory over long periods of time, and then remember it as well as normal controls under certain conditions. Does this pattern of selective memory impairment induced by drugs such as alcohol or benzodiazepines, or in the amnesic patient, imply that explicit and implicit forms of remembering are determined by different psychological and neural mechanisms?

We would argue that the conditions that are necessary to cause an inability to explicitly remember in the benzodiazapine-treated subject or in the amnesic patient are those that require the generation of a combinatorial representational context that is evidence for the binding together of different facets of concurrently experienced information. Additionally, the individuated units of information that are bound together also facilitate the activation of previously experienced related episodes both within and across local neural networks (which all converge to tag that information in experiential time).

In response to the dichotomous approach to studying human memory characterized most recently by the implicit–explicit distinction, a revival of the transfer–appropriate processing position in memory research has developed over the last few years (Roediger et al., 1991; Squire & Butters, 1992; Tenpenny & Shoben, 1992). This approach emphasizes that the compatibility of stimuli and procedures at encoding and retrieval determines what information will be best retrieved. In another guise, this approach was known as *context* or *state-dependent encoding and retrieval.* The implication of this approach is that there are an endless number of "states of memory" that exist depending on environmental demands/encoding and internal–intentional learning/retrieval strategies. Is there a way to reconcile the dichotomous explicit–implicit approach to that of the process-driven context-dependent approach?

In the remainder of this chapter, we offer an outline of an alternative theory of human memory that is representationally driven, contains both unitized and associated memories, and is highly sensitive to the temporal constraints of experience. We have labeled this approach the *Combinatorial Binding and Strength (CBS) model* of memory, and we believe that this conception of human memory makes coherent a set of disparate findings within cognitive neuroscience while demanding an approach to investigating memory that is compatible with its practical foundations.

REPRESENTATIONS OF KNOWLEDGE AND INFORMATION

One of the more profound findings to emerge from recent cognitive neuroscience research is the complexity of information representation in the human cerebral cortex. Whether the study examines motor control or object recognition, the results and discussion inevitably assume that several different components of information processing contribute to a single "function" (such as recognizing a word), and that these components are both topographically (in the brain), operationally, and informationally distinct (Shallice, 1988). For example, different neural networks have been hypothesized to store orthographic and phonological information. Furthermore, these representational stores are considered psychologically "encapsulated" and located in distinct regions of cerebral cortex.

How might information such as orthographic features be represented within a componential domain? Contemporary researchers have debated whether a distributed processing (PDP model) or feature-driven network is superior to represent information. The debate over the nature of the representational architecture is far from concluded. For the purposes of this article, we prefer to designate the elemental form of representational information as a *unit* of information. A unit of information is equivalent to a node in a feature-driven network or a pattern of activation in a distributed processing network. That is, the unit represents a characteristic element that is irreducible within the local cognitive architecture and could be a syntactic frame, a single meaning, a single set of abstract letters that compose a word or grapheme, a single letter, an edge, and so on. The probability of activating this unit of information depends on such things as how often the subject might be exposed to that unit of information via sensory experience, how often it is activated via internalized thought, or even through vicarious activation due to a neighbor unit within the network being activated.

These units of information are connected to each other within a network by a relational metric that can be measured as an associative (e.g., the words *ice* and *cream* appear together more often than *balloon* and *elephant*) or as a similarity value (e.g., the words *drag* and *brag* sharing similar orthographic features; Medin, Goldstone, & Gentner, 1993). A diagram of the CBS model is shown in Fig. 13.1.

Although it appears as if these distinct componential domains of knowledge respect the physical distinctions that appear in the world or internally generated semantic distinctions, the neural and psychological rules that enforce these distinctions remain vague at best. We believe that uncovering the nature of these rules and the number and kinds of componential domains that are stored in spatially distinct regions of brain (the magnitude of this effort can be inferred from Van Essen's description of the number of distinctive operations within the visual information processing stream; Knierim & Van Essen, 1992) will become increasingly important to doing memory research in the 21st century, for the reasons outlined next.

Binding Between Componential Domains

We propose that besides the strengthening of individual units of memory (via activation frequency and other within-network consolidation processes), the second principal method ensuring memory for experienced events is combinatorial binding. We define *binding* as a functional and neuroanatomical linkage between unitized elements of memory residing in cognitively distinctive neural networks. By *cognitively distinctive neural networks* we mean two or more local neural nets that are devoted to specific but different information processing operations (e.g., semantic–lexical knowledge might be stored in a

Combinatorial Binding and Strength Model

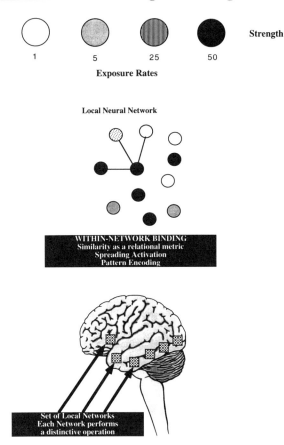

FIG. 13.1. Read from top to bottom. A unit of information's strength in memory is primarily determined by its activation (*or* exposure) rate. The unit is stored within a local network as a pattern of activation across the network or as one of a large number of nodes. The relationship between units of information stored in within a local neural network might be based on relational metrics such as similarity. Although the foundations of a cognitive architecture (e.g., relational metrics and principles of storage) might be constant across local networks, each network performs a distinctive operation based on its particular stored representations.

network that is located in left temporal–parietal cortex, whereas orthographic features might be stored in left-occipital–temporal cortex). Functional binding between units from distinct neural networks is carried out via white-matter fiber bundles (i.e., a structural link). We propose that there are at least three kinds of functional binding that are temporal in nature and neuroanatomically supported: temporal, sequential, and third party (see Fig. 13.2).

<u>Combinatorial Binding and Strength Model</u>

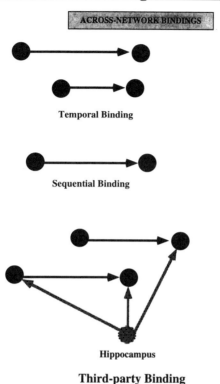

FIG. 13.2. Illustrates the kinds of binding that may occur across neural networks. A single network in the figure is represented by a darkened circle. See text for a description of each kind of binding.

Temporal binding occurs when neural networks that are, at best, only indirectly or weakly linked to one another are activated during information processing and are therefore primarily linked temporally (but not structurally). Sequential binding occurs when neural networks that are ordinarily structurally linked become activated in a set order during information processing. Third-party binding simultaneously activates two or more neural networks via a third-party structure such as the hippocampus, thereby encoding a set of representations as a time- and structurally linked episode.

Temporal binding would serve to strengthen individual units of information within a single componential domain and, by virtue of their temporal coincidence, allow for a complete percept of the world. For example, during reading we normally process both the overall form as well as the individual orthographic features of a word. Novel symbol strings may more strongly activate the form-encoding network while only weakly activating the orthographic-encoding network. As a subject is more frequently exposed to the same letter string and its meaning, the orthographic form of the letter string may take processing precedence over form analysis. The neural networks that are devoted to these processes are topographically distinct, stored in posterior cortex but in different hemispheres, and do not appear to be strongly or directly linked with each other. For effective learning of new visually presented words to occur, these distinct networks must be repeatedly and coincidentally activated. However, because these networks are only weakly linked, damage to one or the other system or their connections minimally affects cortical information processing within either spared functional domain (i.e., reading words or the processing of nonlinguistic forms). The result is an incomplete perception of a stimulus. Furthermore, these coincidentally activated networks are normally only activated together momentarily as a perceptual fragment—the lack of a structural link means that the coincidentally activated networks cannot be intentionally retrieved from memory as an episode. To even reproduce their exact activation configuration, it would be necessary to reproduce the exact environmental conditions that led to their activation in the first place.

Sequential binding is critical for forming an ordered set of associations between units of memory within neural networks that are structurally and functionally linked. Within the CBS framework, structural binding allows for a signal to be sent between two networks that can activate a specific pattern within those distant neural networks that represents an associated cognitive or motor function. For example, in order to learn and remember a complex motor skill such as typing, it is necessary to activate a linked set of visuomotor representations and eventually store this linked set as a single visuomotor procedure. The neural networks that are devoted to this process are also topographically and functionally distinct (e.g., the structures would include the cerebellum, basal ganglia, thalamus, and motor/premotor cortex, and visual processing components), but are directly and sequentially linked with each other as part of a distributed system designed to promote sequential coding of action and movement. For effective speeded and anticipatory typing to occur, these distinct networks must be repeatedly sequentially activated, thereby facilitating the speed of typing words. In the acquired apraxic, the critical process that sequentially and temporally links these networks is disrupted. Sequential (and thus structural) binding is important for both action and perception.

Third-party binding is usually referred to as *episodic memory* and is based on simultaneous activation of distinct cortical regions that may or may not be directly structurally linked. For example, remember the last time you saw ex-President George Bush laughing. The neural networks that are devoted to this process are again topographically distinct, stored throughout the brain, can be directly or indirectly linked with each other, but should be simultaneously activated via each network's structural connection to a third-party binding structure such as the hippocampus and related neural structures. For your memory of George Bush's last laugh, these distinct networks that could include semantic knowledge of George Bush, his face, his expression of laughing, presidential retirement schemas, television news appearances, and so on must be linked co-temporally during encoding. In the amnesic patient with presumed hippocampal damage, the temporal links between these distinct representational networks is broken, which results in a fractionated set of representations each time the patient is exposed to new information or episodes—that is, each neural network remains available for unitized priming but only weakly bound to representational information stored in other "key" networks for the encoding of an episode. Premorbid episodes are spared, because their intact encoding insures the retrieval of an episode. The strength of that premorbid episode in memory is at least partially dependent on its subsequent reactivation frequency.

It is uncertain whether specific neural networks that subserve distinctive cognitive functions when bound together form anatomically "highlighted" distributed processing systems. If so, these networks would, in effect, form functionally "barricaded systems" for the perception and production of behavior. The use of the word *system* here specifies a set of representations that are bound together for a distinct behavioral purpose rather than making a claim for a unique memory process.

Temporal binding may be dominant in posterior regions of cortex where more elemental information processing occurs in parallel, such as object and lexical recognition, and is particularly responsible for our perception of the world as a whole. Sequential binding may be dominant in sensorimotor and prefrontal cortex and is necessary for aspects of perception as well as the execution of a sequence of motor and cognitive actions. The process of sequential binding is just too slow to be able to reevoke an episode. Third-party binding (depicted in Fig. 13.3) may link together posterior cortex with its domains of space, object, and meaning with prefrontal cortex with its domains of plans, execution, actions, and schemas in order to form episodic memories. Furthermore, we suggest that guided (and perhaps even passive) search strategies through various representational domains of memory are dependent on knowledge stored in prefrontal cortex. We suggest here, and in recent papers, that knowledge stored in prefrontal cortex includes structured event-complexes that serve as plans and schemas (Grafman, 1989, 1994; Grafman & Hendler, 1991; Grafman, Sirigu, Spector, & Hendler, 1993; Grafman et al., 1991; Nichelli et al., 1994; Spector & Grafman, 1994). Such plans and schemas are linked by a third-party structure to a wide range of other representational networks so that recognition or execution of a plan would simultaneously activate other unitized knowledge. Such activation would facilitate the subject's awareness that other unitized knowledge de-

Combinatorial Binding and Strength Model

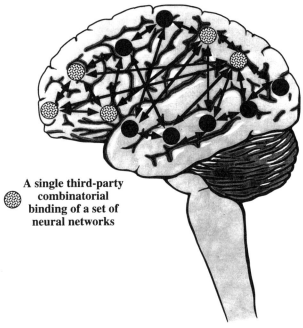

A single third-party
combinatorial
binding of a set of
neural networks

**Should each new bound neural network combination
be considered a memory system?**

FIG. 13.3. Patients with neurological disorders may fail at one or more kinds
of binding. See text for a description of the consequences of a lesion on a
particular type of binding mechanism.

serves attention during a specific instantiation of that plan. This third-party
linked activation of disparate neural networks serves as a memory for the
episode and enables the conscious, effortful retrieval of memory for those
same episodes.

Disorders of Memory

Given this framework, there are a number of ways in which memories can
become inaccessible. For example, posterior cortical damage could directly
affect both the storage of local unit knowledge (e.g., causing an agnosia)
and simple temporal binding of perceptual domains (e.g., causing disconnection or working memory deficits). Damage to the cerebellum, thalamus,
or frontal cortex would directly impair both the storage of local unit knowl-

edge (e.g., specific movement operations) and its organization into sequential actions (e.g., drawing a picture), causing apraxias or impaired working memory. Damage to the hippocampus and related structures would affect the third-party combinatorial binding of unit knowledge with plan/schema knowledge and lead to deficits in episodic memory (as in the case of selectively amnesic patients).

Implications for Memory Research

The goal of much of contemporary human memory research has been to identify distinct types of memory processes and memory systems by demonstrating that they can be dissociated from one another using behavioral manipulations in normal controls, by contrasting the performance of cognitively impaired patients, and by examining the effects on memory resulting from the reversible lesions produced by drugs. Along with an avalanche of findings, we have witnessed the development of all kinds of memory theories, models of memory, and frameworks for the analysis and synthesis of memory findings (Collins et al., 1993; Damasio & Damasio, 1993; Squire & Butters, 1992). Each new theory, model, and framework has proposed yet another set of distinctive memory systems and/or processes. This has also meant that there has developed a rich set of terms and metaphors for describing memory that, after a period of use and acceptance, has become an integral part of how memory researchers think about the nature of memory (Roediger, 1990). The metaphors have become "real" to many researchers and constrain their thinking about memory.

How we categorize what we know about memory has enormous consequences, not only for how knowledge about memory is organized but also for our interpretation and understanding of memory findings. The development of these theories, models, and language for describing memory phenomena during the last half-century has not, in our view, been translated into more information about human memory.

We are arguing that the multiprocess and system views of memory that are currently in vogue are misleading. Our review of this same research has led us to a different conclusion about the interpretation of human memory phenomena and this, in turn, has implications for more effective strategies for studying human memory. We conclude that memory can be characterized in many ways but that there are only two general types of memory processes. One type of process is necessary for the formation, and organization, of memory units within the networks of knowledge that are distributed throughout the brain. There are a very large number of these networks each representing a particular type of information and/or operation. The second process binds, and therefore organizes, information across neural networks in time and results in the storage of an episode. The hippocampus and related structures (e.g., the basal forebrain—see Salazar et al., 1986) play a crucial role in the storage of episodes through a third-party binding procedure (Cohen & Eichenbaum, 1993).

The expression of what is stored in memory is determined not only by the nature of how unitized and bound memories are represented, but by the specific stimulus conditions that are present when we retrieve knowledge. For example, how we explicitly ask people about what they remember about a piece of information they were exposed to earlier will bias their search strategies through memory (Jacoby, 1991).

Therefore, we would conclude, as would many other researchers, that the memory deficit that is ascribed to the amnesic is one of a failure to encode and later activate bound unitized representations. The unitized representations themselves are spared and when activated give the impression of an implicit retrieval.

The study of memory also needs to consider the wider cognitive conditions that are present during storage and retrieval. It is extraordinary how the field of memory research has developed as a discipline separate from other areas of research that make up cognitive neuroscience. For example, attentional and perceptual mechanisms have, until recently, been relatively neglected in considering the "implicit" acquisition of new knowledge (Squire & Butters, 1992). More important, in the context of the model outlined earlier, it would be crucial to cognitively label and map the large number of neural networks devoted to distinctive cognitive functions as researchers in aphasia, agnosia, and perception have begun to do, because it is these networks that are bound together to form episodes in memory. In particular, portions of the anterior temporal lobe and prefrontal cortex that compose over 30% of the human cerebral cortical space remain virtually uncharted (Ruchkin et al., 1994; Rueckert et al., 1994).

Slight changes in experimental and task demands could very well recruit a different configuration of neural networks in the subject (see Fig. 13.4). Such slight modifications could result in an observer's impression that a different memory system was being used (rather than the more mundane explanation of a different network configuration). Nevertheless, the CBS model supports the relevance of the human factors approach to knowledge acquisition and retrieval, because selective neural network configurations are more relevant for the performance of specific tasks.

CONCLUSIONS

The CBS framework implies that there are truly only two types of memory processes. First, local cortical and subcortical network processes that allow for unitized knowledge and feature storage and that are the locus for at least

Combinatorial Binding and Strength Model

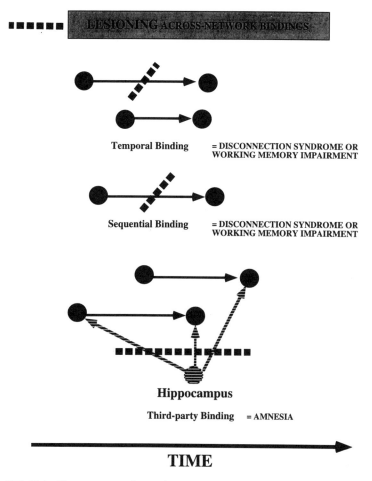

FIG. 13.4. Illustrates a set of neural networks (stipled circles) that are bound together via a third-party mechanism. Only a small number of the possible local networks in just the cerebral cortex are indicated. The possible number of network configurations based on various binding mechanisms is quite large.

certain kinds of perceptual, procedural, and other types of priming phenomena. The second process binds together distinctive domains of features and knowledge. The second process is most affected by hippocampal and related neural structure damage. The first process is most affected by cortical lesions but could be secondarily affected by a hippocampal lesion given that plans/schemas would be less likely to be bound to, and therefore less frequently activate, unitized knowledge. That is, it is probably the case that a stored unit of information that is linked not only to neighborhood units within its own representational network but to units of knowledge in other representational networks (via the hippocampus) will be activated less frequently if it was dissociated from knowledge in other distant representational networks (as might occur in amnesia following hippocampal damage).

The notion of memory "systems" rings shallow given this perspective. That is, in our two-process CBS view of memory, groups of representational networks can be linked together (i.e., bound together) momentarily to perform a function (e.g., planning a vacation by reading a travel guide would incorporate representational networks concerned with visual word recognition, images, topography of location, syntactic processing, semantic processing, planning, etc.). However, given the numerous number of acts that a human being performs in an hour, much less a lifetime, the number of potential representational network combinations is very large, dynamic, and potentially chaotic. Would one dare call each and every combination a system?

REFERENCES

Appollonio, I., Grafman, J., Clark, K., Nichelli, P., Zeffiro, T., & Hallett, M. (1994). Implicit and explicit memory in patients with Parkinson's disease with and without dementia. *Archives of Neurology*, *51*, 359–367.

Boller, F., & Grafman, J. (Eds.). (1989). *Handbook of neuropsychology*. Amsterdam: Elsevier.

Boller, F., & Grafman, J. (Eds.). (1993). *Handbook of neuropsychology*. Amsterdam: Elsevier.

Carroll, L. (1875). Chapter 3, Looking-glass insects. In *Through the looking glass and what Alice found there* [On-line]. Available: http: //192.76.144.75/books/carroll/alice/htm/

Cohen, N. J., & Eichenbaum, H. (1993). *Memory, amnesia, and the hippocampal system*. Cambridge, MA: MIT Press.

Collins, A. F., Gathercole, S. E., Conway, M. A., & Morris, P. E. (Eds.). (1993). *Theories of memory*. Hillsdale, NJ: Lawrence Erlbaum Associates.

Curran, H. V. (1986). Tranquillising memories: A review of the effects of benzodiazepines on human memory. *Biological Psychology*, *23*, 179–213.

Curran, H. V., Schiwy, W., & Lader, M. (1987). Differential amnesic properties of benzodiazepines: A dose-response comparison of two drugs with similar elimination half-lives. *Psychopharmacology*, *92*, 358–364.

Damasio, A. R., & Damasio, H. (1993). Cortical systems underlying knowledge retrieval: Evidence from human lesions studies. In T. A. Poggio & D. A. Glaser (Eds.), *Exploring brain functions: Models in neuroscience* (pp. 233–248). London: Wiley.

Danion, J. M., Zimmermann, M. A., Willard-Schroeder, D., Grange, D., & Singer, L. (1989). Diazepam induces a dissociation between explicit and implicit memory. *Psychopharmacology*, *99*, 238–243.

Fang, J. C., Hinrichs, J. V., & Ghoneim, M. M. (1987). Diazepam and memory: Evidence for spared memory function. *Pharmacology, Biochemistry, and Behavior*, *28*, 347–352.

File, S. E., Sharma, R., & Shaffer, J. (1992). Is lorazepam-induced amnesia specific to the type of memory or the task used to assess it? *Journal of Psychopharmacology*, *6*, 76–80.

Ghoneim, M. M., Dembo, J. B., & Block, R. I. (1989). Time course of sedative and amnesic effects of diazepam by flumazenil. *Anesthesiology*, *70*, 899–904.

Grafman, J. (1989). Plans, actions, and mental sets: Managerial knowledge units in the frontal lobes. In E. Perecman (Ed.), *Integrating theory and practice in clinical neuropsychology* (pp. 93–138). Hillsdale, NJ: Lawrence Erlbaum Associates.

Grafman, J. (1994). Alternative frameworks for the conceptualization of prefrontal lobe functions. In F. Boller & J. Grafman (Eds.), *Handbook of neuropsychology* (pp. 187–202). Amsterdam: Elsevier.

Grafman, J., & Hendler, J. (1991). Planning and the brain. *Behavioral and Brain Sciences, 14,* 563–564.

Grafman, J., Rao, S., Bernardin, L., & Leo, G. J. (1991). Automatic memory processes in patients with multiple sclerosis. *Archives of Neurology, 48,* 1072–1075.

Grafman, J., Sirigu, A., Spector, L., & Hendler, J. (1993). Damage to the prefrontal cortex leads to decomposition of structured event Ccomplexes. *Journal of Head Trauma Rehabilitation, 8,* 73–87.

Grafman, J., Thompson, K., Weingartner, H., Martinez, R., Lawlor, B. A., & Sunderland, T. (1991). Script generation as an indicator of knowledge representation in patients with Alzheimer's disease. *Brain and Language, 40,* 344–358.

Grafman, J., Weingartner, H., Lawlor, B., Mellow, A. M., Thompsen-Putnam, K., & Sunderland, T. (1990). Automatic memory processes in patients with dementia–Alzheimer's type (DAT). *Cortex, 26,* 361–371.

Grafman, J., Weingartner, H., Newhouse, P. A., Thompson, K., Lalonde, F., Litvan, I., Molchan, S., & Sunderland, T. (1990). Implicit learning in patients with Alzheimer's disease. *Pharmacopsychiatry, 23,* 94–101.

Hommer, D. W., Matsuo, V., Wolkowitz, O., Chrousos, G., Greenblatt, D. J., Weingartner, H., & Paul, S. M. (1986). Benzodiazepine sensitivity in normal human subjects. *Archives of General Psychiatry, 43,* 542–551.

Hommer, D. W., Matsuo, V., Wolkowitz, O. M., Weingartner, H., & Paul, S. M. (1987). Pharmacodynamic approaches to benzodiazepine action in man. *Psychopharmacology Service Center Bulletin, 3,* 52–61.

Jacoby, L. L. (1991). A process dissociation framework: Separating automatic from intentional uses of memory. *Journal of Memory and Language, 30,* 513–541.

Knierim, J. J., & Van Essen, D. C. (1992). Visual cortex: Cartography, connectivity, and concurrent processing. *Current Opinion in Neurobiology, 2,* 150–155.

Lister, R. G., & Weingartner, H. (1987). Neuropharmacological strategies for understanding psychobiological determinants of cognition. *Human Neurobiology, 6,* 119–127.

Lister, R. G., Weingartner, H., Eckardt, M. J., & Linnoila, M. (1988). Clinical relevance of effects of benzodiazepines on learning and memory. *Psychopharmacolology Service Center Bulletin, 6,* 117–127.

McKenna, P., & Warrington, E. K. (Eds.). (1993). *The neuropsychology of semantic memory.* Amsterdam: Elsevier.

Medin, D. L., Goldstone, R. L., & Gentner, D. (1993). Prospects for similarity. *Psychological Review, 100,* 254–278.

Moscovitch, M., & Umilta, C. (1991). Conscious and nonconscious aspects of memory: A neuropsychological framework of modules and central systems. In R. G. Lister & H. Weingartner (Eds.), *Perspectives on cognitive neuroscience* (pp. 229–266). New York: Oxford University Press.

Moscovitch, M., Vriezen, E., & Gottstein, J. (1993). Implicit tests of memory in patients with focal lesions or degenerative brain disorders. In F. Boller & J. Grafman (Eds.), *Handbook of neuropsychology* (pp. 133–174). Amsterdam: Elsevier.

Nichelli, P., Grafman, J., Pietrini, P., Alway, D., Carton, J. C., & Miletich, R. (1994). Brain activity in chess playing [letter]. *Nature, 369,* 191.

Pascual-Leone, A., Grafman, J., Clark, K., Stewart, M., Massaquoi, S., Lou, J. S., & Hallett, M. (1993). Procedural learning in Parkinson's disease and cerebellar degeneration. *Annals of Neurology, 34,* 594–602.

Roediger, H. L. (1990). Implicit memory: A commentary. *Bulletin of the Psychonomic Society, 28,* 373–380.

Roediger, H. L., Rajaram, S., & Srinivas, K. (1991). Specifying criteria for postulating memory systems. In A. Diamond (Ed.), *The development and neural bases of higher cognitive function* (pp. 572–595). New York: New York Academy of Sciences Press.

Ruchkin, D. S., Grafman, J., Krauss, G. L., Johnson, R., Jr., Canoune, H., & Ritter, W. (1994). Event-related brain potential evidence for a verbal working memory deficit in multiple sclerosis. *Brain, 117*(Pt 2), 289–305.

Rueckert, L., Appollonio, I., Grafman, J., Jezzard, P., Johnson, R., Jr., Le Bihan, D., & Turner, R. (1994). Magnetic resonance imaging functional activation of left frontal cortex during covert word production. *Journal of Neuroimaging, 4*, 67–70.

Salazar, A. M., Grafman, J. H., Vance, S. C., Weingartner, H., Dillon, J. D., & Ludlow, C. (1986). Consciousness and amnesia after penetrating head injury: Neurology and anatomy. *Neurology, 36*, 178–187.

Schacter, D. L. (1987). Implicit memory: History and current status. *Journal of Experimental Psychology: Learning, Memory, and Cognition, 13*, 501–518.

Spector, L., & Grafman, J. (1994). Planning, neuropsychology, and artificial intelligence. In F. Boller & J. Grafman (Eds.), *Handbook of neuropsychology* (pp. 377–392). Amsterdam: Elsevier.

Squire, L. R. (1992). Memory and the hippocampus: a synthesis from findings with rats, monkeys, and humans. *Psychological Review, 99*, 195–231.

Squire, L. R., & Butters, N. (Eds.). (1992). *Neuropsychology of memory* (2nd ed.). New York: Guilford.

Tenpenny, P. L., & Shoben, E. J. (1992). Component processes and the utility of the conceptually-driven/data-driven distinction. *Journal of Experimental Psychology: Learning, Memory, and Cognition, 18*, 25–42.

Tulving, E. (1985). How many memory systems? *American Psychologist, 40*, 385–398.

Tulving, E., & Schacter, D. L. (1990). Priming and human memory systems. *Science, 247*, 301–306.

Warburton, D. M., & Rusted, J. D. (1992). Drugs as tools for investigating cognition. *Clinical Neuropharmacology, 15 (Supplement 1)*, 329a–330a.

Weingartner, H., Eckardt, M., Molchan, S., Sunderland, T., & Wolkowitz, O. (1992). Measurement and interpretation of changes in memory in response to drug treatments. *Psychopharmacology Bulletin, 28*, 331–340.

Weingartner, H., Grafman, J., Boutelle, W., Kaye, W., & Martin, P. R. (1983). Forms of memory failure. *Science, 221*, 380–382.

Weingartner, H. J., Hommer, D., Lister, R. G., Thompson, K., & Wolkowitz, O. (1992). Selective effects of triazolam on memory. *Psychopharmacology, 106*, 341–345.

Wolkowitz, O. M., Tinklenberg, J. R., & Weingartner, H. (1985). A psychopharmacological perspective of cognitive functions. II. Specific pharmacologic agents. *Neuropsychobiology, 14*, 133–156.

CHAPTER FOURTEEN

Management and Rehabilitation of Memory Problems

Barbara A. Wilson
Medical Research Council, Applied Psychology Unit
Cambridge, England

Memory problems are frequently associated with neurological conditions. More than 30% of patients who have sustained a severe head injury, for example, will experience memory impairment. Those with progressive degenerative disease, particularly dementia, will almost certainly exhibit memory deficits sooner or later. Korsakoff's syndrome, herpes simplex encephalitis, anoxia following cardiac arrest, and carbon monoxide poisoning are just some of the conditions that are likely to result in general memory impairment. A unilateral stroke may lead to material specific memory impairment.

In spite of the fact that there are large numbers of people sustaining brain damage each year, many of whom will be severely handicapped as a result of amnesic deficits, few of them will be offered any help in managing their problems or reducing the effect of their handicap on their everyday functioning. Among neurologists working with amnesic patients, the prevailing attitude seems to suggest that nothing can be done to help brain-damaged people. Holders of this attitude may argue that when the brain is damaged it cannot be repaired, there is no known treatment to restore lost memory functioning, and, therefore, the patient and his or her family must manage themselves as best as they can without assistance from hospital staff. Among the relatives of amnesic patients, the patients themselves, and some paramedical staff the reverse attitude is held: They believe that if the appropriate drug or treatment can be found this will restore the patient to a premorbid level of functioning.

Neither of these attitudes is in fact correct. It is indeed true that there is no known way we can restore lost memory functioning in a patient with an organic amnesia once the period of natural recovery is past. Even in those patients with a transient amnesia following head injury it is far from clear whether any memory therapy can accelerate recovery. On the other hand, there are ways to help patients and their families cope with the difficulties. We can, for example, help patients to find ways to bypass or ameliorate their problems to some degree. Also we can help memory-impaired people use whatever memory skills they do possess more efficiently. Finally, we can find out the best ways for people to learn new information. It is often the inability to learn new information that is the most handicapping aspect of organic memory deficit.

People with organic memory problems are likely to:

- Show normal or near normal immediate memory (i.e., they can repeat back a telephone number) immediately.
- Have difficulty in remembering things after a delay or distraction.
- Have problems when learning new things.
- Remember things that happened some time before their neurological insult better than things that happened a short time before it.
- Remember (usually) how to do things they were good at or had practiced a great deal (e.g., playing the piano, swimming or driving a car).
- Be helped by cues such as giving the first letter of someone's name.

Is Recovery Possible?

"A deficient memory cannot be cured" (Berg, Koning-Haanstra, & Deelman, 1991, p. 101). This was the advice given to Dutch memory-impaired patients. Berg, Koning-Haanstra, and Deelman also reported that the patients were also told: "However, you can make more efficient use of your remaining capacities" (1991, p. 101). If we accept that a deficient memory cannot be cured, does this mean that we can expect no recovery or no improvement of memory functioning?

The answer to this depends, in part, on the cause of the memory impairment. For someone with Alzheimer's disease, we would not expect any recovery or improvement. In this case we can ask another question—"Is it possible to slow down the rate of deterioration?" The answer here is probably "No, at least not at present, but we do not really know." On the other hand, a patient who has sustained a severe head injury and is in posttraumatic amnesia (PTA) may expect considerable improvement and possibly even complete recovery. In a recent long-term follow up of 54 patients (from several diagnostic groups) referred for memory therapy between 5 and 10 years earlier (Wilson, 1991), I looked for evidence of improvement in memory functioning. Using the Rivermead Behavioural Memory Test (RBMT; Wilson, Cockburn, & Baddeley, 1985) to measure improvement in memory, it was found that just under a third of the subjects had improved, a small number had deteriorated, and about 60% showed little or no change since leaving rehabilitation. Although only a third showed marked improvement, most of the subjects had learned to use a number of coping methods to bypass or compensate for their memory problems.

These subjects were originally seen several months postinjury, so they were not in the acute stage. The long-term follow-up study showed that a small but significant number of people continued to improve over a period of time. Head-injured people were more likely to improve than other diagnostic groups. However, as most of the improvers showed residual memory deficits I would be hesitant to apply the term *recovery* in their case.

One exception was T.B., who was 55 years old when he developed a short-term or immediate memory deficit after a series of epileptic seizures. He was seen for a period of a year, and throughout this period his immediate memory span was 2 (Baddeley & Wilson, 1988). When seen at follow up, his span (both forward and backward) had increased to 8. This is above average for his age: His ability to do other working memory tasks had likewise improved (Wilson & Baddeley, 1993). T.B. thought his recovery was due to his wife (who had been very supportive), his computer (on which he played chess and exercised his intellectual abilities), and a relaxation tape made for him at the rehabilitation center several years earlier. T.B., however, is not typical of people with memory difficulties. His was a rare and unusual disorder and the true explanation for his recovery is probably physical, for example, a resolution of some electrical abnormality associated with his original seizure.

For the most part it would appear that, after the acute stages, memory functioning improves in a minority of brain-injured people. For the majority, however, marked improvement is unlikely to occur and, on the whole, the best way forward for these people is that recommended by Berg et al. (1991) and quoted previously. This conclusion is supported by other studies. Schacter and Glisky (1986), for example, reviewed the literature on memory rehabilitation and concluded that there was no evidence to suggest it was possible to improve the memory functioning of amnesic patients.

Group studies, too, suggest that although treating people in groups has certain advantages, improving memory functioning per se is not one of them (Evans & Wilson, 1992). Wilson and Moffat (1992) pointed out that memory groups may have indirect therapeutic value because participants (and their relatives) think or believe such treatment is effective and this creates optimism, it is possible to ensure that every individual succeeds on some occasions, and the groups are enjoyable. Because memory-impaired people frequently fail and are often bewildered and confused by what is happening to them, such indirect value is not to be sneered at. Perhaps the most beneficial aspect of memory groups is the social function they fulfil. Many memory-impaired people are lonely and isolated and enjoy the contact with other similarly impaired people. Evans and Wilson (1992) found that anxiety and depression decreased for some members of the weekly outpatient group they organized and ran for several months. Use of external memory aids increased but there was little evidence of improved memory functioning per se.

To summarize this section, although some improvement in memory functioning may occur in the early stages for those without degenerative diseases, and some head-injured people may continue to improve over a long period, it is unrealistic to expect that the majority of memory-impaired people will recover. In consequence, it is recommended that ways should be sought to help them and their carers cope with their disability.

HELPING PEOPLE WITH MEMORY PROBLEMS

Although restoration of impaired memory functioning is probably not possible in people with brain injury or dementia, this does not mean that nothing can be done to alleviate, bypass, or compensate for problems encountered in everyday life. Memory performance can be improved in a number of ways. Drugs, for example, can, under certain circumstances, improve retention of material, although the effects in people with dementia are at best minimal (see Kopelman, 1992, for a review). Rote learning is commonly used by students, actors, and others. Rhymes are sometimes employed to remember information such as historical dates ("In 1492 Columbus sailed the ocean blue"). A kitchen timer will remind a cook that it is time to check the oven. Harris (1992) described many of these methods. Not all of these techniques can be applied successfully to brain-damaged individuals, but there are some strategies that will be applicable.

General Guidelines

The following guidelines are based on work carried out in cognitive psychology over the past 25 years (Wilson, 1992). They will not *solve* memory problems but may *improve* or *ease* situations for brain-damaged people and their relatives.

1. Getting the Information In. If we are to remember more efficiently, then we need to take in information. For some memory-impaired people this is a problem. Sometimes they have language or perceptual difficulties so the information is distorted initially, sometimes too much information is offered all at once, and sometimes the information being given is too complicated. To help avoid such situations there are rules we should follow. These are:

- Simplify information that we expect the memory-impaired person to remember. It is easier to remember short, simple words than longer, more complicated ones.
- Reduce the amount to be remembered (e.g., ask the person to remember one thing rather than three).
- Make sure that memory-impaired people have understood the information by having them repeat it back or retell it in their own words.
- Try to get them to link the information to something that they already know and to make associations.
- When helping a memory-impaired person to learn or remember something new, use the rule "little and often." Generally, it is better to work for a few minutes several times a day than for an hour once a day.
- Encourage the person to organize the information that is to be remembered. We know, for example, that if people are asked to remember a shopping list they remember more when they group the items into categories such as vegetables, dairy produce, stationery, and cleaning materials than if they simply list the items randomly.

2. Storing the Information. Most people forget new information rather rapidly over the first few days and then the rate of forgetting diminishes. This is also true for people with memory problems, bearing in mind, of course, that in their case relatively little information gets stored in the first place. However, once we have helped get the information in we can help keep it there by testing or persuading the memory-impaired person to rehearse or practice it at intervals. The best way to help here is to test the person immediately after he or she sees or hears information, then test again after a short delay, then again after a slightly longer delay. This process, known as *expanding rehearsal,* is continued with the intervals being lengthened gradually. Such practice or rehearsal usually leads to better retention of information.

3. Retrieving the Information. It is sometimes the case that although you have learned something, you just cannot access it when you want it. This is more often the case for people with memory problems, and if we can provide a hook in the form of a cue or prompt they may well be able to access the correct memory. For example, providing the first letter of a name may well assist the remembering of that name. Perhaps all of us have faced a situation in which we recognize a face but cannot place the person.

This is more likely to happen if the person is seen in a different place from that in which earlier meetings occurred. Retrieval is easier for most of us if the surroundings in which we are trying to remember something are the same as those in which we first learned it. In the case of people with impaired memory we may find they remember better if, when trying to remember something, they are in the same room with the same people as were there when that something was first learned or experienced.

It follows from this that when trying to teach a memory-impaired person new information we should aim to teach that person to remember that information in a number of different settings and social situations. Our aim should be to encourage learning in the many different, everyday situations that are likely to be encountered in daily life. Learning must not be limited to a classroom or hospital setting.

The mood or state of mind we are in may also influence our ability to remember. We know that people who learn things when they are sober remember better when they are sober. This may not seem surprising. However, it is also true that things learned when a person is drunk may be remembered better when that person is drunk again (Baddeley, 1990). There is also some evidence that things learned when one is happy or sad are better recalled when the original emotion is experienced (Baddeley, 1990). Consequently, when helping a memory-impaired person to remember it is probably wise to teach him or her in a number of different moods.

Cues and prompts also help remembering, so sometimes we might supply the first letter or sound or part of a word to enable a memory-impaired person to find the information he or she wants to remember. Sometimes it is possible to help people find their own prompts or cues by systematically going through letters of the alphabet ("Does this person's name begin with A, B, C, etc.?"). Similarly, if a person has mislaid something it often helps to go back to the last time that person remembers possessing the item, then ask the person to go through carefully all the actions that followed. In this way the location of the lost article may be recalled.

Obviously, not all these guidelines will be appropriate for all memory-impaired people. In most cases it will be necessary to augment general guidelines with other strategies such as those described next.

Reality Orientation (RO)

RO was designed to meet the sensory and emotional needs of long-stay patients by encouraging nursing assistants to spend more time with patients, to change staff attitudes, and to provide stimulating activities for patients (Folsom, 1968). Today, most RO programs are used with confused elderly patients either in group work, known as "classroom RO" or on a more informal basis, known as "24-hour RO." Holden and Woods (1982) and

Moffat (1989, 1992) provided summaries of RO treatment and evaluation of RO studies. Moffat concluded from his review that, in general, informal RO does not work because staff do not incorporate the right procedures in their contacts with patients, there are problems because of the lack of specificity as to what staff should do, and there is lack of reinforcement for appropriate staff behavior.

The more formal classroom RO, on the other hand, does appear to lead to specific gains. Moffat (1992) gave an example of teaching specific routes around the ward and teaching orientation items such as the name of the hospital or the year.

Reminiscence Therapy

Reminiscence therapy involves reminding memory-impaired people of times and incidents in their past. Usually, this technique is used with elderly confused people and treatment takes place in groups. Old songs, photographs, and clothes from the 1900s to 1930s, for example, might be presented, and people encouraged to reminisce about old times. As far as we know, this has not been tried with head-injured people. However, it might prove to be useful for those with a memory gap of some years before an accident. Going through songs, scrapbooks, and photographs of a time that a person can remember might bring back some memories and may help in the relearning of past memories.

Brotchie and Thornton (1987) found little evidence to suggest that reminiscence therapy enhanced memory functioning, but there is little doubt that elderly memory-impaired people enjoy the reminiscence groups. They may, therefore, be helpful in reducing some of the emotional consequences of memory impairment.

Environmental Adaptations

One of the simplest ways to help people with memory impairment is to arrange the environment so that they rely less on memory. Examples here include labeling doors for a person who cannot remember which room is which, or labeling beds in a ward or cupboards in the kitchen. Other examples include drawing lines or arrows to indicate routes round a building, or positioning things so that they cannot be missed or forgotten (e.g., tying a front door key to a waist belt). It is also possible to rephrase our own questions or statements in order to avoid a predictable and irritating response. One young man, for example, always said, "Ready, willing, and disabled" when asked if he was ready. Amusing at first, this reply rapidly palled as a result of constant repetition. The problem was solved by avoiding asking the person concerned if he was ready. Thus, the verbal environment or verbal cue that triggered the imitating response was changed to prevent the problem behavior from occurring.

Harris (1980) described a geriatric unit where the rate of incontinence was reduced by the simple strategy of painting all lavatory doors a distinctive color that was strikingly different from other doors. Lincoln (1989) reported how one woman was able to keep track of whether or not she had taken her medication by placing a chart next to the bottle of tablets rather than in another room. Lincoln (1989) also provided suggestions on some other environmental adaptations. She noted that most hospital staff wear name badges that may be too small for elderly people to read and that contain surnames rather than the first names that are usually used on the ward.

For those with very severe intellectual handicap or those with progressive deterioration, environmental changes may be the best we can do to enable people to cope and reduce some of their confusion and frustration. Few studies have discussed ways in which environments can be designed to help people with severe memory impairment, although it would seem a fruitful area for psychologists, engineers, architects, and other designers to join forces.

External Aids

Most people without memory impairments make frequent use of external aids (Harris, 1992), although many head-injured memory-impaired people appear to make less use of external aids than those with no serious problems. However, Wilson (1991) found that when brain-injured people were seen 5 to 10 years after rehabilitation they were using significantly more memory aids and were not very different from the general population.

Given that external memory aids are probably the most important means of compensating for memory deficit, it is worthwhile for therapists, teachers, and relatives to investigate as wide a range as possible, and to be prepared to put considerable effort into teaching the use of such aids. Harris (1992) divided external aids into cuing devices that access internally stored information and systems that record information externally. The former category would include alarm clocks, timers, and tying a knot in one's handkerchief (or a string on one's finger). All of these would remind a person to do something, but they would not specify what it was that had to be done. The latter category would include notebooks, diaries, computers, and tape recorders, all of which record the specific information a person would wish to recall.

For those memory-impaired people who have difficulty reading or writing or who have visual problems, tape recorders and microcassettes are worth investigating for their potential usefulness. One of our patients with cortical blindness and amnesia was unable to read but used a pocket dictaphone to record messages from his wife to staff at the rehabilitation center and vice versa. He also recorded instructions about tasks he was to carry out in occupational therapy, and explanations about memory therapy techniques. Another young man, who was unable to remember how to do certain activities in the woodwork department, recorded the instructions on a personal stereo and wore this during his woodwork sessions. His work rate increased and the number of questions he asked decreased considerably.

Such machines may also be used, of course, by those who can read and write perfectly well. One young man with a pure amnesic syndrome lives alone and attends a furniture-making college. He is able to function independently because he uses a number of external aids very efficiently. One of these is a microcassette. He records ongoing information into this machine at frequent intervals during the day. In the evening at home he listens to the tape and transcribes information he considers to be important into a journal. In addition to his microcassette, he uses a watch with an alarm and a filofax (a personal nonelectronic organizer). He is exceptionally adept at compensating for his severe memory difficulties.

External aids can also be pictorial for patients with aphasia or dyslexia. One example provided by Lincoln (1989) described how recipes were presented pictorially for a 36-year-old head-injured housewife who could not remember how to cook and prepare meals for her family. Wilson (1992) provided a pictorial aid to help an aphasic woman remember how to transfer from her wheelchair to her bed. In both cases, instructions were prepared in the form of pictures. I have also known a globally aphasic man use pictures to refer to the past and to the future with relative ease. This man had no words at all, he could produce one sound ("ba"), and his comprehension of spoken words was at the level of a two-year-old. Yet once he had been taught a simple communication method using a mixture of pictorial and abstract symbols, he could use these to refer to the past and the future. For example, during one of our treatment sessions we tried singing. The patient hummed the melody. A card was made using the "symbols." The message drawn on the card said "B . . . did some singing with Barbara and Philippa." He often retrieved this card from his book to remind us of the occasion. Similarly, he frequently referred to another card "saying" "I am going to stay with my son at Christmas."

The past few years have seen an enormous growth in the use of electronic memory aids. These are essentially electronic calculators or digital watches with extra functions such as alarms or the facility to accept written messages. Harris (1992) described some of them in detail and listed their advantages and disadvantages. These aids range from the simple alarm systems to the complex pocket microcomputers such as the Sharp electronic organizer, which includes the following functions: home and world clock, schedule, calendar, telephone book, memo function, things-to-do list, expense function, calculator, and dictionary. The main disadvantage for memory-impaired people is that such electronic aids are difficult to learn how to use. In order to program the organizers, most people need to remember their previous errors, and it is this, of course, that is beyond the capacity of most memory-impaired people. However, advances are constantly being made and some aids are becoming easier to manage (see Kapur, 1995).

One of the biggest problems with external aids is that many patients are reluctant to use them. Some feel it is cheating and believe they should not rely on aids. This idea should be discouraged. Most non-brain-injured people use memory aids, and anything that helps the memory-impaired person to remember must be regarded in a good light. There is no evidence to suggest that using aids will result in less recovery of memory. If anything, they may result in more efficient use of the memory skills the person does possess.

In the long-term memory study described earlier (Wilson, 1991), it was found that those people using six or more different kinds of aids or strategies were more likely to be independent. Those using none at all were those with the most severe intellectual impairments, and were all in long-term hospital care.

For those people who are reluctant to use, forget to use, or are inefficient at using memory aids, alternative aids can be tried in the hope that they will be more congenial or acceptable. Examples here might include the use of a tape recorder instead of a notebook, or the use of a timer on a stopwatch combined with a printed card.

Teaching the use of an external aid requires patience and ingenuity. For most memory-impaired people it is not enough to simply provide a notebook, organizer, tape recorder, or whatever and expect it to be used. Remembering to use the aid is, in itself, a memory task, so of course problems are to be expected. The people who seem best able to get round such difficulties and use the aids spontaneously are those with a pure amnesic syndrome, that is, those without additional cognitive deficits such as attention, reasoning, and word finding problems and with slow thinking processes. Unfortunately, people with a pure amnesic syndrome are relatively rare. Most of those requiring help will have such additional cognitive deficits, making it harder for them to compensate for their problems without help.

Sohlberg and Mateer (1989) described a detailed and thorough program to train people with severe memory impairments to use compensatory memory books, and provided evidence of its effectiveness. The program is in three stages: acquisition, application, and adaptation. In Stage 1 (acquisition) subjects are taught how to use the book, in Stage 2 (application) they are taught when and where to use the book, and in Stage 3 (adaptation) they are expected to adapt and modify their skills and use the book in novel situations. The books themselves are divided into color-coded sections (e.g., the things-to-do pages might be green, the calendar section might be blue, and the names-of-people section might be yellow). In Stage 1 subjects are taught the meaning and names of the different sections. In Stage 2 subjects are prompted and encouraged to record information in the appropriate section (role playing is also used during this stage). In Stage 3 the subject is monitored to see whether the book is used in everyday situations.

Sometimes it is possible to use an aid as a simple reminder and avoid a lengthy teaching process. For example, some calculators are provided with a repeat alarm that can be programed to sound every 10 minutes, every half an hour, or some other interval. These can be used to remind spinal patients to lift regularly (i.e., push with their arms so that their buttocks leave the wheelchair for several seconds) in order to prevent pressure sores. Dysarthric patients who might "forget" to swallow their saliva can be reminded by a buzzer or alarm that sounds every few seconds. For a full discussion of external memory aids see Kapur (1995).

Mnemonics

Mnemonics are verbal and visual aids to learning. They are sayings, rhymes, or drawings that help us to remember things more easily. Most people have used mnemonics at some time in their life. For example, many people in Britain use the rhyme "Thirty days hath September . . . etc." when trying to remember how many days in each month. Many also use a first letter mnemonic such as "Every good boy deserves fruit" for learning musical notes on the lines of the stave. Mnemonics can be used by those with memory impairment to learn new information (see Wilson & Moffat, 1992, for a description of these). It is unrealistic to expect most people with memory impairment to use mnemonics themselves, because remembering to use them is, in itself, a memory task. Nevertheless, there is considerable evidence that mnemonics result in faster learning of new information than does rote rehearsal (Wilson, 1987). For this reason, we provide the following guidelines for relatives and helpers of memory-impaired people:

1. Use mnemonics to teach particular pieces of information, such as names of people or a new address.
2. It often helps to use two or three strategies to improve learning of one piece of information. For example, if you wanted to teach a memory-impaired person to remember the way to the local shops you could draw a map, describe the way verbally, and accompany the person along the route.
3. New things should be taught one step at a time.
4. Take account of individual preferences and styles. Not everybody likes the same strategy.
5. Be realistic about what is to be learned (i.e., concentrate on relevant material that the memory-impaired person wants to learn).

Rehearsal, Repetitive Practice, and Study Techniques

Repetition by itself is not particularly helpful in aiding memory. Similarly, memory games and exercises will not improve memory functioning, although they may be enjoyable. In order to encourage and indeed *enhance* memory, actions we take or materials we use should be manipulated or structured so that the memory-impaired person has to think about the information rather than be its passive recipient. Craik and Lockhart (1972) showed that the deeper the level of processing, the more likely it is that people will remember.

The method of expanding rehearsal (discussed earlier) is one effective rehearsal strategy. Another, from the field study techniques, is PQRST, first described by Robinson (1970). PQRST is an acronym that stands for preview, question, read, state, and test. These headings refer to a series of steps to work through when trying to retain verbal material. It probably works because it encourages deeper processing of the materials to be remembered, that is, it follows the principle of Craik and Lockhart described earlier. Wilson (1987) reported a series of experiments evaluating PQRST. In all cases, PQRST resulted in better learning than did rote rehearsal.

Computer-Based Memory Rehabilitation

A few years ago there was considerable excitement about the possible uses of microcomputers in rehabilitation. People hoped and indeed seemed to expect that computer-based memory-training programs would revolutionize rehabilitation and improve the memory functioning of brain-injured people. Skilbeck (1984), for example, believed that microcomputers could assist in the management of memory disorders by being applied to assessment, the monitoring of treatment effectiveness, and retraining procedures themselves. Numerous software programs have appeared in the 1980s. However, as Robertson (1990) pointed out, the role of microcomputers in cognitive rehabilitation has not been subjected to controlled investigation until recently. Skilbeck and Robertson (1992) provided a more up-to-date review of computers in memory rehabilitation.

There have been a few encouraging reports about the use of computers in cognitive rehabilitation. Sohlberg and Mateer (1987, 1989) demonstrated improved attention functioning in head-injured people, and three patients described by Robertson, Gray, and Mackenzie (1988) showed less visual neglect after a computer training program. However, given the huge increase in the use of computers in rehabilitation centers around the world, demonstrations of their effectiveness have been negligible. Even the few success stories tend to report changes in test scores rather than improvements in everyday living. Furthermore, several studies have reported the noneffectiveness of computer programs (see, for example, Ponsford & Kinsella, 1988; Robertson, 1988).

Maybe we should not, at this stage, expect computers to have much effect on cognitive rehabilitation programs. As Harris and Sunderland (1981) pointed out, memory is not like a muscle that improves or strengthens with exercise. Practice at a task may well improve performance on that particular activity but will not necessarily improve functioning in other areas. Practice at a memory exercise will not improve general memory functioning. The classic experiments by Ericsson, Chase, and Falcon (1980) demonstrated that students could increase their digit span from the normal 7 (plus or minus 2) to a phenomenal 80 or more with constant drilling and practice. However, posttraining assessment on a similar letter span task revealed normal scores of 7 (plus or minus 2). Thus, no improvement of memory functioning per se had occurred.

Computers can, of course, be of great assistance in the field of rehabilitation. They can save much time and lead to greater efficiency in certain assessment procedures, and they can provide immediate and effective feedback (see Mackey, 1989). Training in the use of computers has led to some exciting results from Schacter and Glisky (1986) and Glisky and Schacter (1987). The Glisky and Schacter studies are probably the best to date in the field of computers in memory rehabilitation. The authors taught a number of amnesic patients computer technology using their Method of Vanishing Cues (identical to the forward and backward chaining used in behavior modification). One of their patients was able to obtain employment as a computer programer following several months of training.

Finally, computers may prove to be important as prosthetic aids. Bergman (1991) and Bergman and Kemmerer (1991), for example, described how a head-injured woman with numerous cognitive problems was taught to control her financial affairs and other aspects of her life through a computer program designed specifically for her needs.

Errorless Learning in Rehabilitation

Current work in Cambridge is concerned with the role of errorless learning in rehabilitation. This work has been influenced by studies of errorless discrimination learning from behavioral psychology (Terrace, 1963, 1966), and by studies of implicit memory and learning in memory-impaired people from cognitive psychology (Graf & Schacter, 1985; Schacter, 1987).

Terrace taught a difficult discrimination task to pigeons. During learning, the pigeons made no (or very few) errors. Glisky and Schacter (1987, 1989) tried to use the implicit learning abilities of amnesic subjects to teach them computer technology. Although some success was achieved, it was at the expense of considerable time and effort. This and other attempts to build on the relatively intact skills of amnesic subjects have been disappointing so far. One reason for the failures and anomalies could be that once amnesic subjects have made an error that error gets repeated. If procedural or implicit learning involves a simple incrementing of habit whenever a response is formed, then an erroneous response will tend to strengthen the error, making trial-and-error learning a slow and laborious process.

Baddeley and Wilson (1994) posed the question, "Do amnesic subjects learn better when prevented from making errors during the learning process?" We tested 16 patients with severe memory disorders and gave each of them two lists of five-letter words. One list was presented in an errorful learning way and the other in an errorless way, with the order and condition counterbalanced across subjects. In the errorful condition subjects were told, "I am thinking of a five-letter word beginning with *br*. Can you guess what it might be?" After three incorrect responses (or 25 seconds), in which the subject might say "brain," "bread," and "brown," the tester said, "No, good guesses, but the word is 'bring.' Please write that down." This was repeated for the remaining words, after which two further learning trials were conducted. Thus altogether the subject wrote down each word three times; the incorrect guesses were not written down. In the errorless condition the subject was told, "I am thinking of a five-letter word beginning with *br*, and the word is 'bring.' Please write that down." Again there were three trials. Thus in one condition the subject was generating guesses and in the other only correct responses were produced. This was followed in both conditions by a further nine trials over a 30-minute period. Each trial involved cuing with the first two letters and correcting any incorrect responses. In addition, we tested 16 young and 16 elderly controls (using a 10-word list).

Of the 16 amnesic subjects, every single one of them recalled more words in the errorless condition than in the errorful. This suggests that learning is indeed better when the subject is not allowed to guess during the learning process. The young controls were almost at ceiling in both conditions, whereas the elderly controls' scores fell between those of the young controls and the amnesic subjects. Looking at individual subjects we find that 10 of the 16 elderly controls did better under the errorless condition and 6 did better under the errorful condition.

Since then we have conducted several single-case studies with amnesic subjects, comparing errorful and errorless learning (Wilson, Baddeley, Evans, & Shiel, 1994). These later studies include teaching an agnosic man to recognize pictures, helping a stroke patient to learn people's names, assisting a Korsakof patient to program an electronic aid, and teaching a head-injured man the names of his therapists, items of orientation, and general knowledge. In each case, errorless learning resulted in superior performance to that of trial and error.

Our continuing work on errorless learning leads us to conclude that it is far from being a perfect tool for remembering. Although it is true that results have been encouraging, they do not match those reported by Terrace in the 1960s. In order to achieve better results we have begun to incorporate other principles from learning theory and memory therapy in our program. These include such strategies as not teaching more than one piece of information at a time and the method of expanding rehearsal. It remains to be seen whether other patients, such as those with Alzheimer's disease, can benefit from errorless learning. Would they be able to learn names, practical skills, routes, vocabulary, and so forth using errorless learning in combination with some of these other principles and strategies?

CONCLUDING REMARKS

The fact that we cannot restore memory functioning should not deter us from pursuing the means of improving patients' well-being. Memory-impaired people and their families need therapy that will enable them to understand and cope with difficulties arising during adjustment to everyday life.

Although the general guidelines and specific strategies offered here do not provide a cure, they may reduce to some extent some of the problems faced by memory-impaired people. Success may come from such strategies as bypassing difficulties through environmental restructuring; using alternative ways of remembering through external aids; using residual skills more efficiently through mnemonics and rehearsal techniques; and improving the emotional well-being of both patients and carers through the provision of information, explanations about the nature of memory deficits, relaxation exercises to reduce anxiety, and role playing to teach people how to explain their memory problems to people with whom they interact.

REFERENCES

Baddeley, A. D. (1990). *Human memory: Theory and practice*. Hillsdale, NJ: Lawrence Erlbaum Associates.

Baddeley, A. D., & Wilson, B. A. (1988). Comprehension and working memory: A single case neuropsychological study. *Journal of Memory and Language, 27*, 479–498.

Baddeley, A. D., & Wilson, B. A. (1994). When implicit learning fails: Amnesia and the problem of error elimination. *Neuropsychologia, 32*, 53–68.

Berg, I. J., Koning-Haanstra, M., & Deelman, D. G. (1991). Long term effects of memory rehabilitation: A controlled study. *Neuropsychological Rehabilitation, 1*, 97–111.

Bergman, M. M. (1991). Computer-enhanced self sufficiency: Part 1. Creation and implementation of a text writer for an individual with traumatic brain injury. *Neuropsychology, 5*, 17–24.

Bergman, M. M., & Kemmerer, A. G. (1991). Computer-enhanced self sufficiency: Part 2. Uses and subjective benefits of a text writer for an individual with traumatic brain injury. *Neuropsychology, 5*, 25–28.

Brotchie, J., & Thornton, S. (1987). Reminiscence: A critical review of the empirical literature. *British Journal of Clinical Psychology, 26*, 93–111.

Craik, F. I. M., & Lockhart, R. S. (1972). Levels of processing: A framework for memory research. *Journal of Verbal Learning and Verbal Behavior, 11*, 671–684.

Ericsson, K. A., Chase, W. G., & Falcon, S. (1980). Acquisition of a memory skill. *Science, 208*, 1181–1182.

Evans, J. J., & Wilson, B. A. (1992). A memory group for individuals with brain injury. *Clinical Rehabilitation, 6*, 75–81.

Folsom, J. C. (1968). Reality orientation for the elderly mental patient. *Journal of Geriatric Psychiatry, 1*, 291–307.

Glisky, E. L., & Schacter, D. L. (1987). Acquisition of domain-specific knowledge in organic amnesia: Training for computer-related work. *Neuropsychologia, 25*, 893–906.

Glisky, E. L., & Schacter, D. L. (1989). Extending the limits of complex learning in organic amnesia: Computer training in a vocational domain. *Neuropsychologia, 27*, 107–120.

Graf, P., & Schacter, D. L. (1985). Implicit and explicit memory for new associations in normal and amnesic subjects. *Journal of Experimental Psychology: Learning, Memory and Cognition, 11*, 501–518.

Harris, J. E. (1980). We have ways of helping you remember. *Concord: The Journal of the British Association of Service to the Elderly, 17*, 21–27.

Harris, J. (1992). Ways to help memory. In B. A. Wilson & N. Moffat (Eds.), *Clinical management of memory problems* (2nd ed., pp. 59–85). London: Chapman & Hall.

Harris, J. E., & Sunderland, A. (1981). A brief survey of the management of memory disorders in rehabilitation units in Britain. *International Rehabilitation Medicine, 3*, 206–209.

Holden, U. P., & Woods, R. T. (1982). *Reality orientation: Psychological approaches to the confused elderly.* London: Churchill Livingstone.

Kapur, N. (1995). External memory aids. In A. D. Baddeley, B. A. Wilson, & F. N. Watts (Eds.), *Handbook of memory disorders* (pp. 533–556). Chichester, England: Wiley.

Kopelman, M. D. (1992). The psychopharmacology of human memory disorders. In B. A. Wilson & N. Moffat (Eds.), *Clinical management of memory problems* (2nd ed., pp. 189–215). London: Chapman & Hall.

Lincoln, N. B. (1989). Management of memory problems in a hospital setting. In L. W. Poon, D. C. Rubin, & B. A. Wilson (Eds.), *Everyday cognition in adulthood and late life* (pp. 639–658). Cambridge, England: Cambridge University Press.

Mackey, S. (1989). The use of computer-assisted feedback in a motor-control task for cerebral palsied children. *Physiotherapy, 75*, 143–148.

Moffat, N. (1989). Home based cognitive rehabilitation with the elderly. In L. W. Poon, D. C. Rubin, & B. A. Wilson (Eds.), *Everyday cognition in adulthood and late life* (pp. 659–680). Cambridge, England: Cambridge University Press.

Moffat, N. (1992). Strategies of memory therapy. In B. A. Wilson & N. Moffat (Eds.), *Clinical management of memory problems* (2nd ed., pp. 86–119). London: Chapman & Hall.

Ponsford, J. L., & Kinsella, G. (1988). Evaluation of a remedial programme for attentional deficits following closed head injury. *Journal of Clinical and Experimental Neuropsychology, 10*, 693–708.

Robertson, I. H. (1988). *Unilateral visual neglect.* Doctoral thesis, University of London.

Robertson, I. H. (1990). Does computerised cognitive rehabilitation work? A review. *Aphasiology, 4*, 381–405.

Robertson, I. H., Gray, J., & McKenzie, S. (1988). Microcomputer-based cognitive rehabilitation of visual neglect: 3 single case studies. *Brain Injury, 2*, 151–164.

Robinson, F. B. (1970). *Effective study.* New York: Harper and Row.

Schacter, D. L. (1987). Memory, amnesia and frontal lobe dysfunction. *Psychobiology, 15*, 21–36.

Schacter, D. L., & Glisky, E. L. (1986). Memory remediation: Restoration, alleviation and the acquisition of domain-specific knowledge. In B. Uzzell & Y. Grosse (Eds.), *Clinical neuropsychology of intervention* (pp. 257–282). Boston: Nijoff.

Skilbeck, C., & Robertson, I. H. (1992). Computer assistance in the management of memory and cognitive impairment. In B. A. Wilson & N. Moffat (Eds.), *Clinical management of memory problems* (2nd ed., pp. 154–188). London: Chapman & Hall.

Sohlberg, M. M., & Mateer, C. A. (1987). Effectiveness of an attention training programme. *Journal of Clinical and Experimental Neuropsychology, 9,* 117–130.

Sohlberg, M. M., & Mateer, C. (1989). Training use of compensatory memory books: A three stage behavioural approach. *Journal of Clinical and Experimental Psychology, 11,* 871–891.

Terrace, H. S. (1963). Discrimination learning with and without "errors." *Journal of Experimental Analysis of Behavior, 6,* 1–27.

Terrace, H. S. (1966). Stimulus control. In W. K. Honig (Ed.), *Operant behaviour: Areas of research and application* (pp. 271–344). New York: Appleton-Century-Crofts.

Wilson, B. A. (1987). *Rehabilitation of memory.* New York: Guilford.

Wilson, B. A. (1991). Long term prognosis of patients with severe memory disorders. *Neuropsychological Rehabilitation, 1,* 117–134.

Wilson, B. A. (1992). Memory therapy in practice. In B. A. Wilson & N. Moffat (Eds.), *Clinical management of memory problems* (2nd ed., pp. 120–153). London: Chapman & Hall.

Wilson, B. A., & Baddeley, A. D. (1993). Spontaneous recovery of digit span: Does comprehension also recover? *Cortex, 29,* 153–159.

Wilson, B. A., Baddeley, A. D., Evans, J. J., & Shiel, A. (1994). Errorless learning in the rehabilitation of memory impaired people. *Neuropsychological Rehabilitation, 4,* 307–326.

Wilson, B. A., Cockburn, J., & Baddeley, A. D. (1985). *The Rivermead Behavioural Memory Test.* Flempton, Bury St. Edmunds: Thames Valley Test Company.

Wilson, B. A., & Moffat, N. (1992). The development of group memory therapy. In B. A. Wilson, & N. Moffat (Eds.), *Clinical management of memory problems* (2nd ed., pp. 243–273). London: Chapman & Hall.

CHAPTER FIFTEEN

Failures of Autobiographical Remembering

Martin A. Conway
University of Bristol, England

What is autobiographical memory *for*? Currently, only commonsense answers are possible to this question. Essentially, autobiographical memory appears to be for almost every major aspect of cognition one might care to consider, but has no specific role in any particular activity, with the possible exception of writing one's memoirs (and even here it informs rather than constrains). To be sure, there have been studies of how autobiographical memories are used in discourse, social interactions, and even problem solving (Hyman & Faries, 1992; Pillemer, 1992; Ross, 1984) and the findings from these studies provide clues to some of the functions of autobiographical remembering, but they do not answer the question "What is it for?" But surely, it might be countered, autobiographical memory is central to the self, to identity, to emotional experience, and to all those attributes that define an individual. A person without an autobiographical memory would have no self, no identity, no way of responding to the world emotionally. Autobiographical memory may, indeed, be critical to self, it may constitute the knowledge base of the self (Conway & Rubin, 1993), and it may function as a resource of the self (Robinson, 1986; Salaman, 1970), but if this is the major function then that function is nebulous, intangible, and intrinsically slippery. There is nothing specific about it, nothing on which one could put one's finger.

Assuming, then, that the function of autobiographical memory is, for the moment, ineffable, how can we proceed with empirical investigations? It seems to me that there is no insuperable problem here; after all, there are many objects, actions, and processes whose functions remain unknown, but those same objects, actions, and processes can still be investigated and their properties described. Obviously, the hope is that in the course of compiling a description many if not all of the functions will become apparent. This is exactly the current stage of research into autobiographical memory. Some properties of this type of remembering have been described, progress is being made on others, and some functions have been considered (Baddeley, 1992; Conway, 1990; Conway & Rubin, 1993; Robinson & Swanson, 1990). Research into autobiographical memory is at a descriptive stage and, as the findings accrue and theories of function move from the inchoate to the articulate, models of autobiographical memory may eventually become predictive. One source of evidence of increasing relevance to this enterprise is that of findings arising from patients with neurological and psychogenic memory impairments (Conway, 1993). The failure of autobiographical remembering reveals much about the structure and retrieval of autobiographical knowledge, and it is findings from these studies that form the main part of this chapter. However, it has been possible to generate a broad outline description of autobiographical memory on the basis of experimental findings with nonimpaired subjects, and it is this that is considered first.

THE CONSTRUCTION
OF AUTOBIOGRAPHICAL MEMORIES

In general outline, the constructivist model of autobiographical memory proposes that there is a pool of autobiographical knowledge containing items at different levels of abstraction. Some items of knowledge are highly specific and relate only to memories of single, unique events, whereas other items are more general and encompass many memories and comparatively lengthy periods of time. Within this autobiographical knowledge base, knowledge is compiled into knowledge structures, and specific information stored at particular levels in knowledge structures provides cues or indices to associated levels. A centrally mediated, complex, and dynamic retrieval process generates access to and coordinates output from the knowledge base. A memory is retrieved once an appropriate stable pattern of activation has been established across some subset of knowledge structures. In this model, memories only exist temporarily, they are unstable dynamic representations that must be effortfully maintained, and they change, sometimes strikingly and sometimes imperceptibly, with each retrieval of the same memory. Some stability is provided by the indices between levels of a knowledge structure, and tightly organized knowledge structures may represent highly stable memories (see Conway, 1994a). However, the main constraints that lead to memory stability in any single episode of retrieval are imposed by a mental model of the retrieval task that also forms the central component of the generative retrieval process.

The following sections briefly consider the autobiographical memory knowledge base and the generative retrieval process (see Anderson & Conway, 1993; Conway 1992, 1994a, 1994b, 1994c; Conway & Rubin, 1993, for further details) and later sections examine failures of autobiographical memory.

Autobiographical Knowledge

Evidence from a number of independently conducted investigations using a wide range of experimental procedures has converged on the view that the autobiographical knowledge base[1] is structured (Anderson & Conway, 1993; Barsalou, 1988; Brown, Shevell, & Rips, 1986; Conway, 1992, 1994b, 1994c; Conway & Bekerian, 1987; Conway & Rubin, 1993; Linton, 1986; Schooler & Herrmann, 1992; Treadway, McCloskey, Gordon, & Cohen, 1992). The evidence suggests that there are at least three levels of knowledge that can be distinguished on the basis of their specificity. The most general type of autobiographical knowledge is that of *lifetime periods*, which refers to periods of time measured in months, years, and decades, and encompasses general *themes* of the self that characterized a period (e.g., "When I lived with X," "When I worked at Y," "When I attended school Z," etc.). More specific than lifetime periods are *general events*, which refer to periods of time measured in days, weeks, and, possibly, months, and represent knowledge of goal attainment and personal themes relating to specific sets of events or to extended events such as "Holiday in Italy," "Friday evenings with X, Y, and Z," "Working on project W," and so on. The final type of knowledge, *event specific knowledge* (ESK), is highly detailed and refers to time periods measured in seconds, minutes, and hours. This knowledge tends to be sensory in nature and is frequently, although not always, instantiated during retrieval in the form of images.

Within the autobiographical knowledge base, lifetime periods, general events, and ESK form hierarchical partonomic knowledge structures (Barsalou, 1988; Conway, 1992) in which different types of knowledge are bound together by temporal and thematic indices. For example, the lifetime period "When I worked at Y" would represent knowledge of actors, activities, locations, self-themes, and goal-attainment outcomes common to that period. This knowledge provides cues that can be used to access general events associated with the lifetime period. General event knowledge, in turn, provides cues that access records of specific events in the form of ESK. In other

---

[1]The phrase *autobiographical knowledge base* is used here to denote autobiographical knowledge in general. It is *not* used to refer to a separate memory system. As becomes clear later, general autobiographical knowledge is conceived as being part of a much wider general-purpose, long-term memory system (Conway, 1990). On the other hand, highly specific autobiographical knowledge could, conceivably, be part of a separate memory system (Conway, 1992).

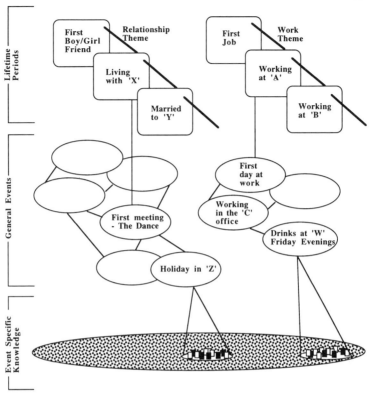

FIG. 15.1. Autobiographical memory knowledge structures for work and relationship themes.

words, general events are part of lifetime periods, and ESK is always part of particular general events. Fig. 15.1 illustrates this scheme for work and relationship themes. (Note that in Fig. 15.1, ESK is depicted as an undifferentiated pool of event features indexed by general event knowledge. The reason for this is to leave open the possibility that the organization of ESK is different from that of more abstract types of autobiographical knowledge; see Conway, 1992. Also, as becomes apparent later in the chapter, some evidence suggests that ESK may be represented separately from other types of autobiographical knowledge.) There are, of course, many other features of these knowledge structures and of the different levels of knowledge (see Conway, 1994b, 1994c; Conway & Rubin, 1993 for reviews) that have not been considered here. Furthermore, there are current investigations into general events and local forms of organization at this level (Anderson & Conway, 1993; Robinson, 1992) that may lead to modifications of this outline. Nevertheless, this brief sketch of the autobiographical knowledge base will be useful when impairments of autobiographical remembering are considered later in the chapter.

Autobiographical Memory Retrieval

One striking fact of autobiographical memory retrieval is that it is slow (i.e., mean retrieval times in excess of three seconds in most studies that have collected retrieval times) in comparison to other types of tasks that also require the access of knowledge in long-term memory (cf. Conway, 1990, 1992). Indeed, verification of factual autobiographical knowledge, which typically takes a little over one second (Conway, 1987), is more than three times as fast as memory retrieval. One reason for this is that memory retrieval is a more complex process involving more intermediate processing stages than the processing sequences underlying fact verification. Norman and Bobrow (1979) first drew attention to this when they proposed that retrieval from long-term memory was mediated by the generation of memory descriptions. According to this view, a cue is first elaborated into a description and the description then used to search memory. As knowledge in memory is accessed the description is fine-tuned until the sought-for knowledge is located.

The memory descriptions model was refined by Williams and Hollan (1981) in a protocol study of autobiographical memory retrieval. They proposed that there were three identifiable stages to the retrieval cycle. In the first stage, a cue is elaborated into a form appropriate to searching the autobiographical knowledge base. Consider a subject in an autobiographical memory cue word experiment (Conway & Bekerian, 1987; Crovitz & Schiffman, 1974; Robinson, 1976) presented with the cue word *ship* and required to retrieve, as quickly as possible, a specific memory of which the cue reminds them. The elaboration phase may involve simply thinking "When would I have been likely to have traveled on a ship?" followed by some plausible inference such as "On a holiday." It might then be further inferred that a foreign holiday would be most likely to involve a journey by ship (at least for U.K. residents). Thus, the elaborated cue or memory description would take the form of "locate autobiographical knowledge of a foreign holiday." The second stage of retrieval can then be initiated, in which the elaborated cue is used to search knowledge structures in autobiographical memory. Assume that the search process first accesses lifetime period information and eventually locates a period that has indices to the general "Trip with X to Paris." This accessed knowledge is then evaluated in the third phase of retrieval, by verification processes that determine whether or not the retrieved knowledge is the sought-for knowledge or whether it is some reasonably close approximation to the sought-for knowledge. In the former case, the search can be terminated and a response executed. In the latter case, the search must cycle through the three-stage process again, using a new memory description generated from the retrieved knowledge. In the second cycle, ESK relating to the general event "Trip with X to Paris" may be accessed, and this knowledge may either support termination of the search (knowledge relating to a cross-channel ferry trip was accessed) or reinitiation of the whole retrieval cycle (knowledge relating to a flight to Paris was accessed).

It is assumed that in most cases the retrieval processes run through many cycles, although in some cases retrieval may be rapid. Moreover, cues may directly access ESK, and activation spreading from this source may make accessible general event and lifetime period knowledge. In this case, the path of activation is channeled by autobiographical memory indices from the many ESK attributes to the single general event and associated lifetime period, and cyclic retrieval is bypassed. This process of direct retrieval may underlie the spontaneous retrieval of autobiographical memories occasionally noted in everyday cognition (Conway, 1992, 1994b, 1994c; Conway & Rubin, 1993). In either case, the main point is that a memory is a temporary pattern of activation established across knowledge structures in the autobiographical knowledge base. Although the memory descriptions approach and cyclic retrieval provide a plausible account of autobiographical memory construction, it is clear that these approaches themselves require further development. Indeed, a critical problem with these approaches is that they, as it were, push the problem of memory retrieval out of the search phase and into the elaboration and verification phases. How can a cue be elaborated without first accessing memory? And how can outputs from long-term memory be evaluated without, again, consulting long-term knowledge?

One way to approach these problems is to view the retrieval process as part of a larger set of central control processes that, among other things, place constraints on memory retrieval. In recent work we (Anderson & Conway, 1993; Conway, 1992, 1994b, 1994c; Conway & Rubin, 1993) proposed that the retrieval process is controlled by the supervisory attentional system, or SAS (Norman & Shallice, 1980; Shallice, 1988), which might also be thought of as the central executive of working memory (Baddeley, 1986). The SAS is conceived as a set of central control processes, part of the function of which is the initiation of memory search and the modulation of output from memory—akin to the cue elaboration and verification stages of cyclic retrieval. In our view, however, the SAS or executive is a knowledge-based system itself, inasmuch as it contains some type of model of the whole cognitive system (Johnson-Laird, 1983) and, in particular, a model of the current state of the self—the working self. With these resources, the SAS can create a temporary model of task demands and specify constraints that must be satisfied prior to execution of a response. For example, in autobiographical memory retrieval one constraint might be that appropriate ESK knowledge must be accessed (cf. Conway, 1994b, for further discussion) when a specific memory is to be retrieved.

In summary: Memory construction involves a structured knowledge base in which knowledge at different levels of abstraction is compiled into hierarchical knowledge structures. A complex and centrally mediated retrieval process samples this knowledge base, gradually establishing a stable pattern of activation that makes accessible the knowledge that satisfies the various constraints of a mental model of current task demands. Disruptions of this system are often striking, and next I consider a variety of single-case studies that illustrate various aspects of the model.

FAILURES OF AUTOBIOGRAPHICAL REMEMBERING

Fragmentary Autobiographical Knowledge

There are a series of single-case studies of brain-injured patients that, in general, demonstrate the preservation of abstract autobiographical knowledge, lifetime periods, and general events, with severely impaired ESK (cf. Conway, 1993). For instance, Cermak and O'Connor's (1983) amnesic patient S.S. had an intact short-term memory but suffered from a dense anterograde amnesia, and his ability to retain knowledge over periods longer than a few minutes was severely impaired. In contrast, S.S. was able to recall and recount many of the events of his life and, when tested with a questionnaire created with the help of his wife and mother, provided elaborate answers for most of the decades of his life. When, however, S.S. was tested with the cue word method, retrieving memories to words naming common objects, activities, and feelings, his performance was dramatically impaired and it became apparent that he could not recall memories for the events of his life. Cermak and O'Connor commented, "Instead, his memories were of generalised events such as jobs he had held, not specific episodes for any one work experience. . . . What he tended to recall was the general idea of a past event or the fact that an event had happened rather than the event itself" (1983, p. 230). S.S. appeared, then, to have a stock of family stories that he could relate and some other general knowledge of the events of his life, but no actual memories. A similar pattern was observed with Tulving, Schacter, McLachlan, and Moscovitch's (1988) patient K.C., who, as a result of a severe closed-head injury, suffered damage to left frontal-parietal and right parietal-occipital lobes. K.C. had both dense anterograde and retrograde amnesia with preserved short-term memory, intellectual skills, and normal intelligence. Tulving et al. found that K.C. was totally unable to recollect any specific event from his life, although he did have access to knowledge of lifetime periods. For instance, he could name the schools he attended, classmates, and some of the companies for which he had worked. In addition to this he could report various other aspects of general personal knowledge. Moreover, in the course of testing more of this knowledge became available to him, especially relating to his job immediately prior to his injury, although as Tulving et al. pointed out that K.C. never reached the point of retrieving a specific memory.

In contrast to S.S. and K.C., Kapur, Ellison, Smith, McLellan, and Burrows' (1992) patient L.T., who suffered a closed-head injury resulting in damage to the anterior portion of both temporal lobes coupled with less extensive injury to both frontal lobes, had a dense retrograde amnesia but only a mild anterograde amnesia. Intellectual performance, IQ, and short-term memory skills were not impaired, but L.T.'s retrograde amnesia for her life prior to her accident was, if anything, more dense than that of K.C. Basically, L.T. was unable to recollect any of the events of her preinjury life and, although she had some knowledge of the facts of her life (e.g., houses she had lived in, holidays taken, etc.), this was far from complete. Indeed, because much of this factual knowledge had been retold to L.T. by her family and friends, it was difficult to determine if any of this knowledge was in fact retrieved from memory or learned anew. In Kapur et al.'s description of her performance L.T. most often commented that the information was not remembered from the past but had been relearned since her accident. It seems that L.T. may have had something approaching a total retrograde amnesia for her preinjury autobiography. Despite this, perceptuomotor skills such as driving and piano playing were retained, but L.T. had no recollection of when or how she had acquired these skills. One intriguing finding was that L.T. claimed to have a feeling of emotional recognition when meeting children she had previously cared for in her job as a nanny, perhaps indicating that her memory of her preinjury life had not been totally lost. Set against this extremely dense amnesia was the remarkable fact that L.T.'s autobiographical memory *since* her injury appeared to be comparatively normal, showing detailed recall of holidays, and of events relating to her treatment and subsequent domestic life.

These three case, S.S., K.C., and L.T., show preservation of lifetime period and general event autobiographical knowledge in the absence of memory for details of unique events. The constructivist account of autobiographical memory is clearly compatible with these findings and suggests a number of possible interpretations. One possibility is that ESK is stored in a separate memory system that, due to brain injury, has in some way become disconnected from the rest of the cognitive system (Warrington & Weiskrantz, 1982). Alternatively, there may be a disruption of the retrieval process such that retrieval terminates prior to accessing ESK. However, autobiographical knowledge can become disrupted in ways other than access failure. Hodges and McCarthy (1993; McCarthy & Hodges, 1994) described a patient, P.S., with bilateral paramedian thalamic damage following a stroke. At the time of his injury, P.S. was a successful garage owner who had been married for a number of years and had three adult children. Following his stroke, P.S. suffered from a very dense anterograde amnesia and a retrograde amnesia covering, virtually, the whole of his adult life. P.S. had no insight into his cognitive disabilities and according to his wife had no memory for any of the events of their married life. He did, however, have some general auto-biographical memory but, although he apparently knew that he was married and had children and grandchildren, he was often confused about specific details (i.e., names of the grandchildren). He also knew that his sons now managed his two garages but, when probed about this aspect of his life, gave stereotypical responses that contained no specific event information. But the most striking aspect of P.S.'s memory impairment was that he had a comparatively good memory for the period covering 1941 to 1946 when he was on active service with the navy. Indeed, the preservation of this lifetime period led P.S. to interpret other autobiographical knowledge in terms of this period and, although he was over 60 years of age during his illness, he still persisted in his claim to be on active naval service. P.S. believed that he was on shore leave and indulged in behavior relating to that time. For instance, he would search for cigarettes although he had not smoked since 1945 and, to his wife's distress, insisted on a nightly blackout (McCarthy & Hodges, 1994).

There are both contrasts and similarities between P.S. and the patients S.S., K.C., and L.T. All these patients had some access to higher levels of autobiographical knowledge structures and could provide some information on periods from their lives and, occasionally, some general event knowledge. None of the patients appeared to be able to fully instantiate detailed, and specific autobiographical memories (with the exception of P.S., who has some preservation of memories from his period of naval service). P.S. is particularly interesting because in his case the disconnection argument cannot be easily sustained and it seems that, for unknown reasons relating to his specific brain injury, the retrieval process could only access a single lifetime period through which all autobiographical knowledge must be processed. One possibility is that for P.S. the period of naval service represented a particularly critical period in his life—one that had far-reaching implications for the self. Such critical periods may be associated with the creation of autobiographical memory knowledge structures that have a central or privileged place in autobiographical memory as a whole and, as a consequence, are represented in some special way (cf. Conway, 1993; Conway & Rubin, 1993). Possibly, such critical periods are multiply represented, being present in both the autobiographical knowledge base and in the knowledge base of central control processes. Thus, when brain injuries lead to a degradation of access to the autobiographical knowledge base but do not affect the retrieval process itself, then becoming "trapped" in time may be a feature of impaired autobiographical remembering, because only autobiographical knowledge held centrally can be used to access the knowledge base.

Interestingly, Treadway, McCloskey, Gordon, and Cohen (1992) recently reported two case studies of amnesics with lifetime period impairments that appear similar to those experienced by P.S. Treadway et al.'s patients, K. and F., were virtually totally amnesic for all memories and skills acquired during a lengthy period in adulthood. K., for example, although 53 years old in 1984, believed himself to be 14 years old and the year to be 1945. Indeed, the last episode K. was able to report was being hit on the head with a baseball bat during a game with some friends. It transpired that this had in fact occurred in August 1945. In a similar vein F., a 39-year-old mother, regained consciousness after undergoing surgery for a cartoid artery aneurysm and believed that the year was 1960 and she was 23 years old. Her most recent family-related memory was of moving into a new house with her husband and three children, whom she believed to be between two and five years old. In fact, she had four children, the youngest being 14 years old, and had lived in the house for 16 years. Both K. and F. had apparently normal memories for events occurring prior to the lifetime period they currently believed themselves to be in and, importantly, good memories for both personal and public events occurring after the onset of their retrograde amnesias. Although there was no evidence of specific neurological injury for either patient, there was evidence of personal trauma associated with the lost lifetime periods. It seems from this that both K. and F. had psychogenic disruptions of autobiographical memory in which traumatic autobiographical knowledge had become inaccessible (cf. Conway & Rubin, 1993, for further discussion). However, both patients were able to retrieve some knowledge from the periods covered by their retrograde amnesias, and this suggests that rather than having become inaccessible, these periods has become clouded. Possibly, these disruptions arise, then, from some (unknown) type of impairment to the retrieval process, which can no longer effectively use the knowledge structures relating to these periods but otherwise functions normally.

Fragmentary Autobiographical Memories

Dense and global retrograde amnesias associated with brain damage and psychogenic illnesses generally show some preservation of lifetime period knowledge and proscribed access to the autobiographical knowledge base. Other types of less severe retrograde amnesias illustrate the breakdown of memory construction. For example, Warrington and McCarthy (1988) reported a study of a 54-year-old amnesic police officer, R.F.R., who, following herpes simplex encephalitis, sustained damage to both temporal lobes resulting in a dense anterograde and retrograde amnesia, although intellectual, language, and perceptual abilities were preserved. According to Warrington and McCarthy, R.F.R.'s knowledge of his own life took the form of an outline C.V., describing the major lifetime periods such as schools attended, periods of employment, and so forth. Occasionally, R.F.R. was able to retrieve a memory, but this was the exception rather than the rule. However, in a subsequent examination (McCarthy & Warrington, 1993), a particularly interesting aspect of R.F.R.'s amnesia became apparent. McCarthy and Warrington observed that R.F.R. was strikingly poor at providing "what happened" information about famous people and public news, but was good at providing superordinate information (e.g., occupation). For example, he identified the *General Belgrano* as a ship but was unable to recall that it had been attacked and sunk during the Falklands War. When responding to personal knowledge he was able to correctly identify the spoken names of friends, he could judge who his oldest and newest friends were, and judge the closeness of friends to his family. He was also able to provide accurate descriptions of friends—descriptions as good as those provided by his wife—but he was unable to describe any specific episodes involving the same friends. R.F.R., then, had good access to knowledge of people but impaired access to knowledge of events in which people have been involved. Indeed, he was able to provide a fairly full character sketch and physical description of a very close friend who had been the best man at his wedding, but he could not recall any events in which he and his friend had participated.

R.F.R. can be contrasted with the patient K.S. described by Ellis, Young, and Critchley (1989). K.S. was a 40-year-old woman who had a lengthy history of epilepsy, culminating in a right anterior temporal lobectomy. Interestingly, K.S. had no history of amnesia, and recall and recognition performance were normal, although she had complained about the mundane quality of her memory both before and after her operation. When tested it turned out that she had an abnormally poor memory for famous people, famous animals, famous buildings, and old product names. On the other hand, her semantic memory appeared normal and her IQ was unimpaired. K.S. was able to give a detailed account of her childhood and adolescence recalling time lifeperiods, general events, and ESK fluently, and described places she had lived and people she had known in some detail. However, her memory for recent events was impaired in that although K.S. could describe events she had experienced, she could not access knowledge concerning people involved in the events. Thus, Ellis et al. described K.S.'s detailed recall of the layout of, and objects in, a consultant's room, as well as her good recall of her conversations with the consultant—but K.S. could not recall any details of the consultant himself. Similarly, she could recall the events of a recent holiday but could not recall people she had met while on holiday. Thus, K.S. provides a contrast to R.F.R., who could recollect in detail the physical appearance of his friends and relatives but could not recall any events.

These types of patients strongly suggest that the autobiographical knowledge base is highly structured, and that autobiographical memories are constructed on the basis of knowledge sampled from different areas of knowledge structures. Thus, R.F.R. might be thought of as a patient who can access lifetime periods and the knowledge represented at this level, but is unable to proceed on the basis of this knowledge to general events and ESK. (Note that the constructivist model proposes that common aspects of significant individuals who featured repeatedly in lifetime periods are stored at this level of knowledge; see Conway, 1992.) K.S. is a more difficult case; she was not clinically amnesic, had good memory for her early life, and her autobiographical memory disorder most clearly related to the period after her operation. Moreover, from the account in Ellis et al. (1989), it seems that her memory impairment may have been very gradually worsening over a period of years. In K.S.'s case, then, we may see the gradual and slow emergence of a dense anterograde amnesia that starts with a disruption to the evaluation and integration component of the generative retrieval process, when this is used in the process of encoding (Conway, 1994b). Thus, for K.S. the problem is one of integrating knowledge of people with preexisting long-term memory knowledge structures and, perhaps, in creating new knowledge structures and indices to ESK.

Disruptions of the ability to use the indices of autobiographical memory knowledge structures may also take a more general form. For instance, Baddeley and Wilson (1986) studied four frontal lobe patients who showed varying types of autobiographical memory impairment. The patients E.W. and J.W. both showed signs of being able to access some autobiographical knowledge and were able to recall, on occasions, autobiographical memories. J.W. showed some signs of confusion about when events occurred, but in general both patients showed what Baddeley and Wilson called a "clouding" of autobiographical memory. Such clouding was shown by other (nonfrontal) amnesic patients tested by Baddeley and Wilson, and generally took the form of an inability to produce the amount of detail one might typically expect a person to have in mind when retrieving a memory.

Interestingly, a related clouding of autobiographical remembering has also been observed in non-brain-damaged patients diagnosed as clinically depressed (Williams & Broadbent, 1986; Williams & Dritschel, 1992; Williams & Scott, 1988; and see Williams, 1994, for a review). The disorder in depressed patients takes a different form from that observed in some frontal lobe patients, but nevertheless suggests an impairment of the retrieval process. Williams (1994) provided an illustration of the problem in recounting a typical interaction between a depressed patient and a therapist in which the therapist probes for memories of specific events:

Therapist: When you were young, what sorts of things made you happy?

Patient: Well, things used to be alright then; I mean, better than they are now, I think. When my dad was there, he used to take me for walks on the Common sometimes after lunch on a Sunday.

Therapist:	Can you tell me about one such walk?
Patient:	Well, we used to go out after lunch, sometimes we would take a ball and play around. Afterwards, we might go and see my granny who lived the other side of the Common.
Therapist:	When you think back, now, can you remember any particular time? I want you to try and recall any one of these times. Any time will do, it doesn't have to be particularly important or special.
Patient:	I remember there used to be other children on the Common sometimes. Sometimes they would be friends of mine and I would stop and chat to them for a while.
Therapist:	Can you remember any particular time when you met any of your friends?
Patient:	If it was winter, there weren't usually many people about. (Williams, 1994, p. 4)

In subsequent formal research, Williams and his colleagues established that clinically depressed patients, when asked to recall memories to cue words, usually were unable to recall memories of specific events. Instead, and as in the previous example, depressed patients recalled *overgeneral* memories typically of repeated or "categoric" experiences (e.g., walks on the common, being criticized by a partner, failing to attain various goals, etc.). Importantly, the overgeneral memories of depressed patients were not dominated by the recall of *extended* events (e.g., "holiday in country X," "day trip to city Y," or "period of illness Z." It would seem from this that depressed patients avoid specific memories and recall general or schematized information abstract from sets of repeated experiences. Williams (1994) proposed that this occurs because the retrieval process terminates prematurely at an intermediate stage of retrieval. Possibly, this malfunction of the retrieval process serves an adaptive function in protecting the depressed individual from retrieving specific memories of negative events that would only exacerbate their already abnormal mood state.

This protective function of disrupted retrieval may also occur in other types of psychogenic disorder. For example, Parkin and Stampfer (1994) described the case of young woman who, after a turbulent and traumatic past, underwent a period of psychosis followed by a period characterized by the "negative" symptoms of schizophrenia. Eventually the patient completely recovered, but during the period of negative symptoms she was strikingly impaired in retrieving autobiographical memories. Possibly, this occurred because of an associated depression and, relatedly, similar disruptions of autobiographical memory in schizophrenics with negative rather than positive symptoms have been reported recently by Baddeley, Thornton,

Chua, and McKenna (1994). At this stage the nature and extent of impairments of autobiographical remembering in schizophrenias is not known, but it seems likely that these too will turn out to be a product of a disrupted retrieval process—perhaps directly associated with a disruption of central control processes themselves.

Taken together, then, these failures of autobiographical remembering suggest disruptions of the retrieval process. Both the neurological and psychogenic patients considered so far clearly can access the autobiographical knowledge base but show marked variability in fully constructing detailed memories. It is as if there is some failure of the retrieval process, perhaps at the verification stage, to further exploit the available indices of the knowledge structures and, in particular, to access and use ESK in any systematic way. One of the most striking cases of this was reported recently by Ogden (1993). Ogden's patient, M.H., was a 24-year-old army Lance Corporal involved in a serious motorcycle accident resulting in extensive orthopaedic injuries and brain damage. The brain damage was mainly confined to the occipital lobes and pathways leading from these areas to temporal and parietal regions. Injury to the occipital lobes is known to give rise to impairments of visual processing, and M.H. had a number of visual deficits including visual object agnosia, prosopagnosia, achromatopsia, and loss of visual imagery. It is worth noting here that although M.H. could not recognize objects on sight, he could recognize objects completely normally when information from other modalities was available. M.H. had a dense retrograde amnesia for his life prior to his injury, although for postinjury events his amnesia was less severe but still outside the range of non-brain-injured controls. Like the patients considered earlier, M.H.'s knowledge of lifetime periods and some general events was less impaired and he could, apparently, even recall one or two specific events. His memory for songs popular prior to his accident was good, and he was able to recognize the horns of different ships in the harbor close by the hospital. He could also recognize friends by their voices. However, his retrograde amnesia was severe and he was, for example, totally unable to recall the extensive celebrations of his 21st birthday that had occurred a few years prior to his accident.

M.H.'s autobiographical memory for events experienced after his accident is particularly interesting. Generally, he could recall some events and was able to provide, for instance, a detailed account of a barbecue he had attended. However, his recall of this and other postinjury events, although specific, did not feature visual images. Instead, his memories consisted of smells, tastes, and feelings associated with an event. Indeed, his recall of learning of traumatic events experienced by a friend was good, and he was able to report his specific feelings and the reasons for them. For experiences prior to his accident he was not able to recall any specific events, although cues such as the sound, smell, and feel of riding a motorcycle could evoke general nonspecific memories of motorcycling. It seems clear, as Ogden (1993) concluded, that M.H.'s retrograde amnesia was a consequence of his loss of the ability to generate visual images. Memories prior to his injury may have been encoded in terms of the visual features of events and these may have formed important indices of autobiographical memory knowledge structures, but M.H.'s visual processing impairments led to an inability to use such information and, hence, his retrograde amnesia. M.H.'s preserved knowledge of the melodies and words of popular songs is particularly revealing here, because these may have been encoded in terms of nonvisual attributes and, consequently, this autobiographical knowledge could still be accessed and used. Postinjury, his autobiographical memory improved, but only because events were now encoded in terms of modality-specific nonvisual cues that could be utilized by the retrieval process.

These intriguing findings have many implications for the constructivist model of autobiographical remembering. The generative or cyclic retrieval process that leads to a stable pattern of activation that constitutes a memory must bind together activation occurring at different of levels of knowledge. For example, knowledge about persons must be bound together with knowledge about events in such a way that the appropriate persons and events become linked in the pattern of activation. Similarly, ESK must be associated appropriately with more abstract lifetime period and general event knowledge. Finally, the retrieval process must be able to represent accessed knowledge in an appropriate form if that knowledge is to be used effectively. Impairments to the retrieval process itself can disrupt these functions and lead to impoverished memories. On the other hand, impairments to peripheral systems not directly part of the retrieval process, such as an image processing system (cf. Kosslyn, 1980), can also impair memory retrieval by removing the ability to temporarily represent whole classes of cues.

Disordered Autobiographical Memories

The failures of autobiographical remembering considered thus far implicate impairments in knowledge access and disruptions to some aspects of the retrieval process. There are, however, much more severe disruptions of autobiographical remembering that are associated with malfunctions of central control processes themselves. These obviously include disruptions of the retrieval process, but with apparent full access to the autobiographical knowledge base preserved. Most notably these have been observed in patients with brain injury to the frontal lobes (Moscovitch, 1989; Talland, 1965), although they are also often present in amnesic patients with Korsakoff's syndrome (Parkin & Leng, 1993). Thus, the patients R.J. and N.W. studied by Baddeley and Wilson (1986) both showed evidence of *confabulation* in fluent autobiographical memory recall. R.J.'s confabulations were striking and fantastic, involving a long account of his brother's death some years previously (his brother was in fact alive and in contact with R.J.), how he had injured his knee in a game of rounders organized by the hospital as part of Christmas Eve activities (in fact, the hospital had been closed on Christmas Eve), and so on. N.W.'s confabulations were not as fantastic as R.J.'s but, nevertheless, were strikingly bizarre. For instance, N.W. provided very detailed and lengthy descriptions of events that had taken place some years previously on his farm in Scotland, including a highly implausible tale concerning a confrontation with another land owner when N.W. was accompanied by his solicitor and a policeman. N.W. claimed this occurred as part of a routine day's work and he just "happened" to be with his solicitor and a policeman. In subsequent retests, N.W. (like R.J.) did not recognize his earlier "memories."

More recently, Dalla Barba, Cipolotti, and Denes (1990) reported a study of a patient, C.A., with amnesia due to alcoholic Korsakoff's syndrome who also confabulated. C.A. showed an apparently unimpaired semantic memory and fairly normal performance on standard laboratory learning tasks. Her main impairment was in autobiographical memory recall and, although she often recalled detailed "memories" that were either true (as far as could be determined) or if not true then highly plausible, these memories were assigned to incorrect time periods. Also, it is worth noting that C.A. only confabulated when recalling autobiographical memories, and no confabulations were noted in her memory performance following standard laboratory learning tasks. C.A.'s errors in dating were often extreme (e.g., she claimed her wedding was in 1964 when in fact it had been in 1943), and she persevered in many of her confabulatory dates, restating them in retest sessions. A patient with purely frontal lobe injuries, R.W., showed a similar problem in assigning correctly recalled events to correct dates (Shallice, 1988). For instance, R.W. accurately recalled the details of a trip he and some friends had made to town some days previously, but incorrectly described his wife trying on a feather boa in a shop they had visited. In fact, his wife had tried the boa on a day following the trip and at their home rather than in a shop.

Dalla Barba (1993, 1994a, 1994b) contrasted the memory performance of two frontal lobe patients, M.B. and S.D., who both confabulated but in different ways. M.B. was a healthy 75-year-old man with a professional background whose performance on a range of neuropsychological tests indicated preserved intellectual functions with some impaired memory performance. M.B., however, frequently confabulated, describing visiting his wife the day previously (in fact, his wife was dead), visiting his mother in hospital who had died just before he arrived, or recounting long stories of shopping trips and being lost in Paris, none of which had actually occurred. As Dalla Barba (1994a) pointed out, it would be difficult for an uninformed observer to detect that these were confabulations as, in principle at least, these and other events could have plausibly occurred. Yet, M.B. did not confabulate public events about which he was well and accurately informed, nor did he confabulate in response to semantic questions probing factual and conceptual knowledge. In short, his confabulations were solely limited to his autobiographical knowledge and he was unaware that his "memories" were confabulations, he could not distinguish between confabulated and nonconfabulated memories, and both types of memories were recollectively experienced (Tulving, 1985).

In contrast, the patient S.D., a 37-year-old man who suffered a severe open-head injury in a skiing accident, confabulated widely and fantastically. S.D.'s performance on neuropsychological tests indicated impaired intellectual function, abnormal memory, and, importantly, impaired semantic processing. S.D. had been a keen runner prior to his accident and the theme of running formed one of the major sources for his confabulations. Unlike M.B., S.D.'s confabulations were semantically inappropriate and wholly implausible and would have been immediately evident to an uninformed observer. For example, on one occasion S.D. claimed to have won a race and been awarded a piece of meat that he placed on his right knee. There were many confabulations of this sort, but S.D. also confabulated when asked the meanings of words (i.e., when asked to define the word *sentence* he replied that it was a high mountain field). When asked where he was (actually in a testing room in a hospital) he commented that he was in a church in Milan dedicated to St. Anthony.

These two cases pose many questions for the model of the construction of autobiographical memories used in this chapter. In the case of M.D., it appears that although he had full access to the knowledge base the retrieval process was unable to appropriately interpret patterns of activation that arose, and dissipated, during retrieval cycles. Instead, an attempt was made to place an interpretation on any activation in the knowledge base, and this was accepted as a "real" memory. The implication here is that there may have been a severe and extensive disruption of the verification stage of retrieval and, almost certainly, in the broader constraints of the mental model of the memory retrieval task generated by executive processes. Indeed, Baddeley and Wilson (1986) conceptualized such confabulations as part of what they termed the *dysexecutive syndrome*. In S.D., the dysexecutive syndrome was clearly far more extensive and S.D. was totally unable to evaluate output from long-term memory. It seems as though this patient had some thematic knowledge of his life and could use this to access autobiographical knowledge, but the interpretation of that knowledge was constrained inappropriately, possibly by cues immediately available in the environment rather than an internally generated task model (cf. Burgess & Shallice, 1995, for further recent discussion of confabulation).

CONCLUSIONS

The constructivist model of autobiographical memory developed from the study of memory performance with non-brain-damaged and nonclinical subjects is broadly compatible with the patterns of impairments seen in a wide variety of patients. Disrupted access to ESK knowledge with the preservation of lifetime period and general event knowledge appears to be common in certain types of amnesic and psychogenic patients. Other patients show patterns of impairment more directly related to impairments of the retrieval cycle or to more extensive disruptions of central control processes. However, although the constructivist model affords some perspective on impairments of autobiographical remembering, it is evident that the mechanisms and processes that underlie this type of remembering have yet to be specified in any detail. In particular, the constructivist model requires a specification of the nature of the self and the role played by the self in central control processing (i.e., in generating constraining mental models for memory tasks). The convergence of evidence from laboratory, neurological, and psychogenic studies at least holds out the promise of further developments of theory in this area.

REFERENCES

Anderson, S. J., & Conway, M. A. (1993). Investigating the structure of specific autobiographical memories. *Journal of Experimental Psychology: Learning, Memory, and Cognition, 19,* 1–19.

Baddeley, A. D. (1986). *Working memory.* Oxford, England: Clarendon Press.

Baddeley, A. D. (1992). What is autobiographical memory? In M. A. Conway, D. C. Rubin, H. Spinnler, & W. A. Wagenaar (Eds.), *Theoretical perspectives on autobiographical memory* (pp. 13–30). The Netherlands: Kluwer Academic Publishers.

Baddeley, A. D., Thornton, A., Chua, S. E., & McKenna, P. (1994). Delusions and the construction of autobiographical memory. In D. C. Rubin (Ed.), *The construction of autobiographical memories* (pp.). Cambridge, England: Cambridge University Press.

Baddeley, A. D., & Wilson, B. (1986). Amnesia, autobiographical memory, confabulation. In D. C. Rubin (Ed.), *Autobiographical memory* (pp. 225–252). Cambridge, England: Cambridge University Press.

Barsalou, L. W. (1988). The content and organization of autobiographical memories. In U. Neisser & E. Winograd (Eds.), *Remembering reconsidered: Ecological and traditional approaches to the study of memory* (pp. 193–243). New York: Cambridge University Press.

Brown, N. R., Shevell, S. K., & Rips, L. J. (1986). Public memories and their personal context. In D. C. Rubin (Ed.), *Autobiographical memory* (pp. 137–158). Cambridge, England: Cambridge University Press.

Burgess, P. W., & Shallice, T. (in press). Confabulation and the control of normal memory. *Memory.*

Cermak, L. S., & O'Connor, M. (1983). The anterograde and retrograde retrieval ability of a patient with amnesia due to encephalitis. *Neuropsychologia, 21,* 213–234.

Conway, M. A. (1987). Verifying autobiographical facts. *Cognition, 25,* 39–58.

Conway, M. A. (1990). *Autobiographical memory: An introduction.* Buckingham, England: Open University Press.

Conway, M. A. (1992). A structural model of autobiographical memory. In M. A. Conway, D. C. Rubin, H. Spinnler, & W. A. Wagenaar (Eds.), *Theoretical perspectives on autobiographical memory* (pp. 167–194). The Netherlands: Kluwer Academic Publishers.

Conway, M. A. (1993). Impairments of autobiographical memory. In F. Boller & J. Grafman (Eds.), *Handbook of neuropsychology* (Vol. 8, pp. 175–191). The Netherlands: Elsevier Science Publishers B.V.

Conway, M. A. (1994a). *Flashbulb memories.* Hove, East Sussex: Lawrence Erlbaum Associates.

Conway, M. A. (1994b). Autobiographical knowledge and autobiographical memories. In D. C. Rubin (Ed.), *The construction of autobiographical memories.* Cambridge, England: Cambridge University Press.

Conway, M. A. (1994c). Autobiographical memories. In E. Bjork & R. Bjork (Eds.), *Handbook of perception and cognition* (Vol. 10). Orlando, FL: Academic Press.

Conway, M. A., & Bekerian, D. A. (1987). Organization in autobiographical memory. *Memory & Cognition, 15,* 119–132.

Conway, M. A., & Rubin, D. C. (1993). The structure of autobiographical memory. In A. E. Collins, S. E. Gathercole, M. A. Conway, & P. E. Morris (Eds.), *Theories of memory* (pp. 103–138). Hove, Sussex: Lawrence Erlbaum Associates.

Conway, M. A., Rubin, D. C., Spinnler, H., & Wagenaar, W. A. (Eds.). (1992). *Theoretical perspectives on autobiographical memory* (pp. 207–221). The Netherlands: Kluwer Academic Publishers.

Crovitz, H. F., & Schiffman, H. (1974). Frequency of episodic memories as a function of their age. *Bulletin of the Psychonomic Society, 4,* 517–518.

Dalla Barba, G. (1993). Confabulation: knowledge and recollective experience. *Cognitive Neuropsychology, 10,* 1–20.

Dalla Barba, G. (1994a). Confabulation: Remembering 'another' past. In R. Campbell & M. A. Conway (Eds.), *Broken memories: Case studies in the neuropsychology of memory.* Oxford, England: Blackwell.

Dalla Barba, G. (1994b). Different patterns of confabulation. *Cortex.*

Dalla Barba, G., Cipolotti, L., & Denes, G. (1990). Autobiographical memory loss and confabulation in Korsakoff's syndrome: A case report. *Cortex, 26,* 525–534.

Ellis, A. W., Young, A. W., & Critchley, E. M. R. (1989). Loss of memory for people following temporal lobe damage. *Brain, 112,* 1469–1483.

Hodges, J. R., & McCarthy, R. A. (1993). Autobiographical amnesia resulting from bilateral paramedian thalamic infarction. *Brain, 116,* 921–940.

Hyman, I. E., & Faries, J. M. (1992). The functions of autobiographical memory. In M. A. Conway, D. C. Rubin, H. Spinnler, & W. A. Wagenaar (Eds.), *Theoretical perspectives on autobiographical memory* (pp. 207–221). The Netherlands: Kluwer Academic Publishers.

Johnson-Laird, P. N. (1983). *Mental models.* Cambridge, MA: Havard University Press.

Kapur, N., Ellison, D., Smith, M., McLellan, L., & Burrows, E. H. (1992). Focal retrograde amnesia following bilateral temporal lobe pathology: A neuropsychological and magnetic resonance study. *Brain, 115,* 515–523.

Linton, M. (1986). Ways of searching and the contents of memory. In D. C. Rubin (Ed.), *Autobiographical memory* (pp. 50–67). Cambridge, England: Cambridge University Press.

McCarthy, R. A., & Hodges, J. R. (1994). Trapped in time: Profound autobiographical memory loss following a thalamic stroke. In R. Campbell & M. A. Conway (Eds.), *Broken memories: Case studies in the neuropsychology of memory.* Oxford, England: Blackwell.

McCarthy, R. A., & Warrington, E. K. (1993). Actors but not scripts: The dissociation of people and events in retrograde amnesia. *Neuropsychologia, 30,* 633–644.

Moscovitch, M. (1989). Confabulation and the frontal systems: Strategic versus associative retrieval in neuropsychological theories of memory. In H. L. Roediger III & F. I. M. Craik

(Eds.), *Varieties of memory and consciousness: Essays in honour of Endel Tulving* (pp. 133–160). Hillsdale, NJ: Lawrence Erlbaum Associates.

Norman, D. A., & Bobrow, D. G. (1979). Descriptions and intermediate stage in memory retrieval. *Cognitive Psychology, 11,* 107–123.

Norman, D. A., & Shallice, T. (1980). *Attention to action: Willed and automatic control of behaviour* (Tech. Rep. No. 99). San Diego: University of California.

Ogden, J. A. (1993). Visual object agnosia, prosopagnosia, achromatopsia, loss of visual imagery, and autobiographical amnesia following recovery from cortical blindness: Case M.H. *Neuropsychologia, 31,* 571–589.

Parkin, A. J., & Leng, R. C. (1993). *Neuropsychology of the amnesic syndrome.* Hove, England: Lawrence Erlbaum Associates.

Parkin, A. J., & Stampfer, H. G. (1994). Keeping out the past. A study of temporary memory loss. In R. Campbell & M. A. Conway (Eds.), *Broken memories: Case studies in the neuropsychology of memory.* Oxford, England: Blackwell.

Pillemer, D. B. (1992). Remembering personal circumstances: A functional analysis. In E. Winograd & U. Neisser (Eds.), *Affect and accuracy in recall: Studies of "flashbulb memories"* (pp. 236–264). Cambridge, England: Cambridge University Press.

Robinson, J. A. (1976). Sampling autobiographical memory. *Cognitive Psychology, 8,* 578–595.

Robinson, J. A. (1986). Autobiographical memory: a historical prologue. In D. C. Rubin (Ed.), *Autobiographical memory* (pp. 19–24). Cambridge, England: Cambridge University Press.

Robinson, J. A. (1992). First experience memories: Contexts and function in personal histories. In M. A. Conway, D. C. Rubin, H. Spinnler, & W. Wagenaar (Eds.), *Theoretical perspectives on autobiographical memory* (pp. 223–239). Dordrecht, The Netherlands: Kluwer Academic Publishers.

Robinson, J. A., & Swanson, K. L. (1990). Autobiographical memory: The next phase. *Applied Cognitive Psychology, 4,* 321–335.

Ross, B. H. (1984). Remindings and their effects in learning a cognitive skill. *Cognitive Psychology, 16,* 371–416.

Salaman, E. (1970). *A collection of moments: A study of involuntary memories.* London: Longman.

Schooler, J. W., & Herrmann, D. J. (1992). There is more to episodic memory than just episodes. In M. A. Conway, D. C. Rubin, H. Spinnler, & W. A. Wagenaar (Eds.), *Theoretical perspectives on autobiographical memory* (pp. 241–262). Dordrecht, The Netherlands: Kluwer Academic Publishers.

Shallice, T. (1988). *From neuropsychology to mental structure.* New York: Cambridge University Press.

Talland, G. A. (1965). *Deranged memory.* London: Academic Press.

Treadway, M., McCloskey, M., Gordon, B., & Cohen, N. J. (1992). Landmark life events and the organization of memory: Evidence from functional retrograde amnesia. In S. Christianson (Ed.), *The handbook of emotion and memory: Research and theory* (pp. 389–410). Hillsdale, NJ: Lawrence Erlbaum Associates.

Tulving, E. (1985). How many memory systems are there? *American Psychologist, 40,* 385–398.

Tulving, E., Schacter, D. L., McLachlan, D. R., & Moscovitch, M. (1988). Priming of semantic autobiographical knowledge: A case study of retrograde amnesia. *Brain and Cognition, 8,* 3–20.

Warrington, E. K., & McCarthy, R. A. (1988). The fractionation of retrograde amnesia. *Brain and Cognition, 7,* 184–200.

Warrington, E. K., & Weiskrantz, L. (1982). Amnesia: A disconnection syndrome. *Neuropsychologia, 16,* 233–249.

Williams, D. M., & Hollan, J. D. (1981). The process of retrieval from very long-term memory. *Cognitive Science, 5,* 87–119.

Williams, J. M. G. (1994). Overgeneral memories. In D. C. Rubin (Ed.), *The construction of autobiographical memories*. Cambridge, England: Cambridge University Press.

Williams, J. M. G., & Broadbent, K. (1986). Autobiographical memory in attempted suicide patients. *Journal of Abnormal Psychology, 95*, 144–149.

Williams, J. M. G., & Dritschel, B. H. (1992). Categoric and extended autobiographical memories. In M. A. Conway, D. C. Rubin, H. Spinnler, & W. A. Wagenaar (Eds.), *Theoretical perspectives on autobiographical memory* (pp. 391–412). The Netherlands: Kluwer Academic Publishers.

Williams, J. M. G., & Scott, J. (1988). Autobiographical memories in depression. *Psychological Medicine, 18*, 689–695.

CHAPTER SIXTEEN

Practical Aspects
of Emotion and Memory

Paula T. Hertel
Trinity University

Can anyone doubt that the study of emotion and memory should have practical implications? Surely not those among us who have had emotional experiences and sometimes try to forget them, to remember them, or to remember other things while having them. Extreme examples include the witness to a robbery and the victim of abuse. Less dramatically but far more commonly, anxious or depressed people perform everyday acts that are memory dependent. Indeed, a practical or useful science of memory should have a great deal to say about how memory works under such emotional conditions.

Research on emotion and memory is also practical for the science at large, because it can extend the usefulness of a general theory. This practical aspect provides the glue for this review. Together with many other researchers in theoretical aspects of emotion and memory, I argue that the memorial correlates and consequences of emotion are best viewed as pertaining to the effects of emotion on the focus and control of attention. This is a fortunate vantage point for practitioners, who want to know what they can and cannot depend on and control when emotion is involved in memorial episodes. Thus, this chapter briefly and selectively describes some recent literature on emotion and memory from the theoretical perspective of attentional control and from the practical perspective of how the findings might be useful to people who have feelings.

The description is restricted to the domain of negative events and states. Elation, passion, other positive states, and the events that produce them also deserve our attention but, apart from being difficult to capture or establish experimentally, they are unfortunately too transient in our culture to cry out for practical approaches. Further, although a wide variety of psychological phenomena, disorders, and practices are related to memory under negatively emotional circumstances, I describe only those that have received the most attention from cognitive psychologists: eyewitness, flashbulb, and possibly repressed memories, and the ubiquitous disorders of anxiety and depression. Even with these restrictions, the bodies of relevant research are still quite large; my description, therefore, often cites recently published reviews instead of the important empirical investigations. Finally, a portion of the literature on depression and memory is examined in greater detail for possible therapeutic applications.

THEORETICAL OVERVIEW

The construct *attention* is central to many theoretical accounts of emotion and memory phenomena. Essentially, these phenomena can be understood as a function of the focus of attention during an initial episode or when it might come to mind on later occasions. The accounts described in this chapter differ according to the phenomena they were designed to address. What they all have in common is reference to a continuum of automatic to controlled mental procedures, as elucidated by early attention theorists like Kahneman (1973), Posner and Snyder (1975), and Shiffrin and Schneider (1977). Briefly stated, automatic procedures are native to the organism or develop from practice. Although they sometimes can be intentionally initiated or interrupted, they do not require attention or intention for their performance. Controlled procedures, in contrast, are those that require attention or conscious focus. In spatial metaphors, controlled mental acts draw on limited attentional capacity. In this chapter, I argue that many accounts of emotion and memory emphasize the control of attention by emotional stimulation as a predictor of performance on memory tasks.

A convenient departure point is found in Bower's (1992) review of the role played by surprising events, both in engendering arousal and in focusing attention on critical aspects of the events. At the time of such focus, arousal activates the autonomic nervous system (ANS) and hormonal systems, which in turn directly affect storage activities in the brain (see Gold, 1992; LeDoux, 1992; McGaugh, 1992). Similarly, Mandler (1992) claimed that "a majority of occasions for visceral (sympathetic nervous system) arousal follows the occurrence of some perceptual or cognitive discrepancy, or the interruption or blocking of some ongoing action" (p. 98). Mandler, as well as other emotion theorists (e.g., Oatley & Johnson-Laird, 1987), stressed the adaptive function of the link between arousal and attention to discrepancies. The link functions to establish immediate resolution or future avoidance (see Bower, 1992). For example, Mineka (1992) suggested that vigilance for sources of threat, augmented by controlled procedures for directing attention away from the event (avoidance), can maintain fearful states on future occasions (see the earlier formulation of emotionally disordered memory by Williams, Watts, MacLeod, & Mathews, 1988). What is ultimately implied by such accounts is that, although unexpected events incur arousal and initially demand attention, the linkage of arousal and attention does not guarantee memory for the initiating events; memory also depends on how attention is subsequently controlled and where it is focused.

Among the first to address matters of attentional control during aroused states was Easterbrook (1959), who contended that increases in arousal are associated with a narrowing in the focus of attention. Later, several accounts of memory during emotional states seem to have combined the Easterbrook hypothesis with the idea that attentional capacity is reduced by arousal (see especially Hasher & Zacks, 1979). In summarizing his earlier work on both emotion and memory, Mandler (1992) stressed the limited capacity of consciousness as the important factor in emotion/memory interactions. His theory of memory makes the distinction between procedures for activating and procedures for elaborating: Activation is automatic, given an external stimulus, and establishes later feelings of familiarity, whereas elaboration requires conscious or deliberate activity and establishes the pathways for retrieval. His theory of emotion stresses two features: arousal and expressed value. The former is visceral and produces internal events, whereas the latter reflects cognitive appraisal and requires attentional capacity. Therefore, "The experience of emotion preempts the limited capacity of consciousness. . . . [When this occurs] other processes that require such capacity will be impaired" (Mandler, 1992, p. 99). Some variant of this position has informed research on emotion and memory for approximately two decades. In particular, memory researchers have emphasized impairments in attention-demanding procedures (e.g., organization and elaboration) that support performance on later tests of deliberate memory.

In short, the limitation on the focus of attention, central to all cognition, is also central to understanding interactions of emotion and memory. Internal stimulation, external stimulation, and related past stimulation all vie for attention; an increase in the strength or distinctiveness of one source should mean that others are less well attended. Therefore, research efforts should—and often do—concentrate on the focus of attention during episodes of possible emotional relevance. This approach has the parsimonious advantage of blending the findings of improved memory for events "in focus" and impaired memory for unattended aspects of experience.

MEMORY FOR EMOTIONAL EVENTS

The nature of memory for emotional events—naturally occurring or simu-lated—depends on the focus of attention in a variety of ways. When events are surprising and therefore arousing: (a) attention is drawn to the central aspects that elicit the arousal via an innate orienting response, (b) those aspects enjoy the retention advantage of physiological arousal, and (c) their distinctiveness incurs elaborative processing that increases the chance that they will later come to mind. These claims have been abstracted primarily from Christianson's (1992) and Reisberg and Heuer's (1992) reviews of both real-world studies of eyewitness memory and laboratory simulations. It is important to keep in mind, however, that the nature of the event itself is often used to classify the memory as emotional. Arousal is sometimes as-sumed, rather than measured, and when arousal can be assumed it is not necessarily accompanied by an evaluative component that, according to Mandler (1992), constructs an emotion. This issue arises in the ensuing synopses of research on eyewitness memory, flashbulb memory, and re-pressed memories.

Eyewitness Memory

Based on the Easterbrook hypothesis, Christianson (1992) and Reisberg and Heuer (1992) argued that arousal restricts the focus of attention to the central details of presumably emotional events and therefore away from peripheral aspects, and thereby produces corresponding facilitation and impairment in memory for the respective aspects. Naturalistic studies of eyewitness testimony frequently show high positive correlations between judged emotionality (in retrospect) and both the reported vividness of the events and accurate memory for their central details. In such studies, however, evidence regarding accuracy is typically obtained through comparisons across repeated tests (with all the accompanying potential confounds) and lacks the appropriate controls. Laboratory simulations have produced somewhat inconsistent results, but the inconsistency might be artifactual of whether accuracy or error is measured. In the latter case, findings of poor memory for arousing events might be due to confabulations to fill in the gaps established by the narrow focus of attention (see Reisberg & Heuer, 1992). On balance, both reviews conclude that laboratory findings are consistent with the attentional-focus account.

Orientation to the central details of arousing events cannot, however, be solely responsible for enhanced memory, according to Christianson (1992). When eye fixations were controlled during initial exposure to emotional or neutral slides, memory for the fixated details was enhanced by emotional content. These findings suggest that ANS arousal and accompanying hor-monal changes increase retention (see Gold, 1992). Christianson also proposed that ongoing arousal might underlie findings of poor performance on immediate tests, due to "the difficulties in refiring of those neurons that are firing repeatedly in the reverberating circuit" (p. 299). In a related vein, Reisberg and Heuer (1992) suggested that the physiological effects of arousal on encoding ultimately slow the rate of forgetting central details. Physiological products of arousal might therefore account for findings of better memory for emotional events only after a delay in testing.

Long-term retention of emotional events might also be facilitated by their distinctiveness, according to both reviews. For example, Christianson (1992) noted that the role of distinctiveness is separable from that of emotional arousal, because parallel findings are obtained with nonemotional but unusual events. The role of distinctiveness, in the sense of the unexpected, however, might not be separable from that of physiological arousal and accompanying retention via ANS mechanisms (see Bower, 1992). Therefore, it might be more important to separate effects of distinctiveness from those of elaboration. When distinctive events are elaboratively processed (compared to when they are not), we typically see a greater advantage on tests of deliberate remembering (Hunt & McDaniel, 1993). Furthermore, the degree of elaborative processing might be limited by the focus of attention on one's aroused state.

In that regard, it is interesting to consider the recent analysis of eyewitness memory for traumatic events by Yuille and Tollestrup (1992). In a manner consistent with Mandler's framework, these authors argued that arousal accompanying "remarkable" events is sometimes associated with an internal focus on the physiological state itself. Under those circumstances, even memory for central details should be impaired. Laboratory research should therefore investigate the conditions that differentiate internal from external attentional foci. This issue is also relevant in investigations of another class of remarkable events: flashbulb memories.

Flashbulb Memories

Flashbulb memories are supposed to be emotional. In fact, a recent volume of papers on the topic was entitled *Affect and Accuracy in Recall* (Winograd & Neisser, 1992). Brown and Kulik (1977) coined the term *flashbulb* to refer to personal memories of finding out about culturally important events (such as the assassinations of public figures) and claimed that surprise and expected consequentiality of the event are their identifying characteristics. These two characteristics have been inconsistently measured (and usually in the absence of appropriate controls), but when they do co-occur the phenomenon might qualify as an emotional memory according to Mandler's criteria (cf. Mandler, 1992). This is because surprise can be counted on to invoke arousal, and expected consequentiality suggests that the arousal is evaluated in a cognitive context. For example, in a recent multinational study, Conway et al. (1994) recruited subjects who were likely to vary in the extent to which the event

(Thatcher's resignation) would be perceived as important and potentially consequential. They found that the initially reported strength of emotional reaction mediated the formation of flashbulb memories *when* the initially perceived importance of the event was high. However, because none of these measures was taken at the time of reception we cannot be sure that the event itself was emotional. This is typically the case.

In general, evidence regarding flashbulb memories is difficult to interpret, at best (see Brewer, 1992). The tradition is to measure memory for the reception event (the subject's own experience) rather than the original event, presumably because people hear the news from others rather than witnessing it firsthand. (Otherwise, of course, the phenomenon would be eyewitness memory.) Reception events usually leave no permanent objective record; therefore, researchers are almost always in the position of measuring memory for a memory, and consistency is not the same as accuracy (see McCloskey, Wibble, & Cohen, 1988). Moreover, appropriate control events are hard to identify (see Brewer, 1992). Another interpretive difficulty is invited by lack of knowledge regarding the focus of attention during reception, although some evidence suggests that central details from the initial report are quite well remembered (see Christianson, 1992). Reisberg and Heuer (1992) suggested that attention is likely to be focused on other people, whose own emotional reactions are unexpected in the context of everyday relations.

Social aspects of *remembering* the flashbulb event were stressed by Loftus and Kaufman (1992); one's audience at the time of remembering directs the nature of the report. Such social functions also remind us that elaborative procedures can easily produce inaccuracies in memory for eyewitness and flashbulb events. In attending to related information (elaborating) during the flashbulb event or its rehearsal, we increase the likelihood that such information will be the focus of attention on subsequent occasions of remembering.

Finally, Brewer (1992) alerted us to consider distinctiveness to be a potentially potent variable in understanding flashbulb memories, given its importance in ordinary personal memories. Events that are considered surprising *and* personally important should undergo elaborative processing for the purpose of reconciliation, according to evolutionary frameworks (see Williams et al., 1988), unless the event is threatening and therefore sets the occasion for avoidance. Although they might sometimes evoke emotions, flashbulb events pose little or no personal threat, unlike the events assumed to be responsible for the next category of emotional memories.

"Repressed and Recovered" Memories

Eyewitness, flashbulb, and presumably repressed memories are all records of distinctive events, although the last category is surely more personally relevant and arousing (Loftus & Kaufman, 1992). Because records of the original flashbulb (reception) event and previously repressed events are rarely obtainable, the conservative stance is to doubt the special status accorded to each class of memory phenomena, and particularly to doubt the accuracy of "recovered" memories of previously repressed events. Loftus (see Loftus & Kaufman, 1992) cautioned us to consider that recovered memories might be replete with error motivated by social context, just like flashbulb memories, and urged us to examine the social functions of such reports.

Compared to recovery, the concept of repression itself has received more attention by memory researchers (see the review by Holmes, 1990). According to Kihlstrom and Hoyt (1990), for example, repression functions to deny controlled access to prior experience, and this function suggests various attention-centered explanations. Guided by ongoing motives (see Simon, 1994), attention can be diverted from the traumatic event and reduce the degree of elaborative processing. Similarly, attention can also be diverted away from later cues for reminding. Kihlstrom and Hoyt (1990) argued that the person might initially be aware of unwanted thoughts produced by such cues and deliberately avoid thinking about them in ways more akin to intentional suppression than to repression. But through practice, they argued, suppression becomes automatic and resembles repression. In a different vein, Bower (1990) suggested that repressionlike failures could also result from retroactive interference by incompatible and much more common experiences in the same domain; later recovery would then arise from the use of appropriate retrieval cues in the therapeutic context. Like Loftus, however, he warned that distortions are likely. In these ways the focus of attention at the time of remembering accounts for repression and possible recovery or confabulation.

Therapists suspect repression when they observe emotional reactions that seem unusual in the client's current context and therefore suggestive of certain kinds of earlier emotional experiences. In this regard, Tobias, Kihlstrom, and Schacter (1992) argued that when emotional responses themselves reflect the effects of past experience, they belong to the category of implicit memory phenomena, because the subject does not intentionally invoke the past in making the response. Although some of the measures used experimentally to support this claim do not qualify as full-blown emotional reactions, they have affective characteristics. Johnson and Multhaup (1992), for example, reviewed studies in the mere-exposure effect on preferences for unfamiliar melodies and people; in Korsakoff patients, such effects are dissociated from recognition judgments. Tobias et al. (1992) described clinical case studies in which a variety of affectively related measures (e.g., judgments of emotional value) showed similar dissociations from traditional measures of intentional remembering. Furthermore, these examples in the literature on human memory are reminiscent of a variety of studies that used truly emotional responses by other organisms as evidence of prior learning. In this regard, LeDoux (1992) reviewed evidence for the "indelibility of emotional memory" (p. 279). This evidence suggests that emotion *as* memory cannot be extinguished, even though the event that gives rise to the emotion might be forgotten.

Finally, perhaps the best developed model of emotion as memory in humans is Johnson's MEM (see Johnson & Multhaup, 1992). Johnson proposed that perceptual and reflective subsystems differentially contribute to affective experiences. "Recapturing affect [emotion as memory] depends on whether it is possible to reinstate the records of the initial processing that led to the initial affective response" (p. 58). If the initial episode was not elaborated in the reflective subsystems, failures in deliberate recall are likely. However, perceptual characteristics of a current context that are similar to those of an earlier traumatic event certainly could evoke arousal along a generalization gradient. Through practice, such arousal could be accompanied by diversion of attention. Moreover, a skillful redirection of attention during emotional episodes might have some small chance of recovering a repressed memory if perceptual memories are sought. In contrast, cuing via reflective subsystems invites dangers of elaborative distortions. In short, the concept of attention is central to understanding that truly traumatic experiences affect subsequent behavior in the absense of aware remembering (the hallmark of suspected repression). It may also be central to designing experimental analogues for the recovery of repressed memories.

Practical Guidelines

What can we tell the practitioner? Because arousal directs, narrows, or redirects the focus of attention in presumably automatic ways, initial control may be difficult, if not impossible. Beyond that point, avenues for self-initiated and environmentally directed control should be examined, particularly in the context of understanding that motives direct attention. In describing the experimental psychologist's approach to understanding repression, for example, Bower (1990) compared it to motivated "unlearning" and forgetting. Presumably, most of us are motivated to remember what we were doing on some culturally important occasion and to forget more personally traumatic events (unless legal or retributional motives exist at the time). Clearly, the motivation to comply with instructions in nonemotional laboratory settings can guide attention during initial exposure and subsequently (see Bower, 1990), but is such control possible when the event is "emotional"? Issues arising from this question concern the effects of arousal on initiating and sustaining attention in ways related to one's motives (fulfilling intentions). For example, if the experience invokes conscious evaluation of arousal, attention should be hard to focus on peripheral aspects potentially relevant to one's prior intentions. In effect, the arousing event may establish new motives that direct attention to their service. Much the same might be said when emotional states are not established directly by the current event.

MEMORY IN EMOTIONAL STATES

There is a fine line between memory for emotional events and memory in emotional states. One way to draw it is to note whether the event produces the state (as is assumed in the research described above). When the state precedes the event to be remembered, I classify the phenomena as memory in emotional states. In this category, the event itself might be emotional (although verbal materials related to emotions often constitute the "events" in such research). If so, researchers usually are interested in mood-congruent and mood-incongruent memories. If not, research is aimed at understanding the conditions for impaired memory in emotional states. In both categories of research, a variety of complicating factors arises from the need to understand the state itself.

Sometimes research participants have been diagnosed as emotionally disordered, sometimes they are selected from nondiagnosed populations according to their responses on various mood inventories, and sometimes they volunteer to be placed in transient moods. To what extent do arousal and its evaluation characterize these states? Although some researchers in the area argue that experimentally induced moods are more intense, others make distinctions between mood and emotion on the basis that arousal characterizes only the latter (see Mandler, 1992). However, the degree of arousal surely varies according to the induction technique or the specific disorder, and within these categories as well. For examples of low arousal, consider endogenous depression without accompanying anxiety, or the lethargic states established by some induction techniques (see Revelle & Loftus, 1992). Regarding the focus of attention on one's aroused state, it is important to know that most clinical disorders are characterized by self-focused attention (see the review by Ingram, 1990). Some mood-induction techniques, however, seem to be characterized by experimental "demand" in ways that are irrelevant to one's state. Subjects might be cued by the nature of the induction to focus attention on particular materials or encouraged to conform to implied expectations for poor attention and performance. (We should also be alert to demand characteristics of some selection procedures.) As well, there are reasons to believe that effects established by inductions differ from those in natural states (e.g., Hertel & Rude, 1991b). That possibility, coupled with a concern for practical value, has led me to emphasize studies on naturally occurring emotional states and disorders in the following description.

Emotion-Congruent Attention and Memory

The ensuing description is guided by Williams et al.'s (1988) evolutionary perspective on attention and memory in anxious and depressed people, because it was developed to address clinical phenomena in the context of traditional cognitive research. The main idea is that anxiety evolved to facilitate detection and subsequent avoidance of potential threat, whereas depression evolved to facilitate reflection on loss and failure. In cognitive terms, "anxiety preferentially affects the passive, automatic aspect of encoding and retrieval, whereas depression preferentially affects the more active, effortful aspects of encoding and retrieval" (Williams et al., 1988, p. 173). The term *preferentially* is the key to understanding emotionally congruent biases in attention and subsequent memory.

Recently, Mathews and MacLeod (1994) reviewed evidence that anxious people have trouble ignoring or inhibiting emotionally congruent aspects of events and show selective detection of these aspects. (Such biases are found in the performance of depressed subjects only to the extent that anxiety is also present.) The bias seems to emerge when the emotional nature of the materials varies within trials, not across, which suggests that the nature of the bias is to prioritize detection. In anxiety the bias is automatic rather than intentional, because it occurs when subjects cannot report the content (e.g., in studies using masked Stroop techniques).

Mathews and MacLeod's (1994) review also concluded that self-referential tasks performed at initial exposure produce better recall for congruent material, but only when they are performed by depressed people. This effect is usually attributed to elaborative processing, achieved by focusing attention on related thoughts and events, particularly when they are perceived as "causally belonging" to one's mood state (Bower, 1992). Elaboration establishes attentional procedures whereby the event can be deliberately brought to mind on later occasions. In fact, evidence of emotional congruence in depression seems to be restricted to performance on tests of deliberate remembering (e.g., Denny & Hunt, 1992). Implicit memory tests—to the extent that they invite more automatic procedures—might be expected to show emotionally congruent effects with anxious subjects (see Williams et al., 1988), but the few studies that have done so have not been replicated (also see Mineka, 1992).

In general, Mathews and MacLeod found no solid evidence for threat-congruent memory in anxiety. This is to be expected if anxious people subsequently focus attention away from detected sources of threat, both during initial exposure and on later occasions, in order to avoid further arousal. Indeed, sometimes impaired memory for threat-related materials is found. The consequence, according to Mineka (1992), is that in natural environments the lack of controlled attention to the source of potential threat prevents an accurate evaluation of its extent and perpetuates anxiety. On the other hand, depression might be exacerbated by attention to negative aspects of current and prior experience (see Williams, 1992).

Depression is characterized by automatic negative thoughts and ruminations (see Beck, 1976; Gotlib, 1992). Ruminations involve sustained attention that is presumably motivated by the urge to resolve discordance associated with the negative thought and to escape the depressed mood. These implicit goals, however, may be almost impossible to reach when the content of the automatic thought is particularly traumatic. Then, the person is motivated to suppress such unwanted thoughts, because they ultimately serve to exacerbate the mood. (Evidence for mood-incongruent recall of less traumatic negative materials may have similar roots in mood regulation; see Parrott & Sabini, 1990.) According to Wegner (1989), thought suppression is achieved initially by focusing attention on random distractors in the environment; however, through repeated attempts and failures, these distractors become associated with the unwanted thoughts and (ironically) serve to cue them. This "rebound" effect appears to be stronger for emotionally charged and unresolved events than for neutral content.

Wegner's (1989) treatment of the rebound effect places it in the category of implicit memory paradigms. The thought comes to mind in the absense of intent to remember—indeed, in the presence of the intent *not* to remember. As such, when past events come to mind against one's will, the memory process can truly be described as automatic (Jacoby, Toth, & Yonelinas, 1993). In this regard, the rebound effect shows evidence of mood congruence (e.g., Howell & Conway, 1992), unlike other paradigms that presumably measure implicit memory.

Impaired Memory

Although depressed people are bothered incessantly by automatic negative thoughts, they complain about poor memory. What they mean is that their deliberate attempts to remember often fail. Indeed, there is little reason to notice that memory functions "normally" in more automatic or implicit ways (provided that the original event had been attended; see Hertel, 1994; Hertel & Hardin, 1990). Similarly, the literature on memory impairments in both anxious and depressed states has concentrated on tests of deliberate remembering. Consider first the case of anxiety.

Anxiety might indeed establish priorities for detecting and subsequently avoiding threatening events, but how should it affect memory when threat is absent? In line with Easterbrook (1959), Eysenck (1982) noted that anxious arousal might impair memory by narrowing the focus of attention during initial exposure in ways that exclude important aspects of more attention-demanding tasks. When arousal has been measured, however, it seems to have contributed little to the relationship between anxiety and performance (see Eysenck & Calvo, 1992). Further, Eysenck and others also noted that arousal is just one component of anxiety. The other component—worry—represents the focus of attention on self-relevant and typically distracting information. Although distraction should impair subsequent memory, anxious subjects sometimes compensate for their distractibility by increasing the effort they expend on the task, because they are motivated to avoid the negative consequences of failure. (In other words, imagined failure can be a source of threat to be avoided by anxious people.) In this regard, Eysenck and Calvo (1992) proposed that processing efficiency (a ratio of effectiveness to effort) is impaired; anxious people expend more effort to maintain a certain level of effectiveness and are therefore less efficient (see Eysenck & Calvo, 1992, for a review of the relevant literature).

This account of performance in anxious states is both similar to and different from typical accounts of performance in depressed states. Both stress the importance of attentional factors, but the latter suggest that depression limits the degree of effort that *can* be applied to cognitive tasks (e.g., Hasher & Zacks, 1979; Williams et al., 1988). (Some research in social cognition is much more consistent with Eysenck & Calvo's framework, however; the review by Weary, Marsh, Gleicher, & Edwards, 1993, suggests that depression is associated with *increased* effort, motivated by the desire for control.)

In one of the more frequently cited accounts of depression and memory, Ellis and Ashbrook (1988) claimed "that being sad ties up some capacity as a result of thinking about one's sad state, so that less capacity is available to be allocated to the criterion task" (p. 27). Their support for this assumption was provided by evidence of impaired recall of materials from more difficult or attention demanding tasks. The key factor in their claim, however, is not "tied-up" or reduced capacity, as stressed by the authors and others (e.g., Hartlage, Alloy, Vazquez, & Dykman, 1993), but the embedded assumption regarding the focus of attention. The experimental support described earlier, for example, was established by mood-induction techniques; in the "depressed" condition, college subjects read statements designed to focus their attention on feeling sad, hopeless, and lethargic. Subsequent experiments on thought listing following such inductions in fact showed that this attentional focus was maintained during a criterion task (Seibert & Ellis, 1991). Therefore, neutral and self-irrelevant materials from "orienting" tasks are peripheral to the focus of attention and should suffer on later tests of deliberate memory, as can be seen in studies of memory for emotional events (see Christianson, 1992).

Can we assume that attention is similarly focused away from neutral aspects when the subjects are naturally depressed? Unwanted thoughts tend to occur on occasions when the mind is not otherwise occupied (Bower, 1992; Wegner, 1989). Such occasions include those during which there is little environmental control of attention, such as Bower's example of falling asleep at night. Probably a large proportion of tasks used in memory research poorly controls the focus of attention. For example, because we generously provide time for subjects to perform incidental orienting tasks, their minds can wander until the next display. Some subjects, however, do show what my colleagues and I have called "cognitive initiative" (see Hertel & Hardin,

1990); they continue to focus attention on the task and related materials in ways that are not required by our instructions. Later, during recall and recognition tasks, we do not tell subjects precisely what to think about, but some subjects voluntarily attend to elements of the past and present that help them perform. Some subjects behave strategically. Of course, these are the processes we want to bring under experimental control so that we can establish their causal importance, but when experimental constraints are imperfect, performance varies as a function of the degree to which such processes are self-initiated. Depressed and dysphoric people are among those who initiate the least.

Depressed subjects comply with stated instructions, but during periods of loose attentional control their minds go blank or wander to task irrelevant matters—perhaps to matters of personal concern. Compared to our typical laboratory tasks, such matters motivate attention. Furthermore, if the focus of attention, rather than reduced capacity, is the key to understanding memory impairments in depression, we ought to be able to sidestep the need for initiative by controlling the focus of attention on the task and thereby reduce or eliminate the impairment. Consider the following experiment with clinically depressed subjects and controls (Hertel & Rude, 1991a). In one condition, attention during the orienting task was poorly constrained (as it was in the research cited by Ellis & Ashbrook, 1988), and subsequent free recall of targets from the more difficult trials was reduced in the depressed sample. In another condition, however, we constrained attention during initial exposure and eliminated the deficit in subsequent recall. The depressed sample performed more slowly on a secondary task during both orienting conditions, and so low task motivation or even reduced capacity might characterize their state. Regardless, the important point is that so-called capacity limitations did not predict recall when initiative was not required.

In the experiments by Hertel and Rude (1991a, 1991b), recall was most likely determined by the degree of initial elaboration (attention to the target's context). Free recall is the classic test of deliberate memory; it encourages a good deal of focus on past events and therefore benefits from such focus during initial exposure (see Jacoby et al., 1993). In contrast, word-identification tests that indirectly measure prior experience (i.e., more old than new words are identified at brief exposures) benefit primarily from prior integration of letters into words. Procedures for activating lexical units are assumed to be automatic under normal reading conditions. Instructions to attend to the perceptual features of the word's display, however, are not normal reading conditions, and under these conditions reading should require some initiative. In this regard, the performance on a subsequent test of word-identification revealed a decreased effect of prior exposure in the depressed sample, compared to the controls (Hertel, 1994). During the perceptual orienting task, the depressed subjects apparently attended less often to the words themselves, because such attention was not required. When the orienting task had instructed them to judge the emotional value of the words, however, the effect of prior exposure on word identification was comparable to that in the control group. In this case, reading was required and other potentially self-initiated procedures during initial exposure would not be expected to improve performance on the test of word identification. Moreover, this and other indirect memory tests are probably less likely to invite self-initiated reflections on the past. For example, a test of homophone spelling showed no depression-related effect of prior exposure to one of the two meanings of each homophone (Hertel & Hardin, 1990).

Compared to indirect tests, recognition tests provide more interesting opportunities for exploring the possible effects of impaired initiative in depression—particularly with regard to the control of attention during the test itself. For example, compared to controls, dysphoric students have shown impairments in recollection—the component of recognition judgments that represents a self-initiated focus on the past context of target items—but comparable reliance on familiarity, the more automatic aspect of recognition (Hertel & Milan, 1994). Further, in our earlier research on recognition, only the nondysphoric subjects appeared to focus attention systematically on remembering the target's context in two prior tasks and to discount familiarity as a basis for judgment (Hertel & Hardin, 1990). When, in a subsequent experiment, we guided the dysphoric subjects to use that attentional strategy, their recognition judgments revealed the same pattern that characterized the unguided judgments by their nondysphoric counterparts. Other studies also support an initiative account of recognition in depressed states (e.g., Channon, Baker, & Robertson, 1993).

Reduced cognitive initiative in depressed states is consistent with symptoms of hopelessness (Abramson, Metalsky, & Alloy, 1989) and perceived lack of control of both internal and external events (Beck, 1976). It can also be understood in neurophysiological terms. In particular, a connection between depression (as well as other emotional disorders) and attentional control should be found in frontal-lobe hypoactivation (see Grafman, 1989). According to Henriques and Davidson (1991), "loss of initiative, impaired concentration, indecision . . . are all symptoms common to patients with left anterior lesions and certain subtypes of depression" (p. 535). Their evidence from EEG recordings of clinically depressed (unlesioned) subjects lends further support to this connection. Mayes (1988) concluded that patients with lesions in the frontal lobes exhibit deficits that "arise when remembering requires the initiation and maintenance of effortful and organized strategies . . . as well as the ability to switch from one strategy to another" (p. 121). In PET studies, hypoactivation in the frontal lobes has been linked to both depression (Resnick, 1992) and reduced attentional control (Posner, 1992). In the context of frontal-lobe hypoactivation, moreover, other brain functions can continue to direct attention and mediate retention of emotionally relevant events (McGaugh, 1992).

In short, at least some evidence from varied research domains paints a picture of depressed people as those who readily attend to emotionally negative events, ruminate about them in ways that exacerbate their depression, and are not motivated to attend to other matters that might not only benefit performance on subsequent memory tasks but aid recovery (see Hertel, 1992). Rather than insisting that this picture is inevitable (e.g., by stressing that depression reduces capacity), however, we should realize that in matters of attentional control, depressed people need a little help from their friends—or at least from their therapists.

Practical Aspects of Memory in Depressed States: Implications for Treatment

The most obvious and perhaps the most frequently discussed avenue for applying research on depression and memory lies in the clinical domain— particularly in the practices of cognitive–behavioral therapy (see Beck, Rush, Shaw, & Emery, 1979). Although this tradition has been "cognitive" only in the loosest sense of the term, recently some attempts have been made to connect the practices with experimental findings and theories in cognitive psychology.

First, experimental evidence regarding the tendency to focus attention on negative aspects of current and prior experience can be used in assessment. For example, vulnerability to depression might be better detected in performance on cognitive tasks than in self-reports (Williams et al., 1988). Similarly, Nasby and Kihlstrom (1986) discussed applications to assess the potential usefulness of particular interventions. Therapists should also take evidence for mood congruent recall into account in evaluating the client's autobiographical reports.

More typically, evidence for biased attention and recall in depression has been related to treatment domains. For example, cognitive–behavioral therapy includes procedures to alter negative thoughts by encouraging clients to use their own behavior to test their beliefs (Beck et al., 1979). In a closer analysis of how that might work, Ingram and Hollon (1986) suggested that such self-monitoring procedures tend to be freer from distortions than is retrospective recall; the results of monitoring can then be elaborated during therapy sessions. In that setting, moreover, Nasby and Kihlstrom (1986) recommended that therapists optimize attention to their feedback by placing clients in happier moods prior to reinterpreting their behavior in less negative terms than the client tends to use.

Evidence for mood-incongruent recall and the suppression of negative thoughts is also relevant to treatment, particularly if one switches therapeutic horses to psychodynamic perspectives. When such mechanisms of "defense" seem ineffective, the therapist might be inclined to encourage clients to reveal early traumatic experiences. Although, as previously described, attempts to recover presumably repressed memories are fraught with reconstructive dangers, Harber and Pennebaker (1992) advocated procedures for encouraging the revelation of suppressed (if not repressed) thoughts. They argued that, in the long run, by virtue of associated increases in ANS and CNS activity, thought suppression is a biological stressor that produces a range of health problems and various cognitive side effects (e.g., stressful dreams). "Confrontation" (by attending to the suppressed memory) should therefore reduce these effects. Support for this latter claim mainly comes from experiments in which college students are randomly assigned to write or speak about either traumatic or mundane events from the past. Outcomes in the "trauma" groups include a subsequently reduced number of physical complaints. With respect to depression, Harber and Pennebaker implied that disclosure should alleviate general distress by focusing attention on the traumatic memory in the presumably safer context of their present lives.

Finally, compared to applications of research on emotionally biased cognition, the literature contains many fewer attempts to address general impairments in depression. One of the few, by Watts, MacLeod, and Morris (1988), documented the remediation of memory and concentration difficulties through imagery training, although subjects did not report a subjectively experienced benefit and therefore might not initiate the procedures in the absense of instructions. In fact, as noted by Williams et al. (1988), there has been little research regarding transfer of remediative strategies outside the therapeutic or experimental setting.

General impairments in depression are typically noted along quantitative dimensions (e.g., fewer words recalled); however, qualitative aspects of recall might be equally important for therapeutic applications. In that regard, Williams and his colleagues (see Williams, 1992) found that the proportion of *specific* memories reported in autobiographical protocols was smaller in groups of patients diagnosed with major depression than in various control groups. Furthermore, this tendency toward overgeneral memories did not depend on the degree of the patients' current mood disturbance. Therapists should, therefore, not assume that overgeneral recall will disappear when mood is temporarily better. Instead, Williams argued, therapists should try to change the processes leading to overgeneral recall. Therapy for depressed clients should include: practice in noticing the tendency toward overgeneral recall, training in procedures for remembering specific aspects of both positive and negative memories (so that the former can be elaborated and the latter reinterpreted), and using diaries for recording specific details, to aid attention at the outset. More generally, Williams (1992) advocated the development of strategies that transfer to nontherapeutic settings.

Cognitive–behavioral therapy sometimes includes "behavioral activation strategies" that are designed to transfer to the real world (Ingram & Hollon, 1986). Specific procedures (e.g., graded tasks) are designed to produce success through the environmental control of attention. Other therapeutic procedures are designed to teach clients to initiate controlled procedures through practice in doing so. And preparation for termination of therapy emphasizes that the skills gained in therapy can be used for future control. Ultimately, such procedures should, according to Ingram and Hollon (1986), decrease self-focused attention that has become maladaptively strong in depressed clients. Moreover, they clearly illustrate that refocusing attention is the key to therapeutic intervention and implicitly assume adequate attentional capacity. The central question, however, is whether the procedures can be initiated during future times of distress, when potentially more powerful motivations guide the focus of attention, impair memory for unattended aspects, and reinstigate the depressive state.

REFERENCES

Abramson, L. Y., Metalsky, G. I., & Alloy, L. B. (1989). Hopelessness depression: A theory-based subtype of depression. *Psychological Review, 96*, 358–372.

Beck, A. T. (1976). *Cognitive therapy and the emotional disorders.* New York: International University Press.

Beck, A. T., Rush, A. J., Shaw, B. F., & Emery, G. (1979). *Cognitive therapy of depression.* New York: Guilford.

Bower, G. H. (1990). Awareness, the unconscious, and repression: An experimental psychologist's perspective. In J. L. Singer (Ed.), *Repression and dissociation* (pp. 209–231). Chicago: University of Chicago Press.

Bower, G. H. (1992). How might emotions affect learning? In S. Christianson (Ed.), *The handbook of emotion and memory: Research and theory* (pp. 3–31). Hillsdale, NJ: Lawrence Erlbaum Associates.

Brewer, W. F. (1992). The theoretical and empirical status of the flashbulb memory hypothesis. In E. Winograd & U. Neisser (Eds.), *Affect and accuracy in recall* (pp. 274–305). New York: Cambridge University Press.

Brown, R., & Kulik, J. (1977). Flashbulb memories. *Cognition, 5,* 73–99.

Channon, S., Baker, J. E., & Robertson, M. M. (1993). Effects of structure and clustering on recall and recognition memory in clinical depression. *Journal of Abnormal Psychology, 102,* 323–326.

Christianson, S. Å. (1992). Emotional stress and eyewitness memory: A critical review. *Psychological Bulletin, 112,* 284–309.

Conway, M. A., Anderson, S. J., Larsen, S. F., Donnelly, C. M., McDaniel, M. A., McClelland, A. G. R., Rawles, R. E., & Logie, R. H. (1994). The formation of flashbulb memories. *Memory & Cognition, 22,* 326–343.

Denny, E. B., & Hunt, R. R. (1992). Affective valence and memory in depression: Dissociation of recall and fragment completion. *Journal of Abnormal Psychology, 101,* 575–580.

Easterbrook, J. A. (1959). The effect of emotion on cue utilization and the organization of behavior. *Psychological Review, 66,* 183–201.

Ellis, H. C., & Ashbrook, P. W. (1988). Resource allocation model of the effects of depressed mood states on memory. In K. Fiedler & J. Forgas (Eds.), *Affect, cognition and social behavior* (pp. 25–43). Toronto: Hogrefe.

Eysenck, M. W. (1982). *Attention and arousal* (pp. 95–123). New York: Springer-Verlag.

Eysenck, M. W., & Calvo, M. G. (1992). Anxiety and performance: The processing efficiency theory. *Cognition and Emotion, 6,* 409–434.

Gold, P. E. (1992). A proposed neurobiological basis for regulating memory storage for significant events. In E. Winograd & U. Neisser (Eds.), *Affect and accuracy in recall* (pp. 141–161). New York: Cambridge University Press.

Gotlib, I. H. (1992). Interpersonal and cognitive aspects of depression, *Current Directions in Psychological Research, 1,* 149–152.

Grafman, J. (1989). Plans, actions, and mental sets: Managerial knowledge units in the frontal lobes. In E. Perecman (Ed.), *Integrating theory and practice in clinical neuropsychology* (pp. 93–138). Hillsdale, NJ: Lawrence Erlbaum Associates.

Harber, K. D., & Pennebaker, J. W. (1992). Overcoming traumatic memories. In S. Christianson (Ed.), *The handbook of emotion and memory: Research and theory* (pp. 359–388). Hillsdale, NJ: Lawrence Erlbaum Associates.

Hartlage, S., Alloy, L. B., Vazquez, C., & Dykman, B. (1993). Automatic and effortful processing in depression. *Psychological Bulletin, 113,* 247–278.

Hasher, L., & Zacks, R. T. (1979). Automatic and effortful processes in memory. *Journal of Experimental Psychology: General, 108,* 356–388.

Henriques, J. B., & Davidson, R. J. (1991). Left frontal hypactivation in depression. *Journal of Abnormal Psychology, 100,* 535–545.

Hertel, P. T. (1992). Improving mood and memory through automatic and controlled procedures of mind. In D. Herrmann, H. Weingartner, A. Searleman, & C. McEvoy (Eds.), *Memory improvement: Implications for memory theory* (pp. 47–65). New York: Springer-Verlag.

Hertel, P. T. (1994). Depressive deficits in word identification and recall. *Cognition and Emotion, 8,* 313–327.

Hertel, P. T., & Hardin, T. S. (1990). Remembering with and without awareness in a depressed mood: Evidence of deficits in initiative. *Journal of Experimental Psychology: General, 119,* 45–59.

Hertel, P. T., & Milan, S. (1994). Depressive deficits in recognition: Dissociation of recollection and familiarity. *Journal of Abnormal Psychology, 103,* 736–742.

Hertel, P. T., & Rude, S. S. (1991a). Depressive deficits in memory: Focusing attention improves subsequent recall. *Journal of Experimental Psychology: General, 120,* 301–309.

Hertel, P. T., & Rude, S. R. (1991b). Recalling in a state of natural or experimental depression. *Cognitive Therapy and Research, 15,* 103–127.

Holmes, D. S. (1990). The evidence for repression: An examination of sixty years of research. In J. L. Singer (Ed.), *Repression and dissociation* (pp. 85–102). Chicago: University of Chicago Press.

Howell, A., & Conway, M. (1992). Mood and the suppression of positive and negative self-referent thoughts. *Cognitive Therapy and Research, 16,* 535–555.

Hunt, R. R., & McDaniel, M. A. (1993). The enigma of organization and distinctiveness. *Journal of Memory and Language, 32,* 421–445.

Ingram, R. E. (1990). Self-focused attention in clinical disorders: Review and a conceptual model. *Psychological Bulletin, 107,* 156–176.

Ingram, R. E., & Hollon, S. D. (1986). Cognitive therapy for depression from an information processing perspective. In R. E. Ingram (Ed.), *Information processing approaches to clinical psychology* (pp. 259–281). New York: Academic Press.

Jacoby, L. L., Toth, J., & Yonelinas, A. (1993). Separating conscious and unconscious influences of memory: Measuring recollection. *Journal of Experimental Psychology: General, 122,* 139–154.

Johnson, M. K., & Multhaup, K. S. (1992). Emotion and MEM. In S. Christianson (Ed.), *The handbook of emotion and memory: Research and theory* (pp. 33–66). Hillsdale, NJ: Lawrence Erlbaum Associates.

Kahneman, D. (1973). *Attention and effort.* Englewood Cliffs, NJ: Prentice-Hall.

Kihlstrom, J. F., & Hoyt, I. P. (1990). Repression, dissociation, and hypnosis. In J. L. Singer (Ed.), *Repression and dissociation* (pp. 181–208). Chicago: University of Chicago Press.

LeDoux, J. E. (1992). Emotion as memory: Anatomical systems underlying indelible neural traces. In S. Christianson (Ed.), *The handbook of emotion and memory: Research and theory* (pp. 269–288). Hillsdale, NJ: Lawrence Erlbaum Associates.

Loftus, E. F., & Kaufman, L. (1992). Why do traumatic experiences sometimes produce good memory (flashbulbs) and sometimes no memory (repression)? In E. Winograd & U. Neisser (Eds.), *Affect and accuracy in recall* (pp. 212–223). New York: Cambridge University Press.

Mandler, G. (1992). Memory, arousal, and mood: A theoretical integration. In S. Christianson (Ed.), *The handbook of emotion and memory: Research and theory* (pp. 93–110). Hillsdale, NJ: Lawrence Erlbaum Associates.

Mathews, A., & MacLeod, C. (1994). Cognitive approaches to emotion and emotional disorders. *Annual Review of Psychology, 45*, 25–50.

Mayes, A. R. (1988). *Human organic memory disorders.* New York: Cambridge University Press.

McCloskey, M., Wibble, C. G., & Cohen, N. J. (1988). Is there a special flashbulb-memory mechanism? *Journal of Experimental Psychology: General, 117*, 171–181.

McGaugh, J. L. (1992). Affect, neuromodulatory systems, and memory storage. In S. Christianson (Ed.), *The handbook of emotion and memory: Research and theory* (pp. 245–268). Hillsdale, NJ: Lawrence Erlbaum Associates.

Mineka, S. (1992). Evolutionary memories, emotional processing, and the emotional disorders. In D. L. Medin (Ed.), *The psychology of learning and motivation* (Vol. 28, pp. 161–206). New York: Academic Press.

Nasby, W., & Kihlstrom, J. F. (1986). Cognitive assessment of personality and psychopathology. In R. E. Ingram (Ed.), *Information processing approaches to clinical psychology* (pp. 217–239). New York: Academic Press.

Oatley, K., & Johnson-Laird, P. (1987). Towards a cognitive theory of emotion. *Cognition and Emotion, 1*, 29–50.

Parrott, W. G., & Sabini, J. (1990). Mood and memory under natural conditions: Evidence for mood incongruent recall. *Journal of Personality and Social Psychology, 59*, 321–336.

Posner, M. I. (1992). Attention as a cognitive and neural system. *Current Directions in Psychological Science, 1*, 11–14.

Posner, M. I., & Snyder, C. R. R. (1975). Attention and cognitive control. In R. L. Solso (Ed.), *Information processing in cognition: The Loyola Symposium* (pp. 55–85). Hillsdale, NJ: Lawrence Erlbaum Associates.

Reisberg, D., & Heuer, F. (1992). Remembering the details of emotional events. In E. Winograd & U. Neisser (Eds.), *Affect and accuracy in recall* (pp. 162–190). New York: Cambridge University Press.

Resnick, S. M. (1992). Positron Emission Tomography in psychiatric illness. *Current Directions in Psychological Science, 1*, 92–98.

Revelle, W., & Loftus, D. A. (1992). The implications of arousal effects for the study of affect and memory. In S. Christianson (Ed.), *The handbook of emotion and memory: Research and theory* (pp. 113–149). Hillsdale, NJ: Lawrence Erlbaum Associates.

Seibert, P. S., & Ellis, H. C. (1991). Irrelevant thoughts, emotional mood states, and cognitive task performance. *Memory & Cognition, 19*, 507–513.

Shiffrin, R. M., & Schneider, W. (1977). Controlled and automatic human information processing. II. Perceptual learning, automatic attending, and a general theory. *Psychological Review, 84*, 127–190.

Simon, H. A. (1994). The bottleneck of attention: Connecting thought with motivation. In W. Spaulding (Ed.), *Nebraska symposium on motivation: Integrated views of motivation, cognition and emotion* (Vol. 41, pp. 1–22). Lincoln: University of Nebraska Press.

Tobias, B. A., Kihlstrom, J. F., & Schacter, D. (1992). Emotion and implicit memory. In S. Christianson (Ed.), *The handbook of emotion and memory: Research and theory* (pp. 67–92). Hillsdale, NJ: Lawrence Erlbaum Associates.

Watts, F. N., MacLeod, A. K., & Morris, L. (1988). A remedial strategy for memory and concentration problems in depressed patients. *Cognitive Therapy and Research, 12*, 185–193.

Weary, G., Marsh, K. L., Gleicher, F., & Edwards, J. A. (1993). Depression, control motivation, and the processing of information about others. In G. Weary, F. Gleicher, & K. L. Marsh (Eds.), *Control motivation and social cognition* (pp. 255–287). New York: Springer-Verlag.

Wegner, D. M. (1989). *White bears and other unwanted thoughts.* New York: Viking.

Williams, J. M. G. (1992). Autobiographical memory and emotional disorders. In S. Christianson (Ed.), *The handbook of emotion and memory: Research and theory* (pp. 451–477). Hillsdale, NJ: Lawrence Erlbaum Associates.

Williams, J. M. G., Watts, F. N., MacLeod, C., & Mathews, A. (1988). *Cognitive psychology and emotional disorders.* New York: Wiley.

Winograd, E., & Neisser, U. (1992). *Affect and accuracy in recall.* New York: Cambridge University Press.

Yuille, J. C., & Tollestrup, P. A. (1992). A model of diverse effects of emotion on eyewitness memory. In S. Christianson (Ed.), *The handbook of emotion and memory: Research and theory* (pp. 201–215). Hillsdale, NJ: Lawrence Erlbaum Associates.

CHAPTER SEVENTEEN

The Aging of Practical Memory: An Overview

Christopher Hertzog
John Dunlosky
Georgia Institute of Technology

Research on aging has been a prominent part of the field of practical or everyday memory. The Second Practical Aspects of Memory Conference contained a set of papers on the topic of aging (Gruneberg, Morris, & Sykes, 1988), and several other recent books have been devoted to aspects of aging and research on practical cognition and memory (Poon, Rubin, & Wilson, 1989; Reese & Puckett, 1993; West & Sinnott, 1992). The healthy synergy between aging research and interests in everyday memory research is far from accidental, for researchers interested in aging have long been interested in how laboratory findings on age differences in cognition translate into implications for everyday life, including functional competence of older adults (e.g., Birren, 1974; Schaie, 1988). In particular, issues associated with how interventions can be designed and implemented to enhance the functioning of older persons, including special populations of older adults (e.g., those with clinical memory disorders), have been discussed by gerontologists since the beginnings of the science of aging earlier in this century (e.g., Talland, 1968).

The purpose of this chapter is to identify some important theoretical issues associated with research on everyday memory and aging, to selectively review some recent research in the area, and to discuss some topics in more detail that are of special interest to us. The two volumes of this book contain chapters by Cavanaugh, Dixon, Park, Rabbitt, and others who have a major or even primary focus on practical memory and aging, and we hope our brief overview will highlight some theoretical issues in gerontology that are relevant to their more focused presentations.

THEORETICAL CONSIDERATIONS

The Third Practical Aspects of Memory Conference took place in the context of some contention between psychologists interested in basic memory mechanisms, as studied in traditional experimental paradigms (Banaji & Crowder, 1989), and psychologists interested in everyday memory phenomena (e.g., Gruneberg, 1992). In Cohen's (1988) overview chapter on aging and practical memory, she commented on the similarities and differences between laboratory and everyday memory research by linking research questions to the context in which the research is conducted. She stated that although both approaches investigate the effects of aging on memory, "there is surprisingly little common ground between them" and suggested that if the aim of research is primarily pragmatic remediation through cognitive training, environmental design, or assessment of "competence to cope with the demands of everyday life," then it was appropriate to "focus on naturally occurring situations" (p. 79).

The idea that applied research benefits from being conducted in naturally occurring situations is hardly surprising. However, the impetus for much of the practical memory movement derives not merely from an interest in applied problems, but also from theoretical assumptions about how best to understand both the structure and function of memory and cognition. Research in the practical memory movement often derives from a contextualist world view (Dixon & Lerner, 1984). This view assumes that cognition is contingent on context, and it seeks to understand the ways in which the dynamic interplay between person and environmental variation influences the creation and utilization of memories. Bruce (1985) described the importance of a functional (evolutionary) theoretical perspective in which memory is understood in the context of its significance for the adaptation and survival of the organism (see also Anderson, 1990; Dixon & Hertzog, 1988). Both views require an understanding of how cognition enables humans to achieve goals effectively against a background of environmental hazards, affordances, and contingencies.

The current controversy regarding the utility of practical memory research exists precisely because healthy theoretical differences exist in the extent to which psychologists believe that memory mechanisms can be isolated from contextual variables in which they occur (Herrmann & Searleman, 1990; Mook, 1983; Petrinovich, 1989). Such differences inform us about our metatheoretical paradigms, theoretical prejudices, and blind spots—and hence should not be disregarded. As psychologists who do basic research on mechanisms of cognition and memory in adulthood, we do not endorse the position that cognitive research must ipso facto be studied in everyday contexts. Conversely, although we are convinced in principle that a laboratory with the proper equipment (e.g., the holodeck on the starship USS *Enterprise*) can dissect virtually any phenomenon with tight experimental control, this does not necessarily imply that well-controlled laboratory research on age differences in experimental tasks (as commonly conducted by earthlings in the late 20th century) will sufficiently characterize how aging affects memory functioning in natural situations. In our view, research on aging will best proceed if we successfully bridge the gap perceived by Cohen (1988) between laboratory and everyday memory research, in large part because the kinds of research questions and theoretical assumptions prevalent in the everyday memory research have not had sufficient impact on gerontology.

Research on everyday memory and aging can be understood in the context of several important premises, which we state in some cases without elaboration:

1. Everyday memory occurs in the context of adaptive, self-regulated, goal-directed behaviors. Everyday memory is seen here as a means toward a goal rather than as an end in itself.

2. Successful and unsuccessful uses of memory represent outcomes of multiple processes, many of which cannot be classified as cognitive mechanisms (e.g., Herrmann & Searleman, 1990; Park & Mayhorn, in press).

3. Understanding everyday memory requires attention both to age changes in cognitive mechanisms and to understanding how adults use knowledge and experience to shape and guide cognitive activity. Normatively, aging is accompanied by decline in the effectiveness of many memory-related processes (Hultsch & Dixon, 1990). However, the aging individual also gains experience, knowledge, and at least a chance for wisdom (Baltes, 1993). Older adults effectively use knowledge and expertise to perform cognitively demanding tasks in everyday life (Rybash, Hoyer, & Roodin, 1986; Salthouse, 1989).

4. Adults can compensate for the effects of aging on cognitive mechanisms by adapting to changing internal conditions (Bäckman, 1989; Bäckman & Dixon, 1992; Baltes, 1993). In everyday life, age-related impairment of various aspects of cognition such as working memory can be offset by the use of compensatory mechanisms such as strategies, external memory aids, or changes in lifestyles to reduce or alter cognitive demands (Cohen, 1988).

5. Everyday memory is influenced by social contexts and social interactions (Best, 1992; Dixon, chap. 18, this volume). Beliefs about self and others (social cognition per se) influence how individuals structure and represent everyday environmental contingencies and hence represent one class of explanations for age changes in laboratory and everyday memory contexts (Hess, 1994).

6. Everyday memory involves a set of complex interrelations between emotion, motivation, beliefs, and cognition. Age changes in how emotion

is experienced can significantly impact memory and effective real-world problem solving (Blanchard-Fields, 1986; Blanchard-Fields, Jahnke, & Camp, 1995; Carstensen & Turk-Charles, 1994).

7. There are individual differences in cognitive ability, in the rates of aging in cognitive mechanisms, in the nature of knowledge and experience gained through life, and in patterns of successful adaptation during adulthood. A complete understanding of aging and everyday cognition will require attending to these individual differences, often through means of research methods uncommon to classical memory research (see Hertzog, 1985).

8. Given the complexity of cognitive phenomena associated with aging, it seems unrealistic to expect that any single construct or class of constructs will account for the successful use of cognition in everyday life (Light, 1991).

RESEARCH ON EVERYDAY MEMORY AND AGING

One trend in everyday memory research is an increased sophistication of both questions being asked and research designs used to address these questions. Concern with general issues such as artificiality of laboratory tasks remains, but the conceptualization of such issues has become more subtle and multifaceted.

Ecological Validity, Familiarity, and Aging

An example of the changing face of everyday memory research in aging involves the construct of task familiarity as part of ecological validity. The artificiality of laboratory memory tasks has been cited as a possible reason for empirical findings of age differences in memory performance (see Kausler, 1991). According to this view, increases in familiarity of task, or increases in motivation of older adults to perform in memory tasks (perhaps by increasing the face validity of the task for everyday memory), will reduce or eliminate age differences in memory performance. Research done over the last two decades has produced little supporting evidence for this hypothesis and a great deal of contradictory evidence. For example, although recently developed batteries of tasks simulate everyday memory (e.g., West, Crook, & Barron, 1992; Wilson, Cockburn, & Baddeley, 1985), age differences on these tasks are typically robust (especially those involving episodic memory where laboratory studies have also indicated significant age differences favoring younger adults). Furthermore, everyday memory tasks correlate with psychometric measures of memory and intelligence (Cockburn & Smith, 1991). Willis and Schaie (1986) showed that older adults' performance on the ETS Practical Skills test, a psychometric test of the ability to perform a variety of simulated everyday tasks (e.g., locate information in the yellow pages), correlates more highly with measures of fluid intelligence than with measures of crystallized intelligence.

Although these studies demonstrate that age differences in memory performance still persist when more ecologically valid measures of cognition are employed, the development and continued use of such alternative measures is important for several reasons. First, they may be more likely to generate cooperation in adults due to their resemblance to naturally occurring situations. Second, everyday memory batteries incorporate a greater variety of tasks that may help to identify additional dimensions of memory and cognition for assessment of age-related change. Finally, these everyday memory batteries may prove especially helpful in clinical assessment, and as such may help to shape the design of cognitive rehabilitation programs.

The evolution of arguments concerning the usefulness of everyday memory measures is reflected in the kinds of hypotheses currently being evaluated in the literature. For example, a valid picture of the accuracy of memory complaints and beliefs about oneself as a rememberer may require comparing beliefs against performance in memory tasks that are familiar to the individuals. Berry, West, and Dennehy (1989) argued that performance predictions, which they treat as measures of memory self-efficacy, are more highly related to performance when the individuals are predicting performance for naturalistic, everyday tasks (e.g., remembering items off a grocery list) than for more artificial tasks (e.g., remembering paired associates of weak semantic relatedness).

Task familiarity may be more complex than originally envisioned in much of this research. West (1992) reported an interesting study of memory for object locations. She manipulated the everyday nature of three dimensions: encoding varied from less familiar line drawings of objects to the objects themselves, context varied from a less familiar table top array of 12 boxes to a room with multiple locations, and retrieval varied from identifying the box an item was located in to subject placement of objects and locomotion in the room to find and identify objects (as operationalized by West, 1992). Older adults were more greatly affected by the manipulation of everyday variables: The condition with everyday encoding, context, and retrieval produced highest recall for older adults and the smallest age differences. However, by having adults place and find the line drawings in the room, West showed that the use of natural objects per se was not the key factor. Use of the artificial stimuli here produced recall that was not different from the completely everyday memory condition. Apparently, the *actions* involved in placing and retrieving a stimulus, not the familiarity of the stimulus, had the greatest benefit for performance. Thus, West's (1992) study serves as a reminder that simulation of everyday conditions is possible in the laboratory, and that the everyday familiarity of stimuli per se is not always the most important determinant of enhanced memory performance in such contexts, when it occurs. Hence, the goal should be uncovering the mechanisms (both cognitive and noncognitive) that enhance performance of older adults in these rather complex, naturalistic situations.

Text Recall: A Prototypical Everyday Memory Task?

Historically, research on text recall in aging increased in the 1970s and 1980s, in part motivated by the belief that it better reflected the everyday use of episodic memory by older adults. What have we learned after two decades of intensive research in this area? Although age differences definitely occur in memory for information presented in texts (Hultsch & Dixon, 1984; Zelinski & Gilewski, 1988), research on text recall shows that age effects vary in magnitude and interact with a host of variables associated with the text, such as type of material (e.g., narrative vs. expository) and quality of organization of the idea units in the text (Meyer & Rice, 1989). Moreover, characteristics of the reader, including intelligence, reading level, and prior knowledge of the topic area, are crucially important in determining memory for text and appear to influence the magnitude of observed age effects. For example, in at least some studies age differences have depended on the verbal ability of the readers (Meyer & Rice, 1989). The literature on text recall supports Bäckman's (1989) arguments that age differences in memory must be understood in the context of the confluence of personal characteristics and task structure.

How the task is structured may influence the magnitude and causes of age differences in text recall, due to the processing demands imposed. Real-time constraints produced by line-by-line presentation of text may maximize relationships of comprehension speed, reading time, and working memory capacity to encoding of textual information, thereby placing older adults at greater disadvantage. Hartley's (1993; Hartley, Stojack, Mushaney, Kiku Annon, & Lee, 1994) analysis of reading times and text recall is interesting in this regard. In her work, both older adults and younger adults were more strategic when pacing their reading than when the pace of exposure was set to be close to the individual's experimentally measured reading speed. However, Hartley et al. (1994) showed that older adults do not necessarily increase self-paced study time sufficiently to improve levels of text learning and recall. Moreover, Hartley's (1993) analysis suggests some qualitative differences in what is recalled under self-paced study. Further work on how older adults use strategies to learn text information under self-paced conditions might shed further light on the causes of age differences in prose retention.

Text recall is typically measured by quantitative coding systems that score the recall protocol for the presence of central ideas and relatively fine-grained details. Labouvie-Vief and Schell (1982) argued that higher levels of recall of information from text by younger adults reflect a processing style emphasizing details and literal meanings. In contrast, older adults process the meaning and more general significance of the story, fueled by growth in the ability to integrate logical (analytic) and emotional (intuitive, expressive) forms of representing meaning. They see age-related shifts not as mere compensation for declines in processing capacity that limit memory for text details, but as reflections of the life tasks of the older adult.

Consistent with this qualitative shift hypothesis, Adams (1991) reported that older adults' recall protocols for metaphorically rich narratives generated qualitative age differences in response pattern, with older adults more likely to recall higher levels of meaning and less likely to recall specific surface-level ideas (see also Jepson & Labouvie-Vief, 1992). This pattern was not found for expository texts, where the goal of reading presumably would be to learn new information more directly related to specific propositions of the text. Furthermore, Adams (1991) showed that story retellings by younger adults contained more details, whereas older adults' retellings were more likely to focus on the higher-order meaning. Although the qualitative shift hypothesis probably cannot account for all age differences in text recall, it serves to remind us that the nature of the processing requirements of the tasks as matched to the abilities and goals of the readers are critical determinants of text recall. Discovering these subtle interactions is of central relevance in evaluating the nature of age changes in underlying cognitive processes.

Applied research has also demonstrated the relationship of knowledge and schema to the comprehension and memory for medical information (Rice, Meyer, & Miller, 1989) and for instructions on how to use medications (Morrow, Leirer, Altieri, & Tanke, 1991). The latter study demonstrated that altering the structure of medication instructions to match the schemas elders have for medication usage boosted comprehension and recall. Subsequent research suggested that framing instructions as categorized lists of actions, rather than presenting them in paragraphs, was preferred by older adults and enhanced their recall of instructions (Morrow, Leirer, & Altieri, 1995). Categorized lists may provide more organizational support for the older adults and minimize the need to identify the organizational structure of the information in the prose passage during reading.

Principles regarding text recall learned in laboratory experiments can be used to enhance text comprehension and recall in everyday life. Meyer, Young, and Bartlett (1989) argued that older adults may not use optimal strategies for reading and remembering text materials because they do not necessarily attend to and use the superordinate structure of the text to organize learning. They trained adults to improve reading comprehension by using a set of planned strategies. Younger and older participants were taught to identify the type of organizational structure present in reading material and to adapt their reading strategy accordingly. They also learned to differentiate the main ideas from the subordinate ideas in the text and to use that hierarchical structure to guide learning. Although age differences in comprehension and recall were not eliminated by strategy training (both groups benefited as compared to same-age controls), older adults showed greater improvements when using the hierarchical structure. At pretest only 12% of the older adults consistently used the top-level structure of text to organize their recalls, whereas 33% of younger adults used the structure. These differences disappeared after training. Meyer et al. (1989) suggested that these initial differences were related to verbal ability: High-verbal older adults are already proficient in using the plan strategy, whereas average-verbal older adults are not.

RESEARCH ON AGING AND METAMEMORY

An area of cognitive aging that we find promising for targeting applications to real-world situations is metamemory. Metamemory has multiple components, including a person's beliefs about his or her own memory system, on-line monitoring of memory, and self-regulated behavior during memory-related activities (for further discussion, see Hertzog & Dixon, 1994; Nelson & Narens, 1990). To better understand aging and metamemory, we have been investigating these components in isolation as well as the interplay between them. In the next sections, we overview selected research in which these components are examined and speculate on how concepts developed from this basic research can be applied so as to enhance everyday memory performance.

Aging and Beliefs About Memory

Self-report questionnaires were one of the first and most prominently used tests to investigate age-related differences in metamemory. Many questionnaires have been developed to measure a person's beliefs about his or her own memory (for reviews, see Gilewski & Zelinski, 1986; Herrmann, 1990). Evidence suggests that age differences exist in adults' perceptions of the ability to remember, of change in ability, and of how much control one has over memory functioning (e.g., Hultsch, Hertzog, & Dixon, 1987; Loewen, Shaw, & Craik, 1990).

Earlier research also showed that self-reports on various questionnaires had little predictive validity for lab-based memory tasks or for memory tasks involved in real-world situations, with correlations between scores on various questionnaires and memory tasks typically being less than +.30 (for exceptions, see Berry et al., 1989; Schlechter, Herrmann, & Toglia, 1990). Measured longitudinal changes in memory self-efficacy and perceived memory change have low-to-nil relations to actual change in memory performance over time (McDonald-Miszczak, Hertzog, & Hultsch, in press). There are several interpretations of such low correlations, with one interesting possibility being that perceived changes in memory are not based on an individual's monitoring of actual changes in memory ability, but instead on an individual's implicit theory of how memory changes during aging in adulthood (McFarland, Ross, & Giltrow, 1992).

Even though the predictive validity of people's beliefs about memory for memory task performance is rather low, these beliefs still have important implications for real-world applications. First, inaccurate, negative beliefs can have dysfunctional impact on individuals' lives. Hence, self-report questionnaires could be used to identify people with extremely low self-efficacy, so as to target these potentially high-risk individuals for appropriate intervention programs (e.g., Best, Hamlett, & Davis, 1992; Lachman, Weaver, Bandura, Elliott, & Lewkowicz, 1992; Neely & Bäckman, 1993; Scogin, Storandt, & Lott, 1985).

Second, memory self-efficacy and related beliefs may play an important role in how individuals utilize various strategies during memory tasks (Berry & West, 1993; Hertzog & Dixon, 1994). Older adults who believe they cannot acquire new memories may be unlikely to utilize effective strategies to acquire new memories (Rebok & Balcerak, 1989), may be more likely to stop rehearsing new material after failure has occurred, or may even avoid challenging tasks that involve learning new material (for further discussion, see Bandura, 1989; Hertzog & Dixon, 1994). That is, people's memory self-efficacy beliefs curtail self-regulated processes that may otherwise compensate for memory problems.

Thus, an important goal in this domain of research is to characterize the relations between people's beliefs about memory and their self-regulated behavior during memory tasks. Research here will need to include procedures wherein people have the opportunity to control various aspects of memory tasks, such as selecting and using various rehearsal strategies (e.g., Belmont, Freeseman, & Mitchell, 1988; Brigham & Pressley, 1988), allocating study time (e.g., Nelson, Dunlosky, Graf, & Narens, 1994), and terminating study (e.g., Murphy, Schmitt, Caruso, & Sanders, 1987). For instance, Belmont et al. (1988) employed a digit-span task in which individuals paced the onset of each digit so as to "discover how to memorize the digits perfectly at non-trivial list lengths" (p. 86). Although many older adults spontaneously used similar chunking strategies to those used by younger adults (as inferred from self-paced pause times), some older adults showed less consistency in the use of these strategies and, hence, had shorter digit spans. Perhaps older adults with low self-efficacy beliefs are less likely to spontaneously use appropriate strategies.

Consistent with this possibility, Riggs, Lachman, and Wingfield (1994) discovered that an older adult's perceived control does affect how he or she regulates study behavior. Each participant was instructed to listen to as many words (individually presented) of a paragraph that he or she believed could be recalled accurately; at this time, the participant stopped the presentation of the paragraph and attempted recall. As compared to older adults who had an internal locus of control (i.e., those believing memory improvement is within their control), those with an external locus of control chose to study more words before stopping the presentation of the paragraph and tended to recall fewer words (cf. Berry, 1987, cited in Berry & West, 1993). One key aspect of this research by Belmont et al. (1988) and by Riggs et al. (1994) is that their procedures include direct measures of processes relevant to self-regulated behavior.

Goals of future research examining the relations between memory self-efficacy beliefs and self-regulated behavior should include evaluating the degree to which higher-memory self-efficacy is needed to elicit regulation of memory-related behavior, and the degree to which improving older adults' beliefs about their memory will produce more effective control and thereby improve memory performance. Evidence shows promise in boosting the first component of this causal chain in which people's beliefs about memory affect control process that in turn affect memory performance. Best et al. (1992) had a group of older adults participate in four sessions wherein beliefs about the negative effects of aging on memory ability were challenged. As compared to control groups, older adults who were involved in these training sessions had fewer memory complaints after training, a reduction that was even maintained until two weeks after training (cf. McEvoy & Moon, 1988). Similarly, Lachman et al. (1992) had older adults participate in sessions that included training memory skills as well as promoting the notion that people have control of their memory. After training, these older adults showed improvements in their self-conceptions of memory, although the effects of this intervention diminished somewhat over three months.

Even though these interventions improved people's beliefs about memory, both Best et al. (1992) and Lachman et al. (1992) reported that changing people's beliefs had little impact on memory performance. (Note, however, that a different treatment in Best et al. and an intervention developed by Neely & Bäckman, 1993, have boosted the memory performance of older adults.) Put differently, boosting memory self-efficacy beliefs per se did not help older adults increase their memory performance. Perhaps in these instances people's enhanced beliefs about memory did affect how they attempted to remember items on the memory tasks (Lachman et al., 1992). An exciting avenue for future research will be to examine how these intervention programs affect various self-regulated strategies (e.g., see Scogin et al., 1985, who reported that training memory skills boosted self-paced study time during several memory tasks), and the degree to which self-regulation mediates memory performance.

Beliefs about memory self-efficacy may also influence other kinds of strategies that aid memory functioning in everyday life. In particular, evidence from daily diaries (Cavanaugh, Grady, & Perlmutter, 1983) and self-report questionnaires (e.g., Hultsch et al., 1987; Loewen et al., 1990) suggest that external aids are used more by older adults than by younger adults (however, see West, 1988). Older adults may use external memory aids more often because they believe their memory ability has declined and are attempting to compensate for this perceived decline (for discussion of this and other hypotheses, see Intons-Peterson & Newsome, 1992; Loewen et al., 1990). Furthermore, because adults prefer to use external aids over internal aids (Cavanaugh et al., 1983), external aids provide a host of strategies that older adults may likely use in enhancing their everyday memory performance.

Several questions related to the notion of compensation have not yet been answered (for others not discussed here, see Intons-Peterson & Newsome, 1992). Does the increased use of a given external aid help older adults compensate for age-related differences in memory performance? Will interventions targeting a given external aid increase its effectiveness in reducing older adults' memory problems? To answer these questions, researchers will need to obtain not only a measure of how frequently a given external aid is used, but also some measure of the effectiveness of that aid (e.g., the proportion of successful memory performance given the use of the aid). To better understand why both measures may be important, consider this example: Even if older adults use a given external aid more frequently after training, their memory performance may remain unchanged (or even get worse) if the increased use of the aid occurs in situations where it is ineffective (e.g., write an appointment in a calendar, but fail to use the calendar later; for further discussion of memory-aid effectiveness, see Harris, 1978). A challenge for future researchers will be to develop procedures in which the effectiveness of an external aid in real-life situations can be compared across various age groups and training conditions. In doing so, basic research here will provide valuable insights into how applications can be targeted at effectively enhancing memory performance of older adults.

Aging and Judgments of Memory Performance

Besides measuring a person's beliefs about his or her own memory system via self-report questionnaires, research has also focused on memory tasks that involve making judgments about memory performance. For instance, after studying a list of 15 face–name associations, a person may predict how many of the 15 items he or she will later correctly recall. In contrast to this global prediction of subsequent memory performance, people may also make item-by-item predictions: Before studying one face–name association, a person would predict the likelihood that he or she will recall the name when later shown that face. As elaborated next, whereas age-related differences have sometimes been found in the accuracy of global predictions, age-related differences have been negligible in the accuracy of item-by-item judgments.

Although research has shown relatively consistent age-related declines in beliefs of memory self-efficacy, research on the accuracy of global predictions of subsequent memory performance shows an inconsistent pattern, with some findings suggesting age-related declines in accuracy (e.g., Bruce, Coyne, & Botwinick, 1982) and others suggesting age-invariance in accuracy (e.g., Perlmutter, 1978; Rebok & Balcerak, 1989). In a more recent series of studies, we have demonstrated both age-related decline and age-invariance in global prediction accuracy when it is measured by signed or unsigned differences between prediction and performance (Connor, Dunlosky, & Hertzog, 1995; Hertzog, Saylor, Fleece, & Dixon, 1994). An apparent resolution of these inconsistent findings is that the accuracy of global predictions is at least partially moderated by age-related differences in memory performance (cf. similar conclusion by Perfect & Stollery, 1993, in relation to the accuracy of other kinds of memory judgments). That is, because both younger adults and older adults typically predict that they will correctly remember about half the items of a list, age-related differences in accuracy depends primarily on the level of memory performance that is yielded by the memory task, with accuracy being better for the group whose memory performance is closer to 50%. By contrast, correlations of before-study predictions and performance (across individuals) are similar for both age groups, even when age-related differences appear in predictive accuracy as measured by difference scores.

One kind of item-by-item prediction that has recently received much attention and may play a causal role in performance during multitrial learning (Nelson et al., 1994) are judgments of learning. These are a person's predictions about the likelihood of his or her own subsequent memory performance for recently studied items. Until recently, a typical procedure used to investigate these kind of judgments was to present an item for study and then to have the participant make the prediction for the item either during or immediately after the presentation of the item. Several studies have demonstrated that the accuracy of immediate judgments of learning are just as accurate for older adults as for younger adults (e.g., Lovelace & Marsh, 1985; Rabinowitz, Ackerman, Craik, & Hinchley, 1982). For instance, Connor et al. (1995) reported that the mean (across individuals) gamma correlation between immediate judgments of learning and eventual recall performance was about +.32 for younger adults and for older adults. Although age-invariance occurred, this somewhat low accuracy may limit the functional utility of these judgments in real-world settings. For example, consider Elizabeth, who is trying to learn people's names at a social gathering. After meeting each person, she asks herself, "Will I remember this person's name later?" If she answers no, then she rehearses the name some more, but if she answers yes, then she stops rehearsing. In this way, Elizabeth is utilizing her judgments to isolate supposedly less well-learned names for restudy. However, because the accuracy of her immediate judgments is so low, she may spend extra time rehearsing names she would have remembered or fail to rehearse names that she will not remember.

In contrast to the limited accuracy of immediate judgments, delaying judgments of learning just a short time until after study (e.g., 30 seconds) can yield nearly perfect accuracy at predicting the likelihood of subsequent recall for one item versus another (Nelson & Dunlosky, 1991; but for a boundary condition, see Dunlosky & Nelson, 1992). Connor et al. (1995) demonstrated that the accuracy of people's delayed judgments of learning is just as high for older adults as for younger adults: Without any special training, older adults almost perfectly predict the likelihood of subsequent memory performance. As discussed by Bäckman (1989), this intact ability of older adults may prove important in helping them overcome memory deficits: "[An] approach might be to focus on those abilities reported to be relatively intact in older adults and to use these well-preserved abilities as triggers for new learning, thereby possibly enhancing the effects of training on deteriorated abilities" (p. 535).

A critical question now arises: Can delayed judgments of learning be used to enhance an older adult's memory performance? Evidence from two lines of research suggest that the answer to this question is affirmative. First, Nelson et al. (1994) reported that younger adults' restudy is allocated more effectively when their own delayed judgments of learning are utilized to allocate restudy as compared to when normative difficulties of items are utilized to allocate restudy, and younger adults also utilize their own meta-cognitive monitoring to effectively allocate restudy. Second, Dunlosky and Connor (1994) found that older adults and younger adults *spontaneously* allocate more restudy time to items that had been given lower delayed judgments of learning than to items that had previously been given higher judgments, which suggests that both age groups utilize the output from monitoring to regulate study time in a way that can yield effective learning. Thus, perhaps training older adults to monitor their memory will be sufficient to help them more effectively learn new material. Consistent with this possibility, Murphy et al. (1987) instructed a group of older adults to monitor their progress by testing themselves during study. These older adults used self-testing at least as much as (uninstructed) younger adults and (relative to uninstructed older adults) spent more time studying as well as recalled more items.

Accordingly, current evidence suggests that older adults' memory performance will benefit from interventions focused on the effective use of various kinds of on-line monitoring, including self-testing and delayed judgments of learning. From this perspective, people would be taught to use on-line monitoring to regulate study when they use any one of a wide variety of specific rehearsal strategies. The possible utility of combining monitoring and self-regulation with other rehearsal strategies is certainly not novel (e.g., Pressley & El-Dinary, 1993). For instance, West (1992) has recently proposed that "a focus on self-regulation may be a prerequisite to systematic practical application of memory aids" (p. 588). Teaching learners of all ages to use these and other kinds of monitoring to regulate study also fits well with multimodal approaches of improving memory, which have been recently advocated by Herrmann and Searlman (1990).

RESEARCH ON PROSPECTIVE REMEMBERING IN LABORATORY AND EVERYDAY LIFE

One fascinating area of research that has been central to research on aging and everyday memory has involved prospective memory: remembering to perform an action in the future. This area illustrates some of the differences and similarities between remembering in everyday contexts and remembering as manifested in laboratory tasks. Craik's (1986) processing view of memory suggests that prospective remembering should be particularly susceptible to aging, because older persons must self-initiate the process of remembering to act (see also Bäckman, 1989). Yet a number of early studies have found minimal age differences in remembering to perform actions like calling the laboratory or returning a postcard (e.g., Maylor, 1990; West, 1988). West (1988) suggested that there was an important difference between performance on tasks in which individuals could use idiosyncratic techniques as cues to perform actions versus prospective tasks that do not provide opportunities for use of external cues to guide remembering, with age differences emerging in the latter tasks.

This distinction has been further supported by recent laboratory studies. Einstein and McDaniel (1990) developed an experimental task measuring prospective remembering in the form of a secondary task—remembering to press a button on a computer keyboard when a particular target stimulus is displayed. They suggested (see also Einstein, Holland, McDaniel & Guynn, 1992) that cue-driven prospective remembering does not change with age unless conditions are manipulated to cause forgetting of the cues (what they term the *retrospective component of prospective memory*). By contrast, time-based prospective remembering (requiring one to respond at a particular time interval), does not involve specific cues for action, and shows robust age differences (Einstein & McDaniel, 1990).

Although time-based tasks may be more prone to age differences than event-based tasks, some recent studies demonstrate that age differences can occur in event-based tasks. Mäntylä (1994) used high and low typicality exemplars of semantic categories as cues, with subjects instructed to respond by pressing a key if any member of the semantic category was displayed. He found age differences for low (but not high) typicality exemplars and argued that this finding supported the self-initiated processing hypothesis. Recently, Park, Hertzog, Morrell, Kidder, and Mayhorn (1994) developed an alternative dual-task approach to investigate event-based and time-based prospective remembering. In their tasks, the event-based cue is a property of the stimulus background rather than an aspect of the target stimulus itself. The primary task was a continuous memory span, which is highly demanding of working memory and attention. Subjects pressed a button either when a previously learned background pattern appeared on the screen or at a specific time interval. Park et al. found age differences in event-based prospective remembering using this paradigm, although they found larger age differences in time-based prospective remembering. This finding is also consistent with Craik's (1986) view, in that age differences emerged in event-based tasks when the cue was not part of the stimulus properties being evaluated to fulfill the requirements of the primary task.

These studies show that age differences exist in mechanisms supporting prospective remembering that can be experimentally isolated. Do these age-related effects translate into prospective remembering problems for older adults in everyday life? West's (1988) study would suggest not necessarily. Where older adults can use external aids and other compensatory strategies (e.g., use of daily routines or scripted activities to guide remembering, Ross & Berg, 1992), everyday prospective remembering can be highly effective (Patton & Meit, 1993). Indeed, Camp and McKitrick (1992) even demonstrated that mild to moderately impaired adults with Alzheimer's disease can be trained to use spaced retrieval and external aids to better remember to perform activities of daily living. Another excellent example of this is provided by work on medication adherence (Park & Kidder, 1995; Park & Mayhorn, in press). Remembering to take one's medicine is a quintessential everyday prospective remembering problem. Park and associates have measured adherence in everyday life through the use of electronic bottle caps and other devices. In one recent study involving older adults, age and performance on standard laboratory memory tasks did not correlate with adherence to a medication schedule, although age differences occurred in cognitive performance. Instead, adherence significantly correlated with measures of coping strategies, affect, and self-reported use of external memory aids (as well as measures of attitudes toward and beliefs about medicines).

CONCLUSIONS

The field of gerontology will continue to benefit from combinations of laboratory tasks and field experiments. Further progress will require renewed attention to issues of compensatory behaviors. Consider the finding that

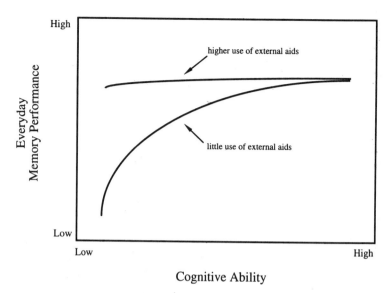

FIG. 17.1. Hypothetical moderation of the functional relationship between basic cognitive abilities and everyday memory performance by compensatory strategies, indicated by high and low use of external aids for everyday remembering. Higher use of external aids eliminates the impact of low ability on everyday memory performance.

everyday prospective remembering, as manifested by taking medications, shows negligible age effects in a sample that simultaneously displays typical age effects in standard cognitive tasks measuring memory and intelligence. The construct of compensation may be critically important in evaluating such outcomes. Perhaps age changes in cognitive ability will not have a strong impact on performance of everyday life tasks that are cognitively demanding, unless individuals fail to develop a set of internal and external compensatory devices that aid cognition as it is manifested in everyday life.

This idea suggests an empirically testable class of interaction hypotheses. As illustrated in Fig. 17.1, the compensation hypothesis predicts that cognitive abilities (as measured by standard laboratory tasks) will relate more highly to everyday performance when compensatory behaviors are either not used (bottom function in Fig. 17.1) or are ineffective for the particular everyday demand (see also Salthouse, 1989). By contrast, cognitive abilities will be less related to everyday memory performance when compensatory behaviors are used effectively (top function in Fig. 17.1). This moderation of the functional relation between abilities and everyday memory by use of compensatory behaviors is hypothesized to occur for adults of all ages. However, this hypothesized interaction would be particularly important for understanding age equivalence in everyday memory functioning. Given that many kinds of cognitive ability decline with age, higher everyday memory performance for older adults (top left quadrant of Fig. 17.1) indicates that effective compensatory behaviors could, in principle, preserve the everyday memory functioning of older adults by reducing their reliance on those abilities that have declined. Accordingly, different levels of everyday memory performance may be determined by qualitatively different processes, with higher-performing older adults often using different procedures for everyday remembering than are used by young adults (who may be more likely to rely on cognitive abilities than on external aids and related compensatory strategies). To successfully evaluate the relations conceptualized in Fig. 17.1, researchers will need to develop independent measures of several constructs (including compensatory behaviors and their effectiveness). Doing so will help to clarify links between laboratory research and everyday life and will, in the long run, lead to more effective interventions that enhance the everyday memory functioning of older adults.

ACKNOWLEDGMENTS

John Dunlosky's work on this manuscript was supported by a Research in Cognitive Aging Training Grant funded by PHS/NIH National Institute on Aging (5 T32 AG00175-07) to the Georgia Institute of Technology. Dunlosky is now at the Department of Psychology, University of North Carolina, Greensboro. We would like to thank John C. Cavanaugh and Cathy McEvoy for helpful comments on an earlier version of this manuscript.

REFERENCES

Adams, C. (1991). Qualitative age differences in memory for text: A life-span developmental perspective. *Psychology and Aging, 6,* 323–336.

Anderson, J. R. (1990). *The adaptive character of thought.* Hillsdale, NJ: Lawrence Erlbaum Associates.

Bäckman, L. (1989). Varieties of memory compensation by older adults in episodic remembering. In L. W. Poon, D. C. Rubin, & B. A. Wilson (Eds.), *Everyday cognition in adulthood and late life* (pp. 509–544). New York: Cambridge University Press.

Bäckman, L., & Dixon, R. (1992). Psychological compensation: A theoretical framework. *Psychological Bulletin, 112,* 259–283.

Baltes, P. B. (1993). The aging mind: Potential and limits. *The Gerontologist, 33,* 580–594.

Banaji, M. R., & Crowder, R. G. (1989). The bankruptcy of everyday memory. *American Psychologist, 44,* 1185–1193.

Bandura, A. (1989). Regulation of cognitive processes through perceived self-efficacy. *Developmental Psychology, 22,* 729–735.

Belmont, J. M., Freeseman, L. J., & Mitchell, D. W. (1988). Memory as problem solving: The cases of young and elderly adults. In M. M. Gruneberg, P. M., Morris, & R. N. Sykes (Eds.), *Practical aspects of memory: Current research and issues* (Vol. 2, pp. 84–89). Chichester, England: Wiley.

Berry, J. M., & West, R. L. (1993). Cognitive self-efficacy across the life-span: An integrative review. *International Journal of Behavioral Development, 16,* 351–389.

Berry, J. M., West, R. L., & Dennehy, D. M. (1989). Reliability and validity of the Memory Self-Efficacy Questionnaire (MSEQ). *Developmental Psychology, 25,* 701–713.

Best, D. L. (1992). The role of social interaction in memory improvement. In D. J. Herrmann, H. Weingartner, A. Searleman, & C. McEvoy (Eds.), *Memory improvement: Implications for memory theory* (pp. 122–149). New York: Springer-Verlag.

Best, D. L., Hamlett, K. W., & Davis, S. W. (1992). Memory complaint and memory performance in the elderly: The effects of memory-skills training and expectancy change. *Applied Cognitive Psychology, 6,* 405–416.

Birren, J. E. (1974). Translations in gerontology—from lab to life. *American Psychologist, 29,* 808–815.

Blanchard-Fields, F. (1986). Reasoning on social dilemmas varying in emotional salience: An adult developmental perspective. *Psychology and Aging, 1,* 325–333.

Blanchard-Fields, F., Jahnke, H., & Camp, C. J. (1995). Age differences in problem solving style: The role of emotional salience. *Psychology and Aging, 10,* 173–180.

Brigham, J. C. N., & Pressley, M. (1988). Cognitive monitoring and strategy choice in younger and older adults. *Psychology and Aging, 3,* 249–257.

Bruce, D. (1985). The how and why of ecological memory. *Journal of Experimental Psychology: General, 114,* 78–90.

Bruce, P. R., Coyne, A. C., & Botwinick, J. (1982). Adult age difference in metamemory. *Journal of Gerontology, 37,* 354–357.

Camp, C. J., & McKitrick, L. A. (1992). Memory interventions in Alzheimer's-type dementia populations: Methodological and theoretical issues. In R. L. West & J. D. Sinnott (Eds.), *Everyday memory and aging: Current research and methodology* (pp. 155–172). New York: Springer-Verlag.

Carstensen, L. L., & Turk-Charles, S. (1994). The salience of emotion across the adult life span. *Psychology and Aging, 9,* 259–264.

Cavanaugh, J. C., Grady, J. G., & Perlmutter, M. (1983). Forgetting and use of memory aids in 20 to 70 year olds everyday life. *International Journal of Aging and Human Development, 17,* 113–122.

Cockburn, J., & Smith, P. T. (1991). The relative influence of intelligence and age on everday memory. *Journal of Gerontology: Psychological Sciences, 46,* 31–46.

Cohen, G. (1988). Memory and aging: Toward an explanation. In M. M. Gruneberg, P. M., Morris, & R. N. Sykes (Eds.), *Practical aspects of memory: Current research and issues* (Vol. 2, pp. 78–83). Chichester, England: Wiley.

Connor, L. T., Dunlosky, J., & Hertzog, C. (1995). *Aging and the accuracy of global predictions and item-by-item predictions.* Unpublished manuscript.

Craik, F. I. M. (1986). A functional account of age differences in memory. In F. Klix & H. Hagendorf (Eds.), *Human memory and cognitive capabilities: Mechanisms and performances* (pp. 409–422). Amsterdam: North Holland.

Dixon, R. A., & Hertzog, C. (1988). A functional approach to memory and metamemory development in adulthood. In F. E. Weinert & M. Perlmutter (Eds.), *Memory development: Universal changes and individual differences* (pp. 293–330). Hillsdale, NJ: Lawrence Erlbaum Associates.

Dixon, R. A., & Lerner, R. M. (1984). A history of systems in devleopmental psychology. In M. H. Bornstein & M. E. Lamb (Eds.), *Developmental psychology: An advanced textbook* (pp. 1–35). Hillsdale, NJ: Lawrence Erlbaum Associates.

Dunlosky, J., & Connor, L. T. (November, 1994). *Aging and the control of self-paced study.* Poster presented at the Thirty-fifth Meeting of the Psychonomic Society of the Psychonomic Society, St. Louis.

Dunlosky, J., & Nelson, T. O. (1992). Importance of the kind of cue for judgments of learning (JOL) and the delayed-JOL effect. *Memory & Cognition, 20,* 373–380.

Einstein, G. O., Holland, L. J., McDaniel, M. A., & Guynn, M. J. (1992). Age related deficits in prospective memory: The influence of task complexity. *Psychology and Aging, 7,* 471–478.

Einstein, G. O., & McDaniel, M. A. (1990). Normal aging and prospective memory. *Journal of Experimental Psychology: Learning, Memory, and Cognition, 16,* 717–726.

Gilewski, M. J., & Zelinski, E. M. (1986). Questionnaire assessment of memory complaints. In L. W. Poon (Ed.), *Handbook for clinical memory assessment of older adults* (pp. 93–107). Washington, DC: American Psychological Association.

Gruneberg, M. M. (1992). The new approach to memory improvement: Problems and prospects. In D. J. Herrmann, H. Weingartner, A. Searleman, & C. McEvoy (Eds.), *Memory improvement: Implications for memory theory* (pp. 1–7). New York: Springer-Verlag.

Gruneberg, M. M., Morris, P. E., & Sykes, R. N. (Eds.). (1988). *Practical aspects of memory: Current research and issues* (Vols. 1 & 2). Chichester, England: Wiley.

Harris, J. E. (1978). External memory aids. In M. M. Gruneberg, P. E. Morris, & R. N. Sykes (Eds.), *Practical aspects of memory* (pp. 172–179). London: Academic Press.

Hartley, J. T. (1993). Aging and prose memory: Tests of the resource-deficit hypothesis. *Psychology and Aging, 8,* 538–551.

Hartley, J. T., Stojack, C. C., Mushaney, T. J., Kiku Annon, T. A., & Lee, D. W. (1994). Reading speed and prose memory in older and younger adults. *Psychology and Aging, 9,* 216–223.

Herrmann, D. J. (1990). Self perceptions of memory performance. In K. W. Schaie (Ed.), *Self directedness and efficacy: Causes and effects throughout the life course.* Hillsdale, NJ: Lawrence Erlbaum Associates.

Herrmann, D. J., & Searleman, A. (1990). The new multimodal approach to memory improvement. In G. H. Bower (Ed.), *Advances in learning and motivation* (Vol. 26, pp. 175–205). New York: Academic Press.

Hertzog, C. (1985). An individual differences perspective: Implications for cognitive research in gerontology. *Research on Aging, 7,* 7–45.

Hertzog, C., & Dixon, R. A. (1994). Metacognitive development in adulthood and old age. In J. Metcalfe & A. P. Shimamura (Eds.), *Metacognition: Knowing about knowing* (pp. 227–251). Cambridge, MA: MIT Press.

Hertzog, C., Saylor, L. L., Fleece, A. M., & Dixon, R. A. (1994). Metamemory and aging: Relations between predicted, actual, and perceived memory task performance. *Aging and Cognition, 1,* 203–237.

Hess, T. (1994). Social cognition in adulthood: Aging-related changes in knowledge and processing mechanisms. *Developmental Review, 14,* 373–412.

Hultsch, D. F., & Dixon, R. A. (1984). Text processing in adulthood. In P. B. Baltes & O. G. Brim, Jr. (Eds.), *Life-span development and behavior* (Vol. 6, pp. 77–108). New York: Academic Press.

Hultsch, D. F., & Dixon, R. A. (1990). Learning and memory in aging. In J. E. Birren & K. W. Schaie (Eds.), *Handbook of the psychology of aging* (3rd ed., pp. 258–274). New York: Van Nostrand Reinhold.

Hultsch, D. F., Hertzog, C., & Dixon, R. A. (1987). Age differences in metamemory: Resolving the inconsistencies. *Canadian Journal of Psychology, 41,* 193–208.

Intons-Peterson, M. J., & Newsome, G. L. (1992). External memory aids: Effects and effectiveness. In D. J. Herrmann, H. Weingartner, A. Searleman, & C. McEvoy (Eds.), *Memory improvement: Implications for memory theory* (pp. 101–121). New York: Springer-Verlag.

Jepson, K. L., & Labouvie-Vief, G. (1992). Symbolic processing of youth and elders. In R. L. West & J. D. Sinnott (Eds.), *Everyday memory and aging: Current research and methodology* (pp. 124–137). New York: Springer-Verlag.

Kausler, D. H. (1991). *Experimental psychology, cognition, and human aging* (2nd ed). New York: Springer-Verlag.

Labouvie-Vief, G., & Schell, D. A. (1982). Learning and memory in later life. In B. B. Wolman (Ed.), *Handbook of developmental psychology* (pp. 826–846). Englewood Cliffs, NJ: Prentice-Hall.

Lachman, M. E., Weaver, S. L., Bandura, M., Elliott, E., & Lewkowicz, C. J. (1992). Improving memory and control beliefs through cognitive restructuring and self-generated strategies. *Journal of Gerontology: Psychological Sciences, 47*, 293–299.

Light, L. L. (1991). Memory and aging: Four hypotheses in search of data. *Annual Review of Psychology, 43*, 333–376.

Loewen, E. R., Shaw, R. J., & Craik, F. I. M. (1990). Age differences in components of metamemory. *Experimental Aging Research, 16*, 43–48.

Lovelace, E. A., & Marsh, G. A. (1985). Prediction and evaluation of memory performance by young and old adults. *Journal of Gerontology, 40*, 192–197.

Mäntylä, T. (1994). Remembering to remember: Adult age differences in prospective memory. *Journal of Gerontology: Psychological Sciences, 49*, P276–P282.

Maylor, E. A. (1990). Age and prospective memory. *The Quarterly Journal of Experimental Psychology, 42*, 471–493.

McDonald-Miszczak, L., Hertzog, C., & Hultsch, D. F. (in press). Stability and accuracy of metamemory in adulthood and aging. *Psychology and Aging*.

McEvoy, C. L., & Moon, J. R. (1988). Assessment and treatment of everyday memory problems in the elderly. In M. M. Gruneberg, P. M., Morris, & R. N. Sykes (Eds.), *Practical aspects of memory: Current research and issues*. (Vol. 2, pp. 155–160). Chichester: Wiley.

McFarland, C., Ross, M., & Giltrow, M. (1992). Biased recollections in older adults: The role of implicit theories of aging. *Journal of Personality and Social Psychology, 62*, 837–850.

Meyer, B. J. F., & Rice, G. E. (1989). Prose processing in adulthood: The text, the reader, and the task. In L. W. Poon, D. C. Rubin, & B. A Wilson (Eds.), *Everyday cognition in adulthood and late life* (pp. 157–194). New York: Cambridge University Press.

Meyer, B. J. F., Young, C. J., & Bartlett, B. J. (1989). *Memory improved: Reading and memory enhancement across the lifespan through strategic text structures*. Hilldale, NJ: Lawrence Erlbaum Associates.

Mook, D. G. (1983). In defense of external invalidity. *American Psychologist, 38*, 379–387.

Morrow, D. G., Leirer, V. O., & Altieri, P. (1995). List formats improve medication: Implications for instruction design. *Educational Gerontology, 21*, 151–166.

Morrow, D. G., Leirer, V. O., & Altieri, P., & Tanke, E. (1991). Elders' schema for taking medication: Implications for instruction design. *Journal of Gerontology: Psychological Science, 48*, 378–385.

Murphy, M. D., Schmitt, F. A., Caruso, M. J., & Sanders, R. E. (1987). Metamemory in older adults: The role of monitoring in serial recall. *Psychology and Aging, 2*, 331–339.

Neely, A. S., & Bäckman, L. (1993). Long-term maintenance of gains from memory training in older adults: Two 3-1/2 year follow-up studies. *Journal of Gerontology: Psychological Sciences, 48*, 233–237.

Nelson, T. O., & Dunlosky, J. (1991). When people's judgments of learning (JOLs) are extremely accurate at predicting subsequent recall: The "Delayed-JOL Effect." *Psychological Science, 2*, 267–270.

Nelson, T. O., Dunlosky, J., Graf, A., & Narens, L. (1994). Utilization of metacognitive judgments in the allocation of study during multitrial learning. *Psychological Science, 5*, 207–213.

Nelson, T. O., & Narens, L. (1990). Metamemory: a theoretical framework and new findings. In G. H. Bower (Ed.), *The psychology of learning and motivation* (Vol. 26, pp. 125–173). New York: Academic Press.

Park, D. C., Hertzog, C., Morrell, R., Kidder, D., & Mayhorn, C. (1994, August). *Event-based and time-based prospective memory: Effects of age and frequency of prospective tasks*. Presented at the Practical Aspects of Memory Conference, College Park, MD.

Park, D. C., & Kidder, D. (1995). Prospective memory and medication adherence. In M. Brandimonte, G. Einstein, & M. McDaniel (Eds.), *Prospective memory: Theory and applications* (pp. 369–390). Mahwah, NJ: Lawrence Erlbaum Associates.

Park, D. C., & Mayhorn, C. B. (in press). Remembering to take medications: The importance of nonmemory variables. In D. J. Herrmann, C. McEvoy, C. Hertzog, P. Hertel, & M. Johnson (Eds.), *Basic and applied memory: Research on practical aspects of memory* (Vol. 2). Mahwah, NJ: Lawrence Erlbaum Associates.

Patton, G. W. R., & Meit, M. (1993). Effect of aging on prospective and incidental memory. *Experimental Aging Research, 19*, 165–176.

Perfect, T. J., & Stollery, B. (1993). Memory and metamemory in performance in older adults: One deficit or two? *The Quarterly Journal of Experimental Psychology, 46A*, 119–135.

Perlmutter, M. (1978). What is memory the aging of? *Developmental Psychology, 14*, 330–345.

Petrinovich, L. (1989). Representative design and the quality of generalization. In L. W. Poon, D. C. Rubin, & B. A. Wilson (Eds.), *Everyday cognition in adulthood and late life* (pp. 11–24). New York: Cambridge University Press.

Poon, L. W., Rubin, D. C., & Wilson, B. A. (Eds.). (1989). *Everyday cognition in adulthood and late life.* New York: Cambridge University Press.

Pressley, M., & El-Dinary, P. B. (1992). Memory strategy instruction that promotes good information processing. In D. J. Herrmann, H. Weingartner, A. Searleman, & C. McEvoy (Eds.), *Memory improvement: Implications for memory theory* (pp. 79–100). New York: Springer-Verlag.

Rabinowitz, J. C., Ackerman, B. P., Craik, F. I. M., & Hinchley, J. L. (1982). Aging and metamemory: The roles of relatedness and imagery. *Journal of Gerontology, 37*, 688–695.

Rebok, G. W., & Balcerak, L. J. (1989). Memory self-efficacy and performance differences in young and old adults: The effect of mnemonic training. *Developmental Psychology, 25*, 714–721.

Reese, H. W., & Puckett, J. M. (1993). *Mechanisms of everyday cognition.* Hillsdale, NJ: Lawrence Erlbaum Associates.

Rice, G. F., Meyer, B. J. F., & Miller, D. C. (1989). Using text structure to improve older adults' recall of important medical information. *Educational Gerontologist, 15*, 187–202.

Riggs, K. M., Lachman, M. E., & Wingfield, A. (1994). *Taking charge of remembering: Locus of control and older adults' memory for speech.* Unpublished manuscript.

Ross, B. L., & Berg, C. A. (1992). Examining idiosyncracies in script reports across the life span: Distortions or derivations of experience. In R. L. West & J. D. Sinnott (Eds.), *Everyday memory and aging: Current research and methodology* (pp. 39–53). New York: Springer-Verlag.

Rybash, J. M., Hoyer, W. J., & Roodin, P. A. (1986). *Adult cognition and aging.* New York: Pergamon Press.

Salthouse, T. A. (1987). Age, experience, and compensation. In C. Schooler & K. W. Schaie (Eds.), *Intellectual functioning, social structure, and aging* (pp. 142–157). Norwood, NJ: Ablex.

Schaie, K. W. (1988). Ageism in psychological research. *American Psychologist, 43*, 179–183.

Schlecter, T. M., Herrmann, D. J., & Toglia, M. P. (1990). An investigation of people's metamemories for naturally occurring events. *Applied Cognitive Psychology, 4*, 213–217.

Scogin, F., Storandt, M., & Lott, L. (1985). Memory-skills training, memory complaints, and depression in older adults. *Journal of Gerontology, 40*, 562–568.

Talland, G. (Ed.). (1968). *Disorders of memory.* New York: Academic Press.

West, R. L. (1988). Prospective memory and aging. In M. M. Gruneberg, P. M., Morris, & R. N. Sykes (Eds.), *Practical aspects of memory: Current research and issues.* (Vol. 2, pp. 119–125). Chichester, England: Wiley.

West, R. L. (1992). Everyday memory and aging: A diversity of tests, tasks, and paradigms. In R. L. West & J. D. Sinnott (Eds.), *Everyday memory and aging: Current research and methodology* (pp. 3–21). New York: Springer-Verlag.

West, R. L., Crook, T. H., & Barron, K. L. (1992). Everyday memory performance across the life span: Effects of age and noncognitive individual differences. *Psychology and Aging, 7,* 72–82.

West, R. L., & Sinnott, J. D. (1992). *Everyday memory and aging: Current research and methodology.* New York: Springer-Verlag.

Willis, S. L., & Schaie, K. W. (1986). Practical intelligence in later adulthood. In R. J. Sternberg & R. K. Wagner (Eds.), *Practical intelligence: nature and origins of competence in the everday world* (pp. 236–268). New York: Cambridge University Press.

Wilson, B. A., Cockburn, J., & Baddeley, A. D. (1985). *The Rivermead Behavioural Memory Test.* Flempton, Bury St. Edwards: Thames Valley Test Company.

Zelinski, E. M., & Gilewski, M. J. (1988). Memory for prose and aging: A metanalysis. In M. L. Howe & C. J. Brainerd (Eds.), *Cognitive development in adulthood: Progress in cognitive development research* (pp. 133–158). New York: Springer-Verlag.

CHAPTER EIGHTEEN

Collaborative Memory and Aging

Roger A. Dixon
University of Victoria, Canada

In this chapter I address four main points. First, evaluating cognitive competence in adults, and perhaps especially older adults, may require attention to everyday contexts of performance not frequently considered in cognitive research. Second, one of the frequent contexts of cognitive performance in everyday life is social, interactional, or, put more functionally, collaborative in nature. Third, research on collaborative cognition in adults—especially developmental research—points to unique issues and faces numerous challenges, but has potential for substantial theoretical and practical implications. Fourth, providing some demonstration of the third point, highlights from a set of studies show that older adults can collaborate effectively on complex remembering tasks; indeed, select older collaborating groups may evince effects of both expertise and compensation.

ISSUES IN EVALUATING THE AGING OF COGNITIVE COMPETENCE

In research on cognitive development in adulthood—which is referred to as the field of *cognitive aging*—typical findings indicate that there is considerable aging-related decline (e.g., Craik & Jennings, 1992), some of which may be related to normal neurological changes (especially slowing; e.g., Salthouse, 1991). Evidence for decline may be seen across a wide range of performance domains, including those in attention, problem-solving, memory, and psychomotor tasks (e.g., Craik & Salthouse, 1992). Not so coincidentally, perhaps, some research indicates that there are also stereotypes and individual beliefs supporting views of widespread aging-related cognitive loss (Heckhausen, Dixon, & Baltes, 1989). Nevertheless, accumulating for decades, but accelerating in recent years, there have been a number of self-reports, anecdotes, and research suggesting that some manner of cognitive competence may be maintained into late life (Schaie, 1990; Willis & Dubin, 1990). Increasingly, cognitive aging research has focused on the conditions under which cognitive competence may be maintained or even improved through practice and training (e.g., Baltes, 1987; Charness, 1989), (re-)arranging critical or deleterious features of the performance environment (Charness & Bosman, 1995), and mechanisms that compensate for aging-related decrements (e.g., Bäckman & Dixon, 1992; Dixon & Bäckman, 1993; Salthouse, 1987).

There is a conundrum lurking in the previous paragraph, one that has puzzled a number of recent observers. Salthouse (1990, p. 310), for example, noted that for the field of cognitive aging: "One of the greatest challenges . . . is to account for the discrepancy between the inferred status of older adults based on their performance in psychometric testing situations and cognitive laboratories and that derived from observations of their successful functioning in everyday situations." How can older adults perform poorly (i.e., as compared to their own previous performance or that of control younger adults) on a wide range of laboratory tasks, and yet appear to be quite competent in a wide range of practical cognitive tasks? Among others, Salthouse identified several steps to consider in resolving this conundrum. First, it is crucial to distinguish between ability and competence. Whereas ability in this common distinction refers to one's actual performance on conventional laboratory tests of cognition, competence refers to the skill with which one can marshal one's abilities in performing in new or demanding situations (Salthouse, 1990). Second, it is important to extend cognitive aging research to a wider range of domains (from theory-based lab tasks to practically significant everyday tasks), indicators (from quantitative measures of production to qualitative measures of production and process), and contexts (from the standard individual to the interactive or social). In this way, competence in late life can be more successfully evaluated (Dixon, 1995; Park, 1992).

This is not to say that all cognitive aging research—whether primarily theoretical or practical—should shift either emphasis (from ability to competence) or position along the continua of domains, indicators, and contexts. The claim is simply that, in order to understand a theoretically puzzling situation with practical implications, the "aging" of both abilities and competencies should be systematically investigated. This position is offered without prejudice to the outcome; that is, it is possible that single, underlying explanatory principles exist for all manner of cognitive aging phenomena (consider the notion of slowing; Salthouse, 1991). It is also possible, and of no small theoretical importance, that other approaches supporting wider ranges of empirical concerns and methodological considerations may yield fruitful results (e.g., Dixon & Hertzog, in press; Hertzog & Dunloskey, chap. 17, this volume).

The topic of this chapter is at the confluence of some of the means through which cognitive aging research could be extended to account for Salthouse's challenge. Specifically, as is seen in subsequent sections, the area of collaborative cognition may be viewed as one way in which domains of everyday competence may be expressed, indicators of performance may include both standard and a wide range of product and process variables, and the context of performance is explicitly interactive. In addition, the role of experience in the aging of cognitive competence may be considered inasmuch as it affects performance in particular domains of evaluation, but also it may affect how well and in what manner the collaboration proceeds. Finally, it is possible to explore the issue of compensation, for example, whether collaborative processes may serve compensatory purposes. In the following section, I elaborate on this view of collaborative cognition—and especially collaborative remembering—and why it is relevant to cognitive aging.

COLLABORATIVE COGNITION AND COGNITIVE AGING

In this section I address two main issues. First, a brief definition of the term *collaborative cognition*, and its association to a number of related terms, is offered. Second, I attempt to specify why collaborative cognition may be of special theoretical and practical interest in adult development.

What Is Collaborative Cognition?

Frequently, observers from a variety of perspectives have noted that a substantial proportion of everyday memory activity occurs in the context of other individuals. These individuals may range from passive listeners to conversational interactants to active collaborators. To be sure, memory per se, and certainly much of everyday remembering, occurs privately, or at least with some distance from the influence of other individuals. Nevertheless, other individuals form the context for considerable cognitive activity, one medium of which is conversation or dialogue. In such interactive, communicative contexts, one or more individuals in a group serve as collaborators, producing accurate recall as well as a variety of other utterances.

I use the term *collaborative cognition* to refer to that cognitive activity that occurs in the context of more than one individual, where the activity is typically directed at an identifiable set of tasks, usually in pursuit of common goals, and performed cooperatively (although not necessarily effectively). Among the characteristics determining the effectiveness of the collaboration are: the individuals involved (varying, e.g., in abilities and motivation), the tasks they perform (varying, e.g., in difficulty and degree to which they can be shared), and the goal(s) they pursue (e.g., the degree to which they are consonant; e.g., Steiner, 1972). Because of the importance of these factors, I use the term *collaborative* such that it is neutral with respect to outcome, but perhaps less so with respect to intent. Whereas collaborating groups may (roughly speaking) share a goal of performing well, collaborative processes can be characterized along such dimensions as cooperative–uncooperative and coordinated–discoordinated (Engeström, 1992). That is, collaborating means working together, but it does not imply that the process is efficient nor that the product is effective or accurate. It is for this reason that researchers in related fields have concerned themselves with evaluating the factors that lead to (or characterize) efficient and effective group performance (e.g., Hill, 1982; Paulus, 1989; Steiner, 1972).

Reflecting perhaps a growing interest in collaborative cognition, there appear to be a growing number of research areas in psychology with interests in related phenomena. Some of these areas have long histories indeed. One of the longest histories belongs to an area called *group cognition* or *group memory*, which dates at least into the 1950s (e.g., Clark & Stephenson, 1989). Other terms for related phenomena include *transactive cognition* (e.g., Wegner, 1986), *socially shared cognition* (e.g., Resnick, Levine, & Teasley, 1991), *collective* or *joint cognition* (e.g., Edwards & Middleton, 1986; Middleton & Edwards, 1990), *conversational cognition* (e.g., Hyman, 1994), *situated cognition* or *learning* (e.g., Greeno & Moore, 1993; Lave & Wenger, 1991), and of course *tutorial* and *peer learning* or *cognition* (e.g., Azmitia, in press; Damon, 1984). The fields in which collaborative cognition phenomena are of interest include educational psychology, cognitive science, social (cognitive) psychology, child developmental psychology, and adult developmental psychology.

Collaborative cognition occurs frequently in multiple everyday situations. Examples include when scientific colleagues attempt to solve a thorny methodological problem in an experiment they are designing or analyzing; when family groups or lineages attempt to reconstruct stories from their shared past; when a spouse is enlisted to help remember a birthday, appointment, or parking place; when peers in school accomplish learning projects together; or when strangers attempt to solve a way-finding or map-reading problem (Dixon, 1992). Theorists as varied as Vygotsky (1978) and Greeno and Moore (1993) argued that such cognition in collaborative situations should be investigated further. Indeed, reflecting an active debate in the cognitive sciences between the symbolic approach (Vera & Simon, 1993) and the situativity approach, Greeno and Moore (1993) claimed that cognitive activities should be considered carefully as interactions between agents and both physical systems and other agents (see also Lave & Wenger, 1991; Resnick et al., 1991). From this perspective, a considerable portion of cognition is situated action, and this portion is not fully explored in the cognitive literature.

Why Study Collaborative Cognition and Aging?

As noted in the previous section, numerous observers have remarked on the frequency with which everyday cognitive activity occurs in interactive contexts. It may, therefore, be an important practical form of cognitive activity in that it is commonly addressed to a wide range of problems, including everyday, pragmatic problems, and it may lead to effective or improved solutions in some circumstances. In the cognitive aging literature, some observers have noted that one potential means for compensating for individual-level aging-related decrements could be through the use of external memory and problem-solving aids, one form of which might be other individuals (e.g., Dixon, 1992). These two still-vague observations lead to some interesting theoretical and practical possibilities. As applied to cognitive aging, these possibilities include collaboration as a means of maintaining or boosting cognitive performance, and collaboration as a means of overcoming individual-level losses or deficits. These possibilities are discussed later in this section.

Selected Research Issues. The initial purpose of investigating collaborative cognition in adults is to discover whether—and to what extent—older groups collaborate effectively on cognitive problems. Most research in the areas noted earlier has been conducted with school-aged children, university students, or adults of unspecified ages and backgrounds. Therefore, it is not an insignificant concern whether older adults, perhaps all of whom will undergo aging-related changes in cognitive abilities, would experience the presence of collaborators as an added layer of (performance-reducing) complexity or as an avenue for facilitating improved performance. Three general research issues circumscribe and, to some extent, define the empirical and theoretical agenda of this research area.

First, as with all research in the broadly defined tradition of collaborative cognition, it is important to identify and document carefully selected characteristics of the group(s) involved in the research. Both the size of the groups (small groups typically range from one to four members) and features of the composition of the groups are relevant. With respect to the latter, whether the group members are acquainted or unacquainted, and of same or different ages, genders, or individual abilities, are key concerns. Second, as would be expected from the earlier comments regarding ability and competence, the cognitive tasks employed are critical, as are the measures on which the researcher evaluates competence. In cognitive aging research, as is shown later in the chapter, it may not be of sufficient theoretical sophistication to compare groups in terms of simply (say) how much is remembered. In addition, researchers examining developmental questions would evaluate performance in terms of other theoretically and practically relevant performance measures. Even such product variables, however, do not capture the potential richness of this paradigm. Also of interest are a variety of indicators of the process through which group members interact in performing their group task. The collaborative cognition paradigm provides a unique window into the manner in which cognitive tasks are solved.

The third general research issue is that the investigator must be prepared to identify key comparisons of interest. For example, in the service of answering specific research questions, the performance of older groups may be compared with older individuals (others, or even themselves); older groups of different sizes; older groups with different membership features; younger individuals; younger groups of different sizes; younger groups with same membership features; nominal groups, or aggregations of data from lower-sized experimental units; and predicted performance based on a variety of mathematical formulae. Clearly, not all of the possible combinations or comparisons can be accomplished in a single study, or even set of studies. My purpose here is to note that there are at least these options—or ranges of issues—available when selecting research foci for given projects. In aging research to date only a few of these issues have been addressed. The situation, however, is quite similar in other areas, where some of the issues have been explored but others remain for future consideration.

Objectives. In a research program on adult collaborative cognition, I and several collaborators focus on the following objectives. The initial objective is to create an opportunity in a controlled setting for collaborative cognitive functioning. At its simplest, more than one person is present in the same room at the same table solving the same problem—together. Once this is accomplished, indicators of performance at both the individual and interactive "levels" can be developed. These may very well differ in their details from one cognitive task to another, but the general classifications of interest may apply across a wide range of tasks. As is summarized later, in addition to characterizing the qualitative aspects of the collaboration summationally, it may be useful to represent the cooperative interactions dynamically. A related concern is to focus on how well collaborative groups perform (we refer to such measures as *product variables*) and how they do whatever they do (termed *process variables*). Because there is such little precedent in life-span research, initial objectives have been more descriptive than explanatory. A sample descriptive research question is: To what extent can and do younger and older adults use collaborators to perform complex cognitive tasks? As noted earlier, collaboration is not uniformly beneficial or effective. It is conceivable that some groups may never effectively coordinate their efforts, some individuals may never contribute an expected share to the group effort, and some individuals may be actually disruptive to the group process. More theoretical questions are presently being posed in some quarters. Our objectives have included consideration of two such theoretical issues, namely, the development of interactive expertise and the role of compensatory mechanisms.

Collaborative Expertise. The first theoretical issue with which our research has been particularly concerned is whether there are experience-related differences in collaborative cognition. With aging, one can pose intriguing questions concerning the hypothesis that collaborative or interactive expertise may develop with practice (e.g., Engeström, 1992). Interactive expertise is associated with sustained practice at interactive problem solving, and may be characterized (not exclusively) in a manner similar to that of individual cognitive expertise (e.g., Ericsson & Charness, 1994; Glaser & Chi, 1988). Of demonstrable and immediate theoretical interest are such general research questions as whether aging interactive expert groups would perform cognitive tasks relatively fast, efficiently, and accurately, with an increase in performance according to practice, and with some signs of heightened self-monitoring (to name a few characteristics of interest). Of derivative interest are such questions as whether the beneficial performance effects would be observed only at the (expert) group level, or whether some boost might occur even for the aging individual.

There are, of course, numerous examples of potential expert collaborative groups, including long-term married couples (Dixon, Hunt-Matheson, & Meers, 1993; Gagnon, Friesen, & Dixon, 1995). Indeed, because of sociohistorical characteristics of the life course in the 20th century, long-term married couples provide a unique and naturally available experimental resource. Simply put, there are many long-term married couples (40 or more years) in the present cohorts of older adults, a resource that may be somewhat less abundant in future generations. There are, of course, numerous influences and sequelae of long-term collaborative associations, and marriage is no exception. Nevertheless, it is possible to begin the investigation of the existence of interactive expertise in older married couples, as compared to younger short-term married couples, older unacquainted dyads, and younger unacquainted dyads. Subsequently, it is of interest to investigate whether the benefits (if any) of interactive expertise would occur exclusively at the couple level, or whether there would be any individual-level boost. That is, the interactively expert couple (qua couple) might be able to solve complex problems together that other interactively novice dyads (or they themselves individually) could not solve, but this boost due to interactive expertise may not extend to their individual (qua individual) competencies, because of individual-level, unreversed, aging-related cognitive decline. These possibilities represent less speculations than empirical questions, some of which have been the topic of initial research. It should be clear, however, that they carry quite different theoretical implications.

Compensation Through Collaboration. A second theoretically intriguing issue is whether compensation (broadly conceived) could occur by older collaborating adults. Compensation may occur when an individual uses an alternative mechanism for performing a given task when the previously used mechanism is unavailable because of an injury-related deficit or aging-related decline (Bäckman & Dixon, 1992; Salthouse, 1990). Despite the loss of the typical or even principal means of performing a complex task associated with a particular skill, a compensatory mechanism can support continued high levels of performance on such skill-related tasks. In general, the possibilities for such alternative mechanisms are wide ranging, depending in part on the nature of the skill in question, as well as the context in which the skill is performed. Compensatory mechanisms have been observed for a wide variety of psychological phenomena (e.g., Bäckman & Dixon, 1992). One well-researched in cognitive aging is transcription typing, in which skilled older typists compensate for losses in reaction time and finger-tapping speed by using large hand–eye previews (e.g., Bosman, 1993; Salthouse, 1987).

Most examples of compensatory mechanisms in cognitive aging are substitutive in nature, that is, a latent developing component of a skill substitutes for a declining component (e.g., Salthouse, 1995). Other forms, however, are possible and may, in fact, be more likely to occur in interactive settings (e.g., Dixon, 1992; Dixon & Bäckman, 1993, 1995). Many older adults are working at the edge of their individual abilities and competencies. Such individuals may have experienced aging-related decrements in fundamental mechanisms that contribute to memory performance (e.g., speed of processing), but through collaboration may be able to compensate by combining their available resources with cooperating individuals. That is, some older adults may use whatever abilities they have left (after subtracting aging-related losses), combine them in some cooperative fashion, and perform competently on complex and demanding cognitive tasks. Successful combinations of resources may be additive (e.g., in the sense of combining like skills or domains), complementary (e.g., in the sense of combining different skills or domains), or perhaps emergent (e.g., performing multiplicatively or at a qualitatively new level). Notably, communication—a competence not necessarily lost with aging (Ryan, Giles, Bartolucci, & Henwood, 1986)—may be a mechanism through which such compensation could occur.

As it may be at the individual level, the probability of compensation may be enhanced by experience. At the group level, however, compensation may be a function of successful communication, which, in turn, may be related to experience at interaction or even interactive expertise. That is, aging collaborative experts may be more likely to compensate for declining individual-level cognitive skills through interactive-level novel behaviors, adjustments, or strategies. In this way, the two main theoretical issues of current interest are closely linked.

COLLABORATIVE MEMORY FOR NARRATIVES

Research focusing on such theoretical and practically relevant issues in collaborative cognition and aging has only recently begun (e.g., Cavanaugh et al., 1989; Dixon, 1992; Gould, Trevithick, & Dixon, 1991). Tasks investigated, however, include standard (ability-like) memory, story-telling, problem-solving, and wisdom tasks (e.g., Dixon & Gould, in press; Staudinger, in press). In fact, a forthcoming volume is devoted to life-span developmental perspectives on collaborative cognition (Baltes & Staudinger, in press). As an illustration of the issues and early results of this avenue of research, I summarize highlights from three sets of studies on collaborative memory for narratives.

Collaborative Story Memory: Initial Issues

Previous theoretical and empirical work on cognition in group situations offers several points relevant to understanding collaborative story recall by adults (e.g., Clark & Stephenson, 1989; Middleton & Edwards, 1990; Resnick et al., 1991; Steiner, 1972). First, whatever the theoretical approach, it is fair to say that much of everyday collaborative cognition is directed at recalling narratives (e.g., news events, personal or shared stories, and autobiographical events) and is conducted through a conversation that takes the form of a narrative. For research purposes, such narratives may be converted to protocols, which can be coded for the presence of a variety of story recall statements. Second, contributions to these collaborative conversations, like individual-based recall, may vary in both the quantity of information recalled and the quality or pattern of the information produced. It is not known whether nonrecall statements would be produced in the equivalent amount and variety as is the case in individual-based recall situations.

Third, some of the activities, individuals, or statements occurring in a collaborative situation may variously promote or detract from the goals of the task or group. That is, collaborative groups may variously experience *process gain* or *process loss*, terms used to refer to the fact that group performance may not be a simple multiple of individual performance (Hill, 1982; Steiner, 1972). Although there are many complications in estimating optimal productivity for a group cognitive process, some tasks (e.g., those easily divisible) and individuals (e.g., those performing consistently at high levels) promote near-optimal group performance. In contrast, other tasks (possibly less well-structured tasks such as narrative recall) and individuals (e.g., social loafers) result in lower-than-optimal levels of group performance. Further research is required to determine the best way to evaluate how close to the optimal level group performance is for complex, if not ill-structured, tasks such as remembering narratives. In addition, the issue of how best to promote higher levels of group performance is pertinent.

Fourth, the process of collaboration may produce observable online evidence of metacognition, which has been defined in cognitive aging research to include a wide range of knowledge and beliefs about cognition and one's own cognitive competence (Hertzog & Dixon, 1994). Metacognitive activities may drive, direct, or influence the process of solving some cognitive problems. For example, metacognitive information regarding strategy use—including the quantity and quality of strategies identified, beliefs about their potential effectiveness, and the outcome of their implementation—may be evident either directly or indirectly in collaborative cognition protocols. The communicative situation makes it necessary to make at least some of them explicit to the collaborating partner(s). In this way, the conversational transcripts may be used as think-aloud protocols to score for the presence of indicators of both productive strategies and counterproductive statements or activities.

Narrative Recall: The Fact and the Figurative

Most of the research conducted on story memory has been at the individual adult level; only recently has the case of interacting, collaborating individuals been considered. The recent work on collaborative memory for narratives, like its individual-level counterpart, attends to accuracy and quantity of memory performance. However, several other aspects of the products and processes of interactive remembering take on special meaning in understanding how groups interact in solving complex cognitive problems. Both issues—accuracy and quantity of the principal product of memory, as well as other products and pertinent processes—are addressed in this section. Following this discussion, the remainder of this chapter is devoted to summarizing a series of recent studies in which we have addressed the questions of how—and how well—younger and older adults collaborate in remembering narrative stories.

Researchers who have begun to examine other forms of information produced by individual adults recalling complex stories have noted that older adults often generate as much or more nonrecall (but story- or task-relevant) information as younger adults (e.g., Adams, 1991; Gould et al., 1991). A critical issue, as yet unresolved, is the extent to which the nonrecall information produced by older adults is productive in the sense of enhancing the story as it is retold by the rememberer. This enhancement could apply to increasing the interest level (to the speaker or listener), the memorability of passages in the story, or the overall cohesion of the story. Arguably, events or stories described verbatim (with all nonverbatim recall information missing) could be less interesting or memorable than stories retold with select elaboration, inferences, or summary statements. On the other hand, stories retold with excessive elaboration (and comparatively little original content) could be less representative or accurate than the alternatives.

There is as yet no precise algorithm for evaluating the overall quality of a recalled or retold story, although some ratings and indicators are available (e.g., Gould & Dixon, 1993; Pratt, Boyes, Robins, & Manchester, 1989). Indeed, it is not yet known how often such statements are produced by younger and older adults, nor how to characterize them in terms of their service to the goal of reproducing an accurate, coherent, informative, and perhaps interesting narrative. Three related perspectives on the potential value of select nonrecall statements as products and indicators of the process of recall are particularly intriguing.

First, some observers have suggested that one possibility is that a greater proportion of older adults rather than younger adults could view the story-recall or storytelling task more as an interpretive than a rote memory one. Such a perspective could result in a substantially different profile of utterances (e.g., Adams, Labouvie-Vief, Hobart, & Dorosz, 1990) than that associated with an assumption that the goal for all participants is to accurately reproduce the original story. If the protocols were to be scored purely for reproductive recall, the results would favor the younger adults. If, however, other statements are scored and evaluated in terms of their contribution to the overall recall task, the older adults would fare considerably better.

The second perspective is similar in that it emphasizes the potential linkage among these two categories of productions. Whether intentionally or not, older adults may produce more nonrecall statements than younger adults in an effort to compensate for decrements in memory ability (Dixon & Bäckman, 1993). Such an individual-level compensatory purpose would be served if the overall integrity of the original story is not impaired by the amount and location of nonrecall statements. Indeed, elaborations and other such statements may be useful in promoting further recall (Gould et al., 1991; Reder, 1982; van Dijk & Kintsch, 1983).

The third perspective on the possible trade-off between recall and other forms of potentially productive information is that an increase in nonrecall information may simply mask an inability to remember original information (van Dijk & Kintsch, 1983). This possibility must be considered seriously for each variety of materials and each set of participants. At the extreme, verbosity (indicated by the presence of excessive off-target statements) can rarely be considered productive (e.g., Gold, Andres, Arbuckle, & Schwartzman, 1988).

For all three perspectives, the important issues are what the balance is between recall and other information produced, and whether the nonrecall information can be usefully categorized into productive and nonproductive statements. There is not yet enough information available to judge whether there is a typical or objectively ideal balance, partly because work on the categorization of statements (and the processes they may represent) is only beginning. These three perspectives are not mutually exclusive, nor are they unique to typical story recall laboratory settings. Much of the research contributing to these perspectives used individual adults varying in age recalling or retelling stories in the laboratory.

COLLABORATIVE MEMORY OF NARRATIVES: RESEARCH HIGHLIGHTS

I summarize several studies on collaborative memory for narratives that have been conducted in the recent past. Details of these studies are available elsewhere (Dixon, 1992; Dixon & Gould, 1994; Gould et al., 1991; Gould, Kurzman, & Dixon, 1994). The general objective of these studies was to explore performance on narrative recall tasks by younger and older individuals in collaborative situations. In order to accomplish this, we first created a situation in which there was an opportunity for same-age adults to collaborate on a story recall task. That is, unlike the standard individual-level paradigm, more than one individual was present in the same room and they were invited to work together in recalling an auditorially presented story. As mentioned earlier, an initial purpose was to investigate the extent to which younger and older adults can and do use collaborators to perform complex cognitive tasks. In order to control for a variety of social effects, in the first study we selected only unacquainted, same-age, and same-gender participants; we varied, however, age (younger and older) and group size (individual, dyad, tetrad). In the second and third studies we investigated collaborative recall among younger and older married couples. In the fourth study we compared communication processes during collaborative remembering by young and old married couples and young and old unacquainted dyads. This research was exploratory in that there was very little previous research with adults in similar tasks on which to base many explicit expectations.

One firm prediction, however, was that younger individuals would perform better than older individuals in gist recall of text. This was based on extensive literature on discourse memory and aging (Hultsch & Dixon, 1990;

Zelinski & Gilewski, 1988). The more challenging question was whether younger or older adults would benefit more (or equally) from the presence of collaborators. For example, would older groups of two individuals (unacquainted dyads or married couples) perform as well as parallel younger groups of two? There was no specific literature on which to base an expectation pertaining to this issue, but because communicative skills are often preserved in later life (Ryan et al., 1986)—and communicative skills may be related to collaborative effectiveness—the hypothesis that older adults would benefit disproportionately from collaborators was considered.

Collaboration Among Unacquainted Adults

The purpose of this first study was to provide initial information about how well individuals and groups perform on a standard story recall task adapted simply for collaborative situations. Younger and older adults were assigned to same-age and same-gender groups of one (individuals), two (dyads), and four (tetrads). All members of the dyads and tetrads were unacquainted with one another. Participants were invited to listen to each of two stories and then to use their own words in remembering as much information as possible from them. The dyads and tetrads were invited to work together to remember the information. Details of the method and analyses are provided in Dixon and Gould (1994).

Although we coded and reported a variety of utterances and behaviors produced during the interaction, we focus here on only those related closely to gist recall. Overall, young adults recalled more correct information from the stories than older adults at all levels of group size: individuals, dyads, and tetrads. Both age groups, however, tended to perform better with additional collaborators, but the difference between the young and old performance remained similar. A more sophisticated analysis of these data, in which recall performance was assessed across levels of information was also conducted. Stories typically contain a variety of levels of information corresponding to a hierarchy of thematic centrality. These levels range from main ideas to incidental details. Several contrasting patterns of performance are possible (see Fig. 18.1). Panel A of the figure shows a pattern consistent with an inference that the remembered story may be relatively well structured; a greater proportion of the main ideas are recalled and they may be served by related but subordinate ideas. Note that Panel A does not present the extreme case in which an excessive proportion of main ideas is recalled, a pattern that would reflect a story that may be too sketchy, somewhat like an outline with main points only. Panel B shows the case in which the proportion of details is much greater than that of main ideas. Although also not the extreme case, it suggests a narrative that may be too densely packed, with recalled details that may be too loosely tied to the most appropriate

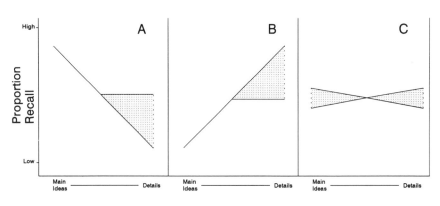

Levels of Information

FIG. 18.1. Schematic representation of three alternative hypothetical results of a levels of information analysis for prose recall.

main ideas. Panel C represents an intermediate case in which the recalled story may also be relatively ill-structured, in that proportion of recall is evenly distributed across the levels of information. This structure does not match that in the original story.

The analysis of the levels of information recalled revealed that, like individuals, both dyads and tetrads tended to display a classic "levels effect" (similar to Panel A). This suggests that, like individuals, unacquainted younger and older dyads and tetrads can identify and remember the themes of narratives. In other words, groups working together appear to be sensitive to the structure of the original story and tend to reproduce this structure in their interactive retelling of the story. Note that this is not a superfluous or necessary outcome. Although the dyads and tetrads recalled more gist information than individuals, they could have attained their overall higher performance by increasing the number of details recalled (Panel B, Fig. 18.1), thereby potentially sacrificing the coherence of the story. For cognitive aging research it is especially noteworthy that the same qualitative pattern (similar to Panel A, Fig. 18.1) was observed for both older and younger dyads and tetrads. This indicated that collaborative story recall was more comprehensive and yet maintained similar qualitative characteristics for both younger and older unacquainted collaborating groups.

Numerous nonrecall product variables were also scored (Dixon & Gould, 1994). Interestingly, a pattern of results not entirely disadvantageous to older adults was observed. For example, older groups produced more macrostatements (correct statements at a thematic level) but actually fewer errors than younger groups. Furthermore, as analyzed in detail elsewhere (Gould et al., 1991), the older groups also produced more elaborations (statements consistent with the content of the story but not actually contained therein) than younger groups. This detailed analysis of elaborations produced a theoretically interesting set of results. We began by dividing all elaborations into two general categories: denotative elaborations, or consistent statements based on information from the story or from world knowledge relevant to the content of the story; and annotative elaborations, or statements based on evaluations and interpretations of the content of the stories or personal experience relevant to the stories. We observed that the number of denotative elaborations was high for individuals and that it increased similarly across group size for both younger and older adults. In contrast, the number of annotative elaborations was relatively low and increased more across group size for older than for younger adults.

What could this mean? Denotative elaborations are conceptually close to gist recall, clearly a form of productive performance that may often be overlooked or uncoded: Younger and older adults produce them similarly in all group size conditions. Regarding annotative—the more personal and evaluative—elaborations, two contrasting arguments could be made. Such elaborations, if produced excessively, could be viewed as tangential, irrelevant, or even harmful to the task of remembering a story. In contrast, if produced judiciously they could be viewed as enriching the storytelling and perhaps even as referencing story information in terms of personal experience. The profile of elaborations in this study led us to conclude that they were more likely positive contributors to the retelling of the story, even though they would not be counted as actual recall statements.

Although generating signs of effective collaborative production, the older tetrads were especially active in a way that is arguably less effective. Specifically, they produced the greatest number of episodes of simultaneous speech. On the one hand, this could indicate a high level of energy and interest in the problem. On the other, it may suggest that there was some less-than-optimal coordination of the efforts and abilities of the individual members of the groups. How well could they have performed had they had more training or experience at collaboration? How would the products and processes of cognitive collaboration by older groups compare to those of younger groups if the groups were equivalent in collaborative expertise?

Collaborative Remembering Among Married Couples

In a subsequent set of two studies, we examined younger and older well-acquainted dyads collaborating on a story recall task (for details, see Dixon & Gould, 1994). We selected one variety of naturally occurring expert collaborative groups, married couples. Our assumption was that such groups frequently work together in solving complex cognitive problems, many of which bear a resemblance to retelling narratives such as those we used in our experiment. Our first two major research interests were similar to those of the first set of studies. Specifically, we were interested in whether there were age differences in absolute levels of recall performance and in some indicators of processes of interaction. One important qualification of the comparisons being made in this experiment should be noted. Our major comparison was between age of couples, and age is obviously confounded with dyadic experience. That is, we compared younger and older couples who varied also in length of marriage. (Although a complete design would have been preferable, it was not practical.) Our solution to this problem was to address the issue of couple expertise directly by examining each individual's knowledge and agreement with their partner on selected issues. We found that, despite the differing lengths of relationship, the younger and older couples did not differ in level of knowledge or agreement. That they were equivalently familiar with one another lent some support to our intention to focus on the age comparison.

Our third major research interest was to begin the examination of the collaborative metacognitive skills of the couples. We asked each couple both before (prediction) and after (postdiction) recalling each story to estimate what percentage of the information contained in the original story they would or had recalled. This prediction paradigm is frequently used in (individual) cognitive aging research to indicate an individual's skill at monitoring their own memory performance and how that performance may change across trials and tasks (e.g., Devolder, Brigham, & Pressley, 1990; Hertzog, Dixon, & Hultsch, 1990). When the tasks remain the same across trials, a successfully monitoring individual might demonstrate some upgrading in pre- and post-diction accuracy. We sought to investigate whether married couples would be able to predict accurately their own performance, improve their accuracy across the two trials, and differ by age in their accuracy.

The procedures, materials, and results of two experiments with younger and older couples were quite similar. Interestingly, in both studies the older and younger couples recalled an equivalent amount of propositions from the stories, a finding of age equivalence not typical in this literature, and one that contrasts with the results of the first collaborative story memory experiment with unacquainted adults. Was this unusual finding accompanied by—or perhaps accomplished through—parallel results in metacognitive performance? Specifically, how well could the younger and older couples monitor their own performance across the two trials? The accuracy of performance predictions and postdictions are relevant to this question. Although accuracy may be measured in a number of ways, for present purposes I use simple correlations (for alternatives, see Devolder et al., 1990; Hertzog et al., 1990). The pattern of trial-specific correlations for younger and older couples was very similar at Trial 1, with younger and older couples showing low and equivalent accuracy at first prediction. The accuracies for both at postdiction in Trial 1 were considerably higher, suggesting that their estimates, like those of individuals, were more accurate after than before a recall task. The next issue concerned whether there would be an upgrading of accuracy for the immediately following prediction (i.e., Trial 2). An apparent upgrading was indeed observed for both younger and older couples. Both maintained a similar and high level of accuracy at postdiction. Indeed, for the older couples, the accuracy of pre- and postdictions at Trial 2 were virtually identical, suggesting a substantial upgrading on their part.

In sum, complex narrative recall tasks, like most episodic memory tasks, rarely result in individual older adults performing as well as individual younger adults. This pattern held for the unacquainted collaborators in the first set of studies, but not for the well-acquainted and presumably well-practiced collaborators in the second experiments. Older couples recalled as much of the stories as younger couples, and in doing so generated a pattern of other recall-related statements that was more similar to that of younger couples and dyads than to the older dyads of the earlier experiment. There were relatively few macrostatements, elaborations, consensus statements, and errors. In many respects, then, their overall memory behavior resembled more younger than older individuals. In a post hoc analysis we sought to explore whether the younger and older couples might differ in the extent to which they shared the burden of recalling the text. Indeed, older husbands and wives on average shared equally in the proportion of propositions recalled, whereas younger husbands (about 40%) and wives (about 60%) did not.

The older couples showed considerable collaborative metacognitive skills, at least as measured by the pre- and postdictions. This may indicate that older experienced couples not only recall complex materials better than their same-age counterparts performing as individuals or dyads, but they also show an ability to arrive collaboratively at a reasonable estimate of how much and how accurate is (and was) their performance. This is notable for such upgrading has not been found for individuals processing discourse materials (Hertzog et al., 1990), although it has been observed for materials such as lists and attributed to the fact that word lists are easier to monitor because of their discrete and countable parts. These stories, in contrast, contained about 300 words in 24 sentences (a fact not known to the participants) and the task was the difficult one of estimating percentage of information recalled. Overall, the suggestion is that there is perhaps both a performance and metacognitive advantage to experienced collaborative cognitive performance.

Communication During Collaboration

In this third study on aging and collaborative prose processing, we compared some aspects of the communication styles of younger and older unacquainted dyads and married couples. Like the previous studies, the task was to listen and remember as much information as possible from a narrative. Unlike the previous studies, however, the research goal was to examine explicitly the process through which the dyads and couples performed this task (see Gould et al., 1994, for details). Thus, after the conversations were transcribed, each statement was coded into one of four categories. These categories were collected into two classifications, story-related statements and conversation-related statements. The two categories in the story-related statements were individual story-based productions (which consisted of correctly recalled information and story-based inferences produced by an individual) and collaborative story-based productions (which consisted of correct recall framed as a dialogue between the partners). The two categories in the conversation-related statements were task discussion productions (which were statements referring to the task itself, e.g., strategies) and sociability and support productions (which contained personal criticisms, references to one's own experience, and statements of agreement with the partner).

A count of the total number of each of these categories of statements revealed that all four groups produced protocols in which about 55% to 60% of the statements were individual story-based productions. Collaborative story-based productions constituted between 15% and 20% of the statements produced by all four groups. However, whereas young and old married couples' statements were constituted by nearly 20% task and strategy discussion, young and old unacquainted dyads' task statements constituted only about 10%. Instead, the latter groups seemed to produce greater proportions of sociability and support statements. Overall, the content of the collaborative recall conversations was similar with respect to story-based productions, in that the largest proportion of statements were recalled propositions and inferences produced by individuals. For all groups, a smaller proportion of the total statements were recall and inferences produced as a direct function of collaboration. The experience factor seemed to differentiate the groups in terms of their conversation-related statements. Whereas younger and older married couples produced task-oriented conversation at a greater rate than unacquainted dyads, the latter groups produced more sociability and support statements. We further examined these conversations by following them as they occurred, that is, across time.

Charting the appearance of statements from each of these categories across the conversations revealed the dynamic quality of these differences (see Gould et al., 1994, for details). This temporal quality is represented schematically in Fig. 18.2. For all groups, individual-based story-related statements predominated in the initial one third of their interactions (between 60% and 70%, with no other category greater than 20%). By the final one third of the conversations, however, individual story-based statements had declined, in most cases, to less than 40% of the total statements in that segment. Increasing for the younger and, especially, the older married couples (to over 40%) were task and strategy-based discussion statements (and

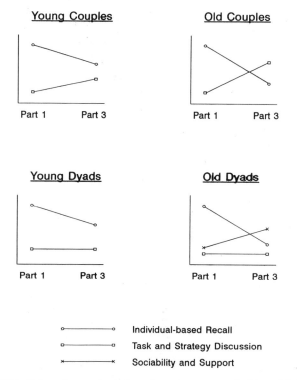

FIG. 18.2. Schematic representation of age (younger and older adults) and collaborative expertise (married couples, unacquainted dyads) effects in story recall conversations (see Gould, Kurzman, & Dixon, 1994, for details).

no other category). Increasing for the old dyads (to over 40%) were sociability and support statements.

In sum, all couples and dyads began with a spurt of recall of information from the narrative—and very little else. As the conversation continued, however, and individual recall began to decline, older couples produced more statements about the task (e.g., strategies for improving performance), whereas older dyads offered more statements of social support (e.g., congratulations for a good effort). Whereas the trend for younger couples was similar to (but lower than) that of older couples, younger dyads did little to compensate for declining recall performance. This dynamic analysis of interactive remembering allows us to identify a potentially theoretically interesting phenomenon worthy of further investigation. Specifically, the pattern of results may be consistent with an effort to compensate for declining individual-level recall, especially by older couples. The older dyads were arguably less productive in their efforts, but they too demonstrated some effort to replace their declining recall production with something. Instead of strategic comments designed to further their performance, however, the older dyads concentrated on helping each other feel comfortable with what was being said and with how well they had already done. It is conceivable that the long-term married couples are experienced enough with each other that they could bypass the sociability concern and concentrate on strategic efforts to improve their performance. Unacquainted dyads, of course, do not have the luxury of such knowledge and so concentrate on other aspects of the interaction. From this perspective, then, it may be important to examine interactive remembering dynamically, as well as summatively, in future research.

CONCLUSION

In order to fully evaluate cognitive competence in older adults, it is valuable to explore a wide range of contexts within which such competence may be expressed. Because one of the frequent everyday contexts of cognitive performance is social or interactional in nature, exploring collaborative processes in older adults is a promising avenue of research. The descriptive questions are important, albeit conventional, within the framework of the larger field of group and collaborative cognition. They include the questions of whether and how well older adults (as a special population) collaborate on solving complex cognitive problems. Approached developmentally, theoretical questions include whether older adults can develop potentially performance-maintaining levels of collaborative expertise and compensatory mechanisms. At a practical level, both the descriptive and theoretical issues have pertinent implications. Much of practical and theoretical utility can be gained if it can be ensured that older adults can benefit from collaboration, develop collaborative expertise with long-term partners, and thereby compensate for individual-level aging-related losses.

Research in this and allied areas is growing rapidly. I summarized some initial projects on collaboration in remembering recently heard narratives. As noted earlier, the goals of this program of research included descriptive issues (e.g., whether older adults could and would collaborate effectively on complex cognitive tasks, the characteristics of the process and products of collaboration, and patterns of aging effects) and theoretical concerns (e.g., experience or expertise effects and possible compensatory mechanisms). In the first set of experiments some degree of collaborative effectiveness was demonstrated for unacquainted dyads and tetrads and for both younger and older adults. In the second set of studies an apparent collaborative and expertise benefit was indicated by high and equivalent narrative recall performance from younger and older married couples.

Remembering narratives is a complex task with multiple indicators of performance. In order to examine the issue of collaborative effectiveness more comprehensively, we interleaved results from a variety of product and process measures and compared a series of performances across group size, age, and collaborative experience. The multiple variables on which we base our inferences about group performance include, but are not limited to, gist recall. For example, the levels of information analyses revealed that this increase in gist recall was not accompanied by a loss in the structural integrity of the retold story for young or old dyads, tetrads, and married couples. In addition, older groups produced significantly more general summary recall statements (macrostatements), more inferences and personal commentary about the stories (elaborations), and fewer recall errors. Such information reveals much about collaborative effectiveness in old age, but it does not tell us precisely whether older (or younger) groups were performing optimally, an issue that is raised frequently in allied literatures. Of more immediate concern in these studies, however, was the theoretically relevant question of how older groups could be collaborating as effectively as they were.

Specifically, why were older married couples not disadvantaged compared to younger couples in overall gist recall, whereas older unacquainted groups improved with group size but did not close the age-related performance gap evident for younger and older individuals? One might surmise that a reason for our results of age equivalence (one that is unusual in the cognitive aging literature) is that, as we had expected, the couples were advantaged with respect to experience at cognitive collaboration. That is, they may have been able to use their unique and shared resources to compensate for individual-level cognitive decline (Dixon, 1992; Gould et al., 1994). The observation that older and younger couples were able to collaboratively monitor their performance on a complex, relatively ill-structured task may support this notion.

Even more direct evidence regarding this potential explanatory variable is available in the final study. Older married couples—who are possibly collaborative experts—engaged in unique and productive strategy-oriented discussions in the final segment of their collaborative recall conversations. The selective increase in such strategic efforts, combined with the general waning of actual recall performance, bodes well for an experienced-based compensation interpretation. Younger married couples had less to compensate for, but also increased slightly such discussion. Older unacquainted dyads, on the other hand, seemed to be trying to develop such experience by providing a friendly foundation for collaborative efforts. These intriguing patterns of performance deserve even further investigation. For example, it is possible (but unlikely) that older long-term married couples are initially better individually at memory tasks than other older adults, or that they have experienced an individual-level boost as a function of their long-term collaborative experience. Either scenario could result in group performance simply reflecting superior individual memory skills. This empirical issue is currently being explored (Gagnon et al., 1995).

These sets of studies were designed to explore the extent to which younger and older adults collaborated effectively in a complex cognitive task. For groups differing in age, size, and collaborative experience, differences and similarities in the products and processes of their performance were observed. The roles of other factors such as gender and other operational definitions of collaborative experience deserve further study. Cognition in collaborative situations appears to be both a common form of the expression of cognitive competence in everyday life, and a form for which older adults may not be uniformly disadvantaged.

ACKNOWLEDGMENTS

This research was supported by grants from the Natural Sciences and Engineering Research Council of Canada and the Canadian Aging Research Network. I appreciate the helpful comments of Christopher Hertzog on an earlier version of this chapter. I also wish to note that Odette Gould and several collaborators made important contributions to the research summarized in this chapter.

REFERENCES

Adams, C. (1991). Qualitative age differences in memory for text: A life-span developmental perspective. *Psychology and Aging, 6,* 323–336.

Adams, C., Labouvie-Vief, G., Hobart, C. J., & Dorosz, M. (1990). Adult age group differences in story recall style. *Journal of Gerontology: Psychological Sciences, 45,* 17–27.

Azmitia, M. (in press). Peer collaborative cognition: Developmental, theoretical, and measurement issues. In P. B. Baltes & U. M. Staudinger (Eds.), *Interactive minds: Life-span perspectives on the social foundation of cognition.* New York: Cambridge University Press.

Bäckman, L., & Dixon, R. A. (1992). Psychological compensation: A theoretical framework. *Psychological Bulletin, 112,* 259–283.

Baltes, P. B. (1987). Theoretical propositions of life-span developmental psychology: On the dynamics between growth and decline. *Developmental Psychology, 23,* 611–626.

Baltes, P. B., & Staudinger, U. M. (Eds.). (in press). *Interactive minds: Life-span perspectives on the social foundation of cognition.* New York: Cambridge University Press.

Bosman, E. A. (1993). Age-related differences in the motoric aspects of transcription typing skill. *Psychology and Aging, 8,* 87–102.

Cavanaugh, J. C., Dunn, N. J., Mowery, D., Feller, C., Niederehe, G., Frugé, E., & Volpendesta, D. (1989). Problem-solving strategies in dementia patient–caregiver dyads. *The Gerontologist, 29,* 156–158.

Charness, N. (1989). Age and expertise: Responding to Talland's challenge. In L. W. Poon, D. C. Rubin, & B. A. Wilson (Eds.), *Everyday cognition in adulthood and late life* (pp. 437–456). New York: Cambridge University Press.

Charness, N., & Bosman, E. (1995). Compensation through environmental modification. In R. A. Dixon & L. Bäckman (Eds.), *Compensating for psychological deficits and declines: Managing losses and promoting gains* (pp. 147–168). Mahwah, NJ: Lawrence Erlbaum Associates.

Clark, N. K., & Stephenson, G. M. (1989). Group remembering. In P. B. Paulus (Ed.), *Psychology of group influence* (pp. 357–391). Hillsdale, NJ: Lawrence Erlbaum Associates.

Craik, F. I. M., & Jennings, J. M. (1992). Human memory. In F. I. M. Craik & T. A. Salthouse (Eds.), *Handbook of aging and cognition* (pp. 51–110). Hillsdale, NJ: Lawrence Erlbaum Associates.

Craik, F. I. M., & Salthouse, T. A. (Eds.). (1992). *Handbook of aging and cognition.* Hillsdale, NJ: Lawrence Erlbaum Associates.

Damon, W. (1984). Peer education: The untapped potential. *Journal of Applied Developmental Psychology, 5,* 331–343.

Devolder, P. A., Brigham, M. C., & Pressley, M. (1990). Memory performance awareness in younger and older adults. *Psychology and Aging, 5,* 291–303.

Dixon, R. A. (1992). Contextual approaches to adult intellectual development. In R. J. Sternberg & C. A. Berg (Eds.), *Intellectual development* (pp. 350–380). Cambridge, England: Cambridge University Press.

Dixon, R. A. (1995). Promoting competence through compensation. In L. A. Bond, S. J. Cutler, & A. Grams (Eds.), *Promoting successful and productive aging* (pp. 220–238). Newbury, CA: Sage.

Dixon, R. A., & Bäckman, L. (1993). The concept of compensation in cognitive aging: The case of prose processing in adulthood. *International Journal of Aging and Human Development, 36,* 199–217.

Dixon, R. A., & Bäckman, L. (1995). Concepts of compensation: Integrated, differentiated, and Janus-faced. In R. A. Dixon & L. Bäckman (Eds.), *Compensating for psychological deficits and declines: Managing losses and promoting gains* (pp. 3–19). Hillsdale, NJ: Lawrence Erlbaum Associates.

Dixon, R. A., & Gould, O. N. (1994). *Story recall by adults in collaborative situations.* Manuscript submitted for publication.

Dixon, R. A., & Gould, O. N. (in press). Adults telling and retelling stories collaboratively. In P. B. Baltes & U. M. Staudinger (Eds.), *Interactive minds: Life-span perspectives on the social foundation of cognition.* New York: Cambridge University Press.

Dixon, R. A., & Hertzog, C. (in press). Theoretical issues in cognition and aging. In T. M. Hess & F. Blanchard-Fields (Eds.), *Perspectives on cognitive changes in adulthood and aging.* New York: McGraw-Hill.

Dixon, R. A., Hunt-Matheson, D. A., & Meers, D. E. (1993, November). *Are there cognitive benefits to long-term marriage?* Paper presented at the Gerontological Association of America, New Orleans, LA.

Edwards, D., & Middleton, D. (1986). Joint remembering: Constructing an account of shared experience through conversational discourse. *Discourse Processes, 9,* 423–459.

Engeström, Y. (1992). Interactive expertise: Studies in distributed working intelligence. *Research Bulletin 83,* Department of Education, University of Helsinki.

Ericsson, K. A., & Charness, N. (1994). Expert performance: Its structure and acquisition. *American Psychologist, 49,* 725–747.

Gagnon, L. M., Friesen, I. C., & Dixon, R. A. (1995, August). *Interactive and transactive expertise in younger and older adults.* Paper presented at the 103rd Annual Convention of the American Psychological Association, New York.

Glaser, R., & Chi, M. T. H. (1988). Overview. In M. T. H. Chi, R. Glaser, & M. J. Farr (Eds.), *The nature of expertise* (pp. xv–xxvii). Hillsdale, NJ: Lawrence Erlbaum Associates.

Gold, D., Andres, D., Arbuckle, T., & Schwartzman, A. (1988). Measurement and correlates of verbosity in elderly people. *Journal of Gerontology: Psychological Sciences, 43,* P27–33.

Gould, O. N., & Dixon, R. A. (1993). How we spent our vacation: Collaborative storytelling by young and old adults. *Psychology and Aging, 8,* 10–17.

Gould, O. N., Kurzman, D., & Dixon, R. A. (1994). Communication during prose recall conversations by young and old dyads. *Discourse Processes, 17,* 149–165.

Gould, O. N., Trevithick, L., & Dixon, R. A. (1991). Adult age differences in elaborations produced during prose recall. *Psychology and Aging, 6,* 93–99.

Greeno, J. G., & Moore, J. L. (1993). Situativity and symbols: Response to Vera and Simon. *Cognitive Science, 17,* 49–59.

Heckhausen, J., Dixon, R. A., & Baltes, P. B. (1989). Gains and losses in development throughout adulthood as perceived by different adult age groups. *Developmental Psychology, 25,* 109–121.

Hertzog, C., & Dixon, R. A. (1994). Metacognitive development in adulthood and old age. In J. Metcalfe & A. P. Shimamura (Eds.), *Metacognition: Knowing about knowing* (pp. 227–251). Cambridge, MA: MIT Press.

Hertzog, C., Dixon, R. A., & Hultsch, D. F. (1990). Relationships between metamemory, memory predictions, and memory task performance in adults. *Psychology and Aging, 5,* 215–227.

Hultsch, D. F., & Dixon, R. A. (1990). Learning and memory in aging. In J. E. Birren & K. W. Schaie (Eds.), *Handbook of the psychology of aging* (3rd ed., pp. 258–274). San Diego, CA: Academic Press.

Hyman, I. E., Jr. (1994). Conversational remembering: Story recall with a peer versus for an experimenter. *Applied Cognitive Psychology, 8,* 49–66.

Hill, G. W. (1982). Group versus individual performance: Are N + 1 heads better than one? *Psychological Bulletin, 91,* 517–539.

Lave, J., & Wenger, E. (1991). *Situated learning: Legitimate peripheral participation.* New York: Cambridge University Press.

Middleton, D., & Edwards, D. (Eds.). (1990). *Collective remembering.* Newbury Park, CA: Sage.

Park, D. C. (1992). Applied cognitive aging research. In F. I. M. Craik & T. A. Salthouse (Eds.), *The handbook of aging and cognition* (pp. 449–493). Hillsdale, NJ: Lawrence Erlbaum Associates.

Paulus, P. B. (Ed.). (1989). *Psychology of group influence.* Hillsdale, NJ: Lawrence Erlbaum Associates.

Pratt, M. W., Boyes, C., Robins, S., & Manchester, J. (1989). Telling tales: Aging, working memory, and the narrative cohesion of story retellings. *Developmental Psychology, 25,* 628–635.

Reder, L. M. (1982). Elaborations: When do they help and when do they hurt? *Text, 2,* 211–224.

Resnick, L. B., Levine, J. M., & Teasley, S. D. (Eds.). (1991). *Perspectives on socially shared cognition.* Washington, DC: American Psychological Association.

Ryan, E. B., Giles, H., Bartolucci, G., & Henwood, K. (1986). Psycholinguistic and social psychological components of communication by and with the elderly. *Language and Communication, 6,* 1–24.

Salthouse, T. A. (1987). Age, experience, and compensation. In C. Schooler & K. W. Schaie (Eds.), *Cognitive functioning and social structure over the life course* (pp. 142–157). Norwood, NJ: Ablex.

Salthouse, T. A. (1990). Cognitive competence and expertise. In J. E. Birren & K. W. Schaie (Eds.), *Handbook of the psychology of aging* (3rd ed., pp. 310–319). San Diego, CA: Academic Press.

Salthouse, T. A. (1991). *Theoretical perspectives on cognitive aging.* Hillsdale, NJ: Lawrence Erlbaum Associates.

Salthouse, T. A. (1995). Refining the concept of compensation. In R. A. Dixon & L. Bäckman (Eds.), *Compensating for psychological deficits and declines: Managing losses and promoting gains* (pp. 21–34). Hillsdale, NJ: Lawrence Erlbaum Associates.

Schaie, K. W. (1990). Intellectual development in adulthood. In J. E. Birren & K. W. Schaie (Eds.), *Handbook of the psychology of aging* (3rd ed., pp. 291–309). San Diego, CA: Academic Press.

Staudinger, U. M. (in press). Wisdom: A prototypical example of the social-interactive and collective foundation of the mind. In P. B. Baltes & U. M. Staudinger (Eds.), *Interactive minds: Life-span perspectives on the social foundation of cognition.* New York: Cambridge University Press.

Steiner, I. D. (1972). *Group process and productivity*. New York: Academic Press.

van Dijk, T. A., & Kintsch, W. (1983). *Strategies of discourse comprehension*. New York: Academic Press.

Vera, A. H., & Simon, H. A. (1993). Situated action: A symbolic interpretation. *Cognitive Science, 17*, 7–48.

Vygotsky, L. S. (1978). *Mind in society: The development of higher psychological processes*. Cambridge, MA: Harvard University Press.

Wegner, D. M. (1986). Transactive memory: A contemporary analysis of the group mind. In B. Mullen & G. R. Goethals (Eds.), *Theories of group behavior* (pp. 185–208). New York: Springer-Verlag.

Willis, S. L., & Dubin, S. S. (Eds.). (1990). *Maintaining professional competence*. San Francisco, CA: Jossey-Bass.

Zelinski, E. M., & Gilewski, M. J. (1988). Memory for prose and aging: A meta-analysis. In M. L. Howe & C. J. Brainerd (Eds.), *Cognitive development in adulthood: Progress in cognitive development research* (pp. 133–158). New York: Springer-Verlag.

CHAPTER NINETEEN

Study Strategies, Interest, and Learning From Text: The Application of Material Appropriate Processing

Mark A. McDaniel
University of New Mexico

Paula J. Waddill
Murray State University

Paul S. Shakesby
Austin Peay State University

The prescription of study activities aimed at increasing students' retention of text information follows from well-established, basic cognitive research. This research supports the idea that good retention is related to both the elaboration of individual pieces of information (e.g., Bellezza, Cheesman, & Reddy, 1977; Einstein & Hunt, 1980; Franks et al., 1982; Hunt & Einstein, 1981; Reder, Charney, & Morgan, 1986; Stein et al., 1982) and the overall organization of information (Bellezza et al., 1977; Bellezza, Richards, & Geiselman, 1976; Einstein & Hunt, 1980; Hunt & Einstein, 1981). In the pedagogical arena, activities like outlining and summarizing, which encourage organization of the text, have been suggested as good activities for helping students remember information that they read (Glynn, Britton, & Muth, 1985). Text adjuncts like embedded questions and reading objectives have long been viewed as promising candidates for encouraging more elaboration or deeper or more meaningful processing of the information presented in a text (Andre, 1979; Faw & Waller, 1976).

A review of the empirical literature, however, reveals apparently inconsistent effects of various study activities on learning from text. Sometimes organizational study techniques improve recall, sometimes they improve recall only for some kinds of information, and sometimes they do not enhance recall at all. Outlining has generally been found to improve overall recall of factual (expository) text relative to reading without outlining (Slater,

Graves, & Piche, 1985; Taylor, 1982; Taylor & Beach, 1984), but Einstein, McDaniel, Owen, and Cote (1990) reported that outlining did not increase overall recall for a narrative. In addition, outlines have been found to increase memory for main ideas but not for facts in expository texts (Eggen, Kauchak, & Kirk, 1978). Rinehart, Stahl, and Erickson (1986) reported that subjects who wrote summaries of an expository passage later demonstrated greater recall of main ideas from the text than did subjects who had not summarized, but summarizing produced no benefit in the recall of facts.

Various ideas have been put forth to try to understand the patterns of effects of organizational study strategies on learning from text. For summarizing, Rinehart et al. (1986) suggested that the skill with which the reader is able to distill the facts and concepts into a brief, organized paragraph affects the degree to which summarization will enhance recall. Yet even with Rinehart et al.'s own trained subjects, summarization showed selective enhancement effects. For outlining, one potentially important factor suggested by basic memory research is whether or not the outline is subject generated (cf. McDaniel, Riegler, & Waddill, 1990; Slamecka & Graf, 1978). In published studies of outlining, however, no clear relationship emerges between retention and whether an outline was constructed by the reader or provided by the researcher.

Research on the effects of elaborative study techniques similarly yields a complex pattern of findings. Halpain, Glover, and Harvey (1985, Exp. 5) embedded factual questions in an expository text. Subjects who read the text with the embedded questions showed no greater overall recall of text information than did subjects who read the same text without embedded questions. Rickards and DiVesta (1974) reported that factual questions embedded in an expository text enhanced recall of the material targeted by the question, but paralleling Halpain et al. overall recall was not enhanced. On the other hand, when Halpain et al. and Rickards and DiVesta embedded conceptual (analysis) questions in their expository texts, overall free recall was enhanced relative to text presentations without embedded questions.

Einstein et al. (1990) found that factual questions enhanced overall recall if embedded in narrative text but not expository text. Ramsel and Grabe (1983) reported a similar result for factual reading objectives: Factual objectives increased total factual recall for a narrative text but not for expository text.

In terms of understanding the effects of adjunct questions, one straightforward notion has been that placement of the questions is important. Questions embedded prior to a text segment containing targeted information may serve to focus the reader's attention on the target information at the expense of other information, whereas no such selective attention is possible when questions are embedded after the segment containing the target information (Andre, 1979). Likewise, specific reading objectives supplied prior to reading a text may engage selective attention similar to that engaged by embedded prequestions. Yet, learning objectives presented prior to reading have been found to facilitate recall (Duchastel, 1979; Muth, Glynn, Britton, & Graves, 1988) as well as produce no facilitation (Ramsel & Grabe, 1983). Recall may be enhanced by prequestions (Rickards, 1976) and not enhanced by postquestions (Halpain et al., 1985; Rickards & DiVesta, 1974). The placement of text adjuncts and students' skills in constructing and utilizing organizational aids undoubtedly play roles in recall, but they are not the whole story. How might we better understand the apparent inconsistencies in enhancement effects across study strategies?

MATERIAL APPROPRIATE PROCESSING

In general, it appears that one overlooked factor in considering the effectiveness of learning strategies is the material to which the strategies are applied. The target material itself may invite or afford a particular type of processing, while discouraging or hindering another type of processing. This idea has received support in the basic memory literature with regard to elaboration of individual constituents of verbal material (which has been termed *individual-item processing*) versus encoding of the relations among those individual constituents (termed *relational* or *organizational processing*). That is, for verbal materials ranging from word lists to connected discourse, certain forms of those materials (e.g., certain types of word lists, Einstein & Hunt, 1980; or certain types of texts, McDaniel, Einstein, Dunay, & Cobb, 1986) will invite predominantly relational processing and other forms will invite individual item processing. As a simple concrete example, structured word lists (word lists in which a number of words are drawn from the same taxonomic categories) will invite relational processing, whereas unstructured word lists invite individual-item processing (see Hunt & McDaniel, 1993).

The import of this idea for present purposes is that a learning strategy may have little benefit for learning to the extent that the learning strategy encourages processing that overlaps or is redundant with the type of processing invited by the material. On the other hand, a learning strategy will be effective if it encourages processing that is not sufficiently invited by the material itself. This view stresses that the learning benefits of a strategy will depend not just on the kind of processing that the strategy encourages but also on whether the processing is material appropriate.

Because the material appropriate processing (MAP) framework has been detailed elsewhere (McDaniel, Blischak, & Einstein, 1995; McDaniel & Einstein, 1989), we limit current discussion to a study that directly demonstrates the potential value of the framework for understanding the inconsistent benefits of the commonly advocated study strategies of outlining and answering adjunct questions. In initial basic work McDaniel et al. (1986) established that during casual reading, expository texts (e.g., describing avalanches in the Kanjenchunga mountains) tended to invite individual-item processing (for texts we assume that the psychological unit or item of encoding is the idea unit or proposition, so that individual-item processing would be processing focused on individual idea units), whereas fairy tales tended to invite relational processing (processing creating coherent and integrated encoding of the set of idea units comprising the text). If one now makes the reasonable assumption that at least some types of adjunct questions (e.g., factual questions) focus processing on individual idea units in the text and that outlining focuses processing on the interrelations of the entire set of idea units, then the MAP framework makes the following novel predictions. Adjunct (factual) questions ought to be an especially effective strategy enhancing free recall of fairy tales but should have little or no benefit for recall of the expository passages. In contrast, outlining should have minimal impact on recall of the fairy tales but should have a robust benefit for recall of the expository texts.

This prediction was confirmed in a study using fairy tales and expository passages that were 14 to 20 sentences in length (Einstein et al., 1990). The proportion of idea units recalled for the fairy tales when subjects casually read the texts (spending about a minute and a half to read) was .45. Recall significantly improved to .59 for subjects who answered adjunct questions (focusing on individual idea units) but did not significantly improve for subjects who outlined the tales (mean = .51). The lack of a significant improvement for outlining subjects is striking in light of the fact that these subjects spent nearly nine minutes (on average) processing the text and doing so with a task presumed to elicit meaningful, integrative processing. The pattern of effects was reversed for the expository passages. Outlining significantly enhanced recall (.46 of idea units recalled) over the level displayed by read-only subjects (.28), but adjunct questions did not (.36).

Supported by the Einstein et al. (1990) results, the MAP framework offers possible insight into the literature mentioned at the outset of the chapter showing that conceptual embedded questions but not factual embedded questions enhanced overall free recall of expository texts. As just mentioned, factual questions would not benefit free recall of expository texts because factual questions focus processing on individual idea units, processing that is redundant with that invited by expository text. In contrast, conceptual questions presumably focus processing on the interrelations of the idea units, processing that is not sufficiently afforded by expository text (at least for casual readers). Accordingly, conceptual questions would enhance free recall of expository texts. An interesting but as yet untested extension of these findings would be to test the companion prediction that conceptual questions should have minimal benefit for free recall of fairy tales or other kinds of text written to tell a story (texts that invite relational processing).

Our framework has thus far focused on material by strategy interactions based on dynamics involving individual item and relational elaboration and using the criterial task of free recall. The present discussion is generally circumscribed by these parameters to reflect the available empirical work. It is important to note, however, that material by strategy interactions are in principle not limited to texts and strategies tapping individual item and relational processing. For instance, when describing scientific concepts, texts can either focus on a literal presentation or they can emphasize an analogical presentation while still presenting the literal details. It appears that literal presentation produces more accurate memory for specific details regarding the concept than does the analogical presentation, whereas texts that include analogical information promote more accurate inferences about the concept than do the literal texts (Donnelly & McDaniel, 1993). Presumably, acquisition of both types of information is a desirable educational objective. Accordingly, on the MAP framework, for literal texts an effective learning strategy would be one that encourages processing leading to better inferencing. For analogical texts, on the other hand, an effective strategy would be one that encourages attention to the details of the concept.

Constructing Text to Invite Relational Processing

The idea that the target text affords a particular type of processing raises questions about the text characteristics that underlie such affordances. Identifying those characteristics defines a research agenda that nicely combines basic and applied concerns. Delineating the text characteristics that are responsible for inviting certain types of processing increases our understanding of basic text processes (e.g, McDaniel, Hines, Waddill, & Einstein, 1994) and simultaneously helps provide insights into how to design texts so that students engage in the kind of processing desired (cf. Britton & Gulgoz, 1991; van den Broek, 1989).

In our laboratory we have been investigating the characteristics of fairy tales that render additional organizational (relational) processing (associated with extra encoding activities like outlining or generating the tale from randomly presented sentences) unnecessary. One hypothesis originates from the observation that narratives typically are rich in causal interconnections (Trabasso & van den Broek, 1985), and when these causal interconnections are present in the text, readers appear to create representations organized around causal relations (Fletcher & Bloom, 1988). Thus, in narratives like folk tales in which these causal interconnections are integrated into a causal structure that links most of the ideas from the inception of narrative to its conclusion, even casual reading should produce a well-organized memory representation of the information in the text. Moreover, existing work has shown that ideas that are components of the causal structure (part of the causal chain of the narrative)

are recalled better than ideas that are not on the causal chain linking the
beginning of the story to the end (Fletcher & Bloom, 1988).

Generally, an integrated causal structure is typically not found in didactic
material, probably in part because the content does not necessarily lend
itself to creating casual links from "beginning" to "end" as a story does.
Recall that the research described earlier showed that expository text benefited from additional organization processing, whereas fairy tales did not.
Thus, it may be that a key feature of text that encourages relational processing
is the presence of causal relations.

To explore the effects of causal structure on learning from text, Robert Hines
and an author of this chapter (M.M.) designed the following study. A social
psychology chapter from an introductory textbook was rewritten such that the
social psychological principles in the chapter were illustrated in the context
of a narrative about the social events in the day of the life of a high school
student. Subjects read either the original version of the chapter or the narrative
version, and then were given free recall, cued recall, and inference level tasks
to assess learning and memory of the text. Encoding strategies were also
manipulated so that some subjects simply read the assigned texts, whereas
others were required to additionally outline the material in the text.

This study allowed examination of several questions bearing on basic
and applied concerns. First, would there be any mnemonic advantage for
the narrative version of the text relative to the textbook version and, if so,
would the advantage be general or selective? Second, would outlining be
an effective strategy for improving performance in the textbook version, as
anticipated by the MAP framework? Third, given an affirmative answer to
the prior question, would the narrative version afford sufficient relational
processing to render superfluous the additional organizational processing
that was presumably prompted in the outlining condition? That is, would
outlining prove not to enhance performance for the narrative version (with
causal structure) although it might do so for the textbook version?

In two experiments using the same materials and procedures, overall free
recall was significantly better for the narrative version than for the textbook
version. This advantage was selective, however. When free recall for the
technical ideas (principles of social psychology) that were common to both
versions was examined, then recall was virtually identical. Furthermore,
performance on inference questions relating to the technical information
was less accurate for subjects given the narrative version than the textbook
version. Thus, even when an attempt was made to integrate the technical
information within a narrative causal structure, although the narrative information itself was well recalled, there was no associated mnemonic benefit
for the technical information (see Kintsch & Young, 1984, for a similar finding
with short passages). It remains to be seen if longer-term retention would
be affected by the present kind of manipulation and whether or not different

approaches to embedding causal structure in technical material would confer mnemonic benefits.

In terms of the effect of the outlining study strategy, for the textbook version outlining produced significant gains over the reading-only condition. These gains were consistently obtained in free recall and cued recall, and outlining subjects outperformed the reading-only subjects on inference-level questions for one of the two experiments. This is the first experimental study of which we are aware that demonstrates the mnemonic benefits of outlining on chapter-length materials taken directly from textbooks. Moreover, as expected by the MAP framework, it is not the case that any study strategy that encourages additional focus on the contents of the chapter would improve memory. A third group of subjects who answered adjunct questions about the chapter during the study phase (with the chapter present) displayed free recall levels equivalent to that observed in the reading-only group.

The final notable finding was that for the narrative version, outlining did not significantly improve learning and retention. This pattern held for overall free recall, free and cued recall of the technical information in the text, and inference-level performance (bearing on the technical information). Paralleling the Einstein et al. (1990) results described earlier, this absence of a benefit is especially noteworthy when the study times are evaluated. Reading-only subjects required 16 minutes on average to read the text, whereas outlining subjects spent three to four times longer in processing the text. Overall, then, the results of the Hines and McDaniel study establish the importance of MAP considerations for educationally relevant materials and associated study strategies.

Further, the study suggests that causal structure, at least narrative-based causal structure, is one factor that influences the extent to which a text will invite relational (organizational) processing, and by so doing modulates the mnemonic effects of organizational study strategies (e.g., outlining). This conclusion must be considered preliminary, however, for several reasons. First, other research has failed to find a similar pattern when manipulating causal structure with much shorter texts (McDaniel et al., 1994). Second, there may have been other differences in the texts used in Hines and McDaniel that were concomitant with the change from textbook version to narrative version. For instance, perhaps the narrative version was more interesting to subjects than the textbook version (see Fernald, 1987). This second possibility dovetails with current work in our research program, to which we now turn.

INTEREST AND COMPREHENSION PROCESSES

The role of interest in facilitating learning from text has been a focus of study for some time (Krapp, Hidi, & Renninger, 1992). Traditionally, research has focused on what the reader brings to the reading encounter, the reader's personal interests, preferences, and prior knowledge (Hidi, 1990; Tobias, 1994). In an evaluation of the relationship among prior knowledge, interest, and learning, Tobias suggested that persons with high knowledge of a topic or domain frequently have high interest in that domain and that such topic interest may engage deeper cognitive processing and activate a more elaborated associative network during the reading of texts related to the topic.

Only recently have instructional researchers begun to extend their focus to include another major aspect of the interest equation: what the text brings to the reading encounter (Hidi & Baird, 1988). A number of factors have been identified as potential sources of such text-based interest (cf. Hidi & Baird, 1988). Kintsch (1980) noted that texts that contain descriptions of events with a direct emotional impact (like violence or sex) or that invite a vicarious experience in the reader are likely to produce emotional interest. Cognitive interest, on the other hand, is created by structural characteristics of the text like unexpectedness, novelty, and overall passage cohesion—the degree to which each unit of the text is meaningfully related to other sections of the text. Readers are also more likely to be interested in texts that contain characters with whom they can identify, events that are unusual, and situations that contain intense feelings or actions (Wade, 1992). Hidi (1990; see also Tobias, 1994) suggested that the comprehension of interesting text might require less overall effort and place a less extensive demand on cognitive resources than uninteresting text. The freed-up cognitive resources might then be involved in integrating the information and creating a more coherent representation of the text. Using the terminology of this chapter, the idea would be that interesting text elicits more relational processing than uninteresting text. If so, then the MAP framework makes an interesting (we hope that the reader will now engage in relational processing!) prediction: Free recall of interesting texts should be significantly enhanced by individual-item but not relational study (encoding) activities, whereas recall of less interesting texts should be significantly enhanced by relational but not individual-item study activities.

This prediction was recently tested in research conducted by one of the authors (P.W.). The materials consisted of two sets of short narratives (383 words on average), each set comprising three stories. The stories in each set differed in the predictability of their plots, with one set consisting of stories in which events unfolded in a relatively linear, predictable fashion and the other set consisting of stories in which events were more interrelated and outcomes contained twists or novel resolutions.

In a separate rating study, subjects read one of the six stories and at several points during the story rated the narrative on characteristics like humor, excitement, surprise, and anticipation (on a scale where 1 corresponded to a low rating on the dimension and 7 to a high rating). The two story sets were found to differ in the level of rated anticipation subjects experienced while reading. When asked to rate the extent to which they wanted to learn more about events yet to come in the story, subjects indicated feeling less overall interest ($M = 3.20$) and excitement ($M = 2.96$) for the predictable stories than for the less predictable stories ($M = 3.99$ and 3.45, respectively).

In the primary experiment, different subjects read one of the six stories under one of three study conditions. One group of subjects engaged in a task suggested by previous work to enhance individual-item processing (cf. McDaniel et al., 1994, Exp. 1): completing words in the story from which letters had been removed. Subjects in this letter-deletion condition received a story with approximately 30% of the letters replaced by blanks (for all words containing two or more letters), and the subjects filled in the missing letters as they read. A second group of subjects engaged in a study task shown previously to require relational processing (McDaniel et al., 1994): reordering randomly presented sentences into a story. Subjects in this sentence-unscrambling condition received a story in which each sentence of the story was typed on a slip of paper and the slips presented in random order; they then reordered the sentences to form a coherent story. Subjects in the read-only control condition read the intact story unaccompanied by any special study task. After processing the story, all subjects were given free recall and cued recall tests to evaluate their memory for the story.

The pattern of results was entirely consistent with the ideas presented earlier. First, comparing the control (reading only) groups for the two kinds of stories, Waddill found no statistically significant difference in overall free recall ($M = .28$ for less interesting stories, $M = .25$ for more interesting stories). At first this finding might seem counterintuitive, but the MAP framework describes processing in terms of qualitative differences rather than quantitative differences. Thus, it is possible to have two identical recall levels resulting from two qualitatively different encoding processes. This situation is just what occurred with the more and less interesting stories. Interesting texts elicited processing that was qualitatively different from less interesting texts. The nature of these processing differences was revealed by an examination of the interaction of encoding strategy and text interest. For stories rated as producing less interest and anticipation, free recall was enhanced by sentence unscrambling (relative to read only) but not by letter deletion. The opposite pattern occurred for the stories rated as eliciting more interest and anticipation: Free recall was enhanced by letter deletion but not by sentence unscrambling. Interesting stories apparently elicited enough relational processing to render superfluous the additional relational processing imposed by a sentence-unscrambling study task. In contrast, less interesting stories apparently did not elicit such extensive relational processing and accordingly benefited from the relational processing induced by sentence unscrambling.

Furthermore, the differential benefits of encoding strategies were not confined to free recall. The pattern of effects observed in free recall was parallelled in cued recall. Subjects were given selected sentences from the story they had read and asked to write down the sentence that had immediately preceded and followed the cue sentence in the original story. Although no statistically significant difference existed between the reading-only controls, (.23 and .20 recalled for less interesting and more interesting texts, respectively), sentence unscrambling improved cued recall for the less interesting stories but not for the more interesting stories (relative to reading only). Letter deletion but not sentence unscrambling enhanced cued recall of the more interesting stories.

Some researchers have suggested that much of the recall improvement found with interesting material can be accounted for by concreteness (Sadoski, Goetz, & Fritz, 1993; Sadoski, Paivio, & Goetz, 1991). Concrete information is rated as more interesting and more comprehensible than abstract information and is better remembered. Other researchers suggest that text coherence is a major contributor to the effects of interest on text recall. When expository texts are rewritten to be more structurally cohesive and organized, readers rate those rewritten texts as more enjoyable than those with seductive details and anecdotes, and they remember more information from them as well (Sawyer, 1991; Wade, 1992). Although concreteness and coherence may underlie some of the effects of interest on text recall, they are not the whole story. The texts used in Waddill's experiment were all simple stories, and the less interesting and more interesting stories were rated as equally comprehensible. It is reasonable to assume, therefore, that the texts were equivalent in both concreteness and coherence (this assumption also gains indirect support from the equivalent levels of recall for the reading-only control groups).

The foregoing results may have important implications for educators concerned with improving students' recall of text information. Conventional wisdom seems to dictate that the recall of text can be improved by making the text more interesting. Yet in Waddill's study, texts that seemed to differ in interest were equally recalled (in the baseline conditions). A more refined approach would suggest that qualitative differences in processing dynamics result from variations in text-based interest. If the processing dynamics for the text differ, then the effects of study strategies will differ. Interesting texts apparently elicit relatively more relational processing than item-specific processing, whereas less interesting texts seem to elicit relatively more item-specific processing than relational processing. The recall of interesting texts should be enhanced by study strategies that elicit item-specific processing, and recall of less interesting texts should be enhanced by relational study strategies.

In the texts used by Waddill, differences in the extent to which readers felt anticipation or interest in the development of the story seemed to produce differences in the relational processing of that text, and as such modulated the benefits to recall of different types of study (encoding) conditions. Clearly, more research is needed to verify this preliminary finding, as well as to explore the possibility that other text-based interest factors (e.g., character identification, action, emotional content) also serve to elicit relational processing (and, by extension, the degree to which certain study activities will effectively enhance recall).

SUMMARY

A popular notion is that the more effort expended in reading or studying a text, the more will be learned from the text. Even if one limits this broad statement to effort directed at semantic or conceptual processing, it is not completely adequate for guiding identification and design of effective study strategies. Strategies for improving students' learning from text must take into account the kind of processing elicited by the text and the kind of processing elicited by the study strategy.

Optimal recall is a result of both item-specific and relational processing. A strategy will be successful in improving recall to the extent that the kind of processing elicited by the strategy does not overlap with that elicited by the text. This principle leads to the following specific suggestions. If the goal is to have students learn information from an expository text, then the use of an additional strategy, like outlining or summarizing, might be necessary. For a narrative, learning objectives or embedded questions might be useful adjuncts for eliciting relatively more item-specific processing and thus improving overall learning.

Text-based interest is another factor that appears to affect text processing and recall. A standard assumption is that overall recall of a text may be enhanced by writing or rewriting the text to make it more interesting. Our preliminary work suggests additionally that there may be processing trade-offs such that interesting texts may elicit relatively more relational processing than uninteresting texts. Thus, the recall of interesting texts may be enhanced by the addition of study strategies that elicit relatively more item-specific processing. In contrast, for relatively uninteresting texts relational study strategies (such as producing an outline) may be more useful.

ACKNOWLEDGMENT

Preparation of this chapter was supported in part by NIA Grant AG05627 to Mark McDaniel.

REFERENCES

Andre, T. (1979). Does answering higher-level questions while reading facilitate productive learning? *Review of Educational Research, 49,* 280–318.

Bellezza, F. S., Cheesman, F. L., & Reddy, B. G. (1977). Organization and semantic elaboration in free recall. *Journal of Experimental Psychology: Human Learning and Memory, 3,* 539–550.

Belleza, F. S., Richards, D. L., & Geiselman, R. E. (1976). Semantic processing and organization in free recall. *Memory & Cognition, 4*, 415–421.

Britton, B. K., & Gulgoz, S. (1991). Using Kintsch's computational model to improve instructional text: Effects of repairing inference calls on recall and cognitive structures. *Journal of Educational Psychology, 83*, 329–345.

Donnelly, C. M., & McDaniel, M. A. (1993). Use of analogy in learning scientific concepts. *Journal of Experimental Psychology: Learning, Memory, and Cognition, 19*, 975–987.

Duchastel, P. (1979). Learning objectives and the organization of prose. *Journal of Educational Psychology, 71*, 100–106.

Eggen, P. D., Kauchak, D. P., & Kirk, S. (1978). The effect of hierarchical cues on the learning of concepts from prose materials. *Journal of Experimental Education, 46*, 7–10.

Einstein, G. O., & Hunt, R. R. (1980). Levels of processing and organization: Additive effects of individual-item and relational processing. *Journal of Experimental Psychology: Human Learning and Memory, 6*, 588–598.

Einstein, G. O., McDaniel, M. A., Owen, P. D., & Cote, N. C. (1990). Encoding and recall of texts: The importance of material appropriate processing. *Journal of Memory and Language, 29*, 566–581.

Faw, H. W., & Waller, T. G. (1976). Mathemagenic behaviors and efficiency in learning from prose materials: Review, critique and recommendations. *Review of Educational Research, 46*, 691–720.

Fernald, L. D. (1987). Of windmills and rope dancing: The instructional value of narrative structures. *Teaching of Psychology, 14*, 214–216.

Fletcher, C. R., & Bloom, C. P. (1988). Causal reasoning in the comprehension of simple narrative texts. *Journal of Memory and Language, 27*, 235–244.

Franks, J. J., Vye, J. J., Auble, P. M., Mezynski, K. J., Perfetti, G. A., Bransford, J. D., Stein, B. S., & Littlefield, J. (1982). Learning from explicit versus implicit texts. *Journal of Experimental Psychology: General, 111*, 414–422.

Glynn, S. M., Britton, B. K., & Muth, K. D. (1985). Text comprehension strategies based on outlines: Immediate and long-term effects. *Journal of Experimental Education, 53*, 129–135.

Halpain, D. R., Glover, J. A., & Harvey, A. L. (1985). Differential effects of higher and lower order questions: Attention hypothesis. *Journal of Educational Psychology, 77*, 703–715.

Hidi, S. (1990). Interest and its contribution as a mental resource for learning. *Review of Educational Research, 60*, 549–571.

Hidi, S., & Baird, W. (1988). Strategies for increasing text-based interest and students' recall of expository texts. *Reading Research Quarterly, 23*, 465–483.

Hunt, R. R., & Einstein, G. O. (1981). Relational and item-specific information in memory. *Journal of Verbal Learning and Verbal Behavior, 20*, 497–514.

Hunt, R. R., & McDaniel, M. A. (1993). The enigma of organization and distinctiveness. *Journal of Memory and Language, 32*, 421–445.

Kintsch, W. (1980). Learning from text, levels of comprehension, or: Why anyone would read a story anyway. *Poetics, 9*, 87–98.

Kintsch, W., & Young, S. R. (1984). Selective recall of text decision-relevant information from texts. *Memory & Cognition, 12*, 112–117.

Krapp, A., Hidi, S., & Renninger, K. A. (1992). Interest, learning, and development. In K. A. Renninger, S. Hidi, & A. Krapp (Eds.), *The role of interest in learning and development* (pp. 3–25). Hillsdale, NJ: Lawrence Erlbaum Associates.

McDaniel, M. A., Blischak, D., & Einstein, G. O. (1995). Understanding the special mnemonic characteristics of fairy tales. In C. Weaver, S. Mannes, & C. Fletcher (Eds.), *Discourse comprehension: Essays in honor of Walter Kintsch* (pp. 157–175). Hillsdale, NJ: Lawrence Erlbaum Associates.

McDaniel, M. A., & Einstein, G. O. (1989). Material appropriate processing: A contextualistic approach to reading and studying strategies. *Educational Psychology Review, 1*, 113–145.

McDaniel, M. A., Einstein, G. O., Dunay, P. K., & Cobb, R. E. (1986). Encoding difficulty and memory: Toward a unifying theory. *Journal of Memory and Language, 25,* 645–656.

McDaniel, M. A., Hines, R. J., Waddill, P. J., & Einstein, G. O. (1994). What makes folk tales unique: Content familiarity, causal structure, scripts, or superstructures? *Journal of Experimental Psychology: Learning, Memory, and Cognition, 20,* 169–184.

McDaniel, M. A., Riegler, G. L., & Waddill, P. J. (1990). Generation effects in free recall: Further support for a three-factor theory. *Journal of Experimental Psychology: Learning, Memory, and Cognition, 16,* 789–798.

Muth, K. D., Glynn, S. M., Britton, B. K., & Graves, M. F. (1988). Thinking out loud while studying text: Rehearsing key ideas. *Journal of Educational Psychology, 80,* 315–318.

Ramsel, D., & Grabe, M. (1983). Attention allocation and performance in goal-directed reading: Age difference in reading flexibility. *Journal of Reading Behavior, 15,* 55–65.

Reder, L. M. Charney, D. H., & Morgan, K. I. (1986). The role of elaborations in learning a skill from an instructional text. *Memory & Cognition, 14,* 64–78.

Rickards, J. P. (1976). Interaction of position and conceptual level of adjunct questions on immediate and delayed retention of text. *Journal of Educational Psychology, 68,* 210–217.

Rickards, J. P., & DiVesta, F. J. (1974). Type and frequency of questions in processing textual material. *Journal of Educational Psychology, 66,* 354–362.

Rinehart, S. D., Stahl, S. A., & Erickson, L. G. (1986). Some effects of summarization training on reading and studying. *Reading Research Quarterly, 21,* 422–438.

Sadoski, M, Goetz, E. T., & Fritz, J. B. (1993). Impact of concreteness on comprehensibility, interest, and memory for text: Implications for dual coding theory and text design. *Journal of Educational Psychology, 85,* 291–304.

Sadoski, M., Paivio, A., & Goetz, E. T. (1991). A critique of schema theory in reading and a dual coding alternative. *Reading Research Quarterly, 25,* 463–484.

Sawyer, M. H. (1991). A review of research in revising instructional text. *Journal of Reading Behavior, 23,* 307–333.

Slamecka, N. J., & Graf, P. (1978). The generation effect: Delineation of a phenomenon. *Journal of Experimental Psychology: Human Learning and Memory, 4,* 592–604.

Slater, W. H., Graves, M. F., & Piche, G. L. (1985). Effects of structural organizers on ninth-grade students' comprehension and recall of four patterns of expository text. *Reading Research Quarterly, 20,* 189–202.

Stein, B. S., Bransford, J. D., Franks, J. J., Owings, R. A., Vye, N. J., & McGraw, W. (1982). Differences in the precision of self-generated elaborations. *Journal of Experimental Psychology: General, 111,* 399–405.

Taylor, B. M. (1982). Text structure and children's comprehension and memory for expository material. *Journal of Educational Psychology, 74,* 323–340.

Taylor, B. M., & Beach, R. W. (1984). The effects of text structure instruction on middle-grade students' comprehension and production of expository text. *Reading Research Quarterly, 22,* 134–146.

Tobias, S. (1994). Interest, prior knowledge, and learning. *Review of Educational Research, 64,* 37–54.

Trabasso, T., & van den Broek, P. (1985). Causal thinking and the representation of narrative events. *Journal of Memory and Language, 24,* 612–630.

van den Broek, P. W. (1989). The effects of causal structure on the comprehension of narratives: Implications for education. *Reading Psychology: An International Quarterly, 10,* 19–44.

Wade, S. E. (1992). How interest affects learning from text. In K. A. Renninger, S. Hidi, & A. Krapp (Eds.), *The role of interest in learning and development* (pp. 255–277). Hillsdale, NJ: Lawrence Erlbaum Associates.

CHAPTER TWENTY

Memory Expertise

John Wilding
Elizabeth Valentine
University of London

In recent years, work on memory expertise, most notably by Ericsson and his colleagues, has strongly supported the case for regarding memory processes as parallel to other types of skill and amenable to similar effects of training and practice. We argue that well-practiced techniques cannot explain all cases of exceptional performance in the literature, and suggest some criteria for discriminating between strategy-based and "natural" superiority in memory performance. These criteria enable us to identify some individuals whose memory is of the latter type. We suggest some research questions following from this conclusion and ways in which these might be pursued. Finally, we consider directions in which research on mnemonics might be developed with advantage.

PRACTICE AND TECHNIQUES: MNEMONICS

In the last decade the most influential work on mnemonics has involved studies of exceptional performance using mnemonic methods, and the development of skilled memory theory to elucidate the processes underlying effective mnemonics. Before turning to those studies we consider briefly work testing the effectiveness of mnemonic methods with a variety of subject groups and tasks.

The Properties of Good Mnemonics

We consider here ease of acquisition, continued usage, fit of mnemonic to task, flexibility and ease in combining mnemonics, and effectiveness of mnemonics in promoting long-term retention. It is generally easy to learn the basics of a mnemonic method by oral instruction and to derive some immediate benefit from its use, but it may be assumed too readily when giving instruction on a mnemonic method that the component skills are already fully present. Carrier, Karbo, Kindem, Legisa, and Newstrom (1983) found that supplying images for a paired-associate word-learning task was superior to asking gifted children to generate them, and suggested some training in this skill might be desirable. Jamieson and Schimpf (1980), however, found that self-generated images were superior to specified images in a group of student nurses learning paired-associate nouns. Richardson (1987, 1992) suggested that effective use of imagery depends on social class, motivation and insight, and Baltes and Kliegl (1992) suggested that older subjects may have difficulty in producing and using images (when employing the method of loci) and may therefore benefit less from their use. The superiority of bizarre images varies with several task variables (Kroll & Tu, 1988; McDaniel & Einstein, 1989).

The meagre evidence that exists suggests that few subjects will continue to use a mnemonic method, however effective, beyond the initial learning session, even in the situation for which it was devised (Anschutz, Camp, Markley, & Kramer, 1987, admittedly in a study of elderly subjects; Herrmann & Searleman, 1990). Herrmann and Searleman argued that continued usage is more likely when a method is task specific, but point to the paucity of evidence on durability over a long period and reasons for abandoning a method. Methods of improving durability need to be investigated.

Evaluation of the effectiveness of mnemonics and comparison of different methods is fraught with problems. Issues of motivation, ease of instruction, and task differences complicate the drawing of general conclusions (see Pressley & Mullally, 1984). Herrmann (1987) reviewed the efficacy of different mnemonics for three tasks and suggested that interactive imagery was most effective with paired associate learning, a story mnemonic (and also the link-word mnemonic) with free recall and the method of loci with serial recall, supporting the view that memory processing differs across different tasks. However, no study is cited that directly compared any of these mnemonics in the case of paired associate or serial learning, and only two direct comparisons were available for free recall (one comparing imagery and a story mnemonic, the other comparing the link and loci mnemonics). Herrmann and Searleman (1990) suggested that task-specific methods can be devised for over 100 everyday memory tasks, so there is scope for further research on task-mnemonic matching. A more challenging and potentially more beneficial task would be to identify general principles which underlie such matching.

Most studies measure effectiveness over a short retention period. Higbee, Markham, and Crandall (1991) found that the pegword mnemonic and imagery aided learning of sentences but were less effective in aiding long-term retention. Generally, however, long-term retention is helped by mnemonics (Scruggs, Mastropieri, McLoone, Levin, & Morrison, 1987; Wilding, Rashid, Gilmore, & Valentine, 1986). The latter study combined first-letter and imagery mnemonics, but combinations may not always be beneficial. Reddy and Bellezza (1980) found that using a pegword mnemonic with a categorizable list of words interfered with the natural strategy of category clustering.

Benefits of Mnemonics with Disadvantaged Populations

Several investigations have found mnemonics to be effective with special populations (Mastropieri & Scruggs, 1989; Scruggs & Mastropieri, 1990; Scruggs et al., 1987) and with the elderly (McEvoy & Moon, 1988), but the effects may be temporary.

Mnemonics in Natural Situations

Can mnemonics help with complex meaningful material and aid storage in a form that permits access from a variety of recall cues? Noice (1992) found that professional actors learn scripts neither by rote nor by use of mnemonics but by identifying underlying meaning and the motivation for the exact words used. Herrmann and Searleman (1990) suggested that general manipulations of the learning environment and state of the learner offer a more promising way of aiding memory than mnemonics. Although there has been relatively little work on the use of mnemonics with prose, there is enough to suggest that, at least in some circumstances, this can be beneficial (Cornoldi & de Beni, 1991; Levin & Levin, 1990; McCormack, Levin, & Valkenaar, 1990; Scruggs et al., 1987). Levin and Levin (1990) found that mnemonics also aided ability to solve problems involving the memorized material, and Scruggs et al. (1987) found that, in a learning-disabled group, mnemonic pictures helped both in learning facts about objects and drawing simple inferences from these facts. However, Haring and Fry (1980) found that giving the first letters of the main points before a concrete (but not an abstract) passage of prose was read aided recall of these points but reduced recall of other points. Giving the mnemonic after reading but before recall was equally effective, suggesting that it aided retrieval.

Mnemonics and Imagery

Is imagery more effective than other memory aids and, if so, why? Which differences in tasks and individuals are relevant to its effectiveness? A study by Hishitani (1985) demonstrated that connecting three nouns by imagery was more beneficial for immediate unexpected recall than relating them by a sentence. However, more forgetting occurred in the first case and both conditions produced equal recall a week later. Vivid imagers (indicated by self-report) performed better than poor imagers under sentence-generation but not image-generation conditions, suggesting that vivid imagers used imagery spontaneously. Vivid imagers also showed less forgetting in the imagery-generation condition than poor imagers. Hishitani suggested that image formation requires more input elaboration than sentence generation and this is more complex in vivid imagers, as shown by their image descriptions. This fails to explain why image generation was not superior to sentence generation after a week's delay.

Although there is ample additional evidence that imagery aids verbal learning (Paivio, 1986), it is not essential to mnemonic methods. Ericsson's subject S.F., discussed later in the chapter, appears to have made no use of imagery. Ernest (1977) reviewed the evidence for relations between individual imagery ability and memory and concluded that they depended both on the task and the measure of imagery employed. The measures can be self-reported vividness of imagery, self-reported control of imagery, or objective tests of visuospatial processing. Vividness of imagery could be seen as one type of memory ability, whereas control of imagery and visuospatial tasks involve other processes.

Ernest noted several studies reporting better incidental recall in subjects scoring high on all three measures, offering some support for a common underlying process mediating retention (Hishitani suggested an encoding process). Self-reported vividness of imagery was not, however, related to deliberate verbal learning, although the other measures were (in certain conditions), suggesting that when controlled strategic processes are engaged, facility in these is more important than the suggested underlying retention process. This conclusion is consonant with the findings that the positive relation between objective spatial ability measures and memory is restricted to situations in which the task encourages imagery or use of imagery is difficult. When verbal processing is encouraged, no relation or a negative relation occurs, especially in female subjects. This is discordant with the view that verbal and spatial ability are independent, but is explicable if subjects who are low in spatial ability tend to concentrate on verbal processing and hence can cope better when this mode of processing is required. However, the case of Rajan Mahadevan, discussed later in the chapter, does imply some trade-off between these two abilities. A better understanding of these issues would aid in devising more effective mnemonics.

PRACTICE AND TECHNIQUES: EXCEPTIONAL
PERFORMANCE

The work of Ericsson and his colleagues, which has led to the development of skilled memory theory, has demonstrated some extraordinary feats of memory achieved by developing mnemonic techniques for specific tasks. They have discussed three tasks in detail: digit span, learning of a number matrix, and memory for dinner orders. Taking our cue from skilled memory theory, we offer suitable mnemonics for the initials of their three expert subjects, Sprint Finish (S.F.), Dated Digits (D.D.), and Just Cooking (J.C.). Training effects in memory are most apparent for tasks requiring learning of unstructured material, especially arbitrary lists of items, this being the type of material which is normally hardest to memorize. Subjects have to learn to convert such material to a form more suited to the way memory works.

Results for the digit span performance of S.F. and D.D. (Chase & Ericsson, 1982; Ericsson, 1985; Ericsson & Chase, 1982) show that vast improvement over untrained subjects can be achieved by encoding groups of three or four digits as meaningful units (such as "a good time for running the mile," "the year 1936," or other codes already present in long-term memory), then building the new units into larger structures. The first of these steps is encapsulated in the first principle of skilled memory theory (Chase & Ericsson, 1982), that information is stored in long-term memory using knowledge already present. Exactly how the order of the digit groups within the larger structure was retained by Ericsson's subjects is not specified in much detail, but seems to be subsumed under the second principle of skilled memory, which is that retrieval structures are associated with a group of items and stored with the memory trace of the group. Retrieval structures are "a featural description of a location that is generated during encoding . . . at recall these features serve as a mechanism for activating the trace when the featural description is attended to" (p. 27). Herrmann and Searleman (1990, p. 179) used the more informative term "alternate record," pointing out that creating this both encourages elaboration and provides a second retrieval route. In the case of S.F., the retrieval structure seems usually to have consisted of simply labeling a set of three item groups as first, middle, and last (Ericsson, 1985, p. 195), but some structures contained more than three groups, so more complex ordinal codes must have been used.

This method does not seem to guarantee accurate recall. Confusion of order seems likely and the variety of encodings for digit groups is restricted. Indeed, in an example discussed by Ericsson (1988) S.F. claimed simply to recall two digit groups without any conversion to a running time or other code, which raises the possibilities that practice had a general effect on memory and/or that S.F. did not fully describe his methods and/or that he had a naturally good memory.

Several of the subjects tested by us, such as T.E. (Gordon, Valentine, & Wilding, 1984; Wilding & Valentine, 1994a), have used a number alphabet, plus imagery, for storing number sequences. Each digit has a prelearned consonant equivalent. Groups of two or three digits are converted into a word by inserting vowels between the consonants. Two words, or a chain of words, if necessary, are linked by images connecting the objects they represent. Another method is to have a prelearned set of imageable associates for each possible sequence of two digits (Wilding & Valentine, 1994b). These methods seem to offer more varied encoding possibilities than does the one used by S.F.

Although the details of these different methods vary, the principles are the same, namely coding groups of items into meaningful chunks already present in long-term memory. For S.F. and D.D., the code for the whole chunk was already present, whereas T.E. first recoded individual digits, then in a further step combined a group of these into a single meaningful code. S.F. (so far as we can tell) retained a sequence of such chunks by ordinal tags, whereas T.E. used a sequence of interactive images to link them.

Chase and Ericsson's third principle is the empirical fact that practice with these methods enables both encoding and subsequent retrieval to become very rapid, just as components of other very different skills come to be executed very rapidly with practice. Kliegl, Smith, Heckhausen, and Baltes (1987), in training two other subjects to improve digit span by recoding digit groups into dates and using the method of loci to create a retrieval structure, found that speeding up of encoding and retrieval required extensive practice but development of meaningful encoding or retrieval structures did not. This finding is reminiscent of the development of automatic, as opposed to controlled processing (Shiffrin & Schneider, 1977), and shows that knowing what to do (recode numbers as dates) does not ensure rapid operation and that repeated application of the knowledge is necessary to achieve this.

Ericsson's discussions of matrix recall (Ericsson, 1985; Ericsson & Chase, 1982) were aimed at discovering how performances on this task described by earlier researchers were accomplished, drawing on the digit-span studies as demonstrating one possible method and arguing that the earlier descriptions of matrix learning do not demonstrate acquisition of an image but rather employment of similar principles to those employed by his own subjects. We return to this issue later.

The third task investigated by Ericsson concerned the ability of the waiter J.C. to recall dinner orders (Ericsson & Polson, 1988). J.C.'s ability to recall orders comprising four items for up to eight people was tested in a laboratory analogue of the normal restaurant situation. J.C. had to recall for each diner one of seven possible steak entrees, cooked to one of five levels, one of five possible salad dressings, and one of three starches. J.C. stored information by type of item rather than by diner and within this scheme individual items were stored clockwise in the order in which the diners were seated. Steak entrees were simply stored as a sequence (noting repetitions or other patterns), temperatures were stored as a spatial pattern, salad dressings by initial letters, and starches as another sequential list. Even if orders were not given in the sequence in which the diners were sitting, J.C. stored the information in the same format. He could generalize, using a similar system, to a set of other categories (animals, flowers, metals, and times of day), although he was never as good with these as with dinner orders.

Ericsson claims that J.C. illustrates the principles of skilled memory, including the use of meaningful encodings. However, the only recodings apparent in this description are first letters for salad dressings and a spatial (five-place) code for temperatures. Consolidation into chunks only occurred if, for example, the initial letters of the salad dressings formed a word; certainly no prelearned set of recodings is apparent, although no doubt some patterns were recognized as familiar. Retrieval cues were basically sequences (spatial or temporal). Although there is no great puzzle over how J.C. retained single orders, his ability to recall later, without warning, most of the orders from the test session or evening's work in the restaurant is not fully explicable in terms of the analysis presented. How were the overlapping sets of orders kept distinct from each other?

J.C. illustrates the general tendency for superior retention of information from a specific sphere of knowledge by experts in that sphere, which has been documented for expertise in areas as diverse as chess (Chase & Simon, 1973), music (Halpern & Bower, 1982) and figure skating (Deakin & Allard, 1991). Experts have instantly available meaningful chunks for coding combinations of smaller elements (patterns of chess pieces, musical phrases, foot movements). Bellezza and Buck (1988) found that experts even recalled better than nonexperts a prose passage that contradicted their knowledge of their field, and argued that expert knowledge provides cues with good mnemonic properties (constructibility, associability, discriminability, invertibility). This suggestion that not only the availability of codings but their effectiveness may be different in experts merits further investigation, and would require elaboration of Ericsson's first principle concerning meaningful recodings.

Our subject T.E. (Gordon et al., 1984; Wilding & Valentine, 1985) showed excellent performance on a range of tasks; perhaps his most impressive feat was on the Atkinson and Shiffrin (1968) continuous paired-associate task in which four nonsense syllables are paired with a different two-digit number on each of a series of trials (e.g. ROQ-52 may appear on trial n and ROQ-08 on trial n + k, with other syllable-number pairs intervening). Intermittent test trials present only a syllable and require the number most recently paired with it to be recalled. Over 140 trials T.E. made only three errors and afterward was able to recall the whole sequence apart from four numbers. He converted each number to a word (see earlier discussion), and used a physical location associated with the sound of each nonsense syllable (a rockery in his garden for ROQ) to anchor a series of images based on the words. Thus, the number 52 yields "line," which he pictured as a ruler lying on the rockery. If ROQ-08 was the next pairing for this syllable, he converted 08 to "sieve" and connected this to the previous number by visualizing rulers being sifted in a sieve. Errors occurred if he made a mistake in identifying which was the last item.

This method conforms to Ericsson's principles. It used associates in long-term memory, first to the nonsense syllable, then to each number by means of the digit-letter alphabet, and created a coherent structure by linking to its predecessor in a chain an image derived from the word representing each new number. In most cases T.E. claimed he achieved direct access to the last item in the appropriate sequence, but if this failed he could retrace through the sequence. In this case the retrieval cue is an image of the preceding item in the chain.

Several of the subjects we have tested have described methods for encoding faces, face–name pairings, lists of words and name–telephone number pairings, which further illustrate the principles. For example, in order to learn names to faces, many successful subjects used the well-known method (Lorayne, 1958) of selecting a prominent feature, exaggerating it, and accessing some associated word (e.g. chubby cheeks evokes "hamster") that can be linked to the person's name via an association found in long-term memory (e.g., from chubby cheeks to the associate "hamster" and then to the name "Hampshire," or from big ears to "oars" to the name "Rowan"). If the order of presentation is to be retained, a peg such as "One is a bun" can be included and a hamster visualized eating a bun, for example. When the subject is only asked to decide if a given face is familiar, the selected feature should evoke the previous association, confirming familiarity of the face. When a name has to be retrieved, the associate to the feature should evoke the name if a suitably vivid association has been devised to link the two. An elaboration of this method enabled Jonathan Hancock, at the Second World Memory Championships, after 15 minutes' study of 100 pictures of faces, each with a name, to recall all the names when subsequently presented with the pictures alone.

Another subject we have studied (Wilding & Valentine, 1994b) had learned the telephone numbers of all Blackpool hotels (some 15,000 in all) by the following method. All two-digit numbers had a prelearned associate (00—bicycle, 57—tomato sauce, 39—Hitler, etc.), and these were used to encode the telephone numbers. Hence, 395700 might become Hitler picking up a bottle of tomato sauce, then riding a bicycle. The order of the numbers is encoded in the temporal order of the pictured event. This subject also found a suitable image for the hotel name (long practice had made this very easy) and then connected it to the composite image representing the numbers.

So "The Beeches" might be represented by a sandy beach and Hitler would ride his bicycle down the beach into the sea. The associates to hotel names would never, of course, include any of those already preempted for the numbers, so it would always be clear which part of the whole image represented the hotel.

In a broad sense these examples conform to Chase and Ericsson's principles because the principles are quite general, but it is apparent that considerable variation occurs and also that some elaboration of the principles may be desirable. The steps common to the different methods are: take a portion of the input (such as a string of four digits, a feature of a face, or the number presented with ROQ); retrieve a verbal or visual associate ("a good mile time," "hamster," "sieve"); link this associate into a larger structure by a label, verbal association, or visual association ("the second group," "hamster"—Hampshire, an image of rulers in a sieve); and adapt the form of this structure to hold any additional information that is to be retained, such as the sequence of occurrence.

The third and fourth steps appear to correspond to what Chase and Ericsson meant by attaching a retrieval structure, although the latter process is only made explicit by them (and not very explicit) for the digit span task. S.F. and D.D. made little use of visual imagery, and therefore there is little discussion of its role, but most of our subjects employed it either in addition to or instead of verbal codes. Retrieval cues are also commonly provided by attaching the products of the second step to an existing memory structure such as a known location (method of loci) or rhyme ("One is a bun," etc.). This helps to ensure that recall is complete and, if necessary, in the correct order. Such a method could have been used by S.F. to encode the order of digit groups (a triumphant runner with a record time eating a bun followed by a dejected runner with a terrible time throwing away his shoe), or by T.E. to encode the sequence of the words derived in the continuous paired associate task. In fact, S.F. appears to have had no problem in retaining order, although it is unclear exactly how he did it.

EXCEPTIONAL PERFORMERS—TRAINING OR TALENT?

Ericsson and Faivre (1988) claimed that there is no evidence that any exceptional performance described in the literature cannot be explained by the use of the type of methods described earlier. In this section we briefly restate the majority of our earlier arguments against this view (Wilding & Valentine, 1991), and also offer some additional examples to strengthen our case, then discuss possible criteria for distinguishing between strategy-dependent and "natural" memory ability.

Ericsson and Faivre (1988) argued that: Superior performance produced by practice is indistinguishable from such performance supposedly due to an exceptional innate memory; the superior performance of memory experts "is primarily limited to a single type of material, such as digits" (p. 449) and hence cannot be due to some general innate ability; trained subjects cannot provide a description of how they achieve their results that is any more explicit than that of subjects whose performance is supposedly dependent on an untrained ability; and in order "to prove exceptionality, the skill must be one that is not attainable by persons through practice" (p. 466).

With reference to the first claim, we discuss later some possible methods for distinguishing strategic and natural memory ability. The second point is considered during the discussion of individual cases. According to the third claim, it should be impossible to find trained subjects whose description of their methods of excelling at a particular task is more explicit than the descriptions of other subjects performing at a similar level without training. We provide some examples of subjects who do not provide detailed description of any method, yet can perform at a high level, and we argue that the absence of a description normally implies the absence of a practiced method and that subjects who are employing a well-practiced method are normally able to describe it in considerable detail. Ericsson and Faivre's fourth argument is clearly faulty. Quality is evaluated by comparison with other performers, not the method used to attain it.

Shereshevskii

We confine our discussion of individual cases to those where there is some doubt as to whether techniques can offer a full explanation. For discussion of other cases, see Ericsson (1985), Brown and Deffenbacher (1988), and Wilding and Valentine (1991). The most intriguing case is Luria's S. Like Ericsson and Chase (1982), we are sceptical of Luria's (1975) claim that S. retained a photographic image of a number matrix, because S.'s patterns of retrieval times for elements of the matrix were so similar to those of subjects using nonvisual encodings. Ericsson and Chase (1982, p. 611) stated, "The data [i.e. the retrieval times referred to earlier] are the only objective evidence supporting Luria's claim that S had a structurally unique memory. The rest of S's memory is based on standard mnemonic techniques." Strictly, this is true; Luria's account is short of numerical records of performance and, where detailed qualitative accounts of recall are given, they clearly report recodings that used associations of the type we have been considering. Perhaps even at his initial meeting with Luria, S. was employing the method of loci (Luria is not specific, p. 31), and later he developed his methods to meet the demands of stage performances and to control the apparently spontaneous activation of multiple associations evoked by sensory inputs (Luria, p. 36). Unfortunately, Luria appears not to have questioned S. concerning his methods at their first meeting, still less attempted to test S.'s own explanations. However, the accounts of some of S.'s achievements, based on notes taken at the time, do suggest that a straightforward explanation in terms of mnemonics is inadequate. The following observations from Luria (1975) suggest there were unusual features to S.'s mental life. For example:

1. Spontaneous synaesthesia such as smudges, splashes, and taste sensations to sounds: "These synaesthetic components of each visual and particularly of each auditory stimulus had been an inherent part of S's recall at a very early age; it was only later, after his faculty for logical and figurative memory had developed, that these tended to fade into the background, though they continued to play some part in his recall" (p. 28).

2. Spontaneous associations achieved with extreme rapidity, for example, to the elements of a meaningless formula.

3. Spontaneous imagery and associations when reading text that blocked extraction of meaning.

4. Retention over many years, without expectation of further recall, of individual tasks, which was "invariably" successful and which included incidental detail: "You were sitting at the table and I in the rocking chair. . . . You were wearing a grey suit and you looked at me like this" (p. 19)—unfortunately, Luria's notes did not enable the accuracy of such details to be checked!

5. Narrow literal interpretation of words. A "hat" was not accepted as having the same referent as a "cap" earlier in a story, indicating that S. did not derive general meanings.

6. Problems in forgetting.

This all sounds very different from the development of careful specific mnemonic methods to master meaningless material. For a long time S. has been regarded as a unique case, but we noted some similarities between his problems over the extraction of general meanings and the behavior of autistic mnemonists who show remarkable abilities for exact reproduction of music or visual scenes or routes (see Wilding & Valentine, 1991) but fail comprehensively to understand "other minds." We ourselves (Wilding & Valentine, 1994b) also studied one other mnemonist who showed a similar but less extreme profile (imagery, rapid associations, mnemonic performances, problems with grasping social conventions and retelling a story). We noted the same pattern of poor recall of meaning combined with superb recall of unstructured material, aided by mnemonics, in at least one other case. Hence, we are inclined to believe that S. does represent an example of a type of memory pathology that merits further investigation.

Aitken, V.P., and T.E.

Other cases that we discussed previously (Wilding & Valentine, 1991) as possible examples of naturally superior memory are Aitken (Hunter, 1977), V.P. (Hunt & Love, 1972), and T.E. (Gordon et al., 1984; Wilding & Valentine, 1985). All of them used methods, although Aitken (who abhorred mnemonics) used rhythm and grouping rather than recoding, but all indicated that methods do not provide a complete explanation of their abilities. Aitken could recall information he had not deliberately encoded (names and numbers of a platoon of soldiers), V.P. knew the street map of Riga at 5 years of age, and T.E. excelled in recalling a story, although his methods were not useful for this task. However, this evidence is largely incidental, fragmentary, and retrospective, and thus is not conclusive.

Rajan

Two studies have recently reported on the memory ability of Rajan Mahadevan (Biederman, Cooper, Fox, & Mahadevan, 1992; Thompson, Cowan, Frieman, Mahadevan, & Vogl, 1991). Rajan recited 31,811 digits of pi in 1981 and Thompson et al. tested him on a digit span task and several other memory tasks. He achieved a 43-item digit span with auditory presentation, and a 28-item span with visual presentation (the latter increased to 60 items later). Letter span was 13 items under both visual and auditory presentation, not very different from his original unpracticed digit span of about 15 items. The authors also established this as his "basic" span by another measure (the list length at which rehearsal time began to increase) and argued that the subsequent longer span was due to methods developed by practice, but that he could hold around 15 items without using any special method.

Thompson and his co-authors argued that Rajan's performance does not support Ericsson's view that practice, using the principles of skilled memory, is necessary to produce exceptional performance. In addition to the evidence for an unusual basic span, Rajan gave no evidence for encoding digit groups into meaningful chunks. Rather, he appeared to encode digits by position in the list; the authors described this as a form of paired-associate learning, although no evidence is offered for explicit pairing other than "he keeps track of the locations of each digit while learning sequences of 14 to 17 digits. He then pieces together the shorter sequences to give the complete string" (p. 705). Thus it seems that Rajan retained sequences of around 15 digits rather in the way that normal subjects retain sequences of about 7 items, but with the important difference that Rajan could retain the sequence in long-term memory and retrieve it later. He could specify the position of short strings in earlier lists and sometimes confused similar strings in the same position in different lists. Rajan was also able to learn number matrices rapidly and recall rows and columns, the latter more slowly than the former apart from the first column, with longer times on the middle columns. Hence, he was not using an eidetic visual image.

As noted earlier, Rajan's letter span was much less than his digit span, although still well above that of control subjects. On several other tasks his performance was, at best, average. On free recall of words he scored somewhat higher than controls but not on lists with a categorical structure, as he made no use of such structure. On all the lists, he memorized the first 12 to 15 items on Trial 1, added a further similar group on Trial 2, and a third group on Trial 3, ignoring the possibility of grouping by category. On story recall he performed about as well as controls, despite studying the visually presented stories for longer. On the Rey-Osterreith figure his performance was virtually identical to that of controls and his own account of his method gave no evidence for the use of imagery.

Thompson et al. argued that Rajan's performance on digit span is due to a combination of practice and innate ability. As well as his unusual letter and digit span, some anecdotal evidence suggested that he had unusual memory for numbers at the age of 5. Biederman et al. (1992) noted that "How Rajan memorizes digits is not clear. He says that he just concentrates on one digit at a time, using no mnemonics or imagery. . . . Another representational system that could support sequential reproduction is, of course, spatial memory" (p. 654).

Biederman et al. (1992) then proceeded to demonstrate that Rajan's memory for spatial relations (position and orientation) was worse than that of controls, and also cited anecdotal evidence that he had difficulty learning the spatial organization of buildings. They argued that spatial processing is carried out in a specialized dorsally located cortical visual system, which is presumably inefficient in Rajan's case. This conclusion is consonant with the view that Rajan's abilities are related to atypical brain organization, but precisely how he stores digit sequences and why his natural ability is apparently limited to retention of digit and letter sequences remains unclear.

Memory Champions

Recently we have reported a study of 10 subjects, 7 of whom took part in the first World Memory Championships in London in 1991 (Wilding & Valentine, 1994a). These subjects were, therefore, on their own assessment, either well-practiced strategists (four cases), possessors of unusual memory ability but not practicing strategists (four or possibly five cases), or intermittent users of strategies (one case). One of the strategists also claimed to have an excellent natural memory. We used the same tasks as in our previous studies (Wilding & Valentine, 1988): recall of a story, recognition of faces, recall of names to faces, free recall of words, recall of telephone numbers to names, recall of spatial and temporal position of a sequence of pictures, and recognition of snow crystals. Comparable data from two subjects studied previously (J.R., a "natural," described by Wilding & Valentine, 1991; and T.M., a strategist, described by Wilding & Valentine, 1994b) were included in our general evaluation. (Results from T.E. were not included, as he did not complete the full battery of tests that we have been using in the later studies.)

First we have to demonstrate that these subjects, or at least some of them, performed well above a sample of the normal population. A control group of 31 subjects (age range 31 to 66 years) provided the baseline data. The mean age of the control group (47) was above that of most of the expert sample (most of whom were in the age range 25 to 35), because the control group had been tested to provide norms for an earlier and older sample, and this point was taken into account in the analysis.

The 12 experts and the 31 controls were rank ordered on each of the seven immediate memory tasks, then summed ranks were obtained and themselves ranked to give an overall ordering. Six of the experts fell in the first seven places (ranks 1 to 4, 6, 7).

In order to evaluate better the level at which these subjects were performing, compared with the control group, scores on the seven immediate memory tasks were converted to z scores, using the means and standard deviations from the control group and adjusting these for the age of the superior subject in each case (see Wilding & Valentine, 1991). Table 20.1 gives the mean z score for the seven subjects in the first seven ranked places, all of whom achieved a mean z score of +1 or greater (at least $2\frac{1}{2}$ standard deviations above the expected mean). One other expert subject also achieved this and is included in the table (the ranking measure undervalues very high scores and this subject also had one very low rank, so his performance was not well represented by the ranks). No other subject approached the level of these eight subjects, the next highest mean z score being only 0.78, so the remainder of the discussion will consider these eight subjects only, of whom four were, by their own account, regular users of strategies, one was an intermittent user, and three made no regular use of strategies. One strategist (Subject G) also claimed to have a good natural memory.

DISTINGUISHING STRATEGISTS FROM "NATURALS"

We have attempted to identify criteria that will distinguish subjects, classified on the basis of self-report as strategists or naturals, by more objective indices. Clearly self-report alone is inadequate, although we reckon it is a useful start. Also, much depends on what our subjects understand by "strategy" and "method." Any adult faced with a memory task will work out some method

TABLE 20.1

Profile of Eight Subjects Categorized as Strategic or Natural Memorizers by Self-Report

Subject	C(MC)	G(MC)	H(MC)	TM	I(MC)	D	JR	36(C)
Strategic/Natural (self-rating)	S	SN	S	S	S?	N	N	N
Immediate memory:								
Overall	1.35	1.74	1.05	1.18	1.39	1.05	1.41	1.03
Strategic tasks	2.46	2.25	2.21	1.65	1.77	0.96	1.31	1.07
Nonstrategic tasks	-0.14	1.06	-0.50	0.56	0.88	1.18	1.53	0.98
Delayed memory	0.62	0.82	-0.02	0.41	—	1.64	4.07	0.81
Near relative	Y	Y	N	N	N	Y	Y	Y
Early awareness	N	Y	Y	N	N	Y	Y	N

Note. (MC = Memory Championship contestant, C = member of control group). Figures are means of z scores over seven immediate memory tasks (four strategic and three nonstrategic) and over four delayed memory tasks.

for tackling it. When does this become a "real" strategy? The solution we have adopted is to ask whether our subjects come to the task with prepared and practiced methods. A number of other criteria are emerging, none satisfactory on its own, but combined use of them seems to offer some promise.

1. Strategists' performance should be exceptional only on those tasks to which they can apply their strategies. In the extreme case this will be only one task (as in the case of S.F.), but many strategists are more flexible, either having several possible methods or being able to adapt a method to several tasks. Hence, superior performance will occur on a group of tasks with common features. Whether, on the contrary, "naturals" can be expected to perform well across the board depends on whether memory systems are subdivided into independent subsystems handling specific types of material or operations, or whether some general neuronal or biochemical process is the main factor in performance. Without offering a definite conclusion on this issue, we have made the more moderate prediction that "naturals" will show high ability over a wider range of tasks than strategists, although the issue of what variables are relevant to defining the range of memory tasks remains a major problem.

2. More specifically, our belief is that strategists will show a marked difference in performance between tasks amenable to strategies and those that are less amenable, whereas those with a good natural memory, who are likely to perform less well than strategists on the strategy-sensitive tasks, may outperform them on the tasks less sensitive to well-prepared strategies.

Use of this criterion depends on ability to categorize tasks in this way; fortunately the broad similarities across subjects in the strategies employed permit some general specifications to be devised. A further problem when attempting to move from strategies to classifying tasks that are or are not amenable to them concerns generality of strategies. S.F. showed no enhanced ability to learn letter sequences after developing a strategy for digit span. T.E., on the other hand, adapted to a variety of tasks, and most of our proficient mnemonists have been able to use their basic methods for faces, face–name pairs, word lists, and name–telephone number pairs. Other tasks we have used, due to unfamiliarity or complexity, are much less amenable—story recall, recognition of snow crystals, and reproducing either the spatial or temporal order of a sequence of pictures without knowing beforehand which will be required. Initially, our judgment on the sensitivity of a task to mnemonic methods was intuitive, but these judgments were later supported by the subjects' descriptions of how they tackled, or tried to tackle, the different tasks. However, several of our subjects claimed that the second time around they would have an effective method for dealing with the snow crystals and the spatial–temporal positions of pictures. For any task, a strategy to improve performance can be constructed, given time.

3. The relation between strategies and long-term retention (LTR) has received only unsystematic consideration. Ericsson argued, correctly we believe, that strategic encoding enables material to be stored rapidly in LTM and this is supported by ability to reproduce without warning after a delay (S., S.F., J.C., T.E.). However, this issue is complicated by the development by some strategists of deliberate strategies for forgetting in order to remove unimportant "clutter," particularly if public performances involving new material are required. We have encountered several cases where unexpected long-term retention was relatively poor in strategic memorizers, who gave this as the reason. Clearly, tests of LTR need to be administered without warning to preclude regular rehearsal or written recording, and to test durability of memory in the face of "normal" interference processes, but the previously cited considerations must be taken into account when attempting to derive any predictions about differences between strategic and non-strategic memorizers. However, if natural memory ability is in part dependent on unusual durability of encoded material, it can be predicted that natural memorizers will show superior retention to strategic memorizers, at least for tasks less amenable to strategies.

4. Superior natural memory ability, if it exists, would presumably depend on some feature or features of the nervous system such as richness of interconnections and efficiency of neuronal excitation or inhibition. Such characteristics might well depend on genetic endowment, and the existence of familial abilities of this kind would strengthen the conclusion that such an ability was natural. Hence we intend, after earlier informal enquiries yielded suggestive indications on this issue, to examine familial patterns of memory ability more systematically.

5. It is likely that naturals will be aware of having a good memory at an early age, whereas strategists develop their methods when somewhat older.

Table 20.1 presents information relating to these criteria in respect of the eight subjects already discussed who performed best in our sample. These subjects are grouped into strategic and natural memorizers according to their self-report. One of them, Subject I., was an intermittent strategist and did not carry out delayed recall.

We would highlight the following points. Strategists perform better than naturals on the four tasks we believe to be most amenable to strategies (face recognition, face–name pairings, word list, and name–telephone number pairings), but perform worse, and mainly below the naturals, on the three tasks that are not so amenable (story, snow crystals, and spatial or temporal positions of pictures). Overall, the best performances were achieved by Subject G. (who regarded himself as having an excellent natural memory but also used strategies), J.R. (who described a strategy only on word recall), Subject I. (intermittent strategies), and Subject C. (a strategist). On delayed testing Subject G. had practiced deliberate forgetting, Subject I. did not carry out the tasks, and Subject C. recalled the story only after about four weeks' delay. With these qualifications, although three of the delayed tests were on tasks amenable to strategies (faces, names, and words), the naturals performed much better than the strategists (a similar pattern is apparent when proportion lost over a week is considered). The only strategist who matches the naturals is Subject G. (despite practicing forgetting), who claimed a good natural memory. The other two criteria, citation of a near relative with an excellent memory and early awareness, are less discriminatory, though T.M., Subject I., and Subject H. (all of whom used strategies) are the only subjects not claiming a near relative, and T.M., Subject I., and possibly Subject C. are the only subjects not claiming early awareness. The general pattern of results suggests that our objective criteria for distinguishing the groups do correlate with self-reported status.

We give one example to illustrate the power of "natural" memory in the absence of any evidence for a special strategy. J.R. recalled 12 out of 13 names to faces at immediate recall and, when asked how she did this, she said, "I just did it." Three subjects achieved the maximum score on this task (two strategists and one natural), so J.R. was not exceptional, but a week later without warning she still recalled all the 12 names, a feat matched only by T.E., whose immediate recall was only 7! J.R.'s delayed performance was calculated to be 8.46 *SD* above the norm (30-year-old norms, calculated from the control data, were used for J.R., this being the lower bound of the age range in that group, and thus her performance may be slightly overestimated). We consider that there is strong evidence for exceptional memory in some subjects who do not use special techniques, and suggest that psychologists should investigate the distinguishing characteristics and causal antecedents of such abilities.

THE NATURE OF MEMORY

Efficiency of memory must depend on some basic parameters of the nervous system, but in practice the study of human memory cannot measure such parameters in isolation, because all memory performance involves a variety of strategic and other processes. In many laboratory tasks the effects of such processes will frequently be much more apparent than any individual differences in basic abilities, and it is tempting to conclude that the strategic effects are the only ones that it is feasible or useful to study. Also, because we know that practice produces extensive improvement, it is tempting to conclude that differences among individuals who have not overtly practiced the task may also be due to learned processes, and differences due to inborn variation in neural processes may be minor.

However, we would argue that if differences between individuals occur consistently over a wide range of tasks, it becomes necessary to postulate some difference in the neural system predating those due to past experience, or to explain what other individual characteristics could generate such general differences. The former alternative is strengthened if parallel differences between individuals also occur in abilities less obviously sensitive to strategic factors than immediate forewarned recall, such as retention without forewarning over a long interval.

We appreciate that such a view is at variance with the prevailing wisdom that there is no single memory system. There is no space here to address this issue in detail, but we suggest that some common processes may operate across several subsystems. One goal of future research must be to understand better the nature of these suggested processes and their relation to other aspects of cognitive ability. There is a growing consensus that speed of neural processing is related to measured IQ (Anderson, 1992), and it has also been suggested that the decline in memory with age is due to a decreased speed of processing (e.g., Salthouse, 1985). However, Nettelbeck and Rabbitt (1992) found that partialing out measures of processing speed eliminated the relation between age and many measures of cognitive performance, but the relation between age and memory performance survived, suggesting that some aspect of memory is related to factors other than processing speed. Such factors could be implicated in the encoding, storage, or retrieval processes of traditional memory models, but these models may be inadequate. Even the mnemonic methods render this rather simple threefold distinction hard to sustain, because these methods are directed at improving encoding, but thereby improve resistance to interference and accessibility to retrieval. Such distinctions are likely to be equally difficult to sustain when attempting to identify sources of natural ability.

The increasing popularity and sophistication of neural net models for cognitive processes provides one possible path toward understanding individual memory differences. Parameters such as those representing the number or pattern of neural interconnections, thresholds, decay, strength of inhibition, and so on, can be varied systematically in an attempt to match observed results, once we have a more substantial body of data. Brain scanning and biochemical sensing techniques will increasingly enable in vivo measurement of the relevant neural parameters in humans.

EFFECTIVE MEMORY TRAINING

In the immediate future a more feasible task may be to address methods of improving memory for complex material rather than mainly lists and associates, of ensuring the durability and automatic implementation of mnemonics so that they operate in incidental as well as intentional memory, and of understanding better the relation between subject state and memory efficiency (Herrmann & Searleman, 1990). Common ground needs to be explored with the investigation of learning styles, where distinctions are made between surface and deep approaches (oriented toward literal or more meaning-related aspects of the input respectively). Attempts to modify surface learning (regarded as an inferior learning style) toward a deeper approach have not proved highly successful. Clearly, these issues involve more than just the study of memory, but they are important if the insights gained from research on mnemonics are to be applied more profitably.

REFERENCES

Anderson, M. (1992). *Intelligence and development: A cognitive theory.* Oxford, England: Blackwell.

Anschutz, L., Camp, C. J., Markley, R. P., & Kramer, J. J. (1987). Remembering mnemonics: A three-year follow-up on the effects of mnemonics training in elderly adults. *Experimental Aging Research, 13,* 141–143.

Atkinson, R. C., & Shiffrin, R. M. (1968). Human memory: a proposed system and its control processes. In K. W. Spence & J. T. Spence (Eds.), *The psychology of learning and motivation* (Vol. 2, pp. 90–195). New York: Academic Press.

Baltes, P. B., & Kliegl, R. (1992). Further testing of limits of cognitive plasticity: Negative age differences in a mnemonic skill are robust. *Developmental Psychology, 28,* 121–125.

Bellezza, F. S., & Buck, D. K. (1988). Expert knowledge as mnemonic cues. *Applied Cognitive Psychology, 2,* 147–162.

Biederman, I., Cooper, E. E., Fox, P. W., & Mahadevan, R. S. (1992). Unexceptional memory in an exceptional memorist. *Journal of Experimental Psychology: Learning, Memory and Cognition, 18,* 654–657.

Brown, E., & Deffenbacher, K. (1988). Superior memory performance and mnemonic encoding. In L. A. Obler & D. Fein (Eds.), *The exceptional brain: Neuropsychology of talent and special abilities* (pp. 191–211). New York: Guilford.

Carrier, C., Karbo, K., Kindem, H., Legisa, G., & Newstrom, L. (1983). Use of self-generated and supplied visuals as mnemonics in gifted children's learning. *Perceptual and Motor Skills, 57,* 235–240.

Chase, W. G., & Ericsson, K. A. (1982). Skill and working memory. In G. H. Bower (Ed.), *The psychology of learning and motivation: Advances in research and theory* (Vol. 16, pp. 1–58). New York: Academic Press.

Chase, W. G., & Simon, H. A. (1973). The mind's eye in chess. In W. G. Chase (Ed.), *Visual information processing* (pp. 215–281). New York: Academic Press.

Cornoldi, C., & de Beni, R. (1991). Memory for discourse: Loci mnemonics and the oral presentation effect. *Applied Cognitive Psychology, 5,* 511–518.

Deakin, J. M., & Allard, F. (1991). Skilled memory in expert figure skating. *Memory & Cognition, 19,* 79–86.

Ericsson, K. A. (1985). Memory skill. *Canadian Journal of Psychology, 39,* 188–231.

Ericsson, K. A. (1988). Analysis of memory performance in terms of memory skill. In R. J. Sternberg (Ed.), *Advances in the psychology of human intelligence* (Vol. 4, pp. 137–179). Hillsdale, NJ: Lawrence Erlbaum Associates.

Ericsson, K. A., & Chase, W. G. (1982). Exceptional memory. *American Scientist, 70,* 607–615.

Ericsson, K. A., & Faivre, I. A. (1988). What's exceptional about exceptional abilities? In L. A. Obler & D. Fein (Eds.), *The exceptional brain: Neuropsychology of talent and special abilities* (pp. 436–473). New York: Guilford.

Ericsson, K. A., & Polson, P. G. (1988). An experimental analysis of the mechanics of a memory skill. *Journal of Experimental Psychology: Learning, Memory and Cognition, 14,* 305–316.

Ernest, C. H. (1977). Imagery ability and cognition: a critical review. *Journal of Mental Imagery, 2,* 181–216.

Gordon, P., Valentine, E., & Wilding, J. (1984). One man's memory: a study of a mnemonist. *British Journal of Psychology, 75,* 1–14.

Halpern, A. R., & Bower, G. H. (1982). Musical expertise and melodic structure in memory for musical notation. *American Journal of Psychology, 95,* 31–50.

Haring, M. J., & Fry, M. A. (1980). Facilitating prose recall with externally-produced mnemonics. *Journal of Instructional Psychology, 7,* 147–152.

Herrmann, D. J. (1987). Task appropriateness of mnemonic techniques. *Perceptual and Motor Skills, 64,* 171–178.

Herrmann, D. J., & Searleman, A. (1990). The new multimodal approach to memory improvement. In G. H. Bower (Ed.), *The psychology of learning and motivation* (Vol. 26, pp. 175–205). New York: Academic Press.

Higbee, K. L., Markham, S. K., & Crandall, S. (1991). Effects of visual imagery and familiarity on recall of sayings learned with an imagery mnemonic. *Journal of Mental Imagery, 15,* 65–76.

Hishitani, S. (1985). Coding strategies and imagery differences in memory. *Japanese Psychological Research, 27,* 154–162.

Hunt, E., & Love, T. (1972). How good can memory be? In A. W. Melton & E. Martin (Eds.), *Coding processes in human memory* (pp. 237–250). New York: Wiley.

Hunter, I. M. L. (1977). An exceptional memory. *British Journal of Psychology, 68,* 155–164.

Jamieson, D. G., & Schimpf, M. G. (1980). Self-generated images are more effective mnemonics. *Journal of Mental Imagery, 4,* 25–43.

Kliegl, R., Smith, J., Heckhausen, J., & Baltes, P. B. (1987). Mnemonic training for the acquisition of skilled digit memory. *Cognition and Instruction, 4,* 203–223.

Kroll, N. E., & Tu, S. F. (1988). The bizarre mnemonic. *Psychological Research, 50,* 28–37.

Levin, M. E., & Levin, J. R. (1990). Scientific mnemonomies: Methods for maximizing more than memory. *American Educational Research Journal, 27,* 301–321.

Lorayne, H. (1958). *How to develop a super-power memory.* Preston, England: Thomas.

Luria, A. R. (1975). *The mind of a mnemonist.* Harmondsworth, England: Penguin.

Mastropieri, M. A., & Scruggs, T. E. (1989). Constructing more meaningful relationships: Mnemonic instruction for special populations. *Educational Psychology Review, 1,* 83–111.

McCormick, C. B., Levin, J. R., & Valkenaar, D. E. (1990). How do mnemonic and thematic strategies affect students' prose learning. *Reading Psychology, 11,* 15–31.

McDaniel, M. A., & Einstein, G. O. (1989). Sentence complexity eliminates the mnemonic advantage of bizarre imagery. *Bulletin of the Psychonomic Society, 27,* 117–120.

McEvoy, C. L., & Moon, J. R. (1988). Assessment and treatment of everyday memory problems in the elderly. In M. M. Gruneberg, P. E. Morris, & R. M. Sykes (Eds.), *Practical aspects of memory: Current research and issues, vol. II: Clinical and educational inferences* (pp. 155–160). Chichester, England: Wiley.

Nettelbeck, T., & Rabbitt, P. M. A. (1992). Aging, cognitive performance and mental speed. *Intelligence, 16,* 189–205.

Noice, H. (1992). Elaborative memory strategies of professional actors. *Applied Cognitive Psychology, 6,* 417–427.

Paivio, A. (1986). *Mental representations.* Oxford, England: Oxford University Press.

Pressley, M., & Mullaly, J. (1984). Alternative research paradigms in the analysis of mnemonics. *Contemporary Educational Psychology, 9,* 48–60.

Reddy, B. G., & Bellezza, F. S. (1980). Interference between mnemonic and categorical organization in memory. *Bulletin of the Psychonomic Society, 24,* 169–171.

Richardson, J. T. E. (1987). Social class limitations on the efficacy of imagery mnemonic instructions. *British Journal of Psychology, 78,* 65–77.

Richardson, J. T. E. (1992). Imagery mnemonics and memory remediation. *Neurology, 42,* 283–286.

Salthouse, T. A. (1985). *A theory of cognitive aging.* Amsterdam: North Holland.

Scruggs, T. E., & Mastropieri, M. A. (1990). The case for mnemonic instruction: From laboratory research to classroom applications. *Journal of Special Education, 24,* 7–32.

Scruggs, T. E., Mastropieri, M. A., McLoone, B. B., Levin, J., & Morrison, C. (1987). Mnemonic facilitation of learning disabled students' memory for expository prose. *Journal of Educational Psychology, 79,* 27–34.

Shiffrin, R. M., & Schneider, W. (1977). Controlled and automatic human information processing: II. Perceptual learning, automatic attending and a general theory. *Psychological Review, 84,* 127–190.

Thompson, C. P., Cowan, C., Frieman, J., Mahadevan, R. S., & Vogl, R. J. (1991). Rajan: A study of a memorist. *Journal of Memory and Language, 30,* 702–724.

Wilding, J., Rashid, W., Gilmore, D., & Valentine, E. (1986). A comparison of two mnemonic methods in learning medical information. *Human Learning, 5,* 211–217.

Wilding, J., & Valentine, E. (1985). One man's memory for prose, faces and names. *British Journal of Psychology, 76,* 215–219.

Wilding, J., & Valentine, E. (1988). Searching for superior memories. In M. M. Gruneberg, P. E. Morris, & R. M. Sykes (Eds.), *Practical aspects of memory: Current research and issues, vol. I: Memory in everyday life* (pp. 472–477). Chichester, England: Wiley.

Wilding, J., & Valentine, E. (1991). Superior memory ability. In J. Weinman & J. Hunter (Eds.), *Memory: Neurochemical and abnormal perspectives* (pp. 209–228). Chur, Switzerland: Harwood.

Wilding, J., & Valentine, E. (1994a). Memory champions. *British Journal of Psychology, 85,* 231–244.

Wilding, J., & Valentine, E. (1994b). Mnemonic wizardry with the telephone directory, but stories are another story. *British Journal of Psychology, 85,* 501–509.

CHAPTER TWENTY - ONE

Updating the Scientific Validity of Three Key Estimator Variables in Eyewitness Testimony

Kenneth A. Deffenbacher
University of Nebraska at Omaha

In their survey of 63 experts on eyewitness testimony, Kassin, Ellsworth, and Smith (1989) determined that there were relatively high consensus levels concerning the reliability of three key phenomena. At least 70% of the experts agreed that data on the following phenomena were reliable enough for psychologists to present in court: nature of the forgetting curve (Ebbinghausian in shape), strength of the accuracy–confidence relation (confidence is not a good predictor), and the effects of stress (very high levels impair accuracy). Actually, the consensus levels were above 80% in two instances— 82.5% in the case of the nature of the forgetting function and 87.1% regarding the predictability of eyewitness accuracy from eyewitness confidence.

Recent critics (Egeth, 1993; Elliott, 1993) argued that such consensus as displayed by the experts in Kassin et al.'s (1989) sample is premature. Premature expert consensus or not, I present theoretical developments that provide reasonably solid underpinning for the scientific validity of the three phenomena characterized previously.

NATURE OF THE FORGETTING FUNCTION

A critical question in any criminal case is identity. Is the defendant the same person as the perpetrator? In cases where eyewitness identification is proffered, the trier of fact must decide whether the identification is accurate. In order to make this decision, the trier of fact requires an estimate of the eyewitness's memory strength for the face of the perpetrator at the time his or her memory was tested. Three pieces of information are necessary to lend a degree of precision to the estimate: an estimate of initial memory strength, the amount of time that has elapsed since original viewing of the perpetrator (retention interval), and the nature of the mathematical function characterizing memory trace strength over time.

What do we know about the nature of the forgetting curve? According to one recent critique, matters are rather muddled. Elliott (1993) summed up one impression of the literature on the subject:

> The Ebbinghaus forgetting curve . . . is another dubious metaphor for most eyewitness circumstances, both because the human face seems to have special properties as a stimulus, and because the retention intervals that are pertinent to identification scarcely ever include the very short ones where most forgetting presumably occurs. There is now a large enough number of results that are null or negative with respect to the Ebbinghaus hypothesis that their presence ought certainly to form a part of any testimony that might be given: They should no longer be treated simply as error. (p. 429)

It would appear that Elliott concluded that there is no firmly established effect of forgetting for the human face. Neither was he convinced of the validity of the Ebbinghaus (1885/1964) prediction of a logarithmic decline of the forgetting function for faces. His explanation for these null conclusions was that the eyewitness should suffer little memory loss for a perpetrator's face, given the special stimulus properties of human faces. Furthermore, he appears to have argued that failure to find a statistically significant effect of forgetting may be due to an investigator not including the very short retention intervals where most forgetting predicted by an Ebbinghausian function would occur. Does Elliott's precis square with the available literature on the topic?

I present the results of meta-analyses and theoretical developments that make it clear that Elliott (1993) was incorrect in his assessment on three counts but correct on one. It turns out that there is a firmly established effect of forgetting for the human face and that the forgetting function is generally Ebbinghausian in that it does show the greatest rate of memory loss right after exposure, with the rate leveling off over time. There is some indication of the human face having at least one special property, but the theoretical forgetting function that perhaps best captures the data over lengthy retention intervals does an equally good job describing the forgetting of words and pictures. Hence, faces are not special in the sense of following a different law of forgetting than for other types of stimulus material. Finally, I argue that Elliott (1993) was indeed correct that failures to find statistically significant effects of forgetting for faces may have been due to failure to include one or more very short retention intervals, ones as brief as one minute, for instance.

In two different meta-analyses of face memory studies, investigators have shown a clear effect of retention interval. Across 18 studies, Shapiro and Penrod (1986) found a modest effect size with respect to face recognition hits ($d = .43$) and a smaller effect size for false alarm responses ($d = .33$). These effect sizes correspond to cumulative z scores (Rosenthal, 1978) of 8.03 and 2.02, respectively. I examined overall proportion correct across retention intervals and found a cumulative z of 8.38 taken across 33 studies (Deffenbacher, 1986). Effect sizes such as these are reasonably impressive, given the relatively large number of null results combined in the analyses. Statistically speaking, then, one can safely say that the strength of a face memory trace will be weaker at longer retention intervals than at shorter ones.

Will this conclusion be much affected by studies yielding null results but which have not yet been reported? It is not likely that "file drawer" studies will soon invalidate this conclusion. Following Rosenthal's (1979) procedure, 825 new, filed, or unretrieved studies averaging null results ($z = 0.00$) would have to exist before the overall results could be reasonably attributed to sampling bias in the 33 studies that I analyzed (Deffenbacher, 1986).

A Power-Exponential Forgetting Function

Of course, the effects size analyses simply demonstrate that there is less memory strength at longer retention intervals than shorter ones. These analyses tell us nothing about the shape of the forgetting function. However, I showed (Deffenbacher, 1986) that Wickelgren's (1974) single-trace fragility theory of memory does a nice job of making predictions regarding the decline and fall of the memory trace of a face, a face seen only once previously. The equation for the forgetting function proposed by Wickelgren is a gamma function, a function with both a power component and an exponential component: $d' = L\ t^{-D}\ e^{-It}$. Three parameters need to be estimated: L, initial trace strength in d' units; D, the time decay parameter which I found to be constant across face recognition studies; and I, an interference parameter that varies inversely with the distinctiveness of the target face. The other two parameters need not be estimated in that e is the base of the system of natural logarithms, and t is the time in seconds since the end of stimulus exposure, the retention interval expressed in seconds.

Table 21.1 illustrates the fit of Wickelgren's (1974) theory of memory to data from an experiment conducted by Wixted and Ebbesen (1991). The data are from an experimental condition wherein observers had 11 seconds to view each of 40 color slides of male faces. At retention intervals of 1 hour, 1 day, 1 week, and 2 weeks, separate groups of observers completed a "yes/no" recognition memory test comprised of 80 color slides of male faces, half being those seen previously. The fit of Wickelgren's power-exponential function is quite good. The small discrepancies in d' units translate

TABLE 21.1
Predicted and Obtained Memory Strength Values (Mean d' Scores)
from Experiment 2 of Wixted and Ebbesen (1991)

	Retention Interval			
	1 Hour	1 Day	1 Week	2 Weeks
Obtained	2.01	1.75	1.46	1.41
Predicted	2.01[a]	1.83	1.57	1.37

[a]The predicted value of d' here is the same as the obtained value, because the latter was used in the equation for Wickelgren's (1974) forgetting function to solve for L, the initial memory strength, here estimated at $d' = 2.47$.

TABLE 21.2
Effect of Time Decay and Interference on Memory Strength
Across Retention Interval

Retention Interval	Time Decay	Interference	Product
1 hour	.815	.999	.814
1 day	.753	.983	.740
1 week	.717	.886	.635
2 weeks	.705	.785	.553

Note. Columns 2 and 3 contain the values of the time decay and interference terms specified by Wickelgren's (1974) theory for the data of Wixted and Ebbesen (1991, Exp. 2). The values in Column 4 were then multiplied by the estimate of initial memory strength to produce the memory strength estimates in the second row of Table 21.1.

into discrepancies in percent correct ranging from less than 0.5% to less than 2.0%. With Wickelgren's (1974) theory of memory, time decay (t^{-D}) is by far the greater contributor to forgetting in the first minutes and hours after initial stimulus exposure, but the amount of forgetting due to decay decreases per unit time. Interference (e^{-It}) has just the opposite effect. Both of these effects are illustrated in Table 21.2. Therein are the values for the time decay and interference terms that were multiplied by the estimate of initial trace strength to yield the predicted values in Table 21.1. As can be clearly seen, time decay is accounting for practically all the loss of memory strength during the first 24 hours after stimulus exposure. In the ensuing days, however, time decay slows considerably, and the rate of loss in memory strength due to interference increases.[1]

---

[1]For retention intervals of as long as a week, Wickelgren's (1974) power-exponential function provides the same degree of fit to empirical data as would the simple power functions of Wixted and Ebbesen (1991). At longer retention intervals, however, the exponential (interference) component of Wickelgren's function would come to dominate the power component and result in different predicted values of memory strength.

Application of Wickelgren's Power-Exponential Forgetting Function

Wickelgren's (1974) theory of forgetting offers us a plausible explanation for frequent failures to find statistically reliable forgetting effects with memory for faces. Often memory is tested at only two intervals, 1 day and 1 week, for example. If we examine Table 21.1, again, we may note that, significant or not, there was an approximately 12% drop in initial memory strength (d' = 2.47) during the six-day interval from Day 1 to Day 7. Nevertheless, the actual amount of loss in fidelity of memory since stimulus exposure was about 41% of original trace strength. Hence, the actual amount of forgetting has been underestimated by a factor of more than three to one, if we consider only the forgetting occurring in the Day 1 to Day 7 interval. Indeed, this is a clear demonstration of the point Elliott (1993) made concerning the need to test memory at very short intervals, if we hope to discover whether the forgetting function for faces shows the rapid descent right after stimulus exposure characteristic of the Ebbinghaus (1885/1964) function.

When one applies Wickelgren's (1974) theory to face memory, one finds that the theory permits plausible estimates of original memory trace strength for target faces in a number of field studies. Consider Pigott, Brigham, and Bothwell's (1990) study of 47 Florida bank tellers who were participants in a 1.5-minute interaction with one of two males who tried to cash a crudely altered U.S. Postal Service money order. The tellers, 77% of whom had training in eyewitness techniques, did not know that their encounter with the perpetrator of attempted bank fraud was not genuine until after their recall and recognition had been measured four hours later. Their average proportion correct across two target-present and two target-absent lineups was 0.55, which for a seven-alternative, forced-choice recognition memory task (cf. tabled values of Hacker & Ratcliff, 1979) is equivalent to a d' of 1.41. Applying Wickelgren's forgetting theory, a very plausible estimate of initial memory strength is d' = 1.79 (equivalent to 67% correct on a seven-alternative, forced-choice recognition memory task). Thus, after only four hours, memory strength was just 79% of what it had originally been. If the tellers had not been tested until a week afterwards, memory strength would likely have been d' = 1.24, equivalent to a performance score of 49% correct.

How does the eyewitness performance just described for the Pigott et al. (1990) field study compare with that for other published field studies? In general, performance by Pigott et al.'s bank tellers was rather similar to that recorded by retail clerks in four other studies (Brigham, Maass, Snyder, & Spaulding, 1982; Krafka & Penrod, 1985; Platz & Hosch, 1988; Read, Tollestrup, Hammersley, McFadzen, & Christensen, 1990). Taken across 19 different photo lineups, 16 different perpetrators, and 365 retail clerks in the aforementioned four studies, the average d' score achieved at a 2-hour retention interval was 1.13, equivalent to 46% correct on a seven-alternative, forced-choice task. Averaging across four different photo lineups, four different perpetrators, and 44 clerks, d' was 1.08 (equivalent to 44% correct) at a 24-hour retention interval for the Krafka and Penrod (1985) study. The highest performance noted thus far in a field study was the average d' of 2.10 (equivalent to 76% correct) achieved by averaging across four different photo lineup conditions and 212 retail clerks in Read et al.'s (1990) study. However, because only one perpetrator was used across the four 48-hour retention interval conditions to which Read et al.'s clerks were exposed, it may well be that the higher performance than that obtained by eyewitnesses in the other studies was due to the single perpetrator having a rather distinctive, and hence memorable, face. Thus, as an approximate rule of thumb, expected probability of making a correct identification response for an eyewitness under conditions similar to these field studies would be 0.50, where testing was by means of a fair, six-person lineup, with "none of these" being an acceptable alternative response. This level of performance is 3.5 times chance but might not inspire confidence that eyewitness accuracy is accurate beyond a reasonable doubt.

No matter what the expected probability of a typical eyewitness making an accurate identification might be, the trier of fact needs reliable information for estimating that probability. Witness confidence in the accuracy of his or her identification would seem likely to be used in this regard. Indeed, Bothwell, Deffenbacher, and Brigham (1987) reviewed empirical evidence of jurors relying heavily on eyewitness confidence to predict eyewitness accuracy.

STRENGTH OF THE ACCURACY–CONFIDENCE RELATION

The notion that eyewitness accuracy is not invariably strongly predicted by eyewitness confidence appears to be generally accepted by researchers interested in the psychology of testimony. In fact, Elliott (1993, p. 431) commented that, "Psychologists in the eyewitness field tend to write about the relation of confidence to accuracy as if the idea of a positive relation between them were one of the great myths of our time, one which we as experts are uniquely equipped to dispel." Elliott went on to state his belief that the true correlation of accuracy and confidence is approximately +.30, and that many jurors would not be unaware of the limited predictability of accuracy from confidence.

Elliott's (1993) estimate of the true accuracy–confidence correlation is quite close to the best available estimates. Bothwell et al.'s (1987) meta-analysis of 35 staged-event studies resulted in a conservative estimate of the population correlation at $r = +.25$ ($d = .52$), an effect medium in size (Cohen,

1977). Correcting for unreliability in the confidence measure, Bothwell et al. arrived at a more liberal estimate, $r = +.34$. It should be pointed out that Bothwell et al. did not try to correct for unreliability in the accuracy measure, because an eyewitness in the reviewed studies was either correct or incorrect on a single identification trial, not a very reliable measure. Correcting for unreliability here would have produced a spuriously high estimate of the interindividual accuracy–confidence correlation.

However, Elliott (1993) was not justified in being so sanguine concerning juror awareness of the limited utility of witness confidence in predicting witness accuracy. Brigham and Bothwell (1983) found that fully 56% of jurors believed that confidence indicates accuracy. Large proportions of persons with whom jurors have courtroom contact also subscribe to the same commonsense notion: Brigham and Wolfskeil (1983) found that 73% of police officers and 75% of prosecuting attorneys hold to the belief that confidence is directly related to accuracy. Furthermore, whether jurors are aware of the limited predictive validity of witness confidence or not, they still rely more heavily on it in making judgments of accuracy than they do on any other variable. Wells, Lindsay, and Ferguson (1979) found that variations in juror perceptions of eyewitness confidence account for as much as 50% of the variance in juror judgments as to witness accuracy. Similarly, Cutler, Penrod, and Stuve (1988) found that of 10 identification variables, only witness confidence had a reliable effect on jurors' judgments as to accuracy.

There is no convincing evidence, either, that jurors are especially sensitive to the possibility that the predictive validity of confidence may vary as a function of the optimality of witnessing conditions. Bothwell et al. (1987) found, for instance, that exposure duration for a target face is a moderating variable, in that the correlation between exposure duration and the accuracy–confidence correlation across their sample of 35 studies was $+.51$. Longer exposures (greater than 75 seconds) were associated with higher accuracy–confidence correlations. The estimated population correlation for accuracy–confidence at longer durations of target face exposure was $+.31$ ($d = .65$); for the shorter durations it was $+.19$ ($d = .39$). Other investigators have likewise found evidence of optimality of witnessing conditions serving to moderate the size of the accuracy–confidence correlation. Brigham (1990) noted a correlation of $+.38$ between target face distinctiveness and the size of the accuracy–confidence correlation for each target face; Cutler and Penrod (1989) found a nearly identical correlation of $+.37$. O'Rourke, Penrod, Cutler, and Stuve (1989) showed that disguise of the perpetrator produced a moderator effect, too. The correlation of accuracy and confidence was $+.40$ in a no-disguise condition but only $+.11$ for witnesses in a high-disguise condition.

These moderator effects provide support for my *optimality hypothesis*, in that certain conditions permit more efficient encodings by eyewitnesses (Deffenbacher, 1980). As the optimality hypothesis would predict, such efficiencies of processing allow for greater predictability of recognition memory from confidence ratings. The optimality hypothesis, then, predicts that the size of the accuracy–confidence correlation is directly related to the optimality of information processing conditions at encoding and retrieval. That is, the accuracy–confidence correlation should vary directly with any bias-free measure of recognition memory accuracy, for instance, signal detection theory's measure, d'.

Recasting the Optimality Hypothesis

In fact, by placing the recognition memory task within the framework provided by signal detection theory, as is often done, one can easily derive the optimality hypothesis. To my knowledge this derivation had not been done until very recently (Ebbesen & Wixted, 1994).

In the traditional analysis of face recognition with signal detection theory, each face, previously seen ("old") or not ("new"), is assumed to have some value on an underlying subjective dimension that reflects the strength of evidence that the face was seen before. The set of strengths for "new" and "old" faces are both assumed to be normally distributed, with the strength of the "old" faces being greater on average than that for the "new" faces. Signal detection theory's measure of discriminability, d', is directly proportional to the distance between the means of the two underlying strength distributions. Correct labeling of faces as "old" or "new" obviously improves the greater the strength of evidence is on average for the "old" faces over that for the "new" faces. The theory also assumes that observers make decisions about whether a face is familiar or not by adopting a particular value on the strength of evidence dimension as a response criterion: If the strength of evidence for a given face is above that criterion point, the observer identifies it as having been seen previously.

Clearly, accuracy of responding by an observer depends both on d', the distance between the means of the two strength distributions, and where the observer places his or her criterion on the strength of evidence axis. Confidence in correctness of an observer's judgment is easily incorporated into the signal detection model by assuming that an observer defines a second set of decision criteria on the strength of evidence continuum (Ebbesen & Wixted, 1994; MacMillan & Creelman, 1991). Here, each level of rated confidence that a face was "old" or "new" represents a band of values on the strength of evidence continuum. Hence, low values on the strength continuum should tend to elicit judgments of "highly confident" that the face is "new," but high values should tend to elicit judgments of "highly confident" that the face is "old." Values midway between the means of the two strength distributions should tend to elicit "just guessing" that a face is "old" or "new."

Derivation of the optimality hypothesis within the framework of signal detection theory is now relatively straightforward. When encoding and retrieval conditions are optimal, d' increases. That is, the distance between strength distributions increases, because "old" faces should have been encoded and retrieved more efficiently, thereby increasing the average strength of evidence that they have been seen before. With less overlap between the strength distributions, fewer highly confident "old" responses will be false alarm errors. Similarly, fewer highly confident "new" responses will be errors due to misses. Hence, the correlation between confidence ratings and accuracy should be enhanced relative to the suboptimal situation wherein d' is lower, there is greater overlap of the two strength distributions, and the likelihood is greater that the same confidence rating will be assigned to "old" and "new" faces.

Ebbesen and Wixted (1994) performed an extensive series of Monte-Carlo simulations of the effect of d' on the size of average within- and between-subjects confidence–accuracy correlations. They examined the confidence–accuracy correlation at each of seven values of d': 0, 0.5, 1.0, 1.5, 2.0, 2.5, and 3.0. Their simulation randomly sampled a strength of evidence value from one of two normal distributions separated by d'. If the value was greater than the value of the response criterion (placed midway between the two distributions), a response of "old" was assumed. Otherwise, the response was considered to be "new." Errors were counted when "old" responses were given to items sampled from the strength distribution with the smaller mean and when "new" responses were given to items sampled from the distribution with the larger mean.

The size of each strength of evidence value sampled also determined into which confidence band it was placed. Ebbesen and Wixted (1994) used a 10-point confidence scale, a 5-point scale ranging from "just guessing old" to "absolutely confident old" in the direction of increasing strength of evidence from the response criterion, and a 5-point scale ranging in the other direction from "just guessing new" to "absolutely confident new." They placed the most extreme confidence cutpoints plus or minus 1.0, 1.5, or 2.0 standard deviations from the response criterion in either direction and the remaining confidence cutpoints were spaced evenly in between. For reasons that will not detain us here, they also varied the ratio of the standard deviation of the "old" distribution to that of the "new" distribution: Ratios used were 1.0, 1.25, and 1.50. Crossing three values of confidence cutpoint placement with these three ratios yields nine separate simulations that were performed at each value of d'.

Let's first consider the simulations relating within-subject confidence–accuracy correlations to the value of d'. For each separate simulation, within-subject correlations were computed between confidence (1 to 5 rating) and accuracy (1 if correct, 0 if not). The correlations were computed over 80

TABLE 21.3
Results of Ebbesen and Wixted's (1994) Monte-Carlo Simulations
of the Effect of d' on the Size of the Average Within-Subjects
Confidence-Accuracy Correlation

	Magnitude of d'						
	0.0	0.5	1.0	1.5	2.0	2.5	3.0
Correlation	−.01	+.12	+.22	+.29	+.34	+.37	+.39

trials in each case, 40 from each distribution, and this was repeated 100 times (equivalent to 100 subjects). Thus, at each value of d' the mean value of the within-subjects correlation coefficient was averaged across the equivalent of 900 subjects. Values obtained by Ebbesen and Wixted (1994) are displayed in Table 21.3. What is striking about these theoretical values is that the relation of the average confidence–accuracy correlation and d' is not linear. Rather, it levels off below a correlation of .40, not reaching the .40 level, even at a rather high d' value of 3.00. Here we can see that when the optimality hypothesis is recast within the framework of signal detection theory, rather specific predictions can be made regarding the expected size of the confidence–accuracy correlation as a function of d'. Ebbesen and Wixted showed that the empirical data from Table 21.1, when combined with corresponding values of the within-subjects correlation coefficient, are fit rather well by the theoretical function of Table 21.3.

When Ebbesen and Wixted (1994) performed similar Monte Carlo simulations by which they attempted to assess the theoretical relation between d' and the between-subjects correlation, results were much the same. The shape of the function was the same, with the mean between-subjects correlation barely above +.40 at a d' value of 3.00.

Implications of Recasting the Optimality Hypothesis

I noted earlier in connection with applying Wickelgren's theory of forgetting to estimates of memory strength that most estimates of d' for retention intervals of two hours to a week were in the range of 1.0 to 1.50. Examining Table 21.3, one may note that predicted values of the correlation between confidence and accuracy should range from +.22 to +.29. Interestingly, a midrange predicted value here would be +.255, remarkably close to Bothwell et al.'s (1987) estimated population value of +.252. The predicted value of the confidence–accuracy correlation for Pigott et al.'s (1990) bank teller eyewitnesses would have been approximately +.28; the obtained value was +.27.

Now, in the real world, police and triers of fact must judge whether a particular witness identification is correct or not, based on whether the witness appears to be high or low in confidence concerning their identification. What one would like to know is the error rate for triers of fact or the police in making these judgments. For the sake of argument, let's assume that Bothwell et al.'s (1987) more liberal estimate of the population correlation of confidence and accuracy, +.34, were true. With a correlation of this size and confidence dichotomized as high or low, approximately 67% of the time the witness's accuracy (correct/incorrect) could be predicted correctly from their expressed confidence level (Ozer, 1985). More generally, the error rate in predicting values on one dichotomous variable from values on another is $(1 - phi)/2$, where *phi* is the correlation coefficient calculated for the case of two dichotomous variables (Levy, 1967). In the present case, the 67% level is certainly above the chance rate of 50% but is not very impressive when one considers that the misclassification rate is 33%. Even in the case of an optimal encoding and retrieval situation wherein the d' score would typically be about 3.0 and phi would be about .40, the misclassification rate would still be 30%—that is, $(1 - .40)/2 = .30$.

Thus, if one were interested in estimating the true score accuracy for an eyewitness, the average accuracy level across a large number of trials, a confidence–accuracy correlation of +.25, +.34, or even +.40 would represent moderate predictability. However, when making predictions in the individual case, as triers of fact must, such values of the correlation coefficient yield an accuracy prediction of questionable value, at best.

EFFECTS OF STRESS OR AROUSAL

Current critics of the scientific validity of the research on this topic have argued that the literature is as much a muddle now as it was when McCloskey and Egeth (1983) made their critique. Egeth (1993) stated: "On the whole, the research is as equivocal as it was a decade ago. It is still the case that some research shows that performance improves as arousal increases, some shows that it gets worse, and some shows that it has no effect. And it is still the case that an attempt to fit this literature, after the fact, to the inverted U of the Yerkes–Dodson (1908) Law is unjustified" (p. 578). Elliott (1993) added, "I think it is true that our knowledge, in the sense of the power to predict the direction and rough extent of arousal or stress effects in the ranged experienced by the large majority of witnesses, has not improved at all since McCloskey and Egeth (1983) made their criticism years ago" (p. 426).

Egeth's (1993) view was correct on both counts. Now, however, we can do a better job of fitting the literature after the fact (Deffenbacher, 1994).

For the same reason, theoretical advance, Elliott's (1993) assertion was not correct. Although considerably more research is needed specifically testing the second stage of the two-process theory I synthesized (Deffenbacher, 1994), the theory is clear in its prediction that there is a sizeable portion of the state-dependent performance space in which combined levels of anxiety (worry) and physiological activation are sufficient to produce a drastic reduction in eyewitness memory performance.

Relation of Arousal and Memory Performance: A New Look

My two-process theory (Deffenbacher, 1994) joins together Tucker and Willamson's (1984) asymmetric neural control system theorizing with Fazey and Hardy's (1988) catastrophe model of the effects of anxiety on performance. An adumbrated presentation of these two theoretical proposals follows.

Asymmetric Neural Control Systems. Tucker and Williamson (1984) presented considerable evidence and cogent argument for the case that there are two principal neural control systems dynamically regulating response to environmental demands. The function of the *arousal* system is to support alert wakefulness and responsivity to novel stimulation. *Activation*, on the other hand, functions to maintain a readiness for action. These two systems are essentially "either/or" in nature: Either one or the other is dominant at any given time. Furthermore, the mode of response, both cognitively and physiologically, is qualitatively different in each case.

The arousal system is organized for processing environmental change; it is biased against unchanging input. Attention is relatively broadly distributed and loosely regulated. Cognitive processing is entrained to external events. The physiological response is very similar to that of the orienting response—deceleration of heart rate, for instance.

Activation is a neural control system that is organized so as to promote a tonic motor readiness and to exhibit a bias against responding to novelty. As compared with the arousal system, attention is relatively focused, and cognitive processing proceeds under tight internal control. Physiological response is "defensive" in nature—acceleration of heart rate, for example.

Catastrophe Model of the Effects of Anxiety. In introducing their catastrophe model, Fazey and Hardy (1988) were concerned with clarifying the relation between different anxiety components and sports performance. They summarized a number of difficulties with the inverted-U hypothesis, the most interesting of which for present purposes relates to anecdotal evidence from sports psychology: When a sports performer "goes over the top," the drop in performance level is sudden and dramatic, not gradual, as implied by the smooth inverted-U curve relating anxiety/stress levels to performance. Once performance has "fallen off the cliff," even a mediocre level of perform- ance is difficult to achieve, at least in the short run. This would imply that small reductions in anxiety would be ineffective in restoring performance level, once the performance catastrophe has occurred. The Yerkes–Dodson (1908) Law and its associated inverted-U curve would, however, predict that performance would be restored to optimum level with such an intervention.

Fazey and Hardy's (1988) catastrophe model corresponds to one of seven fundamental catastrophes, models of naturally occurring discontinuities in functions which are normally continuous (Thom, 1975). Their particular catastrophe (Fig. 21.1) is referred to as a *cusp catastrophe.* It generates a three-dimensional (two predictor variables and a dependent variable), non- linear performance surface that resembles a breaking wave in cross-section. The variable on the *x*-axis is referred to as the normal factor, whereas the variable on the *y*-axis is referred to as the *splitting factor.* Hence, when scores on the splitting factor are high, continuous and gradual increases in scores on the normal factor produce continuous and gradual increases in performance, up to a certain point. Beyond that point, performance suddenly and drastically drops to a much lower value. If scores on the normal factor are then gradually reduced, however, performance does not gradually return to more nearly optimum levels; instead, it jumps back up in discontinuous fashion. The latter point of discontinuity is at a different point on the *x*-axis, though, than is the point of discontinuity when scores are increasing on the normal factor: This is the phenomenon of hysteresis.

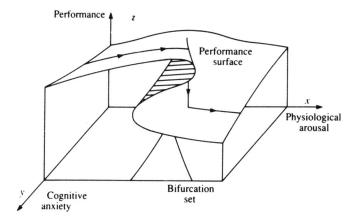

FIG. 21.1. Fazey and Hardy's (1988) catastrophe model of the relation between anxiety and performance. From "A Catastrophe Model of Anxiety and Performance" by L. Hardy and G. Parfitt (1991), *British Journal of Psychology, 82,* p. 167. Copyright 1991 by the British Psychological Society. Adapted by permission.

Given the model implemented in Fig. 21.1, Fazey and Hardy (1988) assumed that state anxiety has two components, a cognitive component (worry) and a physiological component. They proposed that cognitive anxiety is a splitting factor that determines whether increases or decreases in the normal factor, physiological arousal, result in gradual, small performance changes at the one extreme or in catastrophic, large ones at the other extreme.

Hardy and Parfitt (1991) successfully conducted a strong test of this model by testing experienced women's basketball players under conditions of high cognitive anxiety (day before an important tournament) and low cognitive anxiety (day after). Each day, physiological arousal was indexed by heart rate and manipulated by means of physical work such that half of the subjects were testing with physiological arousal increasing during the first session and decreasing the next, with the other half experiencing the other order. Increases and decreases in physiological arousal had little effect on performance when anxiety was low. When anxiety was high, however, high levels of physiological arousal resulted in catastrophic performance decrements, effects on set shot accuracy. Hysteresis occurred as well. The heart rate level at which performance plummeted as heart rate increased was at a higher level than the point at which performance improved dramatically as heart rate decreased.

Theoretical Synthesis. In order to predict whether there will be enhancement or decrement of memory in regard to any aspect of environmental change, one must first determine which of Tucker and Williamson's (1984) two modes of attentional control was dominant at the time of encoding. If the observer were relaxed and the task were one of simple perceptual intake, then the arousal mode would have been dominant. The most novel, surprising, and informative aspects of the stimulus array would have received greater attention relative to other aspects of the array and relative to information already in memory. There should have been enhancement of memory for the information emphasized by attention (Deffenbacher, 1994).

Contrariwise, if the observer were in a state of high cognitive anxiety and/or physiological arousal or the task were one of vigilance, escape, avoidance, or one requiring mental concentration, then the activation mode should have been dominant. Fazey and Hardy's (1988) catastrophe theory could then be used to predict whether memory performance would be facilitated or inhibited (Deffenbacher, 1994).[2] Of course, one would need to know the observer's initial levels of cognitive anxiety and physiological activation and how much each might have increased during performance.

---

[2]It is possible to fit precise catastrophe curves to data using methodologies such as Guastello's (1987) direct difference approach.

Applying the Theoretical Synthesis. Consider first the recent studies wherein researchers have determined that increases in negative emotionality of an event improves memory (e.g., Burke, Heuer, & Reisberg, 1992; Christianson, Loftus, Hoffman, & Loftus, 1991). These studies took place in lab settings where both cognitive anxiety and physiological activation should have been relatively low (baseline heart rates averaged 68 to 82) beats/minute). The tasks presented were those of simple perceptual intake. Negative emotional content of key slides in scenarios presented to observers was neither a threat to their body integrity nor self-esteem (modestly gruesome accident or surgery scene). It was, however, attention-grabbing enough to have elicited an orienting response characteristic of the arousal mode of attention (e.g., Hare, Wood, Britain, & Shadman, 1970). It produced a deceleration in heart rate of 3 to 5 beats/minute and in one case where it was measured (Christianson, 1984), an increase in skin conductance. If pupillary dilation had been measured in any of these studies, the more emotionally involving material should have elicited greater dilation as well. All three of these measures are indicative of an orienting response, characteristic of the arousal mode. The prediction from the current integrative theoretical perspective would have been for memory enhancement for the emotionally colored material. Such enhancement was indeed observed.

I should also note that findings by Lang, Greenwald, Bradley, and Hamm (1993) are consistent with my interpretation here. They found that interest ratings and duration of time a person chooses to view a visual display both load on the same factor as does the magnitude of the skin conductance response.

Finally, let's see how the present approach fares in accounting for the results of an eyewitness memory study done in a field setting (Peters, 1988). Here, 212 university students required to be inoculated for measles and rubella at a Department of Health immunization clinic were asked to provide photo identifications and physical descriptions of a nurse who had recently inoculated them and of a second person whom they had met 2 minutes after getting their shots. A control study had determined both target persons to be equally memorable, and care had been taken to ensure about 15 seconds of eye contact with each. Pulse rates at inoculation (and presumably also the level of state anxiety at this time) were significantly higher than 2 minutes later, 88 versus 71 beats/minute. Both physical descriptions and photo lineup identification of the nurse were less accurate than those of the person encountered under less arousing conditions. Where 20% correct was at chance, identification of the second person was correct 66% of the time, but only 41% of the time for the nurse.[3] If we examine data from just the 20 most and the 20 least physiologically aroused eyewitnesses (39 beats/min-

---

[3]There was a substantial loss of recall memory, too, for personal characteristics of the nurse.

ute vs. 3 beats/minute elevation in heart rate between the two viewing conditions), the difference in identification accuracy of the nurse was 31% versus 59%.

With the current theoretical approach, it is easy to model these differences in identification accuracy. First, persons waiting in line for an inoculation certainly should have been in the activation state of attentional regulation. Second, these same persons should have been in a state of increased cognitive anxiety (worry) as they approached the point of pain infliction, an increase relative to individual baselines, at least. Concomitantly, a moderately large acceleration in heart rate (17 beats/minute) could easily have represented a sufficiently large increase in physiological arousal to have pushed memory performance over the crest of the wave on the catastrophe solid.

Certainly not all types of eyewitness memory are negatively impacted by combined levels of anxiety and physiological activation elicited by real-life events that pose threats to bodily integrity. Typically, witness descriptions are relatively accurate and persistent over time for certain criminal event details such as action, weapon, and clothing (Christianson & Hübinette, 1993; Yuille & Cutshall, 1986). Nevertheless, recall of some details of the target person's physical appearance are often noticeably less accurate under such "catastrophic" conditions (Christianson & Hübinette, 1993; Peters, 1988; Yuille & Cutshall, 1986). Peters (1988) showed quite clearly that the ability to render an accurate face identification suffers serious decrement for those individuals who have "gone over the crest." It is precisely the accuracy of the identification response that is crucial in cases where eyewitness identification evidence is proffered.

REFERENCES

Bothwell, R. K., Deffenbacher, K. A., & Brigham, J. C. (1987). Correlation of eyewitness memory and confidence: Optimality hypothesis revisited. *Journal of Applied Psychology, 72,* 691–695.

Brigham, J. C. (1990). Target person distinctiveness and attractiveness as moderator variables in the confidence–accuracy relationship in eyewitness identifications. *Basic and Applied Social Psychology, 11,* 101–115.

Brigham, J. C., & Bothwell, R. K. (1983). The ability of prospective jurors to estimate the accuracy of eyewitness identifications. *Law and Human Behavior, 7,* 19 30.

Brigham, J. C., Maass, A., Snyder, L. S., & Spaulding, K. (1982). The accuracy of eyewitness identifications in a field setting. *Journal of Personality and Social Psychology, 42,* 673–681.

Brigham, J. C., & Wolfskeil, M. P. (1983). Opinions of attorneys and law enforcement personnel on the accuracy of eyewitness identification. *Law and Human Behavior, 7,* 337–349.

Burke, A., Heuer, F., & Reisberg, D. (1992). Remembering emotional events. *Memory & Cognition, 20,* 277–290.

Christianson, S.-Å. (1984). The relationship between induced emotional arousal and amnesia. *Scandinavian Journal of Psychology, 25,* 147–160.

Christianson, S.-Å., & Hübinette, B. (1993). Hands up: A study of witnesses' emotional reactions and memories associated with bank robberies. *Applied Cognitive Psychology, 7,* 365–379.

Christianson, S.-Å., Loftus, E. F., Hoffman, H., & Loftus, G. R. (1991). Eye fixations and memory for emotional events. *Journal of Experimental Psychology: Learning, Memory, and Cognition, 17*, 693–701.

Cohen, J. (1977). *Statistical power analysis for the behavioral sciences* (rev. ed.). New York: Academic Press.

Cutler, B. L., & Penrod, S. D. (1989). Moderators of the confidence–accuracy correlation in face recognition: The role of information processing and base-rates. *Applied Cognitive Psychology, 3*, 95–107.

Cutler, B. L., Penrod, S. D., & Stuve, T. E. (1988). Juror decision making in eyewitness identification cases. *Law and Human Behavior, 12*, 41–55.

Deffenbacher, K. A. (1980). Eyewitness accuracy and confidence: Can we infer anything about their relationship? *Law and Human Behavior, 4*, 243–260.

Deffenbacher, K. A. (1986). On the memorability of the human face. In H. D. Ellis, M. A. Jeeves, F. Newcombe, & A. Young (Eds.), *Aspects of face processing* (pp. 61–70). Dordrecht, Netherlands: Martinus Nijhoff.

Deffenbacher, K. A. (1994). Effects of arousal on everyday memory. *Human Performance, 7*, 141–161.

Ebbesen, E. B., & Wixted, J. T. (1994). *A signal detection analysis of the relationship between confidence and accuracy in face recognition memory.* Unpublished manuscript, University of California, San Diego.

Ebbinghaus, H. (1885/1964). *Memory: A contribution to experimental psychology.* Mineola, NY: Dover.

Egeth, H. E. (1993). What do we *not* know about eyewitness identification? *American Psychologist, 48*, 577–580.

Elliott, R. (1993). Expert testimony about eyewitness identification: A critique. *Law and Human Behavior, 17*, 423–437.

Fazey, J. A., & Hardy, L. (1988). *The inverted-U hypothesis: A catastrophe for sport psychology* (British Association for Sports Sciences Monograph No. 1). Leeds, England: National Coaching Foundation.

Guastello, S. J. (1987). A butterfly catastrophe model of motivation in organizations: Academic performance. *Journal of Applied Psychology, 72*, 165–182.

Hacker, M. J., & Ratcliff, R. (1979). A revised table of d' for M-alternative forced choice. *Perception & Psychophysics, 26*, 168–170.

Hardy, L., & Parfitt, G. (1991). A catastrophe model of anxiety and performance. *British Journal of Psychology, 82*, 163–178.

Hare, R., Wood, K., Britain, S., & Shadman, J. (1970). Autonomic responses to affective visual stimulation. *Psychophysiology, 7*, 407–417.

Kassin, S. M., Ellsworth, P. C., & Smith, V. L. (1989). The "general acceptance" of psychological research on eyewitness testimony. *American Psychologist, 44*, 1089–1098.

Krafka, C., & Penrod, S. D. (1985). Reinstatement of context in a field experiment in eyewitness identification. *Journal of Personality and Social Psychology, 49*, 58–69.

Lang, P. J., Greenwald, M. K., Bradley, M. M., & Hamm, A. O. (1993). Looking at pictures: Affective, facial, visceral, and behavioral actions. *Psychophysiology, 30*, 261–273.

Levy, P. (1967). Substantive significance of significant differences between two groups. *Psychological Bulletin, 67*, 37–40.

MacMillan, N. A., & Creelman, C. D. (1991). *Detection theory: A user's guide.* New York: Cambridge University Press.

McCloskey, M., & Egeth, H. (1983). Eyewitness identification: What can a psychologist tell a jury? *American Psychologist, 38*, 550–563.

O'Rourke, T. E., Penrod, S. D., Cutler, B. L., & Stuve, T. E. (1989). The external validity of eyewitness identification research: Generalizing across age groups. *Law and Human Behavior, 13*, 385–395.

Ozer, D. J. (1985). Correlation and the coefficient of determination. *Psychological Bulletin, 97,* 307–315.

Peters, D. P. (1988). Eyewitness memory and arousal in a natural setting. In M. M. Gruneberg, P. E. Morris, & R. N. Sykes (Eds.), *Practical aspects of memory: Current research and issues, Vol. 1: Memory in everyday life* (pp. 89–94). Chichester, England: Wiley.

Pigott, M. A., Brigham, J. C., & Bothwell, J. C. (1990). A field study on the relationship between quality of eyewitnesses' descriptions and identification accuracy. *Journal of Police Science and Administration, 17,* 84–88.

Platz, S. J., & Hosch, H. M. (1988). Cross-racial/ethnic eyewitness identification: A field study. *Journal of Applied Social Psychology, 18,* 972–984.

Read, J. D., Tollestrup, P., Hammersley, R., McFadzen, E., & Christensen, A. (1990). The unconscious transference effect: Are innocent bystanders ever misidentified? *Applied Cognitive Psychology, 4,* 3–31.

Rosenthal, R. (1978). Combining results of independent studies. *Psychological Bulletin, 85,* 185–193.

Rosenthal, R. (1979). The "file drawer problem" and tolerance for null results. *Psychological Bulletin, 86,* 638–641.

Shapiro, P. N., & Penrod, S. D. (1986). Meta-analysis of face identification studies. *Psychological Bulletin, 100,* 139–156.

Thom, R. (1975). *Structural stability and morphogenesis* (D. H. Fowler, Trans.). New York: Benjamin/Addison-Wesley.

Tucker, D. M., & Williamson, P. A. (1984). Asymmetric neural control systems in human self-regulation. *Psychological Review, 91,* 185–215.

Wells, G. L., Lindsay, R. C. L., & Ferguson, T. (1979). Accuracy, confidence and juror perception in eyewitness identification. *Journal of Applied Psychology, 64,* 440–448.

Wickelgren, W. A. (1974). Single-trace fragility theory of memory dynamics. *Memory & Cognition, 2,* 775–780.

Wixted, J. T., & Ebbesen, E. B. (1991). On the form of forgetting. *Psychological Science, 2,* 409–415.

Yerkes, R. M., & Dodson, J. D. (1908). The relation of strength of stimulus to rapidity of habit formation. *Journal of Comparative Neurology and Psychology, 18,* 459–482.

Yuille, J. C., & Cutshall, J. L. (1986). A case study of eyewitness memory of a crime. *Journal of Applied Psychology, 71,* 291–301.

Author Index

Subject Index